CARDINAL CLASSICS

CARDINAL CLASSICS

Outstanding Games
From Each of the
St. Louis Baseball Club's
100 Seasons
1882-1981

Robert L. Tiemann

Baseball Histories, Inc St. Louis

Copyright © 1982 by Robert L. Tiemann

Published by
Baseball Histories, Inc.
P.O. Box 15168
St. Louis, MO 63110

Typeset by Delmas, Ann Arbor, MI
Printed by McNaughton-Gunn, Inc., Saline, MI

cover photos:
Top: the 1885 St. Louis Browns. Photo courtesy Missouri Historical Society. Photo by Strauss

Bottom: the 1981 St. Louis Cardinals. Photo courtesy St. Louis Cardinals

ISBN 0-9608534-0-5

*To my father,
who taught me to love his favorite game*

Acknowledgments

After years of haphazardly researching old baseball games and pennant races, the impetus for my writing a book about the Cardinals came from John M. Howard. He and I, along with my sister Elizabeth and my parents, became partners in the venture to publish this and, hopefully, subsequent books on baseball history. Our fledgling corporation, Baseball Histories, Inc., became a reality thanks to the very generous assistance of our attorney, Richard E. Shinners, and the personnel at his firm, Diekemper, Hammond & Shinners.

As for the actual researching and writing of this book, the efficient assistance of the many librarians at the St. Louis Public Library, the St. Louis County Library, and the Missouri Historical Society was invaluable. My other sister, Jane E. Tiemann, saved me much trouble by acting as a research assistant at the University of California Library at Berkeley.

And the assistance and encouragement of the people in the offices of the Cardinal baseball club, especially Robin Monsky, Jim Toomey, and Marty Hendin, helped speed the book to completion.

Introduction

This book is intended to give the reader some feeling for the evolution of Cardinal baseball over the span of the club's first century of play. Although this is not a complete history of the club, it does deal with each of the 100 seasons since the team, originally known as the Browns, was founded as a charter member of the old American Association in 1882. The team transferred to the National League in 1892 and changed its name to the Cardinals around 1900.

Back in 1882, the infielders and outfielders played barehanded. The pitcher had to deliver the ball underhanded. It took seven balls for a walk. Only one umpire was on duty. Twenty-five cents got you into the ballpark. And $2,000 per season was a top salary. But it was still baseball. Teams of nine players (no substitutions were then allowed without the consent of the opposing team) played for nine innings, trying to score the most runs. Three strikes and you were out, and three outs and your team went out to the field.

Rather than analyze the complete history of the St. Louis franchise, its roster, and its progress through 100 years of pennant races, this book focuses on one game from each season, plus one game from each World Series that St. Louis was involved in. In this way, the reader will hopefully be able to note the changes in the team's personnel and fortunes in the context of actual games played.

Although each fan has his or her own personal choices of outstanding games, I have chosen the games for this book using three criteria: 1) that the game itself was particularly exciting, 2) that a Cardinal player or the team as a whole achieved some outstanding record during the game, or 3) that the game was somehow representative of the team's overall season performance.

In a season in which the Cardinals were involved in an exciting pennant race, key games in the race take priority over other outstanding games. Therefore, for example, the dramatic game on September 25th, 1974, in which the Cards rallied for four runs in the bottom of the eleventh inning to beat Pittsburgh and move back into first place ahead of the Pirates, takes precedence over the game a few weeks earlier in which Lou Brock broke Maury Wills's record for stolen bases in a season.

In years in which the Cardinals did poorly, the tendency is to use a game which somehow typifies their losses for the year. For example, in 1965 the Cards were hampered by numerous injuries, and I have chosen a game that year in which they were forced to use an outfielder with no previous catching experience, Mike Shannon, behind the plate because of injuries to their other catchers. But in some lackluster seasons, outstanding individual achivements are the focus of the game chosen. Examples are 1924, when Jim Bottomley drove in a record 12 runs in a game, although the Cardinals finished a distant sixth, and 1978 when Bob Forsch pitched a no-hitter in an otherwise disastrous season.

Sometimes, of course, the choices were difficult. Like 1979, when Lou Brock got his 3,000th hit, but Roger Freed won a game in the most dramatic possible fashion with a grand slam in the bottom of the eleventh, the Cardinals behind by three runs, two men out, the bases loaded, and a 3-and-2 count. Of course, there were other years in which not even one game stood out as dramatically as those two 1979 classics.

In keeping with the aim of giving the reader the flavor of baseball at the time, I have written the stories of the games as if the game had just taken place. At the end of each account, there is a brief summary of the team's fortunes for the remainder of the season. Also, some of the old-time terminology is used. "Cranks," for example, was a term used before the turn of the century to denote what came to be known as "fans." And the word "Pittsburg" was not spelled in the sports pages with an "h" at the end until the World War I era.

I also use the nickname of the team and the name of the ballparks that were current at the time the game was played. This may cause the reader some confusion because St. Louis had three separate teams which were called "the Browns," and there were three different incarnations of "Sportsman's Park" and two Busch Stadiums.

Briefly, the Browns was the traditional name for St. Louis's professional baseball teams starting with the first pro club in 1875. This team played in the National League in 1876 and 1877, then it folded. The next professional team which was also named the

Browns, was formed in 1882, and it played in the American Association. This team moved into the National League in 1892 and changed its name to the Cardinals around 1900. The present-day Cardinals, therefore, were first called the Browns when they were founded 100 years ago. In 1885 and 1886, the National League had a rival team in St. Louis called the Maroons. In 1902, the upstart American League put a team in St. Louis, and it appropriated the old name, the Browns. The American League Browns lasted through 1953 before moving to Baltimore to become the present-day Orioles.

As for the ballparks, the first Sportsman's Park was located on Grand Avenue. The Browns played here from 1882 through 1892. Then they moved to a park on Natural Bridge Avenue. This park was also called Sportsman's Park until 1899. Then its name was changed to League Park. Later, the Natural Bridge grounds were also known as Robison Field and Cardinal Field. Meanwhile, the American League club built a new park on the old Grand Avenue site and named it Sportsman's Park. The Cardinals moved to this park as tenants of the Browns in 1920. When the Cardinals bought this park in 1953, they renamed it Busch Stadium. In 1966, this old park was abandoned in favor of the new downtown Busch Stadium, formally known as Civic Center Busch Memorial Stadium.

Despite changing leagues, names, ballparks, and ownership, the present St. Louis National Baseball Club has played 100 continuous seasons through 1981. There have been some terrible seasons, and there has been quite a lot of success, including 16 pennants. Through it all, baseball has remained the most popular spectator sport in St. Louis and the nation. And this 100th anniversary season seems an appropriate time for the fans to look back through the seasons past.

Table of Contents

EXPLANATION OF BOX SCORES - 4

CHAPTER I - POWERHOUSE OF THE AMERICAN ASSOCIATION - 6
1882 - May 2nd - Professional Baseball Returns, St. Louis Wins Opening Game
1883 - September 21st - Athletics Beat St. Louis in Opener of Critical Series
1884 - July 29th - Rookie Dave Foutz Wins Debut with Browns, Strikes Out 13
1885 - July 16th - Browns Win, 13-11, for 27th Straight Victory at Home
   World Series - Game #2 - Browns Walk Off Field, Forfeit Game to Chicago
1886 - May 29 - Comiskey Removes Sand from Basepaths, St. Louis Runs Wild
   World Series - Game #6 - Browns Rally to Win Game and World Championship
1887 - May 12th - Browns Outslug Orioles to Win by 22-14 Score
   World Series - Games #10 & 11 - Browns Split Two Games, Detroit Clinches Series
1888 - August 3rd - Browns Retain Lead with 10-Inning, 7-6 Win over Bridegrooms
   World Series - Game #1 - Giants Edge Browns, 2-1, in World Series Opener
1889 - September 7th - St. Louis, Leading 4-2, Forfeits Key Game in Brooklyn
1890 - August 16th - St. Louis Overcomes Nine-Run Deficit to Beat Athletics
1891 - October 4th - Breitenstein Pitches No-Hitter as Browns Split Final Games

CHAPTER II - DOORMAT IN THE NATIONAL LEAGUE - 36
1892 - April 17th - Browns Lose in National League's First-Ever Sunday Game
1893 - September 30th - St. Louis Ends Season with Two Wet Wins Over Boston
1894 - May 10th - St. Louis Gets Six Home Runs but Loses to Cincinnati, 18-9
1895 - May 24th - Miller Makes Four Errors in One Inning, Quits as Team Captain
1896 - July 16th - Umpire Leaves Field in Fifth, Rain Halts Game in Ninth
1897 - September 26th - St. Louis Loses Two More for 18 Straight Defeats
1898 - April 17th - Browns Lose, 14-1, on Site of Burned-Down Sportsman's Park

CHAPTER III - THE ROBISON BROTHERS' CARDINALS - 52
1899 - April 15th - St. Louis's New "Perfectos" Trounce Cleveland in Opener
1900 - May 12th - Cardinals Lose Thriller in McGraw's Debut with St. Louis
1901 - July 8th - St. Louis Fans Attack Umpire after Cardinals Lose Tight Game
1902 - August 17th - Spectacular Game with Superbas Ends in 18-Inning Tie
1903 - July 22nd - Cards Win, 8-7, on Smoot's Ninth-Inning, Three-Run Home Run
1904 - October 15th - Cards Win, 10-6, Front Offices Feud, City Series Ends Tied
1905 - October 15th - Cards Lose Twice, Browns Win City Series, 4 Games to 3
1906 - April 12th - Opener Scoreless until 13th, then Pirates Edge Cards, 2-1
1907 - August 11th - Karger Pitches 7-Inning Perfect Game as Cards Win Pair
1908 - April 20th - Cardinals' Raymond Pitches One-Hitter but Loses, 2-0
1909 - May 24th - St. Louis Finally Beats Christy Mathewson after 24 Losses
1910 - September 23rd - Cardinals Get Just Two Hits but Win, 6-2

CHAPTER IV - UPS AND DOWNS IN THE TEENS - 78
1911 - July 26th - Cards Play Great Ball, Edge Phils in Action-Packed Game, 7-6
1912 - May 5th - Cardinals Lose to Reds, 11-9, Despite Rube Ellis's Slugging
1913 - May 4th - Cards Win, 10-8, in Thirteen, Konetchy Gets Pitching Victory
1914 - August 27th - Cards Stop Braves, 3-2, in 10, Trail Giants by One Game
1915 - August 30th - Cards Lose as Home Run Bounces off Bescher and Over Fence
1916 - October 1st - Cards End Season with 14th Straight Loss, Tie for Last
1917 - June 11th - St. Louis Rallies to Win, 5-4, Gonzalez Steals Home in 15th
1918 - July 3rd - Fisher's Hidden Ball Trick Saves 2-1 Victory for Cardinals
1919 - July 17th - Ex-Cardinal Meadows Beats Former Mates in First Meeting, 1-0

CHAPTER V - SAM AND BRANCH BUILD A WINNER #
1920 - July 1st - Cardinals Lose First Game in Sportsman's Park, 6-2 in Ten
1921 - June 13th - Cardinals Humiliate Giants, 10-1, to Win Tenth Straight
1922 - July 22nd - Six-Run Eighth-Inning Rally Moves St. Louis into First Place
1923 - July 10th - Rookie Stuart Wins Both Games of Doubleheader for Red Birds

I

1924 - September 16th - Bottomley Drives In 12 Runs as Cardinals Rout Robins
1925 - April 22nd - Cardinals Score 11 Runs in First Inning of Home Opener

CHAPTER VI - PENNANTS! - 112
1926 - August 31st - Cardinals Take Two from Pirates, Move into League Lead
   World Series - Game #7 - Alexander, Thevenow Star as Cards Win World Series
1927 - September 4th - Triple Play Helps St. Louis Edge Chicago, 2-1
1928 - September 20th - Harper Hits Three Homes in Game as Cards Retain Lead
   World Series - Game #4 - Ruth Hits Three Homers as Yankees Complete Sweep
1929 - July 6th - Cards Lose 11th in a Row, then Crush Phillies, 28-6
1930 - September 16th - Cardinals Take League Lead with Thrilling, 1-0 Victory
   World Series - Game #5 - A's Win, as Foxx's Homer Ruins Masterpiece by Grimes
1931 - July 12th - Overflow Crowd Makes Farce of Games as Cards Split with Cubs
   World Series - Game #7 - Cards Take Series on Base Running, Watkins's Home Run

CHAPTER VII - THE GAS HOUSE GANG - 134
1932 - August 14th - Carleton, Dean Hurl St. Louis to Two Victories over Chicago
1933 - July 2nd - Giants Sweep Cardinals with Brilliant Double Shutout
1934 - September 21st - Paul Dean Pitches No-Hitter after Three-Hitter by Dizzy
   World Series - Game #7 - Cardinals Trounce Tigers, 11-0, to Win World Title
1935 - July 18th - Red Birds Rout Braves, 13-3, for 14th Consecutive Triumph
1936 - April 29th - Cards' Parmelee Beats Giants' Hubbell in 17-Inning Duel
1937 - August 4th - Pinch-Hit by Frisch Caps Ninth-Inning, Game-Winning Rally
1938 - September 11th - P. Dean Returns with Win, 6-4, Frisch Fired as Manager
1939 - August 20th - Cardinals Win Two in Cincinnati, Trail Reds by 3½ Games

CHAPTER VIII - GLORY FOR SAM - 154
1940 - May 8th - Slugging Record Crumbles as Cardinals Crush Dodgers, 18-2
1941 - September 13th - Wyatt Edges M. Cooper, 1-0, Dodgers Retain League Lead
1942 - September 12th - St. Louis Tops Brooklyn, 2-1, to Gain Tie in Pennant Race
   World Series - Game #5 - Cards Beat Yankees Again, Win World Championship
1943 - June 4th - Cooper's Second Straight One-Hitter Gives Cards 5-0 Victory
   World Series - Game #5 - Cards Get Ten Hits but Lose, 2-0, Yanks Win Series
1944 - June 10th - Cardinals Bury Reds' Pitchers in 18-0 Massacre
   World Series - Game #6 - Cardinals Beat Browns, 3-1, Win World Series
1945 - September 25th - Cubs Best Cards, 6-5, Lead St. Louis by 2½ Games
1946 - October 1st - Pollet and Cards Beat Dodgers, 4-2, in First Playoff Game
   World Series - Game #7 - Daring and Defense Win Series for Cards over Red Sox

CHAPTER IX - A SLOW DECLINE - 178
1947 - July 30th - Red Birds Rally from 10 Runs Behind, Then Lose to Dodgers
1948 - June 6th - Schoendienst's Doubles & Cardinal Homers Featured in Sweep
1949 - September 29th - Dickson and Pirates Knock Cardinals out of Lead
1950 - September 3rd - Unorthodox Strategy Backfires, Cards Lose to Bucs, 12-11
1951 - September 13th - Cards Beat Giants by Day, Lose to Braves at Night
1952 - June 15th - Birds Overcome 11-0 Deficit to Win First Game, then Lose, 3-0
1953 - September 25th - Haddix Wins 20th Game, Schoendienst Nears Batting Lead
1954 - May 2nd - Musial Hit Five Home Runs in Doubleheader, Cards Split
1955 - June 1st - Rookie Luis Arroyo Wins Sixth Straight for St. Louis

CHAPTER X - GUSSIE WAITS FOR A WINNER — 198
1956 - September 29th - Cardinals Knock Braves Out of First with 12-Inning Win
1957 - July 28th - Von McDaniel Hurls One-Hitter as Cardinals Win Pair
1958 - May 13th - Musial Gets 3,000th Hit with Pinch-Double, Starts Winning Rally
1959 - April 16th - Cardinals Use 25 Men but Lose to Los Angeles, 7-6
1960 - August 11th - Musial Homer Beats Pirates in 12th, Cards Trail Bucs by 4
1961 - July 18th - Cards Sweep Again, White's Hit Total Up to 14 in Two Days
1962 - July 8th - Musial Hits Three Straight Home Runs as Cards Trounce Mets

CHAPTER XI - BACK ON TOP - 214
1963 - September 16th - Cards Lose to Dodgers, 3-1, in Opener of Critical Series
1964 - September 30th - Redbirds Complete Sweep of Phillies, Grab League Lead
   World Series - Game #7 - Gibson Hangs on to Beat Yanks, 7-5, Cards Win Series
1965 - August 8th - Cards Forced to Use Shannon as Catcher, Lose to Giants
1966 - May 12th - St. Louis Opens New Stadium with 12-Inning Win over Atlanta
1967 - July 25th - Cardinals Hold Off Cubs to Win, 4-3, Regain One Game Lead
   World Series - Game #7 - Gibson's Third Win Gives St. Louis the Series
1968 - July 1st - Scoreless Streak Ends, but Gibson Beats Dodgers Easily, 5-1
   World Series - Game #1 - Gibby Fans 17 Tigers, Cardinals Win Opener, 4-0

CHAPTER XII - RED'S EAST DIVISION BLUES - 234
1969 - September 15th - Carlton Strikes Out 19 for New Record but Loses, 4-3
1970 - August 11th - Taylor's Pinch-Grand Slam Caps Come-from-Behind Victory
1971 - August 14th - Gibson Pitches No-Hitter, Cuts Pittsburgh's Lead to 5 Games
1972 - September 20th - Carlton Bests Wise and Cardinals, 2-1, for 25th Win
1973 - July 22nd - Late Rally Wins for Cards, 5-4, St. Louis Takes Division Lead
1974 - September 25th - Four-Run Rally in Eleventh Puts Birds Back into First
1975 - July 12th - "Mad Hungarian" Gets Win on "Hwe Hlove Hrabosky" Day
1976 - May 22nd - Smith's Three Homers, Great Catch Bring Victory to Cards, 7-6

CHAPTER XIII - ON TO WHITEY BALL - 252
1977 - August 29th - Brock Steals Two Bases to Pass Cobb, Redbirds Lose, 4-3
1978 - April 16th - Forsch No-Hits Phillies, Controversy over Scoring Call
1979 - May 1st - Freed's Dramatic Grand Slam in 11th Wins Game for Cards, 7-6
1980 - May 28th - Bullpen Fails Again, Blows 5-0 Lead, as Mets Beat Cards, 6-5
1981 - September 29th - Big Crowd Sees Cards Win Final Home Game, Regain Lead

APPENDICES - 264

BIBLIOGRAPHICAL NOTE - 268

Explanation of the Box Scores

The box scores in this book are provided as an adjunct to the narrative. The figures in them are not necessarily official. In a few cases, some of the numbers are merely estimated.

Explanation of the Abbreviations:
Names: The last name of the players and umpires are preceded by the initial of their most commonly used first name or nickname. Example: "D. Dean" is Dizzy Dean.
Positions: Standard abbreviations are used for the nine fielding positions and for pinch-hitters and pinch-runners. If a player did not start the game, or he changed positions during a game, the inning he entered the game or changed positions follows the abbreviation. Example: "pr8-rf-lf12" means that a player entered the game as a pinch-runner in the eighth inning, stayed in the game to play right field, then switched to left field in the twelfth inning.
ab: at bats, as counted in the year that the game took place.
h: hits
r: runs scored
bi: runs-batted-in
o: putouts
a: assists
e: errors
ip: innings pitched. For fractional innings, ".1" equals one-third inning, and ".2" equals two-thirds. If a pitcher pitched part of an inning without retiring a batter, that fact is noted below the pitching summary.
h: hits allowed
r-er: runs allowed and earned runs allowed. Earned runs are calculated by applying modern rules.
bb: bases on balls allowed
so: batters struck out
WP: wild pitches
PB: passed balls
HBP: hit by pitch. Listed by pitcher, with the name of the batter hit in parentheses.
(W 1-0): The winning pitcher and his new record are listed
(L 0-1): The losing pitcher and his new record are listed
(sv #1): The pitcher getting official credit for a save (since 1969) and the number of saves for the season are also listed.
2B: two-base hits (doubles)
3B: three-base hits (triples)
HR: home runs
BB: bases on balls. Listed only for 1887, the only year in which walks counted as at bats and hits.
SH: sacrifices. Listed only in years in which sacrifices were officially recognized.
SF: sacrifice flies. Also listed only when they were an official statistic.
SB: stolen bases. Not available for 1882, 1884, and 1885.
CS: caught stealing. Listed only for games in which sufficient data was available.
LOB: number of runners left on base
BE: number of runners who were allowed to reach first base because of errors. Listed only when sufficient data was available.
DP: double plays. Defensive players who were involved in the play are listed in sequence, connected by hyphens.
TP: triple plays
Time, attendance, and *umpires* are also listed, when available.

In the line score, runs scored are listed by innings. The team which batted first is always listed on top. If the winning run was scored in the bottom half of the ninth inning or of an extra inning, the number of outs at the time is noted.

In cases of doubleheaders, a full box score is provided for one game, and a line score is provided for the other. To this line score, each team's final total of runs, hits, and errors are added. Also provided are listing of the batteries for each team. The pitchers are followed by the number of innings pitched, and the winning and losing pitchers, plus their records, are noted. The catchers are listed following the symbol "&".

In the "Today's Results" tables, the scores of all games involving teams in St. Louis's league or division on that day are listed. If there were games postponed ("ppd.") or cancelled, that is also noted.

In the "Standings" tables, the standings following all of the day's games are listed. *W-L* is for games won and lost thus far during the season. *Pct.* is the winning percentage. And *GB* is for games behind the first place club. In a very few cases, a team in second place (by percentage) is ahead in "games behind." In those cases, the second place club has a plus (+) before its number in the GB column.

Chapter I

Powerhouse of the American Association
1882-1891

1882—May 2nd at Sportsman's Park
Professional Baseball Returns to St. Louis, Browns Win Opening Game

1883—September 21st at Sportsman's Park
Athletics Beat St. Louis, 13-11, in Opener of Crucial Series

1884—July 29th at Cincinnati
Rookie Dave Foutz Wins Debut with Browns, Strikes Out 13

1885—July 16th at Sportsman's Park
Browns Win, 13-11, For 27th Straight Victory at Home

1885 World Series—Game #2
Browns Walk off Field, Forfeit Game to Chicago

1886—May 29th at Philadelphia
Comiskey Removes Sand from Basepaths and Browns Run Wild

1886 World Series—Game #6
Browns Are World Champions! Defeat White Stockings in Thriller

1887—May 12th at Sportsman's Park
St. Louis Browns Outslug Baltimore Orioles and Win, 22-14

1887 World Series—Games #10 & 11
Browns and Wolverines Split Two Games, Detroit Clinches Championship

1888—August 3rd at Brooklyn
Browns Retain Lead with Ten-Inning, 7-6 Victory Over Bridegrooms

1888 World Series—Game #1
Giants Edge Browns, 2-1, in Opening Game of World Series

1889—September 7th at Brooklyn
Leading 4-2, Browns Forfeit Critical Game in Brooklyn

1890—August 16th at Sportsman's Park
Browns Overcome Nine-Run Deficit, Beat Athletics, 12-11

1891—October 4th at Sportman's Park
Breitenstein Pitches No-Hitter as Browns and Colonels Split Final Games

The present St. Louis National League club originated in 1882 in the old American Association. That league was formed as a rival to the N.L. with teams in several cities that had been kicked out of the National League. St. Louis had had a team in the N.L. in 1876 and 1877, but it had dropped out after several players it had signed for 1878 were expelled for throwing games while playing for Louisville in 1877.

The American Association franchise was granted to the St. Louis Sportsman's Park and Club Association. This group held the lease on a ballpark, called Sportsman's Park, on Grand Avenue at the southwest corner of Sullivan Avenue. The president and controlling stockholder was Chris Von der Ahe, a German immigrant with little baseball knowledge. Chris owned a grocery store and saloon one block from the park.

The team, called the Browns, played its first championship game on May 2, 1882, defeating the Eclipse club of Louisville, 9-7.

In 1883, they made a run at the pennant but lost two out of three games in a crucial series against the Athletics in late September. The first game of the series, won by the Athletics 13-11, featured 28 errors and an unusual double play.

In 1884, the Browns had pitching troubles and finished fourth out of twelve. But two late-season acquisitions brought pitchers Dave Foutz and Bob Caruthers. Foutz was particularly impressive in his debut, winning, 6-5, in thirteen innings and striking out thirteen batters.

In 1885, the Browns ran away with the pennant. They also set a record, which still stands, by winning 27 consecutive home games. A World Series was arranged with the National League champions from Chicago, but the Browns walked off the field in one game, and the series eventually ended in dispute.

In 1886, the Browns again ran over the rest of the Association. Nothing could stop their aggressive base running, although the Athletics tried piling sand in the basepaths one day. The Browns got the last laugh, however, by removing the sand, running wild, and winning a doubleheader. St. Louis also got revenge against Chicago by winning a World Series rematch, 4 games to 2.

In 1887, the rules allowed for four strikes for the only time in history, and the St. Louis offense went wild. They again dominated the Association, running off an early-season winning streak of 15 games. One victory was an impressive 22-14 drubbing of the strong Baltimore team. But St. Louis played poorly in the World Series and lost to the Detroit Wolverines, five games to ten.

In 1888, St. Louis won its fourth straight pennant, although Von der Ahe had sold several stars over the winter. Captain Charlie Comiskey was able to find replacements and keep the Browns in the race. They had trouble with Brooklyn early in the season, but they turned that around, starting with a 7-6 victory in early August. St. Louis lost the World Series that fall to the New York Giants, four games to six.

In 1889, Brooklyn edged St. Louis in a hotly contested pennant race. Two forfeits in Brooklyn late in the season (one of which was later changed to a St. Louis victory) hurt the Browns.

In 1890, the Browns were unable to contend seriously for the pennant, although they won some high-scoring games. In one they trailed the Athletics by nine runs but rallied to win, 12-11. St. Louis finished the season in third place.

In 1891, St. Louis finished second. On the last day of the season, a young recruit named Ted Breitenstein was given his first major league start, and he pitched a no-hitter.

1882 — Tuesday, May 2nd, at Sportsman's Park, St. Louis
Professional Baseball Returns to St. Louis
Local Club Wins Opening Game in American Association
Browns Beat Eclipse Club of Louisville

After an absence of four years, organized professional baseball returned to St. Louis today with the inauguration of the American Association championship season. The local franchise got off to a good start by beating the Louisville franchise in the first game, 9-7.

St. Louis had its first professional team, the original Browns, in 1875, 1876, and 1877. Then it only had semi-professional outfits until 1882.

In 1881, a German-born grocer named Christian Frederick Wilhelm Von der Ahe

Today's Results
ST. LOUIS 9 - Eclipse 7
Allegheny 10 - Cincinnati 9
Athletic 10 - Baltimore 7

Standings	W-L	Pct.	GB
ST. LOUIS	1-0	1.000	-
Allegheny	1-0	1.000	-
Athletic	1-0	1.000	-
Cincinnati	0-1	.000	1
Eclipse	0-1	.000	1
Baltimore	0-1	.000	1

took over the lease to the baseball grounds on Grand Avenue at Sullivan Ave. This field had been laid out by Gus Solari in 1866 and had been the home of the first professional club. Von der Ahe formed a company, called the Sportsman's Park and Club Association, which improved, expanded, and renamed the grounds. Teams came from as far away as Brooklyn to play against local teams at Sportsman's Park.

In November, 1881, Von der Ahe and five other independent club owners got together to form a league, the American Association. In contrast to the National League's puritanical policies, the new Association authorized Sunday games and the sale of alcoholic beverages at its parks, two institutions which were quite popular in St. Louis. It also adopted a 25¢ minimum admission charge, whereas the League's minimum was 50¢.

Von der Ahe's new team was naturally called the Browns. Veteran Edgar "Ned" Cuthbert was appointed captain and manager. He signed five players from the East, but the key members of the team were St. Louis semi-pros. These included the Gleason brothers, Jack and Bill, pitcher George McGinnis, and outfielder George Seward. A St. Louis native who had been playing in the National League with Buffalo, Tom Sullivan, was also signed. Rounding out the squad was 22-year-old Charlie Comiskey, a Chicagoan who had been playing for a team in Dubuque.

After a dozen exhibition games in April, Cuthbert's squad was ready for the official opening of the season on May 2nd.

Von der Ahe was ready, too. Ever a showman, he arranged for a locally prominent band to serenade the spectators before the game, and he outfitted his men in brand-new uniforms of pure white with brown caps, stockings, and trim. The opposition, the Eclipse club of Louisville, also wore new uniforms.

The weather was beautiful, and a good crowd of about 2,000 was on hand for the game. Betting was light, however, and the visitors were the decided favorites.

By American Association rules, the home club had the choice of the umpire, and a local ballplayer, Charlie Houtz, was assigned the duty. He called the captains together to flip a coin for choice of innings, and Louisville lost. St. Louis captain Cuthbert naturally chose to bat last, and his men took the field. McGinnis occupied the four-by-six-foot pitcher's box, which park superintendent Solari had carefully laid out 50 feet from the middle of the home base. Sullivan went behind the bat wearing the peculiar equipment of his position: a mask, two tight-fitting gloves, and a chest protector. The fielders went to their stations barehanded.

Pete Browning was the first Eclipse batsman. He called for a "high ball," then he watched seven wide ones and was given first base on balls. After Dan Sullivan fouled out on a tip to catcher Tom Sullivan, Tony Mullane singled. But first baseman Comiskey put the next two batters out, one unassisted after a fine stop and one on an assist from

McGinnis.

St. Louis came to bat, and Jack Gleason started with a clean hit past second. After the next two men went out, Comiskey drove a ball to the fence in right field and circled the bases behind Gleason, thanks to some poor handling of the throw-in. So the Browns led, 2-0.

Eclipse scored its first run in the second inning on two singles, an error, and a wild pitch.

A two-base hit by McGinnis and a one-bagger by Seward, along with a fumble and a passed ball, gave St. Louis two more runs in the second.

A new ball was put into play in the third inning. The Eclipse batters could do nothing with it in the next two rounds, while St. Louis scored one run each time.

The Louisville men scored the only run of the fifth inning, but the Browns earned two runs in the sixth on four safe hits.

Each side counted once in the seventh, giving St. Louis a safe lead, 9-3.

But Louisville rallied to make the game close in the last two innings. Hits by Guy Hecker and William "Chicken" Wolf and wild pitches by McGinnis gave the visitors two runs in the eighth. D. Sullivan opened the ninth with a single, but Mullane went out. Phil Reccius hit to right field and was thrown out at first, Seward to Comiskey. Leech Maskrey kept the Eclipse hopes alive with a double, driving Sullivan home. When Hecker hit safe, the Browns let Maskrey canter home. But then Wolf lifted an easy fly to Comiskey, who made the game-ending catch.

The final score was 9-7 in favor of the home team. So the new Saint Louis Browns had won their very first championship game.

Eclipse	ab	r	h	bi	o	a	e	St. Louis	ab	r	h	bi	o	a	e
P. Browning, 3b	4	0	0	0	0	4	1	J. Gleason, 3b	4	2	2	0	0	1	1
D. Sullivan, c	5	3	2	0	2	2	2	B. Gleason, ss	5	0	1	0	1	5	1
T. Mullane, p	5	0	1	0	0	4	1	O. Walker, cf	5	2	2	0	3	0	0
P. Reccius, cf	5	0	2	1	0	0	0	C. Comiskey, 1b	5	1	2	2	12	0	0
L. Maskrey, lf	4	1	1	1	3	0	0	B. Smiley, 2b	5	0	2	2	2	2	1
G. Hecker, 1b	5	1	4	1	15	0	0	T. Sullivan, c	4	0	1	0	8	1	1
C. Wolf, rf	5	2	2	0	1	0	0	N. Cuthbert, lf	4	2	1	0	1	0	1
G. Pearce, 2b	4	0	1	0	3	4	1	G. McGinnis, p	4	1	2	2	0	9	1
D. Mack, ss	4	0	0	0	0	4	0	G. Seward, rf	3	1	0	0	0	1	1
	41	7	13	3	24	18	5		39	9	13	6	27	19	7

Eclipse   010 010 122 - 7
St. Louis   221 102 10x - 9

	ip	h	r-er	bb	so
Mullane (L 0-1)	8	13	9-5	2	2
McGinnis (W 1-0)	9	13	7-5	2	6

WP: McGinnis 6, Mullane 3.
PB: T. Sullivan 2, D. Sullivan 2.

LOB: Eclp 9, StL 5.
DP: T. Sullivan-J. Gleason-Smiley, B. Geason-Comiskey
2B: McGinnis 2, Walker, Cuthbert, Maskrey.
3B: Comiskey, T. Sullivan
Time - 2:10   Attendance - 2,000
Umpire: C. Houtz

The American Association's first season was a big success, although the practice of having the home team choose the umpire was abandoned in mid-season, and the Association hired full-time arbiters.

The Browns finished fifth in the six-team standings, but they did very well financially, drawing about 175,000 customers.

1883 — Friday, September 21st, at Sportsman's Park

Athletics Defeat St. Louis in Opening Game of Crucial Series

Overflow Crowd Sees Browns Lose, 13-11

Errors and Tension Throughout the Wild Contest

Today in St. Louis, the Athletics of Philadelphia, leaders in the American Association, opened a crucial three-game series against the second-place St. Louis Browns. The local team was hoping for a sweep of the series, which would have put them into first place, but the visitors won the opening game by a 13-11 score. The game was hardly an artistic masterpiece, with errors outnumbering hits, but it was filled with action and excitement.

With less than two weeks to go in the pennant race, the Athletics arrived in town leading the Browns by 2½ games. The decisive nature of the series drew an immense weekday crowd of nearly 10,000 people to Sportsman's Park. Grand Avenue was clogged with vehicles transporting spectators, and the park's facilities for parking carriages were overtaxed. The seating capacity was likewise surpassed, and some of the customers had to stand along the edges of the grandstand. The most distinguished onlooker was Governor Thomas T. Crittenden. He occupied the club directors' box along with club president Chris Von der Ahe, Congressman John J. O'Neill, and other notables.

Today's Results
Athletic 13 - ST. LOUIS 11
Cincinnati 10 - Baltimore 2
Allegheny 7 - Eclipse 5 (10 inn.)
Metropolitan 6 - Columbus 1

Standings	W-L	Pct.	GB
Athletic	64-28	.696	-
ST. LOUIS	61-32	.656	3½
Cincinnati	59-35	.638	6
Metropolitan	50-41	.549	13½
Eclipse	47-44	.516	16½
Allegheny	31-62	.333	33½
Columbus	31-62	.333	33½
Baltimore	27-66	.290	37½

The tension of the day was reflected in the shoddy play on the field. Twenty-eight errors were made. Arlie Latham was the leading culprit for St. Louis, making five miscues. Philadelphia catcher Ed Rowan led all players, committing eight errors in his attempts to curb the Browns' base running.

Rowan and Bobby Mathews formed the battery for the Athletics, while Tony Mullane and Tom Deasley occupied the points for St. Louis.

Play was called at 3:13 p.m., and the home team won the toss. St. Louis captain Charlie Comiskey sent the visitors to bat first. Jud Birchal opened with a shot off shortstop Bill Gleason's shins for a single. Harry Stovey followed with a clean hit over third. Alonzo Knight forced Stovey at second. Mike Moynahan hit to short, and Gleason threw wildly home, allowing Birchal to score the game's first run.

Then came one of the most unusual plays ever witnessed. In it the Browns made three errors, yet still pulled off a double play. With runners on first and second, Jack O'Brien hit sharply to Gleason, who fielded cleanly and tossed to Joe Quest in an attempt to force Moynahan at second. Quest, however, muffed the throw. As the ball trickled away, Knight rounded third and raced for home. Quest recovered the ball and made a good throw to catcher Deasley, who tagged Knight out. Meanwhile, Moynahan broke for third, and he reached that base safely when Deasley's throw went wild and got past third baseman Latham. Seeing this error, O'Brien lit out from first toward second. Gleason, who had been backing up third, got the ball and threw it to Quest to head O'Brien off. Once again, Quest muffed the throw, and once again a runner (Moynahan this time) tried to score from third on his error. And, once again, Quest shot the ball to Deasley in time for a putout at home. The tumultuous crowd fell silent for a moment, then, realizing that the play had resulted in two outs and no runs, it split the air with exultant shouts.

Neither team scored again until the third inning, when the Athletics got four runs. They only made two clean hits, but Latham committed three errors, and Deasley made one.

An additional run in the fourth gave the Philadelphians a 6-0 lead.

St. Louis cut the deficit in half with three runs in their fourth at bats. Hard hits past the second baseman by Hugh Nicol and Fred Lewis and Nicol's fine base running gave the Browns their first run. About this time, first baseman Stovey sprained his ankle chasing a foul fly, and the Browns allowed the Athletics to put George Bradley in as a substitute. The new man muffed the first ball that came to him, and two runs scored.

Both sides picked up three tallies in the fifth. Errors did most of the work, although Lewis hit a two-run home run over the right field fence for St. Louis.

The Browns got two more runs in the seventh, despite a bad call by umpire Charles Daniels. The visitors' lead was cut to 9-8.

But the Athletics scored four times in the eighth. Three hits, two errors, one wild pitch, and three passed balls did the trick. Catcher Deasley's hands were very sore from handling Mullane's cannon shots, and Latham tried his luck behind the plate.

The Browns came back with three runs in the bottom of the eighth on two hits, two stolen bases, and three errors. Two of the errors were muffs by Bradley at first, and he was finally moved out to center field.

The weather had turned dark and threatening, and ump Daniels called the game after the third out. But the Browns rushed out and talked him into allowing the contest to continue.

In the ninth, the Athletics allowed Deasley to leave the game, and Tom Dolan came in to catch. The visitors were retired in order.

St. Louis came in for their last chance needing two runs to tie. George Strief started out with a fly that Knight muffed amidst the swirling dust. Although it was Dolan's turn to bat, no one seemed to realize it, and Mullane went up instead. Tony popped out to shortstop. Gleason then came up and hit a terrific drive to deep center field. It looked like a game-tying home run, but Bradley redeemed himself for his earlier errors by making a desperate run and an over-the-shoulder catch. Comiskey then grounded out to end the game.

The Athletics won by a 13-11 score. The level of play was poor, and the outcome of the game was a disappointment to the St. Louis fans. But they got their money's worth today.

Athletic	ab	r	h	bi	o	a	e
J. Birchal, lf	6	3	3	1	4	0	0
H. Stovey, 1b	3	1	2	0	5	1	0
G. Bradley, 1b4-cf8	3	0	0	0	3	0	4
A. Knight, rf	5	2	1	0	2	0	1
M. Moynahan, ss	5	3	0	0	2	2	2
J. O'Brien, cf-1b8	5	2	3	2	2	0	0
F. Corey, 3b	5	0	1	2	2	1	1
F. Rowan, c	4	1	0	0	3	2	8
C. Stricker, 2b	5	1	1	0	4	1	0
B. Mathews, p	5	0	1	0	0	5	0
	46	13	12	5	27	12	16

St. Louis	ab	r	h	bi	o	a	e
B. Gleason, ss	6	1	3	0	0	4	2
C. Comiskey, 1b	6	2	2	0	10	0	1
A. Latham, 3b-c8-3b9	5	0	0	1	1	3	5
H. Nicol, rf	5	3	3	2	4	0	1
F. Lewis, cf	4	3	2	2	3	0	0
J. Quest, 2b	5	1	1	1	1	1	2
G. Strief, lf	5	0	1	1	0	0	0
T. Deasley, c-3b8	4	1	0	0	7	3	1
T. Dolan, c9	0	0	0	0	1	0	0
T. Mullane, p	5	0	0	0	0	5	0
	45	11	12	7	27	16	12

Athletic   104 130 040 - 13
St. Louis   000 330 230 - 11

	ip	h	r-er	bb	so
Mathews (W 30-12)	9	11	11-4	2	2
Mullane (L 34-14)	9	13	13-1	1	7

WP: Mullane 3.
PB: Rowen 3, Deasley, 2, Latham.
Umpire: C. Daniels.

LOB: Athl 7, StL 8. BE: Athl 10, StL 8. DP: Gleason-Quest-Deasley-Gleason-Quest-Deasley.
2B: Strief, Stovey, Birchal, O'Brien 2, Nicol. 3B: Quest
HR: Lewis
SB: Gleason 2, Nicol 3.
CS: Nicol, Stricker, Quest.
Time - 2:45. Attendance - 10,000.

St. Louis won the next game, 9-8, but the Athletics won the final game of the series, 9-2, thereby clinching at least a tie for the pennant. The season ended with the Browns just one game behind. The close pennant race was a tremendous boon to attendance, the Browns drawing almost 300,000 spectators.

1884 — Tuesday, July 29th, at the Western Avenue Park, Cincinnati

Rookie Dave Foutz Wins Debut with Browns, Strikes Out 13

St. Louis Beats Cincinnati, 6-5, in 13 Innings

Latham's Base Running Through the Mud Wins for Visitors

Today the St. Louis club tried its new, high-priced pitcher, Dave Foutz, and he exceeded even the most optimistic expectations by pitching the Browns to a thirteen-inning victory over the Cincinnati Reds. The triumph moved St. Louis back ahead of Cincinnati and into fourth place on the American Association list.

The Reds were utterly baffled by Foutz's serves, and 13 of their batters could do no better than fan the breeze. That they were able to score five runs was largely due to the abominable condition of the playing field. Heavy rains had turned the park into a quagmire, making handling of the ball difficult. The only positive features of the game, aside from Foutz's pitching, were Arlie Latham's base running, Fred Lewis's hitting, and Charley Snyder's throwing to the bases.

Today's Results
ST. LOUIS 6 - Cincinnati 5 (13 inn.)
Metropolitan 6 - Brooklyn 1
Columbus 3 - Toledo 1
Louisville 2 - Indianapolis 1 (10)
Washington at Athletic - ppd., rain
Baltimore at Allegheny - ppd., rain

Standings	W-L	Pct.	GB
Metropolitan	46-18	.719	
Columbus	41-19	.683	3
Louisville	41-20	.672	3½
ST. LOUIS	40-20	.667	4
Cincinnati	40-21	.656	4½
Athletic	35-28	.556	10½
Baltimore	29-27	.518	13
Brooklyn	24-37	.393	20½
Toledo	21-40	.344	23½
Allegheny	20-43	.317	25½
Indianapolis	16-43	.271	27½
Washington	11-48	.186	32½

Cincinnati announced that they were formally protesting the game on the grounds that the required ten days had not elapsed since the official notification of Foutz's release by the Bay City club of the Northwestern League. St. Louis manager Jimmy Williams, however, seemed assured that the required time had passed, even if the A.A. secretary had been tardy in notifying the other clubs.

A Maryland native and resident, Foutz first made a name for himself as a pitcher in Leadville, Colorado, where he had gone to try his hand at mining gold. Pitching for Bay City this season, he had won 17 of 21 games. When the club's owners decided to fold, they put their players on the market. The bidding for Foutz, their prize jewel, was brisk, but St. Louis president Chris Von der Ahe came out the winner. The price of $2000 far exceeded any price previously paid for the release of a ballplayer. Von der Ahe was also rumored to have given Foutz a contract calling for a salary of $1600 for the twelve weeks remaining in the season! This was also unprecedented for an untried minor leaguer.

With only 165 pounds hanging on his 6 foot, 2 inch frame, Foutz's appearance caused sarcastic comments by the Cincinnati cranks. But he appeared cool and collected in the pitcher's box. Using a curious combination of speed and curves, he kept the Reds' hitters constantly off balance. This headwork elicited admiration from veteran observers of the game.

His pitching opponent, the bespectacled veteran Will White, also pitched effectively, but nine errors by the Reds undermined his efforts.

St. Louis, for its part, would have won the game in nine innings had not catcher Tom Deasley dropped a third strike, which allowed the tying run to score.

Threatening weather limited the crowd to 2,400 persons. The field was covered with standing water, but, luckily, it did not rain any more. The ball was slippery throughout the game, and the fielders had difficulty both catching it and throwing it.

St. Louis won the toss and took the field.

After two scoreless innings, the Browns counted the first run of the game in the third. Latham hit a bounder to White, which the Cincinnati pitcher fumbled. Arlie quickly stole second. Lewis then got a clean hit, and Latham scored on a wonderful and daring dash through the slop.

Cincinnati tied the game in the fifth. Tom Mansell was hit by a pitch and given first. A passed ball gave him second, and Snyder's good hit brought him home.

The Reds took the lead briefly with a run in the sixth. A double by Hick Carpenter and a single by Charlie Jones were responsible.

St. Louis came to bat and regained the advantage with two runs. Latham once again started the rally, this time with a one-base hit. Lewis then slugged the ball to right field for a triple and a run. Charlie Comiskey's single drove Lewis across.

Poor fielding by the Browns allowed Cincinnati to tie in the eighth. With one gone, Bid McPhee beat a ball into the mud for a safe hit. He stole for second and wound up on third thanks to Deasley's wild throw. Carpenter followed with a slow bounder, which shortstop Bill Gleason fumbled, losing all chance to retire McPhee at home.

But the Browns once again took the lead with two in their eighth at bats. Lewis was hit by an inside curve from White and went down to first. He moved up on Comiskey's clean single. Both men scored when little Hugh Nicol soaked one to left field for three bases.

Needing two runs to tie, Cincinnati came to bat in the ninth. With one out, Mansell knocked a triple to right field. John Corkhill struck a single, cutting the deficit to one run. Corkhill then took a chance and stole second base. Emboldened, he then tried for third and reached safely when Deasley had trouble throwing the wet ball. Snyder then struck out, but Deasley dropped the third strike and had to throw to first for the out. Corkhill boldly broke for home on the throw and crossed the plate with the tying run.

Foutz and White turned their opposition back for the next three rounds, and Foutz set the Reds down in the thirteenth.

With the contest approaching the three hour mark, and with darkness falling, the end came quickly in the bottom of the thirteenth. Latham, the first man up, hit down to Carpenter and reached base on the third baseman's fumble. Lewis's hit sent him to second, and he sprinted home on Comiskey's safe hit, ending the game.

The final score was 6-5, and the Brown's rookie pitcher Dave Foutz was the hero.

Cincinnati	ab	r	h	bi	o	a	e	St. Louis	ab	r	h	bi	o	a	e
B. McPhee, 2b	6	1	1	0	5	1	2	B. Gleason, ss	6	0	1	0	0	4	1
H. Carpenter, 3b	6	1	2	0	4	4	1	A. Latham, 3b	6	3	1	0	1	3	2
C. Jones, lf	6	0	2	1	1	1	1	F. Lewis, cf	5	2	3	2	2	0	0
J. Reilly, 1b	6	0	0	0	10	0	0	C. Comiskey, 1b	6	1	3	2	14	2	0
T. Mansell, cf	5	2	2	0	4	1	1	H. Nicol, rf	5	0	2	2	2	0	0
J. Corkhill, rf	6	1	1	1	5	0	0	T. O'Neill, lf	5	0	2	0	1	0	0
C. Snyder, c	5	0	2	1	5	5	2	D. Foutz, p	5	0	1	0	1	4	0
J. Peoples, ss	5	0	0	0	2	4	1	T. Deasley, c	5	0	0	0	16	2	2
W. White, p	5	0	0	0	0	0	1	J. Quest, 2b	5	0	1	0	2	1	0
	50	5	10	3	36	16	9		48	6	14	6	39	16	5

Cincinnati   000 011 012 000 0 - 5
St. Louis   001 002 020 000 1 - 6
none out when winning run scored

	ip	h	r-er	bb	so
White (L 22-12)	*12	14	6-4	0	0
Foutz (W 1-0)	13	10	5-2	0	13

*faced three batters in thirteenth
WP: Foutz. PB: Snyder.

LOB: Cinc 7, StL 7.
BE: Cinc 4, StL 5.
2B: Carpenter.
3B: Snyder, Lewis, Nicol, Mansell.
HBP: by Foutz (Mansell),
   by White (Lewis).
Time - 3:00
Attendance - 2,400
Umpire: J. Lawler.

In his first 20 days with the Browns, Foutz pitched ten games and won eight of them, keeping St. Louis in the pennant race. Then he was laid up with a fever for three weeks. The pitching staff collapsed, killing the team's pennant chances.

The Browns finished fourth, 8 games behind the pennant-winning Mets.

1885 — Thursday, July 16th, at Sportsman's Park

St. Louis Outlast Athletics, 13-11, for 27th Consecutive Home Victory

Foutz Relieves McGinnis in Pitcher's Box

Two Runs in Ninth Inning Win Game for Browns

The St. Louis Browns won again today, 13-11, beating the Athletics of Philadelphia and stretching their current winning streak to 12 games. All of these victories came at Sportsman's Park, where the home team hasn't lost since April 25th. Since that date, the Browns have won 27 consecutive home games.

That represents a new record for consecutive championship games won at home. In 1875, the Boston Red Stockings won all 34 National Association games played in Boston, but eight of those games did not count in the official final standings. Earlier this season the Browns set an American Association record for consecutive games won, home and away, with a 17-game streak.

Today's Results
ST. LOUIS 13 - Athletic 11
Mets 7 - Cincinnati 5
Louisville 9 - Brooklyn 6
Pittsburg 12 - Baltimore 1

Standings	W-L	Pct.	GB
ST. LOUIS	47-17	.734	-
Cincinnati	38-27	.585	9½
Louisville	36-28	.563	11
Pittsburg	36-28	.563	11
Athletic	27-36	.429	19½
Baltimore	24-38	.387	22
Brooklyn	23-38	.377	22½
Metropolitan	21-40	.344	24½

Today, "Jumbo" George McGinnis was given a chance to pitch for St. Louis. With Dave Foutz and Bob Caruthers pitching great ball for the Browns, McGinnis had pitched just five times previously this season. Long Bob Emslie started in the box for the visiting Athletics. Last month's rules change, which allowed pitchers to throw the ball overhand, didn't appear to help either man much. Neither was pitching at the end of the game, Foutz and John Coleman having been brought into the box from their positions in the outfield.

Not only were there two pitching changes, two substitutions were made from the benches, one for each team. As required by the rules, these changes were made only because two players complained of illness and could not continue.

Exercising the home team's new prerogative, Capt. Comiskey chose to bat his team first. Emslie was wild at the start, walking the first two men, but then Charlie Comiskey hit into a double play, and Yank Robinson grounded out.

In the Athletics' half of the first, Harry Stovey scored a run. He was to score five times before the game was over. This first time he walked on seven called balls, stole second, went to third on an infield out, and counted on a hit by Coleman.

The Browns scored nine runs in the second inning. They laid into Emslie's delivery for seven hits and a base on balls before the first out. With the score 6-1 and two men on base, Coleman changed positions with Emslie. Robinson was retired, but Sam Barkley, batting for the second time in the inning, singled again. Curt Welch followed with a double, and Barkley moved to third. Owing to sudden illness, he could go no further. Robinson was sent in as a pinch-runner, and he quickly scored on a passed ball. The run was credited to Barkley in the box score. The next two batters went out, leaving Welch on third, but the Browns led, 9-1.

In the last of the second, the Athletics fought back with four runs, aided by some key errors. Sadie Houck started with a single. Jack O'Brien then lifted a fly to center, which Welch dropped. It was the first muff of a fly by the Browns' star outfielder all season. A fly out advanced Houck to third. Emslie hit down to Comiskey, who stepped on first and threw home. Catcher Dan Sullivan dropped the ball, and Houck scored. Three safe hits and a muff by Arlie Latham allowed three more runs to score.

Latham made the circuit for the Browns in the third. He reached first on an error by Cub Stricker, stole second, and scored on a hit by Comiskey.

Foutz, who had taken Barkley's spot in the lineup, scored in the fourth on a double and another error by Stricker.

The Philadelphians scored two in their half of the fourth. After the first two men went out, Stovey doubled and came around on a passed ball an a wild pitch. Harry Larkin then singled to left. Coleman lifted a pop fly behind second base that bounced out of Gleason's hands and rolled past Welch, allowing Larkin to come all the way home from first.

Stovey again doubled and scored in the sixth.

The Athletics' uphill struggle finally reached its summit in the seventh inning, when they scored three time to tie the game, 11-11. O'Brien opened the frame with a single. He moved to third on battery errors. Stricker walked and stole second without a throw. Frank Siffel struck out. Blondie Purcell hit a long fly to center, O'Brien scoring after the ball was caught. Stovey then strode to the plate. In his four previous trips, he had walked once and doubled thrice, so the St. Louis cranks gave him a warm ovation. Harry proceeded to foul pitches far down the left field line. Finally, he hit one fair into the farthest corner of the park and circle the bases with a game-tying home run. McGinnis gave up one more hit, but no more runs.

Foutz took over the pitching duties for St. Louis in the eighth, McGinnis moving to left field. In contrast to his balloon-bellied predecessor, "His Needles" (as Foutz was called) held the Athletics hitless.

The Browns broke the tie with two runs in the ninth. With one out, Welch worked a walk. He went to second on Hugh Nicol's single, then made a fine steal of third. McGinnis lifted a fly to left, and Welch was safe at home when O'Brien muffed Purcell's throw. Nicol, having moved up to third on the steal and the fly out, came home on Sullivan's hit, making the score 13-11.

With Stovey due up fourth in the bottom of the ninth, Foutz disposed of the Athletics in one-two-three fashion to end the game.

St. Louis	ab	r	h	bi	o	a	e
A. Latham, 3b	5	2	2	2	3	3	1
B. Gleason, ss	4	1	1	2	2	1	1
C. Comiskey, 1b	5	1	3	1	15	1	0
Y. Robinson, lf-2b3	5	0	1	0	0	6	0
S. Barkley, 2b	2	2	2	1	0	0	0
D. Foutz, lf3-p8	3	1	1	0	1	1	1
C. Welch, cf	3	2	1	1	2	0	1
H. Nicol, rf	5	2	2	0	0	0	0
G. McGinnis, p-lf8	5	1	2	1	0	5	0
D. Sullivan, c	5	1	2	2	5	2	1
	42	13	17	10	27	19	5

Athletics	ab	r	h	bi	o	a	e
B. Purcell, lf	6	1	1	2	1	0	0
H. Stovey, 1b	4	5	4	2	15	1	0
H. Larkin, cf	5	1	3	0	3	2	0
J. Coleman, rf-p2	5	0	1	1	1	2	0
F. Corey, 3b	5	0	1	1	0	2	0
S. Houck, ss	5	1	1	0	2	4	0
J. O'Brien, c	5	2	2	0	2	2	2
C. Stricker, 2b	4	1	1	0	3	5	2
B. Emslie, p-rf2	1	0	0	0	0	0	0
F. Siffel, rf3	4	0	0	0	0	0	0
	44	11	14	6	27	18	4

St. Louis   091 100 002 - 13
Atheltics   140 201 300 - 11

	ip	h	r-er	bb	so
McGinnis	7	14	11-7	2	4
Foutz (W 20-8)	2	0	0-0	0	1
Emslie (L 3-14)	*1	7	8-8	3	0
Coleman	8	10	5-1	0	1

*faced eight batters in second
WP: McGinnis 2, Coleman. PB: Sullivan. 2.

LOB: StL 6, Athl 8.
BE: StL 4, Athl 5.
DP: Stricker-Stovey.
2B: Latham, Gleason, Welch, Stovey 3, Foutz.
HR: Stovey
Time - 2:30
Attendance - 2,000
Umpire: J. Connelly

The Athletics stopped the Browns' streak in the next game, but St. Louis made a complete runaway of the American Association race and won their first pennant. They finished the 112-game schedule with a 79-33 record, 16 games better than the second-place Reds.

Their .705 final percentage and their early-season 17-game winning streak still stand as franchise records. And their 27 consecutive home victories still stands as the all-time major league record.

1885 World Series—Game #2

Thursday, October 15th, at Sportsman's Park

Browns Walk Off Field, Forfeit Game to Chicago

Fans Threaten Umpire, Forcing His Hasty Exit

Disagreement on Fair or Foul Ball is the Last Straw for Comiskey

The second game in the series for the championship of the world between the champions of the two major baseball leagues ended in a serious row. The American Association St. Louis team forfeited the contest to the National League champions from Chicago. Umpire Dave Sullivan's decisions were very poor throughout much of the game. In the sixth inning, they finally became too much for the Browns' captain, Charlie Comiskey, who pulled his team off the field. The crowd overran the playing area and made threatening movements toward Sullivan. The arbiter had to be hustled away from the grounds. At his hotel, Sullivan declared the game forfeited to Chicago, 9-0.

The series had started the previous day in Chicago with a 5-5 tie. Sullivan was the umpire there, too, and had been satisfactory enough for the Browns to request him to come to St. Louis for today's contest. In the first inning, he gave a bad decision against Chicago, but thereafter it seemed that St. Louis was being penalized by all of his mistakes.

Neither team presented its strongest nine. The Chicago White Stockings were without center fielder George Gore, who had been suspended for imbibing too freely in spirits, and catcher Frank "Silver" Flint, who sat out with sore hands. As a result, Mike Kelly was behind the bat and substitute Billy Sunday and pitcher John Clarkson were in the outfield for the Whites. St. Louis catcher "Doc" Bushong was also out due to a hand injury, and Yank Robinson took his place.

Chicago was sent to bat first, and they scored a quick run. Sunday got a safe hit and went to second on a passed ball. Kelly singled to center, and the speedy Sunday scored. Kelly then stole second, or so it appeared, but he was called out by Sullivan.

The Browns scored three runs with some daring base running in their turn at bat. Bill Gleason hit a fly ball to right, which Clarkson misplayed into a double. Curt Welch then sent an easy grounder to Ned Williamson at third, and the big fielder fumbled it. The runners moved up a base on an infield out. Comiskey followed with a hot hit to second baseman Fred Pfeffer, who threw home too late to head off Gleason. Comiskey boldly headed for second, and Kelly's throw got away from Pfeffer, so Welch broke for home. Pfeffer's return throw was wild, Welch scoring and Comiskey reaching third. The St. Louis captain scored the third run on a passed ball.

Chicago got one run in the second on Pfeffer's two-base hit, a ground out, and a muff by Hugh Nicol.

In the St. Louis second, Dave Foutz hit a ball about a foot fair along the right field line and reached second on Clarkson's fumble of the hit. But Sullivan ruled the ball was a foul, and the cranks in the stands let out a ferocious howl. Foutz then struck out.

In the St. Louis third, Sam Barkley was called out on a pitch that many thought was over his head. The cries of "Get a new umpire" were repeated.

St. Louis managed to add another run in the fourth, using an error and Arlie Latham's double.

The fifth inning passed without incident.

Not so the sixth. Sunday opened for Chicago with a two-base hit over Nicol's head. He moved to third on a passed ball. Kelly then hit a bouncer to Gleason. Billy had a chance for an out at home, but he fumbled the ball. He recovered in time to throw the batter out at first by about ten feet. But Sullivan, who was facing home in anticipation of a play there, called Kelly safe at first.

Everyone, including the runner, was taken by surprise by the ruling. The Browns rushed around Sullivan and argued the decision. Chicago captain Adrian Anson and St. Louis club vice-president John J. O'Neill (a member of the federal congress) also joined the discussion. For ten minutes Comiskey fumed and threatened, while Sullivan kept ordering the Browns back to their positions. Finally he gave them a two-minute deadline and pulled out his watch. This finally produced the desired effect, and the game resumed.

Kelly quickly stole second on a wild pitch and took third on a passed ball. Anson cracked a clean hit to center, and Kelly scored the tying run. Pfeffer forced Anson, then stole second.

The batter, Williamson, kept fouling pitches off. Then came the fateful hit. Ned squibbed yet another roller down the first base line, a foot or so foul. Someone (Anson as it turned out) even called out, "Foul." But as the ball neared first base, it hit a clump of grass and kicked back into fair territory. Sullivan called the ball fair, and Comiskey, taken by surprise, was unable to corral the horsehide before Williamson had sprinted across the base. Meanwhile, Pfeffer raced home with the lead run.

This turn of events was too much for the Browns' leader. He rushed Sullivan and accused him of reversing his foul ball call. Sullivan denied having called the ball foul. Comiskey then declared that by American Association rules, the ball was foul anyway. The game was being played under A.A. rules, although Sullivan had been an N.L. umpire during the season. Sullivan seemed ready to accept Commy's claim, but Anson demanded to see a rule book confirming the rule. Comiskey, who had been bluffing on this point, refused to produce a book, and Sullivan ordered Williamson to first base.

Commy then ordered his men to the bench and refused to play. A large number of spectators jumped onto the field, and they looked as though they intended to mob the umpire and the Chicagos. The visiting players grabbed bats and held the crowd at bay, so attention was turned to Sullivan. But park superintendent Gus Solari and a burly guard hurried the umpire to a nearby carriage and out of the park.

Chicago (NL)	ab	r	h	bi	o	a	e
A. Dalrymple, lf	3	0	0	0	3	0	0
B. Sunday, cf	3	2	3	0	0	0	0
M. Kelly, c	3	1	1	2	4	2	1
A. Anson, 1b	3	0	1	1	7	0	0
F. Pfeffer, 2b	3	2	1	0	0	2	2
N. Williamson, 3b	2	0	0	0	0	4	1
T. Burns, ss	2	0	0	0	0	1	1
J. McCormick, p	2	0	0	0	1	6	0
J. Clarkson, rf	2	0	0	0	0	0	0
	23	5	6	3	15	15	5

St. Louis (AA)	ab	r	h	bi	o	a	e
B. Gleason, ss	3	1	1	0	1	2	1
C. Welch, cf	3	1	0	0	1	0	0
S. Barkley, 2b	2	0	0	0	3	3	0
C. Comiskey, 1b	2	1	0	1	7	0	1
Y. Robinson, c	2	0	0	0	4	1	0
T. O'Neill, lf	2	1	0	0	0	0	0
A. Latham, 3b	2	0	1	1	0	1	0
D Foutz, p	2	0	0	0	0	2	1
H. Nicol rf	2	0	0	0	0	1	1
	20	4	2	2	16	10	4

Chicago   110 003 - 9
St. Louis   300 10x - 0
game forfeited to Chicago with one out in the top of the sixth

	ip	h	r-er	bb	so
McCormick	5	2	4-1	0	3
Foutz	5.1	6	5-2	1	2

WP: Foutz. PB: Robinson 3, Kelly

LOB: Chi 3, StL 1.
BE: Chi 3, StL 2.
DP: Gleason-Barkley-Comiskey.
2B: Gleason, Pfeffer, Latham, Sunday.
SB: Robinson, Pfeffer, CS: Kelly
Time - 1:00
Attendance - 2,500
Umpire: D. Sullivan

The series, originally scheduled for twelve games, was called off after just seven.

The first game was a tie and the second was the forfeit. The Browns won the next two games, but the Whites came back to win the fifth and sixth games.

Since the games were not drawing well, it was announced that the seventh game would be the last and decisive game, with the forfeit not counted. The Browns won the game, 13-4, and claimed the title of World Champions. But the Chicago management claimed that the series was a tie, and the general public agreed with them.

1886 — Saturday, May 29th, at Athletic Park, Philadelphia

Comiskey Removes Sand from Basepaths and Browns Run Wild

St. Louis Wins Two Games, 18-1 & 11-3

Browns' Captain Foils Attempt to Slow His Runners Down

The American Association rivals of the St. Louis Browns have searched desperately for some way to stop the high-flying champions. Several rival owners have proposed suspending Captain Charlie Comiskey for not paying the many fines imposed upon him by the umpires. An Association meeting for that purpose was already scheduled.

Today in Philadelphia, the Athletics, hoping to retain a slim .001 percentage point lead over St. Louis, tried a new method of curtailing the wild base-running tactics of Comiskey's men. When the Browns arrived at the Athletics' grounds for this morning's game, they found sand about a foot thick piled up next to first base. Another pile surrounded second base.

Today's Results
ST. LOUIS 18 - Athletics 1 (morning)
ST. LOUIS 11 - Athletics 3 (afternoon)
Pittsburg 16 - Baltimore 5 (morning)
Pittsburg 4 - Baltimore 0 (afternoon)
Brooklyn 4 - Louisville 0
Mets 11 - Cincinnati 6

Standings	W-L	Pct.	GB
ST. LOUIS	22-13	.629	-
Athletic	17-13	.567	2½
Pittsburg	19-15	.559	2½
Brooklyn	15-12	.556	3
Baltimore	14-16	.467	5½
Louisville	15-18	.455	6
Cincinnati	14-20	.412	7½
Metropolitan	9-18	.333	9

Seeing this, Comiskey informed the Athletics' captain, Harry Stovey, that his team would not play unless the sand was cleared away. Stovey and his team (especially catcher Jack O'Brien) were reluctant to do so, since they had ordered the sand put down to stop the Browns from stealing bases. Finally, umpire George H. Bradley was consulted. Comiskey firmly informed the arbiter that his team would not play on the field if it remained in its present condition. So Bradley ordered Stovey to have the sand removed. Not wishing to lose the gate money already taken from the large crowd, Stovey consented.

Groundskeeper John Ryan came out with a wheelbarrow and some shovels. After he had hauled one load away from first base, Comiskey was still dissatisfied, and he told Ryan to bring back a bigger cart. A couple of the Athletics' players began half-heartedly throwing sand into the cart, but Comiskey grabbed a shovel and worked into the pile with vigor. Harry Larkin of the A's moved to stop him, but the Brown's Arlie Latham grabbed another shovel and went to work, while the other Browns commenced removing sand with their hands, so the Athletics had to acquiesce. Comiskey and his men finished the job to their liking, although they left the sand around second base.

The game finally got under way about 15 minutes later than originally scheduled. Bob Caruthers and Doc Bushong formed the St. Louis battery, with Sam Weaver and O'Brien working for the Athletics. Caruthers had the home team completely under control, while Weaver was battered for 12 hits before being replaced in the fourth inning. Catcher O'Brien was also relieved at that time, having been largely unable to stop the Browns from stealing.

During the game, St. Louis made 22 hits, stole nine bases cleanly, got three more on passed balls, and three more on wild pitches. They might have stolen even more, except that they didn't care to run during the last half of the game.

After the home team had batted and failed to score, the Browns scored once in the opening inning. Latham walked and took second on a passed ball. But he was thrown out trying to steal third. Then Bill Gleason singled and came around on three infield errors.

Brother Jack Gleason tripled for the Athletics with one out in the second, but his teammates could not drive him home.

Then St. Louis came to bat and scored seven runs. Triples by Caruthers and Curt Welch, singles by Latham, Gleason, Tip O'Neill, and Dave Foutz, an error, and assorted stolen bases all contributed to the rally.

After failing to score in the third, the Browns scored seven runs again in the fourth. A triple by Comiskey, single by Welch, and double by Foutz routed Weaver. Stovey and Lou Beirbauer came in to form a new battery. After two more hits were made off Stovey, John Coleman took over the pitching duties.

Three more runs were made off Coleman in the fifth, but thereafter the Browns were content to make outs.

The only run for the Athletics came in the ninth inning, thanks to two errors by the Browns. The final score was 18-1.

An immense crowd of over 12,000 turned out for the afternoon game. The spectators completely filled the stands, and several thousand had to stand behind the rope that was stretched across the outfield.

As had been the case in the morning game, the Browns outplayed the home team completely, although the second game was not quite so one-sided. The fine throwing of Athletic catcher Wilbert Robinson held the Browns down to five stolen bases.

Veteran Bobby Mathews pitched for the Philadelphians. He was poorly supported by his mates and was constantly in disagreement with the umpire. As a result, his pitching got worse as the game wore on.

Rookie Nat Hudson was in the box for St. Louis, and he pitched a splendid game. His "drop ball" was very effective, and the Athletics stupidly persisted in calling for low balls, which they kept beating into the ground.

The Athletics scored their three runs in the first two innings. They made only one safe hit, but errors by the Browns enabled them to score.

St. Louis scored two in the first and two in the third, with bases on balls contributing heavily. During the rest of the game, they hit Mathews's delivery hard. The final score was 11-3.

MORNING GAME

Athletics	ab	r	h	bi	o	a	e	St. Louis	ab	r	h	bi	o	a	e
H. Stovey, 1b-p4-rf4	4	0	0	0	2	0	1	A. Latham, 3b	5	2	4	2	2	0	0
H. Larkin, lf	3	0	0	0	6	0	1	B. Gleason, ss	6	2	2	0	2	0	0
J. O'Brien, c-2b4	4	1	1	0	3	3	1	T. O'Neill, lf	6	1	3	2	3	0	0
G. Shaffer, cf	4	0	2	0	2	1	2	C. Comiskey, 1b	6	2	1	0	6	0	1
J. Coleman, rf-p4	4	0	0	1	3	0		C. Welch, cf	6	2	3	3	2	0	0
J. Gleason, 3b	3	0	2	0	1	0	0	D. Foutz, rf	6	3	4	1	2	0	0
L. Bierbauer, 2b-c4	4	0	0	3	1	4		Y. Robinson, 2b	3	2	0	0	3	8	0
J. Quest, ss	3	0	0	0	0	2	3	B. Caruthers, p	5	3	5	3	0	7	0
S. Weaver, p-1b4	3	0	0	0	6	0	0	D. Bushong, c	5	1	1	1	7	0	1
	32	1	5	0	24	10	12		48	18	23	12	27	15	2

Athletics	000 000 001	-	1	
St. Louis	170 730 00x	-	18	

	ip	h	r-er	bb	so
Caruthers (W 4-2)	9	5	1-0	2	7
Weaver (L 0-2)	*3	12	11-8	1	1
Stovey	#0	2	3-2	1	0
Coleman	6	9	4-2	0	0

*faced three batters in third
#faced three batters in third
WP: Weaver, Coleman 2.
PB: O'Brien 2, Bushong, Bierbauer.

LOB: Athl 6, StL 9.
BE: Athl 1, StL 4. DP: Shaffer-O'Brien, O'Brien-Weaver
2B: O'Brien, Foutz, Caruthers.
3B: J. Gleason, Caruthers, Welch, Comiskey.
SB: Latham 3, B. Gleason, O'Neill, Foutz 2, Robinson, Caruthers, O'Brien. CS: Latham.
HBP: by Coleman (Robinson)
Time - 1:58. Attendance - 5,200.
Umpire: G.H. Bradley.

AFTERNOON GAME

		r	h	e	Batteries
Athletics	120 000 000 -	3	3	7	B. Mathews (L 7-4) & W. Robinson.
St. Louis	202 102 31x -	11	14	5	N. Hudson (W 4-3) & D. Bushong.
					Attendance - 12,066

There was no stopping the Browns. They made a runaway of the A.A. pennant race again, finishing with a 93-46 won-lost record and a 12-game lead over the second place Pittsburgs.

The Association did adopt a rule keeping "coachers" like Comiskey from coming right up behind the plate to rattle the catcher and the umpire. This rule is the origin of the modern coach's box.

As for the threatened suspension of the Browns' captain, Von der Ahe paid Comiskey's fines in order to keep his player-manager on the field.

1886 World Series—Game #6

Saturday, October 23rd, at Sportsman's Park

Browns are World Champions!! Defeat White Stockings in Thriller

Trail 3-0 Until Eighth, Then Win, 4-3, in Ten Innings

Capture Series and All Gate Receipts, Four Games to Two

Today the St. Louis Browns became the champion baseball team of the United States and the world, and no one could dispute it! After a much disputed series last year against the National League champion Chicago White Stockings, the American Association champs have whipped their rivals this year beyond doubt.

Since both St. Louis and Chicago repeated as pennant winners, the challenge series between the two league's champions this year had an added aspect of rivalry. Additionally, at the suggestion of Chicago club president Albert Spalding, the winner of this year's match-up was to receive all of the gate receipts, while the losers were to get nothing.

Since the total receipts were estimated at $13,920, and since St. Louis owner Chris Von de Ahe turned over half of that money to his players, each member of the team was due to receive $580 for his week's work. The St. Louis players also collected from the Chicago players on some fairly heavy private bets.

The local pool sellers estimated that as much as $100,000 changed hands on he result of the series, and that many Chicago backers went home practically destitute.

After losing two of the three games played in Chicago, the Browns won the first two games played in St. Louis, setting the stage for today's clinching victory.

"Parisian Bob" Caruthers was given the pitching assignment by Captain Comiskey. Chicago's Capt. Anson used John Clarkson for the fourth time in six days. Johnny pitched a brilliant ballgame from the beginning, not allowing a safe hit until the seventh inning. But he tired toward the end, and St. Louis rallied to tie the game in the eighth and win it in the tenth. Caruthers pitched his usual heady game and held the big Chicago hitters to just six safeties.

The play was steady and often brilliant through most of the game. For Chicago the heroes were Fred Pfeffer, who scored all three runs, and Jimmy Ryan, who performed miracles in the outfield. Standouts for the home team were Arlie Latham, whose dramatic three-base hit tied the game in the eighth, and Curt Welch, who scored the winning run.

Pfeffer commenced the run-making in the second inning. He opened with a single to right, stole second, and went to third on a passed ball. Caruthers looked like he might avoid damage by striking out both Ned Williamson and Tommy Burns. But Ryan spoiled the St. Louis hopes by driving Pfeffer in with a safe hit to right.

In the Browns' second, Ryan further frustrated the locals by making a wonderful running catch of Dave Foutz's line drive to right center.

Pfeffer once again made the circuit in the fourth. This time he hit a ball into the seats in right field, nearly to the fence, and circled the bases before the ball could be retrieved. Two more hits and a wild pitch put men of second and third, but Welch captured Clarkson's fly to end the inning.

A light rain began to fall in the fifth, and the Browns tried to convince umpire Gracie Pearce to call the game. A large contingent of fans came onto the field. But the rain suddenly ceased, the fans were removed, and the game continued.

No more men reached base until the sixth, when it was Pfeffer's turn again. "Fritz" hit down to second, and the ball rolled through Yank Robinson's legs. Foutz in right field also let the ball get past him, and Pfeffer made it as far as third base. He scored on a long fly out by Williamson.

The Browns finally got a hit in the seventh. With one out, Tip O'Neill drove one far into right center. He made third base, then spoiled his effort by overrunning the sack and being tagged out.

The bottom of the eighth came around, and the Browns still trailed, 3-0. Charlie

Comiskey was first up, and he cracked a hit to right. Welch laid down a fine bunt toward third, and Burns made an unnecessary and disastrous throw past first, Comiskey racing all the way home before the ball could be returned. The partisan St. Louis crowd, which had been quiet up to this time, broke into excited cheering. The game was delayed for five minutes before the tumult died. Foutz went out on a fly to left. Welch moved from second to third on a passed ball. Robinson popped to Anson. Bushong walked.

That brought Arlie Latham to the plate. The usually ear-piercing chatterbox had been particularly quiet all day. Anson had shut him up with an awful mimicry of Arlie's coaching style. This time, with men on first and third and two out, Anson tried to guy him again. The Browns needed two runs to tie, and Latham's only utterance was directed to Bushong. "Stay there, Bush," Arlie called, "and I'll bring you both in." Then he proceeded to drive a liner to left field. Abner Dalrymple misjudged the ball for a moment, and it sailed over his head for a triple, tying the game. The crowd became delirious and began showering the field with coins and pool tickets, some worth hundreds of dollars. Caruthers ended the inning by grounding out.

Neither side scored in the ninth, although O'Neill brought the crowd to its feet with a long drive to right center. It looked good for a home run, but Ryan raced over, leaped several feet into the air, and came crashing to the ground holding the ball. It was a miraculous catch, but the St. Louis cranks gave it very little applause.

The Chicagos were quickly retired in the top of the tenth.

Then the Browns came to bat with Welch leading off. Curt was hit by a pitch. But Anson convinced the umpire that Welch had not tried to avoid the pitch, and he had to bat over. He got his revenge by lining a hit to center. Foutz then hit a slow bounder past the mound, which Williamson fumbled. The crowd wanted Robinson to end the game with a long hit, but Yank laid down a sacrifice, instead, moving the runners up. With Bushong at bat, catcher Mike Kelly signaled for a low ball. But Clarkson delivered very high, and Kelly was unable to stop the ball. It careened to the backstop, and Welch trotted home with the winning run.

The stands swelled with insane shouts of joy, and many fans rushed onto the field. The Browns were engaged in wild celebration, and several of them were carried to the clubhouse on the shoulders of the crowd. As World Champions, they rode in glory.

Chicago (NL)	ab	r	h	bi	o	a	e
G. Gore, cf	5	0	0	0	2	0	0
M. Kelly, c	5	0	0	0	9	2	0
A. Anson, 1b	4	0	0	0	13	0	0
F. Pfeffer, 2b	4	3	2	1	0	1	0
N. Williamson, ss	4	0	0	1	0	2	1
T. Burns, 3b	4	0	2	0	1	5	1
J. Ryan, rf	4	0	1	1	3	1	0
A. Dalrymple, lf	4	0	1	0	0	0	0
J. Clarkson, p	4	0	0	0	0	2	0
	38	3	6	3	28	13	2

St. Louis (AA)	ab	r	h	bi	o	a	e
A. Latham, 3b	4	0	1	2	1	1	1
B. Caruthers, p	4	0	0	0	2	0	0
T. O'Neill, lf	3	0	1	0	5	0	0
B. Gleason, ss	4	0	0	0	0	3	0
C. Comiskey, 1b	4	1	1	0	7	0	1
C. Welch, cf	4	2	2	0	5	0	0
D. Foutz, rf	4	0	0	0	3	0	1
Y. Robinson, 2b	4	0	0	1	3	1	1
D. Bushong, c	2	1	0	0	6	0	0
	33	4	5	2	30	7	4

Chicago   010 101 000 0 - 3
St. Louis   000 000 030 1 - 4
one out when winning run scored

	ip	h	r-er	bb	so
Clarkson (L 2-2)	9.1	5	4-3	2	10
Caruthers (W 2-1)	10	6	3-2	0	5

WP: Caruthers, Clarkson. PB: Bushong, Kelly

LOB: Chi 5, StL 3.
BE: Chi 2, StL 1.
2B: Burns. 3B: O'Neill, Latham,
HR: Pfeffer.
SB: Pfeffer.
Time - 2:20. Attendance - 10,000
Umpire: G. Pearce

1887 — Thursday, May 12th, at Sportsman's Park

St. Louis Browns Outslug Baltimore Orioles and Win, 22-14

Browns Extend Association Lead with 12th Straight Victory

Home Team Scores 12 in Fifth, Visitors Make 10 Runs in Eighth

The champion St. Louis Browns have looked as dominant as ever in the early stages of the American Association pennant race. Today they continued their tremendous batting and defeated the Baltimore Orioles, 22-14. The victory was the twelfth in succession for the champs, while the Orioles dropped to third place in the race.

After losing three of their first five games this season, the Browns have slugged the ball as never before during the last dozen games. During their winning streak they have scored 157 runs, or an average of over 13 runs per game.

Today's Results
ST. LOUIS 22 - Baltimore 14
Brooklyn 17 - Cleveland 12
Mets 19 - Cincinnati 6 (8 inn.)
Louisville 4 - Athletics 2

Standings	W-L	Pct.	GB
ST. LOUIS	14-3	.824	-
Brooklyn	10-5	.667	3
Baltimore	11-6	.647	3
Cincinnati	11-8	.579	4
Louisville	10-8	.556	4½
Athletic	7-9	.438	6½
Cleveland	3-16	.158	12
Metropolitan	2-13	.133	11

The new rules adopted for this season have helped, of course. The most significant changes involved the ball-and-strike counts. The number of balls necessary for a walk was reduced from seven to five, while the number of strikes needed for an out went up from three to four. But the restrictions on the movements of the pitcher and the reduction in size of the pitcher's box have also aided the hitters. As the team with the best batting in circuit, St. Louis had benefitted the most from the changes.

On the other hand, as the team with the best pitching, they have also been most adversely effected. Nat Hudson, their number three pitcher last year with 16 wins, was unable to adapt his hop-step-and-jump delivery to the new rules this spring, and he suffered a sore arm. But the Browns' other pitchers, Dave Foutz, Bob Caruthers, and rookie Charley "Silver" King, have all been effective.

Caruthers was today's pitcher, and he hurled effectively until he let up in the eighth inning and allowed Baltimore to score ten runs. But he retired the visitors in order in the ninth inning.

Ed Knouff, who had starred in the Southern League in 1886, was given a chance to pitch for the Orioles. He showed a fine curveball, but had little speed and even less control. After the Browns gauged his curves, they routed him with twelve runs in one inning. He was then replaced by Bill "Blondie" Purcell, who was also hit hard.

With bases on balls counting as hits under the new rules, the game featured 49 total hits, including 10 "phantoms" (i.e., walks). Three Browns got five hits (although each of them got at least one phantom), while Tom "Oyster" Burns made five solid safeties, including a home run, for the Orioles.

The Browns scored the game's first run in the second inning on errors by Mike Griffin and Tommy Tucker and a stolen base by Curt Welch.

Two hit batsmen, a muff by Chris Fulmer, and a run-scoring sacrifice hit by Doc Bushong produced another St. Louis run in the fourth. The daring base running which has made the team famous, resulted in two men being tagged out at home during this frame.

Baltimore scored once in their fourth at bats, and they also had a man thrown out at home. Bill Greenwood and Burns singled and were on second and third after an out and a steal. Tucker then singled Griffin home, but Welch's fine throw nailed Burns, who was also trying to score.

With the score just 2-1 in their favor, the Browns decided that they had better start scoring more if they wanted to win the game. So, in the fifth inning, they broke through for 12 tallies. They were aided by Knouff's wildness. Billy Gleason and Tip O'Neill opened with walks. Charlie Comiskey flied out. Foutz worked the count to four-and-three, fouled off a couple of pitches, then lined out a clean single. Welch got in front of an inside pitch, forcing Gleason across the home base. Yank Robinson waited for five balls and forced another run home. An error by Tucker on a grounder by Caruthers kept the parade going, as did a base on balls to Bushong. At this point, the Browns had made four runs in the inning on just one solid hit.

Then Knouff started putting the ball over the plate, and the hitters started swinging. Latham, Gleason, and O'Neill singled, and Comiskey doubled. Foutz hit the longest ball of the inning, but center fielder Griffin ran back and caught it. Then Welch and Robinson got safe hits, and Caruthers got a phantom hit. A wild pitch sent Welch across, then Bushong struck out, ending the inning at long last. The total destruction was reckoned at 12 runs on 12 hits (including five bases on balls), with two errors, one hit batsman, and two wild pitches.

Purcell went into the box for the Orioles at the start of the next inning. His error and some hard hitting gave St. Louis three more runs.

For St. Louis in the sixth inning, Arlie Latham went behind the bat to relieve Bushong, whose hands were sore. The "Dude" let a wild pitch and a passed ball get past him, as Baltimore scored three runs. In the seventh, owner Chris Von der Ahe came down to the bench and ordered Bushong to resume catching, which he did. No more battery errors were made by St. Louis.

The Orioles were trailing, 18-4, when they came to bat in the eighth. Then they went to work on Caruther's curves and threatened to win the game. The first batter, Greenwood, flied out to deep center, then the next seven men got singles. Knouff followed with a walk. Greenwood came up again and singled. Burns got his second hit of the inning and fifth of the game when he knocked the ball over the left field fence. That made ten runs for the inning. Purcell also got his second hit of the round, but then Caruthers got back to work and retired the next two men.

The Browns padded their lead with four in the ninth, then Caruthers shut the Orioles out in the bottom half to end the game. The final count was 22-14 in favor of the champions.

St. Louis	ab	r	h	bi	o	a	e
A. Latham, 3b-c6-3b7	7	2	5	1	2	2	2
B. Gleason, ss	6	4	5	1	1	3	0
T. O'Neill, lf	7	4	5	2	0	0	0
C. Comiskey, 1b	7	3	4	3	9	1	0
D. Foutz, rf	7	2	4	3	0	0	1
C. Welch, cf	5	4	3	4	3	1	0
Y. Robinson, 2b	5	1	2	1	6	2	1
B. Caruthers, p	6	1	1	1	2	3	0
D. Bushong, c-3b6-c7	6	1	1	1	4	2	1
	56	22	30	17	27	14	5

Baltimore	ab	r	h	bi	o	a	e
B. Greenwood, 2b	5	3	2	1	4	1	1
T. Burns, ss	5	3	5	4	1	3	1
B. Purcell, rf-p6	5	1	2	0	0	1	2
T. Tucker, 1b	5	1	2	1	5	1	0
C. Fulmer, lf	5	2	2	1	2	0	1
M. Griffin, cf	5	1	2	1	4	0	1
J. Davis, 3b	5	1	2	1	2	2	0
L. Daniels, c	5	1	1	1	9	3	2
E. Knouff, p-rf6	4	1	1	1	0	4	0
	44	14	19	11	27	15	8

St. Louis   010 1(12)3 014 - 22
Baltimore   000 103 0(10)00 - 14

	ip	h	r-er	bb	so
Caruthers (W 6-1)	9	19	14-11	2	3
Knouff (L 0-1)	5	22	14-8	6	2
Purcell	4	8	8-7	2	2

WP: Knouff 2, Caruthers, Purcell.
PB: Latham, Daniels 2.
HBP: by Knoff 4 (Gleason, Welch 2, Robinson)
Umpire: J. McQuaid.

LOB: StL 11, Balt 3.
2B: Comiskey, Welch, O'Neill 2.
HR: Burns.
BB: Latham 3, Gleason, O'Neill, Robinson, Caruthers, Bushong, Griffin, Knouff.
SB: Latham, Comiskey, Welch 2, Caruthers, Greenwood, Burns 2, Purcell, Davis, Daniels.
CS: Latham, Gleason, Caruthers.
Time - 2:30
Attendance - 5,000

The Browns won three more games, extending their winning streak to 15, lost one, then won 14 of their next 15. That gave them a lead of 9 games by June 4th.

After building the lead to 19½ games on September 3rd, the Browns cruised home 14 games ahead on the second-place Cincinnati Reds. Their final record was 95-40 for a .704 percentage.

With walks counting as hits, Tip O'Neill finished with a .492 batting average.

The rule counting walks as hits and the rule allowing four strikes were both repealed before the 1888 season.

1887 World Series—Games #10 & #11

Friday, October 21st, at Washington and at Baltimore

Browns and Wolverines Split Two Games, Detroit Clinches Title

Browns Win Morning Game in Washington, 11-4

Detroit Wins Its Eighth Game in the Series in Baltimore in the Afternoon

After losing seven of the first nine games in the fifteen-game World Series against the National League champions from Detroit, the St. Louis Browns gamely won the first game played today. Then they were thoroughly trounced in the second game, and Detroit clinched the series. After playing an excellent game in the morning, St. Louis played like amateurs in the afternoon, the Wolverines beating them with great ease.

Since the game scheduled for Thursday in Washington had been rained out, the two teams stayed over and played the game this morning. Bob Caruthers, working his sixth game in twelve days, was suffering from a very sore arm, but he pitched well for the Browns. Charley Getzein, the famous "pretzel twirler" of the Detroits, was his opponent. Getzein was not so effective, and the American Association champs hit him freely.

The Capitol Park grounds were soggy from yesterday's rains, and their condition contributed to the sloppy fielding. Since the game was played in the morning, the crowd was sparse.

The Wolverines' famous sluggers started into Caruthers' slants quickly. The first batter, Hardie Richardson, opened the game with a home run over the left field fence. Charlie Ganzel followed with a line single. Jack Rowe also hit the ball hard, but Yank Robinson at second base made a fine stop and forced Ganzel. Rowe stole second, went to third on an infield out, and scored when Arlie Latham's fumble gave Jim "Deacon" White a life.

The Browns tied the game in the bottom of the first on four one-base hits. The last of these, by Dave Foutz, plated two runs.

Richardson, Ganzel, and Rowe all singled to start the third inning. But then the Browns thrilled the crowed and killed the rally by making a triple play. Big Sam Thompson drove a terrific liner that Billy Gleason speared at shortstop. Gleason threw the ball to third to retire Richardson, and Latham relayed the ball to Robinson to catch Ganzel before he could get back to second, completing the play.

After Detroit had taken the lead in the top of the fifth, St. Louis went ahead to stay in the bottom of the inning. Tip O'Neill started with a corker to left field for a base. Charlie Comiskey then beat out a bunt. The runners moved up one station on Caruther's out. Foutz lifted a short fly back of third base, which White caught. After the catch, O'Neill brazenly broke for home, and the startled Deacon's throw to stop him was wild, tying the score. The very next batter, Curt Welch, untied it with a two-run home run over the left field boards.

Arlie Latham hit a homer to deep center field in the next inning, and in the seventh, St. Louis score four more on six hits (one a phantom). They added one more run in the eight, and Detroit scored once in the ninth, making the final score 11-4.

The teams then traveled to Baltimore for the scheduled afternoon game. By winning this game, 13-3, the Wolverines clinched the World Series victory. Although they played a loose game in the field, they hit like champions, and their pitcher, Charles "Lady" Baldwin, was very effective. The lefthander limited the Browns to just four hits, two of them being bases on balls.

On the other hand, the St. Louis pitcher, Dave Foutz, pitched indifferently, at times appearing not to care whether he won or lost. The Browns in general played very poorly, although Yank Robinson fielded in grand style.

The weather was clear but cold, and the attendance was moderate.

Detroit was playing without their regular second baseman, Fred Dunlap, and without their regular first baseman, Dan Brouthers. Dunlap had injured his leg in the morning game in Washington. Brouthers had been out for the entire series after spraining his ankle in the final game of the regular season.

St. Louis went to bat first, and Latham opened with a single to center. After three balls had been called on Gleason, Bill switched over to the lefthanded batter's box and was hit in the arm by the next pitch. Baldwin fielded O'Neill's hard hopper, but then he threw wildly to third base, loading the sacks with none out. Comiskey forced Latham at home. Caruthers hit down to Richardson at second, and the fielder threw poorly home, Gleason scoring. Foutz and Welch hit into force plays, and St. Louis only got one run.

Detroit matched that run in their first ups. After two were out, Rowe's high fly bounced out of Caruthers's hands, giving the batter a base. He took second on a passed ball. When Welch also muffed a fly, he scored.

St. Louis scored another run in the second, this time on no hits and two errors.

Detroit took the lead with three in the fourth. Rowe started with a single and moved to third on two outs. Larry Twitchell, who was playing because of Dunlap's injury, then put his team ahead with a home run over the left field fence. That rattled Foutz. He walked Charlie Bennett, allowed the slow-footed catcher to steal second and third, and then he missed a return throw from his own catcher to allow Bennett to score.

The Browns scored a run in the fifth, again on no hits and two errors.

But the Wolverines broke the game open with four runs in their half of the inning. Four hits and two errors did the trick.

Four more were added to the Detroit score in the sixth. Rowe got a two-run double and then scored all the way from second on a wild pitch. A single, hit batsman, walk, and passed ball added the fourth run.

Richardson scored the game's last run in the seventh.

Baldwin set the Browns down in order over the last three innings.

The final score was 13-3 in favor of the Detroit Wolverines, who became the new world champions.

MORNING GAME, at Capitol Park, Washington

		r	h	e	Batteries
Detroit	200 010 001 -	4	9	3	C. Getzein (L 3-2) & Bennett, Ganzel
St. Louis	200 031 41x -	11	9	5	B. Caruthers (W 3-3) & Boyle

Attendance - 1,261

AFTERNOON GAME, at Oriole Park, Baltimore

St. Louis (AA)	ab	r	h	bi	o	a	e	Detroit (NL)	ab	r	h	bi	o	a	e
A. Latham, 3b	5	0	1	0	0	2	0	H. Richardson, 2b	5	3	4	0	2	5	1
B. Gleason, ss	3	1	0	0	1	2	3	C. Ganzel, 1b-c7	5	1	0	0	7	2	0
T. O'Neill, lf	4	1	0	0	0	0	0	J. Rowe, ss	5	4	2	2	1	6	1
C. Comiskey, 1b	4	0	0	0	10	1	1	S. Thompson, rf	5	0	2	0	0	0	1
B. Caruthers, rf	4	0	1	0	2	0	1	J. White, 3b	5	2	2	0	2	0	2
D. Foutz, p	4	0	0	0	1	5	0	L. Twitchell, lf	4	2	3	2	1	0	0
C. Welch, cf	3	0	0	0	0	1	1	C. Bennett, c-1b7	5	1	2	2	9	1	1
Y. Robinson, 2b	4	1	2	0	4	6	0	N. Hanlon, cf	5	0	3	0	4	0	0
J. Boyle, c	4	0	0	0	6	1	1	L. Baldwin, p	5	0	0	0	1	6	1
	35	3	4	0	24	18	7		44	13	18	6	27	20	7

| St. Louis | 110 010 000 - | 3 |
| Detroit | 100 344 10x - | 13 |

	ip	h	r-er	bb	so
Foutz (L 0-3)	8	18	13-6	4	2
Baldwin (W 3-0)	9	4	3-0	2	2

WP: Foutz. PB: Bennett 2, Boyle 3.
HPB: by Baldwin 2 (Gleason, Welch), by Foutz (Twitchell).
Time - 2:00. Attendance - 2,707
Umpires: J. Gaffney & J. Kelly.

LOB: StL 7, Detr 8.
BE: StL 7, Detr 5.
DP: Gleason-Robinson-Comiskey.
2B: Richardson 2, Rowe, Twitchell.
HR: Twitchell
BB: Robinson 2, Bennett, Hanlon 2. Thompson.
SB: Robinson, Latham, Bennett 2, Caruthers, Twitchell, Richardson 3, Thompson.
CS: Welch, White, Robinson.

Although the outcome was already decided, the two teams played out the remaining four games of the traveling World Series, each side winning two.

The decisive nature of the defeat prompted Von der Ahe to sell and trade some of his high-salaried stars over the winter. Caruthers, Bushong, and Foutz went to Brooklyn, while Welch and Gleason were shipped to the Athletics.

1888 — Friday, August 3rd, at Washington Park, Brooklyn

Browns Retain Lead With Ten-Inning, 7-6 Victory Over Bridegrooms

Make Only Six Hits, But All Figure in the Scoring

Gain Revenge Against Caruthers and Brooklyn

Charlie Comiskey's St. Louis Browns were in a difficult position when they came to Brooklyn today. Their lead over the Bridegrooms was just ½ game, and Brooklyn had already beaten St. Louis in seven of the eight games played between the two teams. The visitors were held to just six hits today, but they made them all count and came out victorious in ten innings, 7-6.

To heighten the sweetness of the victory, the Browns defeated their former teammate Bob Caruthers, who had previously pitched Brooklyn to four victories over St. Louis this season.

The Bridegrooms' lineup included all

Today's Results
ST. LOUIS 7 - Brooklyn 6 (10 inn.)
Athletics 13 - Louisville 1
Cleveland 9 - Cincinnati 8
Kansas City 3 - Baltimore 2

Standings	W-L	Pct.	GB
ST. LOUIS	52-27	.658	-
Brooklyn	52-30	.634	1½
Athletic	48-30	.615	3½
Cincinnati	48-31	.608	4
Baltimore	35-46	.432	18
Cleveland	30-49	.380	22
Louisville	30-50	.375	22½
Kansas City	23-55	.295	28½

three players sold by St. Louis to Brooklyn last winter. Caruthers, who went for $8500, pitched and was supported behind the plate by Albert "Doc" Bushong, who brought $4500. Dave Foutz, a $5000 commodity, played first base.

To replace these stars, Comiskey had found younger players. His canniest move was signing little Tommy McCarthy, who had failed in trials with Philadelphia and Boston in the National League and who had drifted to Oshkosh in the Northwestern League. The pitching burden had fallen on the able shoulders of 21-year-old Silver King, with aid mostly from Nat Hudson.

After trailing Brooklyn for most of the first half of the season, the Browns jelled as a team and took over the league lead on July 20th. Meanwhile, the Bridegrooms have had some troubles. Captain Dave Orr, claiming illness, took a day off yesterday. He was seen at the amusement park at Coney Island, so owner Charles Byrne suspended him and relieved him of the captaincy. "Darby" O'Brien was in charge of the squad today, and Foutz took Orr's place at first base.

Today's contest was characterized by fine play all around. Both pitchers pitched well, although both teams made their hits count for the maximum. The fielding was steady. The crowd was of fair size and was very enthusiastic.

Caruthers started the game in fine fashion, facing the minimum of nine batters through the first three innings. He also made a two-base hit in his first trip to the plate but was left on base.

Brooklyn stranded another man in the second but then bunched four hits in the third inning and scored three runs. Bushong started with a pop-fly single to center. George Pinckney lined a hit to right field, and Bushong legged his way to third ahead of McCarthy's throw, Pinckney taking second on the play. O'Brien cracked a terrific hit to center, scoring both runners. Darby stole second and continued to third on Jocko Milligan's throwing error. Foutz grounded to short, plating O'Brien. George Smith was safe on an error by Comiskey, and George McClellan singled. By clever base running, Smith stole third when Milligan threw to first to try and pick McClellan off. But both runners were left stranded.

St. Louis tied the score in the top of the fourth. Arlie Latham started off with a pretty two-bagger to left. Yank Robinson flied to shortstop. Tip O'Neill then smacked a clean base hit over second, sending Latham home. Comiskey hit behind the runner and into right field, then he took second on the futile attempt to catch O'Neill at third. McCarthy brought both men home with a single to center.

The Bridegrooms answered with three runs of their own in the bottom half of the inning. After Jack Burdock was retired, Bushong strolled on five balls. He advanced to second on Pinckney's grounder to Comiskey. O'Brien then pulled a double over third base, and Bushong scored. O'Brien came in on Caruthers's single up the middle. "Parisian Bob" stole second, and he trotted home on Foutz's long triple to left. The long hitting had the Brooklyn cranks cheering themselves hoarse, and they didn't seem too upset when Foutz was left stranded by a strike out.

The lost run, however, became important when the Browns tied the score in the fifth. After the first two batters had grounded out, Caruthers lost his control and passed both Robinson and O'Neill. Needing to get the ball over the plate, he laid one in to Comiskey. The captain wailed it to farthest center field and circled the base with a three-run home run, tying the game at 6-6.

Then the pitchers, King and Caruthers, settled down. Through the next four innings there were no scoring threats and only one man left on base.

The game went into extra innings, and St. Louis broke the tie. With one out in the tenth, Robinson tattooed one to left field and raced all the way to third with a triple. O'Neill was next, and the champion batsman was equal to the challenge, knocking a fly ball deep enough to allow Robinson to score after the catch. Comiskey went out, but the Browns had the lead for the first time.

King once again set the 'Grooms down in order in the bottom of the tenth. He ended the game with a flourish, striking Smith out for the third time in the game for the final out. The Browns were 7-6 victors and were still in first place.

St. Louis	ab	r	h	bi	o	a	e
A. Latham, 3b	4	1	1	0	0	1	0
Y. Robinson, 2b	4	2	1	0	4	5	0
T. O'Neill, lf	4	2	1	2	2	0	0
C. Comiskey, 1b	5	2	2	3	12	0	1
T. McCarthy, rf	4	0	1	2	4	0	0
H. Lyons, cf	3	0	0	0	0	0	0
B. White, ss	4	0	0	0	0	3	1
J. Milligan, c	4	0	0	0	7	1	1
S. King, p	4	0	0	0	1	7	0
	36	7	6	7	30	17	3

Brooklyn	ab	r	h	bi	o	a	e
G. Pinckney, 3b	5	1	1	0	1	0	0
D. O'Brien, lf	5	2	3	3	1	0	0
B. Caruthers, p	5	1	2	1	2	5	0
D. Foutz, 1b	5	0	1	2	11	1	0
G. Smith, ss	5	0	0	0	2	3	1
B. McClellan, rf	4	0	1	0	4	0	0
P. Radford, cf	4	0	0	0	2	0	0
J. Burdock, 2b	4	0	0	0	2	5	0
D. Bushong, c	3	2	1	0	5	2	0
	40	6	9	6	30	16	1

St. Louis   000 330 000 1 - 7
Brooklyn   003 300 000 0 - 6

	ip	h	r-er	bb	so
King (W 26-12)	10	9	6-5	1	3
Caruthers (L 23-10)	10	6	7-7	4	5

PB: Milligan
Umpire: B. Ferguson

LOB: StL 3, Bkn. 5.
BE: StL 1, Bkn 2.
2B: Caruthers, Latham, O'Brien.
3B: Foutz, Robinson.
HR: Comiskey.
SB: O'Brien, Smith, Caruthers
Time - 1:50
Attendance - 3,700

The Browns held the lead for the rest of the season, winning their fourth consecutive American Association pennant. Their record was 92-43, giving them a final margin of 6½ games over the second-place Bridegrooms.

By winning eight of their remaining nine decisions against Brooklyn, the Browns salvaged a splitt in the season series, ten games to ten.

1888 World Series—Game #1

Tuesday, October 16th, at the Polo Grounds, New York

Giants Edge Browns, 2-1, in Opening Game of World Series

Keefe Bests King in Superb Pitchers' Battle

Only Three Hits for Each Team

The World Series opened today in New York, pitting the National League champion New York Giants against the American Association champion St. Louis Browns. A ten-game series was scheduled. New York won the first game by a 2-1 score.

Today's contest was dominated by the pitchers. Each team presented its best: Tim Keefe for New York and Charles "Silver" King for St. Louis. Each man had led his league in victories by a pitcher, Keefe posting a 35-12 record, while King finished with a 45-21 mark. Today both were in top form, and each allowed just three hits. Although each pitcher walked just one batter, both those bases on balls resulted in runs. King made a costly wild pitch, which helped New York score their other run. Keefe was able to pitch around his worst mistake, a two-base throwing error.

The fielders generally had little to do. They were nervous at the outset and all but one of the errors were made in the first half of the game. The latter part of the game was very well played. Johnny Ward, the New York shortstop, made several fine stops on sharply hit balls. And Tommy McCarthy of the Browns made two fine catches in right field.

The day started cool and rainy, and some early reports announced that the game would be postponed. The weather cleared by game time, but the crowd was smaller than had been originally expected.

Many baseball dignitaries from both leagues were present. President Day of the Giants entertained several magnates in his box, while President Von der Ahe of the Browns was surrounded by a large party of guests from St. Louis. Chris had brought many of them with him on a special train. The St. Louis contingent backed their team liberally, although the Giants were favored by the oddsmakers.

The Browns appeared in new white uniforms with red trim and brown stockings. They kept their famous brown and white striped caps. The Giants wore their usual black suits with white trim.

Captain Buck Ewing of the Giants sent the visitors to bat first. Arlie Latham, with a new stage upon which to perform his "Freshest Man on Earth" act, strutted to the batter's box, jibbering and joking until Keefe had put two strikes over the plate. Then Arlie was forced to swing, and he grounded out weakly. Yank Robinson dribbled a safe hit past the box. He moved to second on Tip O'Neill's infield out but was left on base when Comiskey also bounced out.

The New Yorks were disposed of on three ground balls.

With one out in the second, Harry Lyons tapped a ball down the first base line. Keefe fielded the ball, but this throw hit the runner in the back, and Lyons made second before the ball could be returned. But Keefe struck Bill White out and got Jack Boyle on a grounder to Ward.

New York then came in and scored the first run. Connor, first up, knocked a single to left center. Ward missed one bunt, then laid one down toward third and beat the throw to first. King then made his fateful wild pitch, advancing the runners to second and third. Mike Slattery hit a high fly to Lyons, who wisely threw to third, nipping Ward, who was trying to advance. But Connor scored on the play. Jim O'Rourke grounded out.

The Browns tied the game in the top of the third. King fanned. Latham, however, got a base on balls. Robinson also struck out. Latham then stole second and, when Ewing's throw went into center field, continued to third. O'Neill came through with a pretty single to center, driving Latham home. Comiskey was an easy out.

The Giants untied the score immediately. After the first two batters were retired, Mike Tiernan walked. He broke for second and wound up coming all the way around to score when Boyle threw wildly past second and Lyons let the ball get past him in the outfield. Ewing reached base on a fumble by White, and he stole second and third on successive pitches. But Danny Richardson flied out, ending the inning.

A one-out error and a two-out single gave St. Louis two base runners in the fourth. But King struck out, ending the threat.

The next base runner came in the New York half of the fifth. O'Rourke, leading off, shot a ball down to Latham, which the third baseman was only able to knock down, O'Rourke getting a single. After Art Whitney popped to shortstop, Keefe drove a liner to right that looked like extra bases. But McCarthy raced over for a brilliant catch, and O'Rourke had to beat a hasty retreat to first. After Boyle's bad throw allowed the runner to steal second, Tiernan struck out.

Both sides went out in order in the sixth and seventh.

The Browns mounted a threat in the eighth, but came up short. With one out, Robinson beat out a bunt to third base. A passed ball gave him second with the mighty O'Neill at the plate. But Keefe struck the slugger out. Comiskey found a serve to his liking and drove one solidly down the left field line. The high fly gave the New York partisans a bad scare, but the ball hooked foul by a foot or two. On his next swing, Commy popped out to Ward.

Keefe retired the Browns without trouble in the ninth. He ended the game by striking White out. That brought his total for the game to nine strike outs, and Keefe's team was a 2-1 winner.

St. Louis (AA)	ab	r	h	bi	o	a	e
A Latham, 3b	3	1	0	0	2	3	0
Y. Robinson, 2b	4	0	1	0	0	2	0
T. O'Neill, lf	4	0	1	1	2	0	0
C. Comiskey, 1b	4	0	0	0	7	0	0
T. McCarthy, rf	4	0	0	0	2	0	1
H. Lyons, cf	4	0	0	0	5	1	1
B. White, ss	4	0	0	0	3	2	1
J. Boyle, c	3	0	1	0	3	0	2
S. King, p	3	0	0	0	0	3	0
	33	1	3	1	24	11	5

New York (NL)	ab	r	h	bi	o	a	e
M. Tiernan, rf	3	1	0	0	1	0	1
B. Ewing, c	3	0	0	0	9	1	1
D. Richardson, 2b	3	0	0	0	1	1	1
R. Connor, 1b	3	1	1	0	13	0	0
J. Ward, ss	3	0	1	0	3	3	0
M. Slattery, cf	3	0	0	1	0	0	0
J. O'Rourke, lf	3	0	1	0	0	0	0
A. Whitney, 3b	3	0	0	0	0	2	0
T. Keefe, p	3	0	0	0	0	10	1
	27	2	3	1	27	17	4

St. Louis   001 000 000 - 1
New York   011 000 00x - 2

	ip	h	r-er	bb	so
King (L 0-1)	8	3	2-1	1	3
Keefe (W 1-0)	9	3	1-0	1	9

WP: King. PB: Ewing.
Umpires: J. Gaffney & J. Kelly

LOB: StL 6, NY 2.
BE: StL 3, NY 1.
DP: Lyons-Latham.
SB: Latham, Tiernan, Ewing 2, Robinson.
Time - 2:00
Attendance - 4,876

St. Louis won the next game, but then New York took four in a row. After the Browns won the seventh game, the Giants clinched the series by winning the eighth game, 11-3, with Keefe pitching his fourth victory.

The Browns won the last two meaningless games to make the final count 6 games to 4 in favor of the Giants.

1889 — September 7th, at Washington Park, Brooklyn

Browns, Leading 4-2, Forfeit Critical Game in Brooklyn

Delay for Darkness, Then Walk Off Field in Ninth

Chris Says He Will Forfeit Again Tomorrow if His Men are not Protected

An enormous crowd came out to Washington Park today to see the first game of the final series between the two leading teams in the American Association pennant race, the St. Louis Browns and the Brooklyn Bridegrooms. The spectators were treated to an exciting game of ball until the closing innings. Then the visitors, who held the lead, tried to induce the umpire to call the game on account of darkness. When this failed, they tried to delay the game as much as possible, which only made the ump more adamant in his intention to play the game out. Finally, the St. Louis players walked off the field, forfeiting the game to Brooklyn. As they made their way to the clubhouse, some of the Browns were assaulted by the assemblage.

Today's Results
Brooklyn 9 - ST. LOUIS 0 (Forefeit)
Cincinnati 5 - Baltimore 5 (Tie) (9 inn.)
Athletics 4 - Louisville 4 (Tie) (9 inn.)
Columbus 5 - Kansas City 0

Standings	W-L	Pct.	GB
Brooklyn	76-37	.673	-
ST. LOUIS	72-40	.643	3½
Baltimore	64-45	.587	10
Athletic	61-47	.565	12½
Cincinnati	59-55	.518	17½
Kansas City	46-66	.411	29½
Columbus	47-68	.409	30
Louisville	23-90	.204	53

The day was overcast but warm. The crowd began to gather early and soon overflowed the grandstand. A large number witnessed the game from behind ropes around the outfield incline.

Captain Foutz of the Bridegrooms chose to take first ups, and his men immediately scored two runs. Darby O'Brien hit the first pitch of the game to shortstop and reached first on Shorty Fuller's fumble. O'Brien quickly stole second. Hub Collins lined a ball into the crowd in center field and got a double on the ground rules, O'Brien scoring. Dave Foutz followed with a safe hit for another run and took second when Charlie Duffee fumbled the ball in the outfield. Foutz was caught at third when he tried to advance on a fly out by Tom "Oyster" Burns, Tommy McCarthy making a beautiful throw. George Pinckney doubled, but a fly out by John Corkhill ended the inning. Brookyn didn't score again all day.

In the second inning, six batters struck out.

In the third, each team had a man caught stealing.

In the fourth, each side had two men thrown out at home.

St. Louis pushed a run across in the fifth. Duffee opened with a clean hit to left and raced to second when O'Brien made a poor throw back to the infield. He moved to third on Fuller's tap to pitcher Bob Caruthers. Jocko Milligan then scratched a hit, and Duffee scored. Elton Chambelain also singled, but fine fielding retired the next two batters.

St. Louis took the lead with two runs in the sixth. Tip O'Neill began with a hit over second. Charlie Comiskey bunted him to second. Yank Robinson knocked a long hit to center field. Corkhill did well to cut the ball off, but his throw toward home was wild, and O'Neill scored, while Robinson went to second. Fuller put St. Louis into the lead with a two-out double into the crowd.

Comiskey and the Browns soon began asking to have the game called on account of darkness, even though there was still plenty of light.

The Bridegrooms got the tying run to third in the seventh inning but failed to score. Meanwhile, Comiskey took every occassion to argue with umpire Fred Goldsmith and to otherwise delay the game. His teammates followed his lead, and Goldsmith repeatedly had to impose fines to get the men back to their positions.

The Browns added another run in their seventh. Latham reached on a fumble by Collins and stole second on a bad throw by Bob Clark. An out advanced him to third, and O'Neill's third hit of the game brought him home.

Before the Browns went out into the field, McCarthy took the ball and dunked it into a bucket of water. Goldsmith had not been looking, but the Brooklyn cranks roundly hissed McCarthy for his trick, and the umpire put a new ball into play.

Neither side scored in the eighth, but the Browns' delaying tactics made the inning a long one anyway. The highlight came when President Chris Von der Ahe distributed lighted candles for the Browns to put in front of their bench. This caused a great deal of amusement among the spectators, but it only added to the umpire's determination not to give in to St. Louis.

By this time it was quite dark, but Goldsmith was in no mood to call the game. The first Brooklyn batter in the ninth, Clark, struck out, but Milligan missed the third strike, and Clark reached first. Milligan missed another pitch in the gloaming, and Clark moved to second. At this point, the exasperated Comiskey refused to play any longer, and he ordered his men to come in off the field.

Some of the spectators, thinking the game had been called, came down onto the field, which would have been possible grounds for a Brooklyn forfeit. But the alert Bridegrooms got the cranks back into the grandstand.

Goldsmith, meanwhile, had ordered the Browns back onto the field and had pulled his watch out. As the St. Louis players were heading for the clubhouse, the prescribed five minutes had expired, and Goldsmith declared the game forfeited to Brooklyn. The crowd led out a riotous cheer. A portion of the mob went after the Browns, and some of the players were hit by thrown bottles and stones.

The forfeiture carried with it a penalty of $1500, plus the loss of about half that much in the visitors' share of the gate. But Von der Ahe said that he would also forfeit the upcoming Sunday game. The Bridegrooms played Sundays in Ridgewood, Queens, even though the state laws prohibited Sunday amusements. Because the Queens County sheriff tacitly allowed the games to take place, no police were ever present, and Von der Ahe said that he feared his men could not be protected against the mob. He also wanted to hurt Brooklyn owner Charles Byrne by depriving him of about $4000 in Sunday gate revenues.

Brooklyn	ab	r	h	bi	o	a	e
D. O'Brien, lf	4	1	1	0	2	0	1
H. Collins, 2b	4	1	2	1	4	4	2
D. Foutz, 1b	4	0	2	1	11	0	0
T. Burns, rf	4	0	0	0	1	0	0
G. Pinckney, 3b	4	0	1	0	1	1	1
J. Corkhill, cf	3	0	0	0	0	0	1
B. Clark, c	4	0	1	0	4	4	1
B. Caruthers, p	2	0	0	0	5	0	
G. Smith, ss	2	0	0	0	1	4	0
	31	2	7	2	24	18	6

St. Louis	ab	r	h	bi	o	a	e
A. Latham, 3b	4	1	1	0	2	3	0
T. McCarthy, rf	4	0	0	0	3	1	1
T. O'Neill, lf	4	1	3	1	1	0	0
C. Comiskey, 1b	4	0	0	0	3	2	0
Y. Robinson, 2b	4	1	1	0	0	3	1
C. Duffee, cf	4	1	1	0	4	0	1
S. Fuller, ss	4	0	1	1	3	1	1
J. Milligan, c	3	0	2	1	7	2	1
E. Chamberlain, p	3	0	1	0	1	1	0
	34	4	10	3	24	13	5

Brooklyn   200 000 00* - 9
St. Louis   000 012 10 - 0
*Game forfeited to Brooklyn with one man on base and no one out in the top of the ninth.

	ip	h	r-er	bb	so
Caruthers	8	10	4-1	0	3
Chamberlain	#8	7	2-1	3	4

#faced two batters in ninth
WP: Chamberlain. PB: Clark, Milligan

LOB: Bkn 8, StL 6. BE: Bkn 2, StL 3. Base on Missed Third Strike: Bkn 1.
DP: McCarthy-Latham.
2B: Collins, Pinckney, O'Neill, Fuller.
SB: O'Brien, Corkhill, Latham, Clark. CS: Latham, O'Neill, O'Brien, Chamberlain
Time - 2:25 Attendance - 15,143
Umpire: F. Goldsmith

After the Browns forfeited the game the following day, the final two games of the series were rained out. By the end of the week, St. Louis trailed by 7 games.

On September 23rd, a special Association meeting officially reversed the September 7th forfeit, declaring the Browns victors, 4-2. But the Sunday forfeit remained on the books.

Meanwhile, the Browns put on a tremendous spurt to try and capture their fifth straight pennant. They won twelve games in a row. But they lost a game on their last day and finished with a 90-45 record, two games behind Brooklyn's 93-44 mark.

Before the next season started, the Bridegrooms and the Cincinnati Reds had jumped to the National League, and the players' Brotherhood had set up its own league, the Player's League. Many prominent players, including seven Browns, jumped to the new circuit.

1890 — Saturday, August 16th, at Sportsman's Park

Browns Overcome Nine-Run Deficit, Beat Athletics, 12-11

Ramsey Pitches Great Ball in Relief

Visitors' Behavior Disgusting, Welch Ejected

The St. Louis Browns pulled a victory out of the fire with a long, uphill battle against the Athletics of Philadelphia. After just two innings, the visitors had built up a 9-0 lead against St. Louis pitcher Jack Stivetts. Tom "Toad" Ramsey was then substituted, and he pitched a great game. Meanwhile, his teammates began hitting against two Athletic pitchers and eventually won the game, 12-11.

The Athletics tried to secure their lead by intimidating umpire Bob Emslie into making the game go their way. They ignored the rules and harrassed the arbiter to the limit of human endurance. It was only Emslie's exceptional forbearance that kept them from forfeiting the game.

Today's Results
ST. LOUIS 12 - Athletics 11
Louisville 9 - Rochester 7
Columbus 7 - Syracuse 1
Toledo 9 - Brooklyn 4

Standings	W-L	Pct.	GB
Louisville	59-31	.656	-
ST. LOUIS	54-36	.600	5
Athletic	48-43	.527	11½
Columbus	47-44	.516	12½
Rochester	45-44	.506	13½
Toledo	44-44	.500	14
Syracuse	37-53	.411	22
Brooklyn	26-65	.286	33½

The Athletics were a fine club and held first place in the Association race for eight weeks. But then they began to degenerate in July. Today they looked more like a band of thugs than a baseball nine. Captain Curt Welch, the former Brown, was the champion kicker of all, and he was eventually ejected from the game and fined $50. Sadie McMahon and Blondie Purcell were also fined.

Aided by Stivetts's wildness, the visitors started the game as if they intended to spend the entire afternoon at bat. After St. Louis went out in the top of the first, the Athletics came in and scored three runs. Purcell got a hit, and Jack O'Brien was hit by a pitch. George Shaffer hit a fly to right field that Chief Rossman muffed and then returned wildly, allowing two runs in. Kid Baldwin singled across another run.

The Athletics scored six in the second. Joe Kappel started with a clean home run. After Ed Seward was retired, Stivetts hit both Ben Conroy and Curt Welch with wild serves. Then Purcell walked. Denny Lyons delivered a double, and O'Brien singled. It was at this point that Ramsey replaced Stivetts as the Browns' pitcher. He retired the side, but not before the score stood 9-0 in favor of the Athletics.

St. Louis scored its first run in the third inning, but the Athletics regained their nine-run lead by also counting once in the third.

Tommy McCarthy tripled and scored for the Browns in the fourth, then the visitors were held without a run.

Neither side scored in the fifth.

In the sixth, St. Louis got back into the game with five runs. Two men were out before the rally started. Then Charles "Count" Campau was given a base on balls. Roseman hit for two bases, Ed Cartwright hit for one, Bill Higgins for two, Charlie Duffee for one, John Munyan for two, and Ramsey for one, all of the hits coming in succession.

Seward finally got the last out, but, at the start of the seventh, Welch tried to replace him with Sadie McMahon. The change was in obvious violation of the new substitute rule, since McMahon was not listed on the lineup card as one of the Athletics' two designated substitutes. The Browns argued vigorously with Emslie, but Welch browbeat the umpire into allowing McMahon to pitch. Capt. Campau then formally announced that his club was playing the game under protest. After the Browns won the game, however, the protest became a moot point.

McMahon was off in his form, and the Browns continued their hard hitting against his slants. In the seventh inning, McCarthy walked and stole. Cartwright and Higgins singled with two out to score the run, making the count 10-8 in favor of the Athletics.

St. Louis finally took the lead in the eighth. Munyan walked, and Ramsey sacrificed him along. Shortly Fuller singled. McCarthy then hit a slow one to first baseman O'Brien. The runner and the fielder collided heavily at the base, while Munyan scored. Emslie called McCarthy safe, and the Athletics put up a terrific cry. After a heated discussion, Emslie pulled his watch out and threatened to forfeit the game to St. Louis. Although it took much longer than the minimum time required to forfeit the game, the Athletics finally returned to their positions, and the game continued. The Browns made a couple more hits and piled up four runs in the inning, taking a 12-10 lead. All through the latter part of the round, the Athletics hurled the vilest epithets at poor Emslie.

Welch scored a run for the Athletics in the last of the eighth on a hit, a steal, a wild pitch, and a single by Purcell.

In the ninth inning, Welch became uncontrollable in his accusations to the umpire, and Emslie finally ordered him off the field. For ten minutes he refused to go, but finally, after another threat of a forfeit, he went amidst the loud jeering of the cranks in the stands. Ed Seward was brought back into the game to play center field. This was another illegal substitution, but the Browns saw no point in arguing.

Neither side scored in the ninth, and the game went to St. Louis by a 12-11 final score. The fans left the grounds satisfied with the outcome of the contest, but disgusted with the language and conduct of the visitors. The Athletics left the field cursing Emslie for his work.

St. Louis	ab	r	h	bi	o	a	e
S. Fuller, ss	5	1	1	0	0	0	0
T. McCarthy, 3b	4	3	2	1	2	1	0
C. Campau, rf	4	2	1	1	0	0	0
C. Roseman, lf	5	1	2	2	1	0	3
E. Cartwright, 1b	5	1	2	2	9	1	0
B. Higgins, 2b	5	1	2	1	4	2	0
C. Duffee, cf	5	1	3	0	2	0	0
J. Munyan, c	4	2	3	2	9	3	1
J. Stivetts, p	0	0	0	0	0	0	0
T. Ramsey, p2	5	0	1	0	0	0	0
	42	12	17	9	27	7	4

Athletics	ab	r	h	bi	o	a	e
C. Welch, cf	3	2	2	1	1	0	0
E. Seward, cf9	0	0	0	0	0	0	0
B. Purcell, lf	4	2	3	0	0	0	0
D. Lyons, 3b	5	1	2	2	3	5	0
J. O'Brien, 1b	4	2	1	1	13	0	1
G. Shaffer, rf	4	1	1	0	2	1	0
K. Baldwin, c	5	0	1	1	4	0	0
J. Kappel, ss	5	1	1	1	2	7	1
E. Seward, p	3	1	1	0	0	0	0
S. McMahon, p7	1	0	0	0	0	0	0
B. Conroy, 2b	3	1	0	0	2	2	0
	37	11	12	6	27	15	2

St. Louis	001	105	104	— 12
Athletics	361	000	010	— 11

	ip	h	r-er	bb	so
Stivetts	1.1	5	9-4	1	0
Ramsey (W 23-12)	7.2	7	2-2	1	10
Seward	6	11	7-4	1	1
McMahon (L 24-14)	3	6	5-5	2	0

WP: Seward, Ramsey. PB: Baldwin.
HPB: by Stivetts 3 (O'Brien, Conroy, Welch), by Ramsey (Welch).

LOB: StL 5, Athl 5.
DP: Cartwright-Higgins, Kappel-O'Brien, Shaffer-O'Brien.
2B: Lyons, Munyan 2, Seward, Roseman, Higgins, Purcell.
3B: McCarthy. HR: Kappel.
SB: McCarthy 3, O'Brien, Welch.
Time - 2:30
Attendance - 2,200
Umpire: B. Emslie

Ramsey developed arm trouble a few weeks later, and the Browns were unable to climb in the race, slipping to third place by the finish. Their record was 78-58.

The Athletics, meanwhile, went bankrupt, sold many of their players, and finished the season with a 22-game losing streak, which landed them in seventh place.

After the season, the Players' League collapsed, and stars like Comiskey and O'Neill returned to the Browns.

1891 — Sunday, October 4th, at Sportsman's Park

Breitenstein Pitches No-Hitter as Browns and Colonels Split Final Games

St. Louis Hurler Stifles Louisville in First Start

Colonels Win Second Game on Hoy's Muff

The St. Louis Browns and the Louisville Colonels closed the 1891 championship season by winning one game each today. In the first game, the Browns gave their young pitching recruit, Ted Breitenstein, his first chance to pitch a full game, and he equalled all records by shutting Louisville out without the semblance of a hit. Will McGill pitched effectively for the Browns in the second game. But the Colonels bunched three hits with a walk and a fatal error by William "Dummy" Hoy, and they scored enough runs in one inning to win the game, 4-3.

The Browns finished their season in second place behind the Boston Reds. St. Louis had the satisfaction of knowing that they won the season series from all seven opposing teams. Their record for ten years in the American Association revealed a .644 overall winning percentage (781-432), and at home their percentage was a fantastic .720 (458-178).

Today's Results
ST. LOUIS 8 - Louisville 0 (1st game)
Louisville 4 - ST. LOUIS 3 (8 inn.) (2nd)
Milwaukee 8 - Columbus 4
no other games scheduled

Standings	W-L	Pct.	GB
Boston	92-41	.692	-
ST. LOUIS	85-51	.625	8½
Athletic	72-65	.526	22
Baltimore	69-63	.523	22½
Milwaukee	64-72	.471	29½
Columbus	61-76	.445	33
Louisville	54-83	.394	40
Washington	43-89	.326	48½

Today the Browns gave their patrons two games for the price of one admission for the first time this year. About 2,500 people took advantage of the bargain, despite the cold weather.

Having nothing to lose, the Browns used a 22-year-old Theodore Breitenstein in the box. The St. Louis native had pitched on five occasions since the Browns bought his contract from the Grand Rapids club. On all of those occasions, he had pitched only the latter part of a game. Today he was given his first starting assignment, and he went through the Louisvilles as if he were facing amateurs. It is doubtful if he ever had an easier game, even when he was pitching the "Home Comforts" to the local semi-pro championship a few years back. Only one visiting player reached first (on a walk), and that man was promptly caught trying to steal second. The strawberry blonde lefthander struck out five Colonel batters.

He was given errorless support, with each of the fielders handling at least one chance. Although there were no really spectacular plays, Shorty Fuller, Tip O'Neill, Charlie Comiskey, Jack Boyle, and John Munyan all distinguished themselves for St. Louis.

The Louisville pitcher in the first game was also a rookie, Jouett Meekin. His speed was nearly as hard to hit as Breitenstein's, but his control was poor, and his catchers could not stop his wild pitching. Only two of the Browns' eight runs would have been earned by hitting alone.

St. Louis scored twice in the first inning. Hoy stopped a pitch with his arm and went to first. Tommy McCarthy singled, O'Neill then pounded a long two-bagger, driving two men across.

Munyan scored in the second without the aid of a bat striking the ball. He was given first on four balls and scored on three passed balls. The Louisville catcher, Tom Cahill, was severely handicapped by a hand injury, and he was soon replaced by Al Schellhasse.

Jack Boyle was next to make the circuit. He went around the bases in the sixth inning on a single, stolen base, and two infield outs.

Fuller and McCarthy scored in the seventh. They were helped along by a wild pitch and a throwing error by shortstop Hugh Jennings.

"Bad Bill" Eagan and Munyan counted in the eighth, aided by wild pitching, to bring the final score to 8-0.

Meanwhile, Breitenstein was tying the Louisville hitters into knots in their futile efforts to connect solidly. Mostly they popped feebly to waiting fielders.

When the final out was made, the crowd gave a nice cheer to the remarkable young pitcher.

After a brief interval, the second game got under way. The batteries were McGill and Munyan for St. Louis and John Fitzgerald and "Farmer" Bill Weaver for Louisville. By this time the wind had picked up into a gale, and the players seemed reluctant to swing the bat. As a result, nine of them waited for bases on balls. Twelve hits were made, six by each side. Of the five errors in the game, four were made by the visitors and one by the Browns. But the one St. Louis error proved fatal.

The Browns built an early lead of 2-0 on run-scoring singles by Munyan in the second and fourth innings.

The Colonels scored all of their runs in the bottom of the fourth. With one out, Tim Shinnick waited for a walk. Cahill, playing outfield in the second game, delivered a single. After a force play, Monk Cline rapped a single to left, scoring Shinnick. Weaver lifted a high fly to center field. The wind played tricks with the ball, but Hoy got under it. The ball hit squarely in his hands, and the crowd let out a cheer. But the sphere popped out of his grasp and fell to the ground, Cahill and Fitzgerald scoring and Weaver taking second. While the Browns were arguing that the ball had been held long enough for a legal catch, Weaver, who was standing on second base, grabbed the ball from Fuller and threw it into right field. Then he ran to third, while the crowd howled. The umpire had not been watching, so he allowed Weaver to stay at third. A single by Harry Taylor brought him home.

The Browns got one run in the fifth, making the score 4-3. But that was all they could manage, and the game was called because of darkness and cold in the middle of the eighth inning.

FIRST GAME

St. Louis	ab	r	h	bi	o	a	e	Louisville	ab	r	h	bi	o	a	e
D. Hoy, cf	4	1	0	0	1	0	0	M. Cline, lf	3	0	0	0	3	0	0
S. Fuller, ss	4	1	1	0	2	2	0	F. Weaver, cf	3	0	0	0	0	1	0
T. McCarthy, rf	4	2	2	0	1	0	0	H. Taylor, 1b	2	0	0	0	12	0	0
T. O'Neill, lf	4	0	1	2	1	0	0	H. Jennings, ss	3	0	0	0	2	6	1
C. Comiskey, 1b	5	0	0	1	9	1	0	C. Wolf, rf	3	0	0	0	2	0	0
J. Boyle, 3b	5	1	1	0	4	1	0	W. Kuehne, 3b	3	0	0	0	1	1	1
B. Eagan, 2b	4	1	1	0	1	4	0	T. Shinnick, 2b	3	0	0	0	1	4	0
J. Munyan, c	2	2	1	1	7	1	0	T. Cahill, c	0	0	0	0	2	0	0
T. Breitenstein, p	3	0	0	1	1	0	0	A. Schellhasse, c3	3	0	0	0	4	1	0
								J. Meekin, p	3	0	0	0	0	2	0
	35	8	7	5	27	9	0		26	0	0	0	27	15	2

St. Louis	210	001	220	-	8	LOB: StL 7, Louv 0. BE: StL 1.
Louisville	000	000	000	-	0	2B: O'Neill.

	ip	h	r-er	bb	so	
Breitenstein (W 2-0)	9	0	0-0	1	5	SB: Fuller, O'Neill, Boyle.
Meekin (L 9-17)	9	7	8-6	6	4	Time - 2:00
HPB: by Meekin (Hoy)						Attendance - 2,500
						Umpire: T. Dolan

SECOND GAME

				r	h	e	Batteries
St. Louis	010	110	00 -	3	6	1	W. McGill (L 20-14) & J. Munyan.
Louisville	000	400	0x -	4	6	4	J. Fitzgerald (W 13-16) & F. Weaver.

game called on account of darkness

The American Association and the National League had been engaged in a contract "war" all year, and, after the season ended, most of the Browns' top stars signed with N. L. teams. Von der Ahe was able to sign a few N. L. players, but his team lost heavily. Breitenstein was the only member of the 1891 Browns to play with the team in 1892.

Chris had also lost a great deal of money bankrolling the A. A. in Cincinnati and elsewhere. Finally, he led the Association to make peace with the League.

Chapter II
Doormats in the National League
1892-1898

1892—April 17th at Sportsman's Park
Browns Lose to Reds in National League's First-Ever Sunday Game

1893—September 30th at the new Sportsman's Park
Browns End Season with Two Wet Wins Over Beaneaters

1894—May 10th at Cincinnati
St. Louis Hits Six Home Runs But Loses to Cincinnati, 18-9

1895—May 24th at Sportsman's Park
Miller Makes Four Errors in One Inning, Replaced as Team Captain

1896—July 6th at Sportsman's Park
Umpire Leaves Field in Fifth, Rain Halts Game in Ninth

1897—September 26th at Sportsman's Park
Browns Lose Two More Games for 18 Straight Defeats

1898—April 17th at Sportsman's Park
Browns Lose, 14-1, On Site of Burned-Out Sportsman's Park

In 1891, a contract war between the American Association and the National League broke out. After the season, the Browns lost most of their good players to N.L. raids. In December, St. Louis owner Chris Von der Ahe led the A.A. into a peace agreement with the N.L. The settlement called for four A.A. clubs, including St. Louis, to merge with the N.L., forming a twelve-team league officially called the "National League and American Association of Professional Base Ball Clubs." Thus, St. Louis was admitted to the National League, where it has had a franchise ever since.

As a part of the peace agreement. St. Louis was allowed to retain Sunday games, breaking the N.L.'s traditional stance against games on the Sabbath. The first Sunday game in National League history was played at Sportsman's Park, April 17, 1892, with the Browns losing to the Cincinnati Reds, 5-1. St. Louis did poorly in the new league, finishing ninth and eleventh in the two halves of the split 1892 season.

In 1893, Von der Ahe moved his team to a new ballpark, also called Sportsman's Park, at the corner of Natural Bridge Avenue and Vandeventer Avenue. The Browns were still a weak team. They relied on pitching more than on hitting, and, in 1893, the pitching distance was increased about 5 feet to the present distance of 60½ feet. This helped the hitters greatly, and the Browns were adversely affected. They could not beat the champion Boston Beaneaters until the last day of the season, when St. Louis won two games by lopsided scores.

In 1894, offense reached an all-time high. But St. Louis wasn't helped much. In one game, the Browns hit six home runs, including three in a row, and still lost handily, 18-9.

In 1895, Browns' captain and catcher George Miller set a record by making four throwing errors in one inning. He was so disgusted with himself that he quit as captain after the game. The Browns continued to get worse, finishing the season in eleventh place.

After the 1895 season, Von der Ahe opened Sportsman's Park to horse racing, much to the disgust of the baseball world. In 1896, he added lights for night racing and installed amusement park features like a "shoot the chutes" roller coaster.

In 1896, the Browns were eleventh again. A demoralized lot, they once drove the umpire from the field with their complaining. Apparently they did better without an ump, because they tied the game after having lost 12 games in a row.

In 1897, the team was the worst yet, finishing dead last. Their final winning percentage was a mere .221, still the worst in the history of the franchise. They had a late-season losing streak of 18 games, which also still stands as a franchise record.

In 1898, Chris decided on a rebuilding program for the Browns. A president, B. Stuart Muckenfuss, and a manager, Tim Hurst, were hired with independent authority. The amusement park and racing facilities at Sportsman's Park were removed, and the club was going to work strictly on baseball. But the park burned down on the second day of the season. A makeshift facility was thrown up literally overnight, with the Browns' players helping the construction crews, but St. Louis lost the next day's game in dispiriting fashion, 14-1. The team finished twelfth again.

Since the club had invested most of its money into rebuilding the park, it did not have enough left to pay all its bills. When it failed to retire some bonds on time, a bank had the courts put the club into receivership. So, after 17 years as a big-league magnate, Chris Von der Ahe lost control of his club.

1892—Sunday, April 17th, at Sportsman's Park
Browns Lose to Reds in National League's First-Ever Sunday Game
Cincinnati Players Hit Three Long Home Runs, Win 5-1
Latham, Comiskey, O'Neill Cheered in Debut Here as Visitors

Chris Von der Ahe's St. Louis Browns have moved into the National League and have brought Sunday baseball with them. Today an Easter Sunday crowd of over 15,000 people came to Sportsman's Park to see the first Sunday game of the year.

The Browns, of course, played Sunday games throughout their ten years in the American Association. As a condition to their entering the National League, they were allowed to keep playing Sunday ball, breaking the league's sixteen-year-old prohibition against sport on the Sabbath. Louisville and Cincinnati were the only other N.L. clubs to schedule Sunday games this season, but Cincinnati magnate John T. Brush, after seeing today's fine crowd, predicted that every club in the league would have Sunday games soon.

Today's Results
Cincinnati 5 - ST. LOUIS 1
no other games scheduled

Standings	W-L	Pct.	GB
Boston	2-0	1.000	-
New York	2-0	1.000	-
Pittsburg	3-1	.750	-
Louisville	2-1	.667	½
Brooklyn	2-1	.667	½
Chicago	2-1	.667	½
Philadelphia	1-1	.500	1
Cincinnati	2-3	.400	1½
Cleveland	1-2	.333	1½
ST. LOUIS	1-3	.250	2
Washington	0-2	.000	2
Baltimore	0-3	.000	2½

Despite threatening weather, today's throng overflowed the grandstand, and people had to stand behind ropes in the outfield. Ground rules called for balls hit into the crowd to be two-base hits. Three doubles were hit in the game. And three balls were hit over the fence and into the bleachers. They were home runs, crowd or no crowd.

Many patrons were seeing the new Browns for the first time. In today's lineup, none of the Browns were with the team last year. Six played with National League clubs, two were with other American Association teams, and one spent 1891 in the minors.

The performers most familiar to the spectators were Arlie Latham, Charlie Comiskey, and Tip O'Neill, all now with the Reds. All three were given rousing ovations by the St. Louis cranks when they were introduced for their first turns at bat.

Each of them got hits, with Latham getting two. But the men who did the most for the Reds' victory were Tony Mullane (who pitched a three-hitter) and Bid McPhee, Jocko Halligan, and Bug Holliday (all of whom hit home runs).

Except for the long-distance slugging against him, St. Louis pitcher Bob Caruthers pitched a fine game. Bob had played four years with Brooklyn, but signed with St. Louis this winter. Today he was also lustily cheered when he made his appearance.

Captain Jack Glasscock of the Browns chose to take first bats, and his men went out in order.

For Cincinnati, McPhee led off with an out. Then Latham stepped to the plate amid the acclaim of the fans. He indulged in a hefty round of his famous joking and chattering, then he lined out a single to left field. He stole second and third, but the next two men couldn't bring him home.

In the second, the Browns again went out quickly.

Tip O'Neill, the shy and quiet one, received a great cheer when he came up to lead off the second inning for the visitors. But Latham, who was on the coaching lines, cut off the applause with a sharp gesture, explaining that Tip was liable to get rattled. After O'Neill grounded out, Arlie muttered, "See, I told you he can't stand too much applause."

Comiskey was next up, and the former Browns' captain was also accorded a rousing reception. He too went out.

In the third inning, McPhee found a slow ball to his liking and drove it into the seats beyond the left center field fence for a home run, giving Cincinnati the first run of the game.

The Browns tied it in the fourth. After being retired in order through the first three innings, the home team got its first base runner when Jack Crooks walked to lead off. Cliff Carroll then hit a hot one down to first base. Comiskey made a fine stop and forced Crooks at second. Steve Brodie shot a hit over shortstop, putting runners on first and second. Perry Werden then hit slowly to shortstop. Comiskey plainly bobbled George Smith's throw, and, by good base running, Carroll raced all the way home, while Brodie made third. But Umpire John Sheridan shocked the assemblage by calling Werden out at first. It was the first of many calls that went against the home club today. George Pinckney then ended the inning with an easy fly to left.

In the fifth, the Browns were turned back on three great assists by McPhee.

Thereafter they failed to mount any sustained hitting attack against Mullane's curves and speed.

Caruthers, meanwhile, showed little of his old-time speed but held the Reds down with his curves and headwork.

Cincinnati finally edged into the lead in the seventh inning, with the help of Mr. Sheridan. With one out, George "Germany" Smith singled and went to third on Jerry Harrington's hit down the right field line. Mullane then lifted a fly to Brodie in right, and the runner tried to score after the catch. The throw appeared to the home fans to be in the catcher's hands in plenty of time for the out, but Sheridan called Smith safe, and Cincinnati led, 2-1.

They wrapped the game up with heavy hitting in the eighth. Latham opened with a hit to left, which he stretched into a double with a great slide. Halligan then drove a long four-bagger over the outer fence, driving Latham home ahead of him. Not to be outdone, Holliday, a St. Louis boy playing in front of the home folks for the first time in three years, whacked a line drive into the left field bleachers for another home run.

The Browns failed to score in the ninth, and the Reds won, 5-1. To them went the distinction of winning the first Sunday game in National League history

St. Louis	ab	r	h	bi	o	a	e	Cincinnati	ab	r	h	bi	o	a	e
J. Crooks, 2b	3	0	1	0	2	3	0	B. McPhee, 2b	4	1	1	1	4	5	0
C. Carroll, lf	3	1	0	0	0	0	0	A. Latham, 3b	4	1	2	0	1	1	0
S. Brodie, rf	4	0	1	0	2	0	0	J. Halligan, rf	4	1	1	2	0	0	0
P. Werden, 1b	4	0	0	0	14	0	0	B. Holliday, cf	4	1	2	1	2	0	0
G. Pinckney, 3b	3	0	0	0	0	7	1	T. O'Neill, lf	4	0	1	0	1	0	0
J. Glasscock, ss	2	0	0	0	0	5	0	C. Comiskey, 1b	4	0	1	0	13	2	0
B. Van Dyke, cf	3	0	0	0	2	0	0	G. Smith, ss	3	1	1	0	2	3	1
B. Caruthers, p	3	0	0	0	0	1	0	J. Harrington, c	3	0	1	0	4	2	0
D. Buckley, c	3	0	1	0	4	0	0	T. Mullane, p	3	0	0	1	0	4	0
	28	1	3	0	24	16	1		33	5	10	5	27	17	1

St. Louis   000 100 000 - 1
Cincinnati   001 000 13x - 5

	ip	h	r-er	bb	so
Caruthers (L 0-1)	8	10	5-5	1	3
Mullane (W 1-2)	9	3	1-1	3	3

Umpire: J. Sheridan

LOB: StL 3, Cinc 5. DP: Pinckney-Crooks-Werden, Mullane-Comiskey-Latham, Glasscock-Crooks-Werden. 2B: Buckley, Holliday, Latham. HR: McPhee, Halligan, Holliday. SB: Latham 2.
Time - 1:40 Attendance - 15,200

Von der Ahe's Browns, after ten years as one of the powers of the American Association, had begun seven years as National League doormats.

In the N.L.'s split season in 1892, they finished the first half in ninth place with a 31-42 record. In the second half they slipped to eleventh (out of twelve) with a 25-52 mark.

1893—Saturday, September 30th, at the new Sportsman's Park

Browns End Season With Two Wet Wins Over Beaneaters

First St. Louis Victories Over Boston All Year

Quinn, Shugart, Cooley Lead Slugging in 17-6 & 16-4 Decisions

The St. Louis Browns waited until the last day of the season to post their first victories over the champion Boston Beaneaters, but when they finally won, they did it in a big way. They took a doubleheader, winning both games by lopsided scores.

The condition of the playing field was miserable, and the players had trouble controlling both the wet ball and their slipping, sliding feet. The champs seemed to care little for the outcome of the contests, but the Browns' players made good use of their final chance to raise their season batting averages. Joe Quinn got four hits in each game to lead the hitting. Duff Cooley, who sat out most of the first game, played his greatest game in the nightcap, making six hits in six at bats. Frank Shugart played both games and made seven hits and scored eight runs.

The Bostons came to town on Thursday and beat the local club for the tenth time this season without a defeat. When it rained Friday and this morning, it looked like the Browns would end the year without a single victory over the champions. But the rain stopped around noon, and two games were played, as announced, with the home team winning by scores of 17-6 and 16-4.

Today's Results
ST. LOUIS 17 - Boston 6 (1st game)
ST. LOUIS 16 - Boston 4 (2nd)
Pittsburg 8 - New York 6
Philadelphia 10 - Cleveland 2 (6 inn.)
Washington at Cincinnati - cancelled
Baltimore at Louisville - 2 games
  cancelled due to rain
Brooklyn at Chicago - 2 games
  cancelled due to rain

Standings	W-L	Pct.	GB
Boston	86-43	.677	-
Pittsburg	81-48	.628	5
Cleveland	73-55	.570	12½
Philadelphia	72-57	.558	14
New York	68-64	.515	19½
Cincinnati	65-63	.508	20½
Brooklyn	65-63	.508	20½
Baltimore	60-70	.462	26½
Chicago	56-71	.441	29
ST. LOUIS	57-75	.432	30½
Louisville	50-75	.400	34
Washington	40-89	.310	46

The playing field was in no shape for the sport, and the players on both teams seemed more eager to guard against accidents than to give their fullest efforts to capture batted balls. The infield was especially treacherous, and many attempts by the fielders ended in ludicrous falls. In the first game, Boston's Bobby Lowe covered himself with glory (and a lot of mud) by accepting twelve of the thirteen chances offered to him. His partner, Herman Long, on the other hand, was charged with three errors out of eight chances.

The attendance was light (1,505) owing to the weather. For the year, the Browns drew nearly 200,000 customers to their new grounds on Natural Bridge Avenue at Vandeventer, the third best atteadance in the league. The new Sportsman's Park should be given some of the credit for that, since the Browns finished a lowly tenth in the twelve-team pennant race. To be sure, the St. Louis team played its best in front of the home fans, winning 40 and losing 30 at the new park. On the road they played at a 17-45 pace.

St. Louis presented its regular nine in the first game today. Boston made a few lineup changes. Captain Billy Nash was in Chicago attending the World's Fair, and pitcher Jack Stivetts played third base. Jack committed an error in each game, and it looked as if his future at the hot corner was limited. Boston also used two substitutes in the outfield.

Captain Quinn chose first bats for St. Louis, but Boston scored the first run. It came in the bottom of the first inning.

Boston pitcher Hank Gastright lost his control in the second inning. After issuing some costly bases on balls, he laid the ball over the plate for the hitters. The Browns took full advantage of the opportunity and pounded out nine runs.

Boston scored four in the bottom of the inning, but St. Louis added five in the top of the third.

After that, the pitchers settled down, the fielders began to get their sea legs, and the scoring fell off. By the end of the fifth, the score stood at 17-6 in favor of the Browns, but for the next four innings, not a single man crossed the plate. The most noteworthy incident in the latter part of the game was the dislocation of one of "Old Hoss" Art Twineham's fingers by a foul tip in the sixth inning. He was replaced by Duff Cooley.

When the final ledger was tallied, the Browns had 17 runs, 21 hits, and one error. The Beaneaters had 6 runs, 13 hits, and five misplays. Hugh Duffy of Boston and Joe Quinn of St. Louis each had four hits. The Browns' Ted Breitenstein pitched a good game, although, with the big early lead, he didn't have to give his best effort to win.

Between games, there was a ceremony in which Joe Quinn, Charlie Frank, and Ted Breitenstein, all of the Browns, were presented with medals by the locally-based weekly, *The Sporting News,* for finishing first, second, and third, respectively, in that journal's poll for the most popular baseball player in America.

The regular umpire, John McQuaid, left the grounds after the first game, and St. Louis pitcher Art Clarkson was agreed upon as his substitute for the second game. William "Kid" Gleason was the Browns' pitcher, and Harry Staley worked on the slab for Boston. Hugh Duffy left in the middle of the game to catch a train, and Gastright finished out the game in center field for the Beaneaters.

Once again, Boston scored in the bottom of the first, only to have St. Louis take a good lead in the top of the second.

The field had dried out considerably, and the fielding was sharper than in the opening contest. The hitting was also better. The Browns piled up 25 safeties, while Boston added 13. Quinn, Gleason, and Shugart each smacked four hits for St. Louis. But the biggest hitter was the Browns' Cooley, who collected a triple, a double, and four singles.

The final score of the game was 16-4.

The players dressed quickly after the game, and the Browns disbanded for the season. The Boston team, minus Duffy, left for Milwaukee, where they were scheduled to begin an exhibition tour against an All-American team of stars.

FIRST GAME

		r	h	e	Batteries
St. Louis	095 120 000 -	17	21	1	T. Breitenstein (W 19-20) & A. Twineham, D. Cooley.
Boston	140 010 000 -	6	13	5	H. Gastright (L 15-5) & C. Bennett. Umpire: J. McQuaid

SECOND GAME

St. Louis	ab	r	h	bi	o	a	e
T. Dowd, rf	6	2	3	1	1	0	0
F. Shugart, cf	6	5	4	2	3	0	0
D. Cooley, c	6	1	6	3	3	2	0
C. Frank, lf	5	0	1	1	2	0	0
P. Werden, 1b	5	0	1	1	8	0	1
B. Ely, ss	5	0	0	5	4	0	
J. Quinn, 2b	5	2	4	0	4	2	1
J. Crooks, 3b	5	2	2	1	1	0	0
K. Gleason, p	5	4	4	3	0	3	0
	48	16	25	12	27	11	2

Boston	ab	r	h	bi	o	a	e
H. Long, ss	5	1	2	0	3	5	0
B. Lowe, 2b	5	0	0	0	5	3	0
H. Duffy, cf	3	0	1	0	1	0	0
H. Gastright, cf6	2	0	0	0	0	0	0
T. Tucker, 1b	5	2	2	0	13	0	0
J. Stivetts, 3b	4	1	3	1	1	0	1
C. Ganzel, rf	4	0	2	2	2	0	0
B. Van Dyke, lf	4	0	1	0	2	0	0
C. Bennett, c	3	0	0	0	0	6	3
H. Staley, p	4	0	2	0	0	6	2
	39	4	13	3	27	17	4

| St. Louis | 031 204 402 | - | 16 |
| Boston | 101 020 000 | - | 4 |

	ip	h	r-er	bb	so
Gleason (W 21-25)	9	13	4-3	1	0
Staley (L 19-10)	9	25	16-10	0	0

Umpire: A. Clarkson
Time - 1:40

LOB: StL 5, Bos 9. DP: Quinn-Ely-Werden, Staley-Long-Tucker.
2B: Shugart, Cooley, Gleason, Ganzel.
3B: Cooley, Long, Stivetts.
SB: Cooley, Shugart 2.
Attendance - 1,505

Thus ended another poor season for the Browns. They made only one major move over the winter, acquiring George Miller from Pittsburg. A catcher-infielder, Miller also replaced Bill Watkins as manager.

1894—Tuesday, May 10th, at League Park, Cincinnati
St. Louis Hits Six Home Runs But Loses to Cincinnati, 18-9
Shugart Hits Three, Peitz Two, and Miller One
Long Hits Can't Match Nine Singles in One Inning by Reds

The few fans who came to see the game at Cincinnati today were entertained by a slugging match. Since the pitching box was replaced by the more distant (60½ feet) pitcher's plate in 1893, the hitters have had all the best of it.

Today's game offered a classic study of the two different methods of batting runs around. The St. Louis Browns gave a fine exhibition of long hitting by poling six home runs. However, the Cincinnati Reds gave an even more convincing demonstration of the advantages of bunching short hits when they strung together nine singles, along with a walk, a hit batsman, and a couple of errors, to score eleven runs in one inning. This rally won the game for the home team, 18-9, despite the home runs by the visitors.

The Reds knocked the Browns' two star pitchers, Pink Hawley and Ted Breitenstein, out of the game, and first baseman Charlie Frank finished the game as St. Louis's pitcher. Tom Parrott pitched for Cincinnati, and, while he was hit hard, his batting helped win the game. He got four hits, including his team's only home run.

Today's Results
Cincinnati 18 - ST. LOUIS 9
Cleveland 2 - Pittsburg 1
Philadelphia 9 - Baltimore 3
Boston 7 - Brooklyn 1
New York 6 - Washington 2
Louisville at Chicago - ppd., rain

Standings	W-L	Pct.	GB
Cleveland	13-2	.867	-
Baltimore	12-5	.706	2
Philadephia	11-6	.647	3
Boston	11-6	.647	3
Pittsburgh	10-6	.625	3½
ST. LOUIS	8-8	.500	5½
New York	8-8	.500	5½
Cincinnati	6-8	.429	6½
Louisville	5-9	.357	7½
Brooklyn	6-11	.353	8
Washington	3-15	.167	11½
Chicago	2-11	.154	10

The Brown's home runs were hit by three players. Three came off the bat of Frank Shugart. He also got an ordinary single. Heinie Peitz hit two homers, and George Miller hit one. All of these four-baggers were long flies into the seats beyond the fence and would have been home runs in any park.

Only about 1,800 faithful cranks paid their way into the park today, partly because of the cool weather and partly because of the poor showing of the local team so far this year. Most prominent among the onlookers were the two club owners, John T. Brush and Christian F.W. Von der Ahe. For three innings, Von der Ahe was beaming and chortling, while Brush wore a black expression. Suddenly the Reds made their big rally, and Brush's face brightened, while Von der Ahe began to look like a ripe tomato about to explode.

After Tommy Dowd walked to open the game, Shugart came up for the first time. He took a liking to Parrott's speed right from the start, driving a pitch over the fence for two runs.

Peitz hit his first walk-around shot in the fourth inning, giving St. Louis a 3-0 lead.

Hawley had allowed just one hit, a scratch by McCarthy, through the first three innings. But in the fourth the dam broke suddenly, and the Reds came rushing through. Arlie Latham opened with a base on balls. Bug Holliday bounced an infield hit past the pitcher. Bid McPhee then sent a scorcher whistling past Miller at third base, and Latham scored the first run. Frank Motz squared around to bunt, but Hawley's fastball hit him instead, loading the bases. Captain Miller ordered the infield to play in, and "Farmer" Harry Vaughn guided a ground ball through the defense for a hit. "Germany" George Smith then stroked a pop fly to a spot just beyond the reach of shortstop Bones Ely, putting the Reds ahead.

Hawley was becoming demoralized at this time, and he began laying the ball over the middle of the home base. Parrott, "Dummy" Hoy, and Jack McCarthy all singled in succession, bringing the Cincinnati score up to seven. Latham came up for the second time in the inning and dropped down a bunt, which Hawley fumbled, loading the bases. Holliday finally made the first out of the inning, a fly ball on which Hoy scored. McPhee and Motz added hits. After throwing errors by Duff Cooley and Peitz had brought the total to eleven runs, Vaughn and Smith made outs, ending the agony.

Parrott hit his home run in the next inning with a drive to the terrace in left field. That was the only Reds' run in the fifth, but it convinced "Calliope" Miller to bring Breitenstein in to pitch in the sixth.

Before he got into the game, the Browns gave their most impressive display of power. In the top of the sixth, Shugart, Miller, and Peitz, batting in succession, all reached the seats with long drives for homers. It was the first time in National League history that three consecutive batters had hit home runs.

For a fleeting moment it seemed as if St. Louis might get back into the ball game. But then Breitenstein ruined their chances. He was raked for four singles, two doubles, and walk, giving Cincinnati five more runs.

The Browns got three in the seventh. Breitenstein hit for two bases and scored on a throwing error by McPhee. Dowd was given a life on the misplay and was once again spared when the Cincinnati second baseman allowed him to steal by dropping a throw. Dowd then trotted home for the second time in front of a home run by Shugart.

Breitenstein was told to save his arm for a better day, and Frank was brought in to pitch. He worked the final two innings and was lucky to escape with only one run scored against him.

Parrott held Shugart to a mere one-base hit in the ninth and retired the next three hitters to end the game.

The final score was 18-9 in favor of Cincinnati.

Umpire Ed Swartwood had done such an outstanding job that no one noticed him until the game was over.

St. Louis	ab	r	h	bi	o	a	e
T. Dowd, lf	3	2	0	0	1	0	0
C. Frank, 1b-p7	4	0	0	0	5	1	0
F. Shugart, cf	5	3	4	5	5	0	0
G. Miller, 3b	5	1	2	1	1	0	0
H. Peitz, c	4	2	2	2	1	0	1
J. Quinn, 2b	5	0	1	0	5	3	0
B. Ely, ss	4	0	1	0	3	3	0
D. Cooley, rf	4	0	0	0	2	0	2
P. Hawley, p	2	0	0	0	1	1	1
T. Breitenstein, p6	1	1	1	0	0	1	0
D. Buckley	1	0	1	0	0	0	0
	38	9	12	8	24	9	4

Cincinnati	ab	r	h	bi	o	a	e
D. Hoy, cf	5	2	3	1	2	1	0
J. McCarthy, rf	6	1	3	4	2	0	0
A. Latham, 3b	4	2	1	0	1	2	0
B. Holliday, lf	3	2	1	1	2	0	0
B. McPhee, 2b	5	3	3	2	2	7	2
F. Motz, 1b	4	1	1	1	10	0	0
H. Vaughn, c	5	1	1	2	6	0	0
G. Smith, ss	4	3	2	2	2	2	0
T. Parrott, p	5	3	4	3	0	1	0
	41	18	19	16	27	13	2

St. Louis   200 1 0 3 300 - 9
Cincinnati   000 1(11)5 01x - 18

	ip	h	r-er	bb	so
Hawley (L 2-2)	5	11	12-9	2	0
Breitenstein	1	5	5-5	1	0
Frank	2	3	1-1	2	0
Parrott (W 4-2)	9	12	9-7	3	3

HBP: by Hawley (Motz)

LOB: StL 6, Cinc. 5.
BE: StL 1, Cinc 1.
DP: Smith-McPhee, Ely-Quinn.
2B: Parrott, McCarthy, Breitenstein.
HR: Shugart 3, Peitz, Miller, Parrott. SH: Frank
SB: Hoy.
Time - 1:55
Attendance - 1,800
Umpire: E. Swartwood

It was another lackluster season for St. Louis. The Browns finished in ninth place, one percentage point ahead of the Reds.

That was one notch higher than they had finished in 1893, although their 1894 record of 56-76 was slightly worse than their mark of a year before.

1895 — Friday, May 24th, at Sportsman's Park
Miller Makes Four Errors in One Inning, Replaced as Team Captain
Manager Buckenberger Appoints Peitz
Errors Allow Washington to Beat St. Louis, 8-4

Today's game was lost by the Browns thanks to the errors of Captain George Miller. In the second inning, he made four wild throws into center field, trying to stop opponents from stealing. After the game the foghorn-voiced player was so disgusted with himself that he went to Manager Al Buckenberger and asked to be laid off. Buckenberger then relieved Miller of the captaincy and conferred the position upon Heinie Peitz.

"I do not say we are pennant winners," Buckenberger conceded, "but I think we should make a respectable showing." After today's display, the manager expressed hope that the change in captains would help the team shake its lethargy and also help Miller snap out of his slump.

All who were consulted wished the popular Peitz luck in his new assignment. But, if today's game was any indication, it will take more than luck to help the Browns. The defeat left them just barely ahead of both Washington and Brooklyn, and another lost game might drop them to eleventh place.

Today's Results

Washington 8 - ST. LOUIS 4
Pittsburg 5 - Boston 4 (13 inn.)
Philadelphia 14 - Cincinnati 13 (10)
Cleveland 14 - New York 11
no other games scheduled

Standings	W-L	Pct.	GB
Pittsburg	19-8	.704	-
Chicago	18-10	.643	1½
Cincinnati	18-10	.643	1½
Cleveland	17-10	.630	2
Philadelphia	13-11	.542	4½
Boston	12-11	.522	5
New York	12-12	.500	5½
Baltimore	10-10	.500	5½
ST. LOUIS	10-18	.357	9½
Washington	8-16	.333	9½
Brooklyn	8-16	.333	9½
Louisville	5-18	.217	12

The Browns played a miserable game and made even the lowly Washington Senators look like world-beaters. St. Louis committed nine errors, which ruined a well-pitched game by Harry Staley. Joe Quinn and Tom Brown also played well for the home team, but they were overwhelmed by the bad play of their teammates. Miller, of course, was the worst. Not only did he make the four throwing errors as catcher, he made a fumble of an easy grounder after switching to third base. This error led to yet another Washington run. Peitz made a costly error at third and was charged with a passed ball after changing places with Miller. Duff Cooley dropped a fly in left, and Quinn and Bones Ely made infield errors, but none of these contributed directly to the scoring.

Al Maul pitched for the visitors. He won the game without putting on a very impressive exhibition of hurling. His batting (two doubles) was better than his pitching.

St. Louisans Billy Joyce and Bill Hassamaer made their first appearances of the season in their home town, and they were given a rousing reception, as was former Brown Jack Crooks.

Umpire William Long was unable to work the game due to a foot injury, and the two captains were unable to agree upon a player to take his place. Eventually, Joe Battin, the old third baseman, was brought out of the stands. He did a fine job. His only trouble came in the bottom of the first inning. The leadoff batter, Brown, hit a slow roller to first baseman Ed Cartwright, who fielded the ball and lumbered to the bag just as the speedy Brown raced across the bag. Battin called the runner safe, and Maul let out a howl. The pitcher than came up behind the umpire and gave him a shove. A regular umpire would have banished the player straightaway, but Battin, unsure of his authority, did nothing.

After a scoreless first round, Miller filled center field with bad throws, and Washington scored four runs in the second. Dan Coogan led off with a walk. He was forced at second by Crooks. The new runner then started the parade by stealing second and getting third on Miller's first error. Charlie Abbey singled him home. Abbey stole second and was given third on an overthrow. He scored while Maul was being put out. Kip Selbach hit down to third base and reached first on a fumble. He immediately took off for second and, naturally, made third on Miller's wild throw. Joyce plated him with a base hit, and Billy repeated the stolen base-wild throw routine. Hassamaer then drove a ball between the outfielders, scoring Joyce from third, but the batter foolishly made two bases on the hit. If he had stayed at first, he undoubtedly could have made third on a wild throw. Jim "Deacon" McGuire flied out, ending the inning.

After four errors as a catcher, Miller went to third base, switching positions with Peitz. In the fifth inning, the "Foghorn" proved that he could do damage from his infield position, too. He fumbled Cartwright's easy grounder, giving the batter a base. Cartwright advanced to second on a passed ball and scored on a pair of outs.

In the seventh inning, the Senators upped their score to eight. This time they did it mostly by good hitting. McGuire started with a walk, Cartwright and Coogan singled, and Maul finished with a two-base hit.

St. Louis rallied in their half of the inning, counting three runs. Quinn opened with a safe hit. Ely lifted an easy fly to left center, which Selbach and Abbey allowed to drop for a gift double. Dowd bounced down to Joyce, and the third baseman fumbled, loading the bases. Staley flied out, but Brown rapped a great hit to right field, driving two runs across and sending Dowd to third. Cooley hit into a force play, and Dowd scored.

The Browns made their final rally in the last of the ninth, but it was too little and too late. Dowd opened with a hit. Ted Breitenstein was sent to bat for Staley, and he hit a daisy to right for a base. Brown popped out. Cooley singled, scoring Dowd. Miller made his last contribution to the cause by hitting into a force out at second. Roger Connor ended the game by hitting an easy pop fly to Joyce. The final score was 8-4.

The disheartened Miller then met with Buckenberger, and was demoted to a mere player.

Washington	ab	r	h	bi	o	a	e	St. Louis	ab	r	h	bi	o	a	e
K. Selbach, lf	5	1	2	0	3	0	0	T. Brown, cf	5	0	3	2	2	1	0
B. Joyce, 3b	5	1	2	1	3	1	1	D. Cooley, lf	5	0	1	2	3	0	1
B. Hassamaer, rf	5	0	1	1	3	0	0	G. Miller, c-3b3	5	0	0	0	2	3	5
J. McGuire, c	4	1	0	0	2	2	0	R. Connor, 1b	5	0	1	0	10	0	0
E. Cartwright, 1b	3	2	1	0	7	0	0	H. Peitz, 3b-c3	4	0	1	0	3	0	1
D. Coogan, ss	2	1	1	1	3	4	2	J. Quinn, 2b	4	1	1	0	3	5	1
J. Crooks, 2b	4	1	0	1	6	2	0	B. Ely, ss	4	1	1	0	1	5	1
C. Abbey, cf	4	1	1	1	0	0	0	T. Dowd, rf	4	2	2	0	3	0	0
A. Maul, p	3	0	2	3	0	0	0	H. Staley, p	3	0	0	0	0	1	0
								T. Breitenstein, ph9	1	0	1	0	-	-	-
	35	8	10	8	27	9	3		40	4	11	4	27	15	9

Washington 040 010 300 - 8
St. Louis 000 000 301 - 4

	ip	h	r-er	bb	so
Maul (W 3-3)	9	11	4-3	0	0
Staley (L 2-3)	9	10	8-3	3	3

PB: Peitz

LOB: Wash 5, StL 9.
2B: Dowd, Hassamaer, Maul 2, Ely.
SB: Crooks, Abbey 2, Selbach, Joyce, Cartwright 2.
SH: Coogan, Maul.
Time - 2:10
Umpire: J. Battin

The Browns' cause was pretty hopeless in 1895. Buckenberger was fired in June and replaced by Joe Quinn. Quinn tried reinstating Miller as captain, but it didn't help.

Quinn was relieved as manager in August.

St. Louis finished a sorry eleventh, just 4 games ahead of last-place Louisville. The Browns record was 39-92 for a .298 percentage.

1896 — Monday, July 6th, at Sportsman's Park
Umpire Leaves Field in Fifth, Rain Halts Game in Ninth
Ump Keefe Refuses to Complete Game, But Play Goes On
Giants and Browns Both Rally in Ninth, But Game Reverts to 6-6 Tie

After eight exciting and unusual innings, and a most eventful ninth, nature intervened in the game today between the New York Giants and the St. Louis Browns. Both sides had scored in the ninth, New York getting two runs in the top of the inning and the Browns having one run in, two men on base, and no one out in the bottom of the round. Then a storm broke, and the game had to be called. It went into the books as an eight-inning, 6-6 tie.

Umpire Tim Keefe was not on hand for this non-finish, having left the field in the fifth inning after the kicking of both teams had become too much for him. Despite the entreaties of men from both sides, he positively refused to continue, and the two captains had to assign two players to officiate the rest of the game.

Today's Results
ST. LOUIS 6 — New York 6 (TIE) (8 inn.)
Cleveland 3 - Brooklyn 1
Baltimore 14 - Chicago 13
Cincinnati 10 - Philadelphia 6
Louisville 5 - Boston 2
Washington 6 - Pittsburg 2

Standings	W-L	Pct.	GB
Cleveland	40-19	.678	-
Baltimore	41-20	.672	-
Cincinnati	44-24	.647	½
Boston	37-25	.597	4½
Pittsburg	33-29	.532	8½
Chicago	36-33	.522	9
Washington	30-29	.5085	10
Philadelphia	33-32	.5077	10
Brooklyn	31-33	.484	11½
New York	25-36	.417	16
ST. LOUIS	15-50	.231	28
Louisville	12-47	.203	28

The Browns, who had lost their previous 12 games, played their best ball in weeks today. Although they were not rewarded with a victory, at least they did not lose again. Frank "Red" Donahue pitched a fine game for the home team. Of the ten hits made off his delivery, several were mere scratches. But for a bad error by Roger Connor, Donahue would probably have won the game. Bert Meyers and Monte Cross made good plays behind him, and Cross hit a home run.

For the Giants, Bob Stafford stood out by making two sensational catches. Frank Connaugton made some fine plays, but his slow fielding of two chances cost his team. Willie Clark's failure to cover first base also hurt New York.

The crowd was very sparse, owing to the terrible play of the local team recently. The Browns had won just three of the last 34 games before today.

Neither side scored in the first two innings. The feature of these rounds was a great play by Meyers to rob Stafford of a double.

In the third inning, New York scored three times. After one was out, Mike Sullivan singled. He took second when George Van Haltren nearly tore Meyers in half with a line-drive single. Stafford also singled, loading the bases. Mike Tiernan bounced back to Donahue, who forced Sullivan at home. Kid Gleason then came up. With a count of 2-and-2, Donahue cut the heart of the plate with a pitch and started to walk off the field. But Keefe called the pitch a ball. This was not the first time that Keefe's calls had been questioned, nor would it be the last, but it was the costliest as far as St. Louis was concerned. Gleason was given a base on balls, forcing a run across. George Davis then hit a bouncer to first base. Connor got in front of the ball, then fell down as the ball took a tricky hop and bounced off his hands. By the time the ball was recovered, two runners had crossed the plate.

The Browns cut their deficit to 3-2 in the fourth. Bill Douglas singled and stole second. Monte Cross then hit a long drive to left field that bounced over the fence for a two-run home run.

After some delay in the top of the fifth, caused by Keefe's exit, New York scored two runs. Tiernan opened with a one-bagger. Gleason then hit a ball down the right field line, which Keefe ruled fair, the runners getting to second and third. The Browns put up a vigorous kick, claiming the ball was foul.

The overwrought Keefe had been subjected to arguments and abuse almost from the first pitch of the game, but now Roger Connor, his old friend and teammate, joined the kicking. For Keefe this was the last straw. He went to the bench, emptied the spare balls out of his pockets, and made for the exit. Managers Connor and Art Irwin now began arguing with the umpire to stay, but Keefe's mind was made up, and he positively refused to continue.

After some wrangling, the two managers agreed on two players, Ed McFarland of St. Louis and Jouett Meekin of New York, to provide the umpiring in Keefe's absence.

Play resumed, and Davis drove in two runs with a single. He then stole second, but was thrown out trying to swipe third. Clark singled and was also caught stealing.

Tiernan hit a ball into the lake beyond the right field fence in the seventh, putting New York ahead by 6-2.

It looked like another dreary defeat for the Browns, but they rallied in fine style to tie the contest.

One run came in the sixth. Tom Parrott reached first when Clark was slow in covering. Tiernan then dropped Connor's high fly after a long run, and Parrott scored on the hit.

St. Louis made three runs in the eighth to tie. With two out, no one on base, and threatening clouds on the horizon, it looked bad for the home team. But Morgan Murphy singled, and Donahue and Tommy Dowd followed suit. Bill Hart, a pitcher who was playing left field today, then cracked a long triple, and the score was tied.

The Giants scored twice in the top of the ninth on doubles by Tiernan and Gleason and a single by Davis.

Then the Browns came up. Connor was given third on a terrible throw to first by Gleason. Meyers singled him home. With the wind whipping up and the rain beginning to fall, Tiernan muffed Douglas's high fly, putting two men on base with no one out.

But then the clouds opened in a heavy downpour, and the game had to be called. By the rules, the last complete inning was counted, and the game reverted to an eight inning, 6-6 tie.

New York	ab	r	h	bi	o	a	e		St. Louis	ab	r	h	bi	o	a	e
G. Van Haltren, cf	5	1	1	0	1	0	0		T. Dowd, 2b	5	1	2	0	3	4	1
B. Stafford, lf	4	1	1	0	3	0	0		B. Hart, lf	4	0	1	3	1	0	0
M. Tiernan, rf	4	3	2	1	1	0	0		T. Parrott, cf	5	1	2	0	2	0	0
K. Gleason, 2b	3	1	1	1	4	2	0		R. Connor, 1b	3	0	1	1	8	1	1
G. Davis, 3b	4	0	2	2	4	2	0		B. Meyers, 3b	4	0	0	0	1	3	0
W. Clark, 1b	4	0	1	0	10	0	1		B. Douglas, rf	4	1	2	0	0	0	0
F. Connaughton, ss	3	0	1	0	0	4	0		M. Cross, ss	3	1	1	2	2	1	1
P. Wilson, c	3	0	0	0	1	1	0		M. Murphy, c	4	1	1	0	6	2	0
M. Sullivan, p	4	0	1	0	0	1	0		R. Donahue, p	3	1	1	0	1	2	0
	34	6	10	4	24	10	1			35	6	11	6	24	13	3

New York   003 020 10 - 6
St. Louis   000 200 13 - 6
game called on account of rain

	ip	h	r-er	bb	so
Sullivan	8	11	6-6	2	1
Donahue	8	10	6-4	2	4

HBP: by Sullivan (Donahue)
Time - 2:05
Umpires: T. Keefe; J. Meekin & E. McFarland

LOB: NY 7, StL 9.
2B: Gleason, Connor.
3B: Davis, Hart.
HR: Cross, Tiernan.
SH: Hart, Wilson.
SB: Douglas, Cross, Davis 2, Gleason. CS: Davis, Clark.
Picked Off: Cross.
Attendance - 400

The Browns stretched their losing streak to 14 games before finally winning a game.

They finished the season with a miserable 40-90 won-lost record. That left them in eleventh place, just 2½ games ahead of Louisville, 17½ games out of tenth place, and 50½ games behind the pennant-winning Baltimore Orioles.

1897 — Sunday, September 26th, at Sportsman's Park
Browns Lose Two More Games for 18 Straight Defeats
Cincinnati Wins by 10-4 and 8-6
Haven't Beaten the Reds Since 1895

While the eyes of the baseball-watching public were fixed upon Baltimore, where the Orioles and Boston were locked in a crucial series for first place in the National League, a little noticed and hardly unexpected event took place in St. Louis. The last-place Browns lost two games. The defeats brought their consecutive-game streak to 18 (a club record) and raised their total for the year to 100, making them only the second team in National League history to reach triple figures in games lost.

Today's Results
Cincinnati 10 - ST. LOUIS 4 (1st game)
Cincinnati 8 - ST. LOUIS 6 (2nd)
Cleveland 8 - Louisville 4
no other games scheduled

Standings	W-L	Pct.	GB
Baltimore	88-37	.704	-
Boston	90-38	.703	+½
New York	81-46	.638	8
Cincinnati	74-54	.578	15½
Cleveland	69-59	.539	20½
Brooklyn	60-69	.465	30
Washington	58-69	.457	31
Pittsburg	56-70	.444	32½
Chicago	56-71	.441	33
Philadelphia	54-75	.419	36½
Louisville	51-76	.402	38½
ST. LOUIS	27-100	.213	62

The doubleheader defeat was the second in two days, both of which have come at the hands of the Cincinnati Reds. The Browns have not beaten the Reds since the last game played in 1895 between the two clubs. Cincinnati swept the 12-game season series in 1896 and has won the first 11 games of the series in 1897, with one game left to play.

St. Louis last won a league game on September 2nd in Baltimore, when they defeated the Orioles, 4-3, in ten innings. Rookie Willie Sudhoff was the winning pitcher, and that victory broke an eight-game losing streak. Baltimore got revenge the next day by winning by a 22-1 score. The Browns then traveled to Boston, New York, Cleveland, and Pittsburg, losing three games in each city. They finished the road trip by losing a single game in Cincinnati, giving them 14 consecutive losses. Yesterday at Sportsman's Park they lost two games to the Reds. The Browns led the first game, 5-3, until the Reds scored four runs in the ninth inning to win, 7-5. The second game went to the visitors, 8-7.

A surprisingly good-sized crowd was on hand for the doubleheader today. They came mostly to see two new local men play for the Browns. Pitcher Willie Sudhoff made his first appearance in Sportsman's Park after pitching in nine games on the road. He showed excellent promise, although he was beaten, 10-4. Outfielder Ed Beecher, just recruited from the Moberly Reds but a well-known St. Louis amateur before this season, played his first full National League games today and did well.

Despite the showing of the new men, the Browns came through with their specialty, defeats. They were fairly beaten in the first game, 10-4. In the second game they gave away the lead early, then rallied unsuccessfully and lost, 8-6.

Sudhoff was the Browns' pitcher in the opener, and the cranks were impressed by his performance. He showed a good curveball that broke sharply, some speed, and good control. The most surprising feature of his work was his fine fielding. He also made a base hit and scored a run by good base running.

If his teammates had played half as well as he had, Sudhoff might have been victorious. Unfortunately, his support was poor. Third baseman Fred Hartman was a particular offender. In the fifth inning, with two out and a man on third, Hartman decided to see if a bunt down the third base line would go foul. The ball stayed fair, while the runner scored. The next better, Jake Beckley, then hit a home run that put the game beyond reach. On another occassion, Sudhoff had a man picked off third, but Hartman threw the ball away during the rundown, allowing a run.

Cincinnati's pitcher was veteran Frank Dwyer. He was wild, walking six. His teammates made four errors, but he was good in the pinches. He didn't allow the Browns to score until the seventh inning, by which time his team had a safe lead.

Charlie Irwin offered fine support at third base, and, in the outfield, Bug Holliday and Dummy Hoy made good catches.

But the real star of the game was the Reds' Jake Beckley. He hit three home runs. Two were long drives over the right field fence and into the lake in the amusement park. Both cleared the barrier with plenty to spare, although one was just barely fair. The third homer came on a fly ball to left that Beecher misjudged and allowed to drop. It bounced over the low fence.

The Browns had Percy Coleman and Bill Douglas as their battery in the second game. Cincinnati manager Buck Ewing countered with Billy Rhines and Heinie Peitz. Neither pitcher did particularly well, and hits were the order of the day.

Three catches in center field by Billy Hoy were the feature of the contest. On two very high drives the famous deaf mute ran straight back at full speed and made marvelous grabs. He was heartily applauded for his work.

For St. Louis the feature was the hitting of two men, Tuck Turner and Ed Beecher. Turner made a remarkable record by getting five hits in five times at bat. Two were triples, one a double, and two were singles. He also made a nice running catch near the fence in right field. Beecher, who had looked shaky in the first game, made four hits in the second game. He showed very good speed, two of his hits being infield scratches. He also stole a base and showed a good arm, much to the delight of his friends in the stands.

Cincinnati started the game with a rush, piling up four runs in the first inning. They had built the lead to 7-1 by the middle of the fifth.

Then the Browns battled back. By the ninth inning they had cut the margin to 8-6 and had the tying runs on base. The fans were in a state of excitement, but the rally and the game ended, and another defeat went onto the Browns' record.

FIRST GAME

		r	h	e	Batteries
Cincinnati	012 030 211 -	10	14	4	F. Dwyer (W 17-13) & B. Schriver.
St. Louis	000 000 211 -	4	8	3	W. Sudhoff (L 1-7) & B. Douglas.

SECOND GAME

Cincinnati	ab	r	h	bi	o	a	e
B. Holliday, lf	4	2	2	1	1	0	0
D. Hoy, cf	5	1	1	0	6	0	0
T. Corcoran, ss	5	1	2	2	2	4	0
J. Beckley, 1b	5	2	2	1	8	0	0
C. Irwin, 3b	5	1	1	0	2	2	0
C. Ritchey, rf	5	0	0	1	0	0	0
H. Peitz, c	5	1	3	1	2	1	0
B. McPhee, 2b	3	0	1	0	5	6	1
B. Rhines, p	3	0	1	0	1	1	0
	40	8	13	6	27	14	1

St. Louis	ab	r	h	bi	o	a	e
B. Douglas, c	5	0	1	1	1	0	1
M. Cross, ss	5	0	0	0	4	3	1
F. Hartman, 3b	5	2	2	0	2	0	0
T. Turner, rf	5	3	5	2	2	0	0
M. Grady, 1b	3	0	1	1	7	1	0
J. Houseman, 2b	5	0	0	1	3	5	0
D. Harley, cf	4	0	0	0	5	0	0
E. Beecher, lf	4	1	4	0	4	0	0
P. Coleman, p	4	0	1	0	1	0	0
	40	6	14	5	27	9	2

Cincinnati   400 120 010 - 8
St. Louis   010 011 201 - 6

	ip	h	r-er	bb	so
Rhines (W 19-15)	9	14	6-4	2	2
Coleman (L 1-2)	9	13	8-5	2	1

HBP: by Rhines (Harley)

LOB: Cinc 8, StL 10.
DP: Corcoran-McPhee-Beckley.
2B: Hoy, Beckley, Holliday, Turner.
3B: Turner 2. SH: Rhines.
SB: Irwin, Beecher.
Time 2:00 Attendance - 3,000
Umpire: F. Pears

The next day St. Louis beat Cincinnati, 5-4, behind the pitching on Red Donahue. That ended their losing streak at 18 games and broke the Cincinnati "hoodoo" at 23 games.

The Browns finished the season the following Sunday with a 29-102 record. That left them in last place, 63½ games behind the pennant winning Bostons and 23½ games behind the eleventh-place Louisvilles.

Their 18-game losing streak and their .221 percentage for the season both still stand as franchise records for futility.

1898 — Sunday, April 17th, at Sportsman's Park

Browns Lose, 14-1, on Site of Burned-Out Sportsman's Park

Temporary Seats Thrown Up to Accomodate Large Crowd

St. Louis Players, Exhausted from Night's Work, Make 11 Errors

Yesterday, Chris Von der Ahe's $62,000 Sportsman's Park burned to the ground in less than half an hour. None of the spectators attending the game at the time were killed, but several were seriously injured in the panic to evacuate the stands. The fire destroyed the entire park except for the right field bleachers.

Owner Von der Ahe, who lived above the refreshment saloon, was incoherent in his grief over the loss of his ballpark and nearly all of his personal effects. This spring he had spent several thousand dollars on improvements, had removed the "Shoot the Chutes" and other amusement park attractions, and was committed strictly to baseball. Then, in just the second game of the season, it all went up in smoke.

Today's Results
Chicago 14 - ST. LOUIS 1
Cincinnati 12 - Cleveland 1
Pittsburg 5 - Louisville 4
no other games scheduled

Standings	W-L	Pct.	GB
Chicago	2-0	1.000	-
Boston	1-0	1.000	½
Brooklyn	1-0	1.000	½
Baltimore	1-0	1.000	½
Pittsburg	2-1	.667	½
Cincinnati	2-1	.667	½
Cleveland	1-2	.333	1½
Louisville	1-2	.333	1½
New York	0-1	.000	1½
Philadelphia	0-1	.000	1½
Washington	0-1	.000	1½
ST. LOUIS	0-2	.000	2

The club's new president, Benjamin S. Muckenfuss, and the manager, Tim Hurst, kept their wits about them. Muckenfuss immediately set about the work of collecting the $35,000 insurance and arranging for an architect to make plans for a new structure. He also wired National League president Nick Young to have the game scheduled for today transferred to Chicago. But Hurst objected to the transfer, arguing that a new fence and temporary stand could be thrown up in time for the game. Since the club was in need of quick cash, Muckenfuss agree to Hurst's plan, and, by 7:30 p.m., a gang of about 150 carpenters was busily clearing debris and gathering supplies for construction.

Every possible hand was needed, so Hurst drafted his ball players into the effort.

By this afternoon, the minor miracle had been wrought, and the public turned out in large numbers to see it. The grounds on Natural Bridge Ave. had been enclosed by a new fence, and a temporary stand seating 1,700 had been put up. It extended from the screen behind home plate to well beyond third base. With the existing right field bleachers, there was seating for nearly 4,000 people.

But curiosity to see the ruins, fine weather, and the first Sunday game of the year all combined to attract over 7,000 cranks to the park. When it became obvious that the park would be filled, the management upped the admission fee from 25¢ to 50¢. Although most of the customers got in before the price hike, those who had to pay more were outspoken in their dissatisfaction.

And when the game was played, only the most forgiving partisans could find anything good to say about the home team. The Browns made error after error and, except for Tommy Dowd, didn't hit a lick. The visiting Chicago Orphans won in a walk, 14-1. After the game, Hurst was in a furious mood, threatening wholesale changes in the lineup.

Perhaps some of the blame for the team's poor showing rests with the manager, however. He had his players out at the park until past midnight working on the construction. Even those who didn't do any strenuous work stayed out too late to be in peak form for this afternoon's game.

Look at the example of Wilfred "Kid" Carsey. He had pitched two innings on Saturday before his work was interrupted by the fire. Then he was out at the park at night unloading lumber for the new stands. When he went out to pitch today, he did well for three innings, but he totally gave out in the fourth, allowing ten runs in the inning.

The story was the same for his teammates. Mike Mahoney, the big collegian recruit, played a gallant role in assisting spectators to escape the blaze yesterday. But today he was nearly worthless on the ball field, making two errors and getting nothing close to a base hit. Old Lou Bierbauer played so badly at second base that Hurst pulled him out of the game. The usually reliable Lave Cross made two errors at shortstop, and outfielder "Ducky" Holmes muffed a pair.

With the overflow crowd surrounding the field, the two managers agreed on ground rules which made a hit into the crowd worth three bases. Only one member of the home team was able to reach the throng with a batted ball, but the visitors turned the trick six times.

Tim Donahue, Bill Everett, Barry McCormick, and Jimmy Ryan all tripled in the fatal fourth inning. The Orphans also made two singles and a sacrifice during the rally, while the Browns contributed five fielding errors. By the time the round had ended, the cranks were thoroughly disgusted with the local nine.

Lefthander Pete Daniels replaced Carsey in the fifth for St. Louis. He was hit for three runs in two innings. Jim Hughey pitched the final three innings, and he shut the Chicagos out.

The visiting pitcher, Walter Thornton, pitched a strong game throughout, holding the feeble Browns to one run and six hits.

The lonely St. Louis run came in the sixth inning on a triple by Cross and an infield out by Russ Hall.

The Chicago outfield provided the features of the game. Both Billy Lange and Jimmy Ryan made phenomonal catches in the late innings. Ryan's catch included a jump at the end of a long, hard run, and he got the best applause of the day for his effort.

The Browns got only criticism for their work. After the game Hurst fumed, "We made enough errors to do for a week. Now we'll have winning ball. If not, we'll have other ball players."

Although the team's prospects seemed poor at the start of the season, they could hardly do worse than they did today. Then again, presumably they would not be called upon to help rebuild the ballpark just before any more games.

Chicago	ab	r	h	bi	o	a	e
M. Kilroy, rf	6	2	2	0	0	0	0
B. Lange, cf	5	2	1	0	4	0	0
B. Dahlen, ss	5	0	0	0	2	4	1
B. Everett, 1b	5	2	2	1	10	0	0
J. Ryan, lf	4	3	1	3	3	0	0
B. McCormick, 3b	5	2	2	2	0	1	1
J. Connor, 2b	5	1	0	1	3	3	0
T. Donahue, c	4	1	1	1	5	1	0
W. Thornton, p	4	1	2	1	0	3	0
	43	14	11	9	27	12	2

St. Louis	ab	r	h	bi	o	a	e
T. Dowd, cf	5	0	3	0	1	0	0
T. Turner, rf	4	0	1	0	4	0	0
D. Holmes, lf	4	0	0	0	2	0	2
J. Clements, c	3	0	0	0	6	2	0
L. Cross, ss	4	1	1	0	2	2	2
M. Mahoney, 1b	4	0	0	0	10	0	2
R. Hall, 3b	4	0	0	1	1	3	1
L. Bierbauer, 2b	0	0	0	0	0	1	2
J. Crooks, 2b5	2	0	0	0	1	2	1
K. Carsey, p	2	0	1	0	0	2	0
P. Daniels, p5	0	0	0	0	0	0	1
J. Hughey, p7	2	0	0	0	0	3	0
	34	1	6	1	27	15	11

Chicago 100 (10)12 000 - 14
St. Louis 000 001 000 - 1

	ip	h	r-er	bb	so
Thornton (W 1-0)	9	6	1-1	2	4
Carsey (L 0-1)	4	8	11-5	0	1
Daniels	2	2	3-1	0	2
Hughey	3	1	0-0	2	3

HBP: by Thornton (Clements), by Carsey (Donahue)

LOB: Chi 6, StL 9. BE: Chi 8, StL 2. DP: Mahoney-Clements-Hall. 2B: Kilroy. 3B: Everett 2, Ryan, McCormick 2, Donahue, Cross. SB: Lange. SH: Lange.

Time - 1:45 Attendance - 7,000
Umpires: J. McDonald & H. O'Day

The 1898 season was an unmitigated disaster for the Browns. The team finished a distant last, winning only 39 games while losing 111.

After spending his available funds to rebuild the park, Von der Ahe was beset by creditors and by lawsuits stemming from the fire. The club came under the control of a court-appointed receiver, and it was eventually sold at sheriff's auction in March, 1899, ending Chris's colorful career as a baseball magnate.

Chapter III
The Robison Brothers' Cardinals
1899-1910

1899—April 15th at League Park, St. Louis
New St. Louis Perfectos Trounce Cleveland, 10-1, in Opening Game

1900—May 12th at League Park
Cardinals Lose Thriller in McGraw's Debut with St. Louis

1901—July 8th at League Park
St. Louis Fans Attack Umpire After Cardinals Lose Tight Game

1902—August 17th at League Park
Spectacular Game with Superbas End as 18-Inning Tie, 7-7

1903—July 22nd at League Park
Cards Win, 8-7, on Smoot's Ninth-Inning, Two-Out, Three-Run Home Run

1904—October 15th at League Park
Players and Front Offices Feud, City Series Ends Tied

1905—October 15th at League Park
Cardinals Lose Twice, Drop City Series to Browns, 4 Games to 3

1906—April 12th at League Park
Opening Game Scoreless Until 13th, Then Pirates Edge Cardinals, 2-1

1907—August 11th at League Park
Karger Pitches Seven-Inning Perfect Game as Cardinals Win a Pair

1908—April 20th at League Park
Cardinal's Raymond Pitches One-Hitter but Loses, 2-0

1909—May 24th at New York
St. Louis Finally Beats Christy Mathewson After 24 Losses

1910—September 23rd at Brooklyn
Cardinals Make Just Two Hits but Win, 6-2, Over Dodgers

After a long legal battle, Von der Ahe's club was sold at sheriff's auction in March, 1899. It quickly passed into the hands of two brothers, Frank de Haas Robison and M. Stanley Robison. They were street car tycoons and already owned the Cleveland club in the National League.

In 1899, they moved all the good players from their two teams to the St. Louis club. The city was ecstatic, and about 15,000 St. Louisans braved very cold weather to cheer the new team to an opening-day victory over the Cleveland team, which was made up mostly of old Browns.

The new ownership changed the name of the park at Natural Bridge and Vandeventer from Sportsman's Park to League Park, and it outfitted its players in white uniforms with red caps and socks. After a year or so of being called things like Perfectos and Red Caps, the team became popularly known as the Cardinals, in reference to the shade of red that the wore.

In 1900, the National League was reduced from twelve to eight clubs, and St. Louis acquired two stars from Baltimore, John McGraw and Wilbert Robinson. They at first refused to report but finally signed and played their first game with the Cardinals on May 12th.

The new American League signed McGraw, Robinson, Cy Young, and a few other Cardinals in 1901, but St. Louis was not hurt as much as some N.L. teams. It had a shot at the pennant in the summer of 1901. Fan interest ran high. When umpire Hank O'Day's decision in one game cost the Cards a victory, the crowd attacked him violently. He was only saved by the police, who had to draw their revolvers twice to quell the mob.

In 1902, the American League moved a team into St. Louis called the Browns. The Cardinals lost a lot of stars to the new team, and they dropped into the second division. Even in one of their best games of the season, they could do no better than tie, 7-7, in eighteen innings.

In 1903, the Cards only had one winning streak as long as four games. And it took a two-out, three-run, ninth-inning home run by Homer Smoot to get the streak that far. The Cardinals finished last and then lost a City Series to the Browns.

In 1904, the Cardinals improved, finishing fifth. The City Series ended in a tie, with each front office accusing the other of deception.

In 1905, the Cardinals slipped to sixth in the N.L. and blew the City Series, 4 games to 3, by losing two games on the final day.

In 1906, St. Louis played a very exciting opening-day game with Pittsburg, but they lost in thirteen innings, 2-1. The rest of the season was something of an anticlimax, as the Cardinals finished seventh.

They fell to eighth early in 1907. Even a nine-game winning streak, which featured a seven-inning perfect game by Eddie Karger, could not get St. Louis out of the cellar.

In 1908, the pitching was good, but the offense and fielding were terrible. The Cardinals were shut out a record total of 33 times. Young Bugs Raymond pitched a one-hitter in his first start but lost, 2-0. He wound up on the short end of 11 shutout losses. The team finished last again.

In 1909, Roger Bresnahan was acquired to manage the team. He gave the Cards a new, aggressive style, and they even beat Christy Mathewson for the first time in years. But they could finish no higher than seventh.

In 1910, some of the youngsters Bresnahan was trying began to show some promise, but St. Louis wound up seventh again. Late in the year, Cy Alberts pitched a three-hitter with last-out help from Bob Harmon, and the Cards won the game, 6-2, despite making just two hits themselves.

1899—Saturday, April 15th, at League Park, St. Louis

New St. Louis "Perfectos" Trounce Cleveland, 10-1, in Opening Game

Weather Cold and Play Erratic, But Fans Cheer Both Sides

Largest Crowd Here in Years Sees New Heroes Beat Old

The new century began a few months early for baseball fans in St. Louis. With the prospect of a real, live championship contender to represent the city, expectant spectators came out in vast numbers to see the opening game of the season today. The new St. Louis nine, comprised of players who had played for Cleveland last year, didn't disappoint them. They easily beat the new Cleveland team, which had a line-up including eight members of last year's twelfth-place St. Louis club.

The switching of players was brought about within the last month by the purchase of the St. Louis franchise by the Cleveland owners, Frank de Haas Robison and his brother M. Stanley Robison. Although the deal had been rumored for months, Chris Von der Ahe's legal battle to retain his franchise delayed the sale until late March. Then foreclosure proceedings were finally ordered by the courts, and the assets of the debt-ridden St. Louis Sportsman's Park and Club Association were sold at auction to Edward C. Becker, one of Von der Ahe's creditors. Becker quickly completed a deal with the Robisons, which transferred the top Cleveland players to St. Louis and sent the sorry St. Louis men to the Ohio city.

Today's Results
ST. LOUIS 10 - Cleveland 1
Chicago 2 - Louisville 1
Boston 1 - Brooklyn 0 (11 inn.)
Baltimore 5 - New York 3
Pittsburg 5 - Cincinnati 2
Philadelphia 6 - Washington 5

Standings	W-L	Pct.	GB
Chicago	2-0	1.000	-
Philadelphia	2-0	1.000	-
ST. LOUIS	1-0	1.000	½
Boston	1-0	1.000	½
Baltimore	1-0	1.000	½
Pittsburg	1-0	1.000	½
Brooklyn	0-1	.000	1½
Cincinnati	0-1	.000	1½
New York	0-1	.000	1½
Cleveland	0-1	.000	1½
Louisville	0-2	.000	2
Washington	0-2	.000	2

Besides the new men, the new ownership has attempted to rid itself of the bad image left by seven years of bad teams under Von de Ahe. Therefore, the name "Sportsman's Park" has been dropped, and the plant at Natural Bridge and Vandeventer has been rechristened "League Park." The time-honored brown stockings have also been discarded, and the new men have been outfitted in white uniforms with cardinal red caps and stockings. The debate over a new name for the team started before the opening game. There seemed little enthusiasm for the old Cleveland names, "Spiders" and "Indians." In the eastern press, the name "Perfectos" has come to the fore, and that name has been adopted locally only by *The Sporting News*.

The name "Exiles," which was sometimes applied to the Cleveland team in 1898, has seemed particularly appropriate for the Cleveland team of 1899.

Today's game was preceded by a morning parade downtown, which was enthusiastically cheered. In the head carriage sat the new St. Louis club's president, F.d.H. Robison, Vice-President Becker, and M.S. Robison, who is officially president of the Cleveland club. They were lionized for bringing good baseball back to St. Louis.

At the ball park, civic and sporting dignitaries were numerous. Heading the list was Mayor Ziegenhein, who gave a short address to the players before the game urging new St. Louis manager Patsy Tebeau and his men to win the pennant. The mayor also hoped that the Exiles would come in second in the race.

The crowd was very large, despite the cold weather. Estimates of its size ranged from 12,000 to 18,000. In any case, it was the largest gathering at a baseball game in St. Louis in several years.

Although the fans had come to root for the new home team, they were much more familiar with the visiting players, and they accorded them the larger share of the applause when they came to bat. The only two members of the St. Louis team to get really enthusiastic receptions were Oliver "Patsy" Tebeau and Jack O'Connor. Both these men were born in North St. Louis, and many of their friends from the Goose Hill neighborhood were packed into the left field bleachers. By his fine play, Bobby Wallace of the Perfectos earned some loud cheering. Lave Cross, Willie Sudhoff, Joe Quinn, and Tommy Dowd of the visitors were all cheered lustily.

Big Cy Young was the St. Louis pitcher, and he lived up to his reputation with a fine effort, holding the Exiles to just six hits and one run. Sudhoff, a St. Louis lad who has been exiled, pitched a fair game for Cleveland, but St. Louis bunched its hits and scored ten runs against him.

Neither side got a base runner until the second inning. In the bottom of that round, Wallace drove a long ball to the bleachers in right and was thrown out trying to make third base on the hit. Tebeau also doubled, but he was cut down at home trying to score on a single to left by O'Connor.

St. Louis continued their hitting in the third, and this time scored five runs. Singles by Harry Blake and John Emmett Heidrick and doubles by O'Connor and Young, along with three errors, a walk, and a neat sacrifice by Clarence "Cupid" Childs, were the building blocks of the runs.

The Clevelands got their run in the fourth. Quinn scored, but three other men were left on base.

St. Louis added four more runs in the fifth on five hits, some sloppy fielding, and fine base running.

The Exiles again loaded the bases in the sixth. But Young pitched out of trouble, striking out George Bristow and inducing Sudhoff to pop out to Childs.

Wallace opened the bottom of the sixth with a long triple to right center. With one out, Tebeau walked. With two out, Wallace scored on a double steal before Tebeau could be tagged out.

The best defensive play of the game came in the eighth. Cleveland's Dick Harley made a diving, somersaulting catch in short left field.

The final score was 10-1 in favor of the new St. Louis Perfectos, and the crowd went away with a new image of baseball in the Mound City.

Cleveland	ab	r	h	bi	o	a	e	St. Louis	ab	r	h	bi	o	a	e
T. Dowd, cf	4	0	0	0	1	0	1	J. Burkett, lf	5	1	1	0	1	0	1
D. Harley, lf	4	0	0	0	2	1	0	C. Childs, 2b	3	0	0	0	3	1	0
J. Quinn, 2b	4	1	1	0	2	5	0	E. McKean, ss	5	0	0	1	2	3	1
L. Cross, 3b	4	0	1	1	3	2	1	B. Wallace, 3b	3	2	2	0	2	4	0
J. Clements, c	4	0	1	0	2	2	1	J. Heidrick, rf	4	2	1	0	2	0	0
T. Tucker, 1b	4	0	2	0	10	0	1	P. Tebeau, 1b	3	1	2	0	12	0	2
S. Sullivan, ss	3	0	1	0	2	0	0	J. O'Connor, c	4	1	3	2	3	0	0
G. Bristow, rf	4	0	0	0	2	1	0	H. Blake, cf	4	2	2	1	2	0	0
W. Sudhoff, p	4	0	0	0	0	3	1	C. Young, p	4	1	2	2	0	4	0
	35	1	6	1	24	14	5		35	10	13	6	27	12	4

Cleveland   000 100 000 - 1
St. Louis   005 041 00x - 10

	ip	h	r-er	bb	so
Sudhoff (L 0-1)	8	13	10-6	4	0
Young (W 1-0)	9	6	1-1	1	3

WP: Sudhoff
Umpires: H. O'Day & J. Brennan

LOB: Clev 8, StL 6.
BE: Clev 3, StL 2.
DP: Childs-McKean-Tebeau.
2B: Wallace, Tebeau, Young, O'Connor, Burkett.
3B: Wallace, SH: Childs.
SB: none. CS: Tebeau
Time - 1:50 Attendance - 15,000

The new team was a vast improvement over the Browns, and pennant fever was rampant in St. Louis during the early weeks of the season. But the team fell off the pace in June and finished fifth in the twelve-team league with a 84-67 record.

The Cleveland team was the worst in the history of major league baseball, winning only 20 games but losing 134.

The name "Perfectos" did not sit well with some journalists, and names like "Red Caps" and "Cardinals" soon began appearing in some of the daily newspapers. The latter, of course, is the one that stuck.

1900—Saturday, May 12th, at League Park
Cardinals Lose Thriller in McGraw's Debut With St. Louis
Brooklyn's Late Rally Wins Game, 5-4
McGraw and Robinson Shine in First Game with Cardinals

After ending their combined holdout, John McGraw and Wilbert Robinson played their first game with the local team today. Despite a lack of training, both played well, although McGraw's error in the ninth inning contributed to the rally that won the game for the visiting Brooklyn Superbas. McGraw reached base four times out of five, scored one run, and drove home another. Robinson made three hits in four tries, also scoring one and knocking in another tally.

The debut was a great success until the ninth inning, when the defending champion Superbas spoiled the party with one of their famous "Brooklyn finishes." They scored three runs in their last chance and beat the home team, 5-4.

Today's Results
Brooklyn 5 - ST. LOUIS 4
Philadelphia 8 - Cincinnati 5
Pittsburg 5 - Boston 1
Chicago 13 - New York 3

Standings	W-L	Pct.	GB
Philadelphia	13-5	.722	-
Brooklyn	10-7	.588	2½
Cincinnati	9-8	.529	3½
Pittsburg	9-9	.500	4
Chicago	9-10	.474	4½
ST. LOUIS	8-9	.471	4½
New York	6-10	.375	6
Boston	5-11	.313	7

When the National League agreed to a reduction from twelve to eight clubs, McGraw and Robinson's Baltimore club was one of those eliminated. They became the property of the Brooklyn franchise, but were outspoken in their refusal to play in that city. So they were sold, along with second baseman Bill Keister, to St. Louis for the handsome sum of $16,750. McGraw and Robinson refused to report to the Cardinals, however, until their contract demands were met. After prolonged negotiations, they signed on May 8th. They reportedly were given a $6,000 bonus for signing, of which McGraw got the larger part. "Muggsy" McGraw also signed a contract with the reserve clause stricken from it. He made it known that he would play in St. Louis for just one season.

Despite these contrary developments, the St. Louis cranks were very anxious to see the famous pair perform for the local team, and the new players were loudly cheered when they made their appearance on the field today. The crowd numbered 7,300, which is remarkable considering the fact that a street car strike had the city's transportation virtually stopped. But it was a lovely day for a walk, and people came one way or another.

In the top half of the first, McGraw gave the fans their first chance to cheer him by making a fine stop and sharp throw to retire the fleet Fielder Jones. When Muggsy came to bat in the bottom of the inning, he was given three big bouquets of flowers. Then he scored the game's first run. After McGraw drew a base on balls, Patsy Donovan was also given a free pass by the Brooklyn pitcher, Joe McGinnity. Expecting a bunt, the Brooklyn infield went scurrying about, with shortstop Bill Dahlen trying to sneak in behind McGraw at second. But John Emmett Heidrick ruined the play by hitting a ground ball through the hole left open by Dahlen, and McGraw ran home.

The Superbas tied the score in the second. With one out, Jimmy Sheckard walked. Gene DeMontreville sent him to third with a long single to left center. Then the runners worked the double steal, DeMontreville reaching second on Robinson's low throw and Sheckard scoring on Wallace's high return throw home.

In the St. Louis half of the second, Robinson was presented with flowers, and Cy Young was given a high silk hat. Old Cy was guyed into putting the hat on, and, as it appeared to be several sizes too small, everyone got a good laugh out of the demonstration.

Robinson put St. Louis back in front in the fourth. After Dan McGann walked and Joe Quinn singled, the corpulent catcher got his first hit of the game, driving McGann home. The rally was then killed by Brooklyn's quick work in forcing Quinn at third on an attempted sacrifice.

The Cardinal scored another run in the fifth. With Donovan on third and Jesse Burkett on first, the Cards tried the double steal routine. Catcher Jim McGuire faked a throw to second and then picked Donovan off third. Bobby Wallace reached first on an error by Dahlen, and again the Cardinals tried the double steal. Again McGuire faked a throw, and again a man was hung up between third and home. But this time, McGuire made a wild throw in the rundown, and Burkett scored.

St. Louis threatened in the sixth, but again were stifled by the Brooklyn defense on a bunt play. Again it was Quinn on second, Robinson on first, and Young at bat. Since Quinn had been forced at third once before because Dahlen had faked him back to second base, Joe made sure to get a good jump off second this time. But Young's bunt was in the air, and McGinnity grabbed it and snapped a throw to second, doubling Quinn before he could get back.

Brooklyn scored in the seventh on a hit by DeMontreville, a steal, a long fly out, and McGinnity's single.

Robinson made the circuit in the eighth. He hit a ball that would have been a home run except that it hit the flag pole on the left field foul line and bounced back onto the field. Robbie had to settle for a double. But his comrade, McGraw, brought him home with a sharp single.

The score stood 4-2 against Brooklyn at the start of the ninth. Young walked Dahlen. Quinn made two fine plays to retire the next two batters, while Dahlen worked his way around to third. McGuire then hit a grounder toward the hole between short and third. McGraw ranged far to his left to make the stop, but his throw to first pulled McGann off the bag, Dahlen scoring. Harry Howell went in to run for McGuire, and manager Ned Hanlon sent pitcher Frank Kitson up to hit for McGinnity. Kitson bounced a single over Young, sending Howell to third. A walk loaded the bases. Willie Keeler then chopped one to the right of the mound, which Young lunged for but could only deflect. Shortstop Wallace was moving to his left, and couldn't change directions in time. The ball trickled past him, and the tying and leading runs raced across the plate. Young then struck out Hugh Jennings, ending the inning.

Burkett opened the bottom of the ninth with a single. But Kitson retired the next three batters, and Brooklyn won, 5-4.

Brooklyn	ab	r	h	bi	o	a	e
F. Jones, cf	4	0	2	0	3	0	0
W. Keeler, rf	5	0	1	2	1	0	0
H. Jennings, 1b	5	0	0	0	13	1	0
J. Kelley, 3b	4	0	0	0	3	3	0
B. Dahlen, ss	3	1	0	0	2	6	1
J. Sheckard, lf	3	1	0	0	3	0	0
G. DeMontreville, 2b	4	1	3	0	3	0	0
J. McGuire, c	4	0	0	0	0	1	1
H. Howell, pr9	0	1	0	0	-	-	-
D. Farrell, c9	0	0	0	0	0	0	0
J. McGinnity, p	3	0	1	1	2	3	0
F. Kitson, ph9-p	1	1	1	0	0	0	0
	36	5	8	3	27	17	2

St. Louis	ab	r	h	bi	o	a	e
J. McGraw, 3b	2	1	1	1	1	1	1
P. Donovan, rf	4	0	1	0	0	0	0
J. Heidrick, cf	5	0	1	1	3	0	0
J. Burkett, lf	5	1	2	0	3	0	0
B. Wallace, ss	4	0	0	0	1	2	1
D. McGann, 1b	3	1	0	0	7	1	0
J. Quinn, 2b	4	0	1	0	5	2	0
W. Robinson, c	4	1	3	1	7	2	0
C. Young, p	3	0	0	0	1	1	1
	34	4	9	3	27	9	3

Brooklyn   010 000 103 - 5
St. Louis   100 110 010 - 4

	ip	h	r-er	bb	so
McGinnity (W 4-1)	8	8	4-3	6	0
Kitson	1	1	0-0	0	0
Young (L 3-3)	9	8	5-2	3	6

WP: Young. PB: Robinson.
HBP: by McGinnity 2 (McGraw, Wallace)

LOB: Bkn 7, StL 12.
BE: Bkn 3, StL 1.
DP: Kelley - Jennings, McGinnity-Dahlen.
2B: Robinson, Burkett.
SH: McGann.
SB: Sheckard, DeMontreville 3, McGraw, Donovan, Wallace, Burkett.
Attendance - 7,300. Time - 2:11
Umpire: T. Hurst.

Despite a roster that included five future Hall-of-Famers the Cardinals struggled all year. They finished tied for fifth in the eight-team league with a 65-75 record. That left them 19 games behind the champion Superbas.

After the season was over, half a dozen St. Louis players jumped to the new American League. These included McGraw, Robinson, and Young.

1901 — Monday, July 8th, at League Park

St. Louis Fans Attack Umpire After Cardinals Lose Tight Game
Dubious Call Gives Brooklyn Three Runs in 7-6 Victory
Police Must Draw Revolvers to Protect Ump from Murderous Mob

The scene at the end of today's baseball game looked more like a riot by fanatical Boxers in Peking than it resembled the conclusion of an American sporting event. Thousands of St. Louis partisans, representing all classes of society, swarmed out of the stands at the end of the game with one common objective, to maim the umpire, Hank O'Day.

A decision by O'Day robbed the St. Louis Cardinals of victory. In the eighth inning, he called two visiting players safe when they both appeared to be out on the same play. When the game was over and the mob descended, the home players did their best to protect the arbiter from attack. They were aided by a small contingent of police. The presence of the law did not restrain the mob until the officers finally drew their guns and escorted O'Day to the club offices. The unfortunate umpire was badly beaten around the head and neck.

Today's Results
Brooklyn 7 - ST. LOUIS 6
Pittsburg 5 - Boston 0
New York 9 - Cincinnati 3
Chicago 2 - Philadelphia 1 (10 inn.)

Standings	W-L	Pct.	GB
Pittsburg	38-25	.603	-
New York	31-25	.554	3½
ST. LOUIS	35-30	.538	4
Brooklyn	34-30	.531	4½
Philadelphia	33-30	.524	5
Boston	29-29	.500	6½
Cincinnati	27-35	.435	10½
Chicago	22-45	.328	18

With both St. Louis and Brooklyn fighting to gain in the pennant race, a crowd of nearly 4,000, large for a Monday, came out to the park. Until O'Day's rank decision in the eighth inning, they were entertained by an exciting, seesaw game of baseball.

The pitchers were Jack Powell for the Cardinals and Bill Donovan for the Superbas. Donovan, who earned the nickname "Wild Bill" last year at Hartford because of control problems, had emerged as the top man on the Brooklyn pitching staff this year. Today he was not at his best, and the Cardinals should have beaten him. Powell was effective for most of the contest, but Brooklyn bunched their hits against him and, aided by the umpire, pulled the victory out of the fire.

St. Louis held a 4-3 lead through seven innings. John Emmett Heidrick had scored the first three runs for the Cardinals, stealing three bases along the way. Powell's double drove home Jack Ryan with the fourth run. Bad fielding helped the Superbas to their first run, and Jim McGuire's two-bagger had plated the next two.

Then came the fatal eighth inning. The first batter for Brooklyn, Jimmy Sheckard, popped out. Tom Daly hit safely over second. Bill Dahlen worked a perfect hit-and-run, singling Daly to third.

Then came the play that brought on all the trouble. Cozy Dolan hit weakly down the first base line. Dan McGann fielded the ball about 15 feet in front of the bag and, with his eye on the runner at third, waited for Dolan to run down for a tag out. Cozy was not so obliging, however, and he ran about five or ten feet into the infield to avoid the tag. McGann never touched him, but, by the rules, any runner who goes more than three feet from the base line to avoid a tag is automatically out. Meanwhile, Daly broke for home. McGann's throw was high, but got to catcher Ryan in plenty of time. Jack applied the tag few feet up the line toward third. But, to the consternation of the fans, O'Day called the man safe. Then he shocked them further by ruling that Dolan was safe at first.

That meant that, instead of the inning ending with a double play, the score was tied, there was just one out, and two men were on base. The St. Louis players put up a tremendous kick, and the spectators joined in. One box-seat holder was seen rushing to the concession stand and returning with his arms loaded with beer bottles, which he threw at O'Day in rapid succession. Other fans jumped out of the bleachers and began milling around the outfield.

Cooler heads prevailed, at least temporarily, and the game finally resumed. McGuire was the next batter, and his single sent Dahlen across the pan and put Dolan on third. "Deacon Jim" then bluffed a steal of second, drawing a throw to second and wild relay to first, allowing Dolan to score. The next two men went out, but Brooklyn led, 6-4.

The Superbas added another run in the ninth on singles by Joe Kelley and Wilie Keeler and some daring base running.

In the Cardinals' last chance, they put two men on with two out. Jesse Burkett came up and lined one past shortstop. In center, Dolan let the ball skip by him, and Burkett just kept running. But Daly's perfect relay caught Jesse at the plate, despite a desperate slide, ending the game with Brooklyn winning, 7-6.

Immediately the fans poured onto the field and surrounded O'Day. Three St. Louis players, Patsy Donovan, Dick Padden, and Emmett Heidrick, tried to keep the mob away, but several blows were landed in the vicinity of the umpire's head. Luckily, Capt. Gaffney and a squad of police came to the rescue. With their revolvers drawn, they escorted O'Day to the safety of the club offices. Still, the crowd milled around for nearly an hour. When O'Day emerged from the building, the police had another tense time getting him to Gaffney's carriage.

They left the grounds, but the ordeal was not yet over. An accident involving a wagon and a street car had snarled traffic on Spring Avenue. When Gaffney and his men got caught in the tie-up, the crowd recognized their passenger and began to pelt O'Day with stones. Once again, Gaffney had to order his men to draw their guns to quiet the mob and get O'Day safely to his hotel.

It was announced during the evening that O'Day would not be umpiring at the following day's contest.

Brooklyn	ab	r	h	bi	o	a	e
J. Kelley, 1b	4	0	1	0	9	1	0
W. Keeler, rf	5	1	2	0	2	0	0
J. Sheckard, lf	5	1	0	1	1	0	0
T. Daly, 2b	5	2	2	0	2	3	0
B. Dahlen, ss	5	1	2	0	4	6	0
C. Dolan, cf	4	2	2	2	3	1	1
J. McGuire, c	3	0	2	3	5	1	1
F. Gatins, 3b	4	0	0	0	1	1	0
B. Donovan, p	3	0	0	0	0	0	0
	38	7	12	5	27	14	2

St. Louis	ab	r	h	bi	o	a	e
J. Burkett, lf	4	0	1	1	4	0	0
J. Heidrick, cf	3	3	2	0	1	0	0
D. McGann, 1b	4	0	1	1	10	0	0
D. Padden, 2b	4	0	1	1	2	2	2
B. Wallace, ss	2	0	0	3	3	5	0
O. Krueger, 3b	3	1	1	0	1	1	0
J. Ryan, c	4	1	2	0	6	1	0
A. Nichols, rf	3	0	0	0	1	0	0
J. Powell, p	3	0	1	1	0	0	0
B. Schriver, ph9	1	0	0	0	-	-	-
P. Donovan, pr9	0	1	0	0	-	-	-
	31	6	9	4	27	9	2

Brooklyn 000 102 031 - 7
St. Louis 100 101 102 - 6

	ip	h	r-er	bb	so
Donovan (W 13-7)	9	9	6-4	5	5
Powell (L 10-9)	9	12	7-6	3	4

Time - 2:25
Attendance - 3,800
Umpire: H. O'Day

LOB: Bkn 7, StL 4. BE: none.
DP: Wallace-McGann, Dahlen-Kelley, Dahlen-Daly-Kelley.
2B: McGann, Powell, McGuire.
SH: Nichols.
SB: Keeler, Dahlen 2, Heidrick 3, Wallace.

Despite incidents like this, O'Day's umpiring career lasted until 1927.

St. Louis remained in the pennant chase until late August. The Cardinals finished a respectable fourth with a 76-64 record.

Then the American League moved one of its franchises to St. Louis, calling the team the Browns. Seven of the Cardinals' top players jumped to the crosstown rivals.

It would be another 20 years before the Cardinals had as good a season, percentage-wise, as they had in 1901.

1902—Sunday, August 17th, at League Park

Spectacular Game with Superbas Ends as 18-Inning Tie, 7-7

"Cupid" Currie and "Wild Bill" Donovan Pitch Great Ball

Clutch Fielding and Desperate Base Running are Features of Game

In one of the most brilliantly played games here in years, the St. Louis Cardinals and the Brooklyn Superbas battled to an 18-inning, 7-7 tie. Darkness finally ended the game before a decision could be reached. The game had just about everything: critical errors and game-saving plays in the field, costly bases on balls and clutch pitching, and daring base running and men caught napping on the base paths. Each side had numerous chances to win, but were unable to put the game way.

Alex Pearson, the Cardinals' newest acquisition, made his St. Louis pitching debut today. He did poorly, allowing five runs in just two innings. He was replaced by Clarence "Cupid" Currie, who had been released to St. Louis by Cincinnati in July. Currie pitched brilliantly for the remaining 16 innings.

Today's Results
ST. LOUIS 7 - Brooklyn 7 (TIE)(18 inn.)
Cincinnati 2 - Pittsburg 1
New York 3 - Chicago 2 (14 inn.)(1st)
New York 3 - Chicago 1 (7 inn.)(2nd)
no other game scheduled

Standings	W-L	Pct.	GB
Pittsburg	71-24	.747	-
Brooklyn	55-45	.550	18½
Boston	49-44	.527	21
Chicago	51-47	.520	21½
Cincinnati	45-51	.469	26½
ST. LOUIS	45-53	.459	27½
Philadelphia	38-60	.388	34½
New York	34-64	.347	38½

"Wild Bill" Donovan was on the slab for Brooklyn. He showed all of his famous speed, striking out 13, and also lived up to his nickname by passing seven batters. He allowed four runs in the first two innnings, then pitched great ball for the rest of the game. Despite the intense heat, both he and Currie finished the game.

Pearson, pitching in front of a big crowd for the first time in his life, was nervous at the start, walking three men in the first inning. That he was able to escape with just one run scored against him was mainly due to fine fielding by Otto Krueger.

The Cardinals then scored three in their first at bats. Kitty Brashear's single, a safe bunt by George Barclay, and a walk to Patsy Donovan loaded the bases. John Farrell then smashed a hit past first base for two runs. The third run came on Krueger's out at first.

The first two Brooklyn batters in the second bunted safely, and the next one sacrificed. An unsuccessful attempt to throw a man out at home, two singles, and a stolen base gave the Superbas four runs in the inning.

Jack Ryan's single, a fumble by Cozy Dolan, and two outs gave St. Louis one run in their half, leaving the score 5-4 in favor of the visitors.

Currie was then put in to replace Pearson, and he stopped the Brooklyn attack cold, allowing just four harmless singles over the next six innings.

B. Donovan settled down, too. But he had a streak of wildness in the sixth, and St. Louis took the lead. Barclay and "the other" Donovan were both given free passes, and they scored on Krueger's single and Fred Hartman's long fly.

In the eighth inning, P. Donovan kept his team in the lead with a fine throw. After Bill Dahlen had been retired on a magnificent play by Krueger to open the inning, Tom McCreery walked. Hartman's error gave Duke Farrell a life. Tim Flood then sent a hit to right, and McCreery made for home. Patsy Donovan saved the day with a perfect throw to Ryan, who did a great job of blocking the plate and tagging the runner out. McCreery was hurt in the collision and left the game.

The Cardinals had a 6-5 lead when the ninth inning opened. With one man out, Jimmy Sheckard hit sharply to shortstop. Krueger picked the ball up nicely, but his throw to first pulled Brashear off the bag, allowing Sheckard to reach safely. He quickly stole second and took third on an infield out. Cozy Dolan hit a slow one to Krueger, who bobbled the ball slightly, then threw hurriedly into the dirt near first base. Brashear had caught several similar throws earlier in the game, but, with a putout meaning the ball game, he failed to come up with this one, and the tying run scored.

Brooklyn got the first good chances in extra innings, but good fielding and bad base running turned them back. In the tenth, D. Farrell and Flood singled, but the former was doubled off second after Barclay's nice catch of B. Donovan's sinking liner. In the eleventh, Sheckard was on third and Keeler on second when Brashear made a nice scoop of Krueger's low throw, retiring the side. In the next round, Ryan picked Hugh Hearne off first base.

In the thirteenth, however, Brooklyn managed to push a run across with singles by Sheckard, Keeler, and Dahlen.

After P. Donovan was out to lead off the home half, it looked bad for the Cardinals. J. Farrell grounded to Dahlen at shortstop, but the fielder threw high past D. Farrell at first, and John F. raced all the way to third, arriving with a head-first slide just ahead of the throw. Krueger then lifted a fly to short center. "The Rabbit" (Farrell) made a daring dash for home, again ending in a long slide. Dolan's throw was off line just enough to allow the run to score, and the game was tied again.

In the bottom of the fourteenth, Brashear walked and Homer Smoot singled. Barclay sacrificed, and P. Donovan came to the plate with men on second and third. The crowd was in a uproar, calling on the Cardinal manager to end the game with a hit. But B. Donovan, at the suggestion of his manager, Ned Hanlon, pitched four very wide ones, and Patsy walked. Wild Bill then turned on the speed and got Farrell to tap weakly to the mound for a force at home. Krueger fouled out, and the inning was over.

In the seventeenth, Patsy tried to win the game by sprinting home from second on J. Farrell's single to right. But Keeler's throw to the plate was a perfect one-hopper, and Hearne tagged Donovan out just as he was trying to slide between the catcher's legs.

The moon had already risen and the sun set, so umpire Tom Brown announced that the eighteenth would be the last inning. It passed quickly, the only base runner, Sheckard, being caught stealing, and the game ended as a 7-7 tie.

The fans rushed for the street cars, hoping that their dinners would not be too cold by the time they finally got home.

Brooklyn	ab	r	h	bi	o	a	e	St. Louis	ab	r	h	bi	o	a	e
J. Sheckard, lf	6	4	3	1	4	1	0	K. Brashear, 1b	8	1	1	1	26	0	0
W. Keeler, rf	7	0	2	1	2	1	0	H. Smoot, cf	8	0	2	0	2	0	0
C. Dolan, cf	9	1	1	0	2	0	1	G. Barclay, lf	6	2	1	0	6	1	0
B. Dahlen, ss	7	0	2	2	4	6	2	P. Donovan, rf	5	2	2	0	1	1	0
T. McCreery, 1b	2	0	0	1	11	0	0	J. Farrell, 2b	8	1	2	2	9	9	0
H. Hearne, c9	4	0	2	0	12	0	0	O. Krueger, ss	6	0	2	3	5	13	2
D. Farrell, c-1b9	7	0	2	0	13	2	0	F. Hartman, 3b	7	0	2	1	1	3	1
T. Flood, 2b	8	1	4	0	1	7	0	J. Ryan, c	8	1	2	0	3	4	0
B. Donovan, p	7	1	1	0	1	4	0	A. Pearson, p	1	0	0	0	0	1	0
E. Wheeler, 3b	7	0	0	0	4	3	0	C. Currie, p3	5	0	0	0	0	5	0
								M. O'Neill, ph18	1	0	0	0	-	-	-
	64	7	17	6	54	24	3		63	7	14	7	*53	37	3

Brooklyn   140 000 001 000 100 000 - 7
St. Louis   310 002 000 000 100 000 - 7
game called on account of darkness

*Wheeler out for running out of baseline

	ip	h	r-er	bb	so
Donovan	18	14	7-5	7	13
Pearson	2	4	5-5	3	0
Currie	16	13	2-1	5	1

HBP: by Currie (Sheckard)
Picked Off: Bkn 1.
CS: Bkn 3, StL 2.
Time - 3:30
Attendance - 10,000

LOB: Bkn 14, StL 12. BE: Bkn 3, StL. 1. DP: Krueger-J. Farrell-Brashear, Krueger-Brashear, Currie-Krueger-Brashear, Barclay-J. Farrell, D. Farrell-Wheeler. 2B: Krueger. SH: Wheeler, Hartman, Keeler, Barclay, Krueger. SB: Sheckard 2, Barclay, Dahlen 2, P. Donovan, Krueger.

The Cardinals had been hurt badly by the defections to the American League Browns, and they finished the 1902 season with a 56-78 record. Their .418 percentage left them in sixth place. Poor pitching and fielding were mostly to blame.

1903 — Wednesday, July 22nd, at League Park

Cards Win, 8-7, on Smoot's Ninth-Inning, Two-Out, Three-Run Home Run

Carried Off the Field on the Shoulders of the Crowd

Fourth Consecutive Victory for St. Louis

Homer Smoot did it again today. For the third time in less than two weeks, he turned an apparent Cardinal defeat into a victory. Today he did it with a last-inning home run that turned an apparent 7-5 defeat into an 8-7 triumph. On July 12th, he had scored the go-ahead run in the top of the tenth inning in Philadelphia, then he saved the day with a tremendous, running, jumping catch to turn a potential two-run home run into the game-ending out. And last Sunday he ended the game by scoring the winning run in the tenth inning against the Superbas on his own double and a two-bagger by George Barclay.

Today's Results
ST. LOUIS 8 - Cincinnati 7
Philadelphia 3 - New York 2 (10 inn.)
Boston 5 - Brooklyn 2
no other game scheduled

Standings	W-L	Pct.	GB
Pittsburg	53-26	.671	-
New York	46-30	.605	5½
Chicago	49-33	.598	5½
Cincinnati	41-38	.519	12
Brooklyn	38-37	.507	13
Boston	31-44	.413	20
ST. LOUIS	31-50	.383	23
Philadelphia	24-55	.304	29

Today's victory was the fourth in a row for the Cardinals, their longest winning streak of the year. All four triumphs have been achieved in the team's last turn at bat. On Sunday they beat Brooklyn in ten innings, 5-4. On Monday, they broke a scoreless tie with five runs in the bottom of the eighth and defeated the Cincinnati Reds, 5-1. Yesterday they edged the Reds, 5-4, with a run in the bottom of the ninth. And today, after Cincinnati had scored two in the top of the ninth to take the lead, Smoot's home run gave the Cardinals three runs to win, 8-7.

Between two and three thousand loyalists were at the Vandeventer Avenue grounds today, hoping for a repeat of the home team's recent victories. They were not disappointed, although they had to wait longer than usual (the game lasted nearly 2½ hours) to see it.

The Cincinnati lineup was something of a makeshift affair, owing to the absence of verteran shortstop Tommy Corcoran. Although the Reds made no errors, and Harry Steinfeldt got ten assists at shortstop, several St. Louis hits that regular players might have cut off went through the infield untouched.

St. Louis manager Patsy Donovan was able to put his strongest nine on the field.

Jack Harper, the former Cardinal who had jumped to the Browns in 1902, was the Cincinnati pitcher. He was opposed by Cardinal rookie Mordecai Brown, the three-fingered Indiana coal miner. Brown lasted only four innings before being replaced by Clarence Currie.

Brown retired the Reds in the first inning, despite a leadoff hit by Mike Donlin.

Then St. Louis came in and scored two runs. After John Farrell bounced out, Donovan singled and stole. Smoot knocked a terrific drive past Cy Seymour in center field for a triple and a run. After Dave Brain fanned, Barclay brought Smoot home with a hit past the stumbling Steinfeldt.

Steinfeldt redeemed himself by leading off the Cincinnati second with a home run to the clubhouse wall in center field. After two men went out, light-hitting catcher Bill Bergen walked, and pitcher Harper doubled. Donlin then put Cincinnati ahead, 3-2, with a two-run single.

They made it 5-2 in the fourth. Bergen singled and advanced on Harper's out. Donlin singled him home and moved up on another infield out. Cozy Dolan then singled, plating Donlin.

That was all for Brown, and Currie went to the mound in the next inning. "Cupid" worked effectively until the ninth.

In the meantime, St. Louis tied the score with a three-run rally in the fifth. Farrell opened with a single and stole second. Donovan shot a hit through shortstop, and the "Rabbit" raced home. Patsy stole second and moved to third when Smoot bounced out. Lee DeMontreville, who had replaced Brain when the latter was ejected for saying the wrong thing to the umpire, walked. He stole also, putting St. Louis men on second and third. Barclay was retired, Steinfeldt to Beckley, while Donovan scored. Jimmy Burke's single drove DeMontreville across with the tying run.

The 5-5 deadlock remained until the ninth, although it took a sensational play by Donlin to prevent a Cardinal run in the eighth. With one out, Burke tripled. Then Jim Hackett lifted a fly ball down the left field foul line. Donlin took the ball on the run as he crossed the line and, without stopping himself, threw perfectly to home to nip Burke, who had tagged up after the catch.

The Reds scored two in the top of the ninth. After two were out, Steinfeldt was hit by a pitch. He stole second and scored on Joe Kelley's long single. Peitz also singled, sending Kelley to third. The two then worked the double steal, Kelley scoring when Farrell's return throw to home was wild.

Jack O'Neill struck out to start the home half of the ninth. Donovan then sent Jack's brother Mike up to pinch-hit, and he walked. Harper also gave Farrell free passage. Donovan, however, hit into a force play at second base for the second out.

Now Smoot was the Cardinals' last hope. When Bergen missed a pitch, Donovan made second. With darkness fast approaching, that meant that a long single would give St. Louis a tie. With two strikes, Smoot pulled a lightning shot past old Jake Beckley at first base, and the runners were headed home. Right fielder Dolan apparently didn't see the ball at all, and Beckley had to run out and retrieve it. By the time he had relayed the ball to Harper, Smoot had circled the bases and was across the plate with the winning win. In disgust, the Cincinnati pitcher heaved the ball into the stands with all his might.

Meanwhile, the fans streamed out onto the field to lionize their heroes. Before he knew what was happening, Smoot found himself riding to the clubhouse on the shoulders of the adoring throng. The bashful Homer looked a bit embarrassed by this display, but later he admitted that he had enjoyed the experience.

Cincinnati	ab	r	h	bi	o	a	e	St. Louis	ab	r	h	bi	o	a	e
M. Donlin, lf	5	1	4	3	2	1	0	J. Farrell, 2b	4	1	2	0	0	5	1
C. Seymour, cf	5	0	0	0	0	0	0	P. Donovan, rf	5	3	2	1	4	0	0
C. Dolan, rf	5	0	1	1	1	0	0	H. Smoot, cf	5	2	2	4	2	0	0
J. Beckley, 1b	5	0	2	0	13	0	0	D. Brain, ss	1	0	0	0	0	1	0
H. Steinfeldt, ss	4	2	2	1	1	10	0	L. DeMontrev'le, ss3	2	1	0	0	1	2	1
J. Kelley, 2b	4	1	1	1	1	1	0	G. Barclay, lf	4	0	2	2	1	0	0
H. Peitz, 3b	5	0	2	0	1	3	0	J. Burke, 3b	4	0	3	1	1	3	0
B. Bergen, c	4	2	1	0	7	1	0	J. Hackett, 1b	4	0	0	0	14	0	0
J. Harper, p	3	1	1	0	0	0	0	J. O'Neill, c	4	0	0	0	4	1	0
								M. Brown, p	2	0	1	0	0	0	0
								C. Currie, p5	1	0	0	0	0	2	0
								M. O'Neill, ph9	0	1	0	0	-	-	-
	40	7	14	6	26	16	0		36	8	12	8	27	14	2

Cincinnati   030 200 002 - 7
St. Louis   200 030 003 - 8
two out when winning run scored

	ip	h	r-er	bb	so
Harper (L 5-6)	8.2	12	8-8	3	5
Brown	4	9	5-5	1	0
Currie (W 4-8)	5	5	2-1	2	2

PB: Bergen 2
HBP: by Currie (Steinfeldt)
Umpire: A. Moran

LOB: Cinc 10, StL 5.
DP: Donlin-Bergen.
2B: Harper, Barclay.
3B: Smoot, Burke.
HR: Steinfeldt, Smoot.
SB: Donovan 2, Farrell, DeMontreville, Burke, Steinfeldt, Peitz.
Time - 2:25 Attendance - 2,500

The Cardinals' winning streak was broken in their next game. For the rest of the season, they were never able to win even three games in a row. As a result, they slid into last place, finishing with a 43-94 record.

Smoot finished the season with a .296 batting average, second on the team to manager Donovan's .327. Smoot had four home runs for the year, exactly half of the team's total of eight.

After the regular season, the Cardinals were soundly defeated in a City Series with the American League Browns.

1904 — Saturday, October 15th, at League Park

Players and Front Offices Feud, City Series Ends Tied

Nine Runs in Third Inning Give Cardinals the Game, 10-6

Cardinal Players Refuse to Play Seventh Game on Sunday

The second annual autumn series between the Cardinals and the Browns ended prematurely today, and the championship of St. Louis was left undecided. Today's game was won by the National League Cardinals, 10-6, tying the series at three games apiece.

But the players' contracts were set to expire on midnight, October 15th, and the Cardinal players refused to play the seventh game on Sunday, the 16th, unless they were given all of their club's receipts from the game. This, of course, the Cardinal owners, the Robison brothers, were unwillng to do. They felt that they had already been more than generous by agreeing to pay the players any share of the receipts; after all, they had contracts. They offered the players half of the club's share of the Sunday gate, but were turned down. The Robisons got their revenge by not delivering the final paychecks to those players who left town this evening.

The Cardinals' management tried to get the full seven games in by staging a doubleheader today. At first they thought that the Browns had agreed to this, but yesterday the Browns' owner, Robert L. Hedges, issued a statement in which he stated that he would not ask his players to play two games today.

The Cardinals' business manager, B.S. Muckenfuss, countered with the charge that it had been the Browns who had first suggested the doubleheader, so they could not back out of the deal now. Therefore, he said that two games would indeed be played on Saturday.

Relations between the clubs became so strained that when the Browns' field manager, Jimmy McAleer, went to the Cardinals' offices to consult about the selection of umpires, he was thrown out. Stanley Robison made quite a scene of it, although he did not have to carry out a threat of bodily force.

The Cardinal players were at the grounds, in uniform, at 1:00 p.m., ready to play the first game. But the Browns didn't show up until nearly 3:00, the scheduled starting time for a single game. Only one game was played.

Bad feelings had been generated between the two squads during the course of the first five games, and today two of the principals in the squabbling, Danny Shay and Jesse Burkett, spent most of the afternoon exchanging insults and profanity. It was only due to the one-sided nature of the game that serious trouble was averted.

The only encouraging development of the day was the umpiring. In the first five games, arguing and brawling had gone unchecked. But today, two local men with umpiring experience, Frank Pears and Frank Genins, served as arbiters, and they did very well in keeping the players under control.

Willie Sudhoff was given a chance to pitch for the Browns for the first time in the series. He went to pieces in the third inning, and the Cardinals were given nine runs and the game. Up to that point, the Browns had built up a 4-0 lead.

Manager Kid Nichols put himself onto the mound for the Cardinals.

The Browns got to him for two runs in the first inning. Burkett opened with a single, and John Heidrick doubled. Bobby Wallace then hit safely to center, and Homer Smoot kicked the ball around long enough to allow two runs to score.

The American Leaguers got two more in the top half of the third. Burkett sent a fly to right, which John Dunleavy dropped, and took second on a poor return to the infield. Heidrick's grounder was too difficult for John Farrell to handle. Wallace followed with another hit, Burkett scoring. Tom Jones then hit into a force play, while Heidrick scored. Jones stole second but injured his leg doing so. And Dick Padden hurt his hand hitting one of Nichols's pitches.

When the Browns went out to the field, Harry Howell replaced Jones at first base, and Harry Gleason went in at second for Padden.

Nichols opened the third for the Cardinals with an inconspicuous hit. Farrell's safe drive to center was more impressive. Spike Shannon followed with a double play ball to shortstop, but Wallace fumbled it, and all hands were safe, Nichols racing home from second base.

Then came the key play. Jake Beckley laid a bunt down the third base line. The third sacker, Charlie Moran, charged in for it, but Sudhoff pounced on the ball first. Danny Shay was coaching third, and he tricked Sudhoff into throwing to the uncovered base by standing on third and calling for the ball. When Sudhoff threw it, Shay stepped aside, and the ball sailed down the grandstand wall, while two runs scored.

Burkett came charging into the infield, intent on committing mayhem upon Shay's body, but Jimmy Burke sprang off the Cardinal bench and diverted Burkett's attention. A loud argument ensued, but no blows were struck.

When play resumed, Sudhoff and the Browns went completely up in the air. Hits by Dave Brain and Smoot tied the game. Mike Kahoe dropped Dunleavy's bunt, loading the bases. The next two men went out, with one runner scoring. Wallace then made a terrible throw on Nichols's tap, allowing two more runs in. Three more hits followed, and the Cardinals had nine runs to their credit.

Cy Morgan came in to pitch for the Browns in the fourth, and he held the Cardinals to just one more tally.

The Browns counted twice in the sixth, but otherwise Nichols held them at a safe distance, and the Cardinals won, 10-6.

With the players and management and everyone at each others' throats, the series ended without the decisive seventh game being played.

Browns (AL)	ab	r	h	bi	o	a	e
J. Burkett, lf	5	2	1	0	1	0	0
J. Heidrick, cf	5	2	2	0	0	0	0
B. Wallace, ss	4	0	2	3	2	3	2
P. Hynes, rf	3	1	1	0	3	0	0
T. Jones, 1b	2	0	0	1	4	1	0
H. Gleason, 2b3	2	1	0	0	1	4	0
D. Padden, 2b	2	0	1	0	1	2	0
H. Howell, 1b3	2	0	2	1	6	0	0
C. Moran, 3b	4	0	1	1	1	2	0
M. Kahoe, c	4	0	0	0	5	1	0
W. Sudhoff, p	2	0	0	0	0	1	1
C. Morgan, p4	2	0	1	0	0	0	0
	37	6	11	6	24	14	3

Cardinals (NL)	ab	r	h	bi	o	a	e
J. Farrell, 3b	4	2	2	0	5	3	0
S. Shannon, lf	5	1	1	1	0	1	0
J. Beckley, 1b	5	1	1	2	8	0	0
D. Brain, 3b	5	1	2	0	1	4	1
H. Smoot, cf	4	1	1	1	2	0	0
J. Dunleavy, rf	4	1	0	0	1	0	1
D. Shay, ss	4	0	0	0	3	3	1
M. Grady, c	4	1	1	1	7	1	0
K. Nichols, p	4	2	3	0	0	1	0
	39	10	11	5	27	13	3

Browns	202 002 000	-	6
Cardinals	009 000 10x	-	10

	ip	h	r-er	bb	so
Sudhoff (L 0-1)	3	8	9-2	0	1
Morgan	5	3	1-1	0	2
Nichols (W 1-1)	9	11	6-4	0	4

LOB: Browns 5, Cardinals 7.
2B: Heidrick, Howell.
SH: Hynes.
SB: Jones.
HBP: by Sudhoff 1, by Morgan 1.
PB: Kahoe.
Time - 1:53
Attendance - 3,500
Umpires: F. Pears & F. Genins

The Cardinals had finished the National League season in fifth place with a 75-79 record, while the Browns had finished sixth in the A. L. with a 65-87 mark.

1905 — Sunday, October 15th, at League Park

Cardinals Lose Twice, Drop City Series to Browns, 4 Games to 3

Late Rally Gives A. L. Team First Game, 7-6

Howell Gets Credit for Both Wins, Taylor Charged with Both Losses

Needing to win just one of the two games played today to win the City championship, the St. Louis Cardinals lost both games and, with them, the series to their hometown rivals, the Browns. The National Leaguers were leading the first game by four runs, but the Browns scored five times in the eighth inning to reverse the verdict. The second game was scoreless until the fifth inning, then the Browns scored three runs with the aid of two errors. The game was called after six innings, and the Browns won, 3-0.

In the series, the Cardinals put most of their hopes upon the strong right arm of Jack Taylor, while the Browns used Harry Howell as often as possible. Today these pitchers both relieved in the first game and then pitched the entire second game, shortened as it was.

The Browns never led in the series until they won it today. In the opening game on Monday, Taylor bested Howell, 4-1. The Browns evened the series with an 8-3 victory on Tuesday. But Taylor pitched the Cards to victory on Wednesday, 9-1. Thursday's game ended in a tie, 1-1. On Friday, Howell avenged his opening game defeat by beating Taylor, 2-1. The Cardinals took a 3-2 lead in games on Saturday when "Buster" Brown edged Fred Glade and the Browns in a thrilling, 1-0 game.

That set the stage for today's decision. Because of the tie game, a doubleheader was set up, with the second game to last only seven innings. A large crowd was on hand for the last chance to see baseball here this year. Brown had pitched well the day before, and Captain Danny Shay decided to gamble and put him out there again in the first game today. Barney Pelty, who hadn't pitched since Wednesday, started for the Browns.

The American League curveballer started out very well, retiring the Cardinals in one-two-three fashion in the first three innings.

In the fourth inning the string was broken. Spike Shannon found left fielder George Stone playing shallow, and he sliced a drive over Stone's head for a triple. Shannon got caught in a hot box on Homer Smoot's grounder, but he managed to avoid being tagged out until Smoot had made it all the way around to third. He scored on a hit by Jake Beckley.

The Cards added two runs in the next inning. Art Hoelskoetter and Brown singled, and Shay and George McBride were hit by pitches during the rally.

Meanwhile, Brown had been breezing along. The rookie from Omaha had scattered five hits and a base on balls through the first five innings. But he suddenly lost his stuff in the sixth. Emil Frisk opened the inning with a hot drive that bounced off Shay's chest and gave the batter a double. Bobby Wallace hit the next pitch off the right field fence for a triple. And Tom Jones singled.

Shay removed Brown and brought Taylor in to pitch. "Brakeman Jack" put a stop to the scoring, striking out two batters, hitting one, then retiring Stone on a foul fly.

Spitballer Howell came in to pitch for the Browns in the bottom of the sixth, and the Cardinals hit him hard. Shannon and Smoot hit safely, and an error by Wallace filled the bases. Mike Grady forced Shannon at the plate, but Shay walked, bringing one run in. Hoelskoetter hit sharply to left. As Beckley came home from third, he got tangled up with catcher Tubby Spencer, and the throw home bounced off the pile-up. Rookie umpire Bill Klem ruled that Spencer was guilty of interference, and he motioned Grady in from third. The Browns were incredulous at the ruling and made a bitter protest. But, of course, it was to no avail.

The score remained 6-2 in favor of the Cardinals until the eighth. Then Ben Koehler of the Browns blooped a hit to left. After a pop out, Howell hit a long double to left, scoring Koehler. Stone was given a life on McBride's fumble, and Ike Rockenfield was hit by a pitch. That loaded the bases for Frisk. He worked the count to 3-and-2 then lifted a high drive to center. Smoot misjudged the ball for a fateful instant, and it went for a triple, tying the score. Frisk scored the go-ahead run on Wallace's liner to right.

In the bottom of the eighth, Howell was ejected for arguing too vigorously about Klem's ruling that Shay was hit by a pitch. Willie Sudhoff was brought in with two on and one out. Hoelskoetter greeted him with a solid line drive toward left, but Wallace snared the ball with a great effort and doubled the runner off second.

In the bottom of the ninth, with one man on and two out, Stone saved the game with a sensational falling, rolling catch of Shannon's sinking drive, and the Browns were victors, 7-6.

The second game began almost immediately. Howell was rehabilitated and sent in to pitch for the Browns, while Taylor remained on duty for the Cardinals.

The Cards got men on base in every inning, but could not score. The closest they came to a run was when Beckley was thrown out at home trying to score from second on Harry Arndt's single to center in the fourth.

Taylor held the Browns hitless through three innings and then yielded a harmless baser by Rockenfield in the fourth.

In the fifth inning, Taylor's support abandoned him, and the game was given to the Browns. With one out, Koehler dropped a double into short left. Spencer hit a liner, which McBride muffed, putting men on first and second. Howell forced Spencer on what should have been the third out of the inning. Stone then hit a very high fly to center. Smoot ran under it after a bad start only to have the ball glance off his glove. Two runs scored on the error. A third followed on Rockenfield's double down the left field line.

That was the extent of the scoring. After the sixth inning, Klem called the game on account of darkness.

The Browns won the game, 3-0, and with it the series. They also won some heavy bets from the Cardinal players. Taylor reportedly lost $500 on the outcome.

FIRST GAME

Browns (AL)	ab	r	h	bi	o	a	e
G. Stone, lf	5	1	2	0	1	0	0
I. Rockenfield, 2b	4	1	2	0	3	1	0
E. Frisk, rf	5	2	3	3	1	0	0
B. Wallace, ss	5	1	1	2	4	4	2
T. Jones, 1b	5	0	2	1	8	0	0
H. Gleason, 3b	5	0	0	0	0	3	0
B. Koehler, cf	4	1	1	0	3	0	0
J. Sugden, c	2	0	0	0	2	2	0
I. Van Zandt, ph6	1	0	0	0	-	-	-
T. Spencer, c6	2	0	0	0	3	0	0
B. Pelty, p	2	0	1	0	2	1	0
F. Roth, ph6	0	0	0	0	-	-	-
H. Howell, p6	1	1	1	1	0	0	0
W. Sudhoff, p8	0	0	0	0	0	0	0
	41	7	13	7	27	11	2

Cardinals (NL)	ab	r	h	bi	o	a	e
J. Dunleavy, rf	5	0	0	0	2	0	0
S. Shannon, lf	5	0	2	0	2	0	0
H. Smoot, cf	4	2	1	0	1	0	0
J. Beckley, 1b	4	1	1	1	9	1	1
M. Grady, c	4	1	1	0	5	0	0
D. Shay, 2b	1	1	0	1	1	3	0
A. Hoelskoetter, 3b	4	1	2	2	2	1	0
G. McBride, ss	3	0	0	0	4	5	2
B. Brown, p	2	0	1	1	1	0	0
J. Taylor, p6	1	0	0	0	0	0	0
H. Arndt, ph9	1	0	0	0	-	-	-
	34	6	8	5	27	10	3

```
Browns       000  002  050  -  7
Cardinals    000  123  000  -  6
```

	ip	h	r-er	bb	so
Pelty	5	4	3-3	0	2
Howell (W 2-1)	2.1	4	3-2	1	1
Sudhoff	1.2	0	0-0	0	0
Brown	*5	8	2-2	1	2
Taylor (L 2-2)	4	5	5-3	0	2

*faced three batters in sixth

LOB: Browns 10, Cardinals 5.
DP: Hoelskoetter-McBride-Beckley, Wallace-Rockenfield.
2B: Howell, Frisk.
3B: Shannon, Wallace, Frisk.
SB: Shay, Hoelskoetter, Gleason.
HBP: by Pelty 2 (Shay, McBride), by Taylor 2 (Roth, Rockenfield), by Howell (Shay).
PB: Sugden.
Time - 2:00
Attendance - 10,000
Umpire: B. Klem

SECOND GAME

			r	h	e	Batteries
Browns	000	030 -	3	4	2	H. Howell (W 3-1) & T. Spencer
Cardinals	000	000 -	0	4	3	J. Taylor (L 2-3) & M. Grady

game called after six innings on account of darkness

1906 — Thursday, April 12th, at League Park

Opening Game Scoreless Until 13th, Then Pirates Edge Cardinals, 2-1

Umpire's Decisions & Bad Base Running Foil St. Louis

Brilliant Pitching and Fielding the Features of Exciting Contest

The 1906 National League season opened in St. Louis with as thrilling a game as one could hope for on any day of the year. Through twelve innings the rival pitchers, Jack Taylor and Vic Willis, matched goose eggs, while their teammates gave them flawless support. Then in the thirteenth, the Pittsburg Pirates scored two runs, aided by the first error of the game. The St. Louis Cardinals were able to answer with just one tally in the bottom of the inning and lost, 2-1.

Featured in the breathtaking finish were two calls by umpire Bill Klem, both of which went against St. Louis. On one, in the bottom of the twelfth, a Cardinal runner was called out at home just after most observers thought he had scored the winning run. The other, a "Foul" call on a ball hit by Pittsburg's Otis Clymer, nullified an easy out and allowed the batter to swing again. He did and started the winning rally with a hit.

Today's Results
Pittsburg 2 - ST. LOUIS 1 (13 inn.)
New York 3 - Philadelphia 2
Chicago 7 - Cincinnati 2
Boston 2 - Brooklyn 0

Standings	W-L	Pct.	GB
Pittsburg	1-0	1.000	-
New York	1-0	1.000	-
Chicago	1-0	1.000	-
Boston	1-0	1.000	-
ST. LOUIS	0-1	.000	1
Philadelphia	0-1	.000	1
Cincinnati	0-1	.000	1
Brooklyn	0-1	.000	1

Still, the home team could have won the game despite the umpire if their base running had been better. In each of the last two innings, a man was thrown out at home, and, in the second instance, the man directly behind him only went from first to second on the hit. When the next batter singled on the infield, this runner could not score, and the Cardinals wound up leaving the bases loaded at the end of the game.

With the weather chilly and rain threatening, the opening day crowd was a modest 6,000. Those fans who made it to the park witnessed a ball game they would not soon forget.

The day marked the debut of John McCloskey as the Cardinals' manager.

Jack Taylor pitched a beautiful game for St. Louis. His old-time speed was not in evidence, but his control was impeccable. Mike Grady gave him fine support behind the plate, throwing out all three Pirates who attempted to steal on him. George McBride made two wonderful plays at shortstop, cutting off runs in each case. And the outfielders all made fine catches.

The Pirates didn't shine quite as much in the field, but the throwing of their outfielders was brilliant. Pitcher Willis was found for twelve hits, and he gave three bases on balls. But he was untouchable in the pinches and was rewarded with victory.

Taylor faced only 22 Pirate batters in shutting Pittsburg out through the first seven innings.

Meanwhile, Willis was shutting the Cardinals out. They got two men aboard in the third to no avail, then threatened again in the fourth. With one out, Homer Smoot walked. Jake Beckley and John Himes followed with singles, loading the bases. Harry Arndt was the next hitter, and any sort of safety or long fly would give St. Louis a run. But Harry bounced to Hans Wagner, and the big Dutchman started a double play.

Jim Nealon opened the Pittsburg eighth with a base knock, and Tommy Sheehan bunted him to second. Claude Ritchey then hit a hot shot up the middle on the ground. Nealon had a good jump and seemed sure to score, but McBride came out of nowhere to spear the ball, throw Ritchey out at first, and keep Nealon at third. George Gibson then flied out, ending the inning.

The Cardinals also threatened in the eighth. McBride led off with a hit, and Taylor sacrificed him to second. A wild pitch moved him to third. Pug Bennett was the batter, and he lifted a soft liner over short. It looked like a hit, but the tall, athletic Wagner made a leaping catch. Spike Shannon then popped out to third, and McBride was left at third.

The next three innings passed quickly.

In the bottom of the twelfth, the home team came within an eyelash of winning, but they were foiled by the umpire. Grady opened with a walk, and Smoot bunted him to second. Beckley then pulled a beauty to right field for a hit, and Grady made for home. Clymer had a long throw, but he made it strong and on target, and a very close play ensued. Klem ruled Grady out at home, and the Cardinals put up a tremendous yelp. Even the mild-mannered Smoot screamed his disapproval, an occurrence which surprised his teammates so much that they stopped their arguing. On the play, Beckley alertly went all the way to third, but he was left when Himes flied out.

Pittsburg then came in and scored two runs. Clymer first of all tapped a ball near the plate, which Grady pounced upon and threw to first. But Klem called the ball foul, and again the Cardinals kicked. The reprieved Clymer pulled a single to left. Wagner shot another hit to left. Nealon bunted the runners to second and third. With two strikes, Sheehan boldly dropped a squeeze bunt down toward first base. Beckley fielded in a hurry and threw home. The ball and the runner arrived at just the same moment, and Grady was unable to dig the sphere out of the dirt. As the ball rolled away, Wagner also sprinted home, and Sheehan went to third. Ritchey again hit a shot past shortstop, but McBride snared it and doubled Sheehan off third.

The Cardinals came in needing two to tie. Arndt opened with a hit. McBride flied out. Taylor grounded to short, but Ritchey muffed Wagner's toss to second, and two runners were safe. Bennett singled to right to load the bases. Shannon then singled to short center, scoring Arndt. Taylor also tried to score, but Ganley's throw cut him off at home. Bennett, meanwhile, only went from first to second on the play. After nearly winning the game with a drive that hooked just foul, Grady got an infield hit past Willis, Bennett moving from second to third, not from third to home. With the bases loaded, Smoot could only ground out to first, and the Cardinals were losers by a 2-1 final score.

Pittsburg	ab	r	h	bi	o	a	e		St. Louis	ab	r	h	bi	o	a	e
F. Clarke, lf	4	0	0	0	3	0	0		P. Bennett, 2b	6	0	2	0	3	2	0
B. Ganley, cf	4	0	1	0	4	1	0		S. Shannon, lf	6	0	1	1	5	0	0
O. Clymer, rf	5	1	1	0	0	1	0		M. Grady, c	5	0	1	0	2	4	0
H. Wagner, ss	5	1	2	0	5	4	0		H. Smoot, rf	4	0	0	0	6	0	0
J. Nealon, 1b	4	0	2	0	16	1	0		J. Beckley, 1b	5	0	2	0	13	2	1
T. Sheehan, 3b	3	0	1	0	3	1	0		J. Himes, cf	5	0	2	0	2	0	0
C. Ritchey, 2b	5	0	0	0	2	5	1		H. Arndt, 3b	5	1	2	0	4	1	0
G. Gibson, c	4	0	0	0	5	2	0		G. McBride, ss	5	0	1	0	4	3	0
V. Willis, p	4	0	0	0	1	6	0		J. Taylor, p	3	0	1	0	0	3	0
	38	2	7	0	39	21	1			44	1	12	1	39	15	1

Pittsburg   000 000 000 000 2-2
St. Louis   000 000 000 000 1-1

LOB: Pitts 2, StL 9. BE: Pitts 1, StL 1. DP: Wagner-Ritchey-Nealon, McBride-Arndt. 2B: Nealon. SH: Ganley, Sheehan 2, Taylor, Nealon, Smoot.

	ip	h	r-er	bb	so
Willis (W 1-0)	13	12	1-0	3	3
Taylor (L 0-1)	13	7	2-0	1	1

WP: Willis
Time - 2:00
Umpires: B. Klem & B. Carpenter

SB: Arndt. CS: Clarke, Sheehan, Wagner, Arndt, Ganley.
Picked Off: Taylor.
Attendance - 6,000

The Cardinals had a weak team once again in 1906. The opening day loss was practically the high point of the season.

They finished in seventh place with a 52-98 record. That left them a whopping 63 games behind the pennant-winning Cubs and 11½ games behind the sixth-place Reds.

They also lost the City Series to the Browns, four games to one.

1907 — Sunday, August 11th, at League Park

Karger Pitches Seven-Inning Perfect Game as Cardinals Win Pair

McGlynn Pitches Second Win in Two Days in Opening Game

Last-Place St. Louis Sweeps Five-Game Series from Boston

Behind two remarkable pitching performances, the St. Louis Cardinals today beat the Boston Doves in both games of a doubleheader, 5-4 and 4-0. In the first game, Ulysses Simpson Grant McGlynn, popularly known as Stony, pitched his second complete game victory in two days. In the second game, which was limited to seven innings by mutual agreement, Eddie Karger pitched one of the most outstanding games ever, not allowing a single batter to reach first base safely.

The double victory gave St. Louis a sweep of the five-game series with Boston but still left the last-place Cardinals 13 games behind the seventh-place Doves.

Today it was demonstrated that the Cardinals' weakness was not their front-line pitching. Karger's shutout was the Cardinals' twelfth of the season. But they have won only 16 other games. In runs scored and fielding average, St. Louis lay far at the bottom of the National League list.

Today's Results
ST. LOUIS 5 - Boston 4 (1st game)
ST. LOUIS 4 - Boston 0 (7 inn.)(2nd)
Chicago 1 - Philadelphia 0 (1st game)
Chicago 1 - Philadelphia 0 (7 inn.)(2nd)
Cincinnati 5 - Brooklyn 1 (1st game)
Brooklyn 2 - Cincinnati 1 (8 inn.)(2nd)
no other game scheduled

Standings	W-L	Pct.	GB
Chicago	75-28	.728	-
Pittsburg	58-39	.598	14
New York	58-40	.592	14½
Philadelphia	53-43	.552	18½
Brooklyn	47-55	.461	27½
Cincinnati	45-57	.441	29½
Boston	38-62	.380	35½
ST. LOUIS	28-78	.264	48½

A large throng braved the extreme heat today to watch the Cardinals' last home games before a three-week road trip. The attendance of 12,000 was the largest of the season, and the customers were given a fine show.

With Manager John McCloskey away on a scouting trip, John Burnett and Ed Holly were in charge of the team. Seeing the big crowd, McGlynn went to them and asked to be allowed to pitch the first game. Stony had performed brilliantly on Saturday, pitching a 3-2 victory and driving in the winning run himself. So the captains let him go out there again.

Despite the heat, he pitched a good game. Two other players, however, could not brave the furnace: catcher Pete Noonan and outfielder Red Murray both left the game. Umpire Bob Emslie was only able to last one game, and a player from each team officiated in the second contest. Gus Dorner, the Boston pitcher, quit in the middle of the second game.

The first game was a seesaw affair, which the home team won by scoring two runs in the last of the eighth inning. Vivan Lindaman was McGlynn's mound opponent, and, while neither man was overpowering, both pitched steady ball.

Boston got out on top with a run in the first. Fred Tenney's single and steal, along with a throwing error by Noonan and a hit by Bill Sweeney brought the run around.

St. Louis took the lead with two in the fifth. Two infield hits and a walk loaded the bases. Bobby Byrne's safe pop fly scored one run, and Shad Barry's long fly out drove in the other.

Patsy Flaherty put the Beaneaters back on top with a two-run home run over the right field screen in the sixth.

Red Murray tied the game with a homer in the bottom of the inning. This one, however, was made inside the park, forcing Red to run the circuit at top speed. The effort proved so exhausting that he withdrew from the game, Harry Wolter taking his place.

Boston took the lead again with a run in the eighth.

But the Cardinals scored two in their half to take the game. Ed Konetchy and Burnett singled, and Holly sacrificed them over. Wolter then pulled a hit down the right field line, and both runners scored.

Boston failed to score in the ninth, and the Cardinals won, 5-4.

Umpire Emslie retired before the second game began, and pitchers Fred Beebe and Irv Young were selected to take over his duties. Because of the heat and the necessity of catching a train for Boston, it was agreed before the start of the game to limit the contest to seven innings. As a result, Eddie Karger was deprived of a chance to achieve baseball immortality.

His pitching was perfect. Not a single safe hit, error, nor base on balls marred his record. Indeed, the Cardinal fielders were not called upon to accept anything resembling a difficult chance. The closest thing to a line drive was a soft floater off the bat of Ginger Beaumont, which shortstop Holly gathered in easily. Only four balls were hit out of the infield, and they were all easy flies to the outfielders. And the Texas southpaw's control was so good that he never gave any batter more than two called balls. Karger's only two strikeout victims were Al Bridwell and Bill Sweeney, both in the fourth inning.

Gus Dorner was Karger's initial mound opponent, and he was also effective. Through the first three innings, he held the Cardinals hitless. Then, with one out in the fourth, Konetchy smashed one too hot for Sweeney at third to handle. Dorner, exhausted by the heat, took himself out at this point.

Jake Boultes was brought in, and he lost the game. He hit the first man he faced, then he allowed Koney to steal third. Holly laid down a squeeze bunt, and Big Ed galloped across the plate.

Karger scored the next run. He singled past short with two down in the fifth. Byrne and Barry also singled, bringing the pitcher around.

The Cardinals added two more tallies in the sixth. Hits by Burnett and Murray were sandwiched around a walk, driving one run across. The second followed on Art Hoelskoetter's long fly.

Karger was still going strong in the seventh inning, retiring three men on easy infield chances. The game was then called, with St. Louis getting a 4-0 victory. Too bad Karger didn't get a chance to get a nine-inning perfect game.

FIRST GAME

		r	h	e	Batteries
Boston	100 002 010 -	4	10	1	V. Lindaman (L 8-13) & S. Brown.
St. Louis	000 120 02x -	5	9	1	S. McGlynn (W 8-20) & P. Noonan, D. Marshall. Umpire: B. Emslie.

SECOND GAME

Boston	ab	r	h	bi	o	a	e	St. Louis	ab	r	h	bi	o	a	e
A. Bridwell, ss	3	0	0	0	0	3	0	B. Byrne, 3b	2	0	1	0	0	2	0
F. Tenney, 1b	3	0	0	0	10	0	0	S. Barry, rf	2	0	1	1	1	0	0
B. Sweeney, 3b	3	0	0	0	1	5	0	E. Konetchy, 1b	2	1	1	0	13	0	0
G. Beaumont, cf	2	0	0	0	1	0	0	J. Burnett, cf	2	1	1	0	1	0	0
P. Flaherty, rf	2	0	0	0	2	1	0	E. Holly, ss	1	1	0	1	2	3	0
N. Randall, lf	2	0	0	0	0	0	0	R. Murray, c	3	0	1	1	2	0	0
C. Ritchey, 2b	2	0	0	0	1	2	0	A. Hoelskoetter, 3b	3	0	0	1	0	4	0
T. Needham, c	2	0	0	0	3	1	0	D. Marshal, c	3	0	0	0	2	0	0
G. Dorner, p	1	0	0	0	0	0	0	E. Karger, p	2	1	1	0	0	2	0
J. Boultes, p4	1	0	0	0	0	1	0								
	21	0	0	0	18	13	0		20	4	6	4	21	11	0

Boston	000 000 0	-	0	LOB: Bos 0, StL 4.
St. Louis	000 112 x	-	4	2B: Murray.
game called in the seventh				SH: Barry, Holly.
by mutual agreement				SB: Konetchy.
	ip	h	r-er	bb	so	CS: Byrne.
Dorner	3.1	1	1-1	2	1	HBP: by Boultes (Burnett)
Boultes (L 2-6)	2.2	5	3-3	1	2	WP: Boultes
Karger (W 9-12)	7	0	0-0	0	2	Umpires: F. Beebe & I. Young

The Cardinals traveled to Boston, where they won four more games from the Doves, giving them a nine-game winning streak.

But they were unable to sustain any sort of forward momentum and never got close to escaping the cellar. They finished last with a 52-101 record, 55½ games behind the champion Cubs and 8½ behind the Doves. They did, however, win the City Series from the Browns for the first time.

1908 — Monday, April 20th, at League Park

Cardinals' Raymond Pitches One-Hitter But Loses, 2-0

Cubs' Only Hit Looked Like an Error to Some Observers

St. Louis Offense Weak, Infield Makes Five Errors

In his first start of the young season, Arthur "Bugs" Raymond proved that he was ready to take his place among the better pitchers in the league by holding the hard-hitting Chicago Cubs to just one safe hit. Even that blow went through the hands of the shortstop and might have been ruled an error. Delivered with an easy motion, Raymond's speed and spitball had the opposing batters beating the ball into the ground. However, Bugs was wild, walking six, and his fielders gave him terrible support. In addition, the Cardinals couldn't hit, and Raymond lost, 2-0.

All indications were that it would be another long season for Manager John

Today's Results
Chicago 2 - ST. LOUIS 0
New York 4 - Brooklyn 1
Cincinnati 2 - Pittsburg 1 (10 inn.)
Philadelphia 4 - Boston 3 (10 inn.)

Standings	W-L	Pct.	GB
Chicago	5-1	.833	-
New York	4-1	.800	½
Pittsburg	3-2	.600	1½
Philadelphia	3-2	.600	1½
Cincinnati	2-3	.400	2½
Brooklyn	2-3	.400	2½
Boston	1-4	.200	3½
ST. LOUIS	1-5	.167	4

McCloskey and his Cardinals. Yesterday, Billy Gilbert's error gave Chicago the game. So McCloskey shook up his infield today. He benched Gilbert, moved Chappie Charles from third to second, returned Bobby Byrne to third from short, and inserted Patsy O'Rourke at shortstop. The results were disastrous, the three fielders making five errors. Art Hoelskoetter, who had played every position for the Cardinals over the last few years, was tried at catcher. Today, he threw two men out but let four men steal while he was dropping Raymond's spitters.

The champion Cubs did not hit well, but they played heady ball. They took chances on the bases, and, although they were caught more often than not, their running paid off with two runs. In the field they made only one error. Carl Lundgren, their pitcher, was found for just five hits, which he scattered through as many innings, and he walked just one man.

The visitor's only hit came with one out in the second inning. Harry Steinfeldt shot a screamer up the middle. O'Rourke darted over and got both hands on the ball, but it tore through his grasp, and the batter reached first safely. Official scorer Frank Parker immediately called it a hit, as did the correspondents for the afternoon papers, who were sending running accounts of the contest to their journals.

As the game progressed, and it became apparent that that might be the only hit for Chicago, some sentiment was expressed for ruling the play an error. But Parker stuck with his initial ruling. After the game, McCloskey and Raymond both complained that it should be called an error, and the pitcher should be credited with a no-hitter. Bugs pointed out that, "If a fashionable pitcher like Mathewson of New York" had been the man involved, it probably would have gone down as a no-hit game.

O'Rourke got the first St. Louis hit in the third, a clean drive to left. He was sacrificed to second, but Raymond fanned, and Charles bounced out.

St. Louis put two men on base in the bottom of the fourth. Red Murray singled and Ed Konetchy strolled. But two were out at the time, and Byrne grounded out.

A walk to Johnny Kling and a bunt by Lundgren put a Cub on second in the next round, but he was left.

Chicago's runs came in the sixth. Jimmy Sheckard opened with a walk. Frank Schulte went out at first. Frank Chance was also passed. The runners broke for a double steal, and batter Steinfeldt swung at the pitch. Distracted, Hoelskoetter dropped the ball, giving the runners second and third without a throw. Steiny then hit hard to third, and Sheckard scored on the out at first. Chance had been forced to retreat to second when Byrne made the stop, but he daringly raced to third on the throw to first and beat the return from Konetchy.

Johnny Evers then bounced down to Charles at second, and Chappie fumbled, giving Evers first and allowing Chance to score. Evers swiped second, but Joe Tinker flied out to end the inning.

Joe Delahanty got a two-out single in the bottom of the sixth. But Murray flied out to center.

Konetchy opened the St. Louis seventh with a hit, but he was doubled up after Steinfeldt grabbed Byrne's liner.

Raymond was in trouble again in the eighth. He walked the leadoff batter, Sheckard. O'Rourke then fumbled Schulte's roller. Chance bunted the runners along. Steinfeldt followed with a shot to Byrne, and Sheckard started for home, only to be run down and tagged out. Steinfeldt stole second, and once again there were runners on second and third. But Evers ended the inning by flying to Koney.

O'Rourke's third error gave Kling a life in the ninth. Lundgren moved him to second with a pretty bunt. But Jimmy Slagle grounded out, ending the inning.

The Cardinals then came in for their last try. The first two men made easy outs, but Murray dropped a safe one into short center. Konetchy hit down to Evers, who fumbled away a chance to end the game. With the tying runs on base, Byrne lifted a long one to left, which Sheckard ran under and caught, ending the game.

Chicago was 2-0 winner.

Manager McCloskey said after the game that O'Rourke should have been able to field Steinfeldt's drive in the second, and Raymond should have gotten a no-hitter. But that was just wishful thinking. Discoursing further, McCloskey asserted, "There is nothing wrong with the pitching staff of the Cardinals." Then he added wistfully, "Wish we had a few great infielders."

Chicago	ab	r	h	bi	o	a	e	St. Louis	ab	r	h	bi	o	a	e
J. Slagle, cf	4	0	0	0	1	0	0	C. Charles, 2b	4	0	0	0	2	3	1
J. Sheckard, lf	2	1	0	0	2	0	0	S. Barry, rf	4	0	0	0	1	0	0
F. Schulte, rf	2	0	0	0	0	0	0	J. Delahanty, lf	4	0	1	0	0	0	0
F. Chance, 1b	1	1	0	0	14	1	0	R. Murray, cf	4	0	2	0	2	0	0
H. Steinfeldt, 3b	4	0	1	1	2	3	0	E. Konetchy, 1b	3	0	1	0	14	0	0
J. Evers, 2b	4	0	0	0	1	3	1	B. Byrne, 3b	4	0	0	0	4	2	1
J. Tinker, ss	4	0	0	0	2	2	0	P. O'Rourke, ss	3	0	1	0	2	3	3
J. Kling, c	3	0	0	0	4	0	0	A. Hoelskoetter, c	2	0	0	0	2	4	0
C. Lundgren, p	2	0	0	0	1	3	0	B. Raymond, p	3	0	0	0	0	6	0
	26	2	1	1	27	12	1		31	0	5	0	27	18	5

Chicago   000 002 000 - 2
St. Louis 000 000 000 - 0

	ip	h	r-er	bb	so
Lundgren (W 2-0)	9	5	0-0	1	4
Raymond (L 0-1)	9	1	2-1	6	2

Umpire: H. O'Day

LOB: Chi 8, StL 6. BE: Chi 5, StL 1. DP: Steinfeldt-Chance. SH. Hoelskoetter, Chance 2, Lundgren 2, Schulte. SB: Sheckard, Chance, Evers, Steinfeldt. CS: Sheckard, Evers. Time - 1:33 Attendance - 4,000

The Cardinals of 1908 had the weakest offense in major league history. They averaged just 2.42 runs per game and were shutout 33 times. Both of these are records for offensive ineptness that still stand.

They also had terrible fielding. They made 348 errors, 93 more than any other team in the league in 1908.

So, despite good pitching, they finished a distant last. Their final record was 49-105, which was even worse than the year before.

Poor Bugs Raymond was the losing pitcher in 11 of the Cardinals' shutout defeats. He had a season record of 15-25.

1909 — Monday, May 24th, at the Polo Grounds, New York

St. Louis Finally Beats Christy Mathewson After 24 Losses

Errors and Strange Base-Running Plays Decide Outcome

Gala New York Reception for Cardinals' Bresnahan

New York society turned out today to greet their departed idol, Roger Bresnahan, who has become manager of the St. Louis Cardinals. Roger was presented with numerous gifts from his admirers. Then he and his men showed a great deal of ingratitude by beating the New York Giants, 3-1.

The victory came at the expense of the Giants' ace of aces, Christy Mathewson, whom the Cardinals had not beaten in over five years. Since losing to St. Louis on May 10, 1904, Matty had faced the Cardinals 25 times, and the Giants won every game. Mathewson was credited with 24 of the wins.

Today's Results
ST. LOUIS 3 - New York 1
Pittsburg 6 - Boston 2
Chicago 4 - Brooklyn 3 (11 inn.)
Cincinnati 5 - Philadelphia 1

Standings	W-L	Pct.	GB
Pittsburg	19-11	.633	-
Chicago	20-13	.606	½
Philadelphia	14-13	.519	3½
Cincinnati	16-17	.485	4½
Brooklyn	13-15	.464	5
ST. LOUIS	15-18	.455	5½
New York	12-15	.444	5½
Boston	11-18	.379	8½

But that streak was finally ended today, although Mathewson was not entirely to blame. Good pitching by St. Louis's Johnny Lush and poor fielding by the Giants had more to do with the outcome. All three Cardinal runs came as a result of errors, as did the lone Giant tally.

The game marked the first appearance of Roger Bresnahan in New York since he was traded by the Giants to the Cards last winter. Roger starred with the Giants for seven years and had made a great many friends in Gotham. Those friends came out in force to welcome him back today.

About seven thousands were at the park. Before the game, they were regaled with speeches appreciative of Roger's talents and contributions. The home plate area was the site of a huge floral display. Bresnahan was given a silver loving cup with the names of dozens of distinguished citizens and sports figures from New York on it. Heading the list was Mayor McClellan, and included were actor George M. Cohan, Giants' owner John T. Brush, and manager John J. McGraw.

When it finally came time to play ball, neither side looked like it had its thoughts totally on the game. The fielding was poor, and the base running was downright comical. Only the pitchers played well, and even they were somewhat off, hurling one wild pitch each and walking nine men between them.

The comedy started in the very first inning. With two out and two on, the Cardinals tried to score on a double steal. Catcher Chief Meyers threw down to second, and Larry Doyle returned the throw, which Meyers dropped as the runner, Al Shaw, slid past. But Shaw had neglected to touch the plate. After a moment's hesitation, he decided to take a chance, and he nonchalantly strolled toward the bench. But Mathewson had seen the play, and he yelled to Meyers to tag Shaw. The catcher ran over to the sideline and touched Shaw, and umpire Jim Johnstone called him out with a theatrical gesture.

The Giants had opportunities to score in each of the first two innings, but left two men on each time.

New York pushed a run home in the third. Doyle strolled on four balls. Moose McCormick then sizzled one to Chappie Charles, and the second baseman let it bounce away far enough to allow Doyle to reach third. Red Murray, the former Cardinal, was next up, and he sent a short fly to left. Rube Ellis made the catch, and Doyle broke for home. It seemed like a suicidal chance, but Ellis's throw bounced a dozen times before reaching the plate, and Doyle slid in just ahead of Bresnahan's tag.

Mathewson got some laughs when he tried to shoot a quick pitch past Charles when the latter's back was turned in the fourth. But his pitch was very high, and Matty put on a pained expression.

Lush put himself into a deep hole in the New York fourth, but he pulled himself out of it. With one out, both Meyers and Mathewson walked. Fred Tenney then laid down a perfect bunt single, loading the bases. But Lush got both Doyle and McCormick to foul out.

New York stranded two more men in the fifth, bringing the Giants' total to ten men left in five innings.

St. Louis tied the game in the sixth, thanks to a very strange play. With one out, Ed Konetchy reached on an error by Art Devlin. Steve Evans singled him to second. With a full count on Ellis, Mathewson delivered what looked like a wide one, and the batter headed toward first, while the runners trotted toward the next bases. But Johnstone belatedly called the pitch a strike, and Meyers threw to Tenney, leaving Evans hung up between first and second. Tenney crept towards Evans, acting like a man trying to coax a horse with a piece of sugar. The runner finally broke for second and beat Tenney's late throw. Konetchy, meanwhile, had gone to third. Charles then singled to center, and one run scored, although Evans was thrown out at the plate.

The winning runs came in the seventh. Rudy Hulswitt was passed. Lush singled him to third. Lush moved to second on Byrne's tap to the mound, but Hulswitt had to hold. Shaw was next, and the game was interrupted for a while when Bresnahan came out to argue with Johnstone over a called strike. When play resumed, Shaw hit a grounder toward second. Doyle, who was already playing in, charged the ball but let it trickle past him, allowing both runners to score.

New York lost a chance thanks to some bad running in their half. McCormick was on first when Murray hit a drive to right. Coach Arlie Latham advised Murray to try for third on the hit, but right fielder Evans caught the ball and doubled Murray at first.

The Cardinals gave the Giants an extra opportunity in the eighth. With two on and two out, Tenney lifted an easy foul fly between third and home. It was Byrne's ball, but Bresnahan called him off of it, then dropped it himself. But Tenney could only fly out to center with his next swing.

The game ended on a fine play by Byrne in the ninth, retiring Murray at first, and the Cardinals won, 3-1.

St. Louis	ab	r	h	bi	o	a	e	New York	ab	r	h	bi	o	a	e
B. Byrne, 3b	4	0	2	0	4	4	1	F. Tenney, 1b	5	0	1	0	11	0	0
A. Shaw, cf	3	0	0	0	2	0	0	L. Doyle, 2b	4	1	0	0	1	2	1
R. Bresnahan, c	4	0	0	0	2	0	1	M. McCormick, lf	4	0	1	0	0	0	1
E. Konetchy, 1b	3	1	0	0	13	0	0	R. Murray, rf	4	0	0	1	1	0	0
S. Evans, rf	3	0	1	0	2	1	0	B. O'Hara, cf	4	0	0	0	2	1	0
R. Ellis, lf	4	0	0	0	3	0	0	A. Devlin, 3b	4	0	3	0	3	2	1
C. Charles, 2b	4	0	2	1	1	3	1	A. Bridwell, ss	3	0	1	0	1	3	0
R. Hulswitt, ss	3	1	0	0	0	2	0	C. Meyers, c	2	0	0	0	8	4	0
J. Lush, p	4	1	1	0	0	2	0	C. Mathewson, p	3	0	1	0	0	5	0
	32	3	6	1	27	12	3		33	1	7	1	27	17	3

St. Louis 000 001 200 - 3
New York   001 000 000 - 1

	ip	h	r-er	bb	so
Lush (W 4-5)	9	7	1-0	5	0
Mathewson (L 2-2)	9	6	3-0	4	6

WP: Mathewson, Lush

LOB: StL 6, NY 12. BE: StL 3, NY 2. DP: Evans-Konetchy.
2B: Byrne.
SH: Bridwell. SF: Murray.
SB: Konetchy, Evans.
Time - 1:38 Attendance - 7,000
Umpires: J. Johnstone & S. Cusack

The Cardinals showed some improvement under Bresnahan, but they slumped badly over the last two months of the season.

Their offense was vastly improved over 1908, but their pitching fell to the worst in the league. They finished in seventh place with a 54-98 record.

1910 — Friday, September 23rd, at Washington Park, Brooklyn

Cardinals Make Just Two Hits But Win, 6-2, Over Dodgers

Rookie Pitchers Very Liberal With Free Passes

Bresnahan Returns to Lineup and Delivers Key Hit

The St. Louis Cardinals today outscored the Brooklyn Dodgers, 6-2, in a game in which just five hits were made. The game featured 18 bases on balls and one hit batsman, and it proceeded so slowly that it was called after seven innings on account of darkness.

Manager Roger Bresnahan put himself into the lineup for the first time since he was injured by a foul tip on September 11th. His steadying influence was crucial in getting rookie pitcher Cy Alberts through most of the game. Finally, Bresnahan had to call on Bob Harmon to get the final out.

Alberts, an American Indian recently purchased from the Terre Haute club, was making his first start for St. Louis. He showed plenty of speed and decent control through six innings, allowing just three hits. His best work was in mixing a deceptive slowball in with his fastballs. In the seventh inning, he lost control completely, walking four men before being relieved.

Brooklyn manager Bill Dahlen picked young Sandy Burk to pitch for the home team. The highly regarded recruit from Fort Worth was very wild, walking 11 men and hitting one in seven innings. But his delivery was very fast, and the St. Louis batters were unable to collect a safe hit until the sixth. They got one safety in that frame and one in the seventh for a total of just two hits. But what hits they were. The first was a long single by Bresnahan which drove in two runs, and the second was a three-run double by Steve Evans. They won the game for the visitors.

Threatening weather and experimental pitchers kept the crowd down to just 350.

The pitching, wild but hard to hit, attracted most of the attention during the game. Arnold Hauser, the Cardinal shortstop, also stood out. He walked three consecutive times and made two wonderful fielding plays. Rookie outfielder Ody Abbott stood out by striking out four times.

The first scoring threat came in the home half of the first. Bill Davidson, the leadoff hitter, opened with a long triple. It looked as good as a run, but Alberts put the ball past three big batters and escaped the jam. He fanned Jake Daubert and Zack Wheat, then induced John Hummel to pop to Evans in right field.

Pryor McElveen got the second Dodger hit with one out in the second inning. After advancing to second base, he tried to score on a wild throw past first. But Ed Konetchy recovered the ball and passed it to Bresnahan in time to cut the runner off at home.

In the third, Bresnahan had a hard collision with Bobby Byrne after catching a high pop, but Roger held the ball.

Brooklyn scored the first run of the game in the fourth round. Hummel was the first man up. As he stepped into the box, Bresnahan stopped the game and ostentatiously removed a piece of lint from behind the batter's ear. The ploy didn't distract Hummel one bit, as he drove a long three-base hit off the right field fence. He scored on McElveen's long sacrifice fly.

The Brooklyns were retired in order in the next two frames, thanks to two fine plays by Hauser robbing Bergen and Hummel of hits.

Meanwhile, the Cardinals had been unable to do much against Mr. Burk. Through the first five innings, four men had walked and one had been hit by a pitch, and Hauser had stolen second twice. But the Cards were never able to get a hit to bring the runners

Today's Results
ST. LOUIS 6 - Brooklyn 2 (7 inn.)
New York 6 - Chicago 4
Philadelphia 2 - Pittsburg 1
Cincinnati 8 - Boston 2

Standings	W-L	Pct.	GB
Chicago	92-44	.676	-
New York	81-58	.583	12½
Pittsburg	81-58	.583	12½
Philadelphia	72-68	.514	22
Cincinnati	71-72	.497	24½
ST. LOUIS	56-80	.412	36
Brooklyn	55-84	.396	38½
Boston	48-92	.343	46

home, and Burk was never so obliging as to pass four men in the same inning.

He walked three men in the sixth, and still nearly escaped damage. Rube Ellis and Mike Mowrey, the first two men up, were passed. But Koney grounded into a double play, with Ellis moving to third. Evans was given free transportation, and he quickly stole second.

Still, all Burk needed was one more out. But Bresnahan broke the spell by getting the first hit for his team. It was a long single to left center, scoring both Ellis and Evans easily. Roger stole, but Abbott struck out.

St. Louis clinched the game in the seventh. Hauser walked for the third time, and Alberts bunted him to second. Miller Huggins also bunted, and Burk threw wildly to third in a vain attempt to catch Hauser. Ellis watched four bad ones, and the bases were loaded. Mowrey hit a fly far enough to allow Hauser to score after the catch. Koney walked, filling the sacks again. Then Evans delivered the *coup de grace* with the second St. Louis hit of the day. It was a double to the right field fence, and it cleared the bases. Bresnahan kept the inning alive with a walk, but Abbott struck out again.

Brooklyn threatened in the bottom of the inning. Alberts alternated three walks with two outs. With darkness fast overtaking the field, Bresnahan took every opportunity to go to the mound to settle his pitcher down and to stall for time. Finally umpire Hank O'Day ordered an end to the conferencing, and after a few hot words from Bresnahan, play resumed. Alberts walked Davidson, forcing in a run and forcing Bresnahan to change pitchers. Bob Harmon, who by this time was thoroughly warmed up, came in. He fanned the dangerous Jake Daubert to end the inning.

O'Day then called the game, and the Cardinals had a 6-2 victory.

St. Louis	ab	r	h	bi	o	a	e
M. Huggins, 2b	4	1	0	0	2	1	0
R. Ellis, lf	1	2	0	0	0	0	0
M. Mowrey, 3b	2	0	0	1	2	1	0
E. Konetchy, 1b	2	1	0	0	6	1	0
S. Evans, rf	3	1	1	3	1	0	0
R. Bresnahan, c	3	0	1	2	5	2	0
O. Abbott, cf	4	0	0	0	3	0	0
A. Hauser, ss	0	1	0	0	2	4	1
C. Alberts, p	1	0	0	0	0	0	0
B. Harmon, p7	0	0	0	0	0	0	0
	20	6	2	6	21	9	1

Brooklyn	ab	r	h	bi	o	a	e
B. Davidson, cf	2	0	1	1	1	0	0
J. Daubert, 1b	3	0	0	0	3	0	0
Z. Wheat, lf	3	0	0	0	3	0	0
J. Hummel, 2b	3	1	1	0	4	1	0
B. Coulson, rf	2	1	0	0	1	0	0
P. McElveen, 3b	2	0	1	1	0	1	0
T. Smith, ss	1	0	0	0	0	1	0
B. Bergen, c	2	0	0	0	8	2	0
A. Burch, ph7	1	0	0	0	-	-	-
S. Burk, p	2	0	0	0	1	0	1
J. Dalton, ph7	0	0	0	0	-	-	-
	21	2	3	2	21	5	1

St. Louis 000 002 4 - 6
Brooklyn   000 100 1 - 2
game called after seven innings on account of darkness

	ip	h	r-er	bb	so
Alberts (W 1-0)	6.2	3	2-2	7	2
Harmon	.1	0	0-0	0	1
Burk (L 0-2)	7	2	6-2	11	7

HBP: by Burk (Ellis)

LOB: StL 7, Bkn 6. BE: StL 1, BKN 1. DP: Smith-Hummel-Daubert.
2B: Evans.
3B: Davidson, Hummel.
SH: Alberts. SF: Mowrey, McElveen.
SB: Hauser 2, Evans, Bresnahan.
Time - 1:54
Attendance - 350
Umpires: H. O'Day & B. Brennan

During the final three weeks of the season, the Cardinals and Dodgers seesawed in and out of sixth and seventh places. The Cardinals lost their last game and dropped to seventh, ½ game behind Brooklyn.

St. Louis's record of 63-90 and their percentage of .412 were not very impressive, but they were the club's best since 1904.

Chapter IV

Ups and Downs in the Teens
1911-1919

1911—July 26th at League Park
Cards Play Great Ball, Edge Phils in Action-Packed Game, 7-6

1912—May 5th at Robison Field
Cardinals Lose to Reds, 11-9, Despite Rube Ellis's Slugging

1913—May 4th at Chicago
Cards Win, 10-8, in Thirteen, Konetchy Gets Pitching Victory

1914—August 27th at Robison Field
Cardinals Stop Braves, 3-2 in 10, Trail Giants by 1 Game

1915—August 30th at Philadelphia
Cards Lose as Home Run Bounces Off Bescher's Chest and Over Fence

1916—October 1st at Chicago
Cardinals End Season with 14th Straight Loss, Tie for Last

1917—June 11th at Cardinal Field
St. Louis Rallies to Win, 5-4, Gonzalez Steals Home in 15th

1918—July 3rd at Cardinal Field
Fisher's Hidden-Ball Trick Saves 2-1 Victory for Cardinals

1919—July 17th at Philadelphia
Ex-Cardinal Meadows Beats Former Mates in First Meeting, 1-0

Frank de Haas Robison had retired in 1906 and died in 1908. His brother, M. Stanley Robison, died in March, 1911. The club was inherited by Frank's daughter, Mrs. Helene H.R. Britton.

In 1911, Roger Bresnahan's Cardinals played aggressive ball and were in the pennant race until late July. They were only 4 games out of first place after beating the third-place Phillies, 7-6, on July 26th. But then St. Louis lost 10 of their next 15 games and wound up in fifth place.

A club attendance record was set in 1911 (447,000). For 1912, old League Park was improved and renamed Robison Field in honor of Mrs. Britton's father and uncle.

In 1912, the pitching was poor from the start, and the hitting was not much better. Even when the Cards broke a hitting slump on May 5th, they still lost, 11-9. They finished the season in sixth.

In 1913, Miller Huggins replaced Bresnahan as manager. But no one replaced the pitching staff. Things were so bad one day that first baseman Ed Konetchy had to pitch in relief. He actually got the win in a 10-8, thirteen-inning game. The pitching was bad enough to drop the Cardinals to last place.

In 1914, the Cards pulled a three-for-five man trade with Pittsburgh, and their young pitchers showed remarkable improvement. As a result, they were in the thick of the pennant race in late August. When they edged the hot Boston Braves on the 27th, 3-2 in ten innings, the Cards moved into second place, just 1 game out of first. But then they dropped back and finished third.

In 1915, they didn't get the breaks and finished sixth. One day, they lost when a fly ball bounced off the fence, off outfielder Bob Bescher's chest, then back over the fence to give the Phillies the victory.

In 1916, some veterans did poorly. After struggling most of the year, the Cardinals collapsed at the end of the season, losing their last 14 games and finishing tied for last place. Club president Schuyler Britton, husband of owner Helene Britton, was peeved at this finish and promised a shake-up over the winter. But his wife shook things up by selling the club to a large group of small investors put together by James C. Jones.

The new ownership renamed the park on Natural Bridge at Vandeventer Cardinal Field. By doubling his salary, the new owners induced Browns' vice-president Branch Rickey to jump his contract and become president of the Cardinals. They also instituted the Knot Hole Gang, a program by which young boys were admitted to games free of charge. The newspapers began to call the team the Knot Holers on occasion as a result.

The team made a remarkable turnaround in 1917, even without the housecleaning that Mr. Britton had promised. Manager Huggins had his men playing daring baseball. One day, Mike Gonzalez broke up a beautifully-played, fifteen-inning game with a steal of home. St. Louis finished in third place. But Huggins, who had unsuccessfully tried to buy the club from the Brittons, quit after the season.

Rickey appointed Jack Hendricks as manager for 1918. The Cardinals could not beat the better teams in the league, losing 13 straight to the Cubs at one point before finally beating them with the help of the old hidden-ball trick. St. Louis finished last in the war-shortened season.

In 1919, Rickey managed the team himself. He made a couple of big deals with the Phillies, but the Cardinals were only able to climb to seventh place.

1911 — Wednesday, July 26th, at League Park

Cardinals Play Great Ball and Edge Phillies in Action-Packed Game

Phillie Manager Dooin Breaks His Leg

Fast Fielding and Heavy Hitting in 7-6 Game

The two surprise contenders in the hot National League pennant race, the St. Louis Cardinals and the Philadelphia Phillies, squared off today in St. Louis. The Cardinals won the contest, 7-6, and the Phillies lost more than just the game. They lost their manager and first-string catcher, Charles "Red" Dooin, when his leg was broken in a collison at home plate. The blow was a crucial one to the Phillies' pennant hopes.

Today's defeat dropped the Phils to third place, 2 games behind the league-leading Cubs. The victory kept the Cardinals in fourth place, 4 games back. After a slow start, St. Louis has been playing great ball since mid-May. They have won 44 of their last 66 decisions, a pennant-winning pace of .667.

Today's Results
ST. LOUIS 7 - Philadelphia 6
Chicago 4 - Boston 1 (1st game)
Chicago 7 - Boston 2 (2nd)
New York 5 - Cincinnati 3
Pittsburg 12 - Brooklyn 1

Standings	W-L	Pct.	GB
Chicago	53-31	.631	-
New York	53-34	.609	1½
Philadelphia	53-35	.602	2
ST. LOUIS	51-37	.580	4
Pittsburg	50-37	.575	4½
Cincinnati	36-50	.419	18
Brooklyn	31-55	.360	23
Boston	20-68	.227	35

Today's contest offered a good example of the slashing style of Roger Bresnahan's "Rajahs." Their fielding was flawless, they hit the ball hard, and they ran the bases with abandon. No fewer than five Cardinals were thrown out at home, and three were caught stealing, one at each possible base. But they were successful in pilfering four bases, and only four of their twelve hits did not figure in the scoring.

Rube Geyer was Bresnahan's pitcher. For four innings, he pitched perfect ball. Then he tired out. By the eighth inning he had been found for four runs, and, with the bases loaded, Bresnahan replaced him with Bob Harmon. Two of the runners scored that inning, but Harmon held the lead, and the Cardinals won, 7-6.

The Cards started into Phillie pitcher Earl Moore early, piling up a 4-0 lead by the third inning.

In the first round, Miller Huggins doubled and scored on a triple by Rube Ellis. Ellis was doubled at the plate trying to score on Ed Konetchy's fly out.

In the second, Wally Smith knocked a home run over the screen and into the right field bleachers. Steve Evans, who had been hit by a pitch, scored ahead of Smith.

In the third, Huggins led off with a looper over shortstop for a single. Arnold Hauser duplicated the hit, sending Hug to third. Ellis was then robbed of a hit by second baseman Otto Knabe, but Huggins scored.

In the fourth round, St. Louis failed to score, but Dooin was knocked out of the game. Smith singled, Rebel Oakes walked, and Jack Bliss sacrificed. Smith was thrown out at home on Geyer's grounder. Then Geyer and Oakes tried the double steal. Catcher Dooin shot the ball down to shortstop Mickey Doolan, who immediately returned the throw. The return was high and up the line toward third. Dooin made a lunging catch and sweeping tag, and, in the process, Dooin's leg got tangled up and broken by Oakes's slide.

After going four innings without getting a base runner and then losing their leader, the Phillies suddenly came to life in the fifth. They pounded out two doubles and a single, good for two runs. They might have gotten more but for poor base running. Fred Luderus opened with a walk and took third on Jimmy Walsh's double. Fred Beck doubled two runs home but was thrown out trying for a triple, Evans to Huggins to Smith. Doolan then lined a single to center. But Pat Moran, batting for Dooin, hit into a double play.

Huggins showed great head and leg work in scoring for St. Louis in the bottom of the inning. Hug reached first when Luderus dropped the ball trying to tag him after fielding a bunt. Hauser laid a bunt down toward third, which Hans Lobert came in and fielded, throwing the batter out at first. But no one went back to cover third, and Huggins raced all the way to that station on the sacrifice. He scored on Ellis's infield out. Koney then drove a long one off the wall in left and was thrown out at the plate trying for a home run.

After a scoreless sixth inning, each side made two in the seventh.

The Phillies' runs came on a single by Luderus and a home run into the seats by Beck.

The Cardinals got triples to the opposite extremes of the field. The first one, by Bliss, was a shot past third base and into the left field corner. Geyer followed with a daisy cutter down the right field line, scoring Ellis. Geyer counted on Hauser's single.

The Phillies made their big bid for the lead in the eighth. John Titus, recovering from a broken leg, opened with a pinch single to right. After Titus limped to first, Roy Thomas went in to run. Knabe lined out. Dode Paskert shot one past third for a single, and Lobert walked, filling the bases for Luderus, the Phillies' best hitter. Bresnahan decided that he had to remove Geyer, and Harmon was called in to pitch. He walked Luderus, forcing one run across. Walsh's fly out sent another man home and moved a man to third. Luderus stole second. Harmon wisely passed Beck, loading the bases, to get to the light-hitting Doolan. Mickey's bouncer up the middle was cut off by Hauser for an inning-ending force out.

The Phillies put their ace rookie, Grover Cleveland Alexander, in to pitch the eighth. He shut the Cardinals out, despite a hit, a steal, and a base on balls.

After pinch-hitter Kitty Bransfield was retired in the ninth, Harmon walked Alexander. But Knabe bounced into a double play, Hauser to Huggins to Konetchy, and the Cardinals were 7-6 winners.

Philadelphia	ab	r	h	bi	o	a	e
O. Knabe, 2b	5	0	1	0	3	4	0
D. Paskert, cf	4	1	1	0	0	1	0
H. Lobert, 3b	3	0	0	0	2	1	0
F. Luderus, 1b	2	2	1	1	7	0	1
J. Walsh, lf	3	1	1	1	1	0	0
F. Beck, rf	3	1	2	4	3	1	0
M. Doolan, ss	4	0	1	0	1	5	0
R. Dooin, c	1	0	0	0	5	3	0
P. Moran, ph 5-c	2	0	0	0	2	0	0
K. Bransfield, ph9	1	0	0	0	-	-	-
E. Moore, p	2	0	0	0	0	3	0
J. Titus, ph8	1	0	1	0	-	-	-
R. Thomas, pr8	0	1	0	0	-	-	-
G. Alexander, p8	0	0	0	0	0	0	0
	31	6	8	6	24	18	1

St. Louis	ab	r	h	bi	o	a	e
M. Huggins, 2b	4	3	2	0	4	4	0
A. Hauser, ss	2	0	2	1	1	6	0
R. Ellis, lf	4	0	1	3	1	0	0
E. Konetchy, 1b	3	0	1	0	8	1	0
S. Evans, rf	3	1	0	0	3	1	0
W. Smith, 3b	3	1	2	2	1	1	0
R. Oakes, cf	3	0	2	0	3	0	0
J. Bliss, c	1	1	1	0	5	0	0
R. Geyer, p	3	1	1	1	1	2	0
B. Harmon, p8	1	0	0	0	0	0	0
	27	7	12	7	27	15	0

Philadelphia 000 020 220 - 6
St. Louis   121 010 20x - 7

	ip	h	r-er	bb	so
Moore (L 12-10)	7	11	7-6	2	1
Alexander	1	1	0-0	1	1
Geyer (W 4-3)	7.1	8	6-6	2	3
Harmon	1.2	0	0-0	3	1

HBP: by Moore 2 (Evans, Smith)
Umpires: H. O'Day & B. Emslie

LOB: Phila 4, StL 5. BE: StL 1.
DP: Beck-Dooin, Dooin-Lobert, Huggins-Konetchy-Hauser-Huggins, Doolan-Luderus, Hauser-Huggins-Konetchy.
2B: Huggins, Walsh, Beck.
3B: Ellis, Konetchy, Bliss, Geyer.
HR: Smith, Beck. SF: Walsh.
SH: Hauser 2, Bliss 2.
SB: Oakes 2, Smith, Hauser, Bliss.
CS: Geyer, Hauser, Oakes.
Time - 2:10

Neither the Phillies nor the Cardinals were able to stay in the thick of the pennant race. The Cardinals never got higher than fourth place, and they finished in fifth. Their 75-74 record left them 22 games out of first place.

Still, 1911 was the most successful for the Cardinals in many years, and it showed at the turnstiles. The club's attendance of 447,000 allowed them to pay off most of their debts.

1912 — Sunday, May 5th, at Robison Field
Cards Lose, 11-9, Despite Ellis's Slugging
Late Rally Ends With Bases Loaded
Eleventh Loss in Twelve Games for St. Louis

The St. Louis Cardinals finally broke out of their batting slump today. Unfortunately, they still lost the game, 11-9, to the Cincinnati Reds. After winning four of their first five games this season, the Cardinals have won just one of the next twelve games. The slump has hurt attendance. Today's crowd was one of the smallest Sunday gatherings at the park at Vandeventer Avenue and Natural Bridge in many years.

The team has suffered from the absence of its leader, Roger Bresnahan. He injured his kneecap in the pre-season series with the Browns and was only able to get into two games as a pinch-hitter. Then he came down with pneumonia and had to be confined to a hospital bed. In his absence, the combative spirit of the team has been lacking.

Today's Results
Cincinnati 11 - ST LOUIS 9
Chicago 6 - Pittsburg 2
no other games scheduled

Standings	W-L	Pct.	GB
Cincinnati	14-3	.824	-
New York	11-4	.733	2
Boston	8-8	.500	5½
Chicago	8-9	.471	6
Pittsburg	7-10	.412	7
Brooklyn	6-9	.400	7
Philadelphia	5-9	.357	7½
ST. LOUIS	5-12	.294	9

The Cards have neither been hitting nor pitching well. In their eleven losses before today, their total had been just 19 runs. As for their defense, the opposition had averaged eight runs per game over the last two weeks.

Today the Cardinals broke out of their batting slump, but their pitching was the worst of the year.

Rube Ellis, who hadn't been hitting (like most of his mates), finally broke out of his slump. He got four hits in five trips to the plate. One of the safeties was a mere single, but he also hit a ringing triple and two home runs. His one-day show raised his average from .204 to .254.

Ed Konetchy also slugged the ball, collecting a double, triple, and home run, plus a base on balls.

For Cincinnati, Dick Hoblitzell was 5-for-5 with four singles and a double.

The heavy hitting came against an array of seven pitchers. Only one of them was a real front-line hurler. Reds' manager Hank O'Day threw three pitchers into the fray before bringing in his good man, Rube Benton, to squelch the Cardinals' last-inning rally. Acting-manager Konetchy used three men for St. Louis. The last one, Lou Lowdermilk, was effective in his one inning of work, but by that time the Reds already had 11 runs.

Joe Willis was the first St. Louis moundsman. He struggled through four innings and gave up six runs. The Reds' first tally came in the opening round when Johnny Bates singled, moved to third on Hoblitzell's first hit, and scored on an infield grounder. Bob Bescher walked in the third and scored on a double steal. Cincinnati routed Willis in the fourth. A walk, a bunt single, and a walk loaded the bases with one out. With his team trailing and the pitcher due up, O'Day sent Armando Marsans in as a pinch-batter. He delivered a nice single, driving in two runs. After an out, Bates walked to fill the bases again. Hoblitzell then cut an infield hit through Willis, and two runners scored while the Cardinal infielders stood around wondering who would retrieve the ball. That gave Cincinnati a total of six runs.

Up to this point, St. Louis had scored a run in each of the first three innings. They came at the expense of pitcher Frank Smith, the former Chicago White Sox star. The first tally came on Ellis's first slug, a triple off the right field wall, and a sacrifice fly. The second was made possible by a walk, a hit, and a bad error by outfielder Bates. Koney tripled in the third and scored on Rebel Oakes' infield tap. Reb was called out at first on a close play, and he argued so much about it that he was ejected by umpire Mal Eason.

82

The Cardinals tied the game in the bottom of the fourth with a three-run home run by Ellis off Bert Humphries. A double by Ivey Wingo and a walk to Miller Huggins brought Ellis up with two on and two out. The California Rube dramatically lifted a drive into the right field seats.

Gene Dale took the hill for St. Louis in the fifth, and Cincinnati quickly broke the tie. Dick Egan opened with a free pass to first. He stole second as Art Phelan was striking out. Jimmy Esmond then singled to center, and Egan counted.

Mike Mowrey's wild throw enabled the Reds to add another run in the sixth.

Then, in the eighth, they pounded Dale for three more scores. Bates walked, and Hoblitzell cracked a double off the right field fence. Both men scored on Mike Mitchell's drive to right, which Elmer Miller booted into a triple. Mitchell scored on a fly out.

Meanwhile, young Jim Bagby had shut the home team down for four innings, allowing just one hit.

In the ninth, however, Bagby fell apart. The first batter was slugger Ellis. Rube duplicated his fourth-inning drive into the right field bleachers for another home run. Although the score was now only 11-7, the fans began to make some noise. Mowrey bounced out, and the crowd quieted. Konetchy then pulled a ball into the left field corner. Bescher made little real effort to head the ball off, and Big Ed circled the bases with a home run. This got the crowd excited again. Miller kept the rally going with a single. When Arnold Hauser walked, O'Day decided it was finally time for a decent pitcher.

Lefthander Rube Benton was called in. He was wild at first, walking Lee Magee to load the bases. He put the ball over to Wingo, and Ivey bounced out to Egan, while Miller scored. Jack Bliss waited for four balls, and once again the bases were jammed. The Cardinals now needed only two runs to tie and three to win, and Miller Huggins was the batter, with Rube Ellis on deck. The crowd was in a frenzy at the prospects. But Hug could only lift a short fly to center that Bates gathered in, ending the game.

The final score was 11-9, and the Cardinals fell to nine games behind after having played just 17 games.

Cincinnati	ab	r	h	bi	o	a	e
B. Bescher, lf	5	1	0	0	2	0	0
J. Bates, cf	1	2	1	0	2	0	1
D. Hoblitzell, 1b	5	2	5	2	10	2	0
M. Mitchell, rf	5	1	1	3	2	0	0
D. Egan, 2b	2	2	0	1	2	1	0
A. Phelan, 3b	4	1	0	3	4	0	
J. Esmond, ss	4	0	1	1	2	3	0
L. McLean, c	4	1	2	0	4	0	0
F. Smith, p	1	0	0	0	0	1	1
A. Marsans, ph4	1	1	1	2	-	-	-
B. Humphries, p4	0	0	0	0	0	0	0
E. Grant, ph5	1	0	0	0	-	-	-
J. Bagby, p5	2	0	0	0	0	0	0
R. Benton, p9	0	0	0	0	0	0	0
	35	11	12	9	27	11	2

St. Louis	ab	r	h	bi	o	a	e
M. Huggins, 2b	4	1	0	0	4	3	0
R. Ellis, lf	5	3	4	4	3	0	0
M. Mowrey, 3b	4	0	0	1	1	2	1
E. Konetchy, 1b	4	2	3	1	8	4	0
R. Oakes, cf	2	0	0	1	3	1	0
E. Miller, cf4	3	1	1	0	1	0	0
A. Hauser, ss	3	0	0	0	1	5	0
D. Willie, rf	3	1	0	0	1	0	0
L. Magee, ph9	0	0	0	0	-	-	-
I. Wingo, c	5	1	2	1	5	2	1
J. Willis, p	1	0	0	0	0	0	0
J. Clark, ph4	1	0	0	0	-	-	-
G. Dale, p5	1	0	0	0	0	0	0
W. Smith, ph8	1	0	0	0	-	-	-
L. Lowdermilk, p9	0	0	0	0	0	0	0
J. Bliss, ph9	0	0	0	0	-	-	-
	37	9	10	8	27	17	2

Cincinnati   101 411 030 - 11
St. Louis   111 300 003 - 9

	ip	h	r-er	bb	so
Smith	3	4	3-2	1	0
Humphries	1	2	3-3	1	1
Bagby (W 2-0)	4.1	4	3-3	4	3
Benton	.2	0	0-0	2	0
Willis	4	7	6-5	4	0
Dale (L 0-1)	4	5	5-4	4	4
Lowdermilk	1	0	0-0	0	0

Umpires: J. Johnstone & M. Eason

LOB: Cinc 8, StL 10. BE: Cinc 2, StL 1. DP: Oakes-Hauser.
2B: Konetchy, Wingo, Hoblitzell.
3B: Ellis, Konetchy, Mitchell.
HR: Ellis 2, Konetchy. SH: Bates, Esmond. SF: Mowrey, Egan.
SB: Bescher, Hoblitzell, Egan, Esmond. CS: Bates, Phelan.
Time - 2:30
Attendance - 6,500

The Cardinals lost four more games before breaking their losing streak. They managed to edge back up to fifth place by the end of May, but never got any higher.

They finished sixth with a 63-90 record. Weak pitching and poor fielding were mostly to blame.

1913—Sunday, May 4th, at West Side Park, Chicago

Cardinals Win, 10-8, in Thirteen Innings, Konetchy Gets Pitching Win

St. Louis Runs Out of Pitchers, Then Players

Cubs Build Up 5-0 Lead, But Cards Rally and Win in Seesaw Game

With first baseman Ed Konetchy pitching four and two-thirds innings of scoreless relief, the St. Louis Cardinals outlasted the Chicago Cubs today and won a thirteen-inning decision, 10-8. The Cardinals trailed by a 5-0 count going into the eighth round and were down, 6-2, before rallying for six runs in the ninth inning to take the lead. Then manager Miller Huggins discovered that he had no pitchers left, and he was forced to try rookie outfielder Ted Cather on the mound. Cather proved a failure, and he traded places with Konetchy. Big Ed walked the first man he faced, forcing in the tying run, but a double play saved the game. For the next four rounds Koney's slow balls held the Bruins at bay, while the Cardinals were able to score in the thirteenth and win, 10-8.

Today's Results
ST. LOUIS 10 - Chicago 8 (13 inn.)
Pittsburg 1 - Cincinnati 0
no other games scheduled

Standings	W-L	Pct.	GB
Philadelphia	8-4	.667	-
Chicago	13-7	.650	+1
ST. LOUIS	11-8	.579	-½
Brooklyn	9-7	.563	-1
New York	8-7	.533	-1½
Pittsburg	10-9	.521	-1½
Boston	4-11	.267	-5½
Cincinnati	4-14	.222	-7

Not only did St. Louis run out of pitchers, when a man was ejected in the tenth, they were out of players, period. The only man left in uniform was coach Heinie Peitz, who hadn't played a game since 1906. He was pressed into service as an outfielder and, luckily, had little to do.

St. Louis also had a man, George Whitted, who was playing in his first big league game. He came through with flying colors, getting three hits, including the game-winning triple.

Huggins's troubles could be traced to the National League schedule and the blue laws of Pennsylvania. St. Louis finished a four-game series in Pittsburg Saturday and was due to open another series in Philadelphia on Tuesday. Sunday games being illegal in the Keystone State and elsewhere in the East, the club owners scheduled the Cardinals for a Sunday game in Chicago.

To save expenses, Hug sent six of his pitchers directly from Pittsburg to Philadelphia. He figured that three hurlers would be enough to get him through one game with the Cubs. He figured wrong, but Konetchy made it come out all right.

Pol Perritt was the first Cardinal to essay to pitch. He gave up four runs and seven hits in three innings.

Harry "Slim" Sallee replaced him in the fourth. The cross-fire lefthander did better, allowing just one run in four innings pitched.

Trailing 5-0, St. Louis scored its first two runs in the eighth on a throwing error on a squeeze play.

Joe Willis, the big lefthander, pitched the eighth for the Cardinals, and he was touched for a run.

That left St. Louis four runs down going into the ninth inning. When they had one out and two men on, Huggins had nothing to lose by pinch-hitting for his last pitcher, so he sent Ivey Wingo to the plate. Wingo cracked out a big double, driving both runners in. Hug then contributed a single himself, putting the tying runs on base. Lee Magee singled Wingo home, while Hug went to third. Whitted tapped one on the infield for a hit, but Huggins had to stay at third.

Chicago manager Johnny Evers decided to yank his starting pitcher, Lew Richie. Bert Humphries was brought in. His second pitch was so wild that two runs scored on it, giving St. Louis the lead. Another run scored on Jimmy Sheckard's infield hit.

Now Huggins needed another pitcher and had none. The only player on the bench was rookie Ted Cather. He had started his career as a pitcher in the Tri-State League, so he became the Cardinals' hurler. He quickly showed why he had been converted into an outfielder. He walked the first man he faced and hit the second with a pitch. He retired Heinie Zimmerman somehow, but Vic Saier singled to load the base. Evers was walked forcing a run home.

Cather obviously couldn't get them out, but who could? Konetchy had pitched four innings of a lost game in Brooklyn back in 1910, so he was the choice. Big Ed exchanged gloves and positions with Cather and proceeded to walk the first man he faced, sending home the tying run. Jimmy Archer, however, swung at a serve and flied to center. Saier tried to score after the catch, but Oakes's fine throw nailed him at home, sending the game into extra innings.

In the tenth, Sheckard was ejected for slandering umpire Bill Guthrie in an argument over a close call at second base. Huggins also made some uncomplimentary remarks, but Guthrie let him stay in.

When the Cardinals went out to the field, they had to send Peitz to right field. Chicago was unable to hit any balls in his direction.

On the mound, Konetchy had the Cubs totally baffled. He used no windup and had no speed and precious little control, but the Cubs were able to make just one hit off his slowballs. Each man, it seemed, went up to the plate with the idea that he could knock one of Koney's marshmallows over the fence. But they mostly hit weak pop ups. Three men even struck out. The exhibition was enough to make the Cub fans abandon their home players and root for the visitor's pinch-pitcher.

The Cardinals finally broke the tie in the thirteenth. With one out, Cather singled. Magee singled one out later. Whitted then hit a drive between Otis Clymer and Frank Schulte for a two-run triple. That won the game, as Konetchy shut the Cubs out in the bottom of the thirteenth.

Then the Cardinals had to rush out, in uniform, to taxis to get them to the depot in time to catch their train for Philadelphia.

St. Louis	ab	r	h	bi	o	a	e
M. Huggins, 2b	7	2	3	0	6	1	0
L. Magee, lf	7	3	4	1	2	0	0
G. Whitted, 3b	7	1	3	3	2	2	0
E. Konetchy, 1b-p9	7	0	1	0	9	0	0
J. Sheckard, rf	4	0	1	1	1	0	0
H. Peitz, rf10	0	0	0	0	0	0	0
R. Oakes, cf	5	1	3	0	4	1	0
C. O'Leary, ss	6	1	2	0	2	5	0
L. McLean, c	6	0	1	0	9	1	0
P. Perritt, p	1	0	0	0	0	1	0
S. Sallee, p4	1	0	0	0	0	2	0
S. Evans, ph8	1	0	0	0	-	-	-
J. Willis, p8	0	0	0	0	0	0	0
I. Wingo, ph9	1	1	1	2	-	-	-
T. Cather, p9-1b9	2	1	1	0	4	0	0
	55	10	20	7	39	13	0

Chicago	ab	r	h	bi	o	a	e
O. Clymer, cf	6	2	4	0	3	0	0
F. Schulte, rf	5	3	1	0	3	0	1
W. Miller, lf	4	1	1	1	2	0	0
H. Zimmerman, 3b	6	0	0	1	3	3	1
V. Saier, 1b	4	1	1	0	15	1	0
J. Evers, 2b	5	1	2	3	6	9	0
A. Bridwell, ss	3	0	2	1	2	3	0
W. Good, ph9	0	0	0	1	-	-	-
R. Corriden, ss10	1	0	0	0	1	1	0
J. Archer, c	6	0	1	1	4	2	0
L. Richie, p	4	0	0	0	0	0	0
B. Humphries, p9	2	0	0	0	0	0	0
	46	8	12	8	39	19	2

St. Louis   000 000 026 000 2 - 10
Chicago   310 000 112 000 0 - 8

	ip	h	r-er	bb	so
Perritt	3	7	4-4	2	0
Sallee	4	2	1-1	0	3
Willis	1	1	1-1	1	1
Cather	.1	1	2-2	2	0
Konetchy (W 1-0)	4.2	1	0-0	4	3
Richie	8.1	13	8-7	2	2
Humphries (L 1-1)	4.2	7	2-2	0	2

WP: Richie, Willis, Humphries

LOB: StL 9, Chi 13. DP: Zimmerman-Evers-Saier 2, Oakes-McLean. 2B: McLean, Schulte, Magee, Wingo. 3B: Miller, Whitted. SH: Miller 2, Bridwell, Peitz. SF: Zimmerman. SB: Clymer 2. HBP: by Cather (Miller). Time - 2:45 Attendance - 10,000 Umpires: B. Owens & B. Guthrie

Although Konetchy was not called upon to pitch again, the Cardinals had by far the worst pitching in the majors in 1913. They also had the weakest hitting in the National League.

Not surprisingly, they finished a distant last. Their record was 51-99, leaving them 49 games out of first and 11½ games out of seventh.

1914—Thursday, August 27th, at Robison Field
Cardinals Stop Braves, 3-2, in Ten Innings, Gain Second Place
St. Louis Remains One Game Behind New York
Magee and Cruise Hit Homers, Dolan Wins With Long Double

As the armies of Europe battle across France and East Prussia, the combatants of the National League have been engaged in a bitter struggle at close quarters in their efforts to capture the pennant. The three-time champion New York Giants have held onto the top spot since Decoration Day. But the new forces in the fight, the St. Louis Cardinals and the Boston Braves, have started to press them closely. And the Chicago Cubs have stayed nearby on the flank, trying to mount an assualt of their own.

Today New York beat Chicago, and St. Louis turned back Boston. The Cardinals, as a result, remained one game behind the Giants, and they moved past the Braves and into second place. Miller Huggins's surprising St. Louisans were in the second division until the last day of June. They had been in third place most of July and August but had been gaining steadily.

Today's Results
ST. LOUIS 3 - Boston 2 (10 inn.)
New York 9 - Chicago 2
Cincinnati 3 - Philadelphia 2
Brooklyn 1 - Pittsburg 0 (10 inn.)

Standings	W-L	Pct.	GB
New York	61-49	.555	-
ST. LOUIS	64-54	.542	1
Boston	60-51	.541	1½
Chicago	60-55	.522	3½
Cincinnati	53-60	.469	9½
Brooklyn	52-61	.460	10½
Philadelphia	51-60	.459	10½
Pittsburg	51-62	.451	11½

As surprising as the Cardinals have been, their push toward the front has been eclipsed by the incredible rise of George Stallings's Boston Braves. They were dead last, 15 games behind, on the Fourth of July. They didn't leave the cellar until July 19th, but by August 10th they had risen to second place. On August 23rd they tied New York for the lead. Then they lost their series in Chicago. And today's defeat in St. Louis marked the first time since July 4th that they had lost two consecutive games.

After a crowd of over 27,000 saw the Giants play a doubleheader on Wednesday, today's attendance at Robison Field was much smaller, about 5,500. This was no doubt partially due to the miserable weather. It rained throughout the contest, sometimes rather heavily, and by the end of the game it was so dark and misty that the spectators behind the plate could barely see the outfielders.

As a result, the game was poorly played. Three of the runs were tainted by bad defense. Walton Cruise hit a clean home run, but Lee Magee's round tripper was misjudged by center fielder Les Mann, allowing the ball to get over his head. Boston's runs came on an error and a balk.

Cozy Dolan's tenth-inning double won the game, redeeming the Cardinal outfielder after he had had a very bad day. His error on a fly ball had allowed the Braves' Joe Connolly to circle the bases. And Coze had struck out in one critical situation and had been thrown out stealing another time.

Dick Rudolph and Hub Perdue were the opposing pitchers at the start of the game.

St. Louis scored the first run with a home run off of Rudolph. With two out in the bottom of the second, Cruise, well known as a lefthanded pull hitter, shot one down the left field line. Connolly was playing way over toward center, and by the time he could retrieve the ball, Cruise was headed for the plate. He made it standing up, thanks to an off-line relay by Rabbit Maranville.

The Braves tied the count in the third. Herbie Moran strolled to first, while the Cardinals argued the call on ball four with umpire Bill "Lord" Byron. Johnny Evers sent one down the right field line, which Owen "Chief" Wilson caught in fine style. Connolly then delivered Boston's first hit, but Wilson again was on the ball in a flash, holding Moran to second base. Moran tried to steal third. Catcher Ivey Wingo shot the ball down to Zinn Beck. But the third baseman was asleep and barely aroused himself in time to catch the ball, so Moran slid in safely. Perdue then tried to look the runner back to third and pick the man off first. But he only succeeded in committing a balk, sending Moran home. Connolly was eventually nabbed trying to purloin third.

The first two St. Louis hitters in the third, Perdue and Huggins, singled, and Magee sacrificed. Dolan came up in this key situation and ignominiously fanned. John "Dots" Miller then popped out.

After a scoreless fourth inning, Boston took the lead in the fifth. With two out, Connolly lifted a high one into the rain. Dolan went back for it, circled a few times, got his glove on the ball, dropped it, and kicked it to the fence. Connolly raced all the way around the bases, scoring ahead of Miller's poor relay.

The Cardinals wasted another fine chance in the sixth. Magee opened with a hot single to Red Smith at third. Dolan hit an easy double play ball to Maranville, but the shortstop fumbled both outs away. Miller then tried to sacrifice, but fast fielding by Rudolph forced Magee at third. Wilson fouled out, and Cruise whiffed.

Perdue was lifted for a pinch-hitter in the seventh, and Dan Griner went in to pitch in the eighth. Griner gave up two hits in that inning but struck Maranville out with men on second and third to end the threat.

In the home half, Magee opened with a long liner to center. Les Mann, who had just entered the game, started in on the ball, but the sphere sailed over his head and went to the clubhouse. The speedy Magee easily scored with a game-tying home run. Later in the frame, Wilson singled and Cruise walked, but they were left.

By this time, it was getting very difficult for the outfielders to see, but Byron refused to call the game.

St. Louis got the winning run across in the tenth. Magee started off with a neat single to right, which Moran stopped with some difficulty. Dolan came up to bunt but failed twice. Then he lofted one high into the mist in left field. By the time Connolly found the ball, it was against the fence, and Magee was on his way home with the winning run.

The final score was 3-2.

Boston	ab	r	h	bi	o	a	e
H. Moran, cf-rf8	4	1	1	0	2	0	0
J. Evers, 2b	5	0	1	0	2	2	0
J. Connolly, lf	4	1	1	0	0	0	0
L. Gilbert, rf	3	0	1	0	0	0	0
L. Mann, pr8-cf	0	0	0	0	1	0	0
J. Devore, ph10-cf	1	0	1	0	0	0	0
B. Schmidt, 1b	5	0	1	0	13	1	0
R. Smith, 3b	4	0	0	0	4	1	1
R. Maranville, ss	4	0	1	0	2	3	1
H. Gowdy, c	3	0	1	0	3	2	0
D. Rudolph, p	4	0	0	0	0	4	0
	37	2	8	0	27	13	2

St. Louis	ab	r	h	bi	o	a	e
M. Huggins, 2b	5	0	1	0	1	1	0
L. Magee, 1b	4	2	3	1	6	0	0
C. Dolan, lf	4	0	1	1	2	0	1
D. Miller, ss	4	0	0	0	2	3	0
O. Wilson, rf	4	0	1	0	5	0	0
W. Cruise, cf	3	1	2	1	3	0	0
Z. Beck, 3b	4	0	2	0	1	0	0
I. Wingo, c	4	0	0	0	10	2	0
H. Perdue, p	2	0	1	0	0	0	0
F. Snyder, ph7	1	0	0	0	-	-	-
D. Griner, p8	1	0	0	0	0	0	0
	36	3	11	3	30	6	1

Boston   001 010 000 0 - 2
St. Louis   010 000 010 1 - 3
none out when winning run scored

	ip	h	r-er	bb	so
Rudolph (L 18-10)	*9	11	3-3	2	4
Perdue	7	3	2-1	5	4
Griner (W 5-10)	3	5	0-0	0	2

*faced two batters in tenth.
Balk: Perdue

LOB: Bos 10, StL 9.
BE: Bos 1, StL 1.
DP: Maranville-Evers-Schmidt.
2B: Beck, Dolan.
HR: Cruise, Magee. SH: Magee.
SB: Moran, Schmidt.
CS: Dolan, Connolly, Moran.
Time - 2:34
Attendance - 5,500
Umpires: B. Byron & F. Lincoln

This game was the high-water mark of the Cardinals' pennant drive. They lost the next three games to Boston, then four in a row to Pittsburg, killing their chances.

The Braves, on the other hand, never lost two straight again and swept to the pennant by an incredible 10½-game margin over the Giants.

St. Louis finished with an 81-72 record, 13 games back. That put them in third place, higher than the club had ever before finished in the National League.

1915 — Monday, August 30th, at National League Park, Philadelphia

Cards Lose as Homer Bounces Off Bescher's Chest and Over Fence

Only One Game of Scheduled Doubleheader Played

Phillies Win, 4-3, on Freak Hit in Tenth Inning

The league-leading Philadelphia Phillies have been playing good baseball this summer. But sometimes it helps to be lucky, too. The St. Louis Cardinals haven't played all that badly, but at times the breaks have gone against them. Today Dame Fortune smiled the brightest smile of the year on the Quaker City crew. In a tightly fought game, the Cards and Phils battled through nine innings tied at 3-3. After St. Louis missed a chance to score in the top of the tenth, the Phillies were handed the game when a fly ball hit the fence, bounced off the outfielder's chest, and caromed over the fence for a home run.

The game was the only one played in the National League today, owing to heavy rains over the northeastern section of the country. It rained in Philadelphia all morning, and the first game of the scheduled doubleheader was called off around noon. But the showering ended an hour or so later, and the second game was played, starting at 3:00 p.m.

Today's Results
ST. LOUIS at Philadelphia (1st game) postponed - rain
Philadelphia 4 - ST. LOUIS 3 (10 inn.) (2nd game)
Pittsburg at Brooklyn - postponed - rain
Cincinnati at Boston - postponed - rain
Chicago at New York - postponed - rain

Standings	W-L	Pct.	GB
Philadelphia	65-50	.565	-
Brooklyn	65-56	.537	3
Boston	61-55	.526	4½
Chicago	58-59	.496	8
ST. LOUIS	58-63	.479	10
New York	54-60	.474	10½
Pittsburg	57-64	.471	11
Cincinnati	54-65	.454	13

The playing field was thoroughly soaked, but the heroic efforts of the local groundcrew made conditions tolerable. Considering the weather, the game was well played, with but three errors made. The base running was somewhat off, however. Aside from the decisive home run, the Phillies won the game by better running. Both teams hit well, and the total of just four walks indicated that the pitchers retained command of the ball.

Cardinal manager Miller Huggins had a bad day. He struck out twice, made a critical throwing error on a double play attempt, and was ejected from the game after arguing with the umpires.

Bespectacled rookie Lee Meadows was Huggins's choice as the St. Louis starting pitcher. Pat Moran, the Philadelphia manager, sent out his ace, Grover Alexander. Knowing that Alex the Great would pitch, around 8,000 Philadelphians braved the elements to witness the game.

In the home half of the first, the Phillies made a bid to score. With one out, rookie Dave Bancroft doubled to right. He took third on Dode Paskert's infield out. Slugging Gavvy Cravath was walked. The two runners tried the double steal, but Huggins's return throw to Frank Snyder nailed Bancroft at the plate.

St. Louis loaded the bases in the second but failed to score.

The Cardinals finally broke through in the third. Huggins was first up, and he was called out on strikes. He was not at all pleased with umpire Bill Byron's call, and he argued long and loud before taking his seat on the bench. Art Butler flied out. Bob Bescher smacked a hit to left, and Tommy Long cracked a two-bagger to right. Owen Wilson then came through with a clutch Texas Leaguer that dropped in front of the left fielder, and both runners scored.

The Cards' 2-0 lead lasted for four innings.

Then in the seventh, the Phillies put a rally together. After Bert Niehoff had flied out to Bescher, Bill Killifer singled to left. Beals Becker was sent in to bat for Alexander, and he came through with a safety to center. Milt Stock ripped a shot to left, Niehoff scoring, while Becker stopped at second. Bancroft looped a hit to short left, and the bases were loaded with one out.

Then came a critical play. Paskert grounded down to shortstop. Butler fielded the ball and flipped it to second for the force, and Huggins pivoted and threw to first. Just as he did, however, Bancroft came barreling into him, and the heave went wild. So, instead of an inning-ending double play and a 2-1 St. Louis lead, the Phillies had two more runs and a 3-2 advantage.

Huggins was sure that Bancroft had illegally interfered with him, and the little manager railed at umpire Mal Eason, trying to get Eason to call the batter out on the interference. When it became apparent that he would not get the call, Hug began to rail at Eason's personal characteristics, and the ump waved him out of the game. Dots Miller was shifted from first to second, and Ham Hyatt came in to play first base.

With Alex out of the game, Moran picked his second best pitcher, Erskine Mayer, to try and hold the lead. But he was ineffective in his first inning of work, and St. Louis tied the score. Only the fine throwing of the catcher prevented the Cards from taking the lead. Bescher opened the eighth by walking, but Killifer gunned him down trying to steal second. Long got his second double of the game, this one to center field. Wilson flied deep to center, Long taking third after the catch. Miller then tapped one past the mound for a hit, scoring Long. Dots, too, was caught stealing, ending the round.

The Phillies threatened to win the game in the bottom of the ninth. Hits by Killifer and Bancroft put men on first and third with two out, and Hub Perdue was brought in to relieve Meadows. He hit the first man he faced with a pitch. That loaded the bases for Cravath, but Gavvy popped out.

Hyatt opened the tenth with a double, but was caught off second after Fred Luderus grabbed a popped-up bunt.

With one out in the bottom of the round, George "Possum" Whitted won the game with his freak home run. He hit a long drive to left. Outfielder Bescher went back in pursuit of the ball but pulled up just short of the fence. The drive bounced off the top part of the wall, with Bescher ready to grab it on the rebound. But the carom fooled hm, and the ball hit him on the upper chest. Then it bounced back over the fence, giving Whitted a homer and giving the Phillies the victory, 4-3.

Well, that's the way the ball bounces.

St. Louis	ab	r	h	bi	o	a	e
M. Huggins, 2b	4	0	0	0	2	5	1
H. Hyatt, 1b7	1	0	1	0	3	0	0
A. Butler, ss	5	0	1	0	0	4	0
B. Bescher, lf	4	1	1	0	8	0	0
T. Long, rf	4	2	3	0	2	0	0
O. Wilson, cf	3	0	2	2	2	0	0
D. Miller, 1b-2b7	4	0	1	1	6	2	1
B. Betzel, 3b	4	0	0	0	2	1	0
F. Snyder, c	3	0	0	0	3	1	0
L. Meadows, p	4	0	1	0	0	0	0
H. Perdue, p9	0	0	0	0	0	0	0
	36	3	10	3	28	13	2

Philadelphia	ab	r	h	bi	o	a	e
M. Stock, 3b	4	1	1	1	1	5	0
D. Bancroft, ss	5	0	3	0	3	1	1
D. Paskert, cf	4	0	0	1	3	0	0
G. Cravath, rf	4	0	0	0	0	0	0
F. Luderus, 1b	5	0	1	0	11	1	0
G. Whitted, lf	5	1	1	1	3	0	0
B. Niehoff, 2b	4	0	2	0	5	0	0
B. Killifer, c	4	1	3	0	4	3	0
G. Alexander, p	2	0	0	0	0	5	0
B. Becker, ph7	1	1	1	0	-	-	-
E. Mayer, p8	1	0	0	0	0	0	0
	39	4	12	3	30	15	1

St. Louis   002 000 010 0 - 3
Philadelphia   000 000 300 1 - 4
one out when winning run scored

	ip	h	r-er	bb	so
Meadows	8.2	11	3-2	2	2
Perdue (L 6-10)	.2	1	1-1	0	0
Alexander	7	7	2-2	1	3
Mayer (W 17-12)	3	3	1-1	1	1

HBP: by Perdue (Paskert)

LOB: StL 6, Phil 10. BE: StL 1.
DP: Luderus-Bancroft.
2B: Long 2, Bancroft, Hyatt.
HR: Whitted. SH: Wilson.
SB: none.
CS: Bancroft, Butler, Bescher, Miller.
Time - 2:02
Attendance - 8,000
Umpires: B. Byron & M. Eason

Although the Cardinals played mediocre ball for the rest of the season, they barely missed the first division. By losing their final game of the year, they finished 1 game behind the fourth-place Chicago Cubs.

But the standings were so tightly packed that St. Louis wound up in sixth place. Their record was 72-81, leaving them 18½ games behind the champion Phillies.

1916—Sunday, October 1st, at Weegham Park, Chicago
Cardinals End Season with 14th Straight Loss, Tie for Last
Three Home Runs Pace Cubs to 6-3 Victory
President Britton Promises a Thorough House-Cleaning

While the National League championship remained undecided, and the eastern teams still had four days left on their schedules, the N. L. season ended for St. Louis today with a resounding thud. The Cardinals completed a late-season nose dive tied for last place. They lost their last 14 games. On August 28th, they were 10 games ahead of the cellar-dwelling Cincinnati Reds. After that date, the Cardinals won only five games and lost 28, falling from sixth place into a tie for seventh and eighth, even though the Reds played under-.500 ball.

Today's Results
Chicago 6 - ST. LOUIS 3
Cincinnati 4 - Pittsburgh 0
no other games scheduled

Standings	W-L	Pct.	GB
Brooklyn	91-59	.607	-
Philadelphia	89-58	.605	½
Boston	85-61	.582	4
New York	85-63	.574	5
Chicago	67-86	.438	25½
Pittsburgh	65-89	.422	28
ST. LOUIS	60-93	.392	32½
Cincinnati	60-93	.392	32½

Fortunately for their St. Louis fans, the Cards ended the campaign with an 18-game road trip. The trip opened with a split of four games in Philadelphia. Then came fourteen losses: three in Boston, three in Brooklyn, six in New York, and two in Chicago.

During the streak, they scored just 23 runs, never getting more than four runs in any one game. In only four of those games did they ever have the lead, and in two of those they lost the lead by the bottom of the first inning.

They got some good pitching but wasted it. In one game, Lee Meadows lost to the Giants, 1-0, when rookie Sammy Bohne made two throwing errors in one inning. Meadows was also a 2-0 loser in Boston. Bob Steele lost to New York, 3-2, in ten innings, after carrying a 2-0 lead into the ninth.

The terrible ending caused a strong reaction from Schuyler Britton, the club president and husband of club owner Helene H.R. Britton. Mr. Britton fumed that, "The Cardinals need a thorough house-cleaning. About seven of their regulars have outlived their usefulness in St. Louis." He promised that, after conferring with manager Miller Huggins, the team would have some new faces next spring.

Perhaps the sorest point, from the Brittons' point of view, was that this club had among the highest payrolls in the league. "Eighth place is no position for a club boasting of a $90,000 payroll," Schuyler complained. Although he declined to name any specific names, Britton implied that several high-salaried veterans would be put onto the trading block over the winter. Dots Miller, Owen Wilson, and Bob Bescher, all of whom hit in the .230's, seemed likely to go. The Cardinals had already been able to dispose of Slim Sallee and his large ($6,000) salary to New York on July 23rd. They got a reported $10,000 on the sale.

A couple of the Cardinals' young prospects gave some promise of a brighter future. Rogers Hornsby hit an impressive .313 in his first full year in the league. And pitcher Milt Watson, infielder Bohne, and catcher Tony Brottem all made good impressions in late-season trials.

In today's game, Bohne got three hits and a successful sacrifice bunt in four trips to the plate. And Brottem foiled three attempts to steal bases, two of them being attempted double steals.

Chicago also tried two new recruits today. Scott Perry, recently purchased from Atlanta, pitched. Charlie Deal played second. Deal was with the Browns at the beginning of the season, but he contracted typhoid and was released to Kansas City. The Cubs bought his contract just last week.

The Cardinals got off on top in the first with a run off of Perry. Hits by Bescher and Bohne, followed by a sacrifice fly by Jack Smith, plated the tally.

The lead did not last long. Pitcher Bob Steele was rocked by two home runs in the bottom of the first. Les Mann hit the first one, a drive over the left field wall. With two out, Joe Kelly hit a liner to center, which Smith misjudged. The ball went to the wall, and Kelly circled the bases.

Steele, who took the loss, dropping his record to a dismal 5-15, was knocked out of the box in the second. Deal singled with one out. Chuck Wortman did the same. Perry then pushed a double to left, scoring Deal. Wortman counted on a fly out by Max Flack.

Leon "Red" Ames took over the pitching duties for St. Louis. He was hit for two more runs in the third. Vic Saier led off with a double. Ames sent him home with a pair of wild pitches. Then, with two down, Steve Yerkes homered over the wall, bringing the score to 6-1.

After that, Ames shut the home team out for three innings on just one hit. Rees "Steamboat" Williams succeeded him in the seventh. He managed to keep the Cubs from scoring, despite three hits and a walk in two innings. He was materially aided by the throwing of Brottem.

But the Cardinals could not rally against Perry. They accumulated ten hits off him, but didn't bunch their blows well enough to stage a real threat to the Cubs' lead. Three straight singles yielded one run in the fifth. In the seventh, Bruno Betzel scored after drawing the only pass issued by Perry, but his mates couldn't follow him home.

The feature of the game was the fine fielding of both nines. No errors were made. The perfect support pulled Perry out of trouble a couple of times. Good support also spared Williams.

The game ended with a 6-3 loss going into the St. Louis record. Combined with Cincinnati's 4-0 victory over Pittsburgh, the Cards and Reds finished the season with identical 60-93 records.

That meant that the 1916 Cardinals were tied for last, which caused the management to promise some large-scale changes before the 1917 season.

St. Louis	ab	r	h	bi	o	a	e
B. Bescher, lf	4	1	3	1	2	0	0
S. Bohne, ss	3	0	3	1	2	2	0
J. Smith, cf	1	0	0	1	1	0	0
T. Long, cf4	2	0	0	0	0	0	0
R. Hornsby, 3b	4	0	1	0	3	2	0
O. Wilson, rf	4	0	1	0	0	0	0
D. Miller, 1b	4	0	1	0	11	1	0
F. Snyder, c	2	0	0	0	3	0	0
T. Brottem, c4	2	0	0	0	1	3	0
B. Betzel, 2b	3	1	0	0	1	4	0
B. Steele, p	0	0	0	0	0	0	0
R. Ames, p2	2	1	1	0	0	0	0
M. Gonzalez, ph7	1	0	0	0	-	-	-
S. Williams, p7	0	0	0	0	0	2	0
A. Butler, ph9	1	0	0	0	-	-	-
	33	3	10	3	24	14	0

Chicago	ab	r	h	bi	o	a	e
M. Flack, rf	3	0	0	1	1	0	0
L. Mann, lf	4	1	2	1	1	0	0
V. Saier, 1b	4	1	3	0	13	1	0
J. Kelly, cf	3	1	1	0	0	0	0
A. Wilson, c	4	0	1	0	4	1	0
S. Yerkes, 2b	4	1	1	1	2	3	0
C. Deal, 3b	4	1	1	0	2	6	0
C. Wortman, ss	2	1	1	0	2	2	0
S. Perry, p	3	0	1	1	1	2	0
	31	6	11	5	*26	15	0

*Bescher out, hit by batted ball

St. Louis   100 010 100 - 3
Chicago   222 000 00x - 6

	ip	h	r-er	bb	so
Steele (L 5-15)	1.2	5	4-4	0	1
Ames	4.1	3	2-2	2	1
Williams	2	3	0-0	1	0
Perry (W 2-1)	9	10	3-3	1	3

WP: Ames 2. PB: Brottem

LOB: StL 6, Chi 5.
DP: Deal-Yerkes-Saier.
2B: Perry, Bescher 2, Mann, Saier.
HR: Mann, Kelly, Yerkes.
SH: Bohne. SF: Smith, Flack.
SB: Saier.
Time - 1:45
Umpires: P. Harrison & A. Orth

After the Cardinals lost the City Series to the Browns (4 games to 1), the changes came.

But the shakeup was different than Schuyler Britton had ennvisioned. His wife sold the club to a group of St. Louis businessmen headed by James C. Jones. This group installed Branch Rickey as president. Manager Huggins, who made an unsuccessful bid to buy the club himself, stayed on for one year.

The new ownership made no wholesale changes in player personnel.

1917 — Monday, June 11th, at Cardinal Field

Cardinals Rally To Win, 5-4, as Gonzalez Steals Home in 15th

Doak Allows Four Runs in First, Then Pitches Great Ball

The Only Two Errors Are Costly, But Fast Fielding Enlivens Game

Crippled by injuries and down by four runs before their first time at bat, the St. Louis Cardinals overcame the odds today to beat the Philadelphia Phillies, 5-4. It took them 15 innings to do it, and it took a two-out steal of home by Miguel Gonzalez to bring the winning run home.

Until Gonzalez's final heroics, the game was a battle of pitching and defense. St. Louis pitcher Bill Doak was hit for four runs, three unearned, in the first inning, but he pitched 14 innings of shutout ball thereafter. The Phillies' Joe Oeschger also went the distance. Each side made just one error, but each miscue led to runs. Otherwise the fielders backed both pitchers with fine plays to cut off runs. Both catchers and both shortstops stood out. And the outfielders made some nice catches, in spite of a strong wind.

Today's Results
ST. LOUIS 5 - Philadelphia 4 (15 inn.)
New York 8 - Chicago 2
Cincinnati 3 - Brooklyn 2
Boston 2 - Pittsburgh 0

Standings	W-L	Pct.	GB
Philadelphia	26-15	.634	-
New York	26-16	.619	½
Chicago	29-21	.580	1½
ST. LOUIS	25-21	.543	3½
Cincinnati	23-28	.451	8
Boston	16-22	.421	8½
Brooklyn	16-23	.410	9
Pittsburgh	15-30	.333	13

The hurlers were also greatly aided by umpire Bill "Lord" Byron, who called anything in the vicinity of home plate a strike.

Because of injuries to catcher Frank Snyder and second baseman Bruno Betzel, the Cardinals had to shift their lineup. Dots Miller was moved from first to second base, and Gonzalez, a catcher by trade, covered first. Paddy Livingston, just up from the minors, was the catcher. Walton Cruise played left field despite a charley horse.

The Phillies started their regular lineup. Shortstop Dave Bancroft injured his arm trying to make a tag in the ninth, and he gave way to Patsy McGaffigan.

Philadelphia started out as if it intended to run away with the game. Dode Paskert hit the very first pitch into center field and got a wind-blown single. He quickly stole second. Bancroft walked. Milt Stock bunted the runners to second and third. Gavvy Cravath lifted a fly to right. Tommy Long, battling the wind, dropped the ball, and Paskert scored. George "Possum" Whitted then laid down a squeeze bunt, and Bancroft slid home under Doak's shovel to Livingston. Fred Luderus was passed to fill the bases. Bert Neihoff raised a twister behind third, which shortstop Rogers Hornsby caught after a hard run. The count went to 2-and-2 on Bill Killifer. Doak delivered a spitter that Killifer chased. At the last instant, he brought his bat back. It seemed such an obvious swing that the Cardinals started off the field. But Ump Byron ruled it no swing and ball three. Manager Huggins led the charge to argue, and he was nearly banished for his efforts. When play resumed, Killifer drove the next pitch through the hole and into right field, knocking in two runs.

The Cardinals got a hit in their half of the first, but Byron called Hornsby out on a pitch a foot outside, ending the inning.

After his shaky first inning, Doak was sent back to the mound, and he did a wonderful job for the rest of the game. His spitball was breaking sharply down and across, baffling the hitters. He also showed a good fastball and a dazzling change of pace. Through the final fourteen innings, he allowed just four hits and one base on balls. Only one Philly got as far as third base, and only one other runner got to second against him.

Oeschger also pitched fine ball through the long game. His curve was only fair, but his fastball was excellent, and the St. Louis hitters could do little with it.

Cravath robbed St. Louis of a run in the second by making a running, stretching catch in right center.

In the fourth, the Cardinals finally managed to score. With one out, Hornsby cracked a single down the left field line, his first of four hits. Cruise worked Oeschger (and umpire Byron) for a walk. A wild pitch moved the runners up, and Long's sacrifice fly drove Hornsby home.

The Cards tied the game in the sixth. Gonzalez opened with a long fly to right, which the wind kept in the park and Cravath caught. After some acrimonious discussion about a called strike, Miller singled over second. Hornsby hit safe to left. Miller was forced at third on Cruise's tap to the mound. Long then pushed a double down the right field line. Hornsby scored easily, but the hobbled Cruise had to hold at third. Livingston followed with a shot toward second baseman Niehoff. He got in front of the ball, but it short-hopped under his glove, allowing two runs to score.

With the pitchers in command, the game quickly slipped into extra innings. It looked like darkness would end the game as a tie.

Gonzalez was the second hitter in the bottom of the fifteenth. Mike had made just two hits in his previous 38 at bats. Today he had struck out twice and failed to sacrifice once. But the Cuban was finally ready to do something. He hit a drive to right, which bounded past Cravath for a double. Mike went to third while Stock was making a nice play to retire Miller at first. Hornsby was purposely passed. With Cruise at bat, Hornsby stole second, hoping to draw a throw that might allow Gonzalez to get home. But the catcher held the ball. With Oeschger now pitching from a windup, Gonzalez took matters into his own hands. He took a short lead, bluffed a start while the pitcher was just starting his motion, then sprinted for the plate. The pitch was high. Catcher Killifer got it and tried to make a one-handed, sweeping tag. He put the ball on Gonzalez just as the runner was sliding across the plate. The slide knocked the ball loose, and the Cardinals had the winning run and a 5-4 victory.

It was a fitting climax to one of the best games played in St. Louis in years.

Philadelphia	ab	r	h	bi	o	a	e
D. Paskert, rf	6	1	1	0	2	0	0
D. Bancroft, ss	3	1	1	0	1	2	0
P. McGaffigan, ss9	2	0	1	0	2	2	0
M. Stock, 3b	5	0	1	0	2	3	0
G. Gravath, rf	5	1	0	0	5	0	0
G. Whitted, lf	5	1	1	1	4	0	0
F. Luderus, 1b	5	0	0	0	16	0	0
B. Niehoff, 2b	6	0	0	0	4	3	1
B. Killifer, c	6	0	1	2	8	2	0
J. Oeschger, p	4	0	0	0	0	4	0
	47	4	6	3	44	16	1

St. Louis	ab	r	h	bi	o	a	e
J. Smith, cf	7	0	2	0	2	0	0
M. Gonzalez, 1b	7	1	1	0	19	2	0
D. Miller, 2b	7	0	2	0	2	2	0
R. Hornsby, ss	6	2	4	0	3	7	0
W. Cruise, lf	5	1	0	0	3	0	0
T. Long, rf	5	1	3	2	3	1	1
P. Livingston, c	6	0	0	0	12	1	0
F. Smith, 3b	5	0	0	0	1	1	0
B. Doak, p	6	0	1	0	0	10	0
	54	5	13	2	45	24	1

Philadelphia   400 000 000 000 000 - 4
St. Louis   000 103 000 000 001 - 5
two out when winning run scored

	ip	h	r-er	bb	so
Oeschger (L 3-3)	14.2	13	5-3	2	8
Doak (W 7-4)	15	6	4-1	3	10

WP: Oeschger.
HBP: by Oeschger (F. Smith).

LOB: Phil 4, StL 9.
BE: Phil 1, StL 1.
DP: Bancroft-Niehoff-Luderus.
2B: Long, Gonzalez. SF: Long.
SH: Stock, Whitted, Cravath.
SB: Paskert, Stock, J. Smith, Hornsby, Gonzalez.
Time - 2:55
Attendance - 2,000
Umpires: B. Byron & E. Quigley.

The Cardinals played some exciting ball in 1917. Although they were never a factor in the pennant race, they were in second place briefly in late July and early August.

Huggins had the boys playing over their heads, and they finished third with an 82-70 record.

But Huggins could not resolve his disappointment with the new ownership, and he left the club.

1918 — Wednesday, July 3rd, at Cardinal Field

Fisher's Hidden Ball Trick Saves 2-1 Victory for Cardinals

Ancient Ploy Nabs Paskert in Ninth Inning

Fisher Also Scores Winning Run in Eighth Inning

Having failed with all conventional means to beat the first-place Chicago Cubs, the last-place St. Louis Cardinals resorted to an old schoolyard stunt, the hidden ball trick, to preserve a 2-1 victory over the Chicagoans. Second baseman Bobby Fisher pulled the deception in the ninth inning with one out and men on second and third bases, effectively halting a promising Cub rally. As a result, the Cardinals were able to beat the Cubs for the first time since the opening day of the season. Chicago had beaten St. Louis 13 times since then.

Today's Results
ST. LOUIS 2 - Chicago 1
New York 9 - Brooklyn 4 (1st game)
New York 1 - Brooklyn 0 (2nd)
Philadelphia 5 - Boston 0
Pittsburgh 8 - Cincinnati 5

Standings	W-L	Pct.	GB
Chicago	45-19	.703	-
New York	43-21	.672	2
Philadelphia	30-32	.484	14
Boston	31-35	.470	15
Pittsburgh	30-34	.469	15
Brooklyn	26-37	.413	18½
Cincinnati	25-37	.403	19
ST. LOUIS	25-40	.385	20½

In matching their feeble batting attack against the Cubs' superior pitching and fielding, the Red Birds had never been able to score more than four runs in a game against Chicago. The Cubs hadn't hit the Cardinal pitching hard on all occasions, but they still had managed to win. Five of the 13 games had been decided by one run, three times the final score being 3-2. Today it looked like another 3-2 defeat for St. Louis when the first two Cubs singled in the ninth. But Red Ames was called in to pitch in relief, and he retired the side on a sacrifice, the hidden ball trick, and a strike out to save the game.

The whole game was well pitched. Seventeen hits were made, but both Phil Douglas of the Cubs and Gene Packard of the Cardinals were effective in the pinches. Each showed fine control, Packard issuing the only walk of the game. Only three Cubs got as far as third base. Only two Knot Holers got that far, and they both scored.

In a turnabout from the normal state of affairs, the Cardinals played flawless defense, whereas the Cubs' fielding was responsible for the St. Louis scoring.

A double error by substitute second baseman Charlie McCabe gave the Cards a run on their very first batter. Cliff Heathcote, leading off the bottom of the first, skied a high fly into short right center. McCabe went back and called two outfielders off the play. Then he muffed the ball. By the time he had recovered it, Heathcote was streaking toward third. McCabe uncorked a low throw that skipped past third baseman Charlie Deal, allowing Heathcote to score.

That was the only run of the first four innings. Chicago threatened a couple of times, but were unable to score until the fifth.

In that round, the only base on balls of the game led to a tally. After Deal had been thrown out by Rogers Hornsby, McCabe drew the pass. Bill Killifer hit a liner into right field that scooted past Johnny Beall and went to the fence for a triple, scoring McCabe. Pitcher Douglas was unable to bring his batterymate home, striking out instead. Max Flack's low liner was captured by Heathcote in good style, ending the inning.

Except for McCabe's errors, Douglas, a spitball expert, handled the Cardinals without much trouble for the first four innings.

In the fifth, bad base running killed a promising start for the Cards. Mike Gonzalez was credited with a single when Douglas couldn't pick up his bunt. Packard then pushed a bunt past both Douglas and McCabe, and the ball rolled all the way to the outfield grass. Gonzalez brazenly tried to make third on the hit but was thrown out easily by the right fielder.

Good fielding pulled Packard through a tough spot in the sixth. Charlie Hollocher started the Cubs off with an infield hit. Les Mann tried to bunt him to second, but

Packard made a good play to get a force at second. Fred Merkle, despite a bad leg, beat out a hit to shortstop, putting men on first and second. Fisher stopped the rally by grabbing Paskert's hard grounder and starting a double play.

The Cubs wasted a double by Hollocher in the eighth inning. It came with two out, and Mann followed with a roller to Hornsby.

The Cardinals broke the tie with a run in the last of the eighth. Packard bounced out to Merkle, and Heathcote was retired on a fast play by Deal. Fisher then hooked one just out of Mann's range in left for a single. He tried to steal second. Killifer's throw appeared to beat him to the bag, but McCabe dropped it, and Fisher was safe. Charlie Grimm then slapped a 2-2 pitch past the diving Deal and into left. As Fisher was rounding third, Mann bobbled the ball, and the runner scored easily. Grimm died stealing, but the Cardinals led, 2-1, with just three outs to go.

Merkle opened the ninth by grounding a single just past Doug Baird, the third baseman. Chuck Wortman went in to run. Paskert came up trying to bunt, but he failed on two attempts. Then he lined one into right center for a hit. Heathcote made a fine return·of the ball to hold the runners at second and first.

At this point, manager Jack Hendricks decided that Packard had had enough, and Ames was called in. Deal laid down a bunt, moving the runners up one base while Ames threw to Fisher at first for the out. Fisher and Hornsby then walked to the mound for a conference. Fisher faked handing the ball back to Ames, then he ambled back to his position. Neither Paskert on second, nor Otto Knabe, who was coaching first, nor manager Fred Mitchell, who was stationed at third, were aware of the fact that Fisher still had the ball. Ames went through the motions of taking his stretch and looking in at the batter, McCabe. Paskert stepped away to his lead, and Fisher snuck in behind and tagged him. After Fisher showed umpire Bob Emslie that he had the ball, Paskert was declared out. Ames then did his part by throwing a called third strike past McCabe, and the Cardinals had a 2-1 triumph over the Cubs.

Finally!

Chicago	ab	r	h	bi	o	a	e
M. Flack, rf	4	0	1	0	1	1	0
C. Hollocher, ss	4	0	2	0	1	1	0
L. Mann, lf	4	0	0	0	0	0	0
F. Merkle, 1b	4	0	2	0	16	0	0
C. Wortman, pr9	0	0	0	0	-	-	-
D. Paskert, cf	4	0	2	0	1	0	0
C. Deal, 3b	3	0	0	0	3	2	0
B. McCabe, 2b	2	1	0	0	1	5	2
B. Killifer, c	3	0	1	1	1	2	0
P. Douglas, p	3	0	1	0	0	5	0
	31	1	9	1	24	16	2

St. Louis	ab	r	h	bi	o	a	e
C. Heathcote, cf	4	1	0	0	3	0	0
B. Fisher, 2b	4	1	1	0	2	3	0
C. Grimm, 1b	4	0	2	1	10	0	0
R. Hornsby, ss	3	0	2	0	2	4	0
J. Beall, rf	2	0	0	0	6	1	0
D. Baird, 3b	3	0	1	0	1	1	0
A. McHenry, lf	2	0	0	0	1	0	0
M. Gonzalez, c	3	0	1	0	2	0	0
G. Packard, p	3	0	1	0	0	2	0
R. Ames, p9	0	0	0	0	0	1	0
	28	2	8	1	27	12	0

Chicago   000 010 000 - 1
St. Louis   100 000 01x - 2

	ip	h	r-er	bb	so
Douglas (L 5-1)	8	8	2-1	0	0
Packard (W 3-8)	*8	9	1-1	1	1
Ames	1	0	0-0	0	1

*faced two batters in ninth

LOB: Chi 6, StL 4. BE: StL 1.
DP: Beall-Grimm, Fisher-Hornsby-Grimm.
2B: Hollocher. 3B: Killifer.
SH: Beall, McHenry, Deal.
SB: Fisher.
Time - 1:38
Umpires: B. Klem & B. Emslie

The Cardinals resumed their losing ways the next day, dropping both games of the holiday doubleheader by identical 1-0 scores.

St. Louis was in last place when the season ended on Labor Day (on orders of the War Department). The Cards' record was 51-78 for a .395 percentage.

1919—Thursday, July 17th, at Baker Park, Philadelphia
Ex-Cardinal Meadows Beats Former Mates, 1-0, in First Meeting
Jacobs, Just Acquired by Cards in Same Deal, Gets the Loss
Triple Play and Fast Fielding Also Featured in 12-Inning Duel

In the first game since the two clubs made a big trade, the Philadelphia Phillies and the St. Louis Cardinals tried out some of their new men against their old teams. Gene Paulette and Lee Meadows, the two men who went over to the Phils, both made their first appearances for their new club. The Cardinals had gotten three players in exchange for them, and they used one of them, Elmer Jacobs, as their pitcher today.

If today's game was any indication, Philadelphia got the better of the deal.

Both Meadows and Jacobs pitched great ball, and the game was scoreless until the twelfth inning. Then, aided by the only error of the game, the home team pushed across the run that made Meadows the victor. The bespectacled righthander outpitched Jacobs, allowing just four hits, compared to seven off of Jacobs. Both hurlers walked three, and Jacobs hit a batter. Meadows struck out eight, Jacobs three.

Today's Results
Philadelphia 1 - ST. LOUIS 0 (12 inn.)
New York 2 - Chicago 1
Cincinnati 5 - Brooklyn 1
Pittsburgh at Boston - postponed, street car strike

Standings	W-L	Pct.	GB
New York	47-23	.671	-
Cincinnati	49-25	.662	-
Chicago	42-34	.553	8
Pittsburgh	38-35	.521	10½
Brooklyn	37-36	.507	11½
ST. LOUIS	29-45	.392	20
Boston	26-44	.371	21
Philadelphia	21-47	.309	25

Up until the last inning, both pitchers received perfect fielding support. The Cardinals' work behind Jacobs was often sensational. The high point of their defensive efforts came in the fourth inning, when John "Doc" Lavan turned what looked like a two-run single into a triple play. The St. Louis shortstop also made a sensational stop to rob his former mate Paulette of a hit. Cardinal outfielders Austin McHenry and Cliff Heathcote also shone on defense.

The five-man trade between St. Louis and Philadelphia was announced Monday evening. Both teams were rained out the last two days, but the weather cleared today, allowing the opening game of the Cardinals' series in Philadelphia to be played. Both managers wanted to see right away what they acquired, so Gavvy Cravath sent Meadows out to pitch for the Quakers, and Branch Rickey used Jacobs for the Knot Holers. Each hurler responded with his best game of the year, either because they wanted to get revenge against the clubs that traded them, or because they wanted to make a good impression upon their new employers.

Meadows gave up two hits in the first inning. They were two-out singles by Milt Stock and Rogers Hornby and were wasted.

The Cardinals got only two more hits in the next eleven innings.

In the Phillies' first inning, Paulette sent a sizzler over second base, but Lavan made a marvelous one-handed stop and nipped the batter at first.

Fred Luderus and George "Possum" Whitted singled with one out in the second for the Phils, but they couldn't even get as far as third base.

The Phillies got a man to third and came within an eyelash of scoring in the third inning. With one out, Dave Bancroft walked to first. Lena Blackburne was hit by a pitch. Paulette shot a single to left, and Bancroft tried to score. But Austin McHenry's throw was a beauty, and the runner was out.

Cliff Heathcote singled in the top of the fourth but was left on base.

In the bottom, Jacobs was saved by the triple play. Luderus led off with a walk. Whitted found the gap between right and center for a double, sending Luderus to third. Eddie Sicking then hit a liner to the left of second base, and the runners were off for home. But Lavan scooted over, gloved the ball, and stepped on second, doubling up Whitted. Lavan was well pleased with this feat, and he stood there congratulating himself. But third baseman Hornsby wanted to share the glory, and he yelled to Lavan for the ball. The shortstop obliged, and his throw just beat Luderus back to third, completing the triple killing.

Thus buoyed, Jacobs settled down to some fine pitching. Showing an outstanding curveball, he retired the Phillies in order in each of the next four innings, aided by a couple of nice fielding plays.

Meadows was also sailing along, supplementing his pitching with his own good fielding. The Cardinals threatened to score just once. In the eighth inning, Jacobs opened with a double. Jack Smith followed with the requisite sacrifice, moving Jacobs to third. But the Cardinals couldn't get him home. Dots Miller sent a hot one to third. Blackburne stabbed the ball, ran Jacobs back to the bag, then threw Miller out. Stock ended the inning with a fly to Luderus in back of first.

In the Philadelphia ninth, Paulette singled and Luderus was given a pass. Both were left stranded.

The pitchers continued their good work into extra innings. Meadows walked a man in the tenth but otherwise was perfect. Jacobs set the Phils down in order in the tenth and eleventh.

Then, in the bottom of the twelfth, the break came. Emil "Irish" Meusel, leading off, shot a liner over Stock's head. Milt leaped high for it, but the ball just grazed his glove and went into right for a single. Luderus bunted down the first base line. Catcher William "Pickles" Dillhoefer picked the ball up. Having no chance at second, he threw toward first. But the throw hit Luderus in the head and caromed into right field. By the time it was retrieved, Meusel was on third, and Ludy was on second, rubbing his noggin. First base was open, and Whitted, the next hitter, already had two hits. But the old slugger, Cravath, picked up a bat and stepped into the on-deck position, so the Cardinals elected to pitch to the Possum. Whitted ruined the strategy by delivering a long hit to right field, plating Meusel with the winning run. That meant that the Phillies had a 1-0 victory in one of the best pitched and best played games of the season.

St. Louis	ab	r	h	bi	o	a	e	Philadelphia	ab	r	h	bi	o	a	e
J. Smith, rf	4	0	0	0	1	0	0	D. Bancroft, ss	4	0	0	0	1	3	0
D. Miller, 1b	5	0	0	0	13	0	0	L. Blackburne, 3b	4	0	0	0	1	6	0
M. Stock, 2b	4	0	1	0	0	5	0	G. Paulette, cf	5	0	2	0	1	0	0
R. Hornsby, 3b	5	0	1	0	3	2	0	I. Meusel, rf	5	1	1	0	1	0	0
C. Heathcote, cf	5	0	1	0	7	0	0	F. Luderus, 1b	2	0	1	0	21	1	0
A. McHenry, lf	5	0	0	0	3	1	0	G. Whitted, lf	5	0	3	1	1	1	0
D. Lavan, ss	5	0	0	0	2	3	0	E. Sicking, 2b	4	0	0	0	1	3	0
P. Dillhoefer, c	3	0	0	0	4	1	1	W. Tragresser, c	4	0	0	0	8	1	0
E. Jacobs, p	3	0	1	0	0	3	0	L. Meadows, p	4	0	0	0	1	6	0
	39	0	4	0	33	15	1		37	1	7	1	36	21	0

St. Louis   000 000 000 000 - 0
Philadelphia   000 000 000 001 - 1
none out when winning run scored

	ip	h	r-er	bb	so
Jacobs (L 6-11)	*11	7	1-0	3	3
Meadows (W 5-10)	12	4	0-0	3	8

*faced three batters in twelfth

LOB: StL 7, Phil 8. BE: Phil 1.
TP: Lavan-Hornsby.
2B: Whitted, Jacobs.
SH: Smith, Luderus.
HBP: by Jacobs (Blackburne).

The Phillies got the best of the trade. Jacob and Frank Woodward won only 10 games for the Cardinals before being released in 1920. Meadows went on to win 48 games for the Phils and 88 for the Pirates.

The trade didn't help either club improve much over the remainder of the 1919 season. The Phillies finished last, and the Cardinals wound up in seventh. St. Louis had a poor .394 percentage and finished 40½ games behind the champion Cincinnati Reds.

The Reds' pennant meant that St. Louis was the only one of eight National League clubs that had never won the league championship.

Chapter V
Sam and Branch Build a Winner
1920-1925

1920—July 1st at Sportsman's Park
Cardinals Lose First Game at Sportsman's Park, 6-2 in Ten

1921—June 13th at Sportsman's Park
Cardinals Humiliate Giants, 10-1, to Win Tenth Straight

1922—July 22nd at Sportsman's Park
Six-Run Eight-Inning Rally Moves St. Louis into First Place

1923—July 10th at Boston
Rookie Stuart Wins Both Games of Doubleheader for Red Birds

1924—September 16th at Brooklyn
Bottomley Drives in 12 Runs as Cardinals Rout Robins

1925—April 22nd at Sportsman's Park
Cardinals Score 11 Runs in First Inning of Home Opener

The Cardinals reached a crossroads in 1920. The ownership scheme that James C. Jones had launched in 1917 was inefficient. No one was really in control, and president Branch Rickey operated in a financial vacuum. But in 1920, auto dealer Sam Breadon bought up enough stock to gain a controlling interest. Therefore, he became president, with Rickey becoming vice-president. Rickey was also manager and general manager.

On the field, the team began to look up. Rogers Hornsby won his first of six consecutive batting titles in 1920. Jack Fournier, Milt Stock, and Austin McHenry also provided hard hitting. Bill Doak and Ferdinand Schupp pitched well, as did 26-year-old rookie Jess Haines.

Baseball in general was booming in 1920, and old Cardinal Field, the only wooden park left in the major leagues, was outmoded. At the last game of a homestand (June 6th), spectators stood eight or ten deep in the rear aisle of the grandstand to see the game. While the Cardinals were on the road, Rickey and Breadon negotiated a deal to rent the more modern Sportsman's Park from the St. Louis Browns for Cardinal games. The Cards lost their first game as tenants of the Browns, 6-2, on July 1, 1920.

The new arrangement allowed the Cardinals to sell their old park to the school district. Beaumont High School was built on the site. Some of the money from the sale was invested by the Cardinals in stock in minor league clubs in Houston and Fort Smith. That was the start of what became, at its peak, a 32-team farm system.

The new Sportsman's Park was located on the site of Chris Von der Ahe's first Sportsman's Park: the west side of Grand Avenue between Dodier and Sullivan Avenues.

In 1921, the Cardinals got off to a bad start. But in early June they put together a 10-game winning streak, culminating in a 10-1 humiliation of the New York Giants. The streak put them into the first division. After St. Louis played around .500 ball for most of the summer, the team got hot again at the end of the season and won 30 of its last 39 games to finish third, 7 games out of first.

In 1922, they were pennant contenders. On July 22nd, they actually moved into first place. The Browns were in first place in the American League at the same time, and St. Louis was gripped by double pennant fever. Hornsby won the triple crown, and the seven other Cardinal regulars all hit over .290. But the Cards' pitching was not of championship caliber, and the team finished tied for third, 8 games out.

The Cardinals' fifth-place finish was a big disappointment. Hornsby missed several weeks due to knee problems, the illness of his mother, and a skin rash. Young Jim Bottomley made up some of the slack by hitting .371 in his first full season. And Jess Haines won 20 games. But the pitching staff lacked depth. Rookie Johnny Stuart was even allowed to pitch both games of a doubleheader when manager Rickey was short of arms in July.

In 1924, the Cardinals had some great individual performances. Haines pitched a no-hitter on July 17th, and Herman Bell pitched a six-hit complete doubleheader two days later. Jim Bottomley drove in a record 12 runs in a game in September, and Hornsby finished the season with a .424 batting average. But the Cardinals finished a dismal sixth.

After losing their first three games in 1925, the Cardinals won five in a row. The last of these was their home opener, in which they scored eleven runs in the first inning. But they soon fell to last place. On Memorial Day, Breadon relieved Rickey of his managerial duties, Hornsby taking over. The club did better over the rest of the season, finishing fourth.

1920—Thursday, July 1st, at Sportsman's Park
Overflow Crowd Sees Cardinals' First Game in Sportsman's Park
Benefit Game Draws 20,000
Pittsburgh Wins in Ten Innings, 6-2

The rejuvenated St. Louis Nationals have left their old Cardinal Field for the more commodious facilities of the American League Browns' Sportsman's Park. The team's good showing this season had already overtaxed the capacity of the old wooden park on Natural Bridge Ave., and during their recent, successful road trip, arrangements were perfected to allow the Cardinals to share the Grand Avenue stadium with the Browns. Today even their new home was unable to seat all the fans who turned out to greet the returning heroes.

It was the annual benefit game for the St. Louis Tuberculosis Society, with a full

Today's Results
Pittsburgh 6 - ST. LOUIS 2 (10)
Chicago 1 - Cincinnati 0
Brooklyn 8 - New York 1
no other game scheduled

Standings	W-L	Pct.	GB
Cincinnati	35-27	.565	-
Brooklyn	34-30	.531	2
Chicago	35-31	.530	2
ST. LOUIS	34-32	.515	3
Boston	28-28	.500	4
Pittsburgh	30-30	.500	4
New York	30-36	.455	7
Philadelphia	25-37	.403	10

program of preliminary events to attract an audience. With the added novelties of seeing the Cardinals in a new home and seeing a team that had moved to just three games behind the champion Reds, about 20,000 customers came to the game. The crowd filled the stands and overflowed into foul territory and out onto the fringes of the outfield. They were regaled with music by two military bands and a ball game between teams representing the Great Lakes Naval Training Station and Jefferson Barracks. They also got to witness the finish of the local Junior Marathon Race.

After two and one-half hours of this, the main event, Pittsburgh vs. St. Louis, commenced.

The Pirates, spoiling the party at the end, won the contest, 6-2, in 10 innings. The game was well played, with frequent hitting and clutch fielding. Pittsburgh took the early lead, but the Cards thrilled the fans by scoring in the last two innings to tie. Then the visitors scored four runs in the first extra round to clinch the victory.

Ferdinand Schupp and Vern Clemons were the home battery. Pittsburgh started into them by loading the bases on two walks and a single. But Milt Stock snared Possum Whitted's sharp hopper and started a third-to-home double play. An infield hit loaded the bases again, but Charlie Grimm hit into a force play to end the inning.

St. Louis also loaded the bases in the first inning on two walks and a hit. But Pirate pitcher Hal Carlson coaxed an inning-ending double play ground ball from the bat of Jack Fournier.

Schupp retired the Bucs in order in the second but allowed single runs in the third and fourth innings. A triple by Carson Bigbee and a single by Max Carey produced the first tally. Two-baggers by Buster Caton and Walter Barbare accounted for the second run.

Ferdie settled down after that, although the Pirates threatened in the seventh. A Carlson single with one out was followed by a bid for another triple by Bigbee. But right fielder Joe Schultz made a great running catch in the gap. Max Carey then singled, and Billy Southworth hit a long drive to center, which Cliff Heathcote pulled down at the fence with a marvelous effort.

Meanwhile, the Knot Holers tried without success to break through against Carlson. The Pirate spitballer allowed at least one hit in every inning he worked but, with the help of fine fielding support, continually escaped trouble. In the second, with one man on, Carey robbed Clemons of extra bases with a remarkable catch in deep center. In the fourth, sixth, and seventh innings double plays checked the Red Birds.

In the eighth inning, Heathcote bypassed the Pirate fielders by hitting one into the bleachers in right field for a lead-off home run. Stock followed with a single and, one out later, stole second on a close play. Caton argued the call and even took half a swing at umpire Charlie Rigler, causing the Pirate shortstop to be ejected from the game. But when the smoke cleared, Fournier and Schultz failed to bring the runner home.

In the last of the ninth, Doc Lavan opened with a drive to the right field fence for an apparent triple. But the ball had skirted the edge of the crowd and was ruled a double on the ground rules. Lavan got rather warm disputing the point and was removed, Hal Janvrin taking his place on the basepaths. He moved to third base on Clemons's grounder and scored the tying run on Austin McHenry's pinch single to left. McHenry was out trying to stretch his hit into a double, and Burt Shotton grounded out, ending the regulation innings with a tie, 2-2.

With Schupp gone for the pinch-hitter, manager Branch Rickey called Wee Willie Sherdel into the game. The Pirates took a liking to the lefthander's slants immediately. Carey pulled a single to left. After Southworth was called out on strikes, Whitted stroked a hit to right, Carey racing to third ahead of the throw. Whitted took a wide turn at first, and third baseman Stock threw across to Fournier, trying to catch him off base. With that, Carey broke for home, and the Cards' first sacker's throw to head him off was in the dirt, the ball skipping past catcher Clemons as the winning run scored.

But Pittsburgh wasn't through yet. A walk to McKechnie and a double by Grimm made the score 4-2. Additional runs came across on Barbare's out and Walter Schmidt's double, upping the total to 6-2.

Babe Adams was brought in to pitch the bottom of the tenth. He retired the Knot Holers in order, preserving the victory for Pittsburgh.

Pittsburgh	ab	r	h	bi	o	a	e	St. Louis	ab	r	h	bi	o	a	e
C. Bigbee, lf	4	1	1	0	1	0	0	B. Shotton, lf	5	0	0	0	0	0	0
M. Carey, cf	4	1	3	1	3	0	0	C. Heathcote, cf	5	1	3	1	3	0	0
B. Southworth, rf	5	0	2	0	3	1	0	M. Stock, 3b	4	0	1	0	1	3	0
G. Whitted, 3b	5	1	2	0	1	0	0	R. Hornsby, 2b	4	0	2	0	3	5	0
B. Caton, ss	3	1	2	0	3	5	0	J. Fournier, 1b	4	0	1	0	10	0	1
B. McKechnie, ss8	0	1	0	0	1	2	0	J. Schultz, rf	4	0	2	0	2	0	0
C. Grimm, 1b	5	1	1	1	12	2	0	D. Lavan, ss	3	0	1	0	2	3	0
W. Barbare, 2b	5	0	1	2	3	5	0	H. Janvrin, pr9-ss	0	1	0	0	0	1	0
W. Schmidt, c	4	0	1	1	1	1	0	V. Clemons, c	4	0	1	0	7	1	0
H. Carlson, p	4	0	1	0	2	1	0	F. Schupp, p	3	0	2	0	2	2	0
F. Nicholson, ph10	1	0	0	0	-	-	-	A. McHenry, ph9	1	0	1	1	-	-	-
E. Adams, p10	0	0	0	0	0	0	0	W. Sherdel, p10	0	0	0	0	0	0	0
	40	6	14	5	30	17	0		37	2	14	2	30	15	1

Pittsburgh   001 100 000 4 - 6
St. Louis   000 000 011 0 - 2

	ip	h	r-er	bb	so
Carlson (W 6-5)	9	14	2-2	2	1
Adams	1	0	0-0	0	0
Schupp	9	10	2-2	3	4
Sherdel (L 4-2)	1	4	4-2	1	1

WP: Schupp
Umpires: C. Moran & C. Rigler

LOB: Pitts 9, StL 8. BE: none.
DP: Stock-Clemons, Barbare-Caton-Grimm, Carlson-Grimm, Schupp-Fournier, Grimm-Caton-Grimm.
2B: Caton, Barbare, Lavan, Grimm, Schmidt. 3B: Bigbee.
HR: Heathcote. SH: Lavan, Caton.
SB: Heathcote, Stock.
CS: Whitted, Heathcote.
Time - 2:10 Attendance - 20,000

The move to Sportsman's Park helped the Cardinals draw their best attendance in nine years. But the team was not a serious contender. It finished tied for fifth with a 75-79 record.

1921 — Monday, June 13th, at Sportsman's Park
Cardinals Humiliate Giants for Tenth Straight Victory
Unusual Plays Highlight 10-1 Win
Haines and Mann Star

Ten days ago, St. Louis was in sixth place in the National League pennant race, 11 games behind New York. Ten days and ten victories later, the Cardinals had moved up to third place, trailing the Pirates by 6½ games and the Giants by just 3½ games. The winning streak set a new St. Louis National League record.

The Monday crowd of 11,000, including ladies and Knot Hole Gang youths admitted free, was not only treated to a Cardinals victory, they were also given a chance to witness two rare plays, a triple play and a 15-foot, two-run bunt double. There were other noteworthy accomplishments as well: Leslie Mann hit two home runs, and Jesse Haines pitched his sixth consecutive victory.

Today's Results
ST. LOUIS 10 - New York 1
Pittsburgh 12 - Philadelphia 5
Brooklyn 3 - Cincinnati 1
Chicago 5 - Boston 0

Standings	W-L	Pct.	GB
Pittsburgh	34-16	.680	-
New York	32-20	.615	3
ST. LOUIS	27-22	.551	6½
Boston	25-25	.500	9
Brooklyn	26-29	.473	10½
Chicago	21-26	.447	11½
Cincinnati	21-32	.396	14½
Philadelphia	16-32	.333	17

The home team completely outclassed the New Yorkers in all phases of the game. The Giants collected seven singles and a double, while the Cardinals pounded out eight one-baggers, four two-baggers, a three-base hit, and Mann's two round-trippers. In the field, the Cards turned two double plays and made one error, while the Giants made a triple play and two miscues. On the basepaths St. Louis ran wild, and New York wandered aimlessly.

The Giants got their only run in the first inning. George Burns walked and was forced out by Dave Bancroft. Bancroft then went to third on Frank Frisch's single and scored on another force play. George Kelly also singled in the inning, but no further scoring resulted.

The Giants' lead lasted for just two pitches in the bottom of the first. After taking a ball and a strike, the Cardinal leadoff hitter, Les Mann, lined Art Nehf's third pitch into the right field bleachers for a homer. A walk to Rogers Hornsby and a single by Joe Schultz went for naught, thanks to two fine defensive plays by Frisch. The first inning ended with the score tied at 1-1.

After the Giants failed to score in their second ups, the Cardinals came in and took the lead. With one runner on base and two men out, Mann repeated his act. Once again he watched the first two pitches go by, and once again he hit the third one into the right field bleachers. This home run was a wee bit farther toward center field than the first one, and it made the score 3-1.

In the third inning the New York center fielder, Eddie Brown, entertained the fans with some weird behavior on the bases. With one out, he lifted a pop fly to shortstop and ran down the line to first base. Doc Lavan lost the ball in the sun and dropped it for an error. But Brown headed for the dugout anyhow. Luckily his first base coach, Hugh Jennings, was able to get him back to the base before the Cardinals could catch him napping. They didn't miss him the second time, however. After Kelly struck out, Brown began wandering out toward the outfield, apparently thinking that the inning was over. A quick throw from Vern Clemons to first baseman Hal Janvrin caught Brown before he realized his mistake, and the inning was indeed over.

In the St. Louis third, the Knot Holers routed Nehf and scored four runs. Hornsby started with a one-out triple over Burns's head. He scored, and Schultz raced to second when the latter's pop fly dropped in front of Brown. Austin McHenry singled for another run, spelling the end for Nehf. Rosy Ryan took over the pitching chores and proceeded to give up an RBI single to Clemons and a run-scoring double to Haines before retiring the side.

In the fifth inning Ryan pulled a "Brown" on the bases. After a bunt single, Ryan was on first, while Burns worked the count to 3-and-2. The next pitch was a called strike, but the runner, thinking it was ball four, began walking toward second base. Clemons threw down to Lavan, and Ryan was tagged out for an easy double play.

In the last of the fifth the Giants further embarrassed themselves. With McHenry on third and two out, catcher Earl Smith threw wildly back to the pitcher, allowing the runner to score.

In the seventh the humiliation was completed. Schultz and McHenry started off with singles for St. Louis. Lavan then laid down a bunt, which rolled about 15 feet up the third base line. The new Giant catcher, Alex Gaston, grabbed the ball just when he thought it went foul. However, umpire Ernie Quigley ruled that the ball was fair. Gaston and pitcher Ryan immediately began disputing the call and didn't notice McHenry steaming around third until he was already across the plate. With the damage apparently done, the argument commenced again, and again a Cardinal runner, Schultz this time, was able to sprint past Gaston and Ryan to score. The Giant batterymen were still intent on arguing, but Frisch was finally able to get the ball away from them and to hold Lavan at second with a "double."

With the game well in hand, the Cardinals treated the fans by hitting into a triple play in the eighth. A Jack Fournier single and a Milt Stock walk placed runners on first and second, as Hornsby came to the plate. With the hit-and-run in the works, Rogers lined a wicked shot toward right. But second baseman John Monroe made a leaping catch of the liner and threw to Kelly at first, doubling Stock. Kelly then threw toward second, but Stock intercepted the throw! Fournier was still near third and had no chance of getting back to second, so Milt sheepishly flipped the ball to Bill Patterson, the shortstop, completing the triple killing.

After Haines retired the Giants in the ninth, the fun was over, St. Louis winning by a final score of 10-1.

New York	ab	r	h	bi	o	a	e
G. Burns, lf	4	0	1	0	2	0	0
D. Bancroft, ss	4	1	1	0	2	6	0
B. Patterson, ss8	0	0	0	0	1	0	0
F. Frisch, 3b	4	0	1	0	1	5	0
E. Brown, cf	4	0	1	1	2	0	1
G. Kelly, 1b	3	0	1	0	11	2	0
C. Walker, rf	4	0	0	0	0	0	0
J. Monroe, 2b	3	0	0	0	2	4	0
E. Smith, c	2	0	0	0	2	0	1
A. Gaston, c6	2	0	0	0	0	0	0
A. Nehf, p	1	0	1	0	0	0	0
R. Ryan, p3	2	0	1	0	1	3	0
R. Youngs, ph10	1	0	1	0	-	-	-
G. Rapp, pr10	0	0	0	0	-	-	-
	34	1	8	1	24	20	2

St. Louis	ab	r	h	bi	o	a	e
L. Mann, cf	3	2	2	3	4	0	0
J. Smith, ph6-cf	2	0	1	0	2	0	0
H. Janvrin, 1b	2	0	0	0	3	0	0
J. Fournier, ph4-1b	2	0	1	0	2	0	0
M. Stock, 3b	4	0	0	0	0	1	0
R. Hornsby, 2b	4	1	1	0	7	2	0
J. Schultz, rf	4	2	3	1	1	0	0
A. McHenry, lf	4	3	3	1	1	0	0
D. Lavan, ss	3	0	1	2	1	2	1
V. Clemons, c	4	1	2	1	6	2	0
J. Haines, p	4	1	1	1	0	1	0
	36	10	15	9	27	8	1

New York   100 000 000 - 1
St. Louis   124 010 20x - 10

	ip	h	r-er	bb	so
Nehf (L 7-3)	2.1	7	6-6	1	0
Ryan	5.2	8	4-3	1	1
Haines (W 7-4)	9	8	1-1	3	6

SB: McHenry. CS: Ryan
Umpires: E. Quigley & G. Hart

LOB: NY 9, StL 6. BE: NY 1, StL 1.
DP: Clemons-Janvrin, Clemons-Lavan.
TP: Monroe-Kelly-Patterson.
2B: Schultz, Clemons, Haines, Lavan, Brown. 3B: Hornsby.
HR: Mann 2. SH: Lavan, Fournier.
Time - 1:50   Attendance - 11,000

St. Louis's winning streak ended the next day. The Cardinals fell back into fifth place in late July. But they finished very strongly, winding up in third place. The club's final record was 87-66, giving them their best percentage since the American Association days.

1922—Saturday, July 22nd, at Sportsman's Park
Cardinals Rally to Win, 9-8, Move Into First Place
Six Runs in Eighth Inning Beat Boston
Gives St. Louis Lead in Both Major Leagues for First Time in History

The irresistible Saint Louis Cardinal batting attack did it again this afternoon. After falling behind the Boston Braves, 8-2, the Knot Holers scored one run in the seventh inning and six runs in the eighth inning to win the game, 9-8. It was the second straight day in which they had beaten Boston with six in the eighth and the fourth time in a row that they had overcome a Boston lead to win.

The victory was the fifth in a row for the Cards and moved them into first place in the National League race. Over in the American League, the St. Louis Browns upped their lead over the New York Yankees to 2½ games. Today was the first instance in history that the two local teams had led their respective leagues at the same time. It was also the first time the Cardinals had ever led the N.L. later than the fifth week of the season. Tonight St. Louis fans were dreaming of seeing the World Series.

Today's Results
ST. LOUIS 9 — Boston 8
Cincinnati 3 - New York 2
Brooklyn 7 - Chicago 6
Pittsburgh 8 - Philadelphia 7

Standings	W-L	Pct.	GB
ST. LOUIS	57-35	.620	-
New York	52-33	.612	1½
Chicago	47-42	.528	8½
Cincinnati	48-43	.527	8½
Brooklyn	44-45	.4944	11½
Pittsburgh	43-44	.4943	11½
Philadelphia	31-53	.369	27
Boston	29-56	.341	29½

About 15,000 people were in attendance at Sportsman's Park today to watch the match between the Cardinals and the Braves.

Bill Pertica was the starting pitcher for the home team. He and outfielder Heinie Mueller presented the visitors with a gift run in the first inning. With two out, Walton Cruise was walked. Tony Boeckel followed with a drive to the left field fence, which Mueller misplayed, allowing Cruise to score.

Boston starter Hugh McQuillan injured a finger in the first inning and was replaced in the second.

The Braves scored another run in the second, routing Pertica. Hod Ford opened with a triple past Mueller, and Larry Kopf drove him in with a double. Lou North succeeded to the pitching duties at this point. With the help of a botched hit-and-run play, he retired the side.

The Cardinals rallied in the bottom of the third. Boston changed pitchers twice during the inning, but St. Louis only got one run, that coming on a bases-loaded walk.

Boston upped its lead to 5-1 with five hits in the fourth. Two of the runs came as a result of a pop fly that Rogers Hornsby, Max Flack, and Del Gainor all allowed to drop. But for a double play, the Braves might have scored more.

The home team got one run in the fifth on a walk by Jack Smith, a single by Hornsby, and an infield force out off the bat by Mueller. Heinie was thrown out trying for second on an overthrow, killing the rally.

Jeff Pfeffer came in to pitch for St. Louis in the fifth, and he was touched for two runs in the sixth and one in the seventh. In each of those innings, Boston left runners on second and third. It didn't seem to matter much, however, since they built an 8-2 lead. The Braves ran the bases unmolestedly, stealing four sacks and taking another on a passed ball. The fickle fans loudly derided the Cardinals' rookie catcher, Harry McCurdy.

The Cardinals earned a few cheers by scoring a run in the bottom of the seventh on doubles by Smith and Hornsby. The hit raised Rogers's average to over .400.

Still, the Knot Holers trailed by five runs entering the last of the eighth. Milt Stock led off with a looping single to left, and McCrudy worked pitcher Frank Miller for a walk. Specs Toporcer hit a drive to deep right, which was caught. Joe Schultz was sent up to bat for Pfeffer. With a full count, he hit a deep drive to left. Outfielder Al Nixon slipped slightly as he started for the ball, and it went to the fence for a two-run double. It was Schultz's fourth consecutive hit as a pinch-batter.

Flack popped up for out number two. Smith followed with a grounder that should have ended the inning. But shortstop Ford's throw to first was in the dirt for an error. That brought up the mighty Hornsby, whose home run on Wednesday had beaten Miller in the ninth inning. This time the Rajah stepped into the first pitch and lined it into right field for a double, scoring Schultz and sending Smith to third.

Now it was Mueller's turn to bat. A St. Louis boy, Heinie had gone hitless in three at bats and had looked bad in the field. Now was his chance to redeem himself in front of the home fans. Pitcher Miller fell behind, two balls and nothing, and came in with the third pitch. Mueller cracked it cleanly into center field, knocking in the tying runs.

Pandemonium broke loose. The fans smashed straw hats and tore up scorecards and threw them onto the field. It was the end for Miller, young Tim McNamara taking over on the mound. Les Mann went in to run for Mueller at first. Gainor beat out an infield hit, moving Mann to second. Stock delivered his second hit of the inning, a sharp grounder through the right side, and Mann streaked home with the lead run.

Once again, the cheering was long and loud, and it continued right on through the Braves' ninth. Taking no chances, Cardinal manager Branch Rickey put in his ace battery of Willie Sherdel and Ed Ainsmith. The only trouble was a two-out, infield single by Fred Nicholson. Then Walter Barbare flied out to end the game.

The Cardinals pranced off the field with a 9-8 victory and the league lead. And the fans filed out onto the streets with visions of an all-St. Louis World Series dancing in their heads.

Boston	ab	r	h	bi	o	a	e
R. Powell, cf	3	2	2	2	1	0	0
W. Barbare, ph9	1	0	0	0	-	-	-
A. Nixon, lf	5	0	3	2	1	0	0
W. Cruise, rf	3	1	2	2	4	0	0
T. Boeckel, 3b	4	0	1	1	0	1	0
W. Holke, 1b	5	0	0	0	10	1	0
H. Ford, ss	5	1	3	0	4	5	2
L. Kopf, 2b	5	1	1	1	1	2	0
F. Gibson, c	4	2	2	0	3	2	0
H. McQuillan, p	0	0	0	0	0	1	0
J. Oeschger, ph2-p	1	0	0	0	0	1	0
G. Braxton, p3	0	0	0	0	0	0	0
F. Miller, p3	3	1	1	0	0	0	0
T. McNamara, p8	0	0	0	0	0	0	0
F. Nicholson, ph9	1	0	1	0	-	-	-
	40	8	16	8	24	13	2

St. Louis	ab	r	h	bi	o	a	e
M. Flack, rf	5	1	1	0	2	0	0
J. Smith, cf	4	3	2	0	3	0	0
R. Hornsby, 2b	4	1	3	2	2	6	0
H. Mueller, lf	4	0	1	3	2	0	1
L. Mann, pr8-lf	0	1	0	0	1	0	0
J. Fournier, 1b	1	0	0	3	0	0	0
D. Gainor, ph3-1b	3	0	1	1	5	0	0
M. Stock, 3b	5	1	3	1	2	0	0
H. McCurdy, c	4	1	2	0	2	1	0
E. Ainsmith, c9	0	0	0	0	0	0	0
D. Lavan, ss	1	0	1	0	3	3	0
S. Toporcer, ph6-ss	2	0	0	0	2	0	0
B. Pertica, p	0	0	0	0	0	0	0
L. North, p2	1	0	0	0	0	1	0
B. Shotton, ph4	1	0	0	0	-	-	-
J. Pfeffer, p5	1	0	0	0	0	3	0
J. Schultz, ph8	1	1	1	2	-	-	-
W. Sherdel, p9	0	0	0	0	0	0	0
	37	9	15	9	27	14	1

Boston	110	302	100	-	8
St. Louis	001	010	16x	-	9

	ip	h	r-er	bb	so
McQuillan	1	1	0-0	0	1
Oeschger	1.1	2	1-1	3	0
Braxton	*0	0	0-0	1	0
Miller (L 6-7)	5.1	10	8-4	2	2
McNamara	.1	2	0-0	0	0
Pertica	#1	3	2-2	2	0
North	3	6	3-3	2	2
Pfeffer (W 11-6)	4	6	3-3	2	0
Sherdel	1	1	0-0	0	0

*faced one batter in third
#faced two batters in second
Balk: Oeschger. WP: Miller.
PB: McCurdy.

LOB: Bos 11, StL 10. BE: StL 2.
DP: Lavan-Hornsby-Fournier, Lavan-Hornsby-Gainor, Gibson-Ford, Ford-Holke-Ford, Ford-Kopf-Holke.
2B: Boeckel, Kopf, Cruise, Gibson, Powell, Hornsby 2, Schultz.
3B: Ford, McCurdy.
SB: Smith, Boeckel, Kopf, Powell, Cruise. CS: Lavan.

Time - 2:33
Attendance - 15,000
Umpires: E. Quigley & C. Moran

Alas, the World Series did not come to St. Louis in 1922. The Cardinals fell off the pace in August and wound up tied for third, 8 games behind the pennant-winning Giants.

The Browns finished in second place, 1 game behind the Yankees.

1923 — Tuesday, July 10th, at Braves Field, Boston

Rookie Johnny Stuart Pitches Cards to Two Victories Over Braves

Allows Just 13 Hits in Winning 11-1 & 6-3

His First Starts of Season

For the first game of today's doubleheader, with his team floundering and his pitching staff exhausted, St. Louis manager Branch Rickey gave young Johnny Stuart his first chance to start a game this year. After the youngster breezed through the first game, he gamely volunteered to pitch the second game and proceeded to win that one, too.

The former Ohio State football and baseball star signed a professional contract less than one year ago, and in his only previous major league start, on July 27th, 1922, he failed to retire even one better. After being farmed to Syracuse last year, he completed four of 15 minor league games, but this year he had been used strictly in relief by the Cardinals. Until today, that is. When he was finally given a chance, he used it to carve a niche for himself in the baseball record book by pitching two complete game victories in one day.

Today's Results
ST. LOUIS 11 - Boston 1 (1st game)
ST. LOUIS 6 - Boston 3 (2nd game)
New York 9 - Pittsburgh 8 (10 inn.)
Cincinnati 7 - Philadelphia 2 (10)
Brooklyn 9 - Chicago 0

Standings	W-L	Pct.	GB
New York	50-25	.667	-
Pittsburgh	44-28	.611	4½
Cincinnati	43-29	.597	5½
Brooklyn	39-34	.534	10
Chicago	40-37	.519	11
ST. LOUIS	38-41	.481	14
Philadelphia	22-52	.297	27½
Boston	22-52	.297	27½

Both teams presented makeshift lineups in the opening game. With Jim Bottomley out with arm trouble, Rickey shifted Rogers Hornsby to first base and placed Spec Toporcer at second and Doc Lavan at shortstop. Boston pilot Fred Mitchell had two outfielders in the infield, Gus Felix at third base and Billy Southworth at second. The regular third sacker, Tony Boeckel, was stationed at short.

The game opened with Southworth muffing his first professional infield chance on a ground ball, Max Flack reaching first. Jack Smith walked, and Rogers Hornsby singled to center, plating the first run. Hi Myers's short fly fell between Boeckel and center fielder Ray Powell for a double and another run, and a third run scored on Milt Stock's fly out.

Given a three-run cushion, Stuart took the mound and retired the home team in order in the first inning. In the next frame, Stuffy McInnis hit him for a triple and scored on an infield out, cutting the lead to 3-1.

After Al Nixon's spectacular catch robbed Smith of an extra-base hit in the St. Louis third, Hornsby doubled off the distant left field fence and eventually scored on Toporcer's single.

A four-run rally in the fourth knocked Boston starter Dana Fillingim out of the box. Tim McNamara replaced the spitballer and was charged with one of the runs. Stuart's single started the hitting, and Flack, Smith, Myers, and Stock also contributed safeties.

Hits by Smith, Hornsby, Stock, and Toporcer added up to two more runs in the sixth inning, and Stock's triple and Toporcer's foul out plated the final run in the ninth.

Meanwhile, Stuart disposed of the hapless Braves with little difficulty. He walked only two batters, both in the third inning, and, after McInnis's triple, the only Boston hits were singles by Bill Bagwell in the fourth and McInnis in the sixth. After eliminating the last base-runner on a double play, Stuart retired the Braves in order through the last three rounds. In the eighth, he needed only four pitches to get the job done. The home team failed to get the ball out of the infield in the ninth, and Stuart had himself a three-hit, 11-1 victory.

The first game had gone so easily for Stuart, especially at the end, that he told Rickey he felt strong enough to pitch the second game. The manager gladly accepted the offer, and Johnny went out and won again. This game was not quite as easy, Boston collecting ten hits. The youngster looked mighty tired at the end, but he finished the game.

Once again, he was staked to a three-run lead before he took the mound. The Cardinals used exactly the same starting lineup as in the opening game, and the first five men got singles off Joe Oeschger, the Boston pitcher.

Two singles and Hi Myers's inside-the-park home run to the 500-foot center field fence made the score 6-0 in the second inning. Joe Genewich then relieved Oeschger, and he held the big Cardinal bats at bay for the next six innings, allowing just two hits. Frank Miller shut St. Louis out in the ninth inning.

But Boston couldn't overcome the big deficit against Stuart. They scored one run in the second round on a bunt single by Boeckel and Earl Smith's double. But fine fielding plays by Jack Smith and Stock squelched the rally.

The Braves were held scoreless in the next five innings, but in the eighth it looked as if they might finally finish the Cardinal hurler off. Felix, pinch-hitting, drew a walk, and Frank Gibson, another pincher, popped a hit into short right, which Flack fumbled, putting runners on second and third. Nixon then shot a single to center, scoring Felix. Powell's long fly drove Gibson across, making the score 6-3. After another fly out, McInnis singled, putting men on first and third and bringing the tying run to the plate. But Boeckel's hard smash went straight to Smith in left, ending the inning.

In the ninth, an infield hit and a base on balls gave the few remaining home fans hope, but Stuart retained his composure, and the runners were left on first and second. The final score was 6-3.

The secret of Stuart's success today was his economy of effort. He didn't strike out a single man. Instead, he let his fielders do the work.

FIRST GAME

St. Louis	ab	r	h	bi	o	a	e		Boston	ab	r	h	bi	o	a	e
M. Flack, rf	5	2	1	0	3	0	0		A. Nixon, rf	3	0	0	0	5	0	0
J. Smith, lf	4	2	3	1	2	0	0		R. Powell, cf	4	0	0	1	5	0	0
R. Hornsby, 1b	4	3	3	2	9	0	1		B. Southworth, 2b	3	0	0	0	2	3	1
H. Freigau, 1b8	0	0	0	0	2	0	0		S. McInnis, 1b	4	1	2	0	5	1	0
H. Myers, cf	4	1	2	2	2	0	0		T. Boeckel, ss	4	0	0	0	1	2	0
L. Mann, pr6-cf	1	1	0	0	3	0	0		G. Felix, 3b	4	0	0	1	0	0	0
M. Stock, 3b	3	1	3	3	0	4	0		B. Bagwell, lf	3	0	1	0	4	0	0
R. Blades, 3b9	0	0	0	0	0	0	0		M. O'Neill, c	3	0	0	0	4	2	0
S. Toporcer, 2b	4	0	2	2	5	3	0		D. Fillingim, p	0	0	0	0	0	1	0
H. McCurdy, c	5	0	0	0	0	0	0		T. McNamara, p4	3	0	0	0	1	1	0
D. Lavan, ss	5	0	0	1	2	0										
J. Stuart, p	4	1	1	0	0	2	0									
	39	11	15	10	27	11	1			31	1	3	1	27	10	1

| St. Louis | 301 | 402 | 001 | - | 11 |
| Boston | 010 | 000 | 000 | - | 1 |

LOB: StL 6, Bos. 5. BE: StL 1,
Bos 1. DP: Toporcer-Hornsby,
O'Neill-Southworth.
2B: Myers, Hornsby, Flack, Smith.
3B: McInnis, Stock.
SH: Stock, Torporcer
SB: Myers. CS: Smith.
Time - 1:46 Attendance - 1,500

	ip	h	r-er	bb	so
Stuart (W 3-0)	9	3	1-1	2	0
Fillingim (L 0-4)	3.1	7	6-5	1	1
McNamara	5.2	8	5-5	1	2

HBP: by Fillingim (Stock), by Stuart (Nixon)
Umpires: C. Moran & G. Hart.

SECOND GAME

					r	h	e	Batteries
St. Louis	330	000	000	-	6	11	1	J. Stuart (W 4-0) & H. McCurdy
Boston	010	000	020	-	3	10	1	J. Oeschger (L 2-8) 2.2 IP,
								J. Genewich 5.1 IP, F. Miller 1 IP & E. Smith.

Stuart's iron man performance was not enough to get the Cards out of the second divison. They finished in fifth place with a 79-74 won-lost record. Stuart finished with a 9-5 mark.

1924 — Tuesday, September 16th, at Ebbet's Field, Brooklyn

Bottomley Bats in Twelve Runs as Cardinals Rout Dodgers

Gets Six Hits in 17-3 Victory

Sets New Record for RBI's

The 1924 season was mostly a disappointment for the St. Louis Cardinals. They fell into the second division on the third day of the season, and by mid-July they were stuck in sixth place for good. Their only redeeming moments came from outstanding individual achievements and from beating the teams battling for the pennant. Rogers Hornsby kept his batting average at a record level. Jess Haines pitched a no-hitter. And Herman Bell pitched a complete doubleheader in which he allowed just six hits. Against the contenders this month, they had beaten the Pirates three times and the Giants once.

Then today they got to experience both kinds of satisfaction. Not only did they beat the second-place Dodgers, in addition, Jim Bottomley shattered all records by knocking twelve runs across the plate during the game.

Today's Results
ST. LOUIS 17 - Brooklyn 3
New York 5 - Cincinnati 1 (1st game)
Cincinnati 3 - New York 1 (2nd game)
Philadelphia 6 - Pittsburgh 5 (1st)
Pittsburgh 13 - Philadelphia 7 (2nd)
Chicago 8 - Boston 3 (1st)
Chicago 4 - Boston 2 (12 inn.) (2nd)

Standings	W-L	Pct.	GB
New York	87-56	.608	-
Brooklyn	86-58	.597	1½
Pittsburgh	83-57	.593	2½
Chicago	76-64	.543	9½
Cincinnati	77-66	.538	10
ST. LOUIS	60-83	.420	27
Philadelphia	52-90	.366	34½
Boston	48-95	.366	39

It was a bad day all around for Brooklyn manager Wilbert Robinson. Not only were his "Robins" trounced, 17-3, but he saw his record of 11 RBI's, set back in 1892, finally broken.

The St. Louis attack included 10 singles, two doubles, four triples, and two home runs. Bottomley himself accounted for three one-baggers, a two-baser, and both homers, one of which came with the bases loaded. Pitcher Willie Sherdel was the second-leading Cardinal hitter with two singles and a double.

With the Robins trailing the Giants by just one game, Robinson chose rookie Rube Ehrhardt as his pitcher. The youngster had completed each of his last five starts, winning them all, while allowing a total of just seven runs. Today he couldn't even get one man out in the first inning. Heinie Mueller started off with a walk, and Taylor Douthit beat out a hit to shortstop. Slugger Hornsby caught the defense by surprise by laying down a bunt single. That loaded the bases for the real slugger of the day, Bottomley. Jim started his record assault in somewhat modest fashion, lining a two-run single to center field. When Chick Hafey followed with a two-run triple, Robinson replaced Ehrhardt with Bonnie Hollingsworth. The new man retired the side quickly, leaving Hafey on third.

In the second inning, Hollingsworth was not so effective. Two walks and two outs preceded Bottomley's at bat. This time Jim shot a double past third base, scoring one run.

After the Dodgers scored a run in the bottom of the second, and both teams failed to score in the third, Bottomley came to bat again in the fourth. With men on second and third and one out, the new Dodger pitcher, Art Decatur, gave Hornsby an intentional pass, loading 'em up for Sunny Jim. Not taking kindly to this insult to his hitting ability, Bottomley unloaded the bases with a grand-slam home run over the right field wall.

Decatur was still pitching when the Nokomis, Illinois, slugger came to bat in the sixth. One man was out and one was on base this time, but the result was the same, a homer over the fence and onto Bedford Avenue. To add insult to the injury, Hafey, Mike Gonzalez, and Jimmy Cooney followed with hits (Gonzalez getting a triple) to add two more runs, bringing the count to 13-1.

With the game out of hand, Robinson decided to try his recruit lefthander, Tex

Wilson, in the seventh. Mueller's infield hit, a late throw to second on Douthit's bunt, and Hornsby's sacrifice set the stage for Bottomley. With two "ducks on the pond," he pulled a single to right, scoring both men and bringing his total for the day to 11 RBI's.

In the eighth the Cardinals actually scored a run without the aid of their clean-up hitter. Sherdel's single and Mueller's triple with two out did the trick.

In the home half of the eighth, the first two hitters, Zack Taylor and Andy High, singled, and Taylor scored on a double play.

With Bottomley needing one more run-batted-in to break the record, teammate Rogers Hornsby obligingly opened the ninth inning with a triple into the left field corner. Not wishing to have a winded runner on base, Rickey sent Ray Blades in to take the Rajah's place on third. Facing the fifth Brooklyn pitcher of the day, Jim Roberts, Bottomley singled to right, driving Blades home. Figuring that Jim had done his share for the cause, Rickey then sent Jack Smith in to pinch-run for the slugger. Jack was promptly picked off base.

Rookie Flint Rhem, the South Carolina fastballer, was brought in to show his stuff in the bottom of the ninth. The newcomer was very wild. He walked three men, gave up a hit, and uncorked a two-base wild pitch. A passed ball was thrown in, also, but a lucky double play on a line drive held the Brooklyns to just one run, and the final score was 17-3.

Four different Cardinals had scored three runs each, and six had gotten extra-base hits, but there was definitely one man who stood out from the rest, Bottomley. Sunny Jim finished the game with six hits, three runs scored, twelve runs-batted-in, and the same cheerful disposition he had always displayed, win or lose.

St. Louis	ab	r	h	bi	o	a	e
H. Mueller, rf-1b9	3	3	2	1	4	0	0
T. Douthit, cf	3	3	1	0	2	0	0
R. Hornsby, 2b	4	2	2	0	2	2	0
R. Blades, pr9-2b	0	1	0	0	1	0	0
J. Bottomley, 1b	6	3	6	12	5	0	0
J. Smith, pr9-rf	0	0	0	0	0	0	0
C. Hafey, lf	6	1	2	2	3	1	0
M. Gonzalez, c	4	1	1	1	2	0	0
V. Clemons, c6	2	0	0	0	1	0	0
S. Toporcer, 3b	1	0	0	0	0	0	0
J. Cooney, 3b1	4	0	1	1	0	0	0
T. Thevenow, ss	5	0	0	0	6	4	0
W. Sherdel, p	4	3	3	0	1	0	0
F. Rhem, p9	0	0	0	0	0	0	0
	42	17	18	17	27	7	0

Brooklyn	ab	r	h	bi	o	a	e
A. High, 2b	4	0	2	0	4	0	0
J. Mitchell, ss	4	0	1	0	1	4	0
Z. Wheat, lf	4	0	0	0	3	0	0
J. Fournier, 1b	2	1	0	0	5	1	1
D. Loftus, 1b7	1	0	1	0	3	0	0
E. Brown, cf	4	0	1	0	3	0	0
M. Stock, 3b	3	1	1	0	1	1	0
T. Griffith, rf	2	0	0	0	2	0	0
H. DeBerry, c	3	0	1	1	4	0	0
R. Ehrhardt, p	0	0	0	0	0	0	0
B. Hollingsworth, p1	1	0	0	0	0	0	0
A. Decatur, p4	0	0	0	0	1	1	0
J. Johnstone, ph6	1	0	1	0	-	-	-
T. Wilson, p7	0	0	0	0	0	1	0
Z. Taylor, ph8	1	1	1	0	-	-	-
J. Roberts, p9	0	0	0	0	0	1	0
C. Hargreaves, ph9	1	0	0	0	-	-	-
	31	3	9	1	27	9	1

St. Louis   410 404 211 - 17
Brooklyn   010 000 011 - 3

	ip	h	r-er	bb	so
Sherdel (W 6-9)	8	8	2-2	2	1
Rhem	1	1	1-0	3	0
Ehrhardt (L 5-2)	*0	4	4-4	1	0
Hollingsworth	#3	2	3-3	3	2
Decatur	3	6	6-5	2	0
Wilson	2	4	3-3	0	1
Roberts	1	2	1-1	0	0

*faced five batters in first
WP: Decatur, Rhem. PB: Clemons

LOB: StL 7, Bkn 6. BE: none.
DP: Thevenow-Hornsby,
Thevenow-Hornsby-Bottomley,
Mueller (unassisted).
2B: Bottomley, Sherdel. 3B: Hafey,
Gonzales, Mueller, Hornsby.
HR: Bottomley 2.
SH: Douthit 2, Hornsby.
Time - 1:55
Attendance - 3,000
#faced two batters in fourth
Umpires: B. Klem & F. Wilson

Eleven days later, the season ended for the Cardinals. They finished sixth, 28½ games out. Their final record was 65-89.

Brooklyn finished second, 1½ games behind New York.

Bottomley's record still stands, over 50 years later.

1925 — Wednesday, April 22nd, at Sportsman's Park
Cardinals Score 11 Runs in First Inning of Home Opener
Defeat Cincinnati Reds, 12-3
Set Record with Eleven Singles in One Inning

The St. Louis Cardinals opened the local National League season with a wallop, scoring 11 runs in their very first inning in front of the home crowd and coasting to a 12-3 victory over the Cincinnati Reds. After the first-round burst, the Knot Holers made just two more hits, but Flint Rhem pitched effectively, and his defensive support was brilliant.

Prior to today, the Cardinals had played seven games on the road, losing the first three then winning four in a row.

This afternoon's home opener was preceded by a full program of ceremonies. Newly-elected Mayor Victor Miller was at

Today's Results
ST. LOUIS 12 — Cincinnati 3
New York 6 - Boston 5
Philadelphia 8 - Brooklyn 7
Pittsburgh 6 - Chicago 1

Standings	W-L	Pct.	GB
New York	5-1	.833	-
ST. LOUIS	5-3	.625	1
Cincinnati	5-3	.625	1
Philadelphia	3-2	.600	1½
Pittsburgh	3-5	.375	3
Chicago	3-5	.375	3
Brooklyn	2-4	.333	3
Boston	1-4	.200	3½

the center of the events. First, His Honor led both teams in a march from home plate to the center field flag pole. This being the National League's 50th season, a Golden Jubilee Banner was raised up the staff after Old Glory. For Opening Day, the band struck up "The Star-Spangled Banner," while the players stood, bare-headed, at attention. The athletes then returned to the infield, and the mayor went to the mound to hurl the first pitch. Actually, he held forth for five deliveries, while some irreverent fans pitched a few lemons in his direction. Then the mayor retired to a front-row box occupied by former mayor Henry Kiel and several other distinguished guests.

As the players took the field, delegations of fans presented flowers to manager Branch Rickey and to left fielder Ray Blades.

Obviously inspired by the festivities, the batters then took over the show.

The visiting Reds scored two runs in their first ups. With one out, Babe Pinelli hit a pop fly single behind second base, which Rogers Hornsby got his glove on but dropped. Edd Roush then drove a ball off the right center field fence, which Heinie Mueller misplayed into a triple, Pinelli scoring. Roush counted on Rube Bressler's single to center.

The Red Birds came to bat, trailing 2-0. Pete Donohue was the Cincinnati pitcher. He had shut the Cardinals out in the season opener in Cincy a week before and had beaten Pittsburgh on Saturday, 12-2. But today it was a different story. Ray Blades led off with a single to right and took third on Wattie Holm's single to center. Rogers Hornsby pulled a single to left to drive Blades in. Jim Bottomley singled up the middle to score the second run. Cincinnati manager Jack Hendricks then removed Donohue and brought Tom Sheehan in.

The new hurler retired Les Bell on a weak grounder to short, while the go-ahead run crossed the plate. Then the barrage resumed. Heinie Mueller shot a single to center and wound up on third on Roush's fumble, Bottomley counting. Mike Gonzalez hit a one-bagger to the same sector, Bell sauntering across the dish. Tommy Thevenow smashed a single off Sheehan's glove. Rhem got into the act by dropping a hit to center, with Gonzalez scoring and Thevenow racing to third. Tommy was caught between bases after Blades tapped to the mound, but Holm picked up the assault again with a single to right, good for another run.

Hendricks went back to the mound to remove Sheehan, and Cuban righthander Pedro Dibut came in. After Hornsby delivered yet another run-scoring single, Bottomley varied the pattern by knocking a two-base hit into right, driving in Holm and sending Hornsby to third. Bell then plated two more runs with a single past third. It was the Cardinals' 11th single of the inning, a new all-time record.

It also made the score 11-2 and brought Hendricks trudging out to the mound yet again. Dibut was relieved by Harry Biemiller. Mueller finally brought the rally to an end by hitting a line drive directly into the hands of right fielder Curt Walker.

Thereafter, Biemiller had little trouble with the home team. The only hit he allowed in six innings was a double by Holm in the fifth. Holm's hit, which was fumbled by Elmer Smith, drove in Rhem, who had been hit by a pitch.

With a nine-run lead going into the second inning, Rhem proceeded to walk two Reds. But a great play deep in the hole by Thevenow produced the inning-ending force out, and Cincinnati failed to score.

The Reds were able to score in the third. After Roush was retired on a fine play involving Bell and Bottomley, Bressler doubled down the first base line. He scored on Walker's single to right. A fumble by Thevenow gave Smith a life, but Ike Caveney fanned, and Bubbles Hargrave bounced out.

Rhem was in trouble frequently but pitched out of it using an explosive fastball and a deceptive change of pace. The fielding of his teammates helped him out, too. A fast play by Hornsby nipped Roush at first base in the fourth inning after Pinelli's two-out double. The famous hitter also made a nice play to retire Bressler in the fifth. A fast 4-6-3 double play in the seventh, with two on and one out, again foiled the Reds. Hughie Critz led off the ninth with a hard liner that Hornsby, the fielding star of the day, snared with one hand. Roush got a last-ditch, two-out single, but Bressler ended the game with a pop out to Bell.

The 12-3 victory stretched the St. Louis winning streak to five games and put them into a tie for second place with the Reds. It was an auspicious way to open the home season.

Cincinnati	ab	r	h	bi	o	a	e	St. Louis	ab	r	h	bi	o	a	e
H. Critz, 2b	5	0	0	0	1	5	0	R. Blades, lf	5	2	2	0	1	0	0
B. Pinelli, 3b	5	1	3	0	1	1	0	W. Holm, rf	5	2	3	2	3	0	0
E. Roush, cf	5	1	2	1	1	0	1	R. Hornsby, 2b	5	2	2	2	4	5	0
R. Bressler, 1b	4	1	2	1	14	0	0	J. Bottomley, 1b	5	2	2	2	15	0	0
C. Walker, rf	4	0	1	1	4	0	0	L. Bell, 3b	4	0	1	0	3	3	0
E. Smith, lf	4	0	0	0	0	0	1	H. Mueller, cf	4	1	1	1	1	0	0
I. Caveney, ss	3	0	2	0	1	4	0	M. Gonzalez, c	3	1	1	1	2	0	0
B. Hargrave, c	4	0	0	0	2	2	0	T. Thevenow, ss	4	0	1	0	1	5	1
P. Donohue, p	0	0	0	0	0	0	0	F. Rhem, p	3	2	1	1	0	2	0
T. Sheehan, p1	0	0	0	0	0	1	0								
P. Dibut, p1	0	0	0	0	0	0	0								
H. Biemiller, p1	2	0	0	0	0	1	0								
B. Fowler, ph8	1	0	0	0	-	-	-								
N. Brady, p8	0	0	0	0	0	0	0								
	37	3	10	3	24	14	2		38	12	14	12	27	15	1

Cincinnati   2 0 1   000   000   -   3
St. Louis   (11)00 010   00x   -   12

	ip	h	r-er	bb	so
Donohue (L 2-1)	*0	4	4-4	0	0
Sheehan	.2	5	5-5	0	0
Dibut	#0	3	2-2	0	0
Biemiller	6.1	1	1-1	1	2
Brady	1	1	0-0	0	0
Rhem (W 1-0)	9	10	3-3	3	2

*faced four batters in first
#faced three batters in first

LOB: Cinc 10, StL 4. BE: Cinc 1.
DP: Hornsby-Thevenow-Bottomley.
2B: Bottomley, Bressler, Pinelli, Holm, Caveney.
3B: Roush.
SB: Caveney.
HBP: by Biemiller (Rhem)
Time - 1:47
Attendance - 15,500 total, 14,000 paid
Umpires: C. Moran, F. Wilson, & E. Quigley

The Cardinals lost their next seven games, all at home, and fell to last place. With the team still in the cellar, Rogers Hornsby replaced Branch Rickey as manager on Memorial Day.

The Cardinals did better under their new manager, but didn't get above .500 until the last week of the season. They finished in fourth place with a 77-76 record.

Chapter VI

Pennants!
1926-1931

1926—August 31st at Sportsman's Park
Cardinals Take Two from Pirates, Move into League Lead

1926 World Series—Game #7
Alexander & Thevenow Star as Cardinals Win World Series

1927—September 4th at Chicago
Triple Play Helps St. Louis Edge Chicago, 2-1

1928—September 20th at New York
Harper Hits Three Homers in Game as Cardinals Retain Lead

1928 World Series—Game #4
Ruth Hits Three Homers as Yankees Complete Sweep

1929—July 6th at Philadelphia
Cards Lose 11th in a Row, Then Crush Phillies, 28-6

1930—September 16th at Brooklyn
St. Louis Takes League Lead with Thrilling, 1-0 Victory

1930 World Series—Game #5
A's Win, as Foxx's Homer Ruins Masterpiece by Grimes

1931—July 12th at Sportsman's Park
Overflow Crowd Makes a Farce of Games as Cards and Cubs Split

1931 World Series—Game #7
Cardinals Take Series on Base Running & Watkins's Home Run

In 1926, the Cardinals put it all together, winning the pennant and the World Series. Not rated as contenders before the season, the team got out of the gate slowly. But the pennant was up for grabs. The defending-champion Pirates were plagued by internal dissension and erratic batting. The Cincinnati Reds led the league for most of the summer, but they had troubles at shortstop. The Cards got to within striking distance in June but did not move into first place until August 23rd.

The race was very close, but St. Louis knocked Pittsburgh out of contention by beating them four times out of five decisions on August 30th, 31st, and September 1st.

The Cards and Reds were tied as late as September 16th, but then Cincinnati lost five games in a row, while St. Louis split six games. The Cardinals clinched the pennant on September 24th.

Then they beat the New York Yankees in a stirring, seven-game World Series. Grover Cleveland Alexander and Tommy Thevenow were the stars of the series.

Player-manager Rogers Hornsby was the hero of St. Louis. But owner Sam Breadon could not get along with the outspoken Hornsby, and the slugger was traded to the New York Giants for Frankie Frisch in December, 1926. St. Louis was in an uproar over the deal, but it turned out well for the team.

In 1927, Bob O'Farrell was made manager. But O'Farrell's catching was hurt by arm trouble, and shortstop Thevenow broke his ankle on June 21st. Pitcher Flint Rhem, a 20-game winner in 1926, slipped to 10-12. Still, led by the pitching of Jess Haines, Willie Sherdel, and Alexander and the play of Frisch, the Cardinals were able to stay in the race until the day before the season ended. They finished second, just 1½ games behind the Pirates.

Bill McKechnie took over as manager in 1928. On May 10th and 11th, vice-president Branch Rickey pulled a couple of deals to acquire catcher Jimmie Wilson and outfielder George Harper. They set the club for the race. St. Louis took over first place on June 14th. New York overtook the Cards by sweeping a three-game series in St. Louis in mid-August, but then the Giants went on an eight-game losing streak. The Red Birds built up a 5½-game lead and held on to win the pennant by 2 lengths. Jim Bottomley and Chick Hafey were the big hitters, and Alexander, Haines, and Sherdel once again headed the pitching staff.

In the World Series, the Cards were favored over the New York Yankees, but the Yanks destroyed them in four straight games. Breadon replaced manager McKechnie with Billy Southworth.

Southworth, who had been a member of the team in 1926 and 1927, tried to be an authoritarian manager in 1929, and the players did not respond. A disastrous 11-game losing streak dropped the Cards out of the race, and Southworth was replaced by McKechnie on July 24th. St. Louis finished fourth.

In 1930, Gabby Street became manager, and the team was inconsistent. Tied for last on May 6th, the Cardinals won 17 of their next 18 games to take the league lead. Then they turned right around and lost 12 of 13. They were tied for fifth at the end of July and, on August 8th, trailed the first-place Brooklyn Robins by 12 games. But they got hot and won 39 of their last 49 to win the pennant. A key series was a three-game sweep in Brooklyn in September, beginning with a thrilling, 1-0 victory.

The World Series was lost to the powerful Philadelphia Athletics in six games. The series was tied at two games each until Jimmie Foxx's home run in the ninth inning of the fifth game beat Burleigh Grimes, 2-0.

In 1931, the Cardinals made a runaway of the pennant race. They were out of first place only three days all season and won the flag by a final margin of 13 games. Although the season attendance was well below the record of 761,000 set in 1928, a single-day record was set at a doubleheader with the Cubs on July 12th. The crowd took over the outfield and led to a record number of doubles.

With outfielders Pepper Martin and George Watkins and pitchers Grimes and Bill Hallahan starring, the Cardinals knocked off the Athletics in seven games in the World Series.

1926 — Tuesday, August 31st, at Sportsman's Park
Cardinals Beat Pirates Twice and Take League Lead
Sherdel and Sothoron Winning Pitchers
6-1 and 2-1 Victories Send St. Louis from Third Place to First

A crowd of 24,000 turned out this afternoon to see two crucial games between the St. Louis Cardinals and the Pittsburgh Pirates. They were treated to a doubleheader sweep by the home team that put the Red Birds into the league lead. After one more home game (against the Pirates tomorrow), the schedule dictated that the Cardinals were to play their final 25 games of the season on the road. But, with the home season almost over, the St. Louis fans were expectantly looking forward to the first World Series in St. Louis in 38 years.

Today's Results
ST. LOUIS 6 - Pittsburgh 1 (1st game)
ST. LOUIS 2 - Pittsburgh 1 (2nd)
Chicago 1 - Cincinnati 0
Philadelphia 7 - Boston 2
no other game scheduled

Standings	W-L	Pct.	GB
ST. LOUIS	75-54	.581	-
Cincinnati	74-54	.578	½
Pittsburgh	71-52	.577	1
Chicago	69-58	.543	5
New York	60-64	.484	12½
Brooklyn	60-70	.462	15½
Philadelphia	47-75	.385	24½
Boston	48-77	.384	25

Today's victories, combined with Cincinnati's 1-0 loss in Chicago, put the red-hot Cardinals into first place for only the fourth day all season. But they have built up momentum with 22 victories in their last 28 games. Today they got over two big hurdles in their path by leaping past both the Reds and Pirates in the standings.

The series with Pittsburgh opened on Sunday with a rain-delayed 2-2 tie. Yesterday, the teams split a doubleheader: the Pirates won the first game, 3-0, and the Cards rebounded in the nightcap, winning, 5-3.

Each team had only one regular starting pitcher left for today's doubleheader. In the battle of the regulars, Willie Sherdel pitched the Cardinals to a 6-1 victory over Lee Meadows in the first game. In the second game, Pittsburgh tried veteran John Morrison, while St. Louis got spitballer Allan Sothoron out of mothballs to hurl. Both men did surprisingly well, Sothoron winning, 2-1, to give St. Louis the sweep.

Meadows entered the first game leading the league in pitching wins and carrying a 17-6 record. Sherdel was only at 12-11. But today, Sherdel was effective in the pinches, and Meadows was hit hard.

Bad base running hurt the Cardinals in the first inning. Taylor Douthit led off with a double. After Southworth tapped back to the mound, Douthit was caught in a rundown and tagged out. Southworth, looking for an opportunity to break for second, was then caught off first, completing a double play. Rogers Hornsby bounced out for the third out.

The Birds broke through for a run in the second. A single by Les Bell, a force out, and a hit-and-run single by Bob O'Farrell put Chick Hafey on third with two out. Tommy Thevenow bounced one to shortstop, which Hal Rhyne booted for a run-scoring error.

In the third, St. Louis added three more runs to their lead. Douthit started with a single and moved to third on another hit-and-run safety, this one by Southworth. Hornsby's long fly scored Douthit. After another long fly out, Bell lifted a drive into the left field bleachers for a two-run home run, bringing a shower of straw hats from the delighted fans.

The Cardinals got a run in the sixth on Hafey's home run and counted again in the seventh on singles by Bottomley, Bell, and Hafey.

In the meantime, Sherdel stymied the Pittsburgh attack with his tantalizing slow balls, which induced most of the Buc batters to pop the ball up. The only damage was a fourth-inning home run by Kiki Cuyler. Sherdel walked none, allowed six scattered singles, and was backed by some good defense, especially by shortstop Thevenow. St. Louis won the game, 6-1.

To try and avert a double defeat, Pirate manager Bill McKechnie sent "Jughandle

Johnny" Morrison, the noted curveballer, to the mound in the second game. With the Cardinal pitching staff depleted after nine games in the previous seven days, manager Hornsby turned to Al Sothoron, who had started just two games all season.

Morrison checked the Cardinals through the first six innings. Their most serious threat came in the third. In that frame, St. Louis put men on first and second with one out, thanks to an infield hit by Thevenow and an error by George Grantham. But the runners got no farther, as Douthit and Southworth were retired on easy flies.

Sothoron held the Pirates hitless for three innings. But, in the fourth, Rhyne opened with a single. After fielding Cuyler's bunt, Sothoron put himself into a hole by throwing the ball wildly past first base, allowing runners to get to second and third. He got Pie Traynor to foul out, and he thought he had Clyde Barnhart struck out on a 3-and-2 pitch. But umpire Bill McCormick saw it differently, and the walk loaded the bases. A sacrifice fly plated Rhyne, and a force out ended the inning, with Pittsburgh having taken the lead, 1-0.

Morrison nursed the lead until the seventh, when St. Louis broke through with two runs. Jim Bottomley started with a base on balls. Lester Bell sacrificed him to second. Chick Hafey, normally a pull hitter, went the other way with a curve and lined it to right field for the game-tying single. The event was greeted by thunderous applause and another shower of straw hats. After a delay to clear the field, O'Farrell's single sent Hafey to third. Thevenow then hit a sharp liner up the middle and into center field to put the Cardinals ahead, 2-1. Emil Yde replaced Morrison, and Sothoron grounded into a double play.

Sothoron coolly disposed of the Pirates in the last two innings, allowing only a two-out single by Cuyler in the eighth. He finished with a three-hitter and his first complete game of the year.

And the Cardinals finished the day in first place.

FIRST GAME

				r	h	e	Batteries
Pittsburgh	000	100	000 -	1	7	3	L. Meadows (L 17-7) 7 IP, R. Mahaffey 1 IP & E. Smith, J. Gooch.
St. Louis	013	001	10x -	6	12	1	W. Sherdel (W 13-11) & B. O'Farrell.

SECOND GAME

Pittsburgh	ab	r	h	bi	o	a	e	St. Louis	ab	r	h	bi	o	a	e
P. Waner, rf	4	0	0	0	0	0	0	T. Douthit, cf	3	0	0	0	0	0	0
H. Rhyne, ss	4	1	1	0	4	4	0	B. Southworth, rf	4	0	1	0	5	0	0
K. Cuyler, cf	2	0	1	0	2	0	0	R. Hornsby, 2b	4	0	1	0	1	2	0
P. Traynor, 3b	4	0	0	0	0	1	0	J. Bottomley, 1b	2	1	0	0	9	0	0
C. Barnhart, lf	2	0	1	0	2	0	0	L. Bell, 3b	2	0	0	0	0	1	0
E. Murphy, ph9	1	0	0	0	-	-	-	C. Hafey, lf	2	1	1	1	3	0	0
G. Grantham, 1b	3	0	0	1	11	1	1	B. O'Farrell, c	3	0	1	0	6	1	0
J. Rawlings, 2b	3	0	0	0	2	4	0	T. Thevenow, ss	3	0	2	1	3	2	2
G. Wright, ph9	1	0	0	0	-	-	-	A. Sothoron, p	3	0	0	0	0	3	1
E. Smith, c	2	0	0	0	2	1	0								
J. Morrison, p	3	0	0	0	1	3	0								
E. Yde, p7	0	0	0	0	0	1	0								
	29	1	3	1	24	15	1		26	2	6	2	27	9	3

| Pittsburgh | 000 | 100 | 000 - | 1 |
| St. Louis | 000 | 000 | 20x - | 2 |

LOB: Pitts 6, StL 4.
BE: Pitts 2, StL 1.
DP: O'Farrell-Thevenow, Morrison-Rhyne-Grantham, Rawlings-Rhyne-Grantham, Rhyne-Rawlings-Grantham.
SH: Cuyler, Grantham, Bell.
SB: none. CS: Waner, Hafey.
Attendance - 24,000

	ip	h	r-er	bb	so
Morrison (L 4-8)	6.1	6	2-2	2	1
Yde	1.2	0	0-0	1	0
Sothoron (W 2-3)	9	3	1-0	3	6

Time - 1:40
Umpires: B. McCormick, C. Rigler, E. Quigley, & B. Reardon

The Cardinals won the final game of the Pirate series, 5-2. Then they went on the road. Although they fell behind the Reds twice in the final month, they wound up winning the pennant by two games over Cincinnati and 4½ games over Pittsburgh. St. Louis's final record was 89-65.

Although the Cardinals clinched the pennant on the road, the city of St. Louis went crazy celebrating its first pennant since 1888.

1926 World Series—Game #7

Sunday, October 10th, at Yankee Stadium, New York

Cardinals Win World Series with Dramatic Victory in Seventh Game

New York Errors Pave Way for 3-2 St. Louis Victory

Alexander and Thevenow are Stars of the Game

In one of the most dramatic games of the age, the St. Louis Cardinals defeated the New York Yankees in the seventh and decisive game of the World Series. The score was 3-2. All of the victors' runs came in the fourth inning after two New York errors. The Yankees scored single runs in the third and sixth innings. But their biggest threat came in the seventh, when they loaded the bases against the Cardinals' starting pitcher, Jesse Haines. Grover Cleveland Alexander was brought in to relieve, although he had pitched a complete game the day before. He dramatically struck out rookie Tony Lazzeri, ending the threat. Then he retired the New Yorkers in the eighth and ninth innings to clinch the victory for St. Louis.

St. Louis shortstop Tommy Thevenow was also instrumental in the victory. He drove in the winning runs and made two spectacular plays in the field.

The day was cold and overcast with a threat of rain, and only 38,093 people attended the game. Those who came witnessed a game with just about everything a fan could want. There were costly errors and spectacular catches, dashing base running and questionable chances on the base paths, a clutch home run and a dramatic strike out. And with the world championship in the line, the tension was excrutiating.

Waite Hoyt of the Yankees pitched against Haines. Both men showed good speed and control, but neither was around to finish the game. Herb Pennock replaced Hoyt, and Alexander relieved Haines. Haines was credited with the victory, although Alexander was proclaimed the hero. Hoyt got the loss, although all the runs scored against him were unearned.

There was no scoring in the first two innings. The feature of these frames was a great running catch of Bob O'Farrell's long drive by Babe Ruth on the warning track.

After walking in the first inning, Ruth finally got a slow knuckleball to hit with two out in the third. He lifted it into the right field seats for a home run, giving New York the first run of the game.

St. Louis took over the lead in the fourth. With one out, Jim Bottomley singled to left. Les Bell hit a shot to shortstop Mark Koenig and reached base on an error. Chick Hafey dropped a Texas Leaguer into left field between Bob Meusel and Koenig, loading the bases. It appeared as if Meusel had a chance to catch the ball, but he held up when he saw Koenig coming out. O'Farrell then lofted a fly ball to left center. Earle Combs was under it but, at the last instant, gave way to Meusel, a stronger thrower. Bob muffed the ball, however, Bottomley scored, and the bases remained loaded. Thevenow then stroked a single into right field, scoring Bell and Hafey. The next two men made outs, but St. Louis led, 3-1.

With one on and two out in the New York fourth, Thevenow made the defensive play of the series. Hank Severeid hit a hard liner toward left field that Tommy snared in the top of his glove after a tremendous leap. The catch earned him a hearty cheer from the New York fans.

The Yankees cut their deficit to 3-2 with a run in the sixth. Another great play by Thevenow, however, curtailed the rally. Lou Gehrig led off with a hard smash over the middle, but Thevenow made a brilliant stop and throw to retire the batter at first. Lazzeri struck out for the second time. Joe Dugan then looped a single to center. If Thevenow had been 15 feet tall, he probably would have nabbed that one, too. With a full count and the runner going with the pitch, Severeid hit a low liner to left that Hafey tried to shoestring and missed. The ball got past him, and Dugan scored, and Severeid got a double. Pinch-hitter Ben Paschal bounced out to end the inning.

Herb Pennock took over the Yankee pitching duties, and he managed to keep the Cardinals from scoring during the rest of the game.

It was in the home half of the seventh that the Cardinals changed pitchers. Combs led off with a single and was sacrificed to second. Ruth was intentionally passed, and Meusel hit into a force play at second. After getting two quick strikes on Gehrig, Haines lost control and walked him, loading the bases with two out. Jess had been gripping his knuckleball so tightly that he had rubbed the skin off of the end of his forefinger, and it affected his control. So Hornsby called for Alexander.

When he came in from the bullpen, Alex told Rog, "Well, there's no place to put Lazzeri.... I'll just have to give him nothing but a lot of hell, won't I?" His first pitch to the Yankee rookie was low for a ball. Then he came in with a fastball for a strike. Lazzeri pulled the next pitch deep to left, but it hooked foul. Tony then fanned at the next pitch for strike three. The stadium broke into an uproar with the release of the tension. The fans gave the 39-year-old St. Louis pitcher a great hand. And the entire Cardinals team gave him a hearty round of back slapping as he came off the field.

"Old Pete" retired the Yankees in order in the eighth on a slow roller to short and two infield pop ups.

He retired the first two batters in the ninth before facing Babe Ruth. Hornsby came to the mound and advised Alexander not to let Ruth tie the game with one swing of the bat. So, while the fans booed, Alex gave the slugger a base on balls. It was the fourth time in the game and eleventh time in the series that the Cardinals had passed Ruth. Trying to catch the defense by surprise and get himself into scoring position, Ruth tried to steal second after one pitch to Meusel. But he was cut down, O'Farrell to Hornsby, ending the game. So the Cardinals were winners today, 3-2, and in the series, four games to three.

St. Louis (NL)	ab	r	h	bi	o	a	e
W. Holm, cf	5	0	0	0	2	0	0
B. Southworth, rf	4	0	0	0	0	0	0
R. Hornsby, 2b	4	0	2	0	4	1	0
J. Bottomley, 1b	3	1	1	0	14	0	0
L. Bell, 3b	4	1	0	0	0	4	0
C. Hafey, lf	4	1	2	0	3	0	0
B. O'Farrell, c	3	0	0	1	3	2	0
T. Thevenow, ss	4	0	2	2	1	3	0
J. Haines, p	2	0	1	0	0	4	0
G. Alexander, p7	1	0	0	0	0	0	0
	34	3	8	3	27	14	0

New York (AL)	ab	r	h	bi	o	a	e
E. Combs, cf	5	0	2	0	2	0	0
M. Koenig, ss	4	0	0	0	2	3	1
B. Ruth, rf	1	1	1	1	2	0	0
B. Meusel, lf	4	0	1	0	3	0	1
L. Gehrig, 1b	2	0	0	0	11	0	0
T. Lazzeri, 2b	4	0	0	0	3	1	0
J. Dugan, 3b	4	1	2	0	1	3	1
H. Severeid, c	3	0	2	1	3	1	0
S. Adams, pr6	0	0	0	0	-	-	-
P. Collins, c7	1	0	0	0	0	0	0
W. Hoyt, p	2	0	0	0	0	1	0
B. Paschal, ph6	1	0	0	0	-	-	-
H. Pennock, p7	1	0	0	0	0	1	0
	32	2	8	2	27	10	3

St. Louis	000	300	000	-	3
New York	001	001	000	-	2

	ip	h	r-er	bb	so
Haines (W 2-0)	6.2	8	2-2	5	2
Alexander	2.1	0	0-0	1	0
Hoyt (L 1-1)	6	5	3-0	0	2
Pennock	3	3	0-0	0	0

Time - 2:15
Umpires: G. Hildebrand, B. Klem, B. Dineen, & H. O'Day.

LOB: StL 7, NY 10. BE: StL 3.
2B: Severeid. HR: Ruth.
SH: Bottomley, Haines, Koenig, O'Farrell.
CS: Dugan, Hafey, Ruth.
Attendance - 38,093

Just before Christmas, Cardinal owner Sam Breadon shocked the baseball world (and St. Louis especially) by trading his pennant winning player-manager Rogers Hornsby to the Giants for Frankie Frisch.

1927—Sunday, September 4th, at Wrigley Field, Chicago

Triple Play Enables Cardinals to Edge Cubs, 2-1

Infield Gem Comes in Seventh Inning

Orsatti Shines for Cards in Major League Debut

Bouncing back from two disastrous defeats in Pittsburgh, the St. Louis Cardinals gave their pennant hopes a shot in the arm today by beating the slumping Chicago Cubs, 2-1. The Cubs were held down by a roundabout triple play by the St. Louis infield. The victory kept the fourth-place Cards just 3½ games behind the league-leading Pirates and moved them to just ½ game behind the Cubs, who lost their seventh consecutive game.

St. Louis manager Bob O'Farrell shook up his lineup for today's game. With Wattie Holm not hitting and Billy Southworth still bothered by ear trouble, left-handed hitting outfielders Danny Clark

Today's Results
ST. LOUIS 2 — Chicago 1
Pittsburgh 8 - Cincinnati 4
New York 6 - Philadelphia 0
Boston 3 - Brooklyn 2 (1st game)
Brooklyn 3 - Boston 2 (13 inn.) (2nd)

Standings	W-L	Pct.	GB
Pittsburgh	75-50	.600	-
New York	73-52	.584	2
Chicago	73-54	.575	3
ST. LOUIS	70-52	.574	3½
Cincinnati	57-67	.460	17½
Boston	54-71	.432	21
Brooklyn	55-73	.430	21½
Philadelphia	45-83	.352	31½

and Ernie Orsatti played for St. Louis. They each doubled and scored for the Birds. And Orsatti, who was playing in his first major league game, fielded sensationally.

Willie Sherdel was the St. Louis pitcher, and he was opposed by Chicago's ace, Charlie Root. Both men did fine work. Sherdel yielded seven hits in nine innings, and Root allowed just five safeties in the eight rounds that he worked. Hal Carlson pitched the last inning for the Cubs, allowing two hits.

An overflow crowd of 40,000 turned out to see the Cubs on their return from a three-week eastern trip. The Bruins had been in first place, 5 games ahead, when they left town. They returned in third place, and their fans were in a cross mood, hurling pop bottles and garbage at the visiting players on several occasions.

As the game's first batter, Orsatti quickly showed that he was not awed by the big leagues. He doubled into the standees in left field. Ernie's off-season job as a Hollywood stunt man undoubtedly helped him overcome any first-day jitters. Jim Bottomley, batting in the number two slot for the first time in memory, moved the rookie to third with a ground out. Frankie Frisch drove Orsatti home with a scratch single off of second baseman Clyde Beck's glove. Clark ended the inning by bouncing into a double play.

With two out in the Cubs' half of the first, Orsatti combined with Frisch and Clark in the famous "Alphonse and Gaston" act, allowing Pete Scott's pop fly to drop for a double. Riggs Stephenson fanned, leaving Scott stranded.

Through the next four innings, the two pitchers were in command. Only one hit was made by each team.

The first base on balls of the game was issued to Orsatti in the top of the sixth. But Root got Bottomley to ground into a double play.

Beck initiated the bottom of the sixth with a fly ball into the crowd, good for two bases. Sherdel struck Root out, and Sparky Adams followed with a slow grounder to shortstop. Rabbit Maranville made the pickup and throw to first, but Adams was called safe. The Cardinals descended upon umpire Bill Klem to dispute the call, and objects of many shapes, sizes, and hardnesses descended upon the disputants from the stands. After calm was restored, Sherdel escaped the jam by getting Woody English and Scott on short fly balls.

St. Louis upped their lead to 2-0 in the seventh. With one out, Clark bounced a ball into the stands beyond the right field fence. Under normal circumstances, such a hit would have counted as a home run, but, because of the ground rules instituted with the overflow crowd, Clark was held at second base with a double. The Cardinals put up another argument, and the fans once again exercised their throwing arms. The dispute became academic when Chick Hafey doubled to left, driving Clark home.

The spectators got some legitimate excitement in the bottom of the seventh, which ended with the triple play. Stephenson led off with a single, and Hack Wilson doubled into the crowd, putting the tying runs into scoring position with nobody out. But bad judgement by the base runners and fast work by the infielders halted the rally abruptly. Charlie Grimm bounced to Frisch and was thrown out at first. Wilson ran toward third, but Stephenson had held up there, and Wilson was hung up by Bottomley's throw to Maranville. Rabbit threw the ball home to check Stephenson, then O'Farrell ran Stephenson back and threw to second base, where Frisch tagged a retreating Wilson. Stephenson broke for home again, and Frisch threw to Bottomley, who had run in to cover the plate. Stephenson was again run back toward third, and Bottomley tossed to Les Bell, who administered the tag, which completed the triple killing. The fans generously reacted to the play by covering the field with their summer straw hats.

The Cubs finally managed to score in the eighth. An error by Bottomley on Maranville's assist allowed Gabby Hartnett to reach first. Cliff Heathcote went in as a pinch-runner. He took third on pinch-hitter Chuck Tolson's one-out double. Adams hit a fly to right field, and Heathcote foolishly went part way home before the catch. But Hafey foolishly threw to second base after making the catch, giving Heathcote just enough time to tag up and beat Frisch's throw to the plate.

Wattie Holm, a pinch-runner for the Cardinals, tried his luck at running home in the ninth, but he was thrown out trying to score on an overthrow.

In the bottom of the ninth, Wilson and Sherdel delighted the crowd with a little game of cat-and-mouse. Wilson stepped out of the box just as Sherdel was ready to pitch, then Sherdel stepped off the rubber when Wilson had finally gotten ready to hit. Hack finally walked, but Sherdel got Grimm for the last out of the game, and the Cardinals had won the contest, 2-1.

St. Louis	ab	r	h	bi	o	a	e
E. Orsatti, cf	3	1	1	0	5	0	0
J. Bottomley, 1b	4	0	0	0	7	2	1
F. Frisch, 2b	4	0	1	1	3	3	0
D. Clark, lf	4	1	2	0	4	0	0
W. Holm, pr9-lf	0	0	0	0	0	0	0
C. Hafey, rf	4	0	2	1	3	0	0
L. Bell, 3b	3	0	1	0	2	3	0
B. O'Farrell, c	3	0	0	0	3	1	0
R. Maranville, ss	3	0	0	0	0	5	0
W. Sherdel, p	3	0	0	0	0	1	0
	31	2	7	2	27	15	1

Chicago	ab	r	h	bi	o	a	e
S. Adams, 3b	3	0	1	1	1	3	0
W. English, ss	4	0	0	0	2	5	0
P. Scott, rf	4	0	1	0	2	1	0
R. Stephenson, lf	4	0	1	0	0	0	0
H. Wilson, cf	3	0	1	0	2	0	0
C. Grimm, 1b	4	0	0	0	14	0	0
G. Hartnett, c	3	0	0	0	4	0	0
C. Heathcote, pr8	0	1	0	0	-	-	-
M. Gonzalez, c9	0	0	0	0	1	0	0
C. Beck, 2b	3	0	1	0	1	6	0
C. Root, p	2	0	1	0	0	1	0
C. Tolson, ph8	1	0	1	0	-	-	-
E. Pick, pr8	0	0	0	0	-	-	-
H. Carlson, p9	0	0	0	0	0	0	0
	31	1	7	1	27	16	0

St. Louis   100 000 100 - 2
Chicago   000 000 010 - 1

	ip	h	r-er	bb	so
Sherdel (W 12-10)	9	7	1-0	1	3
Root (L 24-12)	8	5	2-2	1	3
Carlson	1	2	0-0	0	0

Time - 1:45
Umpires: B. McCormick, C. Moran, & B. Klem

LOB: StL 3, Chi 5. BE: Chi 1.
DP: Beck-English-Grimm 2, Bell-Frisch-Bottomley.
TP: Frisch-Bottomley-Maranville-O'Farrell-Frisch-Bottomley-Bell.
2B: Orsatti, Scott, Beck, Clark, Hafey, Wilson, Tolson. SH: Adams.
Attendance - 40,000

The Cardinals finished the season by winning 22 of their remaining 31 games. That was good, but not quite good enough. They finished second, only 1½ games behind Pittsburgh.

Their final record was 92-61.

1928 — Thursday, September 20th, at the Polo Grounds, New York

George Harper Hits Three Homers as Cardinals Win First Game

Shanty Hogan's Late Grand Slam Gives N.Y. a Split

St. Louis Leads by 2 Games with 9 to Play

George Harper's home run hitting led the league-leading St. Louis Cardinals to an 8-5 victory in the first game of today's doubleheader with the second-place New York Giants. The victory assured the Cards of leaving New York in first place in the National League pennant race. But for a fatal fumble with two out in the eighth inning of the second game, St. Louis most likely would have swept the twin-bill, giving themselves a nearly insurmountable 4-game lead. As it turned out, the error allowed New York's Shanty Hogan to hit a grand slam home run, and the Giants won the nightcap, 7-4. That left the St. Louis lead at 2 games with 9 games left for both contenders.

Today's Results
ST. LOUIS 8 - New York 5 (1st game)
New York 7 - ST. LOUIS 4 (2nd)
Pittsburgh 6 - Philadelphia 4
Cincinnati 7 - Boston 2 (1st game)
Boston 9 - Cincinnati 5 (2nd)
no other games scheduled

Standings	W-L	Pct.	GB
ST. LOUIS	89-56	.614	-
New York	87-58	.600	2
Chicago	85-59	.590	3½
Pittsburgh	80-64	.556	8½
Cincinnati	76-67	.531	12
Brooklyn	71-73	.493	17½
Boston	46-97	.322	42
Philadelphia	42-102	.292	46½

A World Series atmosphere prevailed at the Polo Grounds today, and a weekday crowd of 50,000 New Yorkers turned out for the crucial games. The weather was warm, despite a strong breeze blowing toward home plate. The wind did not, however, hold down the long-ball hitting, and a total of eight home runs went into the stands. Besides three homers by Harper in the first game, Hogan and Chick Hafey hit single home runs in both games, and Andy Cohen connected once in the first contest.

In the opening battle, New York manager John McGraw pitched Larry Benton, who held the league lead in both games won and winning percentage. St. Louis manager Bill McKechnie sent Willie Sherdel to the mound. Sherdel was the league's top lefthander in those same two categories. Benton allowed only six hits in seven innings, but he walked four and gave up two home runs, both to Harper. Sherdel was effective throughout, despite the total of twelve hits made against him. But for erratic support, he might have held the Giants to just two runs.

After the two teams were disposed of in order in the first inning, Harper opened the scoring by lining a slowball into the seats in right field for a home run in the second inning.

Fred Lindstrom led off the home half of second with a double and, after two were out, moved to third on Rabbit Maranville's fumble of Bill Terry's grounder. Terry broke for second on the double steal. Catcher Jimmie Wilson decoyed Lindstrom into coming home by faking a throw, then he tagged the embarrassed Giant out, unassisted, to end the inning.

St. Louis was held hitless through the next three frames, although Frankie Frisch and Harper both walked in the fourth.

Meanwhile, Sherdel turned back the Giants. In the third, Jim Bottomley robbed Jimmy Welsh of a hit with a fine one-handed grab of a hot liner. In the fourth, Les Mann was thrown out trying to steal second. In the fifth, Hogan and Terry both singled, but Maranville and Harper turned in fine defensive plays to prevent any scoring.

In the top of the sixth, the Cardinals broke through against Benton for four runs. The first three hitters, Andy High, Frisch, and Bottomley, all singled, scoring a run. After Hafey popped up, Harper strode to the dish. After the count went to 3-and-2, Benton laid one down the middle, and George pulled it into the lower right field stands for a three-run homer. That gave the visitors a 5-0 lead.

The Giants got right back into the game thanks to some poor fielding and Hogan's first home run of the day. After Welsh had flied out, Andy Reese lined one into right field that Harper misjudged and dropped. It was scored a double. Mann fouled out. Lindstrom lifted an easy fly behind shortstop. Maranville, Hafey, or Taylor Douthit could have caught the ball, but all three watched it drop for a run-scoring single. Then Hogan blasted one into the upper tier in left for a two-run home run, cutting the St. Louis lead to 5-3.

The Cardinals added a run in the seventh on Sherdel's walk and a fluke, two-out triple by Frisch. Reese missed an attempted shoestring catch of Frisch's sinking drive to left. The ball rolled about three feet away from him, but Reese couldn't find it, and Frisch got to third before the ball was finally located.

New York got two runs in their half on Terry's single and Cohen's home run. Welsh and Mann also singled in the inning, but Sherdel fanned Lindstrom to end the round.

With Benton gone for a pinch-hitter, McGraw put Jack Scott on the mound in the eighth. He was greeted by homers off the bats of Hafey and Harper. Harper's was the longest of his three, this one landing in the upper deck. It made for a most satisfying game for George, because New York had traded him away in May.

Harper got a chance to tie the all-time record of four home runs in one game in the ninth inning. But, batting against Dutch Henry with the bases loaded, he was called out on a questionable third strike.

With an 8-5 lead, Sherdel easily disposed of the Giants in the last two innings, bringing home his 19th victory of the season.

In the second game, the opposing pitchers were 41-year-old veteran Grover Alexander and 25-year-old rookie Carl Hubbell.

New York nudged its way to a 2-1 lead through five innings, but St. Louis scored single runs in the sixth, seventh, and eighth to lead, 4-2.

In the bottom of the eighth, singles by Lefty O'Doul and Mel Ott and a passed ball scored one run and prompted Alexander to walk Terry with two out. Travis Jackson, hitless on the day, then rolled an easy grounder that Maranville fumbled, loading the bases. Frank "Shanty" Hogan followed with a grand slam to left, giving New York the game, 7-4, and a split in the doubleheader.

FIRST GAME

St. Louis	ab	r	h	bi	o	a	e		New York	ab	r	h	bi	o	a	e
T. Douthit, cf	4	0	0	0	1	0	0		J. Welsh, cf	5	0	1	0	2	0	0
A. High, 3b	4	1	2	0	2	1	0		A. Reese, lf	5	1	2	0	4	0	0
F. Frisch, 2b	4	1	3	1	3	2	0		L. Mann, rf	4	0	1	0	3	0	0
J. Bottomley, 1b	4	1	1	1	8	0	0		F. Lindstrom, 3b	4	1	2	1	2	3	0
C. Hafey, lf	4	1	1	1	3	0	1		S. Hogan, c	4	1	2	2	4	0	0
G. Harper, rf	4	3	3	5	2	0	0		T. Jackson, ss	4	0	0	0	2	4	0
J. Wilson, c	4	0	0	0	6	1	0		B. Terry, 1b	4	1	2	0	8	0	0
R. Maranville, ss	4	0	1	0	2	2	1		A. Cohen, 2b	4	1	2	2	2	2	0
W. Sherdel, p	3	1	0	0	0	3	0		L. Benton, p	2	0	0	0	0	1	0
									J. Cummings, ph7	1	0	0	0	-	-	-
									J. Scott, p8	0	0	0	0	0	0	0
									D. Henry, p9	0	0	0	0	0	0	0
									B. O'Farrell, ph9	1	0	0	0	-	-	-
	35	8	11	8	27	9	2			38	5	12	5	27	10	0

St. Louis   010 004 120 - 8
New York   000 003 200 - 5

	ip	h	r-er	bb	so
Sherdel (W 19-9)	9	12	5-5	0	5
Benton (L 24-8)	7	6	6-6	4	3
Scott	*1	5	2-2	0	0
Henry	1	0	0-0	1	1

*faced two batters in ninth

LOB: StL 8, NY 6. BE: NY 1.
2B: Lindstrom, Reese. 3B: Frisch.
HR: Harper 3, Hogan, Cohen, Hafey.
SH: Douthit, High, Bottomley.
SB: none. CS: Lindstrom, Mann.
Attendance - 50,000
Time - 1:53

Umpires: C. Rigler, B. Klem, E. Quigley, & C. Pfirman.

SECOND GAME

		r	h	e	Batteries
St. Louis	100 001 110 -	4	11	2	G. Alexander (L 15-9) & Wilson.
New York	010 010 05x -	7	8	2	C. Hubbell (W 9-5) & Hogan.

New York won the final game of the series, 8-5. But St. Louis won six of the next seven games to clinch the pennant on the second last day of the season.

The Cardinals' final record was 95-59, leaving them 2 games ahead of the Giants.

1928 World Series—Game #4

Tuesday, October 9th, at Sportsman's Park

Ruth Hits Three Home Runs as Yankees Win, 7-3, for Series Sweep

Heated Argument Precedes Second Homer

Favored Cardinals Overpowered for Fourth Straight Time

Babe Ruth, Lou Gehrig, Waite Hoyt, & Company completed the destruction of the St. Louis Cardinals' World Series hopes today with a 7-3 victory. Supposedly crippled by the loss of Herb Pennock and Earle Combs and by Tony Lazzeri's sore arm, the New York Yankees entered the 1928 World Series as underdogs. But, instead of losing the classic, they rolled over the National League champion Cardinals in four straight games. It was the second year in a row that the Yanks had swept the series in four games.

The star performers were in top form again today. Waite Hoyt pitched a good game, even though eleven hits were made off his delivery. His record for the series was two games and two wins. Today Lou Gehrig walked three times and hit a home run giving him World Series records for slugging percentage (1.727) and runs batted in (9), and a share of the record for most home runs in a series (4). His batting average of .545 would have tied the record, except for one small detail. That detail was the .625 average accumulated in this series by the incomparable Babe Ruth. Today the Bambino outshined the other stars by hitting three home runs and making a spectacular running catch to end the game. The three homers tied the record Ruth set in the same ballpark in the 1926 classic.

After a day off due to rain, both managers started their pitchers from the first game, Hoyt and Willie Sherdel. Both were touched for 11 hits, although Sherdel only pitched 6 1/3 innings. Both did well in critical situations until the top of the seventh. Then Sherdel, perhaps demoralized by losing an apparent third strike on Ruth, was routed by the big New York bats.

Cardinal manager Bill McKechnie changed his lineup today. Looking for more batting punch, he benched slumping hitters Taylor Douthit and Jimmie Wilson and inserted Ernie Orsatti and Earl Smith.

Yankee skipper Miller Huggins used righthanded Ben Paschal in center field, but otherwise stuck to his pat lineup until making defensive changes in the bottom of the seventh.

An early starting time made the sun a handicap to the left fielders, starting in the very first inning. The second St. Louis batter, Andy High, lofted a high fly that Ruth utterly lost, despite his sunglasses. It fell for a double, but Hoyt was able to pitch out of the jam.

In the second inning, Hoyt broke up a hit-and-run play by decking Rabbit Maranville with an inside pitch, allowing catcher Benny Bengough to nail the slow-footed Smith at second. Maranville then doubled but was left stranded.

The Cardinals finally put a run on the board in the third. Orsatti started with a Texas Leaguer to short center and was safe at second on Paschal's wide throw. He moved to third on High's bunt single and scored on a fly out by Frankie Frisch.

New York tied the game almost immediately. Ruth, who had bounced into a double play in the first, led off the fourth. With a count of two balls and one strike, Sherdel threw a curve way inside. Ruth stepped away and lined a home run over the pavilion in right field.

St. Louis regained the lead in the bottom of the inning. Smith singled. Maranville hit a perfect double play ball to Lazzeri, who flipped to Mark Koenig for a force out. But Koenig's relay went into the seats past first base, and Maranville got to second. After Sherdel flied out, Hoyt tried to pick the Rabbit off second. He whirled and fired the ball right over the base, but no one was there to catch it. Maranville sprinted all the way home, despite McKechnie's frantic efforts to stop him at third.

Once again, the lead didn't last. With one out in the seventh, Ruth came up. After two called strikes, Sherdel got the throw back from Smith and immediately returned it right over the heart of the plate, while the St. Louis backstop was distracting the Babe with small talk. Such a "quick pitch" was legal in the National League but illegal in the American, and before the series it had been agree that it would not be allowed in the world championship games. Besides, umpire Cy Pfirman had called time. Still, Sherdel and his teammates gathered around the arbiter and vehemently argued that the batter was out. Meanwhile, Ruth watched the argument wearing a wide grin.

When play resumed, Sherdel pitched two balls wide, then put a slow curve over the inside corner. Ruth, with little apparent effort, stroked a high drive over the pavilion and onto Grand Avenue, tying the game. Lou Gehrig sent a 1-0 pitch onto the same street, this homer being closer to the line, and the Yankees went into the lead. After Bob Meusel singled, Sherdel was replaced by Grover Alexander. He couldn't stop the hitting until the score was 5-2 in favor of the Yankees.

Ruth was roundly booed and made the target of a few pop bottles when he went to left field in the bottom of the seventh.

Cedric Durst lined a homer into the pavilion in the eighth. Ruth followed with a drive to the roof in right center for his third home run, turning the boos to cheers.

Hoyt allowed a run in the ninth. After Smith singled, pinch-runner John "Pepper" Martin was allowed to steal second and score on an infield out without any effort being made to stop him. Orsatti and High singled with two out. Then Frisch popped a high foul down the left field line. Despite a bad knee, Ruth came sprinting along the front of the temporary boxes, and, in spite of the papers thrown in his face by the fans, he reached over a row of seats to make a spectacular, running catch, ending the game. Never breaking stride, the Babe ran to the dugout, triumphantly holding the ball high over his head, while the Cardinals and their fans looked on dejectedly.

The Yankees were too much for the Cardinals this year: too much Ruth and too much Gehrig.

New York (AL)	ab	r	h	bi	o	a	e
B. Paschal, cf	4	0	1	0	3	0	0
C. Durst, cf7	1	1	1	1	0	0	0
M. Koenig, ss	5	0	1	0	4	2	1
B. Ruth, lf	5	3	3	3	2	0	0
L. Gehrig, 1b	2	1	1	1	7	0	0
B. Meusel, rf	5	1	1	0	0	0	0
T. Lazzeri, 2b	4	1	3	0	1	2	0
L. Durocher, 2b7	1	0	0	0	0	0	0
J. Dugan, 3b	3	0	1	0	0	0	0
G. Robertson, ph7-3b	2	0	1	0	0	0	0
B. Bengough, c	3	0	1	0	8	1	0
E. Combs, ph7	0	0	0	1	0	0	0
P. Collins, c7	1	0	1	0	2	0	0
W. Hoyt, p	4	0	1	0	0	2	1
	40	7	15	7	27	7	2

St. Louis (NL)	ab	r	h	bi	o	a	e
E. Orsatti, cf	5	1	2	0	4	0	0
A. High, 3b	5	0	3	0	0	1	0
F. Frisch, 2b	4	0	0	1	3	1	0
J. Bottomley, 1b	3	0	0	0	11	1	0
C. Hafey, lf	3	0	1	0	1	0	0
G. Harper, rf	3	0	0	0	2	0	0
E. Smith, c	4	0	3	0	3	1	0
P. Martin, pr9	0	1	0	0	-	-	-
R. Maranville, ss	4	1	2	0	3	1	0
W. Sherdel, p	3	0	0	0	0	0	0
G. Alexander, p7	0	0	0	0	0	3	0
W. Holm, ph7	1	0	1	-	-	-
	35	3	11	2	27	8	0

New York   000 100 420 - 7
St. Louis   001 100 001 - 3

	ip	h	r-er	bb	so
Hoyt (W 2-0)	9	11	3-2	3	8
Sherdel (L 0-2)	6.1	11	4-4	3	1
Alexander	2.1	4	3-3	0	1

Time - 2:25
Attendance - 37,331

LOB: NY 11, StL 9. BE: none.
DP: Bottomley-Maranville, Koenig-Gehrig.
2B: High, Maranville, Orsatti, Lazzeri, Collins.
HR: Ruth 3, Gehrig, Durst.
SH: Hoyt, Frisch, Combs.
SB: Lazzeri, Maranville.
CS: Smith.
Umpires: C. Pfirman, B. Owens, C. Rigler, & B. McGowan

Over the winter, owner Sam Breadon demoted manager Bill McKechnie to the minor leagues, having him switch places with Rochester manager Billy Southworth.

1929 — Saturday, July 6th, at Baker Bowl, Philadelphia

Cards Lose Eleventh Straight Game, Then Crush Phillies in Nightcap, 28-6

Score Ten Runs in an Inning Twice in Second Game

Bottomley and Hafey Hit Grand Slams

Although it seemed hard to believe 18 days later, the St. Louis Cardinals led the National League on June 18th. Between that date and today, they won only one game, and had lost 13, including their last 10 decisions. Today they tried their luck in a doubleheader against the Philadelphia Phillies. In the first game, St. Louis outhit the Quakers but again came up short on the scoreboard, 10-6. That made it eleven losses in a row. In addition, the Cards added a few casualties to their hospital list. Then in the second game, they broke their bad streak in spectacular fashion, scoring ten runs in the first inning and ten more in the fifth and winning by a score of 28-6. Today was only the second time in history that a big league team had scored in double figures in two separate innings of the same game. St. Louis also got two bases-loaded home runs, tying another record.

Today's Results
Philadelphia 10 - ST. LOUIS 6 (1st game)
ST. LOUIS 28 - Philadelphia 6 (2nd)
Cincinnati 5 - Pittsburgh 3
Boston 3 - Chicago 1
Brooklyn 4 - New York 0

Standings	W-L	Pct.	GB
Pittsburgh	44-26	.629	-
Chicago	42-25	.627	½
New York	41-32	.562	4½
ST. LOUIS	37-36	.507	8½
Brooklyn	33-37	.471	11
Philadelphia	31-41	.431	14
Boston	30-44	.405	16
Cincinnati	26-43	.377	17½

But before the ecstasy there was the agony of the opening game loss. Willie Sherdel was on the hill for the Cardinals, and he did a fine job for three innings. Then his teammates staked him to a four run lead, and Willie fell apart. In the bottom of the fourth, he gave up back-to-back home runs to Pinky Whitney and Chuck Klein. The Phils added four runs in the fifth and one in the sixth. Sherdel was finally driven from the mound in the seventh, when Philadelphia added three more tallies.

Paced by Jim Bottomley's two two-run homers, the Cardinals managed six runs off the Phillies' Ray Benge. Hal Elliott replaced Benge in the eighth, and he shut the Red Birds out in the last two frames.

So the Cardinals lost, 10-6. Eleven straight losses was their longest losing streak since 1916.

In the first game, Earl Smith and Frankie Frisch both pulled leg muscles, and Ernie Orsatti reinjured his ankle. So, St. Louis manager Billy Southworth was forced to improvise a lineup for the second game. Jimmie Wilson went back behind the plate, Carey Selph took Frisch's spot at second base, and Wattie Holm went to center field. This crew was sent out to oppose the Phillies' leading pitcher, Claude Willoughby.

Claude was definitely off form today. After walking the first two batters, the next three (Andy High, Jim Bottomley, and Chick Hafey) all delivered run-scoring singles. After Holm walked, Phillie manager Burt Shotton chose southpaw Elmer Miller as a pitching replacement.

Miller walked the only two men he faced.

Luther Roy was the next nominee, and the Cardinals' pitcher, Fred Frankhouse, greeted him with a two-run single to center. Taylor Douthit, up for the second time in the inning, singled across another run. At this point, the score stood 8-0 and ten men had batted without making an out. But knowing how the last few games had gone, Southworth order Selph to sacrifice the two runners into scoring position. He did, and there was one out. Frankhouse was caught between third and home on High's tap to shortstop, and he eventually wound up trying to share third with Douthit. The latter was tagged out, while High went to second. Bottomley then delivered his second single of the inning, driving in two more runs. Hafey grounded to third, ending the merriment, and the Cards led, 10-0.

Frankhouse went out to pitch with a sore thumb, which hurt his curveball. But that was nothing a little ten-run lead couldn't cure. Two walks and two runs gave the Phils two runs off of him in the first inning.

The two teams traded single runs in the second.

In the fourth, Charley Gelbert doubled, Douthit singled, and Selph tripled, giving St. Louis two more tallies. Selph sprained his ankle sliding into third and had to be assisted from the field. Eddie Delker took his place. With two out in the bottom of the inning, Lefty O'Doul Chuck Klein, and Don Hurst strung singles together for a run, but the Cardinals still had a comfortable lead, 13-4.

They more than doubled their margin in the next inning, posting another 10 on the board in the top of the fifth. Bottomley started with a base on balls and went to third on Hafey's double to center. Holm's sacrifice fly scored Bottomley, and Wilson's single plated Hafey. Gelbert's double sent the Cardinal catcher to third and finally convinced Shotton that Roy had had enough. June Green was the new Philly moundsman, and Frankhouse greeted him exactly the same way he had welcomed Roy: with a two-run single. A single and a walk loaded the bases, and a hit batsman forced another run home. Bottomley then unloaded a grand slam home run over the right field wall. That brought Sunny Jim's RBI total for the doubleheader to 11. Hafey's double, High's infield hit, and Wilson's ground out accounted for the tenth run of the inning.

St. Louis brought its total to 28 runs with five in the eighth. With one out, Douthit walked and scored on hits by Delker and High. Bottomley walked. Hafey then delivered the second grand slam of the game, a drive into the seats in left field.

The Phillies scored harmless runs in the eighth and ninth innings, which made the final score 28-6.

What a way to end a long losing streak!

FIRST GAME

		r	h	e	Batteries
St. Louis	000 400 200 -	6	15	0	W. Sherdel (L 6-7) 6.1 IP, S. Johnson 1.2 IP & E. Smith, B. Jonnard.
Philadelphia	000 241 30x -	10	13	0	R. Benge (W 6-7) 7 IP, H. Elliot 2 IP & B. Lerian.

SECOND GAME

St. Louis	ab	r	h	bi	o	a	e
T. Douthit, cf	6	4	5	2	2	0	0
C. Selph, 2b	2	1	2	1	1	3	0
E. Delker, pr4-2b	3	2	1	0	2	1	0
A. High, 3b	6	4	2	3	0	4	0
J. Bottomley, 1b	5	4	4	7	12	0	0
C. Hafey, lf	7	4	5	5	6	0	0
W. Holm, rf	5	2	1	1	0	1	0
J. Wilson, c	6	2	2	4	3	0	0
C. Gelbert, ss	6	3	2	1	1	4	0
F. Frankhouse, p	7	2	4	4	0	2	0
	53	28	28	28	27	15	0

Philadelphia	ab	r	h	bi	o	a	e
D. Southern, cf	5	2	2	1	3	0	1
L. O'Doul, lf	3	2	2	1	1	0	0
C. Klein, rf	5	0	2	0	2	0	0
D. Hurst, 1b	5	0	2	1	10	0	0
P. Whitney, 3b	4	0	1	0	2	3	1
F. Thompson, 2b	5	1	4	2	3	5	0
T. Thevenow, ss	5	0	1	1	3	6	0
V. Davis, c	3	0	1	0	2	0	0
G. Susce, c6	2	1	1	0	1	0	0
C. Willoughby, p	0	0	0	0	0	0	0
E. Miller, p1	0	0	0	0	0	0	0
L. Roy, p1	2	0	0	0	0	0	0
J. Green, p5	1	0	1	0	0	2	0
	40	6	17	6	27	16	2

St. Louis   10(10) 2(10)0 050 - 28
Philadelphia 210   100   011 - 6

	ip	h	r-er	bb	so
Frankhouse (W 2-1)	9	17	6-6	3	2
Willoughby (L 9-8)	*0	3	6-6	3	0
Miller	#0	0	2-2	2	0
Roy	4.1	13	9-8	1	0
Green	4.2	12	11-11	3	1

*faced six batters in first
#faced two batters in first
Umpires: B. Reardon, G. Hart, & C. Rigler

LOB: StL 10, Phil 11. BE: StL 1.
DP: Thevenow-Hurst, High-Selph-Bottomley, Gelbert-Delker-Bottomley.
2B: Gelbert 2, Hafey 2, Green, Susce, Thevenow. 3B: Selph.
HR: Bottomley, Hafey, Southern.
SH: Selph, Holm, O'Doul
Time - 2:28 Attendance - 10,000
HBP: by Green (High)

Rookie manager Billy Southworth was replaced by Bill McKechnie two weeks later, but the Cardinals couldn't climb out of fourth place.

They finished there, 20 games behind the pennant-winning Cubs, with a 78-74 record.

1930—Tuesday, September 16th, at Ebbets Field, Brooklyn

Cardinals Edge Robins, 1-0, and Regain League Lead

Hallahan Bests Vance in Ten-Inning Duel

High Gets Pinch-Double and Scores Only Run of Senstional Game

With a heart-stopping, ten-inning, 1-0 victory, the St. Louis Cardinals moved past the Brooklyn Robins and back into first place in the hectic National League pennant race. The defeat was the first for Brooklyn in twelve games. For St. Louis it represented the 30th triumph in 38 games since August 8th. This great stretch run had taken them from fourth place, 12 games out of first, into the league lead by last Saturday. On Sunday, the Cards split a doubleheader and dropped back to second place.

The St. Louis pitching rotation called for lefthander "Wild Bill" Hallahan to open the series in Brooklyn, with Flint Rhem and either Jess Haines or Burleigh Grimes to pitch the other two games. However, yesterday Hallahan slammed a car door on the middle finger of his right hand, so manager Gabby Street proposed to pitch Rhem in the first game. When this morning came, however, Flint was missing, and, when he returned later, he was in no shape to pitch. He told the press that he had been kidnapped, taken to a roadhouse, and forced to drink whiskey by gamblers interested in a Brooklyn victory. Street said that no disciplinary action would be taken, but Rhem probably would not pitch against Brooklyn.

Today's Results
ST. LOUIS 1 — Brooklyn 0 (10 inn.)
New York 7 - Chicago 0
Philadelphia 15 - Pittsburgh 14 (10)
no other game scheduled

Standings	W-L	Pct.	GB
ST. LOUIS	83-60	.580	-
Brooklyn	84-61	.579	-
Chicago	82-62	.569	1½
New York	79-65	.549	4½
Pittsburgh	74-69	.517	9
Boston	67-78	.462	17
Cincinnati	55-85	.393	26½
Philadelphia	50-94	.347	33½

The streaking Robins presented a patched-up lineup for today's game. Outfield regulars Rube Bressler and Johnny Frederick were both sidelined by injuries, and their places were taken by Harvey Hendrick and Eddie Moore.

The Cardinals' first-string catcher, Jimmie Wilson, was also out, having sprained his ankle badly on Sunday. He was replaced by Gus Mancuso. And Street had no choice but to pitch Hallahan.

Today's crowd of 30,000 filled Ebbets Field beyond capacity. They were treated to a tension-filled pitching duel. Despite the fact that he had a bandaged finger sticking out of his glove, Hallahan performed brilliantly. Brooklyn's ace, Dazzy Vance, also pitched great ball, fanning eleven batters.

Using his overhand fastball and down-breaking curve, Hallahan set the Robins down in order in each of the first six innings.

In the meantime, the Cardinals threatened several times but failed to score. In the first inning, Sparky Adams dropped a one-out double into short center. Frank Frisch flied out. Jim Bottomley was robbed of a hit by a diving catch of a line drive by first baseman Del Bissonette. In the fifth inning, George Watkins led off with a single off the right field wall. With one out, he went to third on Charley Gelbert's double. After Hallahan fanned, Taylor Douthit hit what looked like an extra-base hit toward the gap in right center. But Babe Herman raced over and made a one-handed catch, saving two runs.

In the sixth inning, St. Louis again came within an eyelash of scoring. Adams opened with a single and moved around to third on two outs. Then, with a 2-and-1 count on Chick Hafey, Adams broke for home. Vance, using his famous exaggerated windup, had no chance of getting the ball to the plate ahead of Adams, but he prevented the run by hitting Hafey with the pitch. Watkins then fouled out, leaving runners on first and third.

Brooklyn finally got a man to first base with two out in the seventh. Babe Herman reached when Hallahan, with his injured hand, fumbled a bouncer back to the mound. Herman got no farther, however, as Glenn Wright flied out to deep center.

Poor base running cost the Robins in both the eighth and ninth innings.

In the eighth, Hendrick singled with one out, ending Hallahan's bid for a no-hitter. Neal Finn missed a hit-and-run sign, and Hendrick was thrown out at second. Finn then knocked a hit to center and tried to stretch it into a double. The throw from the outfield was off line toward first, and Finn and shortstop Gelbert had as head-to-head collision. The ball rolled free, but the dazed Finn wandered off the base and was tagged out.

In the home half of the ninth, rookie Al Lopez started off with a hit. Vance bunted, and Adam's throw to second was late, putting two men on with no outs. Moore also bunted, but he popped the ball into foul territory. Catcher Mancuso snared the ball with a lunge and gunned a throw to second, doubling Lopez off base. An infield single by Wally Gilbert followed, but Herman flied out to end the inning.

In the top of the tenth, Gelbert was removed for pinch-hitter Andy High. High pulled an 0-and-2 curve into right center for a double. With two strikes, Hallahan successfully sacrificed the runner to third. Douthit then looped a single to right to drive in the game's only run.

But the excitement was not over yet. Brooklyn came to bat, High stayed in the game at third base, and Adams moved over to short. Wright doubled to center to start the frame. "Wild Bill" then put the potential winning run on base by walking Bissonette. A sacrifice moved the runners to second and third. Pinch-hitter Jake Flowers was walked, loading the bases with one out. The next batter was Lopez. He sent a shot toward short, which took a high hop. Adams stabbed at the ball, batted it into the air, then grabbed it and flipped it to Frisch at second. The Cardinals pivot man turned it over and launched a lightning throw to first, beating Lopez by an inch, to complete a game-saving and game-ending double play. First baseman Sunny Jim Bottomley leaped for joy and led the charge to the mound to congratulate the big hero of the Cardinals' victory, Bill Hallahan. Then the players charged toward the clubhouse.

Their charge to the pennant had resumed.

St. Louis	ab	r	h	bi	o	a	e	Brooklyn	ab	r	h	bi	o	a	e
T. Douthit, cf	4	0	1	1	6	1	0	E. Moore, cf	4	0	0	0	5	0	0
S. Adams, 3b-ss10	5	0	2	0	1	1	0	W. Gilbert, 3b	4	0	1	0	1	1	0
F. Frisch, 2b	5	0	0	0	4	3	0	B. Herman, rf	4	0	0	0	2	0	0
J. Bottomley, 1b	3	0	0	0	8	1	0	G. Wright, ss	4	0	1	0	1	0	0
C. Hafey, lf	3	0	0	0	2	0	0	D. Bissonette, 1b	3	0	0	0	5	0	0
G. Watkins, rf	4	0	1	0	0	0	0	H. Hendrick, lf	3	0	1	0	3	0	0
G. Mancuso, c	4	0	0	0	6	2	0	N. Finn, 2b	3	0	1	0	1	1	0
C. Gelbert, ss	3	0	2	0	2	3	0	J. Flowers, ph10	0	0	0	0	-	-	-
A. High, ph10-3b	1	1	1	0	1	0	0	A. Lopez, c	4	0	1	0	12	0	0
B. Hallahan, p	3	0	0	0	1	1	1	D. Vance, p	2	0	0	0	0	1	0
	35	1	7	1	30	13	1		31	0	5	0	30	3	0

St. Louis   000 000 000 1 - 1
Brooklyn   000 000 000 0 - 0

	ip	h	r-er	bb	so
Hallahan (W 15-8)	10	5	0-0	2	4
Vance (L 16-14)	10	7	1-1	0	11

HBP: by Vance 2 (Douthit, Hafey)
Time - 2:30

LOB: StL 8, Bkn 5. BE: Bkn 1.
DP: Mancuso-Gelbert, Adams-Frisch-Bottomley
2B: Adams, Gelbert, High, Wright.
SH: Bottomley, Vance, Hallahan, Hendrick.
SB: none. CS: Hendrick.
Attendance - 30,000
Umpires: B. Klem, C. Rigler, C. Pfirman, & B. Clarke

The Cardinals went on to sweep the series from the Robins, then win six of their next seven games to clinch the pennant.

They finished with a 92-62 record and a 2-game margin over the second-place Chicago Cubs. Brooklyn slipped to fourth, 6 games behind.

1930 World Series—Game #5

Monday, October 6th, at Sportsman's Park

Home Run by Foxx Defeats Grimes and Cardinals, 2-0

Ninth-Inning Blast Decides Pitching Duel

Athletics Lead Series, Three Games to Two

Connie Mack's Philadelphia Athletics took a three-to-two game lead in the best-of-seven-game World Series today with a dramatic, 2-0 victory over the St. Louis Cardinals. For eight innings, the game was a scoreless duel between the Cards' Burleigh Grimes and the A's pitching tandem of George Earnshaw and Robert "Lefty" Grove. Then in the top of the ninth, Jimmie Foxx hit a home run with a teammate aboard, and the Red Birds could not answer the runs in the bottom of the inning. The victory sent the Philadelphians home needing just one more victory to wrap up their second straight World Series championship.

After Philadelphia won the first two games of the series, St. Louis bounced back to win the next two. Good pitching characterized the games.

But today's fifth game was the best pitched of the series. Nibbling at the corners, Grimes often fell behind on the count. But his coolness in the pinches kept him in the game until he hung a fatal curveball to Foxx in the ninth. Earnshaw overpowered the National Leaguers with his speed and sharply breaking curve for seven innings, then he left for a pinch-hitter. Lefty Grove took over in the eighth, and, for the first time in the series, pitched with all of his fabled speed.

Each team got one hit in the first inning but did not score. Grimes retired two A's after the count went full.

Both sides went out in order in the second.

The A's went one-two-three again in the third, Joe Boley and Max Bishop striking out.

In the bottom of the third, the Cardinals mounted the first threat of the game. Charley Gelbert, the first man up, walked on four straight pitches. Grimes sacrificed him to second. Taylor Douthit followed with a bouncer to Jimmy Dykes at third. Dykes had Gelbert hung up between second and third and started to run him back toward second. But for some inexplicable reason, he never threw the ball, and Gelbert returned to second safely, while Douthit reached first. But Earnshaw was equal to the crisis, popping Sparky Adams up and inducing Frankie Frisch to ground out.

Both hurlers worked through the fourth inning without serious trouble. Grimes ran the count to three-and-two on all three Philadelphia hitters, but none reached base. Earnshaw walked Chick Hafey, but he didn't get to second.

Foxx opened the fifth with a hit past Gelbert. He was forced by Bing Miller. Mule Haas followed with a hopper that Sparky Adams flagged down, and with an off-balance throw, Adams started a double play.

The Cardinals went out quickly in the bottom of the inning.

Fine infielding helped retire both sides in order in the sixth. Gelbert, Frisch, and Earnshaw made good plays.

Leading off the seventh, Dykes walked on another full count. Mickey Cochrane then lifted a pop near the plate and disgustedly stormed toward the dugout, even though the ball was caught in fair territory. The St. Louis bench made sure that Mickey heard about that mistake, throwing in a few choice comments about Cochrane's big ears. Simmons then sliced a dangerous drive toward the right field corner. But George Watkins snared the ball after a long run, earning a big cheer from the St. Louis fans. The cheering increased when Grimes fanned Foxx to end the inning.

With two out in the home half, Jimmie Wilson hit safely to center and alertly hustled to second when Haas was lackadaisical about fielding the ball. Gelbert was intentionally passed to get to Grimes. Burleigh almost crossed up the strategy with a hot drive to right center, but Haas sprinted over to make the catch.

In the eighth, the A's loaded the bases. With one down, Haas dropped a safe bunt down the third base line. He tried to steal second. Wilson's throw had him beaten, but Frisch dropped the ball, and the runner was safe. Boley then rapped an infield hit off Grimes's glove, putting men on first and third with one out. At this juncture, Mack surprised most observers by pinch-hitting for Earnshaw. The sub, Jim Moore, walked to load the bases. Bishop grounded to Bottomley, who threw home for a force. Dykes then bounced to Gelbert, who flipped to Frisch for another force, ending the inning.

Lefty Grove, who had pitched a complete game just the day before, came in to pitch. After retiring the first two batters, he was hit for a single by Frisch. It was the Cardinal captain's first hit in 15 trips to the plate. Jim Bottomley then struck out for the third time in the game. The St. Louis cleanup hitter's average for the series dropped to .050.

Cochrane walked to open the ninth, and Al Simmons came to the plate. He made a big demonstration of hitching up his pants and tucking in his shirt before stepping into the box. After the first pitch, Grimes sarcastically mimicked Simmons's actions, and the St. Louis bench added derision. The big slugger then popped out weakly.

Grimes then tried to show Foxx a curveball outside. But the pitch didn't break widely enough. It came across the plate belt high, and Foxx lined it deep into the bleachers in left center. The jubilant Cochrane, sauntering around the bases ahead of Foxx, took the occasion to put his hands to his head and flap his ears at Grimes. His teammates added insulting comments and gestures from the bench.

With a 2-0 lead, Grove easily disposed of the Cardinals in the bottom of the ninth. He walked Ray Blades but did not allow the ball to be hit out of the infield. Gelbert ended the game by looking at a called third strike.

So, Grimes's effort was for naught, and the Cardinals fell behind in the series.

Philadelphia (AL)	ab	r	h	bi	o	a	e
M. Bishop, 2b	4	0	0	0	1	0	0
J. Dykes, 3b	3	0	0	0	0	1	0
M. Cochrane, c	3	1	1	0	7	1	0
A. Simmons, lf	4	0	0	0	3	0	0
J. Foxx, 1b	4	1	2	2	12	0	0
B. Miller, rf	4	0	0	0	0	0	0
M. Haas, cf	4	0	1	0	2	0	0
J. Boley, ss	3	0	1	0	2	1	0
G. Earnshaw, p	2	0	0	0	0	4	0
J. Moore, ph8	0	0	0	0	-	-	-
L. Grove, p8	0	0	0	0	0	1	0
	31	2	5	2	27	8	0

St. Louis (NL)	ab	r	h	bi	o	a	e
T. Douthit, cf	4	0	0	0	2	0	0
S. Adams, 3b	4	0	1	0	0	1	0
F. Frisch, 2b	4	0	1	0	3	3	1
J. Bottomley, 1b	4	0	0	0	9	1	0
C. Hafey, lf	3	0	0	0	1	0	0
G. Watkins, rf	3	0	0	0	1	0	0
R. Blades, ph9	0	0	0	0	-	-	-
J. Wilson, c	4	0	1	0	9	0	0
C. Gelbert, ss	2	0	0	0	2	8	0
B. Grimes, p	2	0	0	0	0	0	0
	30	0	3	0	27	13	1

Philadelphia 000 000 002 - 2
St. Louis 000 000 000 - 0

	ip	h	r-er	bb	so
Earnshaw	7	2	0-0	3	5
Grove (W 2-1)	2	1	0-0	1	2
Grimes (L 0-2)	9	5	2-2	3	7

Umpires: G. Moriarty, C. Rigler, H. Geisel, & B. Reardon

LOB: Phil 5, StL 8. BE: none.
DP: Adams-Frisch-Bottomley.
2B: Wilson. HR: Foxx. SH: Grimes.
SB: none. CS: Haas.
Time - 1:58
Attendance - 38,844

After resting one day while the teams traveled back to Philadelphia, George Earnshaw came back on Wednesday and beat the Cardinals in the sixth game, 7-1. That gave the Athletics the series four games to two.

1931 — Sunday, July 12th, at Sportsman's Park
Record Crowd of 45,770 Sees Cards and Cubs Divide Twinbill
Record of 32 Doubles Made
Overflow of Fans Hinders Fielders, Makes Play a Farce

Today was a great day for the St. Louis Cardinals' treasury, but it was a bad day for the game of baseball. A total of 45,770 persons paid a total of $46,629 into the club's coffers in order to watch a doubleheader between the Cardinals and the Chicago Cubs. What they saw was one of the worst excuses for regulation baseball ever staged by professional clubs.

With the crowd occupying every square inch of the stands, the overflow was allowed to stand down the foul lines and around the perimeter of the outfield. Since the club and the police department had not anticipated such a large turnout, the fans easily broke through the restraining ropes and encroached upon the playing area. As a result, several fly balls that traveled a scant 200 feet wound up falling into the crowd for ground-rule doubles. In all, 32 two-baggers were accumulated during the two games, including 23 in the second contest, when all efforts at restraining the throng were abandoned. Of the total, no more than five or six of the hits would have yielded two bases under normal conditions.

At least both teams were equally handicapped, and each side won a game and lost a game. The opener went to the Cubs, 7-5, then the Cardinals took the nightcap, 17-13.

The trouble started long before the beginning of the games. The crowd had filled all the seats and all the potential standing room in the grandstand before noon. Then the gates in the fence were opened, and fans streamed all over the field, interrupting infield practice, grabbing baseballs from players, and surrounding the dugouts.

As the 1:30 game time approached, St. Louis club president Sam Breadon personally led the efforts to clear the field so that the games could start. Sam was greeted with jeers from some box-seat holders, who wanted to know why such a large crowd had been allowed in in the first place.

The police, ushers, players, and umpires were able to get the infield cleared quickly, but the outfield remained a battleground all afternoon. When the ushers would try to push the crowd back in one area, it would surge forward in another sector.

The umpires finally decided to go ahead with the game, despite the crowding. The Cubs scored a run in the second inning on doubles by Hack Wilson and Rogers Hornsby. The Cardinals got three runs in the fourth. There were doubles by George Watkins, Rip Collins, and Ernie Orsatti, plus a single by Frankie Frisch and an error by Wilson. Wilson felt that he had been interfered with by the fans in the outfield, and Chicago manager Hornsby protested that the game should be forfeited by the home team if the crowd could not be restrained.

At this juncture, public address announcer Kelly and manager Street went out to implore the fans to retreat. The appeal was temporarily effective, and play resumed.

Home runs by Kiki Cuyler (in the sixth) and Hack Wilson (in the seventh with two men on) put Chicago into the lead. Charlie Grimm added a two-run single in the seventh to rout Cardinal starter Bill Hallahan.

St. Louis scored two runs in the seventh and threatened again in the eighth. But Guy Bush relieved Jakie May and saved the game for Chicago.

Immediately after the game ended, the crowd occupied the entire field.

The mob once again cleared the infield at the start of the second game. But they gave very little ground in the outfield and in foul territory. With the fans less than 100 feet from the base lines almost all of the way around, the game was a farce. Nine pitchers tried to stop the hitting, but the doubles and runs came hot and heavy. To add to the slaughter, the infielders lost their heads and made seven errors.

Today's Results
Chicago 7 - ST. LOUIS 5 (1st game)
ST. LOUIS 17 - Chicago 13 (2nd)
New York 13 - Philadelphia 6 (1st game)
New York 9 - Philadelphia 4 (2nd)
Brooklyn 7 - Boston 4 (1st game)
Boston 4 - Brooklyn 3 (12 inn.) (2nd)
Cincinnati 14 - Pittsburgh 7 (1st game)
Cincinnati 6 - Pittsburgh 5 (11 inn.) (2nd)

Standings	W-L	Pct.	GB
ST. LOUIS	51-31	.622	-
New York	44-32	.579	4
Brooklyn	45-36	.556	5½
Chicago	43-35	.551	6
Boston	40-39	.506	9½
Philadelphia	34-46	.425	16
Pittsburgh	31-44	.413	16½
Cincinnati	28-53	.346	22½

Chicago scored twice in the first, thanks to errors by Sparky Adams. St. Louis got three in the same round on a couple pop-fly doubles and an error by Footsie Blair. Blair got a three-run homer in the fourth, but the Cards scored seven times in their half, using five two-baggers.

Allan Stout went in to pitch for St. Louis in the fifth, and he failed to retire a batter, as Chicago tied the game at 10-10. But the Cubs sent a new pitcher, Ed Baecht, to the mound in the bottom of the inning, and he walked the only two men he faced. Charley Root, who had started the opener, came in and was hit for doubles by Frisch and Collins, giving the Cardinals three runs and the lead.

Rookie Paul Derringer held the lead for the rest of the game. He allowed three runs, but the Cards got four off "Sheriff" Fred Blake. The final score was 17-13, and the final total was 23 doubles for the game.

Too bad they hadn't been legitimate two-base hits. And too bad the fans hadn't gotten to see legitimate major league baseball.

FIRST GAME

		r	h	e	Batteries
Chicago	010 001 500 —	7	14	2	C. Root 4 IP, J. May (W 3-1) 3.1 IP, G. Bush 1.2 IP & R. Hemsley.
St. Louis	000 300 200 —	5	9	1	B. Hallahan (L 9-7) 6.2 IP, J. Linsey .1 IP, P. Derringer 2 IP & J. Wilson.

SECOND GAME

Chicago	ab	r	h	bi	o	a	e
F. Blair, 2b	6	3	3	4	2	2	1
W. English, ss	6	1	3	2	2	5	1
K. Cuyler, rf	3	0	0	0	1	0	0
H. Wilson, lf	6	0	1	0	1	0	0
R. Hornsby, 3b	4	1	2	0	1	1	0
D. Taylor, cf	4	1	0	0	1	0	1
C. Grimm, 1b	5	2	1	0	8	0	0
G. Hartnett, c	5	3	5	1	8	1	0
P. Malone, p	0	1	0	0	0	0	0
G. Bush, p4	0	0	0	0	0	0	0
L. Bell, ph5	1	1	1	2	-	-	-
E. Baecht, p5	0	0	0	0	0	0	0
C. Root, p5	0	0	0	0	0	0	0
L. Sweetland, ph6	1	0	0	0	-	-	-
S. Blake, p6	0	0	0	0	0	1	0
L. Warneke, p8	0	0	0	0	0	0	0
R. Stephenson, ph9	1	0	0	0	-	-	-
	42	13	16	9	24	10	3

St. Louis	ab	r	h	bi	o	a	e
S. Adams, ss	4	3	1	0	2	3	4
G. Watkins, rf	5	3	1	1	0	0	0
F. Frisch, 2b	5	3	3	1	1	5	0
R. Collins, 1b	6	2	4	4	8	0	0
C. Hafey, lf	5	2	3	3	0	0	0
P. Martin, cf	6	1	3	3	3	1	0
A. High, 3b	4	1	1	1	0	0	0
G. Mancuso, c	5	1	4	2	13	1	0
F. Rhem, p	1	0	0	0	0	1	1
E. Orsatti, ph4	2	1	1	1	-	-	-
A. Stout, p5	0	0	0	0	0	0	0
P. Derringer, p5	3	0	0	0	0	0	0
	46	17	21	16	27	11	5

Chicago	200 441 002	—	13
St. Louis	300 732 02x	—	17

	ip	h	r-er	bb	so
Malone	3.1	10	7-4	0	3
Bush	.2	3	3-3	1	0
Baecht (L 2-3)	*0	0	2-2	2	0
Root	1	2	1-1	0	0
Blake	**2	6	4-4	3	3
Warneke	1	0	0-0	1	0
Rhem	4	7	6-3	3	5
Stout	#0	2	4-3	1	0
Derringer (W 10-3)	5	7	3-3	1	6

Umpires: C. Pfirman, C. Rigler, & B. Clarke

LOB: Chi 9, StL 13. DP: Martin-Mancuso, Frisch-Adams-Collins, English Grimm.
2B: Blair 2, Collins 3, Hafey 2, Hartnett 3, English 3, Mancuso 3, Orsatti, Frisch 2, High, Bell Hornsby, Watkins.
HR: Blair. SH: Malone, Cuyler.
HBP: by Root (High).
WP: Stout, Derringer 2, Blake.
Time - 2:44
Attendance - 45,770
*faced two batters in fifth
**faced three batters in eighth
#faced four batters in fifth

The 1931 Cardinals were a team with great talent and tremendous depth. They won the pennant going away.

Their final record was 101-53, giving them a 13-game margin over the second-place Giants.

1931 World Series—Game #7

Saturday, October 10th, at Sportsman's Park

Cardinals Beat Athletics, 4-2, to Win World Championship

Daring Base Running, Watkins's Home Run Set Pace

Grimes the Winning Pitcher

The St. Louis Cardinals ended the Philadelphia Athletics two-year reign as champions of the world of baseball by winning the seventh and decisive game of the 1931 World Series, 4-2. The victory avenged last year's loss of the series to the A's. Burleigh Grimes, loser of two tough games in the 1930 classic, was the winning pitcher for the second time in the series. And Bill Hallahan, who scored the other two St. Louis victories, saved the game in the ninth inning. To make the victory even sweeter, the Cardinals defeated George Earnshaw, their chief tormentor in the 1930 series.

Gabby Street's men were outhit today, but they won with aggressive base running and flawless fielding. By forcing the Athletics into mistakes, the Cards were able to turn pop-fly singles by Andy High and George Watkins into runs in the first inning. In the third inning their attack was more straightforward, High singling and Watkins homering. Grimes kept the Athletics scoreless until he tired in the ninth. After two runs were in with two out, Hallahan was called in to retire the last batter.

Only 20,805 St. Louis fans made their way to the park today. The chilly weather, the manner of the home team's 7-1 defeat on Friday, and the ridiculously short time alloted for selling tickets were factors in the small draw. And the general feeling around town had been that Earnshaw would stop the Cards once again. Indeed, the Cardinals managed just four hits off the big righthander, bringing their two-year total against him to just 25 safeties in 49 innings. But they made their hits count today.

The Red Birds played without two of their regulars. Batting champ Chick Hafey, who hit only .167 in the series, was benched after injuring a finger dropping a fly ball on Friday. Today he was replaced by Ernie Orsatti, who struck out three times. Sparky Adams was unable to play due to an ankle injury. But handy Andy High filled in in fine style.

After the visitors were retired in order in the top of the first, High led off for St. Louis with a pop to short left center. Al Simmons and Dib Williams converged on the ball. But at the last second, both men pulled up to avoid a collision, and the ball fell safely. George Watkins also hit a high pop, this one down the left field line. Left fielder Simmons was playing well off the line for the lefthanded batter, and shortstop Williams was unable to get under the ball, despite a long run. It fell for another single, putting men on first and second. Frisch sacrificed the runners up one station.

Then the Philadelphia battery began to falter in their execution. Pepper Martin, the hitting star of the series, came to the plate looking for a record-breaking 13th hit. Earnshaw pitched him carefully, working the count to 2-and-2. After two fouls, Earnshaw threw one high and wide, which Cochrane missed. The wild pitch enabled High to score and Watkins to move to third. Martin then walked. He stole second on the first pitch to Orsatti, making a long, head-first slide. Orsatti fanned, but Cochrane dropped the third strike. With first base unoccupied, Orsatti ran down the line, forcing the catcher to throw to first for the out. As soon as the ball left Cochrane's hand, Watkins made a dash for the plate. Jimmie Foxx took the throw for the out at first, but his return to the plate was low and Cochrane couldn't handle it cleanly, allowing Watkins to score on a close play. Jim Bottomley struck out, but St. Louis led, 2-0.

The Athletics threatened in the second inning. Simmons and Bing Miller singled around an out by Foxx. Jimmy Dykes then hit a potential double play ball to High, who got it and threw to Frisch for a force at second. But Miller's hard slide prevented a throw to first, and the A's had men at first and third. Williams hit a dangerous tap past the mound, but Charley Gelbert charged in from shortstop and threw the batter out at first for the third out of the inning.

In the St. Louis second, Jimmie Wilson walked but was wiped out when Gelbert hit into a double play.

With one out in the third, Max Bishop worked a base on balls. But he was immediately picked off by catcher Wilson's snap throw. Mule Haas then hit a long fly to right that Watkins gathered in on the warning track.

The Cardinals then came in and doubled their score. Again it was High and Watkins who scored. High opened with a clean single to center. On the next pitch, Watkins pulled a fastball onto the roof of the right field pavilion for a homer and two runs.

That was all the offense that the Cardinals mounted against Earnshaw, who retired the next 15 hitters.

They got one hit off reliever Rube Walberg in the eighth.

Meanwhile, Grimes held the Athletics safe. Judiciously choosing his pitches and their locations, he retired the Philadelphians without much trouble through the eighth. A double play got him out of his only tight spot in the fifth. In the eighth, he walked two men, but gave up no hits.

The game came down to the ninth inning with St. Louis ahead, 4-0. Grimes walked the first hitter, Simmons. He got Foxx to foul out. Miller then hit to Gelbert, who flipped to Frisch, who in turn threw to first. The Cardinals thought they had a game-ending double play, but umpire Bill McGowan called Miller safe at first. Grimes used his last ounce of energy arguing. When he returned to the mound, he walked Dykes. Williams worked the count full, then scratched a hit off High's glove, loading the bases. Pinch-hitter Doc Cramer lopped a 2-2 pitch to center for a two-run single.

With the tying runs on base, Street had to bring in Hallahan to relieve Grimes. Old Burleigh was barely able to lift his feet as he shuffled to the dugout. Bishop worked the count full against Hallahan, then lifted a fly to short center that Martin caught for the final out.

Grimes looked quite rejuvenated when he ran to the mound to congratulate Hallahan. Then the new champions hustled to the clubhouse for a wild victory celebration.

Philadelphia (AL)	ab	r	h	bi	o	a	e
M. Bishop, 2b	4	0	0	0	2	1	0
M. Haas, cf	3	0	0	0	2	0	0
M. Cochrane, c	4	0	0	0	8	2	0
A. Simmons, lf	3	0	1	0	0	0	0
J. Foxx, 1b	4	0	0	0	11	0	1
B. Miller, rf	4	1	3	0	0	0	0
J. Dykes, 3b	3	1	0	0	1	3	0
D. Williams, ss	4	0	2	0	0	2	0
G. Earnshaw, p	2	0	0	0	0	2	0
P. Todt, ph8	0	0	0	0	-	-	-
R. Walberg, p8	0	0	0	0	0	0	0
D. Cramer, ph9	1	0	1	2	-	-	-
	32	2	7	2	24	10	1

St. Louis (NL)	ab	r	h	bi	o	a	e
A. High, 3b	4	2	3	0	1	4	0
G. Watkins, rf	3	2	2	2	2	0	0
F. Frisch, 2b	3	0	0	0	2	4	0
P. Martin, cf	3	0	0	0	1	0	0
E. Orsatti, lf	3	0	0	0	1	0	0
J. Bottomley, 1b	3	0	0	0	12	0	0
J. Wilson, c	2	0	0	0	7	1	0
C. Gelbert, ss	3	0	0	0	1	4	0
B. Grimes, p	3	0	0	0	0	1	0
B. Hallahan, p9	0	0	0	0	0	0	0
	27	4	5	2	27	14	0

Philadelphia	000 000 002	-	2	
St. Louis	202 000 00x	-	4	

	ip	h	r-er	bb	so
Earnshaw (L 1-2)	7	4	4-3	2	7
Walberg	1	1	0-0	1	2
Grimes (W 2-0)	8.2	7	2-2	5	6
Hallahan	.1	0	0-0	0	0

WP: Earnshaw

LOB: Phil 8, StL 3. BE: none.
DP: Dykes-Bishop-Foxx, Gelbert-Frisch-Bottomley.
HR: Watkins. SH: Frisch.
SB: Martin. Picked Off: Bishop.
Time - 1:57
Attendance - 20,805
Umpires: D. Stark, B. McGowan, B. Klem, & R. Nallin

Photo by Strauss

Courtesy Missouri Historical Society

The 1885 St. Louis Browns of the old American Association, the franchise's first pennant winner.
Front row (left to right): Yank Robison, Arlie Latham, Bob Caruthers, George McGinnis, Dan Sullivan, and Hugh Nicol.
Back row: Doc Bushong, Curt Welch, Sam Barkley, Dave Foutz, Tip O'Neill, and Bill Gleason.
Insets: (left) owner Chris Von der Ahe, (right) captain Charlie Comiskey.
In the background is a view of the grandstand of the original Sportsman's Park.

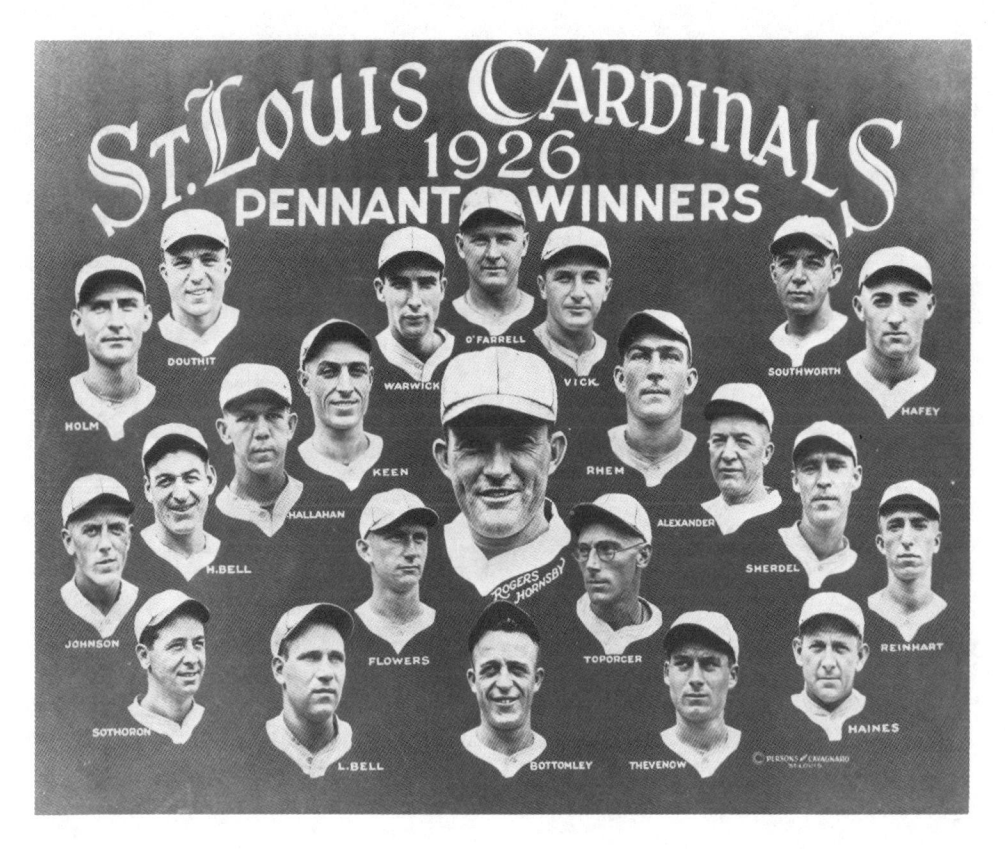

W.C. Persons, Photographer   Courtesy Missouri Historical Society

The 1926 Cardinals, St. Louis's first National League pennant winner.

Photo by W.C. Persons Courtesy Missouri Historical Society

Two views of Sportsman's Park (Grand Avenue at Dodier)
Above: Looking Across the outfield, 1939.
Below: Looking toward home plate from atop the roof of the right field pavilion during the 1948 All-Star Game

St. Louis Chamber of Commerce Photo Courtesy Missouri Historical Society

Photo by Charles Bartlett, Sr.   Courtesy Missouri Historical Society

Above: Fires were the bane of wooden ballparks. This fire at League Park (Natural Bridge Ave. at Vandeventer) took place on May 4, 1901. It destroyed much of the grandstand that had been built following the disastrous fire of April 16, 1898.

Below: Two generations of Cardinal catchers.

    Mike Gonzalez (left), who played for St. Louis off and on from 1915 until 1932 and who coached for the Cardinals from 1934 through 1946.

    Bill DeLancey (right), who caught for the Gas House Gang in 1934 and 1935.

Photo by Hangge   Courtesy Missouri Historical Society

Courtesy Missouri Historical Society

George Watkins's heroics in the seventh game of the 1931 World Series:
Above: Watkins slides home safely in the first inning when catcher Mickey Cochrane couldn't hold a return throw from first base following a dropped third strike. The ball is by Watkins's right hand. The umpire is Albert D. "Dolly" Stark.
Below: Watkins trots across the plate after hitting a two-run home run in the third inning. Frankie Frisch (holding two bats), the batboy, and Andy High are all ready to shake George's hand.

Courtesy Missouri Historical Society

Courtesy Missouri Historical Society

Above: Two leading spirits of the Gas House Gang: Pepper Martin (left) and Dizzy Dean.

Below: Three lesser known heroes:
  (Left) Luis Arroyo, who was a flash-in-the-pan rookie for the Cards in 1955. This picture was taken in 1954, when Arroyo was with the minor league Houston Buffaloes.
  (center) Herm Wehmeier, the St. Louis pitcher whose 12-inning masterpiece knocked Milwaukee out of first place on the day before the 1956 season ended.
  (right) Carl Taylor, Cardinal utility man and pinch-hitter in 1970. His grand slam won a game for St. Louis, 11-10, against San Diego on August 11, 1970.

Courtesy St. Louis Cardinals

Courtesy St. Louis Cardinals

Above: One of the greatest outfields in baseball history: (left to right) Enos Slaughter, Terry Moore, and Stan Musial, pictured here in 1942.
Below: The Cardinals' double play combination in the late 1940's: shortstop Marty Marion (left) and second baseman Red Schoendienst.

Photo by Jack Levy

Courtesy St. Louis Cardinals

Courtesy St. Louis Cardinals

Above: The Cardinals infield of 1963 and 1964. (left to right) third baseman Ken Boyer, shortstop Dick Groat, second baseman Julian Javier, and first baseman Bill White.

Below: Spring training, 1961. Manager Solly Hemus (center) and his coaches (left to right) Howie Pollet, Johnny Keane, Darrell Johnson, and Harry Walker. Keane replaced Hemus as manager on July 6, 1961.

Photo by Levy

Courtesy St. Louis Cardinals

Courtesy St. Louis Cardinals

Above: 1964 World Series - Seventh Game.
Tim McCarver scores on a double steal in the fourth inning. The Yankee catcher is Elston Howard.
Below: August 14, 1971.
Bob Gibson working on his no-hitter. The batter is Gene Clines, who struck out pinch-hitting in the eighth inning.

Courtesy St. Louis Cardinals

Photo by Bill Knight

Courtesy St. Louis Cardinals

Above: Al Hrabosky delivers a fastball.
Below: A banner brought to Busch Memorial Stadium on "We Hlove Hrabosky Hbanner Hday," July 12, 1975.

Courtesy St. Louis Cardinals

Courtesy St. Louis Cardinals

August 29, 1977.
 Above: Lou Brock slides into second base with his record-breaking 893rd stolen base. The fielder is San Diego shortstop Bill Almon.
 Below: The San Diego Stadium message board announces the record.

Photo by The Negative Approach

Courtesy St. Louis Cardinals

Photo by Dennis Davito   Courtesy St. Louis Cardinals

Above: April 16, 1978. Bob Forsch and Ted Simmons about to embrace after the last out of Forsch's no-hitter.
Below: May 1, 1979. Roger Freed (center, without a cap) being greeted at home plate after his grand slam in the eleventh inning won the game for the Cardinals. Keith Hernandez (left) and Ken Oberkfell (24) are the other Red Birds facing the camera.

Courtesy St. Louis Cardinals

Chapter VII

The Gas House Gang
1932-1939

1932—August 14th at Sportsman's Park
Carleton & Dean Hurl St. Louis to Two Victories Over Chicago

1933—July 2nd at New York
Giants Sweep Cardinals With Brilliant Double Shutout

1934—September 21st at Brooklyn
Paul Dean Pitches No-Hitter After Three-Hitter by Dizzy

1934—World Series—Game #7
Cardinals Trounce Tigers, 11-0, to Win World Series Title

1935—July 18th at Sportsman's Park
Red Birds Rout Braves, 13-3, for 14th Consecutive Victory

1936—April 29th at Sportsman's Park
Cards' Parmelee Beats Giants' Hubbell in 17-Inning Duel

1937—August 4th at Sportsman's Park
Pinch Hit by Frisch Caps Ninth-Inning, Game-Winning Rally

1938—September 11th at Sportsman's Park
Frisch Fired as St. Louis Manager, P. Dean Pitches 6-4 Win

1939—August 20th at Cincinnati
Cardinals Win Two in Cincinnati, Trail Reds by 3½ Games

After they won the world championship in 1931, the Cardinals traded batting champion Chick Hafey and World Series hero Burleigh Grimes. Some new faces arrived to help change the image of the team. Rookie pitchers Tex Carleton and Dizzy Dean made the team in the spring of 1932. Manager Gabby Street, however, lost his rapport with the players, and the Cardinals struggled through most of the season. When Carleton and Dean combined to beat the first-place Chicago Cubs in a doubleheader in mid-August, the Red Birds still had a ray of hope in the pennant race. But they soon fell hopelessly out of contention and finished the season tied for sixth.

Dizzy Dean, of course, was a great character as well as a great pitcher. He had two "real names": Jay Hanna Dean and Jerome Herman Dean, and he had an amusing story to tell about it. He also told three different sportswriters three different birthplaces and birthdates. Teamed with Pepper Martin and practical joker Rip Collins, Dean's off-field antics became almost as famous as his pitching accomplishments.

In 1933, Dean won 20 games for St. Louis, and Carleton added 17 wins. The Cardinals were in close contention for first place through most of June. But on July 2nd, they lost a famous doubleheader to the league-leading New York Giants and fell to 5½ games behind. Both Dean and Carleton pitched very well that day, but the Cards were shut out by Carl Hubbell and Roy Parmelee for 27 innings and lost both games by 1-0 scores.

St. Louis fell to fifth place by July 24th, and Street was replaced as manager by Frankie Frisch. The team finished fifth.

In 1934, Dizzy Dean's brother Paul joined the squad. He and his brother headed the pitching staff, and Collins and Joe Medwick led the batting attack. Manager Frisch and his captain, shortstop Leo Durocher, made life difficult for umpiring crews. And the Cardinals began to jell as a team.

They spent much of the summer in third place, and they trailed the league-leading Giants by 7 games with just over three weeks left in the season. But then they made their move. When Dizzy (with relief help from Carleton) and Paul beat the Giants in a doubleheader on September 16th, the deficit was cut to 3½ games. Five days later, the brothers teamed for a double shutout in Brooklyn, Diz hurling a three-hitter and Paul following with a no-hitter. Over the remaining nine days, Dizzy pitched three complete games and relieved twice. Meanwhile, the Giants collapsed, and the Cardinals pulled out the pennant by a 2-game margin. Dizzy finished the season with 30 wins, and Paul wound up with 19.

The Dean boys each won two games in the World Series against the Detroit Tigers, and the Cardinals won the world championship, 4 games to 3. St. Louis took the seventh game, 11-0, behind Dizzy's pitching.

The team picked up the immortal nickname "The Gas House Gang" in 1935. It was quite appropriate. Hard-nosed, quick-fisted, and dirt-caked, they played to the hilt and would do anything to win.

In 1935, they set a club record with a 14-game winning streak. They moved into first place in late August but were overtaken down the stretch by the Chicago Cubs and finished second.

In 1936, the team had problems with the infield and the pitching. Roy Parmelee, acquired from the Giants, started out well, winning his third start, 2-1, with a brilliant, seventeen-inning effort. But he finished the season just 11-11. Paul Dean (5-5) had serious shoulder problems. Brother Dizzy did yeoman's work both starting and relieving, but the team was once again overtaken, this time by the Giants in late August. St. Louis finished tied for second place.

In 1937, Joe Medwick had his greatest year, batting .374 with 154 runs-batted-in. Frisch got his last big league hit on August 4th to win a game. But D. Dean broke his toe in the All-Star Game and was through as a pitching star. Poor pitching led to a fourth-place finish.

In 1938, Medwick slipped to .322, Dean was traded to Chicago, and the team slipped to sixth. Frisch was fired as manager on September 11th.

In 1939, with Ray Blades managing, the Cardinals made a run at first place in August. They got to within 3½ games on the 12th but could not catch the first-place Cincinnati Reds. The Cards finished second.

1932—Sunday, August 14th, at Sportsman's Park
Rookies Carleton and Dean Hurl Cardinals to Two Victories Over Cubs
Tex Pitches 2-0 Shutout in Opener, Dizzy Wins, 2-1, in Ten Innings
Spectacular Fielding Plays Save Each Game

Backing the sensational pitching of two rookies with some clutch fielding gems, the St. Louis Cardinals took both games of a doubleheader from the league-leading Chicago Cubs. The double victory gave the Red Birds seven victories in their last eight games, giving rise to hopes of another miracle pennant drive like the one in 1930. Although the Cards remained in sixth place, they moved to only 6 games behind the leaders. But, with just 42 games left to play, their chances of passing five clubs and grabbing their third consecutive flag could not be called good.

But there was some encouragement for the future. Two youngsters, James Otto "Tex" Carleton and Jerome Herman (or was that Jay Hanna?) "Dizzy" Dean beat established veteran pitchers Pat Malone and Guy Bush with minimal batting support.

Today's Results
ST. LOUIS 2 - Chicago 0 (1st game)
ST. LOUIS 2 - Chicago 1 (10 inn.)(2nd)
Brooklyn 2 - New York 1 (10 inn.)(1st)
New York 8 - Brooklyn 4 (2nd)
Cincinnati 3 - Boston 1 (1st game)
Cincinnati 9 - Boston 3 (2nd)
  no other game scheduled

Standings	W-L	Pct.	GB
Chicago	60-50	.545	-
Pittsburgh	60-51	.541	½
Brooklyn	61-55	.526	2
Philadelphia	59-57	.509	4
Boston	58-58	.500	5
ST. LOUIS	55-57	.491	6
New York	51-60	.459	9½
Cincinnati	51-67	.432	13

St. Louis was outhit in the opener, seven to five, but Carleton kept the Chicago hits well scattered until the late going. He then managed to get out of trouble, thanks to a spectacular catch in the ninth by James "Rip" Collins.

Dean had all the best of Bush in the second game and, except for an error by Jim Bottomley, would have won in regulation time, 1-0. "Sunny Jim" redeemed himself with four hits and with a brilliant stop to save a run in the top of the tenth.

Manager Gabby Street was ejected in the first inning of the opener for disputing a call on a stolen base attempt. About the second inning, he showed up in civilian clothes and stationed himself in a seat behind the Cardinal dugout. He could be seen from the pressbox, but he managed to keep out of the umpires' view. "Old Sarge" remained at that station, surreptitiously directing his troops for the rest of the afternoon.

The Cardinals edged to a 1-0 lead in the second inning of the first game. Ernie Orsatti walked and moved to third on Collins's one-out double to right center. Gus Mancuso's long fly enabled Orsatti to score.

Against Carleton, only two Cubs got past first base during the first seven innings. In the fifth, second baseman Jimmy Reese booted a grounder from the bat of Riggs Stephenson to open the inning. The runner moved to third on two infield outs, then Carleton fanned Gabby Hartnett, leaving Stephenson stranded. Billy Jurges singled to open the sixth and was bunted to second, but he got no farther.

Two double plays complimented Carleton's fine pitching.

St. Louis added a second run in the seventh inning. With one down, George Watkins popped a hit to left. He moved to second on a wild pitch and to third on a ground out. After Mancuso walked, Carleton drove in the insurance run with a single.

The Cubs made bids to score in each of the last two innings.

In the ninth, Stephenson and Johnny Moore singled with one out, putting men on first and third. Charlie Grimm then corked one to deep right, which looked like a game-tying triple. But Collins raced back and made a leaping, glove-handed catch at the fence. The runners had taken off at the crack of the bat, and Collins returned the ball to first base for an easy double play, ending the game.

Dean, a favorite of the fans and writers since he gave himself multiple names and birthplaces, started the second game with a flourish. Billy Herman opened against him with a single, but the next three batters struck out. Diz also fanned the three batters he faced in the second inning. With six strikeouts, he was just one short of the modern major league record. He got two strikes on Jurges, the first batter in the third, but the Cub shortstop popped out.

After the game, Dean fumed that no one had informed him that he as close to a record. Had he known, he said, "A good curve would have put Jurges out on strikes, too."

The Cubs got their only run of the day in the fourth. Woody English, first up, walked. Kiki Cuyler tried to sacrifice but forced English, instead. Dean then had Cuyler picked off first, but Bottomley threw wildly toward second, allowing the runner to reach third safely. He scored easily on a double by Stephenson.

The Cardinals tied the game in their fourth. Bottomley walked, moved up on a wild pitch, and scored on Orsatti's second hit of the game.

The score remained 1-1 through the ninth.

In the final regulation round, Chicago threatened seriously. English opened with a double, and Cuyler was hit by a pitch. Stephenson bunted, and Dean pounced on the ball and threw to third for a force out. After a pop out, another hit batsman loaded the bases. Hartnett hit a hot shot toward right, but Reese knocked it down and recovered in time to throw the batter out at first.

In the top of the tenth, Jurges opened with another two-bagger. he was bunted to third. Herman hit sharply to third, and Frankie Frisch threw Jurges out at the plate. Herman stole second, and English walked. Cuyler chopped one over first base. Bottomley made a leaping stop and dove to the bag just ahead of Cuyler, getting the third out while Herman was steaming home.

The Cardinals then broke the game up in the bottom of the tenth. Charley Gelbert singled with one out and moved to third on Bottomley's two-out hit. Orsatti, the offensive star of the day, then singled home the game-winning run, and the Cardinals had a sweep over the league-leaders.

FIRST GAME

		r	h	e	Batteries
Chicago	000 000 000 -	0	7	0	P. Malone (L 11-12) 7 IP, J. May 1 IP & G. Hartnett, R. Hemsley.
St. Louis	010 000 10x -	2	5	1	T. Carleton (W 6-8) & G. Mancuso

SECOND GAME

Chicago	ab	r	h	bi	o	a	e	St. Louis	ab	r	h	bi	o	a	e
B. Herman, 2b	5	0	2	0	3	3	0	J. Reese, 2b	5	0	1	0	3	2	0
W. English, 3b	3	0	2	0	1	2	0	C. Gelbert, ss	5	1	1	0	5	3	0
K. Cuyler, rf	4	1	0	0	1	0	0	F. Frisch, 3b	5	0	2	0	1	1	0
R. Stephenson, lf	4	0	1	1	0	0	0	J. Bottomley, 1b	4	1	4	0	6	2	1
J. Moore, cf	4	0	0	0	1	1	0	E. Orsatti, cf	5	0	3	2	1	0	0
C. Grimm, 1b	3	0	0	0	12	2	0	G. Watkins, lf	4	0	0	0	3	0	0
R. Hemsley, c	2	0	0	0	3	1	0	R. Collins, rf	4	0	0	0	1	0	0
G. Hartnett, ph7-c	2	0	0	0	3	0	0	G. Mancuso, c	4	0	2	0	9	1	0
B. Jurges, ss	4	0	1	0	3	3	0	D. Dean, p	3	0	0	0	1	3	0
G. Bush, p	3	0	0	0	2	3	0								
	34	1	6	1	29	15	0		39	2	13	2	30	12	1

Chicago 000 100 000 0 - 1
St. Louis 000 100 000 1 - 2
two out when winning run scored

	ip	h	r-er	bb	so
Bush (L 12-10)	9.2	13	2-2	1	5
Dean (W 11-10)	10	6	1-0	2	8

WP: Bush 2. PB: Hemsley.
HBP: by Dean 2 (Cuyler, Grimm).

LOB: Chi 8, StL 10. BE: none.
2B: Stephenson, English, Mancuso, Jurges. SH: Dean, Bush.
SB: Herman 2. CS: Cuyler, Herman.
Time - 2:16 Attendance - 19,000
Umpires: E. Quigley & B. Reardon.

This was about the last hurrah for the Cardinals' pennant hopes in 1932. They edged into fifth place by the end of August but lost ground on the leaders.

Then St. Louis lost 18 of 27 in September and finished in a tie for sixth with a 72-82 record.

The Cubs, on the other hand, rebounded from this double defeat. They won 17 of their next 18 and cruised to the pennant.

1933 — Sunday, July 2nd, at the Polo Grounds, New York

Giants Beat Cards With Thrilling Double Shutout
Both Games Decided by 1-0 Scores
Hubbell Pitches 18-Inning Shutout in Opener

Strong pitching had put the surprising New York Giants into first place in the National League, and today they gave a stunning illustration of that strength. Although three St. Louis pitchers combined to hold the Giants to just two runs in 26 innings, New York's Carl Hubbell and Roy Parmelee each needed only one run to win, and the Giants swept a doubleheader, winning both games by the minimum score, 1-0. Cardinal starters Tex Carleton and Dizzy Dean both pitched great games, only to come up short. The double victory extended the Giants' lead over the second-place Red Birds to 5½ games.

Today's Results
New York 1 - ST. LOUIS 0 (18 inn.)(1st)
New York 1 - ST. LOUIS 0 (2nd game)
Brooklyn 7 - Chicago 3 (1st game)
Brooklyn 4 - Chicago 3 (2nd)
Boston 1 - Cincinnati 0 (1st game)
Cincinnati 3 - Boston 0 (2nd)
no other game scheduled

Standings	W-L	Pct.	GB
New York	43-25	.632	-
ST. LOUIS	39-32	.549	5½
Pittsburgh	37-34	.521	7½
Chicago	37-37	.500	9
Boston	35-37	.486	10
Brooklyn	33-36	.478	10½
Cincinnati	32-41	.438	13½
Philadelphia	29-43	.403	16

Carleton, who beat New York in the opening game of the series on Thursday, started the first game for St. Louis. Pitching on only two days of rest, the side-arming sinkerballer matched zeroes with Hubbell for 16 innings, then gave way to a pinch-hitter. Jess Haines relieved, and the Giants pushed a run across against him in the 18th inning to win the game.

Needing a victory in the second game, manager Gabby Street sent Dean to the mound. Dizzy had pitched on Friday, winning 1-0. Today, with only one day of rest, he came back with a five-hitter. Unfortunately, one of those hits was a home run, and Parmelee shut the Cardinals out to win, 1-0.

Both Parmelee and Hubbell were pitching on three days rest.

Hubbell was truly outstanding in the first game. His screwball, curve, and fastball were all working well. He retired the first twelve St. Louis batters. Rip Collins beat out a slow roller to break the string in the fifth inning. Joe Medwick followed by hitting into a double play. In the sixth, Jimmie Wilson lined one back through the box. Hubbell reached for the ball with his bare hand, and it sizzled through his fingers and into center field for a hit. The Giant pitching ace took some time to rub his hand, then decided that he could continue. He continued for twelve more innings!

After Ernie Orsatti doubled with one out in the seventh, Hubbell set down 19 men in order. With two out in the thirteenth inning, Medwick broke that string by slamming a hit off second baseman Hughie Critz's glove. Ten more St. Louis batters then were retired in a row. Then Wilson got another hit off Hubbell's glove to open the seventeenth. Gordon Slade sacrificed, and Street sent Bob O'Farrell to the plate to pinch-hit for Carleton. This disgusted the crowd, which wanted to see both pitchers stick it through to a decision. O'Farrell struck out, and Pepper Martin bounced to Critz, leavng Wilson stranded.

In the eighteenth, Collins doubled with two out and was tagged out after Medwick hit a bouncer to Johnny Vergez at third.

In the meantime, Carleton was as effective as Hubbell, if not quite as brilliant. New York didn't get a man to third until the eleventh inning. Then three walks (one intentional) loaded the bases with one out. In the crisis, Jo-Jo Moore grounded to Collins, who threw home for a force out. And Gus Mancuso ended the inning by bouncing into a force at second.

Bill Terry tripled with two out in the fifteenth. After Mel Ott was again intentionally passed, Vergez fouled to Wilson, who made a fine catch while leaping into the dugout.

Carleton received a hearty ovation as he headed for the clubhouse in the seventeenth.

Jess Haines took over the pitching duties for the visitors. He allowed a walk and a hit in the seventeenth, but escaped.

In the eighteenth, the Giants won the game. Moore started with a walk and was bunted to second. Pinch-hitter Travis Jackson received New York's fifth intentional pass of the game, and Hubbell forced him at second. With Moore on third and two out, Critz dropped a line single into right center, ending the game with the Giants winning, 1-0.

Hubbell had struck out 12, walked none, and allowed six hits. He had also tied the all-time record for longest shutout by one pitcher.

The second game did not get under way until 6:30. It was a cloudy day, and there seemed little chance of getting a full game in. But with two fastballers, Dizzy Dean and Roy Parmelee, opposing each other in the dusk, the game was over by 7:55.

Dean allowed just three singles, one double, and a home run, but he lost. The homer, by Johnny Vergez in the fourth inning, was not much more than a pop fly. It traveled less than 300 feet from the plate, but it was near the left field foul line and dropped into the upper tier of the grandstand. Parmelee faced the minimum number of batters through the first six innings, thanks to two men getting caught stealing. Orsatti and Pat Crawford got two-out singles in the seventh and eighth innings, respectively, but both were left on base. The Cardinals got their only runner to second in the ninth. Rogers Hornsby led off with a pinch single and was replaced on the bases by Ethan Allen. After Martin fanned, Allen went to second on Frisch's ground out. But Orsatti struck out, becoming Parmelee's 13th victim, and the game was over.

New York had its second 1-0 victory of the day. The Cardinals had just 10 hits and no runs in 27 innings of trying.

FIRST GAME

St. Louis	ab	r	h	bi	o	a	e	New York	ab	r	h	bi	o	a	e
P. Martin, 3b	7	0	0	0	3	6	0	H. Critz, 2b	9	0	3	1	4	12	0
F. Frisch, 2b	7	0	0	0	7	5	0	L. O'Doul, lf	4	0	1	0	0	0	0
E. Orsatti, cf	7	0	1	0	0	0	0	B. James, pr11	0	0	0	0	-	-	-
R. Collins, 1b	7	0	2	0	15	5	0	G. Davis, cf12	2	0	0	0	2	0	0
J. Medwick, lf	7	0	1	0	7	0	0	B. Terry, 1b	6	0	2	0	26	1	0
E. Allen, rf	6	0	0	0	4	0	0	M. Ott, rf	6	0	0	0	2	0	0
J. Wilson, c	6	0	2	0	11	1	0	J. Vergez, 3b	5	0	0	0	3	1	0
L. Durocher, ss	3	0	0	0	3	4	1	J. Moore, cf-lf12	7	1	0	0	3	0	0
R. Hornsby, ph11	1	0	0	0	-	-	-	G. Mancuso, c	7	0	1	0	13	1	0
G. Slade, ss11	1	0	0	0	1	2	0	B. Ryan, ss	6	0	2	0	0	5	0
T. Carleton, p	4	0	0	0	2	3	0	T. Jackson, ph18	0	0	0	0	-	-	-
B. O'Farrell, ph17	1	0	0	0	-	-	-	C. Hubbell, p	7	0	1	0	1	7	0
J. Haines, p17	0	0	0	0	0	2	0								
	57	0	6	0	53	28	1		59	1	10	1	54	27	0

St. Louis   000 000 000 000 000 000 - 0
New York   000 000 000 000 000 001 - 1
two out when winnng run scored
LOB: StL 5, NY 19. DP: Ryan-Critz-Terry. 2B: Orsatti, Collins.
3B: Terry. SH: Carleton, Hubbell, Terry, Slade, Davis, Manucuso.

	ip	h	r-er	bb	so	
Carleton	16	8	0-0	7	7	Time - 4:03 Attendance - 40,000
Haines (L 2-3)	1.2	2	1-1	3	1	Umpires: B. Klem, C. Pfirman,
Hubbell (W 11-5)	18	6	0-0	0	12	& G. Barr

SECOND GAME

		r	h	e	Batteries
St. Louis	000 000 000 -	0	4	0	D. Dean (L 9-8) & B. O'Farrell, J. Wilson
New York	000 100 00x -	1	5	1	R. Parmelee (W 7-2) & G. Mancuso.

The Cardinals continued to slump during the next three weeks. When they fell to fifth place, Gabby Street was fired, and Frank Frisch took over as manager.

They finished fifth, 9½ games behind the pennant-winning Giants. Their final record was 82-71.

1934 — Friday, September 21st, at Ebbets Field, Brooklyn
Dean Brothers Pitch Cardinals to Two Victories over Dodgers
Dizzy's Three-Hitter Wins First Game, 13-0
Paul Pitches No-Hitter in Second Game, Winning 3-0

St. Louis famed pitching brothers, the Deans, gave an unparalleled exhibition of their abilities today against the Brooklyn Dodgers. First, the elder member of the family, Jay Hanna (better known as "Dizzy") stifled the home team on just three hits, winning easily, 13-0. Then Diz was upstaged by his quieter brother, Paul, who stopped the Dodgers without the semblance of a hit in the second game, winning by a 3-0 score.

The double victory shaved ½ game off of the first-place New York Giants' lead over the surging St. Louis Cardinals. The lead was reduced to 3 games, and the Giants had seven games left to play. Nine games were left on St. Louis's schedule.

Today's Results
ST. LOUIS 13 - Brooklyn 0 (1st game)
ST. LOUIS 3 - Brooklyn 0 (2nd)
New York 8 - Boston 1
Pittsburgh 9 - Cincinnati 3 (1st)
Pittsburgh 16 - Cincinnati 3 (2nd)
no other game scheduled

Standings	W-L	Pct.	GB
New York	92-54	.630	-
ST. LOUIS	88-56	.611	3
Chicago	81-61	.570	9
Boston	71-71	.500	19
Pittsburgh	70-71	.496	19½
Brooklyn	65-79	.451	26
Philadelphia	53-86	.381	35½
Cincinnati	51-93	.354	40

Today's games in Brooklyn were added to the slate on what had been an open date for the teams involved.

Casey Stengel's Dodgers started the day with a six-game winning streak, and 18,000 fans came to Ebbets Field hoping to see their heroes beat the famous brothers and put a final crimp in the Cardinals' slim pennant hopes. Instead, the Dean boys stopped the Dodgers cold and, in the end, had the Brooklyn fans rooting for them.

In the opening inning of the opening game, the Cardinals jumped into the lead with two runs. Pepper Martin walked. Jack Rothrock bunted, and pitcher Tom Zachary threw wildly past first, putting men on second and third. An intentional pass filled the bases. Then Rip Collins drove in two runs with a single to right field.

Six hits produced five runs in the St. Louis third inning. And the Cardinals added three more in the fourth, two on a home run by Collins. The Ripper doubled across yet another run in the sixth, then he scored on a single by Chick Fullis. Dizzy Dean singled in the seventh and eventually came around to score, running the count to 13-0.

Collins totaled four hits in five at bats, three runs scored and six batted for the game.

In the meantime, Ol' Diz was untouchable on the mound. Through the first seven innings he held the Dodgers hitless. A fine leaping catch at the scoreboard in right center by Rothrock was the outstanding fielding play behind him. It came in the second inning and robbed Johnny Frederick of an extra-base hit. Diz walked four, and one man reached base on a fumble by Leo Durocher.

Then, with one out in the eighth, Ralph "Buzz" Boyle hit a slow hopper just past substitute third baseman Pat Crawford's glove. Boyle barely beat shortstop Durocher's throw to first base, and the Dodgers had their first hit of the game.

In the ninth, Sam Leslie and Joe Stripp hit legitimate singles, and a Crawford error loaded the bases. But Dizzy struck out the side to win the game, 13-0. The victory was his 27th of the year, tops in the league.

Paul D. Dean, two and one-half years younger than Jay H., was then sent out to pitch for St. Louis in the second game. The rookie had a tougher battle of it, since Ray Benge pitched a good game for Brooklyn. But Paul was absolutely brilliant. Only a two-out walk to Len Koenecke in the first inning kept him from pitching a perfect game. His no-hitter was the first in the major leagues in over three years and the first in the National league since 1929. His curveball was breaking sharply today, and his fastball seemed to gain speed as the game progressed. He fanned six, and all but one or two of the Cardinals' fielding chances were of the most routine type.

Through the first six innings, only one Dodger hit the ball hard. That was pitcher Benge, who twice hit line drives directly at St. Louis fielders.

But only one Cardinal reached first base during the first five innings. That was Dean, who singled in the third. Benge was helped by some fine fielding by Jimmy Jordan, Lonnie Frey, and Tony Cuccinello.

In the sixth inning, St. Louis broke the deadlock. After Durocher fanned, Dean socked a double to left center. Martin drove him home with a double off the left field fence.

A two-bagger by Joe Medwick and a one-baser by Collins added another marker in the seventh.

St. Louis's last run came in the ninth on Medwick's triple and an infield out.

All the while, Paul Dean and his batterymate, Bill DeLancey, were talking about the hurler's chances for a no-hitter. They got the only break they needed in the seventh inning. With two out, Leslie hit a shot into deep left field. But Medwick, who had been fielding very well on the road trip, ran the ball down and made a one-handed catch near the wall. That brought a cheer from the Brooklyn fans, and from there on out, they cheered for Dean.

Paul struck out three batters in the last two innings and got the other three on infield chances. When the game ended, the fans immediately swarmed the field, and Paul needed the assistance of two park policemen to get to the clubhouse.

When he arrived there, he found his older brother praising the younger man's pitching. Then Dizzy complained that he hadn't realized that he, too, had been close to a no-hitter. If he had known, he assured his listerners, "We'd have both had a no-hitter."

FIRST GAME

					r	h	e	Batteries
St. Louis	205	302	100	-	13	17	2	D. Dean (W 27-7) & V. Davis
Brooklyn	000	000	000	-	0	3	2	T. Zachary (L 5-5) 2.1 IP, W. Clark .2 IP, O. Carroll 5 IP, B. Beck 1 IP & A. Lopez.

SECOND GAME

St. Louis	ab	r	h	bi	o	a	e		Brooklyn	ab	r	h	bi	o	a	e
P. Martin, 3b	4	0	1	1	0	1	0		R. Boyle, rf	4	0	0	0	2	0	0
J. Rothrock, rf	4	0	0	0	1	0	0		L. Frey, ss	3	0	0	0	4	3	0
F. Frisch, 2b	4	0	0	0	1	3	0		L. Koenecke, cf	2	0	0	0	1	1	0
J. Medwick, lf	4	2	2	0	6	0	0		S. Leslie, 1b	3	0	0	0	10	1	0
R. Collins, 1b	4	0	1	2	9	1	0		T. Cuccinello, 3b	3	0	0	0	3	0	0
B. DeLancey, c	4	0	1	0	7	0	0		J. Frederick, lf	3	0	0	0	2	0	0
E. Orsatti, cf	3	0	0	0	1	0	0		J. Jordan, 2b	3	0	0	0	1	6	1
L. Durocher, ss	3	0	0	0	1	3	0		A. Lopez, c	2	0	0	0	3	1	0
P. Dean, p	3	1	2	0	1	2	0		J. Bucher, ph9	1	0	0	0	-	-	-
									R. Benge, p	2	0	0	0	1	1	0
									J. McCarthy, ph9	1	0	0	0	-	-	-
	33	3	7	3	27	10	0			27	0	0	0	27	13	1

St. Louis	000 001 101 - 3		LOB: StL 3, Bkn 1. BE: StL 1.
Brooklyn	000 000 000 - 0		2B: Dean, Medwick. 3B: Medwick.
	ip h r-er bb so		SB: none. CS: DeLancey.
Dean (W 18-9)	9 0 0-0 1 6		Time - 1:38
Benge (L 14-12)	9 7 3-3 0 1		Attendance - 18,000

Umpires: B. Klem, Z. Sears, & C. Rigler

With Paul winning one game and Dizzy winning three and saving another game, the Cardinals won seven of their remaining nine games. Meanwhile, the Giants lost six out of seven, and the Cardinals squeezed into first place, winning the pennant by a 2-game margin.

1934 World Series—Game #7

Tuesday, October 9th, at Navin Field, Detroit

Cardinals and Dizzy Dean Trounce Tigers, 11-0, to Win World Series

Unruly Detroit Fans Bombard Medwick

Seven-Run Third Inning Starts Cards to Victory

The St. Louis Cardinals overwhelmed the Detroit Tigers today, 11-0, to win the seventh and decisive game of the World Series. Ten Cardinals contributed to the victors' seventeen-hit attack, while Dizzy Dean held the Tigers to just six safeties.

The one-sided nature of the contest put the Detroit fans into an ugly mood, and, after Joe Medwick was involved in a spike-flashing incident with the Tigers' Marv Owen in the sixth inning, the bleacherites took their frustrations out on the Red Bird left fielder. They hurled all manner of missiles at Medwick when he tried to take his position in the field. The bombardment interrupted play, and finally Commissioner Kenesaw Mountain Landis was forced to order Medwick out of the game.

The victory was truly a team effort. All nine St. Louis starters got hits and scored runs. But the biggest heroes were Dizzy Dean and Frankie Frisch. Diz pitched brilliantly and won his second game of the series, matching his brother Paul's two victories. Diz also got two hits in the decisive third inning, when the Cardinals scored seven runs. Manager Frisch got only one hit in five at bats, but that was a bases-loaded double, which drove in the first three St. Louis runs. After the game, the Cardinal leader said, "You can take all the .800 hitters, but I'll take that two-base hit....That was a million-dollar hit to me."

Rookie Eldon Auker, a submariner pitcher, was the Detroit starter. The Cardinals hit him hard in the first two innings but failed to score.

Assisted by some lackluster fielding, the National League champs broke through in a big way in the third. Leo Durocher led off and flied out. Dean then lifted a foul in back of the plate. Catcher Mickey Cochrane made no effort to pursue the ball, which feel into the front row of box seats and could have been caught. Diz then stroked a hit over the third baseman's head, and, when left fielder Goose Goslin was slow in returning the ball, Dean raced to second with a "hustle" double. Pepper Martin was next, and he hit a bouncer to first baseman Hank Greenberg. The big Tiger started to run to the bag himself, but then he saw he would arrive too late. He flipped the ball to Auker, but Martin outraced the pitcher to the base for a single, Dean moving to third.

The speedy Martin stole second on the next pitch, and Jack Rothrock walked, loading the bases for Frisch. By fouling pitches down both baselines, the veteran worked the count to three balls and two strikes. He finally got the pitch he was looking for and pulled the ball toward the right field corner, driving three runners across the plate.

That finished Auker, and player-manager Cochrane called Lynwood Rowe in to pitch. The "Schoolboy" retired Medwick on one pitch, then James "Rip" Collins singled Frisch home. Collins scored on Bill DeLancey's double off the right field screen.

Rowe was replaced by Elon Hogsett. Ernie Orsatti walked, and Durocher singled, loading the bases again. Dean then got his second hit of the inning on a very high chop to third. The hit scored Collins. When Martin walked on four pitches, Orsatti strolled home with the seventh run.

Tommy Bridges came in and finally put an end to the rally by inducing Rothrock to hit into a force play.

With a big lead, Dean toyed with the Tiger hitters. He mixed a lot of insults in with his fastball and curves. The most serious threat to his shutout came in the fifth innning. Greenberg singled and moved to third on Pete Fox's one-out double. Cochrane let pitcher Bridges bat for himself, and Dean struck him out. Then Jo-Jo White hit a sharp grounder up the middle that Durocher cut off brilliantly, throwing to first to retire the batter.

The Cardinals added two runs in the eventful sixth inning. With Martin on second and two out, Medwick tripled to right center, sliding hard into third baseman Owen. A few kicks were attempted by each man, but peace was restored. Medwick scored moments later of Collins's fourth single of the day.

But when Joe trotted out to left field in the bottom of the inning, the fans started to bombard him with fruit. The barrage soon included soda pop bottles, and Medwick was forced to retreat. After a couple of attempts to regain his position were turned back by the artillery from the bleachers, Joe was called for a talk with Commissioner Landis.

After some discussion, the Judge ordered the Cardinal slugger out of the game. Joe was reluctant to go, but Landis's decision was final. Chick Fullis went into left field. Play resumed after a total delay of about 20 minutes.

The Cards scored two more runs in the seventh. Durocher tripled. Martin reached on an error and stole second. And Rothrock doubled. That made the score 11-0.

Detroit got two hits in the ninth, Charlie Gehringer and Billy Rogell singling around a force out. But Dean struck Greenberg out (for the third time in the game) and got Owen to hit a game-ending grounder, Durocher flipping to Frisch for a force out.

The new champions hustled to the clubhouse for a wild celebration. Manager Frisch was choked-up and said little. But pitcher Dizzy Dean was talking a-mile-a-minute, telling all-and-sundry that his boasts were not idle, and that his teammates were the greatest in the world. They won the World Series, so who could argue with that?

St. Louis (NL)	ab	r	h	bi	o	a	e
P. Martin, 3b	5	3	2	1	0	1	0
J. Rothrock, rf	5	1	2	1	4	0	0
F. Frisch, 2b	5	1	1	3	3	6	0
J. Medwick, lf	4	1	1	1	1	0	0
C. Fullis, lf6	1	0	1	0	1	0	0
R. Collins, 1b	5	1	4	2	7	1	1
B. DeLancey, c	5	1	1	1	5	0	0
E. Orsatti, cf	3	1	1	0	2	0	0
L. Durocher, ss	5	1	2	0	3	4	0
D. Dean, p	5	1	2	1	1	0	0
	43	11	17	10	27	12	1

Detroit (AL)	ab	r	h	bi	o	a	e
J. White, cf	4	0	0	0	3	0	1
M. Cochrane, c	4	0	0	0	2	2	0
R. Hayworth, c9	0	0	0	0	1	0	0
C. Gehringer, 2b	4	0	2	0	3	5	1
G. Goslin, lf	4	0	0	0	4	0	1
B. Rogell, ss	4	0	1	0	3	2	0
H. Greenberg, 1b	4	0	1	0	7	0	0
M. Owen, 3b	4	0	0	0	1	2	0
P. Fox, rf	3	0	2	0	3	0	0
E. Auker, p	0	0	0	0	0	0	0
S. Rowe, p3	0	0	0	0	0	0	0
E. Hogsett, p3	0	0	0	0	0	0	0
T. Bridges, p3	2	0	0	0	0	0	0
F. Marberry, p8	0	0	0	0	0	0	0
G. Walker, ph8	1	0	0	0	-	-	-
A. Crowder, p9	0	0	0	0	0	0	0
	34	0	6	0	27	11	3

St. Louis   007 002 200 - 11
Detroit   000 000 000 - 0

	ip	h	r-er	bb	so
Dean (W 2-1)	9	6	0-0	0	5
Auker (L 1-1)	2.1	6	4-4	1	1
Rowe	.1	2	2-2	0	0
Hogsett	*0	2	1-1	2	0
Bridges	4.1	6	4-2	0	2
Marberry	1	1	0-0	1	0
Crowder	1	0	0-0	0	1

*faced four batters in third

LOB: StL 9, Detr 7.
BE: StL 1, Detr 1.
DP: Owen-Gehringer-Greenberg.
2B: Rothrock 2, Dean, Frisch, DeLancey, Fox 2.
3B: Medwick, Durocher.
SB: Martin 2. CS: Orsatti
Time - 2:19 Attendance - 40,902
Umpires: H. Geisel, B. Reardon, B. Owens, & B. Klem

1935—Thursday, July 18th, at Sportsman's Park
Red Birds Rout Braves, 13-3, for Fourteenth Victory in a Row
Eighteen Hits Help Cards Extend Streak
P. Dean's Pitching, Whitehead's & Collins's Hitting Highlight Game

The surging St. Louis Cardinals and the doormat Boston Braves both extended their streaks today. The Cards won their 14th consecutive game, while the Braves lost their 11th in a row. The victory extended a record for St. Louis in the National League. It also gave the Cardinals an 18-game winning streak at home, dating back to May 29th. The triumph kept the Birds 4 games behind the league-leading Giants. St. Louis was in fourth place, 9½ games behind New York, before starting their streak on July 2nd.

After beating Boston by 2-1 in each of the last two games, the Cardinals had it

Today's Results
ST. LOUIS 13 - Boston 3
New York 5 - Cincinnati 3 (12 inn.)
Chicago 11 - Philadelphia 3
Brooklyn 5 - Pittsburgh 3

Standings	W-L	Pct.	GB
New York	53-24	.688	-
ST. LOUIS	50-29	.633	4
Chicago	47-34	.580	8
Pittsburg	42-41	.506	14
Brooklyn	37-42	.468	17
Cincinnati	38-44	.463	17½
Philadelphia	33-46	.418	21
Boston	21-61	.256	34½

easier today. They scored two runs in the first inning and never lost the lead. The Red Bird bats rang out with 18 safe blows. Burgess Whitehead and Rip Collins paced the attack with four hits each, and Bill DeLancey drove in four runs, three of them with a home run. Pepper Martin contributed a fluke homer and two doubles. In the meantime, Paul Dean held the visitors to just five hits and one base on balls.

Key hits have come from many bats during the Cardinals' hot streak. Rookie Terry Moore won the game yesterday with a home run in the ninth inning. Weak-hitting Leo Durocher hit two homers against Boston on Monday. Virgil Davis's two-out, two-run double in the ninth inning last Thursday beat the Phillies, 5-4.

Today's crowd was under 5,000 persons, and nearly half of those were Knot Hole Gang boys admitted free.

The Braves' manager, Bill McKechnie, shook up his lineup today in an attempt to get more scoring punch. And the Braves scored three runs today, as compared to just one run in each of the previous two games. But the Cardinals, sticking with their successful lineup, buried the Boston team.

After Dean set the Braves down in order in the top of the first, his teammates came to bat and took a two-run lead. Martin started things with a double to right. After Ernie Orsatti flied out, Whitehead ripped a hit off of pitcher Danny MacFayden's bare hand. Joe Medwick then flied deep to center, Martin scoring and Whitehead moving to second after the catch. The speedy Whitehead scored on Collins's single to right.

Rookie Moore scored for St. Louis in the second inning. He singled and stole second, then came around on Martin's two-out double past third base.

The Braves got back into the game with two runs in the top of the third. Joe Coscarart singled and scored on Shanty Hogan's double. Hogan counted on MacFayden's bunt and Billy Urbanski's fly ball.

But Frank Frisch's crew pulled away with four runs in the bottom half of the round. Consecutive singles by Whitehead, Medwick, and Collins plated one run and brought McKechnie out of the dugout to change pitchers. Righthander Bob Smith was brought in to face the lefthanded hitting DeLancey. Bill smacked the new hurler's first pitch to the top of the right field pavilion for a three-run homer, putting St. Louis ahead by a 7-2 margin.

In the fourth, Boston scored one run, but St. Louis again doubled the Braves' score, counting two in the fourth. Wally Berger doubled and scored on two fly balls in the top of the inning. A walk to Orsatti, Whitehead's single, an error, and Moore's two-out single gave the Cardinals their runs.

Smith and Dean settled down for the next three innings, holding the two teams scoreless. Each pitcher gave up just one hit during that period, but two errors by Martin kept Dean in trouble in the fifth and sixth.

Paul himself made an error in the eighth, allowing the Braves' first batter, Baxter Jordan, to reach base safely. Randy Moore added a single with two out, but both runners were left on base when Pinky Whitney fouled out.

Rupert "Tommy" Thompson was put into center field by McKechnie in the bottom of the eighth. He was hurt on the first play of the inning. Martin drove a long fly out to the center field flag pole. Thompson, in hot pursuit, stumbled just as he got to the fence and crashed into the pole with his head. He groggily crawled after the ball, but Martin rounded the bases easily for a home run. Thompson was then led off the field, and Joe Mowry took over in center.

The Cards piled up three more runs before the inning was over. Whitehead had a double, and Medwick, Collins, DeLancey, and Durocher singled. These hits were complimented by some aggressive base running.

Dean nailed down the 13-3 victory by retiring the Braves in order in ninth.

Paul downgraded his performance in the clubhouse afterwards. "How those Cardinals can slug the ball!" he exclaimed. "You've got to give eight men on the team credit for that victory—and I'm not one of them." A reporter informed him that he had pitched a five-hitter. At first Paul didn't believe it, but then he finally had to admit, "I guess you can say nine of us won the game."

Just then a home-cooked snack from Paul's wife arrived, ending the interview. "You know, we southern folks must have our fried chicken," he noted. "And I'm hungry after pitching that game."

Indeed, the Cardinals have been playing like a hungry bunch over the last couple of weeks.

Boston	ab	r	h	bi	o	a	e
B. Urbanski, ss	4	0	0	1	2	0	1
B. Jordan, 1b	3	0	0	0	6	2	0
H. Lee, lf	4	0	0	0	0	0	0
W. Berger, cf	4	1	1	0	5	0	0
T. Thompson, cf8	0	0	0	0	0	0	0
J. Mowry, cf8	0	0	0	0	1	0	0
R. Moore, rf	4	0	2	0	2	0	0
P. Whitney, 2b	4	0	0	1	0	4	0
J. Coscarart, 3b	4	1	1	0	1	1	0
S. Hogan, c	4	1	1	1	6	0	0
D. MacFayden, p	0	0	0	0	0	1	0
B. Smith, p3	2	0	0	0	1	1	0
A. Spohrer, ph9	1	0	0	0	-	-	-
	34	3	5	3	24	9	1

St. Louis	ab	r	h	bi	o	a	e
P. Martin, 3b	5	2	3	2	0	2	2
E. Orsatti, rf	4	0	0	0	2	0	0
B. Whitehead, 2b	5	4	4	0	2	3	0
J. Medwick, lf	5	3	2	2	0	0	0
R. Collins, 1b	5	2	4	2	8	1	0
B. DeLancey, c	5	1	2	4	5	0	0
T. Moore, cf	5	1	2	2	4	0	0
L. Durocher, ss	4	0	1	1	6	2	0
P. Dean, p	5	0	0	0	0	0	1
	43	13	18	13	27	8	3

Boston	002	100	000	-	3
St. Louis	214	200	04x	-	13

	ip	h	r-er	bb	so
MacFayden (L 5-7)	*2	8	6-6	0	1
Smith	6	10	7-5	2	3
Dean (W 10-7)	9	5	3-3	1	3

*faced three batters in third
Umpires: B. Klem, B. Pinelli, & C. Moran

LOB: Bos 6, StL 8.
BE: Bos 3, StL 1.
2B: Martin 2, Hogan, Berger, Whitehead.
HR: DeLancey, Martin.
SH: MacFayden.
SB: T. Moore.
Time - 1:50
Attendance - 2,350 paid 4,650 total

The next day the Cardinals' streak was stopped by Johnny Babich and the Brooklyn Dodgers.

The Cards did finally catch the Giant, moving into first place on August 25th. But St. Louis was overtaken in September by Chicago. The Cubs won 21 straight games and took the pennant.

St. Louis finished in second place, 4 games behind, with a 96-58 record.

The 14-game winning streak is still a Cardinal record.

1936—Wednesday, April 29th, at Sportsman's Park
Cards' Parmelee Beats Giants' Hubbell in 17-Inning Duel
Game Scoreless Until Twelfth Frame
New York Errors in Last Inning Give St. Louis a 2-1 Win

LeRoy Parmelee, acquired by St. Louis in a trade with the New York Giants last winter, got his first chance to face his old team this afternoon. He pitched a great game to beat the Giants, 2-1, although he had to go 17 innings to do it. The Giants' pitcher, Carl Hubbell, was nearly as good on the mound, but two New York errors in the final inning led to his defeat.

Besides coming out ahead on the scoreboard, the Cardinal righthander had the better of his lefthanded opponent in most statistical categories. Parmelee allowed just six hits and struck out nine, while Hubbell yielded eleven hits and fanned six. Both hurlers walked four batsman.

Today's Results
ST. LOUIS 2 - New York 1 (17 inn.)
Chicago 1 - Brooklyn 0
Pittsburgh 10 - Philadelphia 9 (10 inn.)
Boston at Cincinnati - postponed, rain

Standings	W-L	Pct.	GB
New York	8-4	.667	-
Cincinnati	7-6	.538	1½
Chicago	7-6	.538	1½
ST. LOUIS	5-5	.500	2
Philadelphia	7-8	.467	2½
Brooklyn	6-7	.462	2½
Pittsburgh	5-6	.455	2½
Boston	4-7	.364	3½

Last December, the Cards picked up the side-arming fastballer from the Giants in a deal which sent Burgess Whitehead to New York. Today the two clubs met for the first time since the trade. Parmelee held the Giants scoreless until the twelfth inning. Then Whitehead scored a run. The Red Birds matched that run in the bottom of the inning, and the game remained tied until the seventeenth. Then the Cards scored on a double and two errors.

Only one runner got as far as third base through the first eleven innings. That runner was Pepper Martin, who reached the far corner in the first inning. He got to first on Travis Jackson's fumble with two out and advanced two sacks on Joe Medwick's long hit to right. But Johnny Mize ended the inning by bouncing back to Hubbell.

The Cards were retired in order in each of the next four innings before Parmelee singled in the sixth. He was forced by Frankie Frisch, who was then cut down trying to steal.

Mize doubled with two out in the seventh, but Virgil "Spud" Davis followed by flying out to Hank Leiber in center.

Parmelee again singled in the eighth, a two-out scratch, but was left.

Meanwhile, the big Michigander had the Giants handcuffed. Through the first nine innings, he faced only one man over the minimum possible number. Mel Ott hit safely with two out in the first, but was left stranded. Jackson singled in the second but was quickly erased on a double play. And in the fifth, Sam Leslie opened with a single but was caught stealing after Jackson and Harry Danning had struck out.

In the sixth, seventh, eighth, and ninth innings, the Giants went out in one-two-three fashion.

In the tenth, Whitehead became the first New Yorker to reach second base. He led off with a one-baser and moved up on Ott's sacrifice bunt. Parmelee pitched around Leiber, giving him a base on balls, then he retired Leslie and Jackson.

Parmelee and Hubbell clipped through the eleventh without allowing any hits.

New York broke the scoreless tie in the twelfth. Whitehead walked, and Ott again bunted him to second. This time, Parmelee pitched to Leiber, and the Giant strongman delivered a long single to left center, driving Whitehead in. The next two men flied out to center.

Their backs to the wall, the Cardinals came to bat. After Martin was retired, Medwick singled to center. Mize then looped a ball to short right. Ott charged hard, hoping for a shoestring catch, but the ball short-hopped off of his glove and rolled a few feet away. Daring base running by Mize beat the throw to second, and Medwick sprinted hard to third. Stu Martin was sent in as a pinch-runner for Mize, representing the winning run. Davis was intentionally walked, filling the bases. Charley Gelbert then delivered a single to right, scoring Medwick. S. Martin also tried to score, but Ott played the ball perfectly and threw him out at home by several feet. Leo Durocher flied out, and the game went on, now tied 1-1.

The Giants had only two more base runners, and both were picked off base when the next batter failed trying to bunt Parmelee's fastballs. Roy was still humming them at the end.

The Cardinals loaded the bases in the sixteenth, but a nice stop by Dick Bertell kept them from scoring.

In the gathering darkness, the Cardinals took what seemed sure to be their last at bats in the bottom of the seventeenth. Davis opened by lashing a double down the right field line. He was replaced by pinch-runner Lyn King. Gelbert was intentionally passed. Durocher followed with a screamer to deep left center. For a moment, it looked like a sure game-winning hit, but Leiber caught it after a hard run, and the runners had to retreat to their original bases.

Parmelee, with two hits already, was allowed to bat for himself. He hit an easy double play ball to shortstop. But Bertell, in his hurry, fumbled the ball, and the bases were loaded with just one out. With the infield drawn in close, Terry Moore hit a roller to third. Jackson fielded it cleanly and threw to Gus Mancuso at home. The throw arrived ahead of the runner, but it was off line toward first base. Mancuso's foot was pulled off the plate, and King slid across with the game-winning run.

The crowd, most of whom had stayed through the long contest, let out a hoarse shout. Mancuso argued that he had been touching the plate, although photos clearly showed his foot far off the slab. The fans sang their praises of Roy Parmelee as they rushed to their late suppers and the players rushed to their showers.

New York	ab	r	h	bi	o	a	e
J. Moore, lf	7	0	1	0	5	0	0
B. Whitehead, 2b	6	1	1	0	7	2	0
M. Ott, rf	5	0	1	0	3	1	0
H. Leiber, cf	5	0	1	1	7	0	0
S. Leslie, 1b	6	0	1	0	15	2	0
T. Jackson, 3b	6	0	1	0	1	3	2
H. Danning, c	2	0	0	0	2	0	0
G. Mancuso, c5	2	0	0	0	6	2	0
D. Bertell, ss	5	0	0	0	2	8	1
C. Hubbell, p	6	0	0	0	1	1	0
	50	1	6	1	49	19	3

St. Louis	ab	r	h	bi	o	a	e
T. Moore, cf	7	0	0	0	7	0	0
F. Frisch, 2b	7	0	1	0	4	7	0
P. Martin, rf	7	0	1	0	2	0	0
J. Medwick, lf	6	1	2	0	5	0	0
J. Mize, 1b	5	0	2	0	13	1	0
S. Martin, pr12	0	0	0	0	-	-	-
R. Collins, 1b13	2	0	0	0	3	2	0
V. Davis, c	6	0	1	0	11	3	0
L. King, pr17	0	1	0	0	-	-	-
C. Gelbert, 3b	6	0	2	1	1	1	0
L. Durocher, ss	7	0	0	0	3	3	0
R. Parmelee, p	7	0	2	0	2	5	0
	60	2	11	1	51	22	0

New York   000 000 000 001 000 00 - 1
St. Louis   000 000 000 001 000 01 - 2
one out when winning run scored

	ip	h	r-er	bb	so
Hubbell (L 2-1)	16.1	11	2-1	4	6
Parmelee (W 2-1)	17	6	1-1	4	9

Time - 3:41
Attendance - 3,700 paid 4,500 total

LOB: NY 5, StL 13. BE: StL 3.
DP: Durocher-Frisch-Mize
2B: Mize 2, Davis.
SH: Ott 2, Bertell.
SB: none. CS: Leslie, Frisch, T. Moore, J. Moore, Mancuso.
Umpires: B. Reardon, G. Barr, & L. Ballanfant

Despite a lack of pitching depth, St. Louis stayed in the thick on the pennant race through much of the summer. While the Cards were fighting for the lead with the Cubs, the Giants slipped to 10½ games behind in mid-July.

Then New York got hot. They passed St. Louis and moved into first place on August 25th. The Cardinals finished tied for second, 5 games behind. Their record was 87-67.

Parmelee finished the year with an 11-11 mark and was traded during the off-season to Chicago.

1937 — Wednesday, August 4th, at Sportsman's Park

Pinch Hit by Frisch Caps Cards' Winning Rally

Five-Run Ninth Beats Bees, 7-6

Manager's Hit With Two Out Drives in Tying and Winning Runs

Trailing by four runs with two out in the ninth inning, the St. Louis Cardinals staged a last-ditch rally to beat the Boston Bees today, 7-6. The final two runs of the game scored on a single by 39-year-old manager Frankie Frisch. The leader became the hero, and his men rushed onto the field to jubilantly congratulate him for winning the game.

The other highlight of the contest was Joe Medwick's hitting. The league-leading slugger got four doubles, tying the major league record. Two of the two-baggers were flukes. In the first inning, Medwick's clean hit to center took a crazy bounce over Gene Moore's head, enabling Joe to take second. His bouncer in the fifth was misplayed by second baseman Tony Cuccinello, and the ball rolled into short center, Medwick sprinting all the way to second. "Ducky" also hit a drive in the third inning, which was barely missed by Vince DiMaggio. Finally, in the ninth, he found the gap between the right and center fielders.

Today's Results
ST. LOUIS 7 - Boston 6
Philadelphia 2 - Chicago 1
New York 4 - Cincinnati 3
Brooklyn 10 - Pittsburgh 7

Standings	W-L	Pct.	GB
Chicago	60-33	.645	-
New York	55-40	.579	6
ST. LOUIS	50-43	.538	10
Pittsburgh	50-43	.538	10
Boston	45-50	.474	16
Brooklyn	38-54	.413	21½
Cincinnati	38-54	.413	21½
Philadelphia	39-58	.402	23

The slugging raised Medwick's batting average back over the .400 mark, to .403. His two runs-batted-in raised his league-leading total to 102.

Johnny Mize and Gene Moore also had four hits each. A total of 27 hits were made in the game.

The victory lifted the Cardinals into a tie for third place with the Pittsburgh Pirates.

Lou Fette was Boston's starting pitcher. The 30-year-old rookie came within one out of posting his 14th win against just 3 defeats. But two-out hits by Mize and Medwick brought St. Louis within striking distance, and veteran Guy Bush was brought in to pitch. He was rocked for three hits around an intentional walk and was charged with the defeat.

Southpaw Bob Weiland started for St. Louis, and he held Boston scoreless for three innings.

The Cards got their first run in the bottom of the third. Terry Moore singled. Stu Martin bunted a short pop to the mound. Fette cleverly let the ball drop and threw it to first baseman Elbie Fletcher, who tagged Moore and then stepped on the base for a double play. Mize then hit a bases-empty home run onto the roof of the pavilion. Medwick doubled on the bad hop, but Vince DiMaggio ran down Don Padgett's long fly to center.

The Bees came in in the fourth and took a 3-1 lead. Singles by DiMaggio, Cuccinello, and G. Moore tied the game. A costly balk by Weiland moved the runners to second and third and necessitated a walk to Woody English. Fletcher then punched a single to left for two runs.

DiMaggio's RBI single gave Boston another run in the top of the fifth.

St. Louis also scored one in the fifth. With one out, T. Moore and S. Martin singled. Mize hit a double-play ball to short, but Martin's hard slide prevented a twin-killing. Then Cuccinello kicked Medwick's bouncer, Moore scoring and Medwick getting getting credit for his third double.

Ray Harrell pitched a scoreless inning for the Cards in the sixth, and Sheriff Blake blanked the Bees in the seventh.

But, in the eighth, singles by DiMaggio and Cuccinello and Mize's mental error on G. Moore's grounder loaded the bases for Boston. Blake retired English but walked

Fletcher, forcing home a run. Mike Ryba came in to pitch. A run scored on an infield out before he retired the side.

Fette got through the sixth, seventh, and eighth innings without any trouble.

The bottom of the ninth came along with the Red Birds trailing, 6-2. Pinch-hitter Jimmy Brown, leading off, went out. T. Moore walked, but S. Martin made the second out. Moore was allowed to swipe third unmolestedly, but it still didn't look good for the home team. Mize singled to right, driving Moore home. Medwick followed with a double, scoring Mize, and Boston manager Bill McKechnie decided to remove Fette.

Bush, a 35-year-old fastballer, was brought in to get the final out. Medwick was allowed to take third, while Bush got two strikes on Padgett. But the Cardinal right fielder delivered a single to right, making the score 6-5 in favor of the Bees. Don Gutteridge followed with a single to left, also with two strikes; Padgett beat Bobby Reis's throw to third, and Gutteridge moved to second on the play. Frisch sent Pepper Martin up to hit for Leo Durocher, and Bush issued an intentional pass.

Now, with the bases loaded and two out, Frank looked down the bench for another hitter to use in place of rookie catcher Mickey Owen. Having used four pinch-batters already, Frisch's choices were slim. Just then, someone yelled at him, "Why don't you hit, Grandma?" That raised Frisch's dander up. With fire in his eyes, the Cardinal manager grabbed a bat and went to the plate. Jumping on the first pitch, Frisch pulled a hard one-hopper right down the first base line. Fletcher, the first baseman, lunged across the line but could only get the tip of his glove on the ball, and it was deflected into foul territory. Padgett and Gutteridge scored before the ball could be retrieved, and the Cardinals won the game, 7-6.

The ecstatic Red Birds rushed out toward the infield, where they shook manager Frisch's hand, pounded him on the back just like he was one of the boys, and even tried to lift him up onto their shoulders. That was a little too much for a dignified manager and authority figure, but Frankie Frisch sure looked like he was enjoying all the adoration.

Boston	ab	r	h	bi	o	a	e	St. Louis	ab	r	h	bi	o	a	e
B. Reis, lf	3	1	0	0	4	0	0	T. Moore, cf	4	2	2	0	1	0	0
R. Warstler, ss	5	0	0	0	1	4	0	S. Martin, 2b	5	0	1	0	4	4	0
V. DiMaggio, cf	5	2	3	1	2	0	0	J. Mize, 1b	5	2	4	2	13	0	0
T. Cuccinello, 2b	5	2	2	0	3	4	0	J. Medwick, lf	5	1	4	2	3	0	0
G. Moore, rf	4	1	4	2	1	1	0	D. Padgett, rf	4	1	1	1	1	0	0
W. English, 3b	3	0	0	0	3	0	0	D. Gutteridge, 3b	5	1	1	0	1	2	0
E. Fletcher, 1b	3	0	1	2	9	0	0	L. Durocher, ss	3	0	0	0	1	7	0
R. Mueller, c	4	0	0	1	3	0	0	P. Martin, ph9	0	0	0	0	-	-	-
L. Fette, p	4	0	1	0	0	4	0	M. Owen, c	4	0	1	0	3	0	0
G. Bush, p9	0	0	0	0	0	0	0	F. Frisch, ph9	1	0	1	2	-	-	-
								B. Weiland, p	1	0	1	0	0	0	0
								F. Bordagaray, ph5	1	0	0	0	-	-	-
								R. Harrell, p6	0	0	0	0	0	0	0
								R. Moore, ph6	1	0	0	0	-	-	-
								S. Blake, p7	0	0	0	0	0	0	0
								M. Ryba, p8	0	0	0	0	0	0	0
								J. Brown, ph9	1	0	0	0	-	-	-
	36	6	11	6	26	13	0		40	7	16	7	27	13	0

Boston   000 310 020 - 6
St. Louis   001 010 005 - 7
two out when winning run scored

	ip	h	r-er	bb	so
Fette	8.2	13	5-5	3	2
Bush (L 7-13)	*0	3	2-2	1	0
Weiland	5	7	4-4	2	0
Harrell	1	1	0-0	0	0
Blake	1.1	3	2-2	1	1
Ryba (W 4-2)	1.2	0	0-0	0	0

*faced four batters in ninth
Balk: Weiland.
PB: Owen.

LOB: Bos 7, StL 11. DP: Durocher-S. Martin-Mize 2, Fette-Fletcher.
2B: Medwick 4. HR: Mize.
SB: G. Moore.
Time - 2:25
Attendance - 2,393 paid 3,685 total
Umpires: B. Pinelli, L. Goetz, & B. Reardon

The hit was Frisch's last as an active player. On the following day, he pulled a muscle running out a ground ball, ending his playing career.

The Cardinals finished the season in fourth place, 15 games behind the pennant-winning Giants. St. Louis's final record was 81-73.

1938 — Sunday, September 11th, at Sportsman's Park

Frank Frisch Fired as St. Louis Manager

Cardinals Win One Last Game For Him

Paul Dean Returns From Minors to Pitch 6-4 Victory

St. Louis Cardinals' owner Sam Breadon called team manager Frankie Frisch into his office this morning and informed the Dutchman that his services were no longer required. But he also told Frisch that his termination would not be announced until after the game, so Frank got to manage one last contest. With Paul Dean pitching his first National League complete game since 1936, the Red Birds won for Frisch, 6-4, over the Pittsburgh Pirates.

Frisch, the Fordham Flash, had been a favorite of Breadon's since being acquired in December, 1926, in the highly controversial Rogers Hornsby deal. The owner confesses that letting him go was "one of the toughest jobs I've ever had to do."

Today's Results
ST. LOUIS 6 - Pittsburgh 4
Chicago 2 - Cincinnati 0
Brooklyn 3 - New York 0
Philadelphia 11 - Boston 2 (1st game)
Boston 3 - Philadelphia 2 (2nd)

Standings	W-L	Pct.	GB
Pittsburgh	77-54	.588	-
Chicago	75-59	.560	3½
Cincinnati	74-60	.552	4½
New York	73-61	.545	5½
Boston	67-66	.504	11
ST. LOUIS	63-72	.467	16
Brooklyn	61-72	.459	17
Philadelphia	43-89	.326	34½

Before the game, Frisch informed only the team's trustworthy equipment manager, Butch Yatkeman, of his dismissal. But, because of friction between Frisch and general manager Branch Rickey, the move was not unexpected. So rumors began flying through the stands, and Breadon issued a formal confirmation of the firing shortly before the game began. As the news filtered down to the regular box-seat customers behind the home dugout, they began to crowd the aisles, trying to get Frisch to come over and confirm or deny the story. To quell the crowd, the old Flash didn't occupy his accustomed place in the coach's box during the latter part of the game. Instead, he stayed in the dugout and watched his team bat out a victory.

Frisch had become manager on July 24th, 1933. Today's triumph brought his managerial record with St. Louis to 458 games won, 354 lost, and 10 games tied. He of course won one pennant and world championship in 1934. Breadon paid him the remaining salary due him for 1938 and gave him a release to negotiate with any other team. Coach Mike Gonzalez was named to manage the Cardinals for the last three weeks of the season.

Upstaged by the dismissal of Frisch was the successful return of Paul Dean, who hadn't pitched a big league complete game since May 25, 1936. Plagued by shoulder miseries, Paul had gone on the voluntrily retired list twice and had undergone surgery on his damaged wing. He started the 1938 season with the Cardinals' Houston farm club but was cut from the squad. St. Louis then optioned him to the Dallas club. Pitching for a weak team, his Texas League record was 8 wins and 16 losses. But he proved he could pitch again, and that earned him a recall to the Cardinals last week.

Today, Dean was found for twelve hits, but he struck out seven men and was at his best in the pinches. And his teammates, aided by three Pittsburgh errors, rallied to win 6-4.

The defeat cut Pittsburg's league lead to 3½ games. But their margin in the lost column was still 5 games with just 23 games left on the schedule.

The visitors started the game all right, using six hits to build a 3-0 lead through three innings. Lloyd Waner's single preceded Johnny Rizzo's home run in the first frame. Lee Handley doubled with one out in the second, but Dean fanned Al Todd and Jim Tobin. After two were out in the third inning, Rizzo walked and scored on singles by Arky Vaughan and Gus Suhr.

Dean finally retired the Pirates in order in the fourth.

Pittsburgh pitcher Jim Tobin breezed through the first three innings, allowing just one hit and no runs. But the Cardinals went to work on him in a hurry in the fourth, tying the score. Don Padgett and Joe Medwick opened with singles. Then big Johnny Mize cracked a long home run onto Grand Boulevard, driving in three runs. It was Big Jawn's 26th circuit clout of the season. Russ Bauers was rushed in to replace Tobin.

Good fielding helped Dean in the fifth. Mize's glove-hand catch turned Paul Waner's liner into a double play, and Jimmy Brown's diving stop retired Rizzo.

The Cards put men on second and third with one out in their fifth. But Bauers got Padgett and Medwick on harmless fly balls to end the threat.

Vaughan got to third with one out in the Pittsburgh sixth on a double and an infield out. But Dean threw third strikes past Pep Young and Lee Handley.

The Cardinals wasted two more singles in their sixth, and Todd's leadoff single in the Pirate seventh also went for naught.

The home team broke the tie with two runs in the seventh. With one out, Stu Martin walked and Padgett singled him to second. Medwick clouted a long fly to right. Thinking the ball might be caught, the runners held up. But it hit the pavilion screen. P. Waner's throw came in to second base, and Martin belatedly headed for home. Shortstop Vaughan wheeled and threw very wildly past the catcher, allowing Padgett to follow Martin across the plate. That made the score 5-3.

Dean did his best clutch pitching in the eighth, after Rizzo singled and Vaughan doubled him to third. Suhr was retired on a foul pop. Pinch-batter Heinie Manush went out on a fly ball too shallow to drive in a run. And Handley bounced out to shortstop Lynn Myers.

The Cards added an insurance run in their half of the eighth. Myers beat out a bunt. Herb Bremer also bunted, and Bauers's wild throw into the right field corner allowed Myers to come all the way home.

Al Todd homered to open the ninth. But Dean disposed of the next three hitters to end the game. The final score was 6-4.

The last out also ended Frankie Frisch's tenure as the Cardinals' manager.

Pittsburgh	ab	r	h	bi	o	a	e
L. Waner, cf	5	1	2	0	3	0	0
P. Waner, rf	5	0	0	0	0	0	0
J. Rizzo, lf	3	2	2	2	2	0	0
A. Vaughan, ss	4	0	4	0	3	3	1
G. Suhr, 1b	4	0	1	1	10	1	0
P. Young, 2b	3	0	0	0	1	1	0
H. Manush, ph8	1	0	0	0	-	-	-
T. Thevenow, 2b8	0	0	0	0	0	2	0
L. Handley, 3b	4	0	1	0	0	3	0
A. Todd, c	4	1	2	1	5	0	0
J. Tobin, p	2	0	0	0	0	0	0
R. Bauers, p4	0	0	0	0	0	0	1
W. Jensen, ph9	1	0	0	0	-	-	-
	36	4	12	4	24	10	2

St. Louis	ab	r	h	bi	o	a	e
F. Bordagaray, cf	5	0	1	0	3	0	0
S. Martin, 2b	2	1	0	0	1	1	0
D. Padgett, rf	4	2	2	0	2	0	0
J. Medwick, lf	4	1	2	1	3	0	0
J. Mize, 1b	4	1	2	3	9	1	0
J. Brown, 3b	4	0	1	0	0	2	0
L. Myers, ss	4	1	2	0	1	2	0
H. Bremer, c	3	0	0	0	7	2	0
P. Dean, p	4	0	1	0	1	1	0
	34	6	11	4	27	9	0

Pittsburgh   201 000 001 - 4
St. Louis   000 300 21x - 6

	ip	h	r-er	bb	so
Tobin	*3	4	3-3	1	1
Bauers (L 10-13)	5	7	3-1	1	3
Dean (W 1-0)	9	12	4-4	1	7

*faced three batters in fourth

LOB: Pitts 7, StL 8. BE: StL 1.
DP: Mize (unassisted).
2B: Handley, Vaughan 2, Medwick.
HR: Rizzo, Mize, Todd.
SH: Martin, Bauers, Bremer.
SB: L. Waner. CS: Vaughan.
Time - 1:48
Attendance - 15,739
Umpires: G. Magerkurth, T. Parker, & C. Moran

The Cardinals split their last 16 games of the season and finished in sixth place, 17½ games out.
The Pirates, meanwhile, could not even play at a .500 pace and lost the pennant to the Cubs, who won 14 of their last 18 decisions.

1939 — Sunday, August 20th, at Crosley Field, Cincinnati

Cardinals Win Two Games in Cincinnati, Trail Reds by 3½ Games

Eighth-Inning Rallies Give Birds Both Games, 7-1 & 7-5

Have Now Won 19 Out of Last 21 Games

The surging St. Louis Cardinals took two more big steps toward first place today by sweeping a doubleheader from the league-leading Cincinnati Reds. St. Louis extended its current winning streak to seven consecutive decisions. They have also won 19 of their last 21 and 28 of 35. In the short span of three weeks, the Cards have gone from 12 games behind to just 3½ games back. The breathtaking climb has started pennant talk in St. Louis.

After a good start, the Cardinals fell as low as fifth place with a .500 percentage on July 15th. But they have come roaring back into the race. Manager Ray Blades has been juggling his pitchers like a champion circus performer, and the big hitters have been coming through when it counts the most.

Today's Results
ST. LOUIS 7 - Cincinnati 1 (1st game)
ST. LOUIS 7 - Cincinnati 5 (2nd)
Chicago 9 - Pittsburgh 5 (1st game)
Pittsburgh 5 - Chicago 0 (6 inn.)(2nd)
New York 8 - Philadelphia 4 (1st game)
Philadelphia 3 - New York 2 (2nd)
Brooklyn at Boston (2 games) - ppd., rain

Standings	W-L	Pct.	GB
Cincinnati	69-41	.627	-
ST. LOUIS	65-44	.596	3½
Chicago	62-52	.544	9
New York	55-54	.505	13½
Brooklyn	54-54	.500	14
Pittsburgh	50-58	.463	18
Boston	47-61	.435	21
Philadelphia	34-72	.321	33

Today they were tied with the Reds going into the eighth inning of each game and twice rallied to win.

Pepper Martin and Johnny Mize were the hitting heroes. The Wild Horse of the Osage got three hits in each game, started four scoring rallies, and contributed to two others. Big Jawn from Georgia saved most of his heroics for the second game, when he hit two home runs and drove in six of the seven St. Louis runs.

A capacity crowd of 28,432 was on hand to see the leaders try to turn back the Cardinals' onslaught. With all the seats filled, several fans climbed to a perch atop the center field wall. They were removed, however, by order of the umpires.

Martin opened the game by tapping to second and outrunning the throw to first base. Although 35 years old, Pepper showed that he could still fly around the basepaths faster than most teenagers. He went to second on an infield out and scored the game's first run on Enos Slaughter's single to right field.

In the fifth inning, Pepper struck out with a man on second, and he was so disgusted with himself that he threw his bat into the dugout, scattering his teammates.

Pitcher Bob Weiland started the game in grand style, striking out the first three Cincinnati batters. He retired the Reds in order through the first five innings.

Cincinnati broke through in the sixth and tied the game. Harry Craft singled on the first pitch and scored on a two-out single by Eddie Joost.

The score was still 1-1 when the game entered the eighth inning. Then the Cardinals routed Bucky Walters and broke the game open with bunts. After a walk, the Cincinnati infield botched two sacrifices, retiring no one. Jimmy Brown then lined a single to center for two runs. A missed double play (on another bunt), a two-base error by third baseman Billy Werber, and two walks brought in two more tallies. So St. Louis led 5-1.

Three singles and a sacrifice fly gave the Cards two more runs in the ninth.

Weiland had gone out for a pinch-runner in the eighth-inning rally, and Curt Davis took over. He allowed one hit in each of the last two innings but kept Cincinnati from scoring, and St. Louis won the game, 7-1.

"Fiddler" Bill McGee and Lloyd "Whitney" Moore were the starting pitchers in the second game.

Pepper Martin opened with a hit off Lew Rigg's glove at third base. He came around to score on an out, Slaughter's single, and a sacrifice fly.

In the third, Martin singled again. This time he was forced out. Slaughter once again hit safely. Mize followed with his first homer, a tremendous, three-run shot over the wall in right center.

Billy Myers tripled and scored for the Reds in the bottom of the third.

In the sixth, St. Louis temporarily upped their lead to 5-1 on a hit batsman with the bases loaded.

But Cincinnati came in and tied the game. McGee had escaped several jams in the first five innings. But, in the sixth, the first three batters singled for one run. Never one to stick with a pitcher for too long, Blades called Clyde Shoun in to relieve McGee.

He retired the first man he faced but walked the next one to load the bases. Dick West delivered a two-run, pinch single, making the score 5-4 and bringing a shower of cushions from the stands.

Blades changed pitchers again, calling Bob Bowman in. Ernie Lombardi, batting for Lee Gamble, just missed a home run. But his sacrifice fly tied the score.

After a two-out walk in the eighth, Mize found one of Lee Grissom's serves to his liking and drove a two-run home run high into the right field seats, putting St. Louis ahead, 7-5.

The Reds got two hits in the eighth and one in the ninth but couldn't get any runs across against Nate Andrews, so St. Louis won, 7-5.

FIRST GAME

		r	h	e	Batteries
St. Louis	100 000 042 -	7	8	0	B. Weiland (W 8-9) 7 IP, C. Davis 2 IP & D. Padgett, M. Owen.
Cincinnati	000 001 000 -	1	4	1	B. Walters (L 20-9) 7.2 IP, M. Shoffner .1 IP, G. Thompson 1 IP & E. Lombardi.

SECOND GAME

St. Louis	ab	r	h	bi	o	a	e
P. Martin, 3b	5	1	3	0	0	3	0
D. Gutteridge, 3b9	0	0	0	0	1	0	0
J. Brown, 2b	4	1	0	0	2	2	0
E. Slaughter, rf	3	2	2	1	1	0	0
J. Mize, 1b	4	2	3	6	7	2	0
J. Medwick, lf	5	0	1	0	5	0	0
D. Padgett, c	3	0	0	0	3	0	0
M. Owen, ph7-c	2	0	1	0	1	0	0
T. Moore, cf	4	0	0	0	3	0	0
L. Lary, ss	5	0	1	0	2	3	0
B. McGee, p	2	1	1	0	1	1	0
C. Shoun, p6	0	0	0	0	0	0	0
B. Bowman, p6	0	0	0	0	0	0	0
C. Davis, ph7	1	0	0	0	-	-	-
N. Andrews, p7	0	0	0	0	1	0	0
	38	7	12	7	27	11	0

Cincinnati	ab	r	h	bi	o	a	e
L. Gamble, lf	2	0	1	0	2	0	0
E. Lombardi, ph6	0	0	0	1	-	-	-
L. Grissom, p7	0	0	0	0	0	1	0
L. Frey, ph8	1	0	1	0	-	-	-
H. Johnson, p9	0	0	0	0	0	0	0
E. Joost, 2b	5	0	0	0	2	3	0
I. Goodman, rf	5	0	2	0	5	0	0
F. McCormick, 1b	5	1	3	0	8	0	0
W. Hershberger, c	5	1	2	0	4	0	0
H. Craft, cf	5	1	1	1	2	0	0
L. Riggs, 3b	5	0	1	0	1	1	0
B. Myers, ss	3	2	1	0	2	4	0
L. Moore, p	0	0	0	0	0	1	0
N. Bongiovanni, ph3	1	0	1	1	-	-	-
M. Shoffner, p4	1	0	0	0	0	0	0
D. West, ph6-lf	2	0	2	2	1	0	0
	40	5	15	5	27	10	0

St. Louis	103 001 020	-	7
Cincinnati	001 004 000	-	5

	ip	h	r-er	bb	so
McGee	*5	9	4-4	0	1
Shoun	.1	1	1-1	1	0
Bowman	.2	0	0-0	0	0
Andrews (W 1-0)	3	5	0-0	0	1
Moore	3	5	4-4	1	1
Shoffner	3	4	1-1	2	1
Grissom (L 7-6)	2	3	2-2	1	0
Johnson	1	0	0-0	0	1

*faced three batters in sixth

LOB: StL 10, Cinc 11.
2B: Martin, Gamble, Goodman.
3B: Myers.
HR: Mize 2.
SH: Gamble. SF: Mize, Lombardi.
HBP: by Shoffner (Slaughter)
PB: Padgett
Time - 2:35 Attendance - 28,432
Umpires: B. Reardon, L. Goetz, & B. Pinelli

Immediately after these games, the Cardinals' pennant bid got an unexpected jolt: they lost three straight games in Brooklyn.

Still, they had a 27-17 record after leaving Cincinnati. But the Reds outdistanced them to the wire, playing at a 28-16 clip to win the pennant by 4½ games.

St. Louis finished with a record of 92-61.

Chapter VIII

Glory for Sam
1940-1946

1940—May 8th at Sportsman's Park
Slugging Records Crumble as Cardinals Crush Dodgers, 18-2

1941—September 13th at Sportsman's Park
Wyatt Edges M. Cooper, 1-0, Dodgers Retain League Lead

1942—September 12th at Brooklyn
St. Louis Tops Brooklyn, 2-1, to Gain Tie in Pennant Race

1942 World Series—Game #5
Cards Beat Yankees Again, Win World Championship

1943—June 4th at Sportsman's Park
Cooper's Second Straight One-Hitter Gives Cards 5-0 Victory

1943 World Series—Game #5
Cards Get Ten Hits But Lose, 2-0, Yanks Win Series

1944—June 10th at Cincinnati
Cardinals Bury Reds' Pitchers in 18-0 Massacre

1944 World Series—Game #6
Cardinals Beat Browns, 3-1, Win World Series

1945—September 25th at Chicago
Cubs Best Cards, 6-5, Lead St. Louis by 2½ Games

1946—October 1st at Sportsman's Park
Pollet and Cards Beat Dodgers, 4-2, in First Playoff Game

1946 World Series—Game #7
Daring and Defense Win Series for Cardinals Over Red Sox

After a close second-place finish in 1939, the Cardinals started the 1940 season very erratically. Although they won one game 18-2 and hit seven home runs, they had to struggle to stay out of last place. Ray Blades was fired as manager in June and replaced by Billy Southworth. The team did much better under the new skipper and finished third.

In 1941, St. Louis was favored to win the pennant. But Leo Durocher's Brooklyn Dodgers had other ideas. The two teams engaged in a classic pennant race, exchanging the lead 17 times. The Cardinals were hobbled by injuries but hung in gamely.

In the final showdown between the two contenders, the first two games were split. The last game, on September 13th, was a classic pitchers' duel between Whit Wyatt of the Dodgers and Mort Cooper of the Cardinals. Although Cooper held Brooklyn hitless for seven innings, the Dodgers won, 1-0. The Cardinals wound up 2½ games behind.

In 1942, St. Louis was favored again. But this time Brooklyn got out to a big lead early in the season and had boosted their margin to 10 games by August 4th.

Then the Cardinals put on their greatest pennant drive ever. By winning 30 of their next 37 games, they arrived in Brooklyn on September 11th trailing by only 2 lengths. Mort Cooper won the first game of the two-game series, 3-0. In the last game, Max Lanier held the Dodgers to five hits, and Whitey Kuorwski's two-run home run gave St. Louis a 2-1 victory and a share of the lead. By winning 12 of their last 14 games, the Cardinals finished 2 games ahead of the Dodgers.

In the World Series, the Cardinals fell behind the New York Yankees, 7-0, in the opening game. St. Louis rallied for four runs in the ninth inning, and, although they still lost the game, they had turned the series around. The Cards then proceeded to win four games in a row to upset the mighty New Yorkers, 4 games to 1.

Branch Rickey, after 26 years with the club, did not have his contract renewed by owner Sam Breadon after the season. No new general manager was hired, and Sam was in firm control. The next few years were glorious for him.

In 1943, the Cardinals overtook the Dodgers on June 5th and won the pennant easily. They finished 18 games ahead of second-place Cincinnati. Stan Musial won his first batting title and MVP award. The 1942 MVP, Mort Cooper, had a 21-8 record in 1943, including back-to-back one-hitters.

But the World Series was a bitter disappointment. The Cardinals looked bad and lost to the Yankees, 4 games to 1.

With all teams suffering from manpower losses to the military services, the Cardinals, who had the most productive farm system, dominated the league as never before in 1944. They were out of first place only four days all season and took over the lead for good on May 7th. They won games by scores like 18-0 and 16-0 against first-division teams. By August 30th, their lead was 20 games. The final margin was 14½.

In the World Series against the St. Louis Browns, the Cards lost two of the first three games but bounced back to win three in a row and capture another world championship.

By 1945, only five players were left from the 1942 champions, and the Cardinals were finally ousted from first place. They never led the league, and their late-season drive to the top was halted by the Cubs on September 25th. St. Louis wound up 3 games behind.

In 1946, with the stars returned from the war, St. Louis was heavy favorite to win the pennant. But the Cardinals were hurt by the defection of three players to the Mexican League and fell as far as 7½ games behind Brooklyn by July 2nd. But they quickly bounced back, and it was another great race with the Dodgers all the way to the wire.

When the season ended, the two teams were tied. That made a playoff necessary for the first time in major league history. The Cardinals won it in two straight games, taking the opener, 4-2, and the next game, 8-4.

Then they knocked off the heavily favored Boston Red Sox in the World Series, 4 games to 3, by virtue of livelier play.

1940—Tuesday, May 7th, at Sportsman's Park
Slugging Records Crumble as Cardinals Crush Dodgers, 18-2
Cards Pound Out 7 Homers, 2 Triples, 4 Doubles, and 7 Singles
Eleven St. Louis Players Get Hits, Ten Hit for Extra Bases

After the famine, what a feast! The struggling St. Louis Cardinals shook themselves out of the doldrums today and demolished the high-flying Brooklyn Dodgers, 18-2. At the expense of pitchers Hugh Casey and Max Macon, St. Louis set a new club record with seven home runs. That tied the existing National League record first set back in 1886 by the Detroit Wolverines. The major league record of eight was set by the Yankees in 1939. The Cardinals set a new "modern" National League record with 49 total bases. The all-time N. L. mark of 53 was set in 1893. Their 13 extra-base hits tied a modern record, although the Chicago White Stockings made 16 in a game in 1883. Their 29 extra bases on long hits surpassed all previous records. And nine men getting extra-base hits was also believed to be a record achievement. In all, ten Red Birds got safe hits and scored runs, and nine men batted runs in.

Today's Results
ST. LOUIS 18 - Brooklyn 2
Cincinnati 7 - New York 6
Philadelphia 1 - Chicago 0
Boston 11 - Pittsburgh 9

Standings	W-L	Pct.	GB
Brooklyn	11-2	.846	-
Cincinnati	11-3	.786	½
Chicago	9-9	.500	4½
Philadelphia	5-7	.417	5½
New York	5-8	.385	6
Boston	5-8	.385	6
ST. LOUIS	6-10	.375	6½
Pittsburgh	4-9	.308	7

The victory shook the Cardinals loose from a three-way tie for last place in the standings. They began the season as slight favorites to win the pennant. But they've had trouble getting untracked. Poor pitching has been mostly to blame for the slow start, and their batting attack has been responsible for most of their victories. Today, Lon Warneke posted his first win and first complete game of the season, but the hitting made it mighty easy for him.

The defeat was only the second of the young season for Leo Durocher's Dodgers. Hugh Casey, today's starting pitcher, has been charged with both losses. Leo kept him in to take some lumps today. Casey was hit for 13 runs in seven innings, and he showed his displeasure by hitting three batters with pitches. Max Macon, the former Cardinal, was tattooed for five runs in one inning of work against his former team.

The Cardinals did it all with a makeshift lineup. Jimmy Brown was stationed at shortstop, Stu Martin moved over to third, and young Eddie Lake was given a chance at second base. Lake responded with two home runs, the first circuit clouts of his major league career. Johnny Hopp patrolled center field in place of the injured Terry Moore.

Besides Lake's two homers, Johnny Mize blasted a pair of round-trippers, and Stu Martin, Joe Medwick, and Don Padgett each hit one. Brown and Enos Slaughter had triples. And Hopp, Lake, Mize, and Warneke all had two-base hits. Joe Orengo, a late-inning substitution at short, singled and stole the only base of the game.

The biggest cheer of the day was not for any slugging feat, however. It came in the ninth inning when Bill DeLancey went in to catch. Bill had been a star in 1934 and 1935, but a lung ailment had forced him to quit and move to Arizona. The fans lustily cheered his first St. Louis appearance in years.

There was no scoring in the first inning.

Warneke did his best clutch pitching in the second. Cookie Lavagetto opened the round with a hit past Brown. When Hopp fell down trying to field the grounder, it went past him for a triple. But Warneke retired Babe Phelps on a come-backer and struck Dolph Camilli out. Roy Cullenbine was given a base on balls and was forced at second on Durocher's grounder.

The Cardinals took the lead in the bottom of the second on the first home run of the day. Don Padgett hit it into the bleachers just to the right of the center field flag pole, 422 feet from the plate. Brown followed with a triple but did not score.

Brooklyn got a man as far as second base in the third inning, but left him there.

St. Louis then broke the game open with five runs. Lake led off with a homer into the left field bleachers. Martin bunted safely and scored on a triple to left center by Slaughter. Medwick singled Slaughter across. Then Mize unloaded a two-run homer onto Grand Avenue, the ball taking a very high bounce off the pavement. Casey hit the next batter, Padgett, with a pitch, then retired three in a row.

In the fourth, Marin hit a home run, which hit one of the new light towers atop the pavilion.

In the fifth, St. Louis scored three runs without the aid of a home run. Mize was hit in the ribs by a pitch, Brown singled, and Hopp and Lake doubled.

Slaughter was also hit by a pitch, starting a three-run rally in the sixth. Medwick, batting next, homered deep into the seats in left center. Mize followed with a double, and he scored on two outs.

Neither side scored in the seventh, although Camilli got Brooklyn's first hit since the third inning.

With a 13-0 lead, Warneke let up in his work in the eighth and lost his shutout. Pee Wee Reese, Dixie Walker, Jimmy Ripple, and Johnny Hudson all singled, giving the Dodgers two runs.

With Macon on the hill, the Red Bird hitters went to town in the bottom of the eighth. With one out, Mize homered onto the pavilion roof. Orengo singled with two out and stole second. Hopp singled. Warneke then completed the cycle of all starters hitting for extra bases by doubling Orengo home. Lake put the finishing touches on the massacre with a home run down the left field foul line.

Brooklyn got two hits in the ninth but failed to score.

The game went into the books as an 18-2 St. Louis victory. A load of batting records went into the books with it.

Brooklyn	ab	r	h	bi	o	a	e	St. Louis	ab	r	h	bi	o	a	e
C. Gilbert, cf	5	0	0	0	1	0	0	E. Lake, 2b	6	2	3	5	3	1	0
P. Coscarart, 2b	4	1	0	1	0	3	1	S. Martin, 3b	6	2	3	1	4	2	0
J. Ripple, lf	4	0	1	0	4	0	0	E. Slaughter, rf	4	2	2	1	1	0	0
C. Lavagetto, 3b	2	0	1	0	2	1	0	J. Medwick, lf	5	2	2	3	2	0	0
J. Hudson, 3b6	2	0	1	0	1	0	0	P. Martin, lf9	0	0	0	0	1	0	0
B. Phelps, c	4	0	0	0	3	1	0	J. Mize, 1b	4	4	3	3	5	0	0
D. Camilli, 1b	4	0	1	0	14	0	0	D. Padgett, c	4	1	1	1	3	0	0
R. Cullenbine, rf	3	0	1	0	0	0	0	B. DeLancey, c9	0	0	0	0	1	0	0
L. Durocher, ss	1	0	0	0	0	2	0	J. Brown, ss	3	1	2	1	0	2	0
P. Reese, ss4	3	1	1	0	0	3	0	J. Orengo, ss7	1	1	1	0	0	0	0
H. Casey, p	2	0	0	0	0	2	0	J. Hopp, cf	5	2	2	2	7	0	0
D. Walker, ph8	1	0	1	0	-	-	-	L. Warneke, p	5	1	1	1	0	2	0
M. Macon, p8	1	0	1	0	0	0	0								
	36	2	9	2	24	13	1		43	18	20	18	27	7	0

Brooklyn   000 000 020 - 2
St. Louis   015 133 05x - 18

LOB: Bkn 8, StL 5. BE: StL 1.
DP: Lavagetto-Camilli.
2B: Hopp, Lake, Mize, Warneke.
3B: Lavagetto, Brown, Slaughter.
HR: Padgett, Lake 2, Mize 2, S. Martin, Medwick. SH: Brown.
SB: Orengo.
Time - 2:05
Attendance - 2,298 paid
         2,810 total

	ip	h	r-er	bb	so
Casey (L 2-2)	7	15	13-13	0	1
Macon	1	5	5-5	0	0
Warneke (W 1-2)	9	9	2-2	1	1

WP: Casey. PB: Padgett
HBP: by Casey 3 (Padgett, Mize, Slaughter)
Umpires: G. Barr, B. Klem, & B. Campbell

Despite this one day of slugging, the Cardinals continued to struggle through the first eight weeks of the season. With the team in seventh place, Ray Blades was fired on June 11th, and Billy Southworth took over.

St. Louis was still floundering at the All-Star break, but they played very well during the second half of the season and finished third with an 84-69 record.

1941 — Saturday, September 13th, at Sportsman's Park
Wyatt Edges M. Cooper, 1-0, Dodgers Retain League Lead
Each Hurler Allows Just Three Hits in Brilliant Duel
Cardinals Fall to Two Games Behind

With first place at stake in the final meeting between the St. Louis Cardinals and the Brooklyn Dodgers, Mort Cooper and Whitlow Wyatt engaged in one of the tensest and best-pitched contests in years. Wyatt and the Dodgers came out victorious by the minimum possible score, 1-0.

A victory would have given St. Louis a percentage point lead over Brooklyn, but the defeat left them two games behind the Dodgers. St. Louis still was scheduled to play 16 games, while Brooklyn had 14 left. The race for first place had been very close all season, and the two teams had exchanged the lead seventeen times. They had also been tied for first on seven separate occasions.

Today's Results
Brooklyn 1 - ST. LOUIS 0
Cincinnati 6 - New York 4
Pittsburgh 1 - Boston 0
Chicago 5 - Philadelphia 4 (11 inn.)

Standings	W-L	Pct.	GB
Brooklyn	90-50	.643	-
ST. LOUIS	87-51	.630	2
Cincinnati	76-62	.551	13
Pittsburgh	76-64	.543	14
New York	64-72	.471	24
Chicago	64-76	.457	26
Boston	57-81	.413	32
Philadelphia	39-97	.287	49

The three-game series just concluded was the final confrontation between the contenders, and the atmosphere at Sportsman's Park was like the World Series. A packed house was on hand early today. The weather was hot, with a strong breeze blowing from right field.

The two fireballing righthanders, Wyatt and Cooper, were practically untouchable today, and each base runner seemed like potentially the only run that might be scored. Both hurlers worked very slowly, adding to the tension of the game.

Wyatt gave up hits in fifth, sixth, and seventh innings, while Cooper carried a no-hitter into the eighth. Then two doubles plated the only run of the game. Brooklyn added another hit in the ninth, giving each side three safeties for the day. Wyatt walked three men and fanned nine, whereas Cooper passed five and struck out six. Each pitcher hit a batter.

Facing a righthander for the first time in the series, Dodger manager Leo Durocher presented a radically different lineup from the two previous games. Today he had five lefthanded hitters in the order.

St. Louis was missing two star outfielders, Enos Slaughter and Terry Moore. Both took batting practice but did not start the game. Moore had been out of the lineup since being beaned on August 20th. Slaughter got into the game as a pinch-hitter. That marked his first appearance since he broke a bone in his shoulder on August 10th.

Both sides went out in order in the first two innings. Wyatt had some trouble with his control, giving three balls to four St. Louis batters.

Herman Franks walked with one out in the top of the third and became the first base runner of the game. But he got no farther than first.

St. Louis got its first runners in the fourth. With two out, Wyatt walked both Don Padgett and Johnny Mize. Estel Crabtree lifted to right center for the third out.

Frank Crespi opened the St. Louis fifth with the first hit of the game. It was a shot to right center, and he stretched it into a double with some daring running and a head-first slide. Marty Marion's grounder toward left was cut off in the hole by shortstop Pee Wee Reese, who threw to third. The peg hit Crespi and rolled away, allowing Marion to get all the way to second. But Crespi had been stunned by the ball, and he lay motionless on the bag for a minute, unable to score. Still, the Cards had men on second and third and no one out. But Wyatt shut them off with an impressive display of power pitching. Working deliberately and using nothing but fastballs, he blew Gus Mancuso and M. Cooper down on strikes, while the home fans groaned. Jimmy Brown then ended the inning with a feeble grounder to first.

With one out in the top of the sixth, Cooper lost his control and walked Dixie Walker and Billy Herman. Pete Reiser popped out, but Dolph Camilli, the league's leading home run and RBI man, also walked, loading the bases. Lew Riggs hit a difficult roller to Brown, who made a nice play to throw him out by a step, much to the relief of the crowd.

With two out in the bottom of the sixth, Mize singled to left center. A pitch in the dirt hit Crabtree in the foot, and umpire Babe Pinelli waved him to first. Durocher argued the ruling vociferously, but to no avail. A passed ball moved the runners to second and third, and Crespi was walked intentionally. But the Cards once again left the bases loaded when Reese snared Marion's grasser up the middle and flipped to second for a force out.

Jimmy Brown, who singled, was the only man to reach base in the seventh inning.

The scoreless tie was finally broken in the eighth. With one out, Walker lifted a high liner to right center, which fell just beyond Johnny Hopp's reach for a double and Brooklyn's first hit. Hopp was not thought of as a bad outfielder, but the feeling in the stands was that the great Moore would have caught the ball. Herman followed with one to the same sector, a little higher and a little deeper than the first one, and, once again, Hopp couldn't quite run it down. It went for a double, and Walker scored easily. Herman went to third on an infield out, but Camilli fanned to end the inning.

With a new-found lead, Wyatt retired St. Louis in order in the final two innings.

In the eighth, Mize and Crabtree chased outside curves for third strikes after Padgett had bounced to the mound.

In the Brooklyn ninth, Riggs got a hit but was thrown out trying to make second on it. A hit batsman and a line-drive double play followed.

In the last of the ninth, Crespi was retired on a check swing roller, Marion fouled out, and Slaughter, pinch-hitting, fanned. That gave the Dodgers the game, 1-0.

It also gave the unflappable Wyatt his 20th win of the season. It was his sixth shutout, and, from Brooklyn's point of view, it couldn't have come at a better time.

Brooklyn	ab	r	h	bi	o	a	e
D. Walker, lf	3	1	1	0	1	0	0
B. Herman, 2b	3	0	1	1	1	1	0
P. Reiser, cf	4	0	0	0	5	0	0
D. Camilli, 1b	2	0	0	0	7	0	0
L. Riggs, 3b	4	0	1	0	0	1	0
J. Wasdell, rf	3	0	0	0	1	0	0
P. Reese, ss	4	0	0	0	1	2	1
H. Franks, c	2	0	0	0	11	0	0
W. Wyatt, p	3	0	0	0	0	2	0
	28	1	3	1	27	6	1

St. Louis	ab	r	h	bi	o	a	e
J. Brown, 3b	4	0	1	0	2	2	0
J. Hopp, cf	4	0	0	0	4	1	0
D. Padgett, lf	3	0	0	0	5	0	0
J. Mize, 1b	3	0	1	0	7	0	0
E. Crabtree, rf	3	0	0	0	0	0	0
F. Crespi, 2b	3	0	1	0	1	2	0
M. Marion, ss	4	0	0	0	1	1	0
G. Mancuso, c	3	0	0	0	7	0	0
E. Slaughter, ph9	1	0	0	0	-	-	-
M. Cooper, p	3	0	0	0	0	1	0
	31	0	3	0	27	7	0

Brooklyn   000 000 010 - 1
St. Louis   000 000 000 - 0

	ip	h	r-er	bb	so
Wyatt (W 20-10)	9	3	0-0	3	9
Cooper (L 13-7)	9	3	1-1	5	6

PB: Franks.
HBP: by Wyatt (Crabtree), by Cooper (Wasdell).

LOB: Bkn 6, StL 8. BE: StL 1.
DP: Brown-Mize.
2B: Crespi, Walker, Herman.
Time - 2:37
Attendance - 32,691
Umpires: B. Pinelli, A. Barlick, B. Klem, & L. Ballanfant.

The Cardinals won 10 and lost 5 games, with one game cancelled over the last two weeks of the season, and they couldn't catch the Dodgers.

St. Louis finished 2½ games behind with a 97-56 record.

1942 — Saturday, September 12th, at Ebbets Field, Brooklyn

St. Louis Tops Brooklyn, 2-1, to Gain a Tie for First Place

Kurowski's Home Run in Second Inning Scores Two Runs

26th Victory in 30 Games for Red-Hot Red Birds

Billy Southworth's hard-driving St. Louis Cardinals finally caught Leo Durocher's defending-champion Brooklyn Dodgers in the National League pennant race today. By winning both games of a two-game series, St. Louis moved into a tie for first place with Brooklyn with 14 games left to play.

Just over five weeks ago, on August 4th, Durocher's men had an apparently insurmountable 10-game lead over the Red Birds. Since that date, the Dodgers have won 21 and lost 16, while the Cardinals have won 32 and lost only 7. St. Louis has won 26 of their last 30, including five out of six from Brooklyn.

Today's Results
ST. LOUIS 2 — Brooklyn 1
Cincinnati 4 - Philadelphia 1
Boston 4 - Pittsburgh 1 (1st game)
Boston 2 - Pittsburgh 2 (Tie) (11 inn.)
    (2nd game)
no other game scheduled

Standings	W-L	Pct.	GB
ST. LOUIS	94-46	.671	-
Brooklyn	94-46	.671	-
New York	77-62	.554	16½
Cincinnati	69-70	.469	24½
Pittsburgh	62-73	.459	29½
Chicago	64-78	.451	31
Boston	56-82	.406	37
Philadelphia	37-96	.278	53½

The two-game series just concluded marked the end of head-to-head competition between the two contenders. Yesterday, St. Louis's Mort Cooper beat Whit Wyatt, 3-0. Today, Max Lanier pitched the Cardinals to a 2-1 victory over the Dodgers' Max Macon.

Durocher had delayed his pitching selection until just two hours before game time. Then he gave Macon the nod over Curt Davis. Macon pitched well, escaping several tight spots, but his teammates could not score enough runs against Lanier's dazzling speed.

With two lefthanders pitching, the managers shifted their lineups slightly. Rookie Stan Musial was replaced by righthanded hitting Coaker Triplett in left field for St. Louis. Augie Galan was replaced by Johnny Rizzo for Brooklyn. In addition, Pete Reiser was ailing, and Stan "Frenchy" Bordagaray played center field for the Dodgers.

After St. Louis went out in order in the first, Bordagaray singled through the box. He stole second, but was caught trying to pilfer third.

With one out in the second, Walker Cooper singled to left for the Cards. George "Whitey" Kurowski was next up. Macon kept tantalizing him with slow curves. The rookie third baseman pulled three of them foul, the last one with home run distance. Macon tried yet another slow, breaking ball, and this time Kurowski waited long enough to hit it fair and into the lower left field seats for a two-run homer. Johnny Hopp followed with a hit to center. After Marty Marion fouled out, Lanier singled Hopp to second. The runners were left when Jimmy Brown bounced to shortstop.

Brooklyn came right back with one run in the bottom of the second. With one out, Dolph Camilli lined a single to center. Mickey Owen grounded to first baseman Hopp, whose throw to second was very high. But shortstop Marion made a wonderful catch to get a force on Camilli. Pee Wee Reese then socked a double to left center, and Owen raced around to score. Arky Vaughan lifted a high pop foul, which Kurowski nabbed on the run.

Triplett doubled with two out in the third, and Cooper was walked behind him. But Kurowski hit into a force play, and two men were left on.

Brooklyn went out in order.

St. Louis again left two men in the fourth. Hopp led off with a hit through the box. Marion bunted him to second. Hopp took third on Lanier's ground out. Brown walked, then Terry Moore was retired on a fly to center.

Lanier walked both Camilli and Owen with two out in the Brooklyn fourth. Reese then hit a sinking looper into short right, which Enos Slaughter had to charge hard to grab for the third out.

Each side got a man to first with two out in the fifth, but they were unable to score.

Lanier's line drive single to left with two out provided the only base runner in the sixth inning.

St. Louis went down in order in the seventh.

Brooklyn came in and made their closest bid in the bottom of the seventh. The first man up, Owen, hit a bouncer just past Hopp. But Brown ranged far to his left to make the stop, and he threw to Lanier, who was crossing first. The play was very close, but umpire Al Barlick called Owen out. Charley Dressen, coaching first, and Durocher, who came storming out of the dugout, were both ejected for arguing the call. Durocher chased Barlick nearly to the right field wall before getting the thumb.

When play resumed, Reese lifted a fly to center that Moore caught nicely. Vaughan then walked. Galan was sent up to hit for Macon. He rolled to Marion, who threw to Brown just as the hard-sliding Vaughan was reaching second. Jimmy dropped the ball. Unhappy about having to pitch to an extra hitter, Lanier unfurled a wild pitch that went back to the screen. Vaughan tried to score all the way from second, but Cooper's throw to Lanier nipped him at the plate.

Curt Davis went in to pitch for the Dodgers in the eighth. He allowed a two-out triple by Hopp, then walked Marion. Marion was allowed to steal second, but Lanier bounced out, ending the threat.

Musial, who had gone into left as a defensive replacement, ran deep to grab Bordagaray's fly ball leading off the Dodger eighth. Billy Herman then walked. Rizzo hit a long drive to right center, which Slaughter galloped under and caught. Joe Medwick singled to right field, sending Herman to third. But Camilli failed in the clutch, being retired on a weak grounder to second.

An error and a base on balls gave the Cardinals two runners in the top of the ninth, but they did not score.

In the last half, Slaughter made another running catch, this one to get a fly by Owen. Kurowski handled Reese's smash nicely and threw the batter out at first. And Vaughan's pop fly was easy for Hopp, ending the game. The Cardinals were 2-1 winners and tied for first place.

With two weeks to go, their momentum seemed sure to carry them to the pennant.

St. Louis	ab	r	h	bi	o	a	e
J. Brown, 2b	4	0	0	0	1	3	1
T. Moore, cf	4	0	0	0	2	0	0
E. Slaughter, rf	4	0	0	0	4	0	0
C. Triplett, lf	4	0	1	0	2	0	0
S. Musial, lf7	1	0	0	0	1	0	0
W. Cooper, c	3	1	1	0	6	2	0
W. Kurowski, 3b	4	1	1	2	2	1	0
J. Hopp, 1b	4	0	3	0	6	1	0
M. Marion, ss	2	0	0	0	1	2	0
M. Lanier, p	4	0	2	0	2	0	0
	34	2	8	2	27	9	1

Brooklyn	ab	r	h	bi	o	a	e
F. Bordagaray, cf	4	0	2	0	2	0	0
B. Herman, 2b	3	0	0	0	3	4	1
J. Rizzo, rf	4	0	0	0	1	0	0
J. Medwick, lf	4	0	1	0	1	0	0
D. Camilli, 1b	3	0	1	0	11	0	0
M. Owen, c	3	1	0	0	2	0	0
P. Reese, ss	4	0	1	1	4	3	0
A. Vaughan, 3b	3	0	0	0	2	3	0
M. Macon, p	2	0	0	0	1	0	0
A. Galan, ph7	1	0	0	0	-	-	-
C. Davis, p8	0	0	0	0	0	2	0
	31	1	5	1	27	12	1

St. Louis   020 000 000 - 2
Brooklyn   010 000 000 - 1

	ip	h	r-er	bb	so
Lanier (W 13-7)	9	5	1-1	4	5
Macon (L 5-3)	7	7	2-2	3	0
Davis	2	1	0-0	2	1

WP: Lanier
Umpires: L. Ballanfant, A. Barlick, B. Stewart, & B. Pinelli

LOB: StL 12, Bkn 7.
BE: StL 1, Bkn 1.
2B: Reese, Triplett. 3B: Hopp.
HR: Kurowski. SH: Marion, Moore.
SB: Bordagaray, Marion.
CS: Bordagaray.
Attendance - 25,938 paid
            27,511 total
Time - 2:17

The Cardinals kept up their tremendous pace for the next two weeks, winning 12 of the last 14 games. Brooklyn won 10 of 14, but that left them 2 games behind.

St. Louis won the pennant with an impressive 106-48 record for their best N. L. percentage ever, .688.

1942 World Series—Game #5

Monday, October 5th, at Yankee Stadium, New York

Cardinals Beat Yankees Again to Win World Series

Rookies Beazley and Kurowski Pace St. Louis's 4-2 Victory

Southworth's Swifties Win Fourth Straight Game After Losing Opener

The amazing, young St. Louis Cardinals ended the New York Yankees' dominance of baseball's World Series today with a 4-2 victory, which gave the Missourians the world championship. It was the first time since 1926 that the Yankees had lost the fall classic. Since that time, they had won eight championships, losing only four games total in those eight series.

New York won the opening game on this year's series, 7-4. Their pitching ace, Red Ruffing, had a no-hitter for 7-2/3 innings, but the Cardinals put a scare into the Yanks by rallying for four runs in the ninth. Then the National League champs proceeded to win four games in a row. They outplayed the American Leaguers at every point, beating them with daring base running, superb pitching, clutch fielding, and late rallies.

Today's victory even featured big home runs by the Red Birds. George "Whitey" Kurowski provided the winning margin with a two-run, ninth-inning homer. Enos Slaughter had homered earlier in the game for St. Louis's first round-tripper of the series.

Sharing the spotlight with Kurowski was another rookie, pitcher Johnny Beazley, who won his second complete game of the classic. Four Cardinal errors had him in trouble in much of today's game, but the 24-year-old righthander showed remarkable poise through the various crises and came out as the winner.

Facing elimination, Yankee manager Joe McCarthy put Ruffing on the mound today. The 38-year-old righthander pitched a good game, but Kurowski & Company did him in.

Ruffing started the game wildly, walking Jimmy Brown on four pitches. But he struck out Terry Moore, and his infield turned Slaughter's hard grounder into a double play.

With a 1-1 count, New York's leadoff hitter, Phil Rizzuto, lined a ball about 310 feet down the left field line and into the seats for a home run, quickly giving the Yankees the lead.

There was no scoring in the second and third innings. In the third, the St. Louis infield stopped New York with a snappy 3-6-4 double play on an attempted sacrifice bunt.

Enos Slaughter hit Ruffing's first pitch in the fourth inning far into the seats in right field for a home run, tying the game. The next three batters were retired.

New York came in and regained the lead in the bottom of the fourth. Beazley put himself into a hole by throwing wildly past first base after fielding Red Rolfe's bunt. Rolfe was credited with a single, and Beazley drew an error for allowing him to get second. Rolfe moved to third on Roy Cullenbine's long fly to right center. Joe DiMaggio lined the next pitch into center for a run-scoring single. DiMag took third on Charlie Keller's hard single into right. Manager Southworth then came out to the mound to talk to Beazley. Apparently steadied, Johnny struck out Joe Gordon on a tantalizing, slow curve. Bill Dickey then ended the inning by hitting into a force play, leaving two men on base.

Two St. Louis errors gave the Yankees a golden opportunity to break the game open in the bottom of the fifth, but the Bronx Bombers failed in the clutch. Jerry Priddy, the first man up, was retired on a pretty play by shortstop Marty Marion. Ruffing then beat out a slow roller to third for a hit. Johnny Hopp, the first baseman, speared Rizzuto's hot smash but threw low to second, allowing Ruffing to reach that base safely. Rolfe followed with a perfect double play ball, but Brown kicked it, loading the bases with one out. Southworth again went to the mound, and again Beazley responded. Although he fell behind Cullenbine three balls and one strike, he retired him on a soft fly to shortstop. The great DiMaggio ended the inning with a routine grounder to Kurowski, who stepped on third base for a force out.

Buoyed by this narrow escape, the Cardinals tied the score in the sixth. Moore singled to left on the first pitch. Slaughter sent him to third with a hit on the next pitch. Stan Musial also swung at the first pitch, but he popped out. Walker Cooper waited for a pitch to drive, and he hit a long fly to right, scoring Moore. An error on the cutoff allowed Slaughter to take third, but Hopp made the third out with a long fly to center.

The game remained tied until the ninth.

Cooper opened the last inning with a single to center. Hopp sacrificed him to second. Kurowski then waited just long enough on an inside pitch and lined it deep down the left field line. The ball could not be seen from the stands, owing to the darkness and haze, but two umpires signalled that it had stayed fair, and Kurowski had a two-run home run.

It was Whitey's first homer since his clutch shot in Brooklyn on September 13th. This one gave the Cardinals a two-run lead.

The Yankees came in needing two runs to stay alive. Gordon, leading off, broke a string of 14 hitless at bats with a single. Dickey followed with a double play ball to second, but Brown took his eye off it and made an error, putting the tying runs on base. Priddy, the next batter, bluffed a bunt. Catcher Cooper caught the pitch and immediately gunned the ball down to second base, where Marion had slipped in behind Gordon. The runner was picked off easily, taking the steam out of the rally. Priddy then hit a weak looper that Brown lunged for and caught. George Selkirk, batting for Ruffing, ended the game with a ground out to second.

When Hopp squeezed the throw, the Yankees had been replaced by the amazing Cardinals as world champions. The St. Louis players mobbed Beazley, then ran to the clubhouse for a joyous celebration. The happiest man among them was manager Southworth. He praised his players, summing up their season with the statement, "Those kids never knew when to quit."

St. Louis (NL)	ab	r	h	bi	o	a	e
J. Brown, 2b	3	0	2	0	3	4	2
T. Moore, cf	3	1	1	0	3	0	0
E. Slaughter, rf	4	1	2	1	2	0	0
S. Musial, lf	4	0	0	0	2	0	0
W. Cooper, c	4	1	2	1	2	1	0
J. Hopp, 1b	3	0	0	0	9	2	1
W. Kurowski, 3b	4	1	1	2	1	1	0
M. Marion, ss	4	0	0	0	3	5	0
J. Beazley, p	4	0	1	0	2	0	1
	33	4	9	4	27	13	4

New York (AL)	ab	r	h	bi	o	a	e
P. Rizzuto, ss	4	1	2	1	7	1	0
R. Rolfe, 3b	4	1	1	0	1	0	0
R. Cullenbine, rf	4	0	0	0	3	0	0
J. DiMaggio, cf	4	0	1	1	3	0	0
C. Keller, lf	4	0	1	0	1	0	0
J. Gordon, 2b	4	0	1	0	3	3	0
B. Dickey, c	4	0	0	0	4	0	0
T. Stainback, pr9	0	0	0	0	-	-	-
J. Priddy, 1b	3	0	0	0	5	1	1
R. Ruffing, p	3	0	1	0	0	1	0
G. Selkirk, ph9	1	0	0	0	-	-	-
	35	2	7	2	27	6	1

St. Louis   000 101 002 — 4
New York   100 100 000 — 2

	ip	h	r-er	bb	so
Beazley (W 2-0)	9	7	2-2	1	2
Ruffing (W 1-1)	9	9	4-4	1	3

Attendance - 69,052
Umpires: G. Magerkurth, B. Summers, G. Barr, & C. Hubbard

LOB: StL 5, NY 7. BE: NY 3.
DP: Gordon-Rizzuto-Priddy, Hopp-Marion-Brown.
HR: Rizzuto, Slaughter, Kurowski.
SH: Moore, Hopp.
SB: none. Picked Off: Gordon.
Time - 1:58

Several Cardinal players entered the military service before the start of the 1943 season. They included Moore, Slaughter, and Beazley.

1943—Friday Night, June 4th, at Sportsman's Park
Cooper's Second Straight One-Hitter Gives Cardinals a 5-0 Victory
Only Two Phillies Reach Base Against Mort
Musial and Walker Extend Hitting Streaks

Last year's Most Valuable Player, pitcher Mort Cooper, hurled his second consecutive one-hit shutout tonight, pacing the defending-champion St. Louis Cardinals to a 5-0 victory over the Philadelphia Phillies. The first two St. Louis runs were driven in by Stan Musial and Harry Walker, as each man extended his current hitting streak. The victory kept St. Louis just ½ game behind the league-leading Brooklyn Dodgers.

Cooper had stopped the Dodgers on just one hit in the first game of a doubleheader last Monday. The hit was an opposite-field, pop-fly double by Billy Herman, which landed just barely fair. In that game, Cooper walked three batters.

Today's Results
ST. LOUIS 5 — Philadelphia 0
Brooklyn 18 - Chicago 5
Pittsburgh 9 - New York 8
no other game scheduled

Standings	W-L	Pct.	GB
Brooklyn	27-15	.651	-
ST. LOUIS	25-14	.650	½
Pittsburgh	20-17	.541	4½
Cincinnati	20-18	.526	5
Boston	16-18	.471	7
Philadelphia	18-21	.462	7½
New York	15-25	.375	11
Chicago	13-26	.333	12½

Tonight he walked no one, but he made an error to allow a batter to reach first base. The only hit by the Phillies was a clean single by Jimmy Wasdell, leading off the eighth inning. Cooper struck out five batters. He also singled and scored during the Cardinals' third-inning rally.

Mort raised his won-lost record to 6-3 with his third shutout of the season. Two of his losses have been eleven-inning complete games, 1-0 and 4-3.

Charley Fuchs pitched a decent game for the losers, allowing eight hits and walking one. But St. Louis bunched three hits in each of their two scoring innings, giving them five runs. Fuchs' record dropped to 1-6, despite some good pitching this year.

The Cardinals' third baseman, Whitey Kurowski, was still sidelined with an eye injury, and veteran Jimmy Brown took his place in the lineup. Ken O'Dea caught for the Red Birds, giving Mort's brother Walker Cooper a day off. Otherwise, the teams were pretty much at full strength.

A crowd of 6,984 was on hand for the night game. Of that number, 569 were military men in uniform, and 197 were blood donors admitted free.

Danny Murtaugh, the first man to face Cooper, popped out to Lou Klein at second base. Ron Northey fanned. Former Cardinal Buster Adams fouled to O'Dea.

The Cardinals also went out in order in the first.

Wasdell struck out to open the second. Babe Dahlgren, who entered the game with a league-leading .382 batting average, grounded to shortstop Marty Marion and was thrown out at first. Glen Stewart was retired on a come-backer to Cooper.

Once again, the Cardinals also went out in order.

Pinky May opened the third with an easy fly to Musial in right field. Mickey Livingston then hit the longest ball of the day off Cooper, but Johnny Hopp caught it in front of the left field fence. Fuchs tapped to Cooper for the third out.

St. Louis broke through with two runs in the bottom of the third. Brown grounded to shortstop, and Steward fumbled the ball for an error. Marion hit a long fly to left center, which Adams caught on the run. Cooper then stroked a single to right. Klein fanned for the second out. But Walker and Musial followed with RBI singles, putting the Cardinals ahead, 2-0. Walker's hit extended his hitting streak to 13 consecutive games. Musial's streak was upped to 21 games. Walker finished the day with a .346 average, Musial with a .357 mark.

For the next four innings, neither team mounted any real scoring threats, although the Cardinals got two hits and a walk.

Cooper continued to mow down the Phillies.

In the fourth, Murtaugh was out on a long foul and a fine catch by Johnny Hopp. Northey bounced out to second. And Adams fouled to first.

In the fifth, Wasdell led off with a pop out. Dahlgren then made a bid to break up the no-hitter with a hard-hit grounder to third. But Brown made a fine stop of the difficult grass-cutter and threw the batter out at first. Stewart fanned.

The Phillies got their first runner in the sixth. May opened with a high bouncer to the mound. Cooper gloved the ball, then dropped it and twice failed to pick it up again. May reached first on the error. Livingston flied to right, and Fuchs bounced into a double play, Klein to Marion to Sanders.

The visitors tried bunting in the seventh, but to no avail. Ray Sanders retired Murtaugh and Northey on unassisted plays, and Cooper fielded Adam's bunt and tossed him out.

Cooper's streak of hitless innings was ended at twelve in the eighth. Jimmy Wasdell, leading off, lined the second pitch of the frame into left field for a single. But he got no farther than first. Dahlgren struck out, Stewart popped out, and May flied out to center.

The Cardinals iced the decision with three runs in the bottom of the eighth. Walker singled with one out. With two down, Sanders delivered a long double for a run. O'Dea then hit his first home run of the year to make the count 5-0 St. Louis. The homer was a long shot into the right center field section of the pavilion, just past the end of the screen.

Cooper dispatched the visitors easily in the ninth. Livingston was thrown out by Marion. Coaker Triplett, recently acquired by the Phillies from the Cardinals, batted for Fuchs and watched a third strike. Murtaugh then ended the game with a foul fly to Brown.

Cooper became the only Cardinal and only the eighth National League pitcher to allow two or fewer hits in two consecutive complete games.

Philadelphia	ab	r	h	bi	o	a	e
D. Murtaugh, 2b	4	0	0	0	2	3	0
R. Northey, rf	3	0	0	0	3	0	0
B. Adams, cf	3	0	0	0	3	0	0
J. Wasdell, lf	3	0	1	0	4	0	0
B. Dahlgren, 1b	3	0	0	0	6	1	0
G. Stewart, ss	3	0	0	0	1	2	1
P. May, 3b	3	0	0	0	2	1	0
M. Livingston, c	3	0	0	0	3	1	0
C. Fuchs, p	2	0	0	0	0	0	0
C. Triplett, ph9	1	0	0	0	-	-	-
	28	0	1	0	24	8	1

St. Louis	ab	r	h	bi	o	a	e
L. Klein, 2b	4	0	0	0	1	2	0
H. Walker, cf	4	1	2	1	1	0	0
S. Musial, rf	4	0	1	1	2	0	0
R. Sanders, 1b	4	1	1	1	12	0	0
K. O'Dea, c	4	1	1	2	6	0	0
J. Hopp, lf	3	0	0	0	2	0	0
J. Brown, 3b	3	1	1	0	2	1	0
M. Marion, ss	3	0	1	0	1	3	0
M. Cooper, p	2	1	1	0	0	3	1
	31	5	8	5	27	9	1

Philadelphia 000 000 000 - 0
St. Louis   002 000 03x - 5

LOB: Phil 1, StL 4. BE: StL 1, Phil 1. DP: Klein-Marion-Sanders.
2B: Brown, Sanders.
HR: O'Dea. SH: Cooper.
Time - 1:42
Attendance - 6,098 paid
    6,984 total

	ip	h	r-er	bb	so
Fuchs (L 1-6)	8	8	5-3	1	2
Cooper (W 6-3)	9	1	0-0	0	5

Umpires: J. Conlan, G. Barr, & L. Jorda

The Cardinals took over first place on the very next day and ran away with the pennant, winning by 18 games over the second-place Cincinnati Reds. St. Louis's record was 105-49, just one game off their 1942 pace.

Cooper gave up seven hits in winning his next game, 4-3, over Pittsburgh. Mort finished the year with a 21-8 record, down just a mite from his 22-7 record in 1942.

1943 World Series—Game #5

Monday, October 11th, at Sportsman's Park

Cards Get Ten Hits but Lose, 2-0, Giving Yankees the Series

Can't Hit Chandler With Men on Base

New York Avenges Last Year's Defeat With Five-Game Win of Series

    The New York Yankees turned the tables on the St. Louis Cardinals this year, winning the World Series, four games to one, by taking the fifth game today, 2-0. Last year, the Cardinals had beaten the Yankees in the series by the same four-to-one margin. They did it then with clutch hitting and dashing play, making the Yankees look flat. This year, it was the New Yorkers who hit in the clutch, flashed in the field, and careened around the bases. And it was the St. Louisans who looked listless.
    The defending-champion Cardinals were a closed-mouthed, grim bunch before today's game started. Manager Billy Southworth closed the clubhouse to reporters prior to the game and tried to inspire his men behind closed doors. Johnny Beazley, the star of last year's series but a U.S. Marine this year, gave the team a pep talk after yesterday's defeat. And soldiers Jimmy Brown and Enos Slaughter donned Red Bird uniforms today and took practice with the team. But nothing helped.
    Spurgeon "Spud" Chandler and Mort Cooper were the starting pitchers today. Chandler had pitched the Yankees to victory in the opening game, 4-2. Cooper had pitched and won the second game for the Cards, 4-3. Today St. Louis had runners in every inning but the fifth, but Chandler kept turning them back in the pinch. The Cardinals wound up stranding eleven men. The Yankees left nine on, but a two-run home run by Bill Dickey in the sixth inning gave them the game.
    The crowd at Sportsman's Park was smaller than the day before, but it was more vocal. Mary Ott, the Cardinals' number one fan, was in her seat just minutes after the gates opened at 10:00 a.m., and her famous lungs cheered the locals' every move.
    The desperate Southworth shook up his lineup in an attempt to end the team's batting slump. He benched outfielders Harry Walker and Danny Litwhiler, both of whom had started the first four games, and used Johnny Hopp and Debs Garms, instead. The changes failed. Garms and Hopp both went hitless, while Walker and Litwhiler both singled in pinch-hitting roles.
    Cooper started the game in great style. He struck out the first five Yankees he faced. Then he walked Nick Etten before retiring Joe Gordon on a grounder to end the top of the second.
    St. Louis got an infield hit, a sacrifice, and a base on balls in their first. But Walker Cooper and Whitey Kurowski bounced out, leaving two men on.
    A single by Ray Sanders opened the Cardinal second. Hopp bounced back to Chandler, who threw to shortstop Frank Crosetti trying for a force at second. Umpire Joe Rue called Sanders out, but Crosetti dropped the ball as he started to throw to first, and Rue changed his call to safe. The Yankees argued the call vigorously, manager Joe McCarthy even coming out from the dugout. But the ruling stood. Marty Marion followed with a nice sacrifice bunt, putting runners on second and third with just one out. But Chandller turned on the heat and fanned M. Cooper. Klein's long fly to right was caught by Bud Methany, and the runners were stranded.
    Walker Cooper, batting with two out in the St. Louis third, hit safely down the left field line, but he was thrown out trying to get a double on the hit.
    St. Louis stranded two more in the fourth. Kurowski bunted safely, and Sanders walked with no one out. Chandler fell behind on the count to Hopp, 3-and-0, then came back to strike him out. Marion hit into a force out at second. M. Cooper hit a high bouncer toward short, which Crosetti nabbed with a high leap and turned into another force play.
    Tuck Stainback singled with one out in the New York fifth and moved to third on a sacrifice and a wild pitch. With Crosetti at bat, a foul tip split Walker Cooper's finger. The frustrated catcher, who had had a dispiriting series, was forced to leave the game. He gave his mitt a big kick as he disgustedly headed for the clubhouse. Ken O'Dea took

his place. Crosetti popped to Garms in left, ending the inning.

The Cardinals were retired in order in the fifth.

With two down in the top of the sixth, second baseman Lou Klein shifted over toward second base, despite the fact that the batter was a lefthanded hitter, Charlie Keller. Sure enough, Keller singled through the big hole and into right field. On the very next pitch, Bill Dickey hit a long drive onto the roof of the pavilion in right field for a two-run homer.

O'Dea singled to open the bottom of the inning, but he was wiped out on a double play.

In the seventh, St. Louis wasted a pinch single by Walker.

Max Lanier pitched the eighth for St. Louis, blanking New York with the help of a double play. Lanier and Murry Dickson shut the Yankees out in the ninth, although the bases were left loaded. Dickson, who was inducted into the army late in the season, was on a special leave to enable him to be in the World Series.

In the home half of the eighth, O'Dea and Kurowski both singled. But their hits came with two outs, and Sanders followed by bouncing out to Gordon.

St. Louis again threatened in the last half of the ninth. After Hopp flied out, Marion slapped a single to left. Litwhiler, pinch-hitting, singled over shortstop. But, once again, Chandler shut the door, fanning Klein and getting Garms to ground to Gordon for the last out.

That gave the Yankees the victory, 2-0, and with it, their tenth World Series championship.

It left the St. Louis fans shaking their heads and wondering, "What happened to the Cardinals?"

New York (AL)	ab	r	h	bi	o	a	e
F. Crosetti, ss	4	0	1	0	0	5	1
B. Methany, rf	5	0	1	0	1	0	0
J. Lindell, rf9	0	0	0	0	0	0	0
B. Johnson, 3b	4	0	1	0	1	2	0
C. Keller, lf	3	1	1	0	1	1	0
B. Dickey, c	4	1	1	2	7	0	0
N. Etten, 1b	3	0	1	0	11	1	0
J. Gordon, 2b	2	0	0	0	6	6	0
T. Stainback, cf	3	0	1	0	0	0	0
S. Chandler, p	3	0	0	0	0	2	0
	31	2	7	2	27	17	1

St. Louis (NL)	ab	r	h	bi	o	a	e
L. Klein, 2b	5	0	1	0	3	1	0
D. Garms, lf	4	0	0	0	1	0	0
S. Musial, rf	3	0	0	0	1	0	0
W. Cooper, c	2	0	1	0	6	0	1
K. O'Dea, c5	2	0	2	0	2	0	0
W. Kurowski, 3b	4	0	2	0	3	3	0
R. Sanders, 1b	3	0	1	0	7	2	0
J. Hopp, cf	4	0	0	0	1	0	0
M. Marion, ss	3	0	1	0	2	3	0
M. Cooper, p	2	0	0	0	0	1	0
H. Walker, ph7	1	0	1	0	-	-	-
M. Lanier, p8	0	0	0	0	0	1	0
M. Dickson, p9	0	0	0	0	1	0	0
D. Litwhiler, ph9	1	0	1	0	-	-	-
	34	0	10	0	27	11	1

New York   000 002 000 - 2
St. Louis 000 000 000 - 0

	ip	h	r-er	bb	so
Chandler (W 2-0)	9	10	0-0	2	7
M. Cooper (L 1-1)	7	5	2-2	2	6
Lanier	1.1	2	0-0	2	1
Dickson	.2	0	0-0	1	0

Umpires: E. Rommel, B. Reardon, J. Rue, & B. Stewart

LOB: NY 9, StL 11. BE: StL 1.
DP: Crosetti-Gordon-Etten, Klein-Marion-Sanders.
HR: Dickey. SH: Garms, Marion, Chandler, Stainback
Attendance - 33,872
WP: M. Cooper
Time - 2:24

1944 — Saturday, June 10th, at Crosley Field, Cincinnati

Cardinals Bury Reds' Pitchers in 18-0 Massacre

Two Reds Make Big League Debuts, One a 15 Year Old

St. Louis Makes 21 Hits, Scores in Eight of the Nine Innings

The St. Louis Cardinals broke out of their recent batting slump in a very big way today. They piled up 21 hits and 18 runs while shutting the Cincinnati Reds out. It was the most one-sided shutout victory in the club's history and their most one-sided victory since they beat Philadelphia 28-6 in 1929. The Cardinals also tied a league record today by leaving 18 men on base.

In their previous twenty-five innings of batting, the Red Birds had scored just one run. In the last two games, they had totaled just eight hits, losing to the Phillies' Bill Lee, 1-0, and to the Reds' Bucky Walters 2-1.

Today's Results
ST. LOUIS 18 — Cincinnati 0
Pittsburgh 9 - Chicago 4
Boston at Brooklyn - postponed, rain
Philadelphia at New York - ppd., rain

Standings	W-L	Pct.	GB
ST. LOUIS	30-15	.667	-
Pittsburgh	25-17	.595	3½
Cincinnati	25-20	.556	5
New York	22-23	.489	8
Brooklyn	22-24	.478	8½
Philadelphia	18-24	.429	10½
Boston	21-28	.429	11
Chicago	14-26	.350	13½

Today, however, the opposing pitchers were not of that caliber. Bill Lohrman, recently signed by the Reds after Brooklyn released him, started for Cincinnati. He had nothing on the ball and was pounded for five runs in just 1-1/3 innings. Ed Heusser pitched next, and he failed to retire any of the four men he faced. Buck Fausett then took over on the mound. He was a third baseman by trade, but had been known to pitch on occasion. He lasted through the eighth, allowing six runs. Then with his team down by 13 runs, Reds' manager Bill McKecknie decided to give young Joe Nuxhall a look in the ninth. The youth, who had not yet reached his 16th birthday, gave up five runs before being relieved by 21-year-old Jake Eisenhardt, who was also making his league debut.

Against this motley crew of hurlers, all eleven Cardinals who got into today's game got hits. Ten of them scored runs, and nine of them drove runs in. St. Louis was also given 14 bases on balls and scored in eight of the nine innings.

While all this was going on, Mort Cooper let the Reds down on just five hits and two walks. Only one Cincinnati runner got as far as third base. Mort had their hitters popping up easy chances, including an impressive total of seven foul pop outs.

The Cardinals' victory kept them 3½ games in front of the second-place Pirates, and it shoved the third-place Reds to 5 games back.

Johnny Hopp, the game's first batter, flied out. Debs Garms walked. Stan Musial forced Garms, then went to third on Ray Sanders's single. Walker Cooper also singled, plating the first run.

The Cardinals broke the game open with six runs in the second. Marty Marion began with a single, and George Fallon walked. M. Cooper popped out trying to bunt, but it didn't matter much. Hopp and Garms singled, routing Lohrman. Heusser came in and yielded consecutive single to Musial, Sanders, W. Cooper, and Danny Litwhiler. That made the score 7-0 and brought Fausett into the game. The 36-year-old-rookie, who last season had been manager, third baseman, and pitcher for Little Rock, retired the side without further scoring.

St. Louis failed to score in the third, despite a base on balls on which Musial went to second (ball four being a wild pitch).

W. Cooper singled in the fourth and scored on a double by Fallon.

Hopp opened the fifth with a double, and Augie Bergamo pinch-ran for him. Bergamo scored on two fly outs.

In the bottom of the fifth, the Reds got two hits for the only time in the game. But Max Marshall and Gee Walker both fouled out, leaving runners on first and second.

The Reds were retired in order in the last four innings.

Marion walked in the sixth and came home on hits by Fallon and M. Cooper.

In the seventh, Musial walked, and Sanders's single sent him to third. He scored on Litwhiler's fly to left.

After four innings on scoring single runs, the Cards got two tallies in the eighth. M. Cooper and Bergamo both singled to center. Garms bunted, and Fausett bobbled, loading the bases. Musial sent two men home with a base hit to center. Sanders walked, again filling the sacks, but W. Cooper and Litwhiler popped out, and Marion grounded out.

In the ninth, Nuxhall was given a chance. The youngster became the youngest player to ever get into a major league game, being 15 years, 10 months and 11 days old. A big boy, Joe had already grown to a height of 6 feet and 3 inches. He had been signed out of nearby Hamilton, Ohio, High School. He was obviously nervous and was very wild. The first man he faced, Fallon, was retired on a good play by shortstop Eddie Miller. M. Cooper walked and went to second on a wild pitch. Bergamo popped to Miller. But Garms walked, and Musial singled home a run. Then Nuxhall lost all control, passing Sanders, W. Cooper, and Litwhiler, forcing home two runs. After Emil Verban delivered a two-run single, McKechnie mercifully took Nuxhall out.

Lefthander Jake Eisenhardt was brought in. He had been signed recently out of Juniata College in Huntington, Pa. Eisenhardt walked Fallon, but got Mort Cooper to foul out, ending the inning.

Cooper disposed of the Reds in order in the bottom of the ninth, and the Cardinals won the game, 18-0. The 5,469 fans may have been disappointed by the one-sided defeat suffered by the home team, but they had seen a couple of records set.

St. Louis	ab	r	h	bi	o	a	e
J. Hopp, cf	4	1	2	1	2	0	0
A. Bergamo, pr5-cf	3	2	1	0	0	0	0
D. Garms, 3b	4	2	1	1	1	1	0
S. Musial, rf	4	4	3	3	1	0	0
R. Sanders, 1b	5	2	3	2	5	0	0
W. Cooper, c	6	1	2	3	7	0	0
D. Litwhiler, lf	6	1	2	3	4	0	0
M. Marion, ss	5	2	2	0	4	3	0
E. Verban, 2b	1	0	1	2	0	0	0
G. Fallon, 2b-ss8	4	1	2	1	3	1	0
M. Cooper, p	6	2	2	1	0	0	0
	48	18	21	17	27	5	0

Cincinnati	ab	r	h	bi	o	a	e
W. Williams, 2b	3	0	2	0	2	3	0
M. Marshall, rf	4	0	0	0	5	0	0
G. Walker, cf	3	0	0	0	1	0	0
D. Clay, cf8	1	0	0	0	0	0	0
E. Tipton, lf	3	0	0	0	2	0	0
T. Criscola, lf8	1	0	0	0	0	0	0
F. McCormick, 1b	4	0	0	0	8	0	0
R. Mueller, c	0	0	0	0	2	0	0
J. Just, c3	3	0	1	0	2	0	0
S. Mesner, 3b	3	0	0	0	1	0	0
E. Miller, ss	3	0	1	0	4	3	1
B. Lohrman, p	0	0	0	0	0	0	0
E. Heusser, p2	0	0	0	0	0	0	0
B. Fausett, p2	3	0	1	0	0	2	1
J. Nuxhall, p9	0	0	0	0	0	0	0
J. Eisenhardt, p9	0	0	0	0	0	0	0
	31	0	5	0	27	8	2

St. Louis   160 111 125 - 18
Cincinnati   000 000 000 - 0

	ip	h	r-er	bb	so
M. Cooper (W 5-3)	9	5	0-0	2	2
Lohrman (L 0-1)	1.1	5	5-5	2	0
Heusser	*0	4	2-2	0	0
Fausett	6.2	10	6-6	6	2
Nuxhall	.2	2	5-5	5	0
Eisenhardt	.1	0	0-0	1	0

*faced four batters in second

LOB: StL 18, Cinc 6. BE: StL 1.
DP: Marion-Sanders.
2B: Fallon, Hopp. SH: Garms.
SB: W. Cooper, Litwhiler.
Time - 2:23
Attendance - 3,510 paid
    5,469 total
Umpires: L. Goetz, L. Jorda, & B. Reardon
WP: Fausett, Nuxhall

The Cardinals had their biggest run-away with the pennant in 1944. By July 8th their lead was 10 games. On August 30th, the margin peaked at 20 games. They slumped in September, but still won the flag by a 14½-game margin.

Their record was 105-49, the same as in 1943.

As for the Cincinnati pitchers, Lohrman quit baseball immediately, and Nuxhall didn't get back into a major league game until 1952. Eisenhardt never did get into a second big league game. Fausett played a few more games at third base, but Cincinnati never put him in to pitch again. Heusser, who failed the worst on June 10th, wound up leading the N. L. in E.R.A. in 1944 with a 2.38 mark.

1944 World Series—Game #6

Monday, October 9th, at Sportsman's Park

Cardinals Beat Browns, 3-1, Win World Series

Third Straight Victory Gives Cards Series in Six Games

Score All Three Runs in Fourth Inning, Lanier and Wilks Hold Lead

The powerful St. Louis Cardinals defeated their crosstown rivals, the St. Louis Browns, in the World Series by winning today's game, 3-1. The Cards margin in the series was four games to two.

The defeat spoiled the last act for the Cinderella Browns, who had just won their very first American League pennant with a dramatic finish. The Brownies then got off to a two-to-one lead in the World Series, but the Cardinals regained their composure and won the last three games. The National Leaguers were rated as a vastly superior team, and the fact that the Browns won even two games against them was seen as something of an upset.

Pitching dominated the series. A total of 92 batters struck out in the six games, and the combined earned run average for both squads was 1.73. The Browns' two victories came on strong pitching efforts by Denny Galehouse and Jack Kramer. But the Cardinals' pitching was a match for the Browns', and the National Leaguers were superior with the bat and glove, spelling the difference in the series. the Red Birds hit a mild .240, but the Browns were held down to .183. And the winners made only one fielding error, whereas the losers made ten.

The stars of the classic were Marty Marion and George McQuinn. The Cardinal shortstop was brilliant in the field, as usual, handling 29 chances without an error. In fact, the Cardinals' infield was errorless in all 124 chances offered to it. McQuinn, the Browns' first baseman, was the leading hitter in the series with a .438 average. He also led with 5 RBI's. For the Cardinals, Emil Verban led in average with .412, and Stan Musial led as a slugger, getting two doubles and a home run.

The weather throughout the series was pleasant but a mite chilly. Today was no exception. The thermometer hovered around the 60° mark, but the sky was overcast, and a brisk breeze kept the fans bundled up. The sentiments of the spectators were mixed, naturally, but the underdog Browns seemed to have a slightly stronger hold on the emotions of the customers.

Nelson Potter was manager Luke Sewell's choice to pitch for the Browns. Cardinal skipper Billy Southworth tabbed Max Lanier. Both pitchers had done well but gotten no decision in the second game of the series. Both pitched good ball at the outset today, but neither lasted through the sixth inning. Lanier mixed a nice assortment of curves and slow stuff with his best pitch, the fastball. Potter relied heavily on his money pitch, the screwball.

Being the "home" team, the Cardinals wore white uniforms and batted last.

The Browns could not hit a fair ball off Lanier in the first inning.

The first batter in the second, Vern Stephens, struck out. But Chet Laabs came through with a big hit, booming a triple off the 422-foot mark in right center. McQuinn bounced the next pitch through a drawn-in Cardinal infield, and the Browns had the lead. Mark Christman and Red Hayworth both flied out to short center.

The Browns threatened again in the third. With two out, Mike Kreevich doubled when Johnny Hopp missed a shoestring catch. Gene Moore walked, but Stephens bounced toward the hole, and Marion made a clutch stop and quick throw to second for a force out.

Potter faced only six batters in the first two innings.

In the third, however, he got into trouble. Verban and Lanier got singles with one out. But Potter fanned Danny Litwhiler and Hopp on screwballs to escape the jam.

In the fourth, Potter suddenly lost his control. After going to three balls and no strikes on Musial, he retired the Cards' big hitter on a fly to right center. But Walker Cooper walked on four pitches. Ray Sanders sent Cooper to third with a single to right. Nels now needed a double play. He got Whitey Kurowski to hit a grounder, but the Browns' infield botched its chance. Stephens, the shortstop, fielded the ball in the hole, but his throw to second was off line. Don Gutteridge, the second baseman, was unable to stay on the bag, and his relay to first was also late. So no outs were made, and a run scored. Marion fouled out. Verban then dribbled one just beyond the third baseman's reach, Sanders streaking home with the go-ahead run. Lanier followed with a line single to drive Kurowski home and send Potter to the showers.

Bob Muncrief took over the pitching chores. Litwhiler bounced to Stephens, who tossed to Gutteridge. The second baseman stomped on second base several times, making sure the runner was called out.

In the sixth, Lanier lost his control. With one out, he passed both Laabs and McQuinn. Southworth visited the mound but left the lefthander in. On the very next pitch, however, Lanier bounced one well in front of the plate, and the runners moved to second and third. Southworth decided to lift Lanier and bring in righthander Ted Wilks. The reliever was very effective. He got Christman to ground to Kurowski, who threw Laabs out at home. Then Hayworth flied to center, ending the Browns' last threat.

Wilks sent the American Leaguers out in order through the last three innings. He struck out four batters, all pinch-hitters, and needed only one difficult fielding feat in support. That was provided by Musial, who made a hard-charging catch to grab Kreevich's fly in the seventh.

The Cardinals had a runner in the sixth against Muncrief and put men on in the seventh and eighth against Kramer, but they did not score.

But they didn't need to, winning the game, 3-1.

The Browns were glum in their clubhouse, but the champion Cardinals were riotously happy. Southworth had praises for everyone, but he especially lauded the catching of W. Cooper and Hayworth, which he credited for making the pitching so great in the series.

St. Louis AL	ab	r	h	bi	o	a	e
D. Gutteridge, 2b	3	0	0	0	3	2	0
F. Baker, ph7-2b	1	0	0	0	1	0	0
M. Kreevich, cf	4	0	1	0	3	0	0
G. Moore, rf	3	0	0	0	0	0	0
V. Stephens, ss	4	0	0	0	3	3	1
C. Laabs, lf	2	1	1	0	1	1	0
G. McQuinn, 1b	2	0	1	1	6	1	0
M. Christman, 3b	3	0	0	0	1	1	0
M. Byrnes, ph9	1	0	0	0	-	-	-
R. Hayworth, c	2	0	0	0	5	0	1
M. Chartak, ph9	1	0	0	0	-	-	-
N. Potter, p	2	0	0	0	1	1	0
B. Muncrief, p4	0	0	0	0	0	1	0
A. Zarilla, ph7	1	0	0	0	-	-	-
J. Kramer, p7	0	0	0	0	0	1	0
	29	1	3	1	24	11	2

St. Louis NL	ab	r	h	bi	o	a	e
D. Litwhiler, lf	5	0	0	0	2	0	0
J. Hopp, cf	4	0	1	0	3	0	0
S. Musial, rf	4	0	0	0	2	0	0
W. Cooper, c	3	1	2	0	10	0	0
R. Sanders, 1b	3	1	1	0	7	1	0
W. Kurowski, 3b	3	1	1	1	0	1	0
M. Marion, ss	3	0	0	0	0	2	0
E. Verban, 2b	3	0	3	1	2	2	0
M. Lanier, p	2	0	2	1	1	1	0
T. Wilks, p6	1	0	0	0	0	1	0
	31	3	10	3	27	8	0

Browns (AL)   010 000 000 - 1
Cardinals (NL) 000 300 00x - 3

	ip	h	r-er	bb	so
Potter (L 0-1)	3.2	6	3-1	1	3
Muncrief	2.1	2	0-0	1	0
Kramer	2	2	0-0	2	2
Lanier (W 1-0)	5.1	3	1-1	5	5
Wilks	3.2	0	0-0	0	4

LOB: Browns 7, Cardinals 10.
BE: Cardinals 1.
2B: Kreevich. 3B: Laabs.
SH: McQuinn, Wilks, Marion.
SB: none. Picked Off: Kurowski.
Time - 2:06
Attendance - 31,630
WP: Lanier
Umpires: B. McGowan, T. Dunn, G. Pipgras, & Z. Sears

1945 — Tuesday, September 25th, at Wrigley Field, Chicago

Cubs Edge Cardinals, 6-5, Lead St. Louis By 2½ Games

Chicago Beats St. Louis for Only 5th Time in 21 Games

Four-Run Seventh-Inning Rally Gives Bruins Victory

The St. Louis Cardinals' drive to win their fourth consecutive National league pennant received a body blow today in the form of a 6-5 defeat at the hands of the league-leading Chicago Cubs. The result left the Red Birds 2½ games behind with just five to play. The Cubs' schedule showed six games remaining. With only one game left against the Cubs themselves, the Cards' only hope lay in the Cincinnati Reds and Pittsburgh Pirates beating Chicago at least twice.

Still, the Cardinals were convinced that they were a better team than the Cubs. Even after today's game, St. Louis held a 15-6 edge in head-to-head play against Chicago.

Today's Results
Chicago 6 - ST. LOUIS 5
Brooklyn 7 - New York 4
Pittsburgh at Cincinnati - postponed, rain
no other games scheduled

Standings	W-L	Pct.	GB
Chicago	93-55	.628	-
ST. LOUIS	91-58	.611	2½
Brooklyn	84-67	.556	10½
Pittsburgh	80-68	.541	13
New York	77-72	.517	16½
Boston	66-84	.440	28
Cincinnati	60-87	.408	32½
Philadelphia	46-106	.303	49

In today's game, the most important contest of the year, the Cards just made too many mistakes, and the Cubs got a few breaks and won by one run. Two of the three St. Louis errors hurt, and the Cards' base runners made crucial mistakes. An error and two walks helped the Cubs get four runs in the decisive seventh inning.

The weather was unpleasant and drizzly today, limiting the crowd to around 20,000. The playing field was soggy. As a result, play was less than perfect, especially in the early innings.

The Cubs started their new pitching ace, Hank Borowy. He had pitched eleven complete games in twelve starts since being acquired on waivers from the Yankees on July 27th. He was opposed by lefthander Harry Brecheen, who had beaten Borowy, 1-0, in their only previous meeting. Neither starter finished the game, but Borowy got the win, and Brecheen took the loss.

Each team scored twice in the first inning.

For St. Louis, Johnny Hopp singled past third baseman Stan Hack with one out. Buster Adams smashed one to third. Hack fielded it neatly but threw wide to second, and all runners were safe. Whitey Kurowski punched the next pitch into right field for a single, scoring Hopp. Ray Sanders, after fouling off a couple of pitches, singled over second. Adams scored, but Kurowkski gambled and was thrown out at third. Emil Verban lined a single to center. He and Sanders were left stranded when Marty Maion struck out.

Hack opened the bottom of the first by walking on four pitches. Don Johnson singled him to second. Peanuts Lowrey bunted the runners along. Phil Cavarretta then dropped a squeeze bunt toward the mound. Brecheen juggled it, then threw wildly past first base, two men scoring. Andy Pafko lined into a double play.

Both sides loaded the bases but failed to score in the second. The Cards got two-out hits from rookie Albert "Red" Schoendienst and Hopp, and Adams walked. But Kurowski hit into a force play. The Cubs got three straight singles, all with two out, by Roy Hughes, Borowy, and Hack. But Johnson fouled to catcher Del Rice.

St. Louis finally broke the tie in the fifth. Adams opened with a solid single to left. Kurowski bunted him to second. Sanders then lined a single to right center, and Adams slid home just ahead of the throw.

The score remained 3-2 in the Cardinals' favor until the bottom of the seventh. It was about that time that rain, which had been threatening all afternoon, started to come down.

Hughes opened the Cubs' big inning with a grounder to deep short. Marion made a great stop, but could not get quite enough on his throw to catch the man at first. Borowy bunted, but Hughes was forced at second. Brecheen then made his worst mistake, walking Hack. Johnson followed with a line single to left, which Schoendienst bobbled. By the time the ball was returned to the infield, Borowy was across the plate, Hack was on third, and Johnson was on second. It was decided to give Lowrey a base on balls, loading the bases for Cavarretta, the league's leading hitter. Brecheen got him to hit the ball softly, but his looper dropped safely into short center field, putting the Cubs ahead and keeping the bases loaded.

At this point, manager Billy Southworth put George Dockins in to replace Brecheen. Dockins jammed the first batter he faced, Pafko, breaking his bat. But Pafko had enough of a swing to lift the ball over third base and down the left field line for a two-run double. If the bat hadn't broken, the ball probably would have hooked foul. Dockins got Bill Nicholson on a short fly to right, and Ken Burkhart came in and got the last out of the inning. But Chicago had taken a 6-3 lead.

The Cardinals gamely rallied in the eighth, but they came up one run short. Marion got an infield hit with one out. Debs Garms came through with a pinch-hit triple into the gap in right center. A single by pinch-hitter Augie Bergamo scored Garms and routed Borowy. Jack Creel was put in to run for Bergamo, and Ray Prim, a 38-year-old lefthander, was the new pitcher. Schoendienst, the first man to bat against Prim, smacked a hard grounder that skipped past Cavarretta for an error. Southworth, in the coaching box, frantically waved to Creel to come to third, but much to Southworth's displeasure, the runner held up at second. At this time, the sun was breaking through, and the momentum was with the Cardinals. So the veteran Nicholson thought it would be a good time to break the pace. He came into the dugout from right field to get a pair of sunglasses. When play resumed, Prim retired Hopp and Adams in infield pop flies.

The Cardinals got only a two-out single by Verban in the ninth and went down to defeat, 6-5.

Oh well, after three straight pennants, sometimes the breaks have to go the other way.

St. Louis	ab	r	h	bi	o	a	e		Chicago	ab	r	h	bi	o	a	e
R. Schoendienst, lf	5	0	1	0	2	0	1		S. Hack, 3b	3	2	1	0	2	0	1
J. Hopp, rf	5	1	2	0	2	0	0		D. Johnson, 2b	4	2	2	1	3	4	0
B. Adams, cf	4	2	1	0	2	0	0		P. Lowrey, lf	2	1	0	0	5	0	0
W. Kurowski, 3b	4	0	2	1	1	1	1		P. Cavarretta, 1b	3	0	2	2	6	0	1
R. Sanders, 1b	5	0	2	2	8	1	0		A. Pafko, cf	3	0	1	2	0	1	0
E. Verban, 2b	5	0	3	0	1	2	0		B. Nicholson, rf	4	0	0	0	2	0	0
M. Marion, ss	5	1	1	0	3	3	0		M. Livingston, c	4	0	0	0	4	0	0
D. Rice, c	3	0	0	0	4	1	0		D. Williams, c9	0	0	0	0	1	0	0
D. Garms, ph8	1	1	1	1	-	-	-		R. Hughes, ss	4	0	2	0	4	5	0
G. Crumling, c8	0	0	0	0	1	0	0		H. Borowy, p	3	1	1	0	0	1	0
H. Brecheen, p	3	0	0	0	0	0	1		R. Prim, p8	1	0	0	0	0	0	0
G. Dockins, p7	0	0	0	0	0	0	0									
K. Burkhart, p7	0	0	0	0	0	0	0									
A. Bergamo, ph8	1	0	1	1	-	-	-									
J. Creel, pr8	0	0	0	0	-	-	-									
A. Lopatka, p8	0	0	0	0	0	0	0									
	41	5	14	5	24	8	3			31	6	9	5	27	11	2

St. Louis   200 010 020 - 5
Chicago   200 000 40x - 6

LOB: StL 11, Chi 7.
BE: StL 2, Chi 1.
DP: Marion-Sanders.
2B: Pafko.
3B: Garms.

	ip	h	r-er	bb	so
Brecheen (L 14-4)	6.1	8	6-5	4	3
Dockins	.1	1	0-0	0	0
Burkhart	.1	0	0-0	0	0
Lopatka	1	0	0-0	0	1
Borowy (W 10-2)	7.1	13	5-4	1	3
Prim	1.2	1	0-0	0	1

SH: Lowrey, Cavarretta, Kurowski.
Time - 2:38
Attendance - 20,438
WP: Borowy
Umpires: B. Pinelli, D. Boggess,
  L. Ballanfant, & W. Henline

The Cardinals stayed in the race by beating the Cubs the next day, 11-6. But Chicago won its last five games and took the pennant by a 3-game margin.

St. Louis finished with a 95-59 record.

1946 — Tuesday, October 1st, at Sportsman's Park
St. Louis Defeats Brooklyn, 4-2, in First Playoff Game
Cardinals Lead Best-of-Three-Game Pennant Series
Pollet's Pitching, Great Defense, and Garagiola's Hits Win for Cards

The best two-out-of-three playoff to decide the National League pennant opened today in St. Louis. The hometown Cardinals won the first game over the Brooklyn Dodgers, 4-2. The game was slow but exciting, featuring fast fielding by both sides.

The tension was in keeping with the exciting pennant race, which had ended in a tie for first place. Brooklyn and St. Louis alternated in the lead through the first month of the season. The Dodgers held the lead through June, most of July, and the first three weeks of August. Then the Cardinals caught and passed them, holding the lead from August 28th until they fell back into a tie on September 27th. Both teams won on Saturday, September 28th, but then they both lost on the final day of the schedule, Sunday the 29th. That left them with identical 96-58 records for the 154-game slate.

Today's Results
ST. LOUIS 4 — Broooklyn 2
(St. Louis leads best-of-three-game playoff, 1-0)

Standings	W-L	Pct.	GB
ST. LOUIS	97-58	.626	-
Brooklyn	96-59	.619	1
Chicago	82-71	.536	14
Boston	81-72	.529	15
Philadelphia	69-85	.448	27½
Cincinnati	67-87	.435	29½
Pittsburgh	63-91	.409	33½
New York	61-93	.396	35½

So a playoff was necessary. The Dodgers won the coin toss and decided to play the second and third games at home. So the team spent Monday riding from the East Coast out to St. Louis for the first game today (Tuesday). The squads left again tonight for Brooklyn.

Leo Durocher, the Dodger manager, picked 20-year-old fireballer Ralph Branca to pitch today. The former New York University star had been used sparingly this year, compiling a 3-0 record. But he had beaten St. Louis twice, so his selection was not unexpected.

Manager Eddie Dyer of the Cardinals deferred his choice until just before game time. He had both Howie Pollet and Murry Dickson warm up. Pollet, a 20-game winner, had been suffering from an injured muscle in his back. But he told Dyer that he was okay, and he got the assignment. Dickson, however, remained in the bullpen and stayed warmed up through the entire contest.

Pollet completed the game. He was not at his best, but he pitched with a lot of head and a lot of heart. He worked slowly but made only 94 pitches. He threw 45 called balls, but he made his strikes count, fanning only two men and letting his fielders do the work. The Cards turned three double plays, with Marty Marion making the pivot each time. And the outfield played great ball. Harry Walker made two fine, running catches, and Enos Slaughter made a great throw to cut a Brooklyn runner down at third. Pollet himself made the game's only fielding error.

The Cardinals scored the game's first run in the first inning. Two strikeouts surrounded Terry Moore's single. Slaughter sent the Red Bird captain to third with a single, and a walk to Whitey Kurowski loaded the bases. Rookie Joe Garagiola then sent a bouncer to deep short and just barely beat Pee Wee Reese's long throw to first for an RBI single. A force play ended the inning.

Brooklyn tied the game in the third. Howie Schultz hit the first pitch of the inning into the left field bleachers for a home run. With one out, Eddie Stanky singled. But Pollet knocked down Cookie Lavagetto's liner and started a 1-6-3 double play, with Marion making a very quick relay.

The Cardinals then came in and scored two runs to regain the lead. With one out, Stan Musial worked Branca for a walk, and Slaughter lined one off the screen in right field. A fine play by Dixie Walker held the batter to first, but Musial scooted to third.

With the infield back at double play depth, Kurowski hit a grounder to deep short, and after the force at second, he barely beat the relay to first, allowing the go-ahead run to count. Garagiola singled to right center, Kurowski stopping at second. Harry Walker then rolled a single up the middle to drive Kurowski home and send Garagiola to third. Branca was replaced by veteran Kirby Higbe. With Walker running on a 2-1 pitch, Marion hit a hot shot up the middle. But second baseman Stanky had come over to cover the bag, and he made a clever stop and threw Marion out at first, ending the rally.

There were no runs in the fourth, fifth, or sixth. A nice catch by H. Walker robbed brother Dixie of a hit in the fourth. Brooklyn loaded the bases in the fifth on two singles, a sacrifice, and a walk. But second baseman Red Schoendienst captured Stanky's crisp grounder and started a double play, Marion making a strong throw to first despite a hard slide by Stan Rojek. Another 4-6-3 double play nullified a walk in the Dodger sixth.

Brooklyn managed one run in the seventh, but once again the St. Louis defense cut them short. After Carl Furillo was retired on a fine catch by H. Walker, Reese and Bruce Edwards singled. Schultz then looped a hit to right. Reese scored, but Slaughter's pretty throw cut Edwards down at third. A tap back to the mound retired the side.

Musial opened the Cardinal seventh with a long triple to right center. He remained at third until two were out. Then Garagiola popped a single just beyond the reach of shortstop Reese, scoring the run.

Stanky walked to open the Dodger eighth. Lavagetto flied out on a 3-2 pitch. Joe Medwick singled to right. D. Walker hit into a force play, putting men on first and third. Furillo then hit a terrific, sinking line drive, but Marion was able to glove it at his shoetops for the third out.

Pollet looked strong for the first time in an hour when he retired the Dodgers in order in the ninth, nailing down the 4-2 victory.

In the clubhouse, the Cardinals seemed confident of winning the next game and, with it, the pennant.

Brooklyn	ab	r	h	bi	o	a	e
E. Stanky, 2b	3	0	1	0	3	2	0
C. Lavagetto, 3b	3	0	0	0	1	2	0
J. Medwick, lf	4	0	1	0	1	0	0
J. Tepsic, pr8	0	0	0	0	-	-	-
D. Whitman, lf8	0	0	0	0	1	0	0
D. Walker, rf	4	0	0	0	0	0	0
C. Furillo, cf	4	0	0	0	5	0	0
P. Reese, ss	4	1	2	0	2	2	0
B. Edwards, c	4	0	2	0	5	1	0
H. Schultz, 1b	3	1	2	2	6	0	0
R. Branca, p	1	0	0	0	0	0	0
K. Higbe, p3	0	0	0	0	0	0	0
S. Rojek, ph5	0	0	0	0	-	-	-
H. Gregg, p5	0	0	0	0	0	0	0
B. Ramazotti, ph7	1	0	0	0	-	-	-
V. Lombardi, p7	0	0	0	0	0	0	0
R. Melton, p7	0	0	0	0	0	0	0
	31	2	8	2	24	7	0

St. Louis	ab	r	h	bi	o	a	e
R. Schoendienst, 2b	5	0	2	0	1	7	0
T. Moore, cf	5	1	3	0	1	0	0
S. Musial, 1b	4	2	1	0	10	0	0
E. Slaughter, rf	4	0	2	0	4	1	0
W. Kurowski, 3b	2	1	0	1	1	2	0
J. Garagiola, c	4	0	3	2	2	0	0
H. Walker, lf	3	0	1	1	3	0	0
M. Marion, ss	4	0	0	0	5	4	0
H. Pollet, p	4	0	0	0	0	2	1
	35	4	12	4	27	16	1

Brooklyn   001 000 100 - 2
St. Louis   102 000 10x - 4

	ip	h	r-er	bb	so
Branca (L 3-1)	2.2	6	3-3	2	3
Higbe	1.1	1	0-0	0	0
Gregg	2	1	0-0	1	1
Lombardi	.1	1	1-1	0	0
Melton	1.2	3	0-0	1	0
Pollet (W 21-10)	9	8	2-2	3	2

WP: Melton

LOB: Bkn 6, StL 11.
BE: Bkn 1.
DP: Pollet- Marion-Musial, Schoendienst-Marion-Musial 2.
3B: Musial.
HR: Schultz.
SH: Schultz.
SB: none. CS: Schoendienst.
Time - 2:48
Attendance - 26,012 paid
   26,332 total
Umpires: B. Reardon, B. Pinelli,
   L. Goetz, & D. Boggess

The Cardinals won Game #2 on Thursday in Brooklyn, 8-4, to win the playoff and pennant. St. Louis pounded out eight singles, two doubles, and three triples to build up an 8-1 lead going into the bottom of the ninth. Then starter Murry Dickson faltered. But with three runs in and the bases loaded, Harry Brecheen struck out the final two batters to preserve the victory.

1946 World Series—Game #7

Tuesday, October 15th, at Sportsman's Park

Daring and Defense Win World Series for Cardinals Over Red Sox

Brecheen, in Relief of Dickson, Gets Third Series Victory

Win Final Game, 4-3, on Slaughter's Daring Running in Eighth

It was supposed to be no contest. The powerful Boston Red Sox, winners of the American League pennant by a ridiculously large margin, were pitted against the St. Louis Cardinals, who had had to go into a post-schedule playoff to win the National League flag. The Beantowners entered the series as prohibitive favorites.

Even after the underdogs had extended the series to seven games, the Bosox were still quoted as 13-20 favorites. After all, they had Dave "Boo" Ferriss, a 25-game winner, well rested and ready to pitch. And Ferriss had shut St. Louis out in the third game of the classic.

But the Cardinals beat the odds by beating the Red Sox today, 4-3, to win the World Series. In a way, it was a mismatch. But not in the way that the sportswriters and bookmakers had expected. The staid Bostonians, for all their hitting and pitching strength, were unable to cope with the Red Birds' tactics and defense. Harry Brecheen's screwball baffled the Red Sox hitters, and he won three games, including today's game in relief. Three fast outfielders and a radical defensive alignment against slugger Ted Williams kept the Boston offense at bay. And the Cardinal base runners ran rings around the Sox' defense, cashing in on chances that it would never had occurred to the Beantowners to try. Today's winning run was scored when Enos Slaughter caught the Boston infield by surprise and dashed home while Johnny Pesky was wondering what to do with the ball.

Murry Dickson started the game today for St. Louis. He pitched great ball from the first inning, when he allowed a run, until the eighth, when he was removed with no outs and two on.

The first two Boston batters, Wally Moses and Johnny Pesky, singled in the first. Moses scored on Dom DiMaggio's sacrifice fly to right. Williams, who didn't have an extra base hit in the entire series, followed with a long, high fly to right center. Terry Moore, playing way over toward right in the shift, ran back to make a nice catch for the second out. Rudy York then popped out.

St. Louis got two hits in their first but did not score. Red Schoendienst, leading off, singled to left but was thrown out trying for second after Williams had momentarily bobbled the ball. Stan Musial doubled down the left field line one out later, but he was left on second.

The Cards managed to tie the score in the second. Whitey Kurowski doubled to left center to start the inning, and he came home on outs by Joe Garagiola and Harry Walker.

Dickson pitched around an error in the second and set the Red Sox down in order in the third, fourth, and fifth innings. Another great catch, this one by left fielder Walker in nearly straightaway center, robbed Williams in the fourth. In the fifth, Moore made the best catch of the series and one of the best of his sterling career. Despite a sore knee, Terry caught up to a long drive by Pinky Higgins, making the grab right at the wall while running at top speed.

The Cardinals took the lead in the bottom of the fifth. Walker lined a hit just past shortstop Pesky's glove. Marion bunted him to second. Dickson, a good-hitting pitcher, then looped a double over the third baseman to score Walker. Schoendienst sent a hot grounder up the middle for a single and another run. When Moore followed with another hit, Boston manager Joe Cronin took Ferriss out and brought Joe Dobson in to pitch. The Cardinals left the bases loaded, but they had taken a 3-1 advantage.

Dickson walked a man in the sixth, but he came into the eighth with a three-hitter and a two-run lead. Rip Russell, pinch-hitting for the catcher, led off with a line single back up the middle. George "Catfish" Metkovich, also a pinch-batter, doubled to left, sending Russell to third and Dickson to the showers.

Manager Eddie Dyer called in Brecheen, who had allowed just one run in 18 innings against the Red Sox. Harry "The Cat" fanned Moses and got Pesky on a liner to right. But he fell behind DiMaggio, 3-and-1, and the Sox center fielder jumped on the next pitch, a screwball. He drove it to the right field fence for a two-run double. DiMaggio might have made third on the hit, but he pulled a leg muscle and could only limp to second. Leon Culberson ran for him and was left on base when Williams popped out.

Having used up his front-line pitchers in the last two games, Cronin elected to use Bob Klinger in the eighth. Slaughter greeted him with a single to center. The next two men flied out. With Walker at the plate, Slaughter broke for second. Walker lined the pitch over shortstop and toward the gap. Knowing that Culberson did not have as good an arm as DiMaggio, Slaughter streaked for third, and Walker for second. Culberson made a good play to cut the ball off before it went to the wall and returned it to the cutoff man, shortstop Pesky. Slaughter kept coming toward home, but Pesky didn't know it for a moment. By the time he turned around and threw home, it was too late. Enos slid across the plate ahead of the belated throw, which was weak and up the line toward third.

The Cardinals had the lead, 4-3, but the excitement wasn't over yet. The first two Boston hitters in the ninth, York and Bobby Doerr, singled. Playing their usual, conservative game on the bases, this only put Red Sox on first and second. Huggins tried to sacrifice, but Kurowski alertly threw to second for a force out on Doerr. Still, the tying run, in the person of pinch-runner Paul Campbell, was on third with one out. Roy Partee, the new catcher, was next up. Brecheen got ahead of him on the count, then got him on a weak pop to first. Two out. Tom McBride, a pincher, came up. He rapped a twisting grounder toward second. Schoendienst got in front of it, but the ball bounced off his wrist and rolled up his arm. He clamped his armpit onto the ball, then managed to shovel it to Marion at second base just in time for a game-ending force out.

The Cardinals had done it! They were Champions of the World! After mobbing Brecheen on the mound, the boisterous players went into the clubhouse to celebrate. And they celebrated just like they played ball, with enthusiasm and desire.

Boston (AL)	ab	r	h	bi	o	a	e
W. Moses, rf	4	1	1	0	1	0	0
J. Pesky, ss	4	0	1	0	2	1	0
D. DiMaggio, cf	3	0	1	3	0	0	0
L. Culberson, pr8-cf	0	0	0	0	0	0	0
T. Williams, lf	4	0	0	0	3	1	0
R. York, 1b	4	0	1	0	10	1	0
P. Campbell, pr9	0	0	0	0	-	-	-
B. Doerr, 2b	4	0	2	0	3	7	0
P. Higgins, 3b	4	0	0	0	0	1	0
H. Wagner, c	2	0	0	0	4	0	0
R. Russell, ph8	1	1	1	0	-	-	-
R. Partee, c8	1	0	0	0	0	0	0
B. Ferriss, p	2	0	0	0	0	0	0
J. Dobson, p5	0	0	0	0	0	1	0
G. Metkovich, ph8	1	1	1	0	-	-	-
B. Klinger, p8	0	0	0	0	1	0	0
E. Johnson, p8	0	0	0	0	0	0	0
T. McBride, ph9	1	0	0	0	-	-	-
	35	3	8	3	24	12	0

St. Louis (NL)	ab	r	h	bi	o	a	e
R. Schoendienst, 2b	4	0	2	1	2	3	0
T. Moore, cf	4	0	1	0	3	0	0
S. Musial, 1b	3	0	1	0	6	0	0
E. Slaughter, rf	3	1	1	0	4	0	0
W. Kurowski, 3b	4	1	1	0	3	1	1
J. Garagiola, c	3	0	0	0	4	0	0
D. Rice, c8	1	0	0	0	0	0	0
H. Walker, lf	3	1	2	2	3	0	0
M. Marion, ss	2	0	0	0	2	1	0
M. Dickson, p	3	1	1	1	0	1	0
H. Brecheen, p8	1	0	0	0	0	0	0
	31	4	9	4	27	6	1

Boston	100 000 020	-	3
St. Louis	010 020 01x	-	4

	ip	h	r-er	bb	so
Ferriss	4.1	7	3-3	1	2
Dobson	2.2	0	0-0	2	2
Klinger (L 0-1)	.2	2	1-1	1	0
Johnson	.1	0	0-0	0	0
Dickson	*7	5	3-3	1	3
Brecheen (W 3-0)	2	3	0-0	0	1

LOB: Bos 6, StL 8. BE: none.
2B: Musial, Kurowski, Dickson, Metkovich, DiMaggio, Walker.
SH: Marion.
Time - 2:17
Attendance - 36,413
*faced two batters in eighth
Umpires: A. Barlick, C. Berry, L. Ballanfant, & C. Hubbard

Chapter IX
A Slow Decline
1947-1955

1947—July 30th at Sportsman's Park
   Red Birds Rally From 10 Runs Behind, Then Lose to Dodgers, 11-10

1948—June 6th at Sportsman's Park
   Schoendienst's Doubles & Cardinal Homers Featured in Sweep of Phils

1949—September 29th at Pittsburgh
   Dickson and Pirates Knock Cardinals Out of Lead

1950—September 3rd at Pittsburgh
   Unorthodox Strategy Backfires, Cards Lose to Bucs, 12-11

1951—September 13th at Sportsman's Park
   Cards Beat Giants by Day, Lose to Braves at Night

1952—June 15th at New York
   Birds Overcome 11-0 Deficit to Win First Game, 14-12

1953—September 25th at Chicago
   Haddix Wins 20th Game, Schoendienst Nears Batting Lead

1954—May 2nd at Busch Stadium
   Musial Hits Five Home Runs in Doubleheader, Cardinals Split

1955—June 1st at Pittsburgh
   Rookie Luis Arroyo Wins Sixth Straight For St. Louis

After winning their third World Series and fourth pennant in five years in 1946, the Cardinals won only two of their first eleven games in 1947. Stan Musial was suffering from an inflamed appendix, and he was put on a liquid diet. He slowly regained his batting eye, and the team slowly rose in the standings. They left the cellar for good on June 12th and got within 3½ games of the top by mid-July. But the first-place Brooklyn Dodgers swept a three-game series in St. Louis at the end of the month, and the Cardinals, who rallied from a 10-0 deficit in one of the games only to lose, 11-10, in extra innings, were pushed 10 games behind. St. Louis wound up the year in second place, 5 games behind.

Sam Breadon was beginning to lose his health, and he sold the club over the winter to Bob Hannegan and Fred Saigh.

The Cardinals finished second again in 1948, despite a great year by Musial. Stan reached his career high in runs, hits, home runs, and batting average and won his third MVP award. During his worst slump of the year, his road roommate, Red Schoendienst, took up the slugging, making eight doubles and a home run in a three-game stretch in early June. But the team's pitching was not good enough to put them over the top.

In 1949, Hannegan sold out to Saigh because of ill health.

On the field, the veteran pitchers did much better, and the Cardinals found themselves in another hot pennant race with the Dodgers. As it came down to the wire, St. Louis held a 1½-game lead with just five games to play. But they let the pennant slip away. Playing the lowly Pirates and Cubs, the Cardinals lost four games in a row and finished 1 game behind the Dodgers.

In 1950, the pitching again reverted to mediocrity, and the Cardinals were unable to stay in the race. Unable to win close games in the latter part of the season, St. Louis slipped from first place on July 24th to the second division by September 2nd. On September 3rd, a game in Pittsburgh was lost after St. Louis used the questionable strategem of walking the potential winning run intentionally with no one else on base. St. Louis finished fifth.

In 1951, Marty Marion replaced Eddie Dyer as manager. Although the Cards were never pennant contenders, they did better than expected by finishing third, thanks to an early September hot streak. The surge ended with a victory in a day game over the Giants on the 13th, which was followed by a night game loss to another team, the Braves.

Eddie Stanky became manager in 1952, and the team finished third again. With Al Brazle and Eddie Yuhas, St. Louis had a fine bullpen. In one of the most amazing victories in its history, the team rallied from 11 runs behind to win, 14-12, in a June 15th doubleheader.

In 1953, Musial failed to win the batting title for the first time since 1949. Brooklyn's Carl Furillo took the honors, although the Cardinals' Red Schoendienst gave him a run for the money at the end of the season. Rookie pitcher Harvey Haddix won 20 games, and the Red Birds finished tied for third.

In February, 1953, Saigh sold the club to Anheuser-Busch, Inc. The brewery, headed by the energetic August A. Busch, Jr., bought Sportsman's Park from the Browns (renaming it Busch Stadium). This insured that the Cardinals would remain in St. Louis. The Browns moved to Baltimore after the season.

In 1954, the new ownership rebuilt the ballpark and started a youth movement on the ballclub. Veteran Enos Slaughter, who had been with the Cardinals since 1938, was traded. The veteran pitchers continued to decline in 1954, but a new man, Brooks Lawrence, did well. On one day in May, Stan Musial hit five home runs in a doubleheader. But the team was not up to snuff, despite a potent offense, and it finished below .500 for the first time since 1938.

In 1955, the emphasis was even more on rookies. Bill Virdon and Ken Boyer were the best of the lot, although pitcher Luis Arroyo got off to a hot start, winning his first six decisions. But the youth could not sustain the team, and St. Louis fell to seventh place in the final standings.

1947 — Wednesday Night, July 30th, at Sportsman's Park
Red Birds Rally From 10 Runs Behind, Then Lose to Dodgers in Tenth
Reese's Single Scores Winner for Brooklyn
Cards Score Six Runs With Two Out in the Ninth to Tie

In a wild finish, the St. Louis Cardinals rallied to tie the Brooklyn Dodgers 10-10, only to lose the game in extra innings. St. Louis spotted the visitors a 10-run lead tonight. Then the Red Birds came back with four runs in the sixth inning and six more in the ninth to knot the score. St. Louis scored all its runs with two out. Brooklyn scored in the top of the tenth. The game ended when Stan Musial was thrown out trying to steal second, and the Dodgers won, 11-10.

The defeat dropped the Cardinals into third place. The triumph was the 12th in a row for Brooklyn.

A large crowd was on hand for the night game. Many of the spectators left before the exciting finish. With all the scoring and changing of pitchers, the game did not end until twnty minutes past midnight. Even at that late hour, the temperature was over 80°.

Today's Results
Brooklyn 11 - ST. LOUIS 10 (10 inn.)
New York 5 - Cincinnati 4 (10 inn.)
Pittsburgh 5 - Boston 3 (1st game)
Boston 8 - Pittsburgh 5 (2nd)
Philadelphia 9 - Chicago 2

Standings	W-L	Pct.	GB
Brooklyn	62-36	.633	-
New York	49-41	.544	9
ST. LOUIS	51-43	.543	9
Boston	50-45	.526	10½
Cincinnati	46-52	.469	16
Chicago	44-51	.463	16½
Pittsburgh	40-56	.417	21
Philadelphia	39-57	.406	22

Ten pitchers saw action in the game. The Cards also used five pinch-hitters and a pinch-runner. One of the pinch-hitters, Joe Garagiola, batted twice and made two outs in one inning.

In the top of the first, the Dodgers scored a run while the Cardinals were making a fancy double play. With one out, rookie Jackie Robinson singled. Pete Reiser followed suit, and Carl Furillo walked, loading the bases. Dixie Walker hit a sinking liner to right center, which Terry Moore grabbed with a spectacular, sliding, seat-of-the-pants catch. His throw home was too late to get Robinson, but catcher Del Rice relayed to shortstop Marty Marion in time to nab Furillo sliding into second base.

Brooklyn got three runs in the third. Furillo hit a two-run double, then scored. That was all for Cardinal starting pitcher Harry Brecheen. He was removed for a pinch-hitter in the bottom of the inning.

George Munger was on the mound at the start of the fourth. A two-out single by Furillo drove in a run and put Reiser on second. Reiser broke for third while Munger was still holding the ball. Any kind of throw to shortstop Marion would have picked the runner off, but Munger threw very wildly, and the ball went into center field, allowing Reiser to score. Unsettled, Munger walked the batter, then fumbled Bruce Edwards's scratch hit. A walk to Pee Wee Reese forced a run home and heralded Munger's exit from the scene. Alpha Brazle came in in relief. His first pitch to Spider Jorgensen was hit deep to left center for a three-run triple, making the score 10-0.

Despite the big cushion, the Dodgers were very contrary with the umpires. The arguing continued. In the sixth inning, Walker and coach Clyde Sukeforth were ejected from the game for arguing for a catcher's interference call. They didn't get it.

The Dodgers' feistiness seemed to rub off on the Cardinals about this time. With two out in the bottom of the sixth, the home team erupted for four runs. Stan Musial, Enos Slaughter, and Ron Northey singled in succession, scoring one run. Then Whitey Kurowski hit a long fly to left. The ball hit the top of the fence, bounced off a fan's hands, and came back onto the field. It was ruled a home run, despite a vigorous protest by outfielder Reiser.

A single and a walk knocked Dodger starter Ralph Branca out of the box in the seventh, but St. Louis did not score.

Hank Behrman pitched into the ninth for Brooklyn. With the Cards needing to score at least six runs, Rice led off with a single and gave way to a pinch-runner, Jeff Cross. Garagiola was sent to the plate, and he flied out. After Red Schoendienst fanned, the game looked as good as over. But the Birds scratched back to tie. Chuck Diering and Musial both legged out infield hits. Slaughter lined a clean single to right, scoring two men. Northey scratched a hit off Behrman's glove, good for another run.

At this point, Hugh Casey, the famed relief pitcher, came in. Big Hugh didn't have it tonight. Kurowski was given a base on balls, and Marion and Del Wilber (batting for the pinch-runner) followed with solid singles, tying the game and putting the winning run on third.

Clyde King came in to pitch. He retired Garagiola, batting for the second time, on a grounder to deep short, sending the game into extra innings.

Jim Hearn was the St. Louis pitcher in the tenth. With one out, Gene Hermanski tied into one of his serves for a double to left center. With two out, Reese delivered a single to left, and Hermanski scored.

King got the first two Cardinals out of the way in the bottom of the tenth. The next batter was Musial, who already had four hits on the night, raising his average to .282. King gave him a walk and then fell behind on the count to Slaughter, 3-and-1. On an apparent hit-and-run play on the next pitch, Musial broke for second. Slaughter missed the pitch, however, and Stan was thrown out stealing, ending the game.

So despite their two-out rallies and their big comeback, the Cardinals were beaten, 11-10.

Brooklyn	ab	r	h	bi	o	a	e
E. Stanky, 2b	5	1	3	0	2	3	0
J. Robinson, 1b	4	2	2	0	11	1	0
P. Reiser, lf-rf-lf	4	2	1	0	5	0	0
C. Furillo, cf	5	2	2	3	1	0	0
D. Walker, rf	2	1	0	1	2	0	0
Hermanski, ph6-lf-rf	3	1	2	0	0	0	0
B. Edwards, c	6	1	2	1	6	1	0
P. Reese, ss	4	1	1	2	2	3	0
S. Jorgensen, 3b	2	0	1	3	0	3	0
R. Branca, p	4	0	0	0	1	0	0
H. Behrman, p7	0	0	0	0	0	0	0
H. Casey, p9	0	0	0	0	0	0	0
C. King, p9	1	0	0	0	0	0	0
	40	11	14	10	30	10	0

St. Louis	ab	r	h	bi	o	a	e
R. Schoendienst, 2b	6	0	1	0	5	1	0
T. Moore, cf	2	0	0	0	1	1	0
C. Diering, cf5	3	1	1	0	0	0	0
S. Musial, 1b	5	2	4	0	10	0	0
E. Slaughter, lf	5	2	3	2	1	0	0
R. Northey, rf	4	2	2	2	3	0	0
W. Kurowski, 3b	4	2	2	3	0	0	0
M. Marion, ss	5	0	1	2	2	4	0
D. Rice, c	3	0	1	0	6	1	0
J. Cross, pr9	0	1	0	0	-	-	-
D. Wilber, ph9-c	1	0	1	1	2	0	0
H. Brecheen, p	0	0	0	0	0	1	0
D. Sisler, ph3	1	0	0	0	-	-	-
G. Munger, p4	0	0	0	0	0	1	1
A. Brazle, p4	0	0	0	0	0	0	0
J. Medwick, ph5	1	0	0	0	-	-	-
K. Burkhart, p6	0	0	0	0	0	1	0
E. Dusak, ph7	1	0	0	0	-	-	-
T. Wilks, p8	0	0	0	0	0	1	0
J. Garagiola, ph9	2	0	0	0	-	-	-
J. Hearn, p10	0	0	0	0	0	0	0
	43	10	16	10	30	11	1

Brooklyn   103 600 000 1 - 11
St. Louis   000 004 006 0 - 10

	ip	h	r-er	bb	so
Branca	6.2	8	4-4	3	3
Behrman	2	6	5-5	0	0
Casey	*0	2	1-1	1	0
King (W 2-2)	1.1	0	0-0	1	0
Brecheen	3	5	4-4	4	0
Munger	.2	3	6-1	3	0
Brazle	1.1	2	0-0	1	2
Burkhart	2	2	0-0	1	1
Wilks	2	0	0-0	1	1
Hearn (L 7-4)	1	2	1-1	1	2

LOB: Bkn 13, StL 8. BE: none.
DP: Moore-Rice-Marion, Jorgensen-Stanky-Robinson, Stanky-Reese-Robinson Marion-Schoendienst-Musial.
2B: Musial, Furillo, Stanky, Kurowski, Hermanski 2, Schoendienst.
3B: Jorgensen. HR: Kurowski.
SH: Robinson, Behrman.
SB: none. CS: Musial.
*faced three batters in ninth
HPB: by Wilks (Stanky)
Time - 3:34
Attendance - 31,709
Umpires: G. Barr, L. Jorda, & D. Boggess

After they lost to the Dodgers the next day, the Cardinals got hot and pulled within 3 games of the Dodgers by August 11th.

But they never got any closer, and they finished in second place, 5 games behind Brooklyn. St. Louis's final record was 89-65.

1948—Sunday, June 6th, at Sportsman's Park
Schoendienst's Doubles & Cardinal Homers Featured in Sweep of Phils
Four Home Runs in Sixth Inning of Opener
Red Hits Five Two-Baggers, Giving Him Eight in Three Games

The St. Louis Cardinals swept back into first place today with a doubleheader victory over the Philadelphia Phillies. The scores of the games were 11-1 and 2-0. Red Schoendienst, taking up the slack for his slumping road roommate, Stan Musial, led the St. Louis attack. When the Cardinals hit a club record four home runs in the sixth inning of the first game, Schoendienst got one of them. He also got three doubles in the opener and two more two-baggers in the nightcap. Added to the three doubles he hit on Saturday, Schoendienst set a new record by accumulating eight two-base hits in three games.

In the nightcap, Al Brazle hurled a shutout, and Nippy Jones drove in both runs with a bases-loaded single in the sixth inning.

Today's Results
ST. LOUIS 11 — Philadelphia 1 (1st game)
ST. LOUIS 2 - Philadelphia 0 (2nd)
New York 16 - Pittsburgh 4 (1st game)
Pittsburgh 4 - New York 3 (2nd)
Boston 1 - Chicago 0
Brooklyn 5 - Cincinnati 0 (5 inn.) (1st)
 (2nd game postponed - rain)

Standings	W-L	Pct.	GB
ST. LOUIS	24-17	.585	-
New York	23-17	.575	½
Pittsburgh	23-19	.548	1½
Boston	20-19	.513	3
Philadelphia	23-22	.511	3
Brooklyn	19-22	.463	5
Cincinnati	20-24	.455	5½
Chicago	15-27	.357	9½

Musial broke a string of 14 hitless at bats with a single in the eighth inning of the second game. The slump had dropped his batting average from .392 to .362. On the other hand, Schoendienst raised his average from .244 on Saturday morning to .289 by Sunday night. As Whitey Kurowski put it after the games today, "The power of the Musial-Schoendienst room has shifted."

The Cardinals' pitcher in the first game was Jim Hearn. He turned in a fine performance, stopping the Phillies on four hits. He also walked four men. And he stopped rookie Richie Ashburn's 23-game hitting streak.

The only Phillie run of the day came in the fourth inning of the opening game. After Hearn had hurled three hitless innings, Ralph "Putsy" Caballero opened the fourth with a single. Johnny Blatnik followed with another hit. After Dick Sisler flied out, Del Ennis walked to load the bases. Eddie Miller then lined out to deep left, driving Caballero in.

But by that time, the Cards had built up a comfortable lead.

Erv Dusak led off the bottom of the first by walking. Schoendienst then doubled off the fence in right field for a run.

In the second, the Red Birds used four extra-base hits to count four tallies. Jones and Schoendienst got two-base hits, and Marty Marion and Del Rice hit three-baggers. Phillie starter Ken Heintzelman was knocked out of the game. He was replaced by Charlie Bicknell, a 19-year-old rookie recently called up from Class B ball.

Bicknell pitched well until the sixth inning. In the fourth, he even got Schoendienst on a grounder to first. That ended a string of six straight hits by the redhead, which included five doubles and a single.

The home team unfurled its heavy artillery in the sixth frame. Rice opened with a single. With one out, Dusak unloaded one into the left field bleachers for a two-run homer. Schoendienst was next, hitting one off a light tower atop the right field pavilion. It was Red's second home run of the year and sixth of his career, but it was the first one he had ever hit onto the pavilion roof. Musial was given a base on balls. Kurowski forced him at second. Enos Slaughter then deposited a drive onto the roof in right for two more runs. Jones then came up with a blast into the seats in left for the Birds' fourth home run of the inning. That left them one short of the all-time record, which was set by the Giants in 1939. Jones and Slaughter had also both homered in the third inning on Saturday.

Bicknell decked the next hitter, Marion, on the next pitch. The umpires came out to warn the youngster, then Marion made his own reply by lining a hit just past the rookie's ear. Manager Ben Chapman then removed Bicknell and brought Sam Nahem in.

Nahem shut the Cardinals out in the seventh and eighth, although Schoendienst got another double off of him.

In the meantime, Hearn had no trouble with the Phillies, and the Cards won easily, 11-1.

The second game was a pitchers' duel between Alpha Brazle and Nick Strincevich.

Brazle was in trouble often in the early going, but he got through each crisis and finished strongly to post his first shutout since August 12, 1946. The Phillies got men to second base in three of the first four innings, but Brazle turned them back. The Phils got their only man to third in the fifth. Al Lakeman doubled and moved over on Granny Hamner's grounder. But Brazle got both Strincevich and Ashburn to bounce back to the mound for outs.

The Cards got back-to-back doubles in the first inning but did not score. Dusak opened with a drive to deep left center, but he was thrown out trying to make third on the hit. Schoendienst then doubled off the right field screen but was left on base.

The Cardinals scored the game's only runs in the sixth. Another Schoendienst double (his fifth of the day) opened the rally. Red's drive went off the right field fence. Musial walked behind him. Slaughter popped out, but Kurowski beat out a hit to deep short, filling the bases. Jones then came through with a single to center, driving the star roommates, Schoendienst and Musial, across the plate.

Brazle protected the lead and his shutout over the last three innings, finishing with a five-hitter and a 2-0 victory.

FIRST GAME

Philadelphia	ab	r	h	bi	o	a	e
R. Ashburn, cf	2	0	0	0	6	0	0
R. Caballero, 3b	3	1	1	0	0	3	0
J. Blatnik, lf	4	0	2	0	1	0	0
D. Sisler, 1b	4	0	0	0	9	0	0
D. Ennis, rf	3	0	0	0	0	0	0
E. Miller, ss	3	0	0	1	1	2	0
B. Rowell, 2b8	1	0	0	0	1	0	0
A. Seminick, c	3	0	0	0	3	0	0
G. Hammer, 2b-ss8	3	0	1	0	3	2	0
K. Heintzelman, p	0	0	0	0	0	0	0
C. Bicknell, p2	2	0	0	0	0	0	0
S. Nahem, p6	1	0	0	0	0	0	0
	29	1	4	1	24	7	0

St. Louis	ab	r	h	bi	o	a	e
E. Dusak, cf	3	3	2	2	6	0	0
R. Schoendienst, 2b	5	1	4	3	1	3	0
S. Musial, lf	2	0	0	0	4	0	0
W. Kurowski, 3b	5	1	0	1	0	1	0
E. Slaughter, rf	4	1	1	2	3	0	0
N. Jones, 1b	5	2	2	1	10	0	0
M. Marion, ss	4	1	2	1	0	4	0
R. LaPointe, ss7	1	0	0	0	0	1	0
D. Rice, c	5	2	2	1	3	0	0
J. Hearn, p	3	0	1	0	0	1	0
	37	11	14	11	27	10	0

Philadelphia	000 100 000	-	1
St. Louis	140 600 00x	-	11

	ip	h	r-er	bb	so
Heintzelman (L 3-1)	1.1	5	5-5	3	1
Bicknell	4.1	7	6-6	2	0
Nahem	2.1	2	0-0	1	1
Hearn (W 4-2)	9	4	1-1	4	2

Umpires: L. Goetz, J. Conlan, & B. Reardon

LOB: Phil 6, StL 9.
DP: LaPointe-Schoendienst-Jones.
2B: Schoendienst 3, Jones.
3B: Marion, Rice.
HR: Dusak, Schoendienst, Slaughter, Jones.
SH: Caballero, Hearn.
Time - 2:06
Attendance - 22,450

SECOND GAME

		r	h	e	Batteries
Philadelphia	000 000 000 -	0	5	0	N. Strincevich (L 0-1) 7 IP, E. Heusser 1 IP & A. Lakeman.
St. Louis	000 002 00x -	2	7	0	A. Brazle (W 3-2) & J. Garagiola.

St. Louis lost the league lead the next day and never regained it. But they remained in contention for most of the year. They finished second, 6½ games behind the pennant-winning Boston Braves. St. Louis's final record was 85-69.

Schoendienst finished the season with a .272 average and 21 doubles. Musial had his best year, hitting .376.

1949 — Thursday, September 29th, at Forbes Field, Pittsburgh

Dickson and Pirates Knock Cardinals Out of First Place

Cards Lose, 7-2, While Dodgers Win Pair in Boston

Errors and Walks Help Give Pittsburgh the Game

After holding the National League since August 20th, the St. Louis Cardinals fell from first place in the pennant race today. The Brooklyn Dodgers moved into the top spot with just two games left to play. The Cards fell to ½ game back with three left.

For the second consecutive game, the lowly Pittsburgh Pirates took advantage of St. Louis mistakes to beat the leaders. On Tuesday night, the Bucs won, 6-4. Five of their runs came in the second inning on a single, two walks, an error by Red Schoendienst, and a two-out grand slam home run off the foul pole by Tommy Saffell. Today, the Pirates scored in three innings in which the leadoff man walked. In addition, two errors allowed runners to score.

Today's Results
Pittsburgh 7 - ST. LOUIS 2
Brooklyn 9 - Boston 2 (1st game)
Brooklyn 8 - Boston 0 (5 inn.) (2nd)
no other games scheduled

Standings	W-L	Pct.	GB
Brooklyn	96-56	.632	-
ST. LOUIS	95-56	.629	½
Philadelphia	80-72	.526	16
New York	73-79	.480	23
Boston	73-79	.480	23
Pittsburgh	69-82	.457	26½
Cincinnati	61-90	.404	34½
Chicago	59-92	.391	36½

The two victories gave the sixth-place Pirates the season series over the Cardinals, 12 games to 10. St. Louis had already won the series against every other team in the league.

Despite the setbacks, it was still possible for the Cards to assure themselves at least a tie for first by sweeping their three remaining games against the cellar-dwelling Cubs in Chicago.

After a slow start, the Cardinals moved into pennant contention in June. On the 24th of that month, they took over first place. They lost the lead the next day. They remained in second place until July 24th, when they edged ahead of the Dodgers again. After holding the lead for two weeks, the Cards fell back into a tie. The lead seesawed for the next four weeks, then St. Louis finally broke ahead on August 20th. From that date until today, the Cardinals held the lead, but the Dodgers never fell farther than 2½ games behind. In short, it had been a close and exciting race.

The Red Birds came to Pittsburgh with a 1½-game lead and just five games to play. So they looked like pennant winners for sure. But in baseball nothing is certain until the last out is made.

Today's defeat came at the hands of former Cardinal pitcher Murry Dickson. Last winter he had been sold to Pittsburgh for a reported $125,000. In spring training, Cardinals manager Eddie Dyer said that he thought the sale was a mistake. But owner Fred Saigh thought differently. He pointed to Dickson's age (he turned 33 in August) and his poor 1948 record (12-16 and 39 home runs allowed). Today, Dickson raised his 1949 mark to 12-14, including 5-3 against St. Louis.

The Cardinals scored a run off old Murry in the first inning. After Schoendienst flied out deep to open the game and Marty Marion was robbed of a hit by shortstop Stan Rojek, Stan Musial legged out an infield hit. It was Musial's 200th safety of the season. Enos Slaughter slashed a double down the left field line, scoring Musial. Ron Northey flied out.

In the bottom of the first, slugger Ralph Kiner barely missed his 54th home run of the season. His drive hit about a foot from the top of the screen in left field and bounced back onto the field. Kiner got a double but was left on base.

The Cardinals left two men on in each of the next two rounds. In the second, an error, a hit batsman, and a sacrifice put men on second and third. But Schoendienst's two-out liner went right to second baseman Monte Basgall. In the third, Marion opened with a double and moved up on an infield out. With two out, Ron Northey walked. But Rocky Nelson's liner was also caught, this time by right fielder Wally Westlake.

A walk and a sacrifice went for naught in the top of the fourth.

In the bottom half, the Pirates tied the score on a walk, a bad hop, and an error. Kiner, leading off, walked. He was forced out by Johnny Hopp. Westlake fanned. Pete Castiglione's hopper down to third base took a bad bounce and skipped off Tommy Glaviano's glove, rolling into left field. Slaughter picked the ball up in the outfield and started to throw to third. Then he changed his mind and started to throw to second. But as he was throwing, the ball slipped out of his hand, allowing Hopp to round third and score. Basgall fanned, but the damage was done.

A walk to Kiner in the sixth started another rally. A great play by Schoendienst retired Hopp. But Marion failed to come up with Westlake's smash, and it trickled away for a single, sending Kiner to third. Castiglione singled cleanly to center, putting the Pirates into the lead.

Dyer removed his starting pitcher, Gerry Staley, and brought in his ace, Howie Pollet. Monte Basgall, the first batter to face Pollet, slapped a double past first base, driving in two runs. And when Schoendienst's relay bounced past catcher Joe Garagiola, Basgall came all the way home himself. That made the score against the Cardinals 5-1.

Dickson, in the meantime, had settled down. Marion opened the fifth with a single, but he was eliminated by a double play. Dickson set the Cards down in order in the sixth, seventh, and eighth.

Against Ted Wilks in the eighth, the Pirates added two runs. Once again, a walk started things, Hopp strolling this time. Westlake followed with a long home run over the scoreboard in left field.

Trailing 7-1, the visitors scored a meaningless run in the ninth on a double by Rocky Nelson and a pinch-single by Billy Howerton. But another pinch-batter, Steve Bilko, looked at a called third strike for the last out, and the Cardinals lost, 7-2. When the final result of the Dodgers' second game arrived, the Cardinals were in second place.

St. Louis	ab	r	h	bi	o	a	e
R. Schoendienst, 2b	4	0	0	0	2	5	1
M. Marion, ss	4	0	2	0	1	1	0
S. Musial, cf	4	1	1	0	5	0	0
E. Slaughter, lf	4	0	1	1	1	0	1
R. Northey, rf	3	0	0	0	0	0	0
R. Nelson, 1b	4	1	1	0	11	0	0
J. Garagiola, c	4	0	0	0	3	1	0
T. Glaviano, 3b	1	0	0	0	1	3	0
B. Howerton, ph9	1	0	1	1	-	-	-
G. Staley, p	0	0	0	0	0	2	0
H. Pollet, p6	0	0	0	0	0	0	0
R. Derry, ph7	1	0	0	0	-	-	-
T. Wilks, p7	0	0	0	0	0	0	0
S. Bilko, ph9	1	0	0	0	-	-	-
	31	2	6	2	24	12	2

Pittsburgh	ab	r	h	bi	o	a	e
S. Rojek, ss	4	0	2	0	2	1	0
T. Saffell, cf	4	0	0	0	2	0	0
R. Kiner, lf	2	1	1	0	0	0	0
J. Hopp, 1b	3	2	0	0	11	2	1
W. Westlake, rf	4	2	2	2	5	0	0
P. Castiglione, 3b	4	1	3	1	1	0	0
M. Basgall, 2b	3	1	1	2	3	5	0
C. McCullough, c	4	0	0	0	3	0	0
M. Dickson, p	3	0	0	0	0	1	0
	31	7	9	5	27	9	1

St. Louis	100	000	001	-	2
Pittsburgh	000	104	02x	-	7

	ip	h	r-er	bb	so
Staley (L 10-10)	5.1	7	4-3	2	2
Pollet	.2	1	1-0	0	0
Wilks	2	1	2-2	2	0
Dickson (W 12-14)	9	6	2-2	2	2

HBP: by Dickson (Glaviano)
Umpires: D. Robb, B. Pinelli, F. Dascoli, & A. Gore

LOB: StL 7, Pitts 4. BE: StL 1.
DP: Hopp-Rojek, Schoendienst-Marion-Nelson.
2B: Slaughter, Kiner, Marion, Basgall, Nelson.
HR: Westlake. SH: Staley 2.
SB: none. CS: Castiglione.
Attendance - 9,573 paid
    12,196 total
Time - 2:06

The Cardinals left Pittsburgh for Chicago, but the story was the same. They failed in the clutch, losing Friday, 6-5, and Saturday, 3-1. They won their final games, 13-5, but lost the pennant to the Dodgers by 1 game. St. Louis's record was 96-58.

The exciting race led to a home attendance record of 1,430,676, which stood until the Cardinals moved to the new downtown stadium in 1966.

1950 — Sunday, September 3rd, at Forbes Field, Pittsburgh
Unorthodox Strategy Backfires, Cards Lose to Bucs, 12-11, in Ten
Eight Home Runs Highlight Seesaw Battle
Kiner Given Intentional Walk With No One On, Scores Winning Run

An intentional walk with no one on and two out and the score tied in the bottom of the tenth inning? An unorthodox and unusual strategy, to be sure. Nonetheless, that was exactly the tactic tried by Cardinal manager Eddie Dyer today in Pittsburgh. It cost the Cardinals the game. Needless to say, the second-guessers had a field day afterwards.

There were extenuating circumstances. After all, the man walked was Ralph Kiner, the reigning home run king of the world, and he had hit two homers earlier in the game. Besides, pitcher Harry Brecheen had given up two home runs earlier in the inning. So, why let Kiner beat you with his bat? But he wound up scoring the winning run moments later on a double by Gus Bell, so why not let him beat you with his bat? Bell, after all, had tripled twice previously.

Today's Results
Pittsburgh 12 - ST. LOUIS 11 (10 inn.)
Cincinnati 7 - Chicago 5 (11 inn.)
Philadelphia at Boston - postponed, rain
New York at Brooklyn - postponed, rain

Standings	W-L	Pct.	GB
Philadelphia	80-47	.630	-
Brooklyn	70-51	.579	7
Boston	68-56	.548	10½
New York	66-58	.532	12½
ST. LOUIS	65-60	.520	14
Chicago	54-72	.429	25½
Cincinnati	51-73	.411	27½
Pittsburgh	45-82	.354	35

The upshot of it all was that the Cardinals lost a wild game, 12-11. It was their fifth straight loss and dropped them farther from the first division.

They had been in the top half of the standings from May 7th until September 1st. They had even been in first place for 30 days. They led the league as late as July 24th. But since then they have won only 15 of 38 games. In that stretch of time, they were just 3-11 in one-run decisions. Eight of those losses, including today's, came in the last inning.

Today's defeat was perhaps the worst of the many heartbreakers. Three times the Cardinals came from behind to take the lead, but they fell behind again each time. The failure of the pitching was particularly galling in the extra inning. The Red Birds scored two runs in the top of the tenth, only to give up three runs on two home runs, the intentional pass, and the game-winning double.

All the pitching today was weak. Eight home runs spiced the 30 hits that echoed around the yard. There were also six doubles and half a dozen triples. The Pirates had 16 hits, including five circuit blasts, while the Cardinals had 14 hits and three homers. Seven Red Birds were walked, as were six of the Buccaneers. The only two errors of the contest were made by Pirate shortstop Danny O'Connell.

The cannonading started in the bottom of the first. O'Connell and Kiner hit back-to-back home runs off of George Munger, who was making his first start for St. Louis since July 20th. Bell followed with a triple but was left on third.

After being held hitless in the first two innings, the Cardinals broke through for three runs in the third against the Pirates' Murry Dickson. Three-baggers by Tommy Glaviano and Billy Howerton were the big blows.

But the Pirates came in, routed Munger, and regained the lead in their half of the third. Kiner opened with a walk, and the next three men hit safely. Two runs scored although one man was thrown out trying to take an extra base. Munger was yanked, and Alpha Brazle took over. An intentional walk and singles by Dickson and Bob Dillinger gave the home team two more runs and a 6-3 lead.

Bell and Wally Westlake tripled in the fourth, making the score 7-3.

Cloyd Boyer, who replaced Brazle in the fourth, doubled for St. Louis with two out in the sixth. Glaviano then homered, getting the Cardinals back within striking distance, 7-5.

Hits by Stan Musial and Joe Garagiola and an error by O'Connell gave the Red Birds another run in the seventh. Garagiola's hit was his first since being sidelined on July 1st with a shoulder injury.

With two out and a man on first (via a base on balls) in the eighth, Musial put the Cards ahead with a long home run into the right center field seats. When Enos Slaughter followed with a double, Dickson was finally taken out of the game. Frank Barrett came in and got the last out.

Boyer had been pitching good ball since those two triples in the fourth. He got the first two men out in the bottom of the eighth. But he made the mistake of walking O'Connell in front of Kiner. Big Ralph then cracked his 42nd homer of the season over the left field screen, and the Pirates were back on top, 9-8.

James "Junior" Walsh was sent in to hold the lead in the top of the ninth. The first and only man he faced, Howerton, tied the score with a home run into the upper deck in right. Bill Werle was brought in, and he got the next three men out.

Harry Brecheen pitched a 1-2-3 bottom of the ninth.

The game went into extra innings.

The Cardinals went to work on Werle in the top of the tenth. With one out, Red Schoendienst doubled. His roommate Musial singled him home. Stan the Man rode home on Slaughter's triple. Del Rice fanned, and Howerton flied out, but the Cardinals had an 11-9 lead.

It didn't hold up. After getting the first man out, Brecheen served up two straight "gopher balls," one to pinch-hitter Pete Castiglione and one to Dillinger. The homers tied the score again. Brecheen retired O'Connell, bringing the ever dangerous Kiner to the plate. Going against "The Book," manager Dyer ordered the slugger intentionally passed. Bell then ruined the decision and ended the game with a drive high off the screen in right, Kiner scoring easily as the ball bounded far from the outfielders.

The final score was 12-11 Pittsburgh, and they'll talk about that final bit of strategy for some time.

St. Louis	ab	r	h	bi	o	a	e
T. Glaviano, 3b	5	3	2	2	2	2	0
R. Schoendienst, 2b	6	1	2	0	1	0	0
S. Musial, lf	4	4	4	3	2	0	0
E. Slaughter, rf	6	1	2	2	3	0	0
J. Garagiola, c	4	0	1	0	3	0	0
C. Diering, pr7	0	0	0	0	-	-	-
D. Rice, c7	2	0	0	0	1	0	0
B. Howerton, cf	5	1	2	3	4	0	0
R. Nelson, 1b	3	0	0	0	11	0	0
E. Miller, ss	3	0	0	0	1	2	0
M. Marion, ss6	2	0	0	0	1	2	0
G. Munger, p	1	0	0	0	0	0	0
A. Brazle, p3	0	0	0	0	0	0	0
H. Rice, ph4	0	0	0	0	-	-	-
C. Boyer, p4	2	1	1	0	0	2	0
E. Kazak, ph9	1	0	0	0	-	-	-
H. Brecheen, p9	0	0	0	0	0	0	0
	44	11	14	10	29	8	0

Pittsburgh	ab	r	h	bi	o	a	e
B. Dillinger, 3b	6	1	3	3	2	2	0
D. O'Connell, ss	5	2	1	1	4	4	2
R. Kiner, lf	4	4	2	3	4	0	0
G. Bell, rf	6	1	4	1	2	0	0
W. Westlake, cf	4	1	2	2	3	0	0
J. Phillips, 1b	4	1	1	1	10	1	0
J. Berardino, 2b	5	0	0	0	2	3	0
C. McCullough, c	4	1	1	0	3	0	0
M. Dickson, p	3	0	1	0	0	0	0
F. Barrett, p8	0	0	0	0	0	0	0
J. Hopp, ph8	1	0	0	0	-	-	-
J. Walsh, p9	0	0	0	0	0	0	0
B. Werle, p9	0	0	0	0	0	0	0
P. Castiglione, ph10	1	1	1	1	-	-	-
	43	12	16	12	30	10	2

St. Louis   003 002 121 2 - 11
Pittsburgh   204 100 020 3 - 12
two out when winning run scored

	ip	h	r-er	bb	so
Munger	2.1	7	5-5	2	0
Brazle	.2	2	1-1	1	0
Boyer	5	4	3-3	2	4
Brecheen (L 7-11)	1.2	3	3-3	1	0
Dickson	7.2	10	8-6	7	1
Barrett	.1	0	0-0	0	0
Walsh	*0	1	1-1	0	0
Werle (W 8-12)	2	3	2-2	0	1

LOB: StL 10, Pitts 8. BE: StL 1.
DP: O'Connell-Berardino-Phillips.
2B: Phillips, Schoendienst 2, Boyer, Slaughter, Bell.
3B: Bell 2, Glaviano, Howerton, Westlake, Slaughter
HR: O'Connell, Kiner 2, Glaviano, Musial, Howerton, Castiglione, Dillinger.
Attendance - 12,736
Time - 3:06
*faced one batter in ninth
Umpires: A. Donatelli, L. Ballanfant, L. Warneke, & A. Barlick

The Cardinals' losing streak climbed to seven games before ending. St. Louis limped through the rest of the season at about a .500 pace and finished with a 78-75 record.

That left them in fifth place. It was the first time since 1940 that the Cardinals failed to finish either first or second. The glory years were over.

1951 — Thursday, September 13th, at Sportsman's Park

Cardinals Beat Giants by Day, Lose to Braves at Night

Put Crimp in New York's Pennant Hopes with 6-4 Victory

Stopped by Boston's Warren Spahn on One Hit in Night Game

In a doubleheader unprecedented in the major leagues in this century, the St. Louis Cardinals hosted two different clubs on the same day. On what had originally been an open date on the schedule, the New York Giants played in St. Louis in an afternoon game, and the Boston Braves played the Cardinals a few hours later in a night game.

St. Louis and Boston had planned to play a night game to make up a rained-out contest from July 23rd. Since the Braves finished a series in Chicago on Wednesday and were scheduled to start a two-game set in St. Louis on Friday, there seemed little reason not to schedule a make-up for Thursday.

But yesterday the final game between the Giants and the Cardinals here was rained out. New York was trying desperately to catch the front-running Brooklyn Dodgers in the National League pennant race, and they wanted every possible victory to pressure the Bums. Since Thursday had originally been an open date, New York owner Horace Stoneham claimed that the team already in town had precedence for a make-up game, and he wired league president Ford Frick to get the Boston-St. Louis game set aside.

After much long-distance debate, Frick approved a compromsie, which allowed the Cardinals to play both rival teams on the same day. The arrangement was not altogether a success. Less than 9,000 fans came to the two games, and the Giants wound up losing their cherished game. Then the Cardinals rolled over and played dead for the Braves, losing 2-0.

This was the first time since 1899 that a National League team had played two different clubs on the same day. In that year, it happened nine times. Most of these split doubleheaders involved the Cleveland Exiles, the worst team in major league history. They were so bad that they had to play nearly all of their games in the second half of the season on the road, and they often doubled up with other games, since no one would pay to see them alone.

St. Louis won today's opening game, 6-4, with a six-run second inning.

Sal "the Barber" Maglie was the starting pitcher for New York. He lived up to his nickname right away, shaving leadoff man Solly Hemus in the first inning, giving Hemus first base. But Red Schoendienst bounced into a double play, and Stan Musial grounded out to first.

Then came the Cards' big inning. Walks to Enos Slaughter and Del Rice and hits by Vern Benson and Harry Walker produced two runs. After a sacrifice, pitcher Tom Poholsky knocked Maglie out with a single. Southpaw Monte Kennedy was brought in. He proceeded to knock down each of the first three hitters he faced with "purpose pitches." But each man (Hemus, Schoendienst, and Musial) got up and singled, driving in a run apiece. Poholsky was badly spiked by catcher Wes Westrum while sliding home, and he had to leave the game. The inning ended when Schoendienst was tagged out at home.

Another rookie pitcher, Dick Bokelmann, replaced Poholsky in the third. He held the Giants safe until the sixth. Then Don Mueller doubled, Monte Irvin tripled, and Whitey Lockman hit a run-scoring fly ball, giving New York its first two runs.

Bokelmann lasted until Irvin hit a two-run home run in the eighth. Gerry Staley came in and retired the side with the tying runs on base.

Staley pitched a perfect ninth inning, and the Cardinals won, 6-4.

The St. Louis bats, which had little effect against the New York relievers after the second innning of the afternoon game, were almost completely silent in the night game against Boston. The Braves' Warren Spahn had to face only 29 Cardinal batters, allowing just one bloop hit and one base on balls.

Al Brazle pitched a fine game for the Red Birds but lost. He allowed runs in the first and last innings, the first tally being unearned. The first two Braves, Sibby Sisti and Sam Jethroe, singled

Today's Results
ST. LOUIS 6 - New York 4 (day game)
Boston 2 - ST. LOUIS 0 (night game)
no other games scheduled

Standings	W-L	Pct.	GB
Brooklyn	88-49	.642	-
New York	84-57	.596	6
ST. LOUIS	73-65	.529	15½
Boston	70-68	.507	18½
Philadelphia	66-74	.471	23½
Cincinnati	61-80	.433	29
Chicago	58-82	.414	31½
Pittsburgh	58-83	.411	32

in the opening inning. Sisti scored on catcher Del Rice's wild throw trying to pick Jethroe off first. In the ninth inning, Walker Cooper doubled and advanced on an infield out. After an intentional walk to Roy Hartsfield, Spahn delivered his second hit of the game, driving Cooper home.

The only Cardinals to reach base were Chuck Diering and Brazle. Diering walked in the third inning and got as far as second base, thanks to a wild pitch. Brazle got the only hit off Spahn. It came with one out in the sixth, and it wasn't much of a drive. Brazle reached down for a low fastball and popped it weakly into short right field, just beyond the reach of the backpedaling second baseman, Hartsfield. Brazle was stranded on first.

The one-hitter gave Spahn his 20th win of the season.

DAY GAME

New York	ab	r	h	bi	o	a	e		St. Louis	ab	r	h	bi	o	a	e
E. Stanky, 2b	3	0	0	0	2	6	0		S. Hemus, ss	2	1	1	1	2	7	0
A. Dark, ss	5	0	0	0	1	4	1		R. Schoendienst, 2b	4	0	1	1	7	2	0
D. Mueller, rf	4	2	2	0	2	0	0		S. Musial, 1b	4	0	1	1	10	0	0
M. Irvin, lf	3	2	3	3	1	0	0		E. Slaughter, rf	2	1	0	0	3	0	0
W. Lockman, 1b	3	0	0	1	11	4	0		H. Rice, lf	3	1	0	0	1	0	0
B. Thomson, 3b	4	0	1	0	0	1	0		C. Diering, lf9	0	0	0	0	1	0	0
W. Mays, cf	4	0	1	0	0	0	0		V. Benson, 3b	4	1	2	1	0	2	0
W. Westrum, c	1	0	1	0	1	1	1		B. Johnson, 3b9	0	0	0	0	0	1	0
H. Schenz, pr5	0	0	0	0	-	-	-		H. Walker, cf	4	1	3	1	1	0	0
A. Konikowski, p5	0	0	0	0	1	0	0		D. Rice, c	3	0	1	0	2	0	0
B. Rigney, ph7	1	0	0	0	-	-	-		T. Pohlosky, p	1	1	1	1	0	1	0
A. Corwin, p7	0	0	0	0	0	0	0		D. Bokelmann, p3	2	0	0	0	0	0	0
H. Thompson, ph8	1	0	0	0	-	-	-		G. Staley, p8	1	0	0	0	0	0	0
G. Spencer, p8	0	0	0	0	0	0	0									
S. Maglie, p	1	0	0	0	1	0	0									
M. Kennedy, p2	0	0	0	0	1	1	0									
R. Noble, ph5-c	3	0	0	0	3	1	0									
	33	4	8	4	24	18	2			30	6	10	6	27	13	0

New York	000	002	020	-	4		LOB: NY 7, StL 6.
St. Louis	060	000	00x	-	6		DP: Dark-Stanky-Lockman, Hemus-Schoendienst-Musial, Hemus-Musial, Lockman-Dark-Lockman.

	ip	h	r-er	bb	so
Maglie (L 20-6)	1.1	3	5-5	2	0
Kennedy	2.2	4	1-1	1	0
Konikowski	2	2	0-0	0	1
Corwin	1	0	0-0	1	1
Spencer	1	1	0-0	0	0
Poholsky	2	2	0-0	2	0
Bokelmann (W 3-3)	5.1	5	4-4	3	2
Staley	1.2	1	0-0	0	0

2B: Mueller. 3B: Irvin.
HR: Irvin. SH: D. Rice
HBP: by Maglie (Hemus).
Time - 2:26
Attendance - 4,160
Umpires: B. Stewart, A. Gore,
    J. Conlan, & F. Dascoli

NIGHT GAME

						r	h	e	Batteries
Boston	100	000	001	-		2	9	0	W. Spahn (W 20-12) & W. Cooper.
St. Louis	000	000	000	-		0	1	1	A. Brazle (L 6-3) & D. Rice.

Attendance - 4,705

The Cardinals held onto third place, finishing 5 games ahead of the Braves. St. Louis's final record was 81-73.

The Giants, after losing in St. Louis, won 12 of their final 13 regular-season games to wind up tied for first with the Dodgers. If they hadn't played the make-up game in St. Louis, they would have won the pennant outright. Instead, the Giants went into a playoff with the Dodgers, which New York won on a very dramatic home run by Bobby Thomson.

1952 — Sunday, June 15th, at the Polo Grounds, New York

Birds Overcome 11-0 Deficit to Win First Game, Then Lose Second

Set New National League Record in 14-12 Victory

Slaughter and Hemus Lead the Cardinals Back with Key Hits

With a record-setting comeback, the St. Louis Cardinals won the first game of today's doubleheader with the New York Giants. The Giants built up an 11-0 lead after just three innings and had their ace pitcher, Sal Maglie, on the mound. Starting with seven runs in the fifth inning, the Red Birds fought back and won, 14-12.

Enos Slaughter and Solly Hemus got the biggest hits of the game, but nine different St. Louis players contributed hits and runs to the cause. Slaughter drove in five runs with a home run, single, and double. Hemus homered in each of the last two innings, driving in three runs.

The major league record for largest deficit overcome to win, 12 runs, was made in the American League. The old National League record was 10, set all the way back in 1876, and the Cardinals beat that mark today.

St. Louis lost the second game, however, 3-0.

Today's Results
ST. LOUIS 14 - New York 12 (1st game)
New York 3 - ST. LOUIS 0 (7 inn.) (2nd)
Cincinnati 7 - Brooklyn 4
Boston 2 - Chicago 1 (1st game)
Boston 2 - Chicago 0 (2nd)
Pittsburgh 6 - Philadelphia 0 (1st game)
Philadelphia 6 - Pittsburgh 3 (2nd)

Standings	W-L	Pct.	GB
Brooklyn	37-15	.712	-
New York	33-18	.647	3½
Chicago	34-21	.618	4½
ST. LOUIS	28-28	.500	11
Cincinnati	25-29	.463	13
Boston	22-31	.415	15½
Philadelphia	21-30	.412	15½
Pittsburgh	15-43	.259	25

The first game started innocently enough. Each side failed to score in the first inning, and the Cardinals were disposed of in the second.

The Giants tore into St. Louis starting pitcher Joe Presko for five runs in the bottom of the second. After five singles, one walk, and an error, Cardinal manager Eddie Stanky replaced Presko with Jack Crimian, who got the last out.

But Crimian was totally ineffective in the third inning. The first Giant batter, Hank Thompson, hit a home run. A walk and two singles scored another run, then Wes Westrum delivered a three-run homer. Three more singles brought the score to 11-0, and still no one was out. Stanky yanked Crimian and brought in Bill Werle. The big southpaw stopped the Giants' scoring through the sixth inning.

New York manager Leo Durocher decided that this would be a good time to give some of his veterans a rest. He took Westrum and Bob Elliott out of the lineup. Stanky contemplated the same thing, but, as he said later, "Something inside me told me not to make the changes... call it a silly hunch."

The Cardinals went to work on Maglie in the fifth. Sal was making his third try to get win #10 for the season, and with an 11-0 lead, it seemed that he only needed to get through one more inning to be eligible for an easy victory. Tommy Glaviano started the Cards' comeback with a home run. Singles by Werle and Red Schoendienst and a walk to Hemus loaded the bases for Stan Musial. He singled home two runs. Dick Sisler followed with another single, scoring a fourth run. Durocher stuck with Maglie, hoping to get him through the inning for a win. When Peanuts Lowrey flied out, it looked like Sal would make it. But Slaughter pumped a shot into the upper deck in right field for a three-run homer, and Durocher was forced to call in his rookie relief ace, Hoyt Wilhelm.

Wilhelm protected the 11-7 lead through the fifth and sixth. But the Cardinals routed him in the seventh. Musial singled, and with one out, Lowrey reached on an error. Slaughter doubled one run home, and Glaviano singled another runner across. George Spencer relieved Wilhelm and retired the next two men, while one more run scored. It was now 11-10.

Leadoff man Hemus was the first Cardinal up in the eighth. He slammed Spencer's first pitch into the seats in right for a game-tying home run. Ex-Cardinal Max Lanier was then rushed into the breech by Durocher. He retired the next two hitters. But Sisler singled, Lowrey walked, and Slaughter singled, putting the Cardinals ahead, finally, 12-11.

In the ninth, Hemus hit a two-run home run off Monte Kennedy, upping the lead to 14-11.

Eddie Yuhas, who had shut New York out in the seventh and eighth, got the first two men out in the bottom of the ninth. But he walked the next two, and Stanky called Willard Schmidt in to finish up. He got the next two hitters to hit routine ground balls, but both were fumbled, allowing one run to score. Then with the bases loaded, Schmidt induced Davey Williams to foul out to the catcher, and the Cardinals had an incredible, 14-12 victory.

The second game offered quite a contrast to the first. Gerry Staley of the Cardinals and Dave Koslo of the Giants both pitched good ball. The only runs of the game came in the fifth, on Wes Westrum's three-run home run.

The game was called on account of darkness after just seven innings.

FIRST GAME

St. Louis	ab	r	h	bi	o	a	e	New York	ab	r	h	bi	o	a	e
S. Hemus, ss	5	3	2	3	2	1	1	D. Williams, 2b	6	0	3	1	2	4	1
R. Schoendienst, 2b	6	1	2	0	1	0	0	W. Lockman, 1b	5	0	3	3	10	0	1
S. Musial, cf-lf3	6	2	2	2	2	0	0	B. Thomson, 3b	5	0	0	0	0	3	0
D. Sisler, 1b	5	2	2	1	11	0	0	H. Thompson, cf	4	2	1	1	6	0	0
P. Lowrey, lf-cf3	4	1	1	0	5	1	0	B. Elliott, lf	2	1	0	0	0	0	0
E. Slaughter, rf	5	2	3	5	2	0	0	C. Diering, lf4	1	0	0	0	3	0	0
T. Glaviano, 3b	5	1	2	2	0	5	2	B. Howerton, ph9	1	0	0	0	-	-	-
D. Rice, c	5	1	3	1	4	0	0	D. Mueller, rf	4	3	2	1	2	0	0
J. Presko, p	0	0	0	0	0	0	0	A. Dark, ss	4	2	2	2	1	1	0
J. Crimian, p2	1	0	0	0	0	0	0	W. Westrum, c	2	2	2	3	1	0	0
B. Werle, p3	2	1	1	0	0	1	0	R. Noble, c4	2	0	0	0	2	1	0
H. Rice, ph7	1	0	0	0	-	-	-	B. Rigney, ph9	1	0	0	0	-	-	-
E. Yuhas, p7	0	0	0	0	0	1	0	S. Maglie, p	1	2	1	0	0	1	1
W. Schmidt, p9	0	0	0	0	0	0	0	H. Wilhelm, p5	1	0	0	0	0	0	0
								G. Spencer, p7	0	0	0	0	0	0	0
								M. Lanier, p8	0	0	0	0	0	0	0
								G. Wilson, ph8	1	0	0	0	-	-	-
								M. Kennedy, p9	0	0	0	0	0	0	0
								S. Yvars, ph9	1	0	0	0	-	-	-
	45	14	18	14	27	9	3		41	12	14	11	27	10	3

St. Louis   000 070 322 - 14
New York   056 000 001 - 12

	ip	h	r-er	bb	so
Presko	1.2	6	5-4	1	0
Crimian	*.1	7	6-6	1	0
Werle	4	0	0-0	0	3
Yuhas (W 3-2)	2.2	1	1-0	2	0
Schmidt	.1	0	0-0	0	0
Maglie	4.2	9	7-7	1	1
Wilhelm	1.2	4	3-1	0	1
Spencer	#.2	1	1-1	0	0
Lanier (L 1-4)	1	2	1-1	1	0
Kennedy	1	2	2-2	0	0

LOB: StL 7, NY 7.
DP: Williams-Dark-Lockman, Hemus-Sisler.
2B: Slaughter. 3B: D. Rice
HR: Thompson, Westrum, Glaviano, Slaughter, Hemus 2.
SH: Maglie, Yuhas.
Time - 3:22
Attendance - 41,899
*faced eight batters in third
#faced one batter in eighth
Umpires: T. Gorman, A. Donatelli,
  L. Ballanfant, & A. Barlick

SECOND GAME

					r	h	e	Batteries
St. Louis	000	000	0	-	0	5	0	G. Staley (L 9-4) & L. Fusselman.
New York	000	030	0	-	3	5	1	D. Koslo (W 3-3) & W. Westrum.

game called after seven innings on account of darkness

Although none of its other victories were as stirring as its June 15th win, St. Louis played good ball under Stanky, finishing a respectable third.

Their record of 88-66 left them 8½ games behind the champion Dodgers.

1953 — September 25th, at Wrigley Field, Chicago
Haddix Wins 20th Game of Year, Schoendienst Nears Batting Lead
Cardinals Crush Cubs, 11-2
Schoendienst Trails Furillo By .002 With Two Games Left

As the National League season began its final three days, there were still some achievements within the reach of the St. Louis Cardinals. In today's game, rookie lefthander Harvey Haddix posted his 20th victory of the season, and Red Schoendienst kept his hopes of winning the league batting title alive by getting four hits in six at bats. And the team edged ahead of the Philadelphia Phillies and into sole possession of third place.

Schoendienst raised his average to .34234. The leader, Carl Furillo of Brooklyn, has been at .34447 since he was sidelined with a broken bone in his hand on September 6th. The injury occurred in a fight with New York manager Leo Durocher.

Today's Results
ST. LOUIS 11 - Chicago 2
Brooklyn 4 - Philadelphia 3
New York 6 - Pittsburgh 2
no other games scheduled

Standings	W-L	Pct.	GB
Brooklyn	104-48	.684	-
Milwaukee	91-61	.599	13
ST. LOUIS	83-69	.546	21
Philadelphia	82-70	.539	22
New York	69-83	.454	35
Cincinnati	67-85	.441	37
Chicago	63-89	.414	41
Pittsburgh	49-103	.322	55

Stan Musial, who went 2-for-4, also maintained a very slim chance to catch Furillo. His average went up to .33562, and he would have to get hits in his last eight at bats to have a chance at his fourth straight batting crown. Even though his prospects became slim, Stan has been the hottest hitter in the league in recent weeks. He extended his current hitting streak to 13 games, during which he has hit at a .473 pace. But for a prolonged slump early in the season, Stan might have walked away with the batting title. But his average didn't get above the .250 mark until mid-June.

Schoendienst, on the other hand, had been among the league leaders for most of the season. He topped the list most of July, then fell behind New York's Monte Irvin on August 8th. For the next month, Schoendienst, Irvin, and Furillo exchanged the lead. Red was at .341 when Furillo went on the shelf but slumped to .329 with eight games left. Then the Cardinal second baseman turned around and hit .652 over the next six games to move within range of the lead. After today's performance, Schoendienst still needed to go 4-for-8 to pass Furillo. Luckily, the Cards' last two games were scheduled for Wrigley Field, Chicago, where Red has hit at a .595 clip so far this season.

Musial and Schoendienst were abetted in today's game by the hitting of Solly Hemus and Dick Rand, each of whom made three hits, and by Enos Slaughter, Ray Jablonski, and Rip Repulski, who each got two safeties. Steve Bilko got one hit, leaving Haddix as the only starting player for St. Louis to fail to get a base knock. Harvey did, however, score a run after reaching base by being hit by a pitch.

All the hitting made it easy for the young hurler to win number 20. He became the first Cardinal rookie to win that many since Johnny Beazley won 21 games in 1942. He also became the first 20-game winner for the Red Birds since 1949, when Howie Pollet turned the trick.

Haddix turned 28 years of age last week. He spent all of 1951 and most of 1952 in the military service. Prior to that, he had spent three years with Columbus in the American Association, and he was deemed ready to make the big club when the Uncle Sam drafted him. In fact, he had signed with the Cardinals near the end of World War II, but had delayed his entrance into organized baseball until 1947 in order to maintain an agricultural deferment and avoid the draft.

Today's win was his fifth of the year over the hapless Cubs. All of the victories came on complete game efforts. One other time, Haddix was knocked out by the Cubs but got no decision. Today he wasn't scored upon until his team had an 8-0 lead.

Schoendienst got the St. Louis offense started with a single with one out in the first inning. After Musial fouled out, Slaughter doubled the redhead home.

Schoendienst also started the next scoring rally. With one out in the third, he pushed a double down the left field line. Musial singled him home. Stan then came around on hits by Slaughter and Jablonski. The RBI was the 111th of the year for the Cards' rookie third baseman.

In the fourth, Rand singled and Hemus doubled. Howie Pollet was brought in to relieve starter Bob Rush for the Cubs. The switch-hitting Schoendienst moved to the other side of the plate and greeted the ex-Cardinal southpaw with a two-run single to left.

St. Louis scored three more runs in the next inning, with Schoendienst getting another two-run single. That made Red 4-for-4 and gave the Cards an 8-0 lead in the middle of the fifth.

All the while, Haddix had had little trouble with the Cub hitters, allowing just one single through the first four innings.

In the fifth, Chicago strung three hits together for a run. And they scored again in the sixth. This time, Gene Baker beat out a bunt, Ralph Kiner singled, and Hank Sauer delivered a run-scoring fly ball.

But St. Louis had scored two runs in the top of the sixth at the expense of the third Cub pitcher, Dutch Leonard. Musial started the rally with a home run. Jablonski followed with a double, and he scored on a hit by Repulski.

Hemus homered for the last run of the game in the seventh.

Schoendienst was retired in his last two at bats. In the seventh, he was thrown out by shortstop Ernie Banks on a close play at first. And in the ninth, he lined out to right field.

Haddix faced the minimum number of batters in the final three innings. He finished the game with a seven-hitter, no walks, and 10 strikeouts. The 11-2 victory gave him a record of 20 wins and 9 losses.

And, when the Phillies lost a night game to the Dodgers, the Cardinals moved into undisputed possession of third place. And all the St. Louis players were rooting for Red Schoendienst to win the batting crown.

St. Louis	ab	r	h	bi	o	a	e
S. Hemus, ss	6	2	3	2	3	1	0
R. Schoendienst, 2b	6	2	4	4	0	3	0
S. Musial, lf	4	2	2	2	2	0	0
E. Slaughter, rf	5	0	2	1	1	0	0
R. Jablonski, 3b	4	1	2	1	1	2	0
E. Phillips, pr8	0	0	0	0	-	-	-
P. Castiglione, 3b8	0	0	0	0	0	0	0
S. Bilko, 1b	5	0	1	0	9	0	0
R. Repulski, cf	5	1	2	1	1	0	0
D. Rand, c	5	2	3	0	10	1	0
H. Haddix, p	4	1	0	0	0	2	0
	44	11	19	11	27	9	0

Chicago	ab	r	h	bi	o	a	e
F. Baumholtz, cf	4	0	1	0	1	0	0
G. Baker, 2b	4	1	2	0	3	4	0
D. Fondy, 1b	4	0	0	0	9	1	0
R. Kiner, lf	4	0	1	0	2	1	0
H. Sauer, rf	4	0	0	1	4	0	0
R. Jackson, 3b	4	1	1	0	1	2	0
E. Banks, ss	3	0	1	0	1	6	0
C. McCullough, c	3	0	1	1	5	1	0
B. Rush, p	1	0	0	0	0	0	0
H. Pollet, p4	0	0	0	0	0	0	0
T. Brown, ph5	1	0	0	0	-	-	-
D. Leonard, p6	0	0	0	0	1	0	0
B. Serena, ph7	1	0	0	0	-	-	-
B. Moisan, p8	0	0	0	0	0	0	0
	33	2	7	2	27	15	0

St. Louis 102 232 100 - 11
Chicago   000 011 000 - 2

	ip	h	r-er	bb	so
Haddix (W 20-9)	9	7	2-2	0	10
Rush (L 9-14)	3.1	9	5-5	0	2
Pollet	1.2	4	3-3	1	2
Leonard	2	5	3-3	0	1
Moisan	2	1	0-0	1	0

WP: Pollet, Haddix
HBP: by Pollet (Haddix)

LOB: StL 9, Chi 4.
DP: Baker-Fondy, Haddix-Hemus-Bilko
2B: Slaughter, Schoendienst, Hemus 2, Jackson, Jablonski.
HR: Musial, Hemus.
Time - 2:27
Attendance - 2,706
Umpires: B. Engeln, B. Stewart, D. Boggess, & B. Pinelli

Schoendienst went 3-for-9 in the last two games, finishing .002 behind Furillo with a .342 average. Musial went for 4-for-9 to finish at .337. The Cardinals lost the last two games and finished tied for third with the Phillies.

1954—Sunday, May 2nd, at Busch Stadium

Musial Hits Five Home Runs in Doubleheader, Cards & Giants Split

Stan Has Three in First Game Victory, Two in Defeat in Nightcap

Thirty-Two Runs and Twelve Homers Keep the Fans Entertained

What a Man! After twelve years of heroics on the St. Louis diamond, Stan (The Man) Musial may have outdone himself today at Busch Stadium. In ten trips to the plate, he blasted five home runs, breaking the all-time record for a doubleheader. He also singled once, walked twice, flied out to deepest left center, and, in his last at bat, popped out to first base.

Led by Musial's slugging, the Cardinals outbatted the New York Giants in the first game of the twin-bill, 10-6. In the second game, however, St. Louis's rally fell short, and New York won, 9-7.

Besides the five by the veteran Musial, rookies Wally Moon and Tom Alston and second-year man Ray Jablonski homered for the Cards. Four different Giants also hit for the circuit. The total damage to the pitching was 32 runs, 46 hits, and 93 total bases.

Today's Results
ST. LOUIS 10 - New York 6 (1st game)
New York 9 - ST. LOUIS 7 (2nd)
Philadelphia 4 - Cincinnati 3 (1st)
(2nd game postponed - rain)
Chicago 5 - Pittsburgh 2 (1st game)
Pittsburgh 18 - Chicago 10 (2nd)
Brooklyn at Milwaukee - ppd., rain

Standings	W-L	Pct.	GB
Philadelphia	9-6	.600	-
ST. LOUIS	9-7	.563	½
Brooklyn	9-7	.563	½
Cincinnati	10-8	.556	½
New York	9-8	.529	1
Chicago	6-7	.462	2
Pittsburgh	7-12	.368	4
Boston	5-9	.357	3½

A fine crowd of 26,662 came out to newly renovated Busch Stadium (formerly Sportsman's Park) for the first doubleheader of the young season. The customers were given a performance they wouldn't soon forget. Musial's 6-for-8 with five homers, six runs scored and nine batted in overshadowed all other efforts. Nonetheless, Alston had the best day of his young career, going 4-for-4 in the opening game and clubbing a three-run double in the nightcap. He also made some fine stretches of his long frame to pull in wide throws at first base. On the visiting side, Don Mueller had a 5-for-5 second game, incuding two hits and two runs scored in the Giants' big eight-run fourth-inning rally.

The homers started in the home half of the first inning in the first game. Cardinal leadoff man Wally Moon hit a 400-foot drive into the seats in left center field. Moon, a lefthanded hitter, connected off of southpaw Johnny Antonelli. The Cardinals added another run on a walk to Musial and hits by Red Schoendienst and Alston.

Stan began his slugging in the third inning, lifting one of Antonelli's off-speed deliveries onto the roof of the right field pavilion.

The Giants got two singles and two doubles off of Cardinal starter Gerry Staley, tying the score at 3-3 in the top of the fourth.

But in the bottom of the round, Alston lifted a wind-blown fly to deep center. The ball eluded the desperate lunge of Willie Mays and bounced toward left field. By the time it had been returned, the gangly Alston had circled the bases with an inside-the-park home run.

Whitey Lockman and Wes Westrum hit over-the-fence homers in the fifth, giving the Giants a 5-4 lead.

But Musial put St. Louis back on top with a two-run shot in the bottom of the fifth. Stan golfed a low inside fastball onto the pavilion roof.

Al Brazle took the mound for the Cardinals in the sixth. He yielded a game-tying home run to Monte Irvin.

Reliever Jim Hearn held Musial to a line-drive single in the sixth, and the game remained tied until "The Man" came up again in the eighth.

Moon was on second and Schoendienst was on first this time. Hearn tried to get a slider past Musial on the inside, but Stan whipped it to right. The ball just made it to the roof near the foul line. It was Stan's shortest home run of the day, but it put St. Louis into the lead.

The Cardinals added another run before the end of the inning, and Brazle shut the Giants out in the ninth, giving St. Louis a 10-6 victory.

In the second game, the Cardinals jumped out to 3-0 lead in the first inning against the Giants'

Don Liddle. Alston's bases-loaded double drove in the runs.

Musial, who had walked in the first, was finally retired in the third. Stan hit perhaps his longest drive of the day, 410 feet to left center, but Mays made a fine running catch on the warning track.

Apparently buoyed by getting Musial out, the Giants sent twelve men to the plate and scored eight runs in the top of the fourth. A triple and two singles knocked starter Joe Presko out. Pinch-hitter Bobby Hofman greeted reliever Royce Lint with a three-run homer. Mueller later got a two-run single to rout Lint, and Mays greeted Mel Wright, the new pitcher, with a two-run single, making the score 8-3.

In the fifth, Musial hit a slow curve from Hoyt Wilhelm onto Grand Avenue for a two-run home run. Jablonski followed with another homer, and the Cardinals were back in the game, trailing 8-6.

Musial picked a Wilhelm knuckleball and deposited it onto the street car tracks beyond the pavilion in the seventh inning for his fifth homer of the day. That prompted a change of pitcher, Larry Jansen coming in.

Jansen batted in an insurance run for New York in the ninth.

Then he faced Musial, leading off the bottom of the last. Stan was a bit anxious, and, on the second pitch, he chased a high fastball, popping an easy fly to first base. It was the only ball he hadn't hit hard all day.

Nearly all of the fans had stayed around to see Stan's last at bat. Now they streamed out, hardly caring to see the final two outs that spelled defeat for the Cardinals. Jansen was given credit for the Giant's 9-7 victory.

But, win or lose, the big show had been the record-setting home run punch of Stan Musial.

FIRST GAME

New York	ab	r	h	bi	o	a	e
D. Williams, 2b	4	1	1	0	2	1	0
A. Dark, ss	4	0	1	0	0	2	1
H. Thompson, 3b	4	1	1	1	1	4	1
M. Irvin, lf	3	2	2	2	2	0	0
D. Mueller, rf	4	0	1	1	0	0	0
W. Mays, cf	3	0	0	0	2	0	0
W. Lockman, 1b	4	1	1	1	9	1	0
W. Westrum, c	4	1	2	1	7	2	0
J. Antonelli, p	2	0	0	0	1	1	0
J. Hearn, p5	0	0	0	0	0	0	0
M. Picone, p8	0	0	0	0	0	0	0
B. Hofman, ph9	1	0	0	0	-	-	-
	33	6	9	6	24	11	2

St. Louis	ab	r	h	bi	o	a	e
W. Moon, cf	5	2	2	1	2	0	0
R. Schoendienst, 2b	3	3	0	0	3	3	0
S. Musial, rf	4	3	4	6	4	0	0
R. Jablonski, 3b	5	0	1	0	0	2	0
R. Repulski, lf	5	1	2	0	2	0	0
T. Alston, 1b	4	1	4	2	8	1	0
A. Grammas, ss	2	0	0	0	1	1	0
S. Hemus, ph5-ss	3	0	1	1	0	0	0
D. Rice, c	3	0	0	0	6	1	0
G. Staley, p	1	0	0	0	1	2	0
P. Lowrey, ph5	1	0	0	0	-	-	-
A. Brazle, p6	1	0	0	0	0	0	0
	37	10	14	10	27	10	0

New York 000 321 000 - 6
St. Louis 201 120 04x - 10

	ip	h	r-er	bb	so
Antonelli	*4	6	6-5	3	4
Hearn (L 0-2)	3.1	8	4-4	2	2
Picone	.2	0	0-0	0	0
Staley	5	7	5-5	0	3
Brazle (W 1-0)	4	2	1-1	2	3

*faced three batters in fifth

LOB: NY 3, StL 9.
DP: Schoendienst-Grammas-Alston, Jablonski-Schoendienst-Alston.
2B: Thompson, Irvin, Repulski.
HR: Moon, Musial 3, Alston, Lockman, Westrum, Irvin.
SH: Staley, Hearn.
Time - 2:43
Attendance - 26,663
Umpires: A. Donatelli, L. Ballanfant, A. Barlick, & L. Warneke

SECOND GAME

		r	h	e	Batteries
New York	000 800 001 -	9	13	0	D. Liddle 3 IP, H. Wilhelm 3 IP, L. Jansen (W 3-0) 3 IP & B. St. Claire, W. Westrum.
St. Louis	300 030 100 -	7	10	0	J. Presko 3.1 IP, R. Lint (L 1-1) .1 IP, M. Wright 2.1 IP, T. Poholsky 1 IP, C. Deal 2 IP & B. Sarni, D. Rice.

Musial finished the 1954 season with 35 home runs and a .330 batting average. The Cardinals had the most potent offense in the league, but lacked pitching and finished a lowly sixth.

Their record was 72-82. It was their first sub-.500 year since 1938.

1955 — Wednesday Night, June 1st, at Forbes Field, Pittsburgh

Rookie Luis Arroyo Wins Sixth Straight Game for St. Louis

Puerto Rican Southpaw's E.R.A. Drops to 1.55

Rookies Virdon and Boyer Get Three Hits Apiece in 6-2 Victory

The St. Louis Cardinals, with rookies playing a prominent part, defeated the slumping Pittsburgh Pirates tonight, 6-2, It was the second victory in five games for St. Louis since Harry Walker replaced Eddie Stanky as manager. For Pittsburgh it was the 18th defeat in the last 20 decisions.

The winning pitcher was the Cardinals' rookie sensation Luis Arroyo, who raised his won-lost record to 6-0 and lowered his earned run average to a league-leading 1.55. The six Arroyo victories represent almost one-third of the team's season win total of 19.

Today's Results
ST. LOUIS 6 - Pittsburgh 2
Brooklyn 11 - Milwaukee 8
Philadelphia 3 - Chicago 1
Cincinnati 5 - New York 2

Standings	W-L	Pct.	GB
Brooklyn	33-11	.750	-
Chicago	27-18	.600	6½
New York	24-22	.522	10
Milwaukee	21-23	.477	12
ST. LOUIS	19-22	.463	12½
Cincinnati	19-23	.452	13
Philadelphia	19-25	.432	14
Pittsburgh	13-31	.295	20

Two other rookies, center fielder Bill Virdon and third baseman Ken Boyer, split half of the Cardinals' twelve hits. Each man got three singles. Both Virdon and Boyer scored, Virdon drove in two men, and Boyer contributed one RBI. Boyer was a teammate of Arroyo's last year in Houston. Virdon was at Rochester, where he led the International League in batting.

Arroyo, the oldest of the three at age 28, was born in Puerto Rico. He first pitched in the United States in 1948, and he reached the Triple A level in 1950. But he sat out the entire 1952 and 1953 seasons with a mysterious arm ailment. Last year he came back and split time between Columbus, Georgia, and Houston, Texas, posting an overall record of 16-9. He finished the season very strongly, pitching a no-hitter and games in which he struck out 17 and 15 batters. In the Texas League, opposing hitters were only able to hit .188 against his delivery.

Although he had a terrible spring training this year (his E.R.A. was 7.00) he was brought north with the parent club. When he was given a chance to start a regular-season game, he made the most of it, hurling 7-1/3 shutout innings in Cincinnati. His next start didn't come for another three weeks, but Luis was ready. He went the distance in a ten-inning victory over the Phillies. Virdon won that game for him with a home run. Since then, Arroyo has been a regular part of the pitching rotation, and he had shut out the Pirates and beaten the Reds two more times before posting his sixth win tonight. His best pitch has been a lively fastball that runs away from righthanded hitters. He has also shown a decent curve, a change-up, and good control.

Tonight, the Cardinals gave him a lead even before he went to the mound. In the top of the first, Red Schoendienst singled and moved to second on a passed ball. He eventually scored on Virdon's single to left.

Arroyo walked the first man he faced in the bottom of the first, but that runner was quickly wiped out by a double play. The little lefthander did not issue another free pass all night.

Arroyo himself drove in the second Red Bird run. It came in the second inning. With two outs, Boyer was on second base after an error, a force play, and a stolen base. Luis then bounced one up the middle. Second baseman Dick Cole made a nice stop behind the bag. Nonetheless, Walker, coaching third, waved Boyer home. Cole's throw was weak, and catcher Jack Shepard had to stretch out to get it while still trying to block the plate. Boyer ran him over, football style, and the ball rolled away as the run scored. Shepard was so shaken up by the collision that he left the game.

The Cardinals added three more runs off Pittsburgh starter Bob Purkey in the third. After two men were out, Rip Repulski was given a base on balls. Virdon followed with another single. Catcher Bill Sarni then doubled the two runners home. Boyer singled Sarni across the pan, and St. Louis led 5-0.

Given the big lead, Arroyo let up a little in the bottom of the third. Dick Groat and Dale Long opened the Pirate rally with one-base hits. After pinch-hitter Felipe Montemayor struck out, Roberto Clemente, Pittsburgh's prized Puerto Rican rookie, singled Groat home. Long advanced to third on an error and scored on an infield out.

That was the only trouble Arroyo had. He allowed just six hits, three of which came in the third. The last Pirate to reach base safely was Roman Mejias, who doubled with one out in the sixth. After that, Arroyo set the last eleven Pittsburghs down in order.

Nellie King of the Pirates pitched five scoreless innings of relief, then was removed for a pinch-hitter in the eighth.

Vernon Law pitched the ninth and was touched for the Cardinals' final run. Law's own error gave Wally Moon a life. A two-out single by Virdon drove Moon home. Three hits on the night raised the bespectacled Virdon's average to a healthy .348.

The Cardinals won by a fine score of 6-2.

If the rookies could perform that well against first-division opposition, the new Harry Walker regime could turn out to be successful.

St. Louis	ab	r	h	bi	o	a	e
W. Moon, rf	5	1	0	0	2	0	0
R. Schoendienst, 2b	5	1	1	0	2	2	0
S. Musial, 1b	4	0	0	0	10	2	0
R. Repulski, lf	3	1	1	0	3	0	0
B. Virdon, cf	4	1	3	2	6	0	1
B. Sarni, c	5	1	1	2	2	0	0
K. Boyer, 3b	4	1	3	1	0	4	0
A. Grammas, ss	4	0	1	0	1	3	1
L. Arroyo, p	4	0	2	1	1	3	0
	38	6	12	6	27	14	2

Pittsburgh	ab	r	h	bi	o	a	e
R. Clemente, rf	3	0	1	1	2	0	0
D. Cole, 2b	4	0	0	1	2	3	0
R. Mejias, lf	4	0	1	0	1	1	0
F. Thomas, cf	4	0	0	0	5	0	0
Geo. Freese, 3b	4	0	1	0	2	3	0
J. Shepard, c	0	0	0	0	0	0	0
H. Peterson, c2	3	0	0	0	1	3	1
D. Groat, ss	3	1	2	0	5	4	1
D. Long, 1b	3	1	1	0	8	3	0
B. Purkey, p	0	0	0	0	0	0	0
F. Montemayor, ph3	1	0	0	0	-	-	-
N. King, p4	0	0	0	0	1	0	0
Eug. Freese, ph8	1	0	0	0	-	-	-
V. Law, p8	0	0	0	0	0	0	1
	30	2	6	2	27	17	3

St. Louis   113 000 001 - 6
Pittsburgh   002 000 000 - 2

	ip	h	r-er	bb	so
Arroyo (W 6-0)	9	6	2-1	1	2
Purkey (L 2-5)	3	6	5-4	2	1
King	5	5	0-0	1	0
Law	1	1	1-0	1	0

Umpires: L. Ballanfant, A, Barlick, B. Jackowski, & S. Landes

LOB: StL 9, Pitts 3.
DP: Schoendienst-Grammas-Musial, Long-Groat-Long.
2B: Sarni, Mejias. SH: King.
SB: Boyer.
PB: Shepard.
Time - 2:27
Attendance - 7,580

Arroyo lost his next start to the Dodgers, 5-4, on a ninth-inning home run by Jackie Robinson. Luis was 10-3 at the All-Star break and was named to the National League squad.

But he lost his effectiveness in the second half of the season and finished with an 11-8 mark and a 4.19 E.R.A.

Boyer and Virdon both did well throughout the year, and Virdon won the Rookie-of-the-Year Award.

But St. Louis's youth and lack of pitching depth added up to a dismal seventh-place finish, which cost Walker his job as manager. The Cardinals' record was 68-86, their worst since 1924.

Chapter X
Gussie Waits For a Winner
1956-1962

1956—September 29th at Busch Stadium
Cardinals Knock Braves Out of First Place with 12-Inning Win

1957—July 28th at Busch Stadium
Von McDaniel Hurls One-Hitter as Cardinals Win Pair

1958—May 13th at Chicago
Musial Gets 3,000th Hit, Pinch Double Keys Winning Rally

1959—April 16th at Los Angeles
Cardinals Use 25 Men but Lose to Los Angeles, 7-6

1960—August 11th at Pittsburgh
Musial Homer Beats Pirates in 12th, Cards Trail Bucs by 4

1961—July 18th at Sportsman's Park
Cards Sweep Again, White's Hit Total to 14 in Two Days

1962—July 8th at New York
Musial Hits Three Straight Home Runs as Cards Trounce Mets

After the Cardinals had fallen to seventh place in 1955, club president Gussie Busch hired a veteran baseball man, Frank Lane, as general manager. Lane brought in Freddie Hutchinson to manage the team and made a flurry of trades. The moves didn't pan out in 1956, however, and the Cardinals were not serious contenders for the pennant, finishing fourth. They did, however, knock the Milwaukee Braves out of first place on the final weekend of the season.

In 1957, Lane's moves began to bear fruit, and the Cardinals were in the thick of the race that summer. The pitching staff had no real "ace," but two bonus-baby brothers, Lindy and Von McDaniel, pitched well and caught the public's fancy, especially 18-year-old Von. He was fresh out of high school, yet he pitched a two-hit shutout and a one-hit shutout. The Cardinals were in first place as late as August 5th, but then they fell behind the Braves. St. Louis finished second, 8 games behind.

Lane wanted his contract extended after the successful season, but was fired instead. Bing Devine, who had started with the club in the days of Branch Rickey, was made general manager.

In 1958, the Red Birds got off to a horrible start (3-14). But that was overshadowed by Stan Musial's assault on the 3,000 hit plateau. Stan the Man reached the milestone in Chicago on May 13th. In a closely-packed race, St. Louis rose to second place, just 1½ games out of first, by the Fourth of July. But the team swooned in July and was in last place by August 3rd. It wound up the season tied for fifth.

Solly Hemus replaced Hutchinson as manager in 1959. The team started poorly again and never recovered. Hemus tried everything, even using 25 men in one loss, but his roster was not balanced, and the Red Birds finished seventh.

In 1960, the Cards lost their first five games and did not get over .500 to stay until July 2nd. But with Larry Jackson and Ernie Broglio pitching well as starters and Lindy McDaniel starring in relief, the Birds moved into contention. With youngsters Julian Javier, Curt Flood, and Bill White developing, the St. Louis lineup was good, too. The Cardinals got as close as 3 games of the top by winning games in Pittsburgh on August 11th and 12th, but then the first-place Pirates beat them three straight times, and St. Louis never got close again. The Cardinals finished third.

Jackson started the 1961 season with a broken jaw, and Broglio and McDaniel both slumped. The Cardinals got off to another slow start, and Hemus was fired on July 6th. Coach Johnny Keane became manager, and the team quickly improved. On July 17th and 18th, the Cards won back-to-back twi-night doubleheaders from the Cubs, with Bill White making 14 hits in the two days. But St. Louis was too far behind to threaten the league-leaders, and the Cardinals finished the year in fifth place.

In 1962, the Cardinals won their first seven games, but a slump in May killed their pennant chances. The National League had expanded to ten clubs, and the St. Louis offense was helped. Bill White drove in 102 runs, and Stan Musial had a great year at age 41, batting .330. Against the Mets in early July, he hit home runs in four consecutive at bats, including three in one game. The Cardinals' pitching was improving, with young hurlers like Bob Gibson and Ray Washburn showing up well. But the team had troubles in the bullpen and at shortstop and only finished sixth.

1956—Saturday, September 29th at Busch Stadium

Cardinals Knock Braves Out of First Place with 12-Inning Triumph

Wehmeier Bests Spahn in Brilliant Pitching Duel, 2-1

Doubles by Musial and Repulski Account for Winning Run

The St. Louis Cardinals had been in fourth place since July 13th. They were assured of finishing in that spot a week ago. But their final three-game series of the season against the Milwaukee Braves gave them a chance to affect the outcome of the pennant race. By winning the first two games of the series, yesterday and today, the Cards knocked the Braves off the top rung of the standings.

The two defeats at the hands of St. Louis, coupled with a doubleheader sweep by Brooklyn today, dropped Milwaukee from 1 game ahead with three to play to 1 behind with just one game left. In other words, the Braves' chances of bringing Milwaukee its first major league pennant suddenly went from good to very slim, despite the fact that the Braves had been in first place for 121 of the 166 days in the season.

Today's Results
ST. LOUIS 2 - Milwaukee 1 (12 inn.)
Brooklyn 6 - Pittsburgh 2 (1st game)
Brooklyn 3 - Pittsburgh 1 (2nd)
Cincinnati 9 - Chicago 6
New York 2 - Philadelphia 0

Standings	W-L	Pct.	GB
Brooklyn	92-61	.601	-
Milwaukee	91-62	.595	1
Cincinnati	90-63	.588	2
ST. LOUIS	76-77	.497	16
Philadelphia	70-82	.461	21½
New York	66-86	.434	25½
Pittsburgh	66-87	.431	26
Chicago	60-93	.392	32

Friday's game was a tense affair. The Cardinals won, 5-4, when three relievers held off the Braves' desperate efforts to tie the game.

In today's game, a crowd of over 25,000 was treated to one of the finest pitching duels of the season. Harm Wehmeier, pitching for the home team, gave up a home run to the Braves' second batter in the first inning. Then he shut the visitors out for eleven rounds. Milwaukee's Warren Spahn, the perennial 20-game winner, held the Cardinals to just two hits through the first nine innings. But those hits, back-to-back doubles in the sixth, tied the game. The Cards finally broke through with one out in the bottom of the twelfth with two more doubles for the winning run. Spahn ended with a five-hitter, but that wasn't good enough to avoid defeat. Milwaukee found Wehmeier for nine hits, although only four of them came after the third inning.

Both pitchers received good fielding support. No errors were made, and several fine plays cut off potential hits.

After Johnny Logan, leading off the top of the first, was retired, Bill Bruton drove the next pitch from Wehmeier onto the roof in right field for a home run. Hank Aaron scratched a hit, but the next two batters went out.

The Braves wasted a leadoff single by Bobby Thomson in the second.

Logan opened the third with a single. Bruton followed with a bouncer up the middle, which second baseman Don Blasingame stopped in fine style. Being off balance, Blasingame did not throw to first. But Logan, who evidently thought the ball went through to center field, rounded second base. He quickly realized his mistake, but Blasingame's toss to shortstop Al Dark was in time to nip Logan as he dove back to the base. That killed a potentially big inning.

St. Louis got a man to first base on a walk in the third, but he was left.

Both sides went out in order in the fourth, and a walk to Logan provided the only base runner in the fifth.

Aaron opened the sixth with a single, but Eddie Mathews bounced into a double play.

The first two Cardinals in the bottom of the sixth went out. Then Blasingame got the first hit against Spahn. It was a double into the gap in right center. Dark followed with a long drive to the wall in left center. It was good for another two bagger and St. Louis tied the score, 1-1.

Thomson got another leadoff hit in the seventh, but, once again, nothing came of it.

The Braves hit the ball hard in the ninth, but were turned back by some fine fielding by Bobby Del Greco. The Red Bird center fielder went crashing into the fence in deepest center to make a catch of Mathews's liner. Joe Adcock followed with a single, and Thomson looked at a third strike. Jack Dittmer then drove one deep to right center, but Del Greco got the ball with a running, one-handed catch just in front of the warning track.

Spahn, in the meantime, was in command for the Braves. He shut St. Louis out from the seventh through the eleventh. Ken Boyer, who singled in the tenth, was the only Cardinal to reach base. Two Cards hit the ball hard in the eleventh. Del Greco hit a liner over shortstop, but Logan leaped high and speared the ball. Blasingame smashed one up the middle, but Spahn knocked it down with a fine effort and tossed the batter out at first.

Milwaukee had threatened in the top of the eleventh. Aaron singled, and Mathews walked with one out. But Adcock and Thomson hit into force plays, leaving a runner on third.

Dittmer walked to open the Braves' twelfth, but no trouble resulted.

With one out in the bottom of the twelfth, Stan Musial got his first hit of the day, a long double off the fence in right center. The Braves decided to walk Boyer intentionally to get to Rip Repulski, who was hitless in four at bats. The strategy almost resulted in a force out at third. But Repulski's hard shot down the line glanced off Mathews's glove as the third baseman made a desperate stab at it. The ball deflected to the tarpaulin against the grandstand fence, and Musial steamed around third and scored the game-winning run standing up.

Spahn was so disgusted that he threw his glove at a photographer who attempted to take a picture of the dejected hurler as he trudged off the mound. It was a bitter defeat for the Braves and a most satisfying victory for the Cardinals.

Milwaukee	ab	r	h	bi	o	a	e	St. Louis	ab	r	h	bi	o	a	e
J. Logan, ss	5	0	1	0	4	6	0	D. Blasingame, 2b	5	1	1	0	2	5	0
B. Bruton, cf	5	1	2	1	3	0	0	A. Dark, ss	5	0	1	1	5	3	0
H. Aaron, rf	5	0	3	0	4	0	0	S. Musial, 1b	5	1	1	0	9	2	0
E. Mathews, 3b	4	0	0	0	2	1	0	K. Boyer, 3b	4	0	1	0	2	2	0
J. Adcock, 1b	5	0	1	0	11	0	0	R. Repulski, lf	5	0	1	1	5	0	0
B. Thomson, lf	5	0	2	0	2	0	0	W. Moon, rf	4	0	0	0	1	0	0
J. Dittmer, 2b	4	0	0	0	3	3	0	R. Katt, c	4	0	0	0	3	0	0
F. Mantilla, pr12	0	0	0	0	-	-	-	B. Del Greco, cf	3	0	0	0	8	0	0
D. O'Connell, 2b12	0	0	0	0	0	0	0	H. Wehmeier, p	4	0	0	0	1	3	0
D. Crandall, c	4	0	0	0	5	0	0								
W. Spahn, p	5	0	0	0	0	1	0								
	42	1	9	1	34	11	0		39	2	5	2	36	15	0

Milwaukee   100 000 000 000 - 1
St. Louis   000 001 000 001 - 2
one out when winning run scored

	ip	h	r-er	bb	so
Spahn (L 20-11)	11.1	5	2-2	2	3
Wehmeier (W 12-11)	12	9	1-1	3	3

Umpires: F. Dascoli, F. Secory, B. Engeln, & L. Goetz

LOB: Milw 9, StL 5.
DP: Blasingame-Dark-Musial.
2B: Blasingame, Dark, Musial, Repulski.
HR: Bruton.
SH: Crandall.
Time - 2:38 Attendance - 25,587

Milwaukee beat St. Louis on the final day of the season, 4-2, but Brooklyn outlasted Pittsburgh, 8-6, and the Dodgers won the pennant by 1 game.

St. Louis finished fourth, 17 games out, with a 76-78 record.

1957 — Sunday, July 28th at Busch Stadium
Von McDaniel Hurls One-Hitter as Cardinals Sweep a Pair
Youngster Allows Only One Man to Reach Base in Winning Opener, 4-0
Birds Rally in Nightcap and Win Thriller, 9-8

With their 18-year-old pitching sensation Von McDaniel back on the beam, the St. Louis Cardinals defeated the Pittsburgh Pirates in the first game of today's doubleheader, 4-0. Then they came back in the second game and won in eleven innings, 9-8. The double victory put the Cards just ½ game out of first place in the red-hot National League pennant race. They have shaken off a mid-July slump, which had dropped them from the lead, and have now won seven of their last nine games.

Von McDaniel raised his record to 5-2 with an impressive one-hitter. The only hit off his deliveries was a fly-ball double, which fell just fair in the left field corner. McDaniel walked no one and faced just 28 batters. He needed only 99 pitches to complete the game.

Today's Results
ST. LOUIS 4 - Pittsburgh 0 (1st game)
ST. LOUIS 9 - Pittsburgh 8 (11 inn.)(2nd)
New York 2 - Milwaukee 0 (1st game)
Milwaukee 5 - New York 3 (2nd)
Brooklyn 7 - Cincinnati 2
Philadelphia 3 - Chicago 2 (1st game)
Philadelphia 7 - Chicago 1 (2nd)

Standings	W-L	Pct.	GB
Milwaukee	57-41	.582	-
ST. LOUIS	55-40	.579	½
Brooklyn	54-41	.568	1½
Philadelphia	54-43	.557	2½
Cincinnati	54-43	.557	2½
New York	43-54	.443	13½
Pittsburgh	36-62	.367	21
Chicago	32-61	.344	22½

The second game was a seesaw affair. The Cardinals got out to an early 3-0 lead but trailed, 8-5, before rallying for three runs in the ninth inning to tie the game. They won it in the eleventh, 9-8, on a home run by Joe Cunningham.

Von McDaniel, younger brother of Cardinal pitcher Lindy McDaniel, was in high school in Oklahoma just two months ago. After signing a $50,000 bonus contract with St. Louis, he made his professional debut on June 13th, pitching in relief. He got his first win on the 17th, also in relief. On June 21st he got his first starting assignment, and he shut out the powerful Brooklyn Dodgers on just two hits, 2-0. He won his next two starts, beating Philadelphia and Milwaukee, with relief help from Hoyt Wilhelm each time. After a seven-inning effort in which he got no decision, Von was rocked for defeats in his last two outings.

But today he came back strong. Before the game he had carefully gone over the Pittsburgh hitters with his brother. He had also worked on rotating his hips more during his windup, thereby reducing the strain on his arm. And manager Fred Hutchinson and pitching coach Al Hollingsworth convinced him to use his breaking ball more today. All the advice paid off.

It all added up to the best pitched game by a Cardinal this year. The only hit against McDaniel came off the bat of Gene Baker. Batting with two out in the second inning, Baker lifted a fly ball down the left field line. The defense was not expecting him to pull the ball, and left fielder Del Ennis could not get to it. The ball fell safely into the corner, just a few feet fair. Baker was left on second base when Bill Mazeroski popped to first base.

McDaniel then set the Pirates down in order in the last seven innings. The only difficult chances for his fielders came in the seventh, when Don Blasingame made two fine plays. On one he dove to his left to short-hop a shot by Dick Groat, throwing the batter out at first by a step. The next batter, Bob Skinner, hit one up the middle, but Blasingame knocked it down and threw Skinner out on another close play.

Meanwhile, the Cardinals pushed single runs over the plate in four different innings against the Pirates' Vernon Law. Blasingame scored in the first on a single, a stolen base and throwing error, and a sacrifice fly. Singles by Ennis and Ken Boyer and an infield out produced a run in the fourth inning. Eddie Kasko and Blasingame singled around a sacrifice by McDaniel for a tally in the seventh. The final run came in the eighth on hits by Al Dark, Wally Moon, and Boyer.

In the second game, the Cardinals jumped ahead with two runs in the first inning. Boyer drove them both in with a bases-loaded single.

A double by Blasingame and a single by Dark made the score 3-0 in the second.

Then Pittsburgh routed Cardinal starter Larry Jackson with five runs in the third inning. Home runs by Bill Virdon (with two men on) and George Thomas (with one on) were the big blows.

The Cardinals came back to tie the game in the fourth on an error by Dee Fondy followed by a home run by Stan Musial.

But the Pirates went ahead again in the sixth, 7-5, on a two-run single by Mazeroski.

An error by pitcher Herm Wehmeier game the visitors an additional run in the ninth.

Ron Kline, who had pitched three hitless innings in relief of Bob Friend, was still on the mound in the bottom of the ninth. He walked Musial, then allowed hits by Moon and Boyer, plating one run. Joe Cunningham walked, filling the bases, and Pirate manager Bobby Bragan brought in Art "Red" Swanson to try and put out the fire. He got the first man he faced, Hal Smith, to hit into a double play. The score was 8-7 with two out when Kasko came through with a clutch double, knocking in the tying run.

Hoyt Wilhelm, pitching for St. Louis, escaped trouble in both the tenth and eleventh. A good grab by Kasko of a liner saved the bacon in the latter inning.

Then Cunningham, leading off the bottom of the eleventh against Nellie King, plastered the first pitch onto the roof in right field for a home run, winning the game, 9-8.

It was a thrilling victory for the Cardinals. But most of the talk afterwards centered around the first game and the phenomenal pitching of 18-year-old Von McDaniel.

Pittsburgh	ab	r	h	bi	o	a	e	St. Louis	ab	r	h	bi	o	a	e
D. Fondy, 1b	4	0	0	0	10	1	0	D. Blasingame, 2b	4	1	2	1	0	6	0
B. Virdon, cf	3	0	0	0	1	0	0	A. Dark, ss	4	0	1	0	0	3	0
D. Groat, ss	3	0	0	0	1	2	0	S. Musial, 1b	3	0	0	1	14	1	0
B. Skinner, lf	3	0	0	0	4	0	0	W. Moon, rf	4	1	3	0	1	0	0
G. Thomas, rf	3	0	0	0	2	1	0	D. Ennis, lf	4	1	1	0	1	0	0
G. Baker, 3b	3	0	1	0	0	1	0	E. Miksis, pr8-lf	0	0	0	0	1	0	0
B. Mazeroski, 2b	3	0	0	0	2	5	0	K. Boyer, cf	4	0	2	1	4	0	0
H. Foiles, c	2	0	0	0	4	0	1	H. Landrith, c	4	0	1	1	4	0	0
P. Smith, ph9	1	0	0	0	-	-	-	E. Kasko, 3b	2	1	1	0	1	2	0
V. Law, p	2	0	0	0	0	5	0	V. McDaniel, p	2	0	0	0	1	1	0
E. Freese, ph9	1	0	0	0	-	-	-								
	28	0	1	0	24	15	1		31	4	11	4	27	13	0

Pittsburgh	000	000	000	-	0
St. Louis	100	100	11x	-	4

LOB: Pitts 1, StL 6. BE: none.
DP: Law-Mazeroski-Fondy.
2B: Moon, Baker, Landrith.
SH: McDaniel. SF: Musial.
SB: Blasingame.
Time - 2:13
Attendance - 21,319

	ip	h	r-er	bb	so
Law (L 7-4)	8	11	4-4	1	2
McDaniel (W 5-2)	9	1	0-0	0	4

Umpires: J. Conlan, A. Donatelli, V. Delmore, & V. Smith

SECOND GAME

		r	h	e	Batteries
Pittsburgh	005 020 001 00 -	8	14	1	B. Friend 5 IP, R. Kline 3 IP, R. Swanson 1 IP, N. King (L 2-1) 1 IP & H. Peterson, D. Rand.
St. Louis	210 200 003 01 -	9	16	3	L. Jackson 2.2 IP, W. Schmidt 2.1 IP, L. Merritt 3 IP, H. Wehmeier 1 IP, H. Wilhelm (W 1-4) 2 IP & H. Smith.

none out when winning run scored

The Cardinals won their next six games, to take a 1-game lead. But after splitting a doubleheader, they then lost nine in a row to fall 8½ games behind the Braves. They closed to within 2½ games in mid-September, but finished 8 games behind Milwaukee.

St. Louis wound up in second place with an 87-67 record.

Von McDaniel finished with a 7-5 mark.

1958—Tuesday, May 13th at Wrigley Field, Chicago
Musial Cracks Pinch Double for 3,000th Hit, Keys Winning Rally
Stan's Sixth-Inning Double off Drabowsky Drives in a Run
Congratulations Interrupt Game, Then Cards Win, 5-3

Inspired by Stan Musial's history-making 3,000th base hit, the St. Louis Cardinals rallied to defeat the Chicago Cubs today, 5-3. Musial had been held out of the starting lineup by manager Freddie Hutchinson in order to allow him to reach the milestone in front of the hometown St. Louis fans. But, with his team behind, a man in scoring position, and the pitcher due up, Hutchinson called on Stan The Man in a pinch-hitting role in the sixth inning. The old pro delivered an opposite-field double to score the runner. There followed a mob scene at second base, as Hutchinson and a small army of photographers ran out to congratulate the hero. Musial was then removed for a pinch-runner, and he and the press corps retreated to the clubhouse for interviews and more pictures.

Today's Results
ST. LOUIS 5 - Chicago 3
San Francisco 16 - Los Angeles 9
Philadelphia 5 - Milwaukee 2
Pittsburgh 6 - Cincinnati 3

Standings	W-L	Pct.	GB
San Francisco	17-9	.654	-
Milwaukee	15-8	.652	½
Pittsburgh	16-9	.640	½
Chicago	13-14	.481	4½
Cincinnati	9-12	.429	5½
Philadelphia	10-15	.400	6½
ST. LOUIS	9-14	.391	6½
Los Angeles	9-17	.346	8

Meanwhile, back on the field, the Cardinals continued to hit the ball and finished the inning with four runs, which were enough to win the game.

After winning his seventh National League batting championship in 1957, Musial, traditionally a slow starter, made a remarkable assault on the 3,000-hit plateau this season. He started the year 43 hits short of the goal. It took him just 23 games to make those 43 hits. He started off with a 17-game hitting streak. After two straight hitless games, he came back with six hits in the three games immediately previous to today, bringing his lifetime total to 2,999.

With the Cardinals due to return home for a game tomorrow, it was decided to save Stan's 3,000th hit for the home fans. But, with an opportunity to turn the game around and with baseball's hottest hitter on the bench, Hutchinson played his ace in the pinch. Musial, of course, delivered in fine style, helping the Cardinals win. The hit brought Stan's average for the season to .489.

With Musial out of the starting lineup, Hutchinson shifted Joe Cunningham to first base from the outfield and inserted Gene Green into right field. The Cubs presented their regular lineup. Sam Jones pitched for St. Louis, and Moe Drabowsky was on the hill for Chicago.

Chicago scored once in the first inning on Lee Walls's double, a wild pitch, and a sacrifice fly.

The Cardinals tied the score in the third, thanks to two errors. But they missed Musial's big bat when they had the bases loaded with no one out. One run scored on a hit by Irv Noren, but Wally Moon, Ken Boyer, and Green all failed to bring in another run, and the bases were left loaded.

Walls put the Cubs ahead with a home run over the left field fence in the bottom of the third. And he drove in another run with a long fly in the fifth.

The Cardinals were trailing, 3-1, entering the sixth. Green opened with a double to right field. He had to hold second while shortstop Ernie Banks was throwing Hal Smith out. With Jones due up next, Hutchinson decided to use Musial. Stan had been sunning himself in the bullpen, and he received a great cheer when he came to the dugout to pick out a bat.

Anticipation was high as The Man strode to the plate. Chicago manager Bob Scheffing didn't want to put the potential tying run on base, so he ordered Drabowsky to pitch to Musial with first base open. Moe worked carefully, running the count to two balls and two strikes.

The next pitch was a curveball on the outside corner. It came in a little bit higher than

Drabowsky had hoped. Using his classic swing, Musial uncoiled from out of the deepest corner of the batter's box. Keeping his hands back as he pivoted his hips, he stroked the ball into the left field corner for a hit and got to second base easily, while Green scored.

Hit #3,000! Suddenly all else was forgotten. Third base umpire Frank Dascoli got the ball and gleefully trotted over and presented it to Musial. Hutchinson, followed by photographers, ran out from the dugout to congratulate his star. After much glad-handing at second base, a pinch-runner, Frank Barnes, took Stan's place on the bases, and the great man headed for the clubhouse. On the way, he stopped to give a kiss to his wife, Lillian, who was seated behind the visitors' dugout.

When play resumed, Drabowsky walked Dick Schofield, and Don Blasingame singled Barnes home, tying the score. Blasingame and Schofield moved up to second and third on the throw to the plate. Cunningham was given an intentional pass. Noren forced Cunningham at second but beat the throw to first, and Schofield crossed the plate with the go-ahead run. Moon followed with a double to deep right. Blasingame scored easily, but Noren was thrown out trying to get all the way home from first, ending the inning. St. Louis led, 5-3.

Billy Muffett was called in to protect the lead. He gave up two hits in the bottom of the sixth, but there was a double play in between them. He then pitched hitless ball over the last three innings, and the Cardinals won, 5-3.

It was St. Louis's sixth victory in a row, after the team had started the season winning only 3 of its first 17 games.

Meanwhile, in the clubhouse, Musial was fielding questions and posing for pictures. It seemed a little early in the season to talk about hitting .400, he thought, especially at age 37. But Honus Wagner's National League record of 3,430 hits definitely seemed within reach. More immediately, Stan said he was glad the quest for his 3,000th hit was over. And he wondered about the game. "Please turn on the radio," he requested. "What's the score?"

St. Louis	ab	r	h	bi	o	a	e
D. Schofield, ss	2	2	0	0	1	4	0
D. Blasingame, 2b	5	1	1	1	1	2	0
J. Cunningham, 1b	3	0	0	0	8	0	0
I. Noren, lf	4	0	2	2	3	0	0
W. Moon, cf	4	0	1	1	3	0	0
C. Flood, cf6	1	0	1	0	2	0	0
K. Boyer, 3b	4	0	1	0	1	2	0
G. Green, rf	5	1	1	0	1	0	0
H. Smith, c	4	0	1	0	7	0	0
S. Jones, p	2	0	0	0	0	1	0
S. Musial, ph6	1	0	1	1	-	-	-
F. Barnes, pr6	0	1	0	0	-	-	-
B. Muffett, p6	0	0	0	0	0	1	0
	35	5	9	5	27	10	0

Chicago	ab	r	h	bi	o	a	e
T. Taylor, 2b	4	0	1	0	3	5	1
L. Walls, rf	3	2	2	2	2	1	0
E. Banks, ss	3	0	0	1	1	7	0
W. Moryn, lf	4	0	1	0	1	0	1
D. Long, 1b	4	0	0	0	11	0	0
S. Taylor, c	3	0	2	0	4	0	0
B. Thomson, cf	3	1	0	0	2	0	0
J. Goryl, 3b	3	0	1	0	3	1	0
C. Tanner, ph9	1	0	0	0	-	-	-
M. Drabowsky, p	2	0	0	0	0	3	0
P. Smith, ph7	1	0	0	0	-	-	-
T. Phillips, p8	0	0	0	0	0	0	0
	31	3	7	3	27	17	2

St. Louis	001	004	000	-	5
Chicago	101	010	000	-	3

	ip	h	r-er	bb	so
Jones (W 2-3)	5	5	3-3	1	5
Muffett	4	2	0-0	1	2
Drabowsky (L 1-3)	7	8	5-4	5	3
Phillips	2	1	0-0	2	0

WP: Jones

LOB: StL 11, Chi 5. BE: StL 2.
DP: Banks-T. Taylor-Long 2, Muffett-Schofield-Cunningham.
2B: Walls, H. Smith, Green, Musial, Moon, Flood.
HR: Walls. SF: Banks, Walls.
HBP: by Drabowsky (Noren).
Time - 2:27 Attendance - 5,692
Umpires: A. Donatelli, S. Crawford, V. Smith, F. Dascoli.

The next night, in front of the St. Louis crowd, Musial homered in his first at bat and added two more hits, raising his average to an even .500. For the remainder of the season, however, he hit just under .300 and finished with a .337 mark.

The Cardinals climbed to second place and were just 1½ games behind the Braves on the Fourth of July. But then they faded badly and finished tied for fifth with a 72-82 record.

1959 — Thursday Night, April 16th at Memorial Coliseum, Los Angeles

Cardinals Use 25 Men in 7-6 Loss to Dodgers
Hemus Sends in All But Four of the Players on his Roster
Short Left Field Screen Gives Los Angeles Its Runs

Using a record-breaking cast of 25 characters, manager Solly Hemus and his St. Louis Cardinals closed out an unsuccessful three-day run in the movie capital of the nation, Los Angeles. The use of 25 men broke the old major league record for players used in a game. Eight of those men were used in cameo pinch-hitting roles, tying another big league record. When the curtain rang down, Hemus had used all of his players except for four pitchers, one of whom was not even in town tonight. But all the king's horses and all the king's men couldn't keep the hometown Dodgers from beating the Cardinals, 7-6.

For the losers, the most galling part of the

Today's Results
Los Angeles 7 - ST. LOUIS 6
Milwaukee 7 - Philadelphia 3
Chicago 11 - San Francisco 3
no other game scheduled

Standings	W-L	Pct.	GB
Milwaukee	4-0	1.000	-
Cincinnati	3-1	.750	1
San Francisco	4-2	.667	1
Chicago	3-2	.600	1½
Los Angeles	3-2	.600	1½
Philadelphia	1-2	.333	2½
ST. LOUIS	1-5	.167	4
Pittsburgh	0-5	.000	4½

performance was that they were beaten not so much by the opposing players as they were by the set designer. The Coliseum in Los Angeles was not designed for baseball, and when the Dodgers started playing here last year, the field was set up so that the left field fence was just 251 feet from the plate. A 42-foot screen was put up in left, but short pop flies could still become home runs. Today, the Cardinal pitchers held the Dodger batters to just four outfield flies. But three of those went over the barrier, and another bounced off it for a double, accounting for all the L.A. runs. The Cardinals got only one ball over the screen.

The Dodgers grabbed the lead in the bottom of the first inning and held it throughout the game. The Cardinals used all their available hitters in an unsuccessful attempt to catch up.

The Dodgers went to work on St. Louis starter Ernie Broglio in the bottom of the first. Ron Fairly, their lefthanded hitting leadoff man, lifted a fly ball over the screen for a quick run. Wally Moon walked and was forced out by Johnny Roseboro. Don Demeter then popped one over the nearby barrier, making the score 3-0.

Ken Boyer, leading off the second for the Cards, retaliated with a "Chinese" home run of his own. With one out, Curt Flood singled, Hal Smith doubled, and Alex Grammas walked. With the bases loaded, righthanded Bobby Gene Smith was announced as the game's first pinch-hitter. Dodger manager Walt Alston yanked southpaw Sandy Koufax out of the game and called in righthander Art Fowler. Hemus switched pinch-hitters, but Fowler struck out lefthanded hitting Irv Noren and also got Don Blasingame on strikes, retiring the side.

Los Angeles scored three runs off Howie Nunn in the fourth. Demeter opened with a hit. Charlie Neal fanned. Gil Hodges followed with a double play ball back to Nunn, but the pitcher bobbled it momentarily and had to settle for a force out. Then he made another mistake, walking Don Zimmer. That brought up Jim Baxes, a 30-year-old rookie. Nunn threw him a curve, and Baxes hit a pop fly that carried over the screen in left for a three-run homer. That made the score 6-1 in favor of the Dodgers.

The Cardinals got right back into the game in the fifth. Hemus sent himself up to bat for Nunn, bringing a small chorus of boos from the audience. Solly waited out a walk. With one out, Gino Cimoli singled. Stan Musial hit an easy DP ball to short, but Zimmer's high throw to second prevented anything more than a force out. Boyer took advantage of the mistake by driving Hemus in with a single. Chuck Essegian then pounded a 420-foot triple to straightaway center field, scoring two more runs. Johnny Klippstein replaced Fowler on the mound, and he retired Flood for the third out.

Rookie Bob Gibson, making his second appearance for the Cardinals, went in to pitch in the bottom of the fifth. He retired only one man and gave up a run on two singles and a double by Demeter off the screen.

With the score 7-4, the game settled down for three innings. Hemus tried four pinch-hitters and a pinch-runner, but they couldn't produce any runs against Klippstein.

In the ninth inning, Klippstein walked the first batter, Cimoli, and fell behind on the count to Musial, 2-and-0. Alston changed to Clem Labine, who had always been bothersome to Musial. But Clem threw two quick balls, and Stan walked. Boyer struck out, but Essegian drove in a run with a sharp single over third. With young Flood due up, Hemus used his last remaining hitter, Ray Jablonski, in the pinch. Labine walked him, loading the bases. The next three men in the order were two defensive replacements and the pitcher. Gene Green, who had taken over as catcher after Hal Smith had gone out for a pinch-hitter, tapped to the mound. Labine threw to second for a force, while Musial scored. The score was now 7-6. Two were out, and light-hitting infielder Lee Tate was due up. Hemus looked down the bench, but the only players left were pitchers. So Tate went up to the plate. He bounced to shortstop for a game-ending force out, and the Cardinals, for all their players and all their efforts, had come up one run short.

St. Louis	ab	r	h	bi	o	a	e
D. Blasingame, 2b	5	0	0	0	3	2	0
G. Cimoli, rf	4	1	2	0	0	0	0
S. Musial, 1b	3	2	0	0	7	0	0
K. Boyer, 3b	5	2	2	2	0	1	0
C. Essegian, lf	5	0	2	3	0	0	0
C. Flood, cf	4	0	2	0	0	0	0
R. Jablonski, ph9	0	0	0	0	-	-	-
H. Smith, c	2	0	1	0	8	0	0
G. Crowe, ph8	1	0	1	0	-	-	-
L. Jackson, pr8	0	0	0	0	-	-	-
G. Green, c8	1	0	0	1	2	0	0
A. Grammas, ss	2	0	0	0	2	4	0
B. White, ph8	1	0	0	0	-	-	-
L. Tate, ss8	1	0	0	0	1	0	0
E. Broglio, p	0	0	0	0	0	0	0
B. Smith, ph2	0	0	0	0	-	-	-
I. Noren, ph2	1	0	0	0	-	-	-
H. Nunn, p2	0	0	0	0	0	1	0
S. Hemus, ph5	0	1	0	0	-	-	-
B. Gibson, p5	0	0	0	0	1	0	0
P. Clark, p5	0	0	0	0	0	0	0
J. Durham, ph6	1	0	0	0	-	-	-
G. Blaylock, p6	0	0	0	0	0	0	0
J. Cunningham, ph8	0	0	0	0	-	-	-
J. Brosnan, p8	0	0	0	0	0	0	0
	36	6	10	6	24	8	0

Los Angeles	ab	r	h	bi	o	a	e
R. Fairly, rf	4	2	2	1	3	0	0
W. Moon, lf	3	0	0	0	4	0	0
J. Roseboro, c	4	1	1	0	6	0	0
D. Demeter, cf	4	1	3	3	1	0	0
C. Neal, 2b	3	0	0	0	4	0	0
G. Hodges, 1b	4	1	0	0	8	0	0
D. Zimmer, ss	2	1	0	0	0	8	0
J. Baxes, 3b	3	1	1	3	1	1	0
S. Koufax, p	0	0	0	0	0	0	0
A. Fowler, p2	2	0	0	0	0	0	0
J. Klippstein, p5	1	0	0	0	0	2	0
C. Labine, p9	0	0	0	0	0	1	0
	30	7	7	7	27	12	0

St. Louis   010 030 002 - 6
Los Angeles 300 310 00x - 7

	ip	h	r-er	bb	so
Broglio (L 0-2)	1	2	3-3	1	0
Nunn	3	2	3-3	1	6
Gibson	.1	3	1-1	0	0
Clark	.2	0	0-0	1	0
Blaylock	2	0	0-0	0	2
Brosnan	1	0	0-0	0	2
Koufax	1.1	3	1-1	1	0
Fowler	3.1	5	3-3	1	4
Klippstein (W 2-0)	3.1*	1	2-2	5	1
Labine	1	1	0-0	1	1

*faced two batters in ninth

LOB: StL 11, LA 2.
DP: Grammas-Blasingame-Musial.
2B: H. Smith, Demeter. 3B: Essegian.
HR: Fairly, Demeter, Boyer, Baxes.
Umpires: S. Landes, E. Sudol, D. Boggess, & T. Gorman
Time - 2:48
Attendance - 14,274

It was a long, trying season for Hemus and the Cardinals. They never got to the .500 mark and were never higher than tied for fifth. They finished seventh in the league in offense (runs scored), seventh in defense (runs against), and seventh in the standings. Their final record was 71-83.

The pinch-hitter-used record lasted only until September, 1959.

The players-used record was not broken until the Cardinals did it in a 25-inning game in New York on September 11, 1974.

1960 — Thursday Night, August 11th, at Forbes Field, Pittsburgh

Homer by Musial Beats Pirates in Twelfth, Cards Trail Bucs by 4 Games

Broglio and Friend Both Pitch Great Ball

Stan's Two-Run Shot Breaks 1-1 Tie, Ernie Holds On for 3-2 Victory

In one of the most dramatic games of the season, the St. Louis Cardinals edged the Pittsburgh Pirates in twelve innings, 3-2. The winning runs came on a two-run home run by veteran Stan Musial. The Pirates rallied for one run in the last of the twelfth, but they left the tying run on second base.

Aside from the dramatic finish, the feature of the game was the excellent pitching of St. Louis's Ernie Broglio and Pittsburgh's Bob Friend. Each man went the distance, Broglio allowing eight hits and Friend yielding seven. They struck out nine batters each. Friend had a streak of 18 consecutive hitters retired, and Broglio had a string of 20 in a row set down. The win raised Broglio's record to 14-5, including 8-1 since July 1st. Friend's record fell to 12-9.

Today's Results
ST. LOUIS 3 - Pittsburgh 2 (12. inn.)
Los Angeles 3 - Cincinnati 0
San Francisco 8 - Milwaukee 7
  no other game scheduled

Standings	W-L	Pct.	GB
Pittsburgh	65-41	.613	-
ST. LOUIS	62-46	.574	4
Los Angeles	58-46	.558	6
Milwaukee	57-47	.548	7
San Francisco	52-52	.500	12
Cincinnati	47-60	.439	18½
Philadelphia	42-65	.393	23½
Chicago	39-65	.375	25

The game was the opener of a five-game series between the league-leading Pirates and the second-place Cardinals. By winning tonight, St. Louis closed to within 4 games of first place. Pittsburgh has led the league since Memorial Day, except for one day in late July. St. Louis got off to a slow start. On June 29th, they were in fifth place, 10 games behind the Pirates. Since that date, St. Louis has won 30 games and lost only 11.

Today's triumph was the 13th in 15 games for the Cards, and it snapped a seven-game Pittsburgh winning streak. The game was very well played. Besides the brilliant pitching, the fielding was excellent. The Cardinals made the only error of the game, but they also turned four double plays, all in the first five innings. For the Pirates, Bill Virdon stood out in center field. He handled nine chances, several of them difficult. Twice he robbed Ken Boyer of hits. The other big play turned in by the Bucs' defense was a relay play in which Boyer was cut down at the plate in the ninth inning.

Friend retired the Cardinals in order in the first inning.

Virdon opened for the Pirates with a single. With one out, he was put out as part of a fancy 3-6-1 double play by the Cardinals.

Musial doubled with one out in the second for St. Louis's first hit. He was left on base.

Rocky Nelson opened the bottom of the second with a safety, but Gino Cimoli bounced into a double play. Smoky Burgess followed with a hit, but he was left.

Pittsburgh wasted a single by Bill Mazeroski in the third.

An error by Julian Javier in the next round allowed the Pirates to get their leadoff man to first for the fourth straight time. But once again a twin-killing turned them back.

Leading off the fifth, Burgess avoided any possible double play by slamming Broglio's first pitch for a home run. The hanging slider was about the only mistake Ernie made all night. Don Hoak followed with a single, but another DP wiped him out.

After the fifth, Broglio settled down and retired the Pirates in order in each of the next six innings.

In the meantime, Friend was having no trouble with the Cardinals. He upped his streak of consecutive batters retired to 18 when he got Musial out to open the eighth inning.

But then the Cardinals broke through. Walt Moryn, who had been swinging a hot bat of late, got a drive into the slot between right and center for a triple. Carl Sawatski then shot a single past the drawn-in infielders, scoring pinch-runner Charlie James and tying the game. Broglio walked with two out, but George Crowe, hitting for Javier, struck out, leaving two men on base.

St. Louis made a bid to score in the ninth. With two out, Boyer beat out an infield dribbler. Musial then smacked a double to right field. Third base coach Johnny Keane gambled and waved Boyer home. But the relay from Cimoli to Mazeroski to Burgess was perfect, and the runner was out.

Both sides went out in order in the first two extra innings.

Then Bill White, leading off the twelfth, singled. Facing Musial, Friend tried to put a fastball over the outside corner. But he got the ball just a little too far over the plate, and Stan The Man parked it into the upper deck in right field for a two-run home run. The next three batters went out, but St. Louis had a 3-1 lead.

But the Pirates weren't quite ready to call it quits. One of the trademarks of their team had been their ability to rally late in the game. Tonight was no exception, although their rally fell short. Virdon opened the bottom of the twelfth with a single up the middle, snapping Broglio's string of 20 straight batters retired. The big righthander bounced back and struck out Dick Groat, a noted contact hitter, for the fourth time in the game. Bob Skinner bounced out to first. Nelson kept the Pittsburgh hopes alive with a double off the right field screen, scoring Virdon. Manager Danny Murtaugh then sent power-hitting Dick Stuart up to the plate. With the count at 2-and-2, Broglio threw a fastball past the slugger for a game-ending strikeout, Ernie's ninth "K" of the night.

St. Louis was looking like a solid contender for the pennant, and the Cardinals were a happy bunch in the clubhouse after their 3-2 victory, especially Musial and Broglio.

St. Louis	ab	r	h	bi	o	a	e
J. Javier, 2b	3	0	0	0	2	1	1
G. Crowe, ph8	1	0	0	0	-	-	-
H. Smith, c8	1	0	0	0	5	0	0
D. Spencer, ss	5	0	0	0	5	4	0
B. White, 1b	5	1	1	0	8	2	0
K. Boyer, 3b	5	0	1	0	1	3	0
S. Musial, lf	5	1	3	2	1	0	0
J. Cunningham, rf12	0	0	0	0	0	0	0
W. Moryn, lf	3	0	1	0	1	0	0
C. James, pr8-rf-lf12	2	1	0	0	2	0	0
C. Sawatski, c	3	0	1	1	4	1	0
B. Gibson, pr8	0	0	0	0	-	-	-
A. Grammas, 2b8	2	0	0	0	0	0	0
C. Flood, cf	4	0	0	0	4	0	0
E. Broglio, p	3	0	0	0	3	3	0
	42	3	7	3	36	14	1

Pittsburgh	ab	r	h	bi	o	a	e
B. Virdon, cf	5	1	2	0	9	0	0
D. Groat, ss	5	0	0	0	0	6	0
B. Skinner, lf	5	0	0	0	3	0	0
R. Nelson, 1b	5	0	2	1	11	0	0
J. Christopher, pr 12	0	0	0	0	-	-	-
G. Cimoli, rf	4	0	0	0	2	1	0
D. Stuart, ph12	1	0	0	0	-	-	-
S. Burgess, c	4	1	2	1	10	0	0
D. Hoak, 3b	4	0	1	0	0	2	0
B. Mazeroski, 2b	4	0	1	0	1	4	0
B. Friend, p	3	0	0	0	0	1	0
	40	2	8	2	36	14	0

St. Louis   000 000 010 002 - 3
Pittsburgh   000 010 000 001 - 2

	ip	h	r-er	bb	so
Broglio (W 14-5)	12	8	2-2	0	9
Friend (L 12-9)	12	7	3-3	1	9

Attendance - 34,212

LOB: StL 4, Pitts 3. BE: Pitts 1.
DP: White-Spencer-Broglio, Broglio-Spencer-White, Sawatski-Spencer, Spencer-White.
2B: Musial 2, Nelson. 3B: Moryn.
HR: Burgess, Musial. SH: Friend.
Time - 2:57
Umpires: A. Barlick, B. Jackowski, S. Landes, & C. Pelekoudas

St. Louis won the next game, 9-2, getting a big home run by Boyer. But Pittsburgh won the final three games of the series, and the Cardinals left town trailing by 6 games. They never got closer than 5½ games thereafter.

St. Louis finished in third place, 9 games out, with an 86-68 record.

1961—Tuesday Night, July 18th, at Busch Stadium
Cards Sweep Again, White's Hit Total Up to 14 in Two Days
First Baseman Gets Six Hits Today After Eight Hits Yesterday
Jackson and Gibson Pitch St. Louis to 8-3 & 7-5 Victories Over Chicago

Swinging smoking bats and leaving their starting pitchers in to work out of their own troubles, the St. Louis Cardinals have won two doubleheaders from the Chicago Cubs in two nights. Tonight the scores were 8-3 and 7-5. The Cardinals have won nine games and lost just four since Johnny Keane replaced Solly Hemus as manager.

Larry Jackson pitched a complete game to win the twilight game tonight, and Bob Gibson went the distance in the nightcap. On Monday night, Curt Simmons and Ernie Broglio pitched 10-6 and 8-5 victories, although both received relief help from Lindy McDaniel in the ninth inning.

Today's Results
ST. LOUIS 8 - Chicago 3 (1st game)
ST. LOUIS 7 - Chicago 5 (2nd)
Milwaukee 12 - Cincinnati 8
 no other games scheduled

Standings	W-L	Pct.	GB
Cincinnati	56-34	.622	-
Los Angeles	52-37	.584	3½
San Francisco	47-41	.534	8
Pittsburgh	43-39	.524	9
Milwaukee	41-42	.494	11½
ST. LOUIS	42-45	.483	12½
Chicago	38-50	.432	17
Philadelphia	26-57	.313	26½

After pounding out 33 hits on Monday, the Cardinals added 27 safeties in tonight's games. Julian Javier and Bill White had led the attack on Monday by collecting eight hits each. Tonight, Javier slipped to two hits, but White continued his hot streak by getting six hits in eight trips to the plate. His total of 14 hits in consecutive doubleheaders tied the major league record set by Ty Cobb in 1912. White missed a chance to break the record when Cub reliever Barney Schultz set the Cardinals down in order in the last inning of each game, leaving White on deck each time.

After Monday's twin-bill, which didn't end till after midnight, White had gotten home at about 3:00 a.m. He was unable to get to sleep, and he was out in University City at 10 o'clock in the morning for an instructional clinic for youngsters. He finally got a 45 minute nap before batting practice this afternoon, but that was his only sleep between the two doubleheaders. Still, he played his usual flawless game in the field and got six hits.

He was retired in the first inning of the first game by Glen Hobbie. But the Cardinals already had taken a 1-0 lead on a homer by Joe Cunningham.

The Cubs tied the score in the third on a triple by Ed Bouchee and a fly out by Al Heist.

Singles by Cunningham, White, and Ken Boyer put the Cards back on top, 2-1, in the bottom of the inning.

The Cubbies came right back and tied the score again in the fourth. George Altman opened the rally with a drive off the facing of the pavilion in right field. A long rebound and fast fielding held him to a single. Two more singles brought him around anyway.

Heist put the Cubs ahead in the fifth with a home run to right.

But St. Louis came in and took the lead back in the bottom of the inning. White opened with a single and took third on Heist's wild throw. Boyer doubled him home. Then Stan Musial put the Cardinals into the lead with a double past Altman in right.

St. Louis clinched the game with four runs in the sixth. Carl Sawatski led off with a double and eventually scored on Cunningham's two-out, infield single. White then unloaded his biggest hit of the day, a two-run homer into the seats in right center. Boyer knocked the very next pitch out of the park and onto Sullivan Avenue beyond the left field bleachers.

Jackson pitched around a couple of doubles and shut the Cubs out over the last four innings. The Cardinals won, 8-3.

Dick Drott and Bob Gibson were the opposing pitchers at the start of the second game. After a scoreless first inning, in which White popped out, Drott left the game with a pulled muscle in his side. Gibson stayed in through the whole game, despite difficulties in the sixth and seventh innings.

Gibson helped his own cause by driving in the first two runs of the game with a single off Mel Wright in the third inning.

In the fourth, White's triple led to two more St. Louis runs.

White tripled again in the fifth but was left on base.

Gibson's troubles started in the sixth. Altman homered, and three subsequent singles cut the Cardinal lead to 4-2.

The Cubs continued to hit in the seventh, taking a 5-4 lead. Gibson bulled his way past further trouble by striking out Jerry Kindall and Ed Bouchee.

The Cubs' brain trust sent Bob Anderson to the mound to try and hold the led, but he failed. After Bob Lillis bounced out, Cunningham singled. White followed with his sixth hit of the day, a double down the right field line. Boyer was intentionally passed. With the bases loaded, Keane inserted Musial as a pinch-hitter. Stan drove in the tying run with a line out to center field. Don Taussig then put St. Louis ahead with a base hit to right, Altman kicked the ball, and an insurance run also scored.

Given the lead back, Gibson responded by shutting Chicago out in the last two innings, and St. Louis won, 7-5.

After the game, White was not impressed by having set an esoteric record, but he was happy that the Cardinals were able to rack up four victories in two days.

TWILIGHT GAME

		r	h	e	Batteries
Chicago	001 110 000 -	3	8	1	G. Hobbie (L 7-10) 6 IP, B. Schultz 2 IP & S. Taylor, D. Bertell.
St. Louis	101 024 00x -	8	13	0	L. Jackson (W 5-8) & C. Sawatski.

NIGHT GAME

Chicago	ab	r	h	bi	o	a	e
R. Ashburn, cf	4	1	0	0	4	0	0
D. Zimmer, 2b	5	1	1	0	5	1	0
R. Santo, 3b	5	0	2	0	1	2	0
G. Altman, rf	4	2	2	2	1	0	1
B. Williams, lf	3	1	1	0	1	0	0
D. Bertell, c	4	0	2	2	3	2	0
J. Kindall, ss	4	0	0	0	3	1	0
E. Bouchee, 1b	3	0	1	1	4	1	0
D. Drott, p	0	0	0	0	0	0	0
M. Wright, p2	1	0	0	0	2	0	0
S. Taylor, ph5	0	0	0	0	-	-	-
D. Elston, p5	0	0	0	0	0	0	0
B. Will, ph6	1	0	0	0	-	-	-
J. Brewer, p6	0	0	0	0	0	0	0
B. Anderson, p7	0	0	0	0	0	1	0
A. Heist, ph8	1	0	0	0	-	-	-
B. Schultz, p8	0	0	0	0	0	0	0
	35	5	9	5	24	8	1

St. Louis	ab	r	h	bi	o	a	e
B. Lillis, ss	5	0	1	0	2	3	0
J. Cunningham, rf	5	2	3	0	1	0	0
B. White, 1b	4	2	3	1	7	0	0
K. Boyer, 3b	3	1	0	0	0	0	0
C. James, lf	3	1	2	1	2	0	0
S. Musial, ph7	0	0	0	1	-	-	-
C. Flood, cf8	0	0	0	0	0	0	0
D. Taussig, cf-lf8	4	0	2	1	4	0	0
J. Javier, 2b	3	1	2	0	1	4	0
T. McCarver, c	2	0	0	0	6	0	0
C. Warwick, ph6	1	0	0	0	-	-	-
J. Schaffer, c7	1	0	0	0	3	0	0
B. Gibson, p	4	0	1	2	1	0	0
	35	7	14	6	27	7	0

Chicago   000 002 300 - 5
St. Louis 022 000 30x - 7

	ip	h	r-er	bb	so
Drott	1	1	0-0	0	0
Wright	3	8	4-4	0	0
Elston	1	1	0-0	0	1
Brewer	1	1	0-0	0	1
Anderson (L 4-7)	1	3	3-2	2	0
Schultz	1	0	0-0	0	1
Gibson (W 7-6)	9	9	5-5	5	9

Umpires: A. Barlick, M. Steiner, B. Jackowski, E. Vargo, & S. Crawford

LOB: Chi 9, StL 7. BE: none.
DP: Javier-Lillis-White.
2B: Altman, White.
3B: White 2.
HR: Altman.
SF: Musial.
SB: none. CS: James, Javier.
Time - 2:35 Attendance - 12,889
HBP: by Gibson (Taylor)

The Cardinals showed a definite improvement under Keane's leadership. After compiling a 33-41 record under Hemus, they were 47-33 under Keane. Still, they finished in the second division (fifth) with an overall mark of 80-74.

1962—Sunday, July 8th, at the Polo Grounds, New York

Musial Slams Three Home Runs as Cardinals Romp, 15-1

Ties Record With Homers in Four Consecutive At Bats

Gibson Pitches Three-Hitter at Mets, Gets Three Hits Himself

Led by the incredible slugging of their 41-year-old left fielder, the St. Louis Cardinals today destroyed the hapless New York Mets, 15-1. The Cardinals pounded out six home runs, three by the oldest player in the National League, Stan Musial. Musial's home runs came in his first three official at bats today. Added to a homer in his last at bat Saturday, they gave Stan a share of the major league record of four home runs in consecutive at bats. On his final trip to the plate, Musial showed he was still human by striking out on a wild pitch. Bill White, Fred Whitfield, and Bob Gibson also homered for the winners.

Taking a back seat to the slugging was a fine pitching performance by Gibson. Although he walked six and struck out only four, Gibson allowed only three hits. He made that many hits personally, and he outscored the Mets, crossing the plate three times and driving in two runs.

Today's Results
ST. LOUIS 15 - New York 1
Los Angeles 2 - San Francisco 0
Philadelphia 8 - Pittsburgh 4 (1st game)
Pittsburgh 6 - Philadelphia 5 (2nd)
Cincinnati 12 - Houston 8 (1st game)
Cincinnati 12 - Houston 11 (13 inn.)(2nd)
Chicago 7 — Milwaukee 5 (1st game)
Milwaukee 5 - Chicago 3 (2nd)

Standings	W-L	Pct.	GB
Los Angeles	58-31	.652	-
San Francisco	57-31	.648	½
Pittsburgh	52-34	.605	4½
Cincinnati	46-36	.561	8½
ST. LOUIS	47-38	.553	9
Milwaukee	42-43	.494	14
Philadelphia	36-49	.424	20
Houston	33-49	.402	21½
Chicago	32-56	.364	25½
New York	23-59	.280	31½

The Mets contributed to their own downfall with four errors, all of which figured in the St. Louis scoring. The Cardinals' fielded flawlessly.

Musial broke an 0-for-14 slump on Friday night against the Mets. His average had dipped to .324, but with the aid of one of his favorite parks and of expansion-team pitching, his mark moved up to .333 in four games. Yesterday he won the second game of a doubleheader with a home run off Craig Anderson in the eighth inning. He also had two singles earlier in the day.

Today, Jay Hook was the starting pitcher for Casey Stengel's Amazing Mets. He induce the first two Cardinals to bounce back to the mound. But the third batter, Bill White, drove a home run deep into the seats in right field. Musial was next. He watched two balls go by, then picked on a change-up and parked it into the stands near the right field foul line. This home run had a slightly "Chinese" flavor to it, owing to the nearness of the fence down the line (257 feet). But the ball went well up into the seats.

After the Cards went down in order in the second inning, Gibson opened the third with a drive into the upper deck in left. It was the second homer of the big pitcher's career. The first one came on July 5, 1961, off of Johnny Podres in the Los Angeles Coliseum. Curt Flood followed the blast with a single. He stole second when Felix Mantilla was late in covering. After the next two men went out, Musial was walked. Ken Boyer then drove Flood home with a single.

The Cardinals were given five unearned runs in the fourth inning. Three infield errors, along with a hit by Gibson, gave the Cards the first two runs in the round. White then doubled with two out for another score, bringing Stan The Man up. Hook fell behind on the count, 3-and-1, and came in with a slider. Musial jumped on it and drove it into the upper deck in right for a two-run homer.

Willard Hunter, a lefthander, took over as the Mets pitcher in the fifth. He got through two innings without incident.

Then Musial led off the seventh. With the count 2-and-2, Hunter got a fastball up and in. The pitch was probably out of the strike zone, but Stan tomahawked it against the facing of the roof in right field for his third home run of the day. It marked the second time in his National League career that Musial had hit three homers in one game. He also became the eleventh major leaguer to hit home runs in four consecutives at bats. Mickey Mantle had become the tenth just two days before.

Former Cardinal Bob Miller, the second player selected by the Mets in the expansion draft, was on the mound in the eighth. Fred Whitfield, who had replaced White at first, pounded Miller for a two-run homer. That brought Musial to the plate again. The New York fans were rooting for a record-shattering home run. Stan was going for one, too. Miller missed with his first two pitches, then threw a fastball over the plate. Stan let it go, although he later said that it would have been a good pitch to hit. Then he chased a low breaking ball for strike two. Miller came with another curve, which broke into the dirt. Overanxious, Musial swung at it and missed, striking out. But the ball got past the catcher, and Musial got to first base safely. Manager Johnny Keane then sent Bobby Gene Smith out as a pinch-runner. Stan got a nice round of applause as he left, the strikeout notwithstanding.

A triple by Charlie James, a hit batsman, singles by Gibson and Whitfield, and a helpful infield bobble combined to give the Cardinals three more runs in the ninth, making the score 15-0. If he had been left in the game, Musial would have gotten another chance to bat. As it was, Smith flied out to end the inning.

The Mets finally scored in the bottom of the ninth. Mantilla tripled and scored on an infield out. The Mets' faithful fans yelled as if it was the game-winning run. Previously, Joe Christopher (in the second inning) and Marv Throneberry (in the fourth) had gotten the only New York hits off of Gibson. The Cardinal fireballer lost his shutout, but he struck out Cliff Cook and retired Richie Ashburn on a fly to center to nail down the victory. The final score was a lopsided 15-1.

St. Louis	ab	r	h	bi	o	a	e
C. Flood, cf	6	2	3	0	3	0	0
J. Javier, 2b	6	1	0	0	2	4	0
B. White, 1b	3	2	2	2	4	0	0
F. Whitfield, 1b4	3	1	2	3	10	0	0
S. Musial, lf	4	3	3	4	1	0	0
B. Smith, pr8-lf	1	0	0	0	0	0	0
K. Boyer, 3b	5	0	2	1	1	1	0
C. Sawatski, c	4	0	0	0	2	0	0
J. Schaffer, c7	1	0	0	0	2	0	0
C. James, rf	5	1	1	0	2	0	0
D. Maxvill, ss	4	1	0	0	0	3	0
J. Gotay, ss7	0	1	0	0	0	1	0
B. Gibson, p	5	3	3	2	0	4	0
	47	15	16	12	27	13	0

New York	ab	r	h	bi	o	a	e
R. Ashburn rf	4	0	0	0	2	0	0
R. Kanehl, 2b	3	0	0	0	0	0	1
G. Woodling, lf	3	0	0	0	1	0	0
J. Hickman, lf8	0	0	0	0	2	0	0
F. Thomas, 3b	4	0	0	0	0	3	2
S. Taylor, c	2	0	0	0	5	0	0
C. Cannizzaro, c8	1	0	0	0	3	0	0
M. Throneberry, 1b	4	0	1	0	9	1	0
F. Mantilla, ss	3	1	1	0	0	2	1
J. Christopher, cf	3	0	1	1	4	0	0
J. Hook, p	2	0	0	0	0	2	0
W. Hunter, p5	0	0	0	0	1	0	0
G. Hodges, ph7	0	0	0	0	-	-	-
B. Miller, p8	0	0	0	0	0	0	0
C. Cook, ph9	1	0	0	0	-	-	-
	30	1	3	1	27	8	4

St. Louis	202	500	123 -	15
New York	000	000	001 -	1

	ip	h	r-er	bb	so
Gibson (W 10-6)	9	3	1-1	6	4
Hook (L 6-9)	4	8	9-4	1	3
Hunter	3	3	1-1	0	2
Miller	2	5	5-3	0	4

HBP: by Gibson (Kanehl), by Miller (Gotay)
WP: Miller. PB: Sawatski

LOB: StL 7, NY 9. BE: StL 3.
Base on Missed 3rd Strike: StL 1.
2B: White. 3B: James, Mantilla.
HR: White, Musial 3, Gibson, Whitfield.
SB: Flood.
Time - 2:47 Attendance - 12,460
Umpires: P. Pryor, A. Donatelli, F. Secory, & T. Venzon

The Cardinals couldn't seem to play consistent ball, and they had slipped to sixth place by the end of the season. Their 84-78 record left them 17½ games out of first.

Musial finished the season with a .330 average, third best in the league.

Chapter XI

Back On Top
1963-1968

1963—September 16th at Busch Stadium
Cards Lose to Dodgers, 3-1, in Opener of Critical Series

1964—September 30th at Busch Stadium
Red Birds Complete Sweep of Phillies, Grab League Lead

1964 World Series—Game #7
Gibson Hangs on to Beat Yankees, 7-5, Cards Win Series

1965—August 8th at Busch Stadium
Cardinals Forced to Use Shannon as Catcher, Lose to Giants

1966—May 12th at Busch Memorial Stadium
St. Louis Opens New Downtown Stadium with 12-Inning Victory

1967—July 25th at Busch Memorial Stadium
Cardinals Hold Off Cubs to Win, 4-3, Regain 1-Game Lead

1967 World Series—Game #7
Gibson's Third Win Gives St. Louis the Series

1968—July 1st at Los Angeles
Scoreless Streak Ends, but Gibson Beats Dodgers Easily, 5-1

1968 World Series—Game #1
Gibby Fans 17 Tigers, Cardinals Win Opener, 4-0

The Cardinals improved themselves at shortstop after the 1962 season by acquiring veteran Dick Groat. And young Tim McCarver developed rapidly enough to solve the catching problems in 1963.

The Red Birds held first place until they lost a three-game series in Los Angeles in July. They slipped to third place, 7 games behind by August 29th. Then they electrified the baseball world by winning 19 out of 20 games to pull within 1 game of the first-place Dodgers. But Los Angeles halted the St. Louis pennant run by sweeping a three-game set at Busch Stadium on September 16-17-18. Johnny Podres won the first game, 3-1, as the Dodgers scored two runs in the ninth inning off of reliever Bobby Shantz. Sandy Koufax shut St. Louis out in the second game, 4-0. And Los Angeles rallied to take the third game, 6-5, in thirteen innings. St. Louis finished 6 games behind the Dodgers.

In 1964, the Cardinals swooned in June and had problems in the bullpen and the outfield. General manager Bing Devine traded Shantz and Ernie Broglio to Chicago and got young speedster Lou Brock in return on June 15th. On July 7th, Mike Shannon was called up from the minors. He and Brock flanked Curt Flood, and the outfield was suddenly set. On August 1st, veteran knuckleballer Barney Schultz was called up to shore up the relief corps.

Still, the Cardinals' pennant chances looked very slim, and on August 17th, Devine was fired. Bob Howsam succeeded him. It was widely understood that manager Johnny Keane would be let go after the season. But the Cardinals got hot and climbed into second place. They trailed the league-leading Phillies by 6½ games with 13 to play when the Phillies suddenly collapsed. The Cardinals, meanwhile, went on a winning streak. The spurt was capped by a three-game sweep of the Phils, which put St. Louis into first place with just three games left to play. The Cards hung on to win he pennant by 1 game.

Then they outlasted the New York Yankees to win the World Series, 4 games to 3.

Manager Keane unexpectedly quit the day after the series ended, much to the embarrassment of the Cardinal ownership. Red Schoendienst was hired as a replacement.

In 1965, the Cardinals' pitching fell into disarray, and the lineup was riddled with injuries. Things got so bad that one day Schoendienst had to use outfielder Mike Shannon at catcher. The team fell to seventh place in the standings.

In 1966, general manager Howsam began a rebuilding program, trading away most of the older players. The young pitchers did well, but the offense was weak, and the Cardinals finished sixth. The club moved to a big, new ballpark downtown and set a club attendance record.

In 1967, the team jelled. The pitching staff, although short on experience, was long on talent. Even a broken leg that sidelined Bob Gibson for eight weeks didn't seem to hurt the team. The offense, led by Orlando Cepeda, was steady enough to keep the team winning. Cepeda also led the cheering in the clubhouse, and the Cardinals, dubbed "El Birdos," were a remarkably close bunch.

The Cubs challenged them a few times in July, but the Cards pulled away from them, starting on July 25th, and won the pennant easily.

Gibson was healthy for the World Series, and he beat the Boston Sox three times. Nelson Briles beat them once, and the Cards won the world championship, 4 games to 3.

In 1968, St. Louis got out to the lead early, then slumped in May. But led by Gibson's pitching, they pulled out to a 6½-game lead by the end of June. Gibson had a string of five straight shutouts stopped in Los Angeles on July 1st, but he won nevertheless. By August 1st, St. Louis had upped their lead to 15 games, and then the team waltzed to the pennant.

In the opening game of the World Series, Gibson struck out 17 Detroit Tigers and won, 4-0. The Cardinals got out to a 3-to-1 lead in games in the series, but then the Tigers rallied back to take three straight, and the Cardinals lost their hold on the world championship.

1963 — Monday Night, September 16th, at Busch Stadium
Cardinals Lose to Dodgers in Opening Game of Critical Series, 3-1
Defeat Halts St. Louis Winning Streak at 10 Games
Two Runs Off Shantz in Ninth Inning Win for Visitors

By winning 10 straight games and 19 of their last 20, the St. Louis Cardinals had moved to within 1 game of the first-place Los Angeles Dodgers in the standings. And the Dodgers arrived in St. Louis today to start a crucial three-game series. In the opening game tonight, the leaders halted the Cardinals' charge with a 3-1 decision, snapping the St. Louis winning streak.

A World Series atmosphere pervaded Busch Stadium tonight. The crowd of 32,442 was the largest of the season here, and the press box was filled with reporters from out-of-town newspapers.

Today's Results
Los Angeles 3 - ST. LOUIS 1
San Francisco 4 - Milwaukee 3
Pittsburgh 1 - Chicago 0
  no other games scheduled

Standings	W-L	Pct.	GB
Los Angeles	92-59	.609	-
ST. LOUIS	91-62	.595	2
San Francisco	82-69	.543	10
Milwaukee	80-72	.526	12½
Philadelphia	79-72	.5232	13
Cincinnati	80-73	.5229	13
Chicago	75-76	.497	17
Pittsburgh	71-79	.473	20½
Houston	58-93	.384	34
New York	49-102	.325	43

The game was tense throughout. Johnny Podres and Ernie Broglio, the opposing starting pitchers, both did very well, and, after eight innings, the score was tied, 1-1. St. Louis manager Johnny Keane chose to lift Broglio for a pinch-hitter in the bottom of the eighth, and he put Bobby Shantz on the mound in the ninth. Shantz gave up two hits and a walk, which, with an error, gave Los Angeles two runs and the game.

The defeat dropped the Cardinals to 2 games behind the Dodgers and three behind in games lost.

When the Red Birds had headed east from their last western road trip on August 29th, the race looked over for St. Louis. The Cards were in third place, 7 games behind the Dodgers.

But then they turned things around. They won nine in a row before dropping the second game of a doubleheader in Pittsburgh on September 6th. They bounced right back and won ten straight before tonight. In five of their last eight wins, the Cardinal pitching staff turned in shutouts.

The stars of the Cardinal streak were many, but Ken Boyer, Stan Musial, and Curt Simmons stood out. Boyer swung the hottest bat on the team, with Bill White not far behind. Musial, who had announced that this would be his last season, became a grandfather on September 10th, and he celebrated by hitting a home run in his first at bat that night. Simmons pitched four complete game victories, the last three being shutouts.

Tonight's pitchers, Broglio for St. Louis and Podres for Los Angeles, both started out well. Podres, relying mostly on his fastball, retired the Cardinals in order in each of the first five innings. Broglio also shut his opposition out through five, although he was touched for three hits over that span. A base-running error cost the Dodgers in the second inning. Johnny Roseboro hit an apparent triple with two out, but he missed second base, and the alert St. Louis bench saw it. On an appeal to the umpires, Roseboro was called out. Maury Wills singled and stole second base in the fourth inning, and Willie Davis did the same thing in the fifth, but neither could score.

Los Angeles pushed the first run of the game across the plate in the sixth. Broglio got an inside fastball up too high to Wills, and Maury doubled to right center. Jim Gilliam popped up for the first out of the inning, but Wills stole third. After Wally Moon walked, Tommy Davis got jammed by an inside pitch and looped it to center field. Curt Flood, the center fielder, was deceived by Davis's big swing, and he took a step backwards before charging in. The ball fell safely just in front of him for a run-scoring single.

That put the Cardinals behind in the score for the first time in ten games.

Tim McCarver's solid single with one out in the bottom of the sixth gave St. Louis its first base runner. But the next two men went out.

W. Davis singled and stole again in the seventh. He moved to third with one out, but Podres fanned and Wills bounced back to the mound.

With one out in the bottom of the seventh, St. Louis tied the score on a home run by Stan Musial. After throwing him a curve inside, Podres tried to jam Stan with a fastball. But Musial got good wood on it and sent it onto the pavilion roof. An error by Wills and a single by Flood put Podres into more trouble later in the inning, but he retired Charlie James on a fly to center to end the threat.

Both sides went out in order in the eighth. Broglio, who had been experiencing some elbow trouble in the last few weeks, was removed for a pinch-hitter, Bob Gibson. It was Gibson's first pinch-hitting appearance ever, and he popped out to short.

With three lefthanded batters due up in the ninth for the Dodgers, Keane sent Bobby Shantz in to pitch. The little lefty had not worked in eight days, and his control was off, especially on his curveball. His first pitch, a high breaking ball, was lined off the right field screen by Ron Fairly for a double. Roseboro, next up, failed trying to bunt, and he struck out. But Willie Davis lined a low curve to right field for a hit, and Fairly just barely beat James's strong throw to the plate, putting the Dodgers ahead. Shantz walked Ken McMullen, then was removed from the game.

Ron Taylor took over, facing pinch-hitter Bill Skowron. Skowron hit a sharp grounder toward right field. Julian Javier made a diving stop but threw the ball away trying for a force at second, allowing W. Davis to score. After Wills walked to load the bases, Gilliam hit into a force play at home, and Moon struck out.

In the bottom of the ninth, Dodger manager Walt Alston sent in star reliever Ron Perranoski to protect the 3-1 lead. Dick Groat, first up, grounded out to shortstop. Musial worked the count to full, but he, too, bounced to short. And Ken Boyer struck out on four pitches, ending the game.

The Cardinals' incredible pennant drive had been halted.

Los Angeles	ab	r	h	bi	o	a	e
M. Wills, ss	4	1	2	0	3	5	1
J. Gilliam, 2b-3b9	5	0	0	0	1	0	0
W. Moon, rf	4	0	0	0	1	0	0
T. Davis, lf	4	0	1	1	2	0	0
R. Fairly, 1b	4	1	1	0	9	0	0
J. Roseboro, c	4	0	1	0	7	0	0
W. Davis, cf	4	1	3	1	4	0	0
K. McMullen, 3b	2	0	0	0	0	1	0
D. Tracewski, pr9-2b	0	0	0	0	0	0	0
J. Podres, p	3	0	0	0	0	2	0
B. Skowron, ph9	1	0	0	0	-	-	-
R. Gleason, pr9	0	0	0	0	-	-	-
R. Perranoski, p9	0	0	0	0	0	0	0
	35	3	8	2	27	8	1

St. Louis	ab	r	h	bi	o	a	e
J. Javier, 2b	4	0	0	0	3	2	1
D. Groat, ss	4	0	0	0	2	1	0
S. Musial, lf	4	1	1	1	1	0	0
K. Boyer, 3b	4	0	0	0	1	2	0
B. White, 1b	3	0	0	0	8	2	0
C. Flood, cf	3	0	1	0	3	0	0
C. James, rf	3	0	0	0	0	0	0
T. McCarver, c	3	0	1	0	7	0	0
E. Broglio, p	2	0	0	0	2	4	0
B. Gibson, ph8	1	0	0	0	-	-	-
B. Shantz, p9	0	0	0	0	0	0	0
R. Taylor, p9	0	0	0	0	0	0	0
	31	1	3	1	27	11	1

Los Angeles	000	001	002	-	3
St. Louis	000	000	100	-	1

	ip	h	r-er	bb	so
Podres (W 14-10)	8	3	1-1	0	6
Perranoski	1	0	0-0	0	1
Broglio	8	6	1-1	2	4
Shantz (L 6-4)	.1	2	2-1	1	1
Taylor	.2	0	0-0	1	1

LOB: LA 9, StL 3. BE: LA 1, StL 1.
2B: Wills, Fairly.
HR: Musial.
SB: Wills 2, W. Davis 2.
Attendance - 32,442
Time - 2:31
Umpires: S. Landes, E. Sudol, T. Gorman, & A. Forman

The Dodgers went on to sweep the series, killing the Cardinals' pennant hopes. Sandy Koufax won the next game, 4-0. In the final game, St. Louis blew a 5-1 lead and lost a thirteen-inning thriller, 6-5.

The Cards then lost three more games in a row, allowing the Dodgers to clinch the pennant. St. Louis finished second, 6 games behind, with a 93-69 record.

The home run against Podres was the last of Stan Musial's career.

1964 — Wednesday Night, September 30th, at Busch Stadium

Cardinals Complete Sweep of Phillies, Grab League Lead

Eighth Straight Win for Red Birds, Tenth Loss in a Row for Phillies

In First Place for First Time All Year, Only Three Games Left to Play

The incredible collapse of the Philadelphia Phillies and the late-season drive of the St. Louis Cardinals both reached their logical goals tonight: the Cardinals took over first place, while the Phillies were all but eliminated from the pennant race.

Just ten days ago, the Quaker City team was apparently certain of the pennant. They led St. Louis and Cincinnati by 6½ games with just twelve games remaining on their schedule. But since then, the Phils have lost ten games in a row, including three each to the Cardinals and Reds. The Cincinnati team ran off a nine-game winning streak to take the lead. But the Reds lost a heartbreaker today, and the Cardinals, who upped their own winning streak to eight games, moved past them and into first place.

Today's Results
ST. LOUIS 8 - Philadelphia 5
Pittsburgh 1 - Cincinnati 0 (16 inn.)
San Francisco 2 - Houston 1 (11 inn.)
Milwaukee 6 - New York 5 (12 inn.)
Los Angeles 2 - Chicago 0

Standings	W-L	Pct.	GB
ST. LOUIS	92-67	.579	-
Cincinnati	91-68	.573	1
Philadelphia	90-70	.563	2½
San Francisco	88-70	.557	3½
Milwaukee	84-73	.535	7
Pittsburgh	79-78	.503	12
Los Angeles	78-80	.494	13½
Chicago	73-85	.462	18½
Houston	65-93	.411	26½
New York	51-107	.323	40½

Today was the first time that the Cards have led the league all year. On July 24th, they were under .500 with a 47-48 record, which had them tied for seventh. By August 23rd, they were up to fourth place, but they had fallen to 11 games behind the Phillies. Until a week ago, they hadn't been closer than 5 games behind the leaders since June 12th.

But then strange things began to happen. Especially to the Phillies. They lost three straight to the Reds, starting with a 1-0 setback in which the only run scored on a steal of home. There followed four tough losses to Milwaukee.

Meanwhile, the Reds swept five from the lowly Mets, and the Cardinals took five games in Pittsburgh.

When the Phillies arrived in St. Louis for Monday night's game, they had fallen a game behind the Reds and were only ½ game ahead of the Cards. In the opening game of the three-game series, Bob Gibson got his 18th win for the Cardinals, 5-1, with last-inning help from Barney Schultz. On Tuesday night, St. Louis jumped to a quick 3-0 lead, and Ray Sadecki and Schultz held on for a 4-2 victory. Sadecki was credited with his 20th win of the season. At the same time, Pittsburgh scored two in the ninth to edge Cincinnati, 2-0. That put the Cards and Reds into a flat-footed tie for first place.

Tonight, the Cardinals got out to an 8-0 lead and held on to win, 8-5. The Reds, meanwhile, lost 1-0 on a sixteenth-inning squeeze bunt by Pittsburgh rookie Jerry May. The loss dropped the Reds out of a tie, and put the Cardinals on top all by themselves.

They'd come a long way since July.

So had the Phillies. With tonight's defeat, Philadelphia could only hope to tie for first place and then win the pennant in a playoff. And that could only happen if the last-place Mets swept three games in St. Louis over the weekend.

Tonight, in desperation, Phillie manager Gene Mauch put his ace, Jim Bunning, on the mound. Bunning was pitching with only two days of rest for the third time this month. All three times, including tonight, he was knocked out of the box early.

Curt Simmons, whom the Phillies released as washed up back in May, 1960, pitched for the Cardinals. Tonight he beat his old team for the 16th time in 18 decisions since they let him go.

Julian Javier set the tone of the game by making two brilliant plays in the top of the first to shut off the Phillies.

The Cardinals scored their first two runs in the second inning. Dick Groat singled, and Tim McCarver followed with a home run.

A double by Curt Flood, an error on a bunt (the first of four Philadelphia miscues), a two-bagger by Bill White, and singles by Ken Boyer and Groat added up to two more runs in the third. The Cards might have had more, but White tried to take third while Brock was still on that base.

One-out singles by Flood and Brock routed Bunning in the fourth. Bobby Locke relieved, and he was greeted by consecutive singles off the bats of White, Boyer, and Groat. These, along with a wild pitch and an outfield throwing error, made the score 8-0.

In the meantime, Simmons was sailing along. Using a lot of slow stuff, he retired the first 13 Philly batters. When Boyer bobbled a grounder in the fifth, Alex Johnson became the first base runner for the visitors.

Simmons carried a no-hitter into the seventh. But with two out, rookie sensation Richie Allen muscled a single to center. Johnson then blasted a change-up deep into the seats in left center for two runs.

A single by Bobby Wine, a force out, and a triple by Cookie Rojas gave the Phillies another run in the eighth.

An error gave Callison a life to open the ninth. Allen followed with a double, and St. Louis manager Johnny Keane relieved Simmons with righthander Ron Taylor. The new pitcher retired Wes Covington on a pop fly, but Clay Dalrymple delivered a two-run single. When lefthanded-hitting Tony Gonzalez was announced as a pinch-hitter, Keane called in lefthander Gordon Richardson. Mauch switched pinch-hitters, but Richardson got Frank Thomas on a fly to right. Another fastball got Wine to ground to shortstop, where Groat fielded the ball and flipped to Javier for a game-ending force out.

The Cardinals were winners, 8-5, and a few hours later, the Reds lost. So the Cardinals were all alone at the top of the heap.

Philadelphia	ab	r	h	bi	o	a	e	St. Louis	ab	r	h	bi	o	a	e
C. Rojas, cf	4	0	1	1	2	0	0	C. Flood, cf	5	2	3	0	2	0	0
T. Taylor, 2b	4	0	0	0	2	3	1	L Brock, lf	4	2	2	0	1	0	0
J. Callison, rf	4	1	0	0	0	0	1	B. White, 1b	5	1	2	2	11	0	0
R. Allen, 3b	4	2	2	0	1	4	1	K. Boyer, 3b	5	1	3	1	1	1	1
A. Johnson, lf	3	1	1	2	2	0	0	D. Groat, ss	4	1	3	1	1	4	1
W. Covington, ph9	1	0	0	0	-	-	-	T. McCarver, c	4	1	1	2	2	0	0
V. Power, 1b	3	0	0	0	7	0	0	J. Javier, 2b	4	0	0	0	4	6	0
C. Dalrymple, ph9	1	0	1	2	-	-	-	M. Shannon, rf	4	0	0	0	5	0	0
G. Triandos, c	3	0	0	0	6	1	0	C. Simmons, p	4	0	0	0	0	2	0
T. Gonzalez, ph9	0	0	0	0	-	-	-	R. Taylor, p9	0	0	0	0	0	0	0
F. Thomas, ph9	1	0	0	0	-	-	-	G. Richardson, p9	0	0	0	0	0	0	0
B. Wine, ss	4	0	1	0	4	3	1								
J. Bunning, p	1	0	0	0	0	0	0								
B. Locke, p4	0	0	0	0	0	1	0								
D. Cater, ph6	1	0	0	0	-	-	-								
R. Wise, p6	0	0	0	0	0	0	0								
A. Phillips, ph8	1	1	0	0	-	-	-								
M. Steevens, p8	0	0	0	0	0	0	0								
	35	5	6	5	24	12	4		39	8	14	6	27	13	2

Philadelphia 000 000 212 - 5
St. Louis   022 400 00x - 8

	ip	h	r-er	bb	so
Bunning (L 18-8)	3.1	8	6-5	0	2
Locke	1.2	5	2-2	0	1
Wise	2	1	0-0	0	1
Steevens	1	0	0-0	0	1
Simmons (W 18-9)	*8	5	5-4	0	2
R. Taylor	.3	1	0-0	0	0
Richardson	.2	0	0-0	0	0

*faced two batters in ninth

LOB: Phil 3, StL 8.
BE: Phil 2, StL 3.
2B: Flood, White, Allen.
3B: Rojas.
HR: McCarver, Johnson. SH: Brock.
Time - 2:25 Attendance - 29,920
Umpires: A. Forman, B. Jackowski, S. Crawford, & E. Vargo
WP: Locke

The Cardinals nearly blew the pennant, losing their first two games against the Mets. But the Phillies saved them from disaster by snapping their losing streak and beating the Reds twice.

When St. Louis beat New York on the final day of the season, 11-5, it was able to squeeze home 1 game ahead of both Cincinnati and Philadelphia. The Cardinals' final record was the same as it had been the previous year, 93-69.

1964 World Series—Game #7

Thursday, October 15th, at Busch Stadium

Gibson Hangs on to Beat Yankees, 7-5, Cardinals Win World Series

Sets Strikeout Record, Wins Despite Three Home Runs

Boyer, Brock, & Base Running Pace St. Louis Attack

The St. Louis Cardinals won their first World Series championship since 1946 today by taking the seventh and decisive game of the series from the New York Yankees, 7-5. The Cards outplayed the Yanks in all phases of the game today. They outhit the New Yorkers, 10-9, made fewer errors, 2-1, outran the opposition, and Bob Gibson outpitched five Yankee hurlers.

Gibson was the big hero of the triumph. He won his second game of the series, following a 19-win regular season. Pitching today with just two days of rest, he tired noticeably at the end of the game, giving up two home runs in the ninth inning, but he stayed in and won. Gibby struck out nine batters, upping his total for three games to 31, a new World Series record.

The opportunistic Red Birds scored their first run on a New York error and counted their second tally on a double steal. Two additional runs were scored by challenging the great Mickey Mantle's arm. And the Cardinals got solo home runs from Ken Boyer and Lou Brock.

All the Yankee's runs came on three homers.

It was a seesaw series. St. Louis won the first game, 9-5. But New York, behind rookie pitcher Mel Stottlemyre, beat the Cards and Gibson in the second encounter, 8-3. In the third game, Mantle's ninth-inning home run gave the Yankees a 2-1 victory and the lead in the series. The Yanks jumped out to a quick 3-0 lead in Game #4, and it looked bad for St. Louis. But Ken Boyer hit a grand slam, and Roger Craig and Ron Taylor pitched eight shutout innings in relief to bring the Red Birds a 4-3 victory. Gibson put the Cards back into the series lead by taking the fifth game, 5-2, on Tim McCarver's tenth-inning home run. With their backs to the wall, the Yankees clouted three homers to win Game #6, 8-3.

That set up today's match. Managers Yogi Berra of the Yankees and Johnny Keane of the Cardinals chose to go with Stottlemyre and Gibson as the starting pitchers, although both had worked just three days before. Today, the Yankee youngster was undone by poor fielding and an injury suffered while diving for an errant throw. Then the Yankee relievers could not hold the Cardinals down.

The game was scoreless until the Cardinals' fourth. Ken Boyer opened with a solid single to center. Dick Groat walked. Then came the fatal play for Stottlemyre. McCarver rapped a grounder, which first baseman Joe Pepitone gloved. He threw to second, forcing Groat, but shortstop Phil Linz's return throw to first got past the lunging Stottlemyre, who was covering. Boyer steamed all the way around from second on the play, and Stottlemyre hurt his shoulder.

The rookie stayed in, and Mike Shannon, a rookie himself, knocked a long single to right center, sending McCarver to third. Dal Maxvill, subbing for the injured Julian Javier, was the next batter. On an apparent hit-and-run play, Shannon broke for second as Maxie swung and missed. Catcher Elston Howard took a glance at McCarver at third, then threw to second. McCarver broke for home on the throw, and Shannon slid into second. Bobby Richardson, the second baseman, made a quick but futile swipe at Shannon before returning the ball to the plate, giving McCarver just enough time to slide home safely. Maxvill then dropped a single into short right, and Shannon scored ahead of Mantle's throw. St. Louis now led 3-0.

Shannon made a nice play in the field in the fifth. With two men on and one out, he got a good jump on a looper by Linz and made a charging catch to start a double play.

With Stottlemyre gone for a pinch-hitter, Al Downing was the Yankee pitcher in the bottom of the fifth. The Cardinals routed him after just four pitches. Lou Brock, leading off, hit the first serve on a line to the roof of the pavilion in deep right field for a home run. Bill White lined the next pitch into center for a hit. Boyer looked at one pitch, then slammed the next one off the wall in right center for a double. Rollie Sheldon was rushed into the game by Berra. He got Groat on a grounder, while White scored. McCarver hit a fly to short right, and Boyer scored ahead of a weak throw by Mantle, upping the Cardinal lead to 6-0.

The Yankees quickly halved the margin. Richardson opened the sixth with an infield hit. Roger Maris grounded a hit to right. Mantle then lined an opposite-field home run into the bleachers in left center, scoring three runs. Keane went to the mound to talk with Gibson but left him in. When Gibby walked Tom Tresh with two out, catcher McCarver went out and told his pitcher to stick with his best pitch, the fastball. Gibson blew one past Clete Boyer for the third out.

He got through the seventh and eighth innings without trouble.

Ken Boyer lined a home run into the bleachers off Steve Hamilton in the seventh, padding the lead a little.

Gibson took a four-run advantage into the ninth. Ray Sadecki and Roger Craig were warming up in the bullpen, just in case. Tresh, the first batter, struck out on a foul tip. Clete Boyer (Ken's brother) ran the count to 3-and-2, then he connected with a fastball for a home run to left. Johnny Blanchard, pinch-hitting, struck out, again on a foul tip. Linz lifted a long fly to left, which just barely cleared the fence for a homer, cutting the lead to 7-5. Keane came out to the mound and told Gibson that, safe or out, the next batter, Richardson, would be the last that the pitcher would face. Maris and Mantle were due to follow, and Richardson had just set a new World Series record by getting his 13th hit. But Gibson got him to pop weakly to second base for the final out.

There was a wild celebration in the clubhouse, featuring champagne and shaving cream. The Cardinals were champions! A month before, no one would have thought it possible.

New York (AL)	ab	r	h	bi	o	a	e
P. Linz, ss	5	1	2	1	2	0	1
B. Richardson, 2b	5	1	2	0	1	3	0
R. Maris, cf	4	1	1	0	1	0	0
M. Mantle, rf	4	1	1	3	2	0	0
E. Howard, c	4	0	1	0	6	1	0
J. Pepitone, 1b	4	0	0	0	8	2	0
T. Tresh, lf	2	0	1	0	2	0	0
C. Boyer, 3b	4	1	1	1	1	5	1
M. Stottlemyre, p	1	0	0	0	1	1	0
M. Hegan, ph5	0	0	0	0	-	-	-
A. Downing, p5	0	0	0	0	0	0	0
R. Sheldon, p5	0	0	0	0	0	0	0
H. Lopez, ph7	1	0	0	0	-	-	-
S. Hamilton, p7	0	0	0	0	0	0	0
P. Mikkelsen, p8	0	0	0	0	0	1	0
J. Blanchard, ph9	1	0	0	0	-	-	-
	35	5	9	5	24	13	2

St. Louis (NL)	ab	r	h	bi	o	a	e
C. Flood, cf	5	0	0	0	2	0	0
L. Brock, lf	4	1	2	1	0	0	0
B. White, 1b	4	1	2	0	6	0	0
K. Boyer, 3b	4	3	3	1	1	2	0
D. Groat, ss	3	0	0	1	1	1	1
T. McCarver, c	2	1	1	1	9	0	0
M. Shannon, rf	4	1	1	0	3	1	0
D. Maxvill, ss	3	0	1	1	5	3	0
B. Gibson, p	4	0	0	0	0	1	0
	33	7	10	5	27	8	1

New York 000 003 002 - 5
St. Louis 000 330 10x - 7

	ip	h	r-er	bb	so
Stottlemyre (L 1-1)	4	5	3-3	2	2
Downing	*0	3	3-3	0	0
Sheldon	2	0	0-0	0	2
Hamilton	1.1	2	1-1	0	2
Mikkelsen	.2	0	0-0	0	0
Gibson (W 2-1)	9	9	5-5	3	9

*faced three batters in fifth

LOB: NY 6, StL 6. BE: NY 1, StL 1.
DP: Groat-Maxvill-White. Shannon-Groat.
2B: White, K. Boyer
HR: Brock, Mantle, K. Boyer, Linz, C. Boyer.
SH: Maxvill. SF: McCarver.
SB: McCarver, Shannon.
Time - 2:40 Attendance - 30,346
Umpires: F. Secory, B. McKinley, K. Burkhart, H. Soar, V. Smith, & A. Smith

On the very next day, a note of bitterness was injected into the Cardinal camp. Manager Johnny Keane, whose job had been in jeopardy before the Red Birds' race to the pennant, resigned at a press conference that had been called to announce his being rehired.

Coach Red Schoendienst was hired to take Keane's place.

1965—Sunday, August 8th, at Busch Stadium

Cardinals Forced to Use Shannon as Catcher, Lose to Giants, 6-4

Uecker Suffers Split Finger in First Inning

Simmons Loses 11th Game of Season, Spahn Gets Win

The injury jinx struck the St. Louis Cardinals again today. After regular catcher Tim McCarver injured his left thumb on Friday night, the team had just one catcher active, Bub Uecker. This afternoon, the very first batter of the day tipped a foul that split Uecker's right thumb, necessitating 12 stitches and forcing his removal from the game. With no catchers left, manager Red Schoendienst chose to use outfielder Mike Shannon behind the plate.

Shannon, who was sitting on the bench with a .193 batting average, had no previous professional catching experience. The last game he had caught had been when he was a kid in South St. Louis. But he had worked out behind the plate some this season, so he was the obvious choice. He did remarkably well today. His strong arm deterred the opposition from attempting to steal any bases, and he handled even the tricky deliveries of Barney Schultz and Hal Woodeshick well. To top it off, he was the Red Birds' leading hitter, pounding out a double and a triple. The two hits raised his average to over .200.

Today's Results
San Francisco 6 - ST. LOUIS 4
Cincinnati 18 - Los Angeles 0
Milwaukee 8 - Houston 5 (1st game)
Milwaukee 8 - Houston 3 (2nd)
Pittsburgh 7 - Philadelphia 1 (1st)
Philadelphia 5 - Pittsburgh 2 (2nd)
Chicago 7 - New York 6 (1st game)
Chicago 14 - New York 10 (2nd)

Standings	W-L	Pct.	GB
Los Angeles	65-48	.575	-
San Francisco	61-46	.570	1
Milwaukee	61-48	.560	2
Cincinnati	62-49	.559	2
Philadelphia	58-52	.527	5½
Pittsburgh	59-55	.518	6½
ST. LOUIS	55-56	.495	9
Chicago	55-60	.478	11
Houston	46-64	.418	17½
New York	34-78	.304	30½

But Shannon's good work was not enough to keep the Cards from losing their third straight game to the San Francisco Giants. Curt Simmons, a major disappointment this year, was knocked out of the box in the third inning and took his eleventh loss of the year, against just seven wins. Bob Purkey, pitching in relief, allowed two home runs, which provided the Giants with their winning margin, the final score being 6-4.

The St. Louis pitching staff, which allowed 133 home runs in 162 games in 1964, has yielded 127 round-trippers in just 112 games so far this year.

Today's winning pitcher was 44-year-old Warren Spahn. It was win number 361 of his career. The veteran lefthander pitched only 5 1/3 innings, but he snapped a personal losing streak of nine straight decisions, the longest of his career. It was also his 64th win over the Cardinals. Masanori Murakami, the man who relieved him today, was only 2 years old when Spahn won his first game over St. Louis on July 27, 1946.

The Cardinals' troubles started at the very beginning of the game. On the fourth pitch to the Giants' leadoff man, Dick Schofield, Uecker's thumb was split by a foul, and Shannon came in. Schofield grounded out, but the next batter, Jesus Alou, slammed a home run into the left field bleachers. Willie Mays walked and went to third on a double by Jim Ray Hart. But Simmons escaped further damage by inducing Willie McCovey to hit a high pop foul near the plate. Shannon staggered a little bit under the ball, but he made the catch. Cap Peterson bounced out, ending the inning.

The Giants routed Simmons in the third. J. Alou opened with a double, and Mays's single moved him to third. Hart's single scored Alou. After McCovey bounced out, Peterson was intentionally passed to load the bases. Run-scoring singles by Hal Lanier and Dick Bertell ruined the strategy and knocked Simmons out of the game. Barney Schultz came in and got the next two batters, leaving the bases loaded, but San Francisco lead, 4-0.

The Cardinals were given a run in the bottom of the third. Curt Flood walked with two out, and Hart's throwing error on Ken Boyer's grounder let Flood streak all the way home.

A great play featuring catcher Shannon ruined the Giants' chances in the fourth. With one out, Mays singled. Hart then crashed one to the fence in right center. Mays tried to score, but Dick Groat's relay and Shannon's lunging tag retired him at the plate. Then with Hart trying to take third, Shannon got up and gunned the ball to Boyer, completing a double play.

In the bottom of the inning, Shannon doubled to right center. A pinch double by Bob Gibson drove him home.

Bob Purkey came in to pitch for St. Louis in the fifth, and he was greeted by McCovey, who lined a homer onto the pavilion roof. Mays also homered off Purkey in the sixth, giving the Giants a 6-2 lead.

Hal Woodeshick and Don Dennis were able to shut San Francisco out over the last three innings.

The Cardinals threatened against Spahn in the sixth, but Murakami came in with two on, struck Lou Brock out, and got Groat on a liner to second baseman Lanier.

The Cardinals rallied against the Japanese lefthander in the seventh. The first two batters, Flood and Boyer, walked. Bill White then lined one to center, which Mays trapped. Flood, thinking the ball had been caught, held second base, and Mays's throw to third resulted in a force out. Murakami then uncorked two wild pitches, allowing Boyer to score. After Phil Gagliano struck out, Shannon blasted one off the top of the left center field fence for a triple, scoring White. That was all for Murakami, and Jack Sanford came in and retired Ted Savage on a grounder, ending the inning.

Sanford also disposed of the Cardinals easily over the last two innings. The only man to reach base against him was Brock, who walked in the eighth. Sanford promptly picked him off first with a great move. The Cards went out in order in the ninth, and the Giants won, 6-4.

The Cardinals may have lost the game, but they may have found a new catcher, and Mike Shannon may have found his long-lost batting eye.

San Francisco	ab	r	h	bi	o	a	e		St. Louis	ab	r	h	bi	o	a	e
D. Schofield, ss	5	0	0	0	1	5	0		L. Brock, lf	4	0	0	0	3	0	0
J. Alou, rf	5	2	3	1	0	0	0		D. Groat, ss	5	0	1	0	2	3	0
W. Mays, cf	4	2	3	1	3	1	1		C. Flood, cf	2	1	0	0	1	1	0
J. Hart, 3b	5	1	3	1	3	0	1		K. Boyer, 3b	3	1	1	0	2	6	0
J. Davenport, 3b9	0	0	0	0	1	0	0		B. White, 1b	5	1	1	0	8	1	0
W. McCovey, 1b	5	1	1	1	9	1	0		P. Gagliano, 2b	4	0	0	0	2	3	0
C. Peterson, lf	1	0	0	0	0	0	0		B. Uecker, c	0	0	0	0	0	0	0
M. Alou, pr3-lf	1	0	1	0	2	0	0		M. Shannon, c1	3	1	2	1	6	1	0
H. Lanier, 2b	4	0	1	1	3	4	0		T. Savage, rf	4	0	0	0	2	0	0
D. Bertell, c	4	0	2	1	5	0	0		C. Simmons, p	1	0	0	0	0	0	0
W. Spahn, p	3	0	0	0	0	1	0		B. Schultz, p3	0	0	0	0	0	0	0
M. Murakami, p6	0	0	0	0	0	0	0		B. Gibson, ph4	1	0	1	1	-	-	-
J. Sanford, p7	1	0	0	0	0	1	0		B. Purkey, p5	0	0	0	0	1	0	0
									B. Skinner, ph6	1	0	1	0	-	-	-
									H. Woodeshick, p7	0	0	0	0	0	0	0
									T. Francona, ph8	1	0	0	0	-	-	-
									D. Dennis, p9	0	0	0	0	0	0	0
	38	6	14	6	27	13	2			34	4	7	2	27	15	0

San Francisco   103 011 000 - 6
St. Louis   001 100 200 - 4

	ip	h	r-er	bb	so
Spahn (W 5-13)	5.1	6	2-1	4	0
Murakami	1.1	1	2-2	2	2
Sanford	2.1	0	0-0	1	0
Simmons (L 7-11)	2.1	8	4-4	2	0
Schultz	1.2	2	0-0	0	2
Purkey	2	2	2-2	1	0
Woodeshick	2	1	0-0	0	1
Dennis	1	1	0-0	0	1

WP: Murakami 2

LOB: SF 8, StL 10. BE: StL 1.
DP: Flood- Groat-Shannon-Boyer, Boyer-Javier-White.
2B: Hart 2, J. Alou, Shannon, Gibson. 3B: Shannon.
HR: J. Alou, McCovey, Mays.
SB: none. CS: Brock.
Time - 3:11
Attendance - 21,983
Umpires: B. Williams, V. Smith, T. Gorman, & E. Sudol.

Dave Ricketts was called up from Jacksonville to ease the catching emergency before the next game, and McCarver was back in action by the end of the week. Shannon was used behind the plate on three more occasions before the end of the season.

The team went nowhere. They stayed in seventh place for the rest of the season, finishing with an 80-81 record.

1966 — Thursday Night, May 12th, at Busch Memorial Stadium
St. Louis Opens New Downtown Stadium with 12-Inning Win
Buchek's Blooper Ties Game in 9th, Brock's Dribbler Wins It in 12th
Opening Night Crowd Sets New Record for St. Louis

The largest crowd yet to see a sporting event in the history of St. Louis came out to the opening night of the fancy new stadium downtown. The park drew rave reviews from fans, dignitaries, and players, and the first game was an exciting affair, the hometown Cardinals winning in twelve innings, 4-3.

Oh, there were a few inconveniences to keep it from having been a perfect evening. The weather was unseasonably cold, and because the gas had not been installed at the concession stands as yet, there was no hot food to warm the shivering throng. And the field had not been covered from yesterday's rains because the mechanical tarpaulin was not working. So the ground was rather soggy.

But, all in all, the new Busch Memorial Stadium compared favorably to any park in the country. It proved much more spacious than the old Busch Stadium/Sportsman's Park, and there were no seats with obstructed views. The bullpens were located beyond the outfield fence, and a new electronic scoreboard impressed the fans.

Today's Results
ST. LOUIS 4 - Atlanta 3 (12 inn.)
San Francisco 3 - Pittsburgh 0
Philadelphia 5 - Los Angeles 1
Houston at New York - postponed, rain
 no other game scheduled

Standings	W-L	Pct.	GB
San Francisco	21-7	.750	-
Houston	16-11	.593	4½
Pittsburgh	14-11	.560	5½
Los Angeles	15-13	.536	6
Philadelphia	12-11	.522	6½
Atlanta	14-16	.467	8
New York	9-11	.450	8
ST. LOUIS	10-14	.417	9
Cincinnati	10-15	.400	9½
Chicago	6-18	.250	13

Built by a private, non-profit group called The Civic Center Redevelopment Corporation, the stadium was named after the largest single contributor to the $26,000,000 building costs: Anheuser-Busch, Inc. The brewing company, which owns the Cardinals, had also agreed to allow the stadium to keep all of the revenues from parking and concession sales. This assisted the project in obtaining financing.

Just about every prominent St. Louis businessman and politician was in attendance tonight. The most prominent among them, naturally enough, was August A. Busch, Jr., the head of the brewery and the president of the ballclub. Also on hand was a large delegation of baseball's ruling class. Commissioner William D. Eckert, National League president Warren Giles, and Atlanta club owner William C. Bartholomay were all present. They had nothing but praise for the new park.

The attendance of 46,048 was a few thousand below capacity, but it still exceeded the old record of 45,770 set at Sportsman's Park in 1931. Jazz combos seranaded the crowd as it passed through the turnstiles, and each fan received a scroll attesting to the fact that he or she had been present at the stadium's opening game. There was the usual throwing out of the ceremonial first ball, a large choral group sang the Star-Spangled Banner, the spectators bundled themselves up against the wind, and the game was begun.

Ray Washburn of the Cardinals delivered the first pitch (a ball, low and outside) to the Braves' Felipe Alou, and the baseball was promptly given to President Giles for shipment to the Hall of Fame in Cooperstown, N.Y. Gary Geiger, the second man up, got the first hit in the new park, a single to right. Mike Shannon got the first hit for the Cardinals, a one-out single in the bottom of the first.

Shannon also drove in the first run. In the third inning, he tripled to right center with two out, sending Jerry Buchek, who had singled, home. Curt Flood smacked a Wade Blasingame change-up for a single, driving Shannon home. That put the Cardinals ahead, 2-0.

The Braves got one of those runs back in the fourth. Geiger got his second hit, a double, to open the inning. Henry Aaron was walked. Joe Torre hit a grounder to second baseman Julian Javier, who flipped the ball to shortstop Buchek. But Aaron beat the throw to second, so, even though Buchek's relay to first nipped Torre, there was no double play. Lee Thomas then flied out, and Geiger scored after the catch.

Atlanta tied the game in the sixth inning on a long home run by Alou.

With Tracy Stallard on the mound for the Cardinals in the top of the eighth, Alou put the

Braves into the lead with his second home run of the game, a drive deep into the bleachers in left center field.

Joe Hoerner kept the Braves from any further scoring in the eighth and ninth, but the Cards trailed, 3-2, going into the bottom of the last. With one out, Alex Johnson pulled a pitch from Billy O'Dell into left field for a hit, and he continued to second base when Marty Keough fumbled the ball. He took third on Tim McCarver's ground out to second base. With two now out, it was up to Buchek. The St. Louisan got jammed on a 2-and-2 pitch, but his blooper to short right parachuted safely to the ground just out of the reach of three fielders, and Johnson scored the tying run. Bob Gibson followed with a pinch-single past third, but Javier grounded out to end the inning.

The game remained tied until the twelfth.

Hal Woodeshick walked two men in the top of that frame, and Don Dennis was brought in. He got Alou to fly to right for the third out.

The first batter in the bottom of the twelfth, Flood, was hit by a knuckleball from pitcher Phil Niekro. Orlando Cepeda, playing in his first home game as a Cardinal, bunted. Catcher Torre tried to get a force at second, but his throw skipped into center field, allowing Flood to take third and Cepeda second. Charley Smith was intentionally passed, loading the bases. Lou Brock then dribbled a 1-and-2 pitch just past Niekro and through the drawn-in infield for the game-winning hit. The final score was 4-3.

Because it was a school night and the weather was so cold, much of the crowd had left before the game ended.

Atlanta	ab	r	h	bi	o	a	e	St. Louis	ab	r	h	bi	o	a	e
F. Alou, lf-rf8	6	2	2	2	3	0	0	J. Javier, 2b	5	0	0	0	2	9	0
G. Geiger, cf	4	1	3	0	2	0	0	M. Shannon, rf	6	1	3	1	2	0	0
H. Aaron, rf	3	0	0	0	3	0	0	C. Flood, cf	4	1	1	1	5	0	0
B. O'Dell, p8	0	0	0	0	0	0	0	O. Cepeda, 1b	5	0	1	0	19	2	0
C. Olivo, p10	0	0	0	0	0	0	0	C. Smith, 3b	5	0	1	0	0	2	0
G. Oliver, ph11	0	0	0	0	-	-	-	A. Johnson, lf	4	1	1	0	0	0	0
S. Alomar, pr11	0	0	0	0	-	-	-	B. Skinner, ph10	1	0	0	0	-	-	-
P. Niekro, p11	0	0	0	0	0	0	0	L. Brock, lf11	1	0	1	1	0	0	0
J. Torre, c	5	0	0	0	6	1	1	T. McCarver, c	5	0	0	0	4	1	0
L. Thomas, 1b	4	0	1	1	15	0	0	J. Buchek, ss	4	1	2	1	3	4	0
E. Mathews, 3b	4	0	1	0	0	3	0	R. Washburn, p	2	0	0	0	1	3	0
F. Bolling, 2b	4	0	0	0	1	3	0	P. Gagliano, ph7	1	0	0	0	-	-	-
W. Woodward, ss	5	0	0	0	2	5	0	T. Stallard, p8	0	0	0	0	0	0	0
W. Blasingame, p	3	0	0	0	0	1	0	J. Hoerner, p8	0	0	0	0	0	0	0
M. Keough, lf8	0	0	0	0	0	0	1	B. Gibson, ph9	1	0	1	0	-	-	-
R. Carty, ph10-lf	1	0	0	0	1	0	0	H. Woodeshick, p10	1	0	1	0	0	1	0
								D. Dennis, p12	0	0	0	0	0	0	0
	39	3	6	3	33	13	2		45	4	12	4	36	22	0

Atlanta   000 101 010 000 - 3
St. Louis   002 000 001 001 - 4
none out when winning run scored

	ip	h	r-er	bb	so
Blasingame	7	5	2-2	1	3
O'Dell	2.1	5	1-1	1	1
Olivo	.2	0	0-0	0	0
Niekro (L 2-3)	*1	2	1-0	2	0
Washburn	7	5	2-2	1	3
Stallard	.2	1	1-1	1	0
Hoerner	1.1	0	0-0	0	0
Woodeshick	2.2	0	0-0	3	2
Dennis (W 1-0)	.1	0	0-0	0	0

*faced four batters in twelfth
HBP: by Niekro (Flood)

LOB: Atlta 7, StL 14. BE: StL 1.
DP: Javier-Buchek-Cepeda.

2B: Geiger 2, Woodeshick.
3B: Shannon. HR: Alou 2.
SH: Bolling, Cepeda. SF: Thomas.
Time - 3:28 Attendance - 46,048
Umpires: J. Kibler, B. Jackowski,
E. Sudol, & P. Pryor

WP: Blasingame

The Cardinals won 9 of the first 12 games played in the new stadium, but they were unable to rise above sixth place. They made a run toward the top in late July, moving as high as fourth place, but then they fell back.

They finished the season in sixth with an 83-79 record. Their pitching was very good, but they were last in the league in runs scored.

The new stadium helped the club set a new season attendance record, however.

1967—Tuesday Night, July 25th, at Busch Memorial Stadium

Cardinals Hold Off Cubs to Win, 4-3, Regain One-Game Lead

Washburn and Willis Make Early Lead Stand Up

Potential Tying Run Tagged Out at Plate to End Game

The St. Louis Cardinals tonight regained sole possession of first place in the National League standings by beating the Chicago Cubs, 4-3. The Cubs had come to town trailing the Cards by 1 game. On Monday night, Ray Culp pitched Chicago into a tie by winning the game, 3-1. That set up tonight's battle for the lead.

The Cardinals had taken over the league lead from Cincinnati on June 18th. The Cubs tied them on three occasions but never managed to get past them.

St. Louis entered this series without the services of Curt Flood and Bob Gibson. The little outfielder was sidelined with a shoulder injury on July 6th. He was expected to be back in action in a couple of days. The big pitcher suffered a broken bone in the leg on July 15th, an injury that was thought might keep him out for eight weeks.

Today's Results
ST. LOUIS 4 - Chicago 3
Atlanta 1 - Cincinnati 0
San Francisco 5 - New York 4
Los Angeles 3 - Pittsburgh 1
Philadelphia 12 - Houston 7

Standings	W-L	Pct.	GB
ST. LOUIS	57-40	.588	-
Chicago	56-41	.577	1
Atlanta	50-43	.538	5
Cincinnati	52-46	.531	5½
San Francisco	51-47	.520	6½
Pittsburgh	47-47	.500	8½
Philadelphia	46-47	.495	9
Los Angeles	42-53	.442	14
New York	38-55	.409	17
Houston	39-59	.398	18½

In Gibson's absence, manager Red Schoendienst established a pitching rotation with only one veteran, Ray Washburn, in it. The other starting pitchers included 29-year-old rookie Dick Hughes, young lefthanders Larry Jaster and Steve Carlton, and righty Nelson Briles.

Today it was Washburn's turn to pitch. He was making only his second start since suffering a broken thumb last month in Los Angeles. He did a fine job, pitching until the ninth inning. Then he was relieved by Hal Woodeshick, who hit the only batter he faced with a pitch, and Ron Willis, who got the final three outs on two fly balls and a relay play.

The Cubs, who had finished last in the league in 1966, had made a remarkable turnabout in manager Leo Durocher's second year at the helm. With a talented, young lineup, the Cubs were the surprise of the league. Their main weakness appeared to be a lack of pitching depth. After using veteran Culp to win last night's game, Durocher played a hunch and started lefthander Rob Gardner tonight. Gardner had started only one game previously this year, but Durocher was counting on him because the Cardinals owned a sub-.500 (15-16) record against southpaws. But "El Birdos" evened their record against lefties tonight.

St. Louis jumped on Gardner for three runs in the first inning. Lou Brock bounced the first pitch up the middle for a single. Julian Javier lined the next pitch to left for another hit. Roger Maris fouled out. Orlando Cepeda then singled, scoring Brock. Durocher hastily removed Gardner, who had only thrown eight pitches. Bob Shaw, the veteran spitballer recently acquired from the Mets, became the Chicago pitcher. He was greeted by a run-scoring single to center by Mike Shannon and an RBI double to right by Tim McCarver. Alex Johnson fouled out, and Dal Maxvill was purposely walked. Washburn then bounced into a force play, ending the inning.

Shaw was again in hot water in the second. Javier singled with one out, and Maris walked. But Cepeda grounded into a double play.

Two Red Birds got on again in the third, Shannon and Maxvill singling. But Washburn once again ended a rally by going out.

The Cardinals managed a run in the fourth, thanks to a questionable defensive play by the Cubs. Brock opened with a hit. Javier sacrificed him to second. Maris then hit a grounder to shortstop Don Kessinger. Thinking that he could nab the speedy Brock,

Kessinger threw to third. But Lou slid in ahead of the tag, and there was still only one out. When Cepeda flied out, Brock was able to score after the catch. That gave St. Louis a 4-0 lead.

Meanwhile, Washburn held the Cubs down to no runs and three hits through four innings. A great running catch by Brock saved a run in the second. Ernie Banks was on base, via a walk, when Randy Hundley sent a two-out liner to deep left center. Brock raced over, reached across his body, caught the ball, and held it after colliding slightly with center fielder Johnson. In the third, the Cubs wasted two-out singles by Kessinger and Glenn Beckert. A leadoff single by Ron Santo in the fourth also went for naught.

After both teams went out in order in the fifth, the Cubs broke through for two runs in the sixth. Washburn retired the first two batters on ground balls. Then Santo singled again. Banks hit a liner to right center, which Bobby Tolan (who had replaced Johnson) tried to shoestring. He missed it, the ball went to the fence, and Banks had a run-scoring triple. Clarence Jones singled Banks home. Washburn then fanned Hundley.

The Cubs went down in order in the seventh and eighth.

But they rallied desperately in the ninth. Banks opened with a hit to left off Washburn. With the lefthanded batting Jones due up, Schoendienst brought in southpaw Hal Woodeshick to pitch. Durocher sent Ted Savage, a righty, up as a pinch-hitter, and he was hit by a pitch. That was all for Woodeshick, and righthanded sidewinder Ron Willis came in. He got Hundley on a fly to left and Adolpho Phillips on a pop to short. As a last ditch, Al Spangler was sent up to bat. The count went full. With the runners going on the pitch, Spangler lined a single to center, scoring Banks. Savage had a good jump off first, and third base coach Pete Reiser waved him around to the plate. But the Cardinals were alert; Javier took Tolan's throw and quickly relayed it to home. The throw short-hopped into McCarver's glove in plenty of time to nab Savage, who made a desperate, head-first slide. The putout ended the game.

The final score was 4-3, and the Cardinals moved out to a game ahead of the Cubs.

Chicago	ab	r	h	bi	o	a	e	St. Louis	ab	r	h	bi	o	a	e
D. Kessinger, ss	4	0	1	0	2	6	0	L. Brock, lf	4	2	2	0	2	0	0
G. Beckert, 2b	4	0	1	0	2	4	0	J. Javier, 2b	3	1	2	0	2	6	0
B. Williams, lf	4	0	0	0	0	0	0	R. Maris, rf	3	0	0	0	3	0	0
R. Santo, 3b	4	1	2	0	2	1	0	O. Cepeda, 1b	3	1	1	2	11	0	0
E. Banks, 1b	3	2	2	1	9	1	0	M. Shannon, 3b	3	0	2	1	2	1	0
C. Jones, rf	3	0	1	1	0	0	0	T. McCarver, c	4	0	1	1	4	0	0
T. Savage, ph9	0	0	0	0	-	-	-	A. Johnson, cf	1	0	0	0	0	0	0
R. Hundley, c	4	0	0	0	5	0	0	B. Tolan, ph3-cf	3	0	0	0	1	0	0
A. Phillips, cf	4	0	0	0	4	0	0	D. Maxvill, ss	3	0	1	0	3	4	0
R. Gardner, p	0	0	0	0	0	0	0	R. Washburn, p	4	0	0	0	0	1	0
B. Shaw, p1	2	0	0	0	0	0	0	H. Woodeshick, p9	0	0	0	0	0	0	0
L. Thomas, ph7	1	0	0	0	-	-	-	R. Willis, p9	0	0	0	0	0	0	0
B. Hands, p7	0	0	0	0	0	0	0								
A. Spangler, ph9	1	0	1	1	-	-	-								
	34	3	8	3	24	12	0		31	4	9	4	27	13	0

Chicago   000 002 001 - 3
St. Louis   300 100 00x - 4

	ip	h	r-er	bb	so
Gardner (L 0-2)	.1	3	3-3	0	0
Shaw	5.2	6	1-1	2	3
Hands	2	0	0-0	1	1
Washburn (W 6-4)	*8	7	3-3	1	3
Woodeshick	#0	0	0-0	0	0
Willis	1	1	0-0	0	0

*faced one batter in ninth
#faced one batter in ninth

LOB: Chi 6, StL 8.
DP: Kessinger-Beckert-Banks.
2B: McCarver. 3B: Banks.
SH: Javier. SF: Cepeda.
Time - 2:33
Attendance - 37,918 paid
44,996 total
Umpires: S. Crawford, D. Harvey, J. Kibler, & M. Steiner
HBP: by Woodeshick (Savage)

Starting with this victory, the Cardinals pulled away from the rest of the league. They won the following game from the Cubs, 4-2, behind the pitching of Nelson Briles.

Then, playing mostly first division teams, St. Louis won 18 of its next 22 games to build an 11½-game lead by August 19th. From there they cruised to the pennant, winning by 10½ games over the second-place Giants. The Cardinals' final record was 101-60.

The St. Louis fans loved it, and a record 2,090,145 paid to see "El Birdos."

1967 World Series—Game #7

Thursday, October 12th, at Fenway Park, Boston

Gibson's Third Win Gives Cardinals the World Series

Red Sox Stopped on Only Three Hits, Cards Win, 7-2

Maxvill, Gibson, Javier, and Brock Lead Rout of Lonborg

The St. Louis Cardinals and Bob Gibson stopped the Cinderella dream of Boston Red Sox just one game short of the world championship. The Cards, behind the three-hit pitching of Gibson, won the seventh and decisive game of the World Series today, 7-2, and took the championship themselves. That gave the Cardinals eight World Series triumphs to go with their eleven National League pennants. It was also the sixth time in six tries that the Red Birds had won the decisive seventh game of the World Series.

Before today's game, the Cardinals were a bit irked by some of the statements made by the Red Sox in the newspapers. One Boston paper quoted Bosox manager Dick Williams as saying that today the Sox would have "Lonborg and Champagne." Another paper quoted Red Sox first baseman George Scott to the effect that, "Gibson won't survive five." The St. Louis players did not pop off to the press about this, they just went out and won the big game.

Despite having lost the fifth and sixth games, the Cardinals approached the seventh game in their usual, i.e., casual, style. They joked and horsed around at the batting cage and showed little outward sign that this game was going to be for all the marbles. The only real problem seemed to be that Gibson had been unable to get any breakfast. But sportswriter Bob Broeg came to the rescue with a couple of ham-and-egg sandwiches just before the start of batting practice. Apparently, a sandwich was all Gibby needed, because he was overpowering today.

Not so Jim Lonborg. The Red Sox' ace pitcher had shut the Cards out on just one hit in the second game of the series, and he had won the fifth game on a three-hitter, 3-1. But today, pitching with just two days of rest, he was found for ten hits and seven runs in just six innings. The lower end of the Cardinal batting order hit him especially hard. Dal Maxvill started the slugging with a triple in the third inning. Gibson hit a home run in the fifth, and Javier added a three-run shot in the sixth.

The big Cardinal heroes of the series were Gibson and Lou Brock. Gibson, with complete game victories in the first, fourth, and seventh games, was voted the *SPORT* magazine most valuable player of the series, winning a sports car. Brock was also outstanding, batting .414 and stealing seven bases, a new series record. He didn't win the *SPORT* award, but KMOX radio, which broadcast the Cardinal games in St. Louis, announced that it would give Lou a car, too.

Old Fenway Park was jammed early with enthusiastic fans today. They were hoping to see the Red Sox complete the "Impossible Dream" by winning the World Series after finishing in ninth place just a year before. The dream, however, didn't come true.

Gibson was wild at the start of the game, walking leadoff man Joe Foy. Mike Andrews sacrificed. Gibby then jammed the Sox' big hitter, Carl Yastrzemski, and he popped to short. Ken Harrelson struck out on three pitches. Gibson was now rolling, and he set the Red Sox down in order through the next three innings.

The Cardinals, in the meantime, hit Lonborg steadily harder. They scored their first two runs in the third inning. Maxvill led off with a long drive off the center field fence for a triple. Gibson was out when he hit a savage liner that went right into third baseman Foy. Brock popped out, and it looked like Lonborg might escape the jam. But Curt Flood lined a single to center, and Maxie trotted home. Maris singled Flood to third, and a wild pitch brought him home with the second run.

Gibson, batting with one out in the fifth, pounded a 2-1 pitch into the corner of the bleachers in center field for a home run. Brock then popped a single to left. The Cardinal speedster quickly stole second and third, while catcher Elston Howard was unable to handle Lonborg's pitches. Flood walked, and Maris delivered a sacrifice fly, making the score 4-0.

George Scott got Boston onto the scoreboard in the bottom of the fifth. He tattooed an outside pitch to the center field fence. When Flood had a little trouble picking the ball up and Javier's relay to third base skipped into the dugout, Scott circled the bases. But Gibson was not rattled. He retired the next six hitters without trouble.

The Cardinals clinched the victory in the sixth. Right fielder Harrelson, trying for a diving catch, dropped Tim McCarver's line drive, and it went for a double. Foy couldn't handle Shannon's shot to third, and the batter reached on the error. Williams went to the mound to talk to his pitcher, but left him in. Lonborg then hung a 1-2 curve to Javier, and Hoolie lifted it into the screen above the left field fence for a three-run homer. Lonborg finished the inning, then he was lifted for a pinch-hitter.

Gibson tired a little at the end, allowing base runners in each of the last three innings. He walked Yastrzemski in the seventh, but after manager Red Schoendienst came out to talk to him, he got the next three batters. Rico Petrocelli opened the eighth with a double and took third on a wild pitch. Dalton Jones walked, but Gibson then retired the side on three ground balls, while Petrocelli scored. Yaz opened the ninth with a hit, but Harrelson followed by bouncing into a double play. Scott then struck out, and the Cardinals had won, 7-2.

El Birdos were El Champos! With Orlando "Cha-Cha" Cepeda leading the cheers, the jubilant Cardinals celebrated in the clubhouse by yelling, "Lonborg and Champagne, cha-cha-cha," while they sprayed the bubbly stuff around. After flying back to St. Louis and being lionized by the crowd at the airport, the team went to a private victory party at the general manager's place, Stan Musial and Biggie's Restaurant.

St. Louis (NL)	ab	r	h	bi	o	a	e
L. Brock, lf	4	1	2	0	1	0	0
C. Flood, cf	3	1	1	1	0	0	0
R. Maris, rf	3	0	2	1	1	0	0
O. Cepeda, 1b	5	0	0	0	6	2	0
T. McCarver, c	5	1	1	0	12	0	0
M. Shannon, 3b	4	1	0	0	0	0	0
J. Javier, 2b	4	1	2	3	4	4	1
D. Maxvill, ss	4	1	1	0	3	3	0
B. Gibson, p	4	1	1	1	0	1	0
	36	7	10	6	27	10	1

Boston (AL)	ab	r	h	bi	o	a	e
J. Foy, 3b	3	0	0	0	2	3	1
D. Morehead, p9	0	0	0	0	0	0	0
D. Osinski, p9	0	0	0	0	0	0	0
K. Brett, p9	0	0	0	0	0	0	0
M. Andrews, 2b	3	0	0	0	1	2	0
C. Yastrzemski, lf	3	0	1	0	2	0	0
K. Harrelson, rf	4	0	0	3	3	0	0
G. Scott, 1b	4	1	1	0	9	0	0
R. Smith, cf	3	0	0	2	0	0	0
R. Petrocelli, ss	3	1	1	0	3	2	0
E. Howard, c	2	0	0	4	1	0	
D. Jones, ph8-3b	0	0	0	0	0	0	0
J. Lonborg, p	1	0	0	0	0	0	0
J. Tartabull, ph6	1	0	0	0	-	-	-
J. Santiago, p7	0	0	0	0	0	0	0
N. Siebern, ph8	1	0	1	0	-	-	-
R. Gibson, c9	0	0	0	0	1	0	0
	28	2	3	1	27	8	1

St. Louis 002 023 000 - 7
Boston   000 010 010 - 2

	ip	h	r-er	bb	so
B. Gibson (W 3-0)	9	3	2-2	3	10
Lonborg (L 2-1)	6	10	7-6	1	3
Santiago	2	0	0-0	0	1
Morehead	.1	0	0-0	3	1
Osinski	.1	0	0-0	0	0
Brett	.1	0	0-0	0	0

WP: Lonborg, B. Gibson

LOB: StL 7, Bos 3. BE: StL 1.
DP: Maxvill-Javier-Cepeda.
2B: McCarver, Brock, Petrocelli.
3B: Maxvill, Scott.
HR: B. Gibson, Javier.
SH: Andrews. SF: Maris.
SB: Brock 3. CS: Javier.
Time - 2:23 Attendance - 35,185
Umpires: J. Stevens, A. Barlick, F. Umont, A. Donatelli, E. Runge, & P. Pryor

1968 — Monday Night, July 1st, at Dodger Stadium, Los Angeles

Scoreless Streak Ends, but Gibson Beats Dodgers Easily, 5-1

Wild Pitch in First Inning Allows Los Angeles to Score

Seventh Win in a Row for Gibby

Bob Gibson's approach toward the record for consecutive scoreless innings pitched ended in the very first inning tonight, much to the delight of the Los Angeles Dodgers and their fans. But Gibson, who hadn't been known to care much about records, pitched an effective game and did what he had set out to do, i.e., win the game for the St. Louis Cardinals.

With pitching dominating the game more this year than any time since 1908, the focus has been on spectacular achievements of individual pitchers. Jim "Catfish" Hunter of the Oakland A's pitched a rare perfect game on May 8th. Both Denny McLain of the Tigers (14-2) and Juan Marichal of the Giants (14-3) were in positions to possibly become 30-game winners.

Today's Results
ST. LOUIS 5 - Los Angeles 1
Atlanta 5 - San Francisco 1
Cincinnati 3 - Houston 2 (11 inn.)
Philadelphia 6 - Chicago 4
  no other game scheduled

Standings	W-L	Pct.	GB
ST. LOUIS	47-30	.610	-
Atlanta	40-36	.526	6½
San Francisco	40-38	.513	7½
Cincinnati	38-37	.507	8
Los Angeles	40-39	.506	8
Pittsburgh	36-36	.500	8½
New York	36-38	.4865	9½
Philadelphia	34-36	.4857	9½
Chicago	33-42	.440	13
Houston	32-44	.421	14½

But perhaps the most impressive individual accomplishment in the first half of the season was turned in by the Dodger's Don Drysdale. Starting on May 14th, he ran off six consecutive shutouts. That broke a major league record that had stood since 1904. When he pitched 4 1/3 scoreless innings in his next game, Drysdale's 58 1/3 consecutive scoreless innings pitched broke the old mark of 56 set by Walter Johnson in 1913.

About the time that Drysdale's streak was ending, St. Louis's Bob Gibson was starting a string of his own. He had started the season slowly, winning three games and losing five through May, but he got hot in June. On the 2nd of that month, he beat the Mets, 6-3, allowing two runs in the sixth inning and a leadoff home run by Ed Charles in the seventh. Then he became untouchable. He shut out the Astros, the Braves, the Reds, the Cubs, and the Pirates. That gave him five straight shutouts and 48 scoreless innings in a row.

Tonight, he started in Los Angeles against Drysdale and the Dodgers. Another shutout would tie Drysdale's record and put Gibson into a position to break the consecutive scoreless innings record. Naturally, Dodger Stadium was filled to capacity. Unfortunately for the Los Angeles front office, 11,000 of the fans came on free admissions given to Straight-A students (an idea the Dodgers borrowed from the Cardinals). The seats could easily have been sold.

The drama of the occasion lasted only one inning. After Gibson had retired the first two Dodger batters in the first inning, Len Gabrielson singled to right. Tom Haller then hit a sharp grounder toward second. Julian Javier backed up on the ball, but it took a bad hop, kicked off his glove, and rolled into right field. Gabrielson took third on the hit. Ron Fairly, who had a reputation of being able to hit Gibson, was up and the Los Angeles fans cheered. The first pitch was a strike. Gibson rocked and fired the next pitch, a fastball, into the dirt. Catcher Johnny Edwards got only the edge of his glove on the ball, and it kicked off umpire Shag Crawford's shin guard and went to the screen. Gabrielson ran home, leaped up, and landed on the plate with both feet, ending Gibson's shutout streak. Pandemonium broke in the stands. It continued even after Fairly bounced out.

The stands were still buzzing when the Cardinals tied the game in the top of the second. With one out, Bobby Tolan looped a single to right center. The speedster raced to third on Mike Shannon's hit to right. Javier then lined out to left field deeply enough to allow Tolan to tag up and score.

Gibson went back out and shut the Dodgers out for the rest of the game. He was not at his best, allowing nine hits and striking out only four batters, but he was still effective in the pinches.

Drysdale was also effective for five innings, holding the Cardinals to just the one run.

Then St. Louis broke the tie in the sixth. Curt Flood began with a single to left. He took third on Edwards's base hit to right field. Orlando Cepeda flied deep to center, and Flood scored after the catch.

The Red Birds knocked Drysdale out of the box and clinched the victory by scoring three times in the seventh. Javier led off with a hit to left. Maxvill tried to bunt but missed on two attempts. Swinging away, Maxie bounced a single up the middle, sending Hoolie to third. Javier scored on an infield out by Gibson. Lou Brock followed with a hit to left, Maxvill scoring and Brock taking second on the throw to the plate. A passed ball moved Lou to third. Flood brought him home with a hit, making the score 5-1. Manager Walter Alston then relieved Drysdale with Jim Brewer, who retired both Edwards and Cepeda on fly balls to center field.

The Dodgers threatened in each of the last two innings but could not get even one more run. In the eighth, Jim Fairey opened with a pinch single, and, with one out, Paul Popovich moved him to third with a hit. But Gibson got Gabrielson on a short fly to left and Haller on a ground ball. In the ninth, the Dodgers again got men to first and third with one out. Ken Boyer walked and took third on Jim Lefebvre's smash past second. But Wes Parker popped out to third, and Bob Bailey struck out, ending the game. The final score was 5-1.

Gibson was a winner for the seventh straight time, which was really what he cared about. After the game, he discounted any pressure because of the record, saying that that sort of thing was for fans and sportswriters. For the players, "The important thing is to win." But, being a champion clubhouse agitator, Gibby couldn't help needling Edwards about the fateful wild pitch. "It was the catcher's fault, he loused it up," he said loudly. Everyone knew he wasn't serious. He only got serious about important things, like winning games.

St. Louis	ab	r	h	bi	o	a	e
L. Brock, lf	5	1	2	1	2	0	0
C. Flood, cf	5	1	2	1	2	0	0
J. Edwards, c	4	0	1	0	4	1	0
O. Cepeda, 1b	3	0	0	1	8	3	0
B. Tolan, rf	4	1	1	0	0	0	0
M. Shannon, 3b	4	0	1	0	2	0	0
J. Javier, 2b	3	1	2	1	3	4	0
D. Maxvill, ss	4	1	1	0	4	1	0
B. Gibson, p	2	0	0	1	2	1	0
	34	5	10	5	27	10	0

Los Angeles	ab	r	h	bi	o	a	e
W. Davis, cf	3	0	0	0	5	0	0
P. Popovich, ss	3	0	2	0	1	1	0
L. Gabrielson, lf	4	1	1	0	3	0	0
T. Haller, c	4	0	1	0	6	1	0
R. Fairly, rf	4	0	2	0	0	0	0
K. Boyer, 3b	3	0	0	0	1	1	0
J. Lefebvre, 2b	4	0	1	0	2	6	0
W. Parker, 1b	4	0	1	0	8	1	0
D. Drysdale, p	2	0	0	0	1	0	0
J. Brewer, p7	0	0	0	0	0	0	0
J. Fairey, ph8	1	0	1	0	-	-	-
J. Purdin, p9	0	0	0	0	0	0	0
B. Bailey, ph9	1	0	0	0	-	-	-
	33	1	9	0	27	10	0

St. Louis	010	001	300	- 5
Los Angeles	100	000	000	- 1

	ip	h	r-er	bb	so
Gibson (W 10-5)	9	9	1-1	2	4
Drysdale (L 10-5)	6.1	10	5-5	1	4
Brewer	1.2	0	0-0	0	1
Purdin	1	0	0-0	1	0

WP: Gibson. PB: Haller.
Umpires: S. Crawford, C. Pelekoudas, D. Harvey, & J. Kibler.

LOB: StL 6, LA 8.
DP: Cepeda-Maxvill-Cepeda.
2B: Parker. SH: Popovich.
SF: Javier, Cepeda.
SB: Javier, CS: Boyer.
Picked Off: Brock.
Attendance - 42,603 paid, 54,107 total
Time - 2:21

After his 6-0 record paced the Cardinals to a 22-9 record in June, Gibson was again 6-0 in July (allowing just three runs), and the Red Birds were 24-6 for that month.

That gave them a whopping 14½-game lead, and they cruised to their second straight pennant, finishing with a 97-65 record and a 9½-game final margin over the second-place Giants.

Gibson ran his personal winning streak to 15 games before losing to Pittsburgh on August 24th. He finished the season with a 22-9 record, 13 shutouts, and an incredible 1.12 E.R.A. He won both the Cy Young and MVP awards.

1968 World Series—Game #1

Wednesday, October 2nd, at Busch Memorial Stadium

Gibby Fans 17 Tigers, Cardinals Win Series Opener, 4-0

Cards Score Three in Fourth, Brock Homers in Seventh

Gibson Bests McLain in Battle of Pitching Stars

The World Series between the American League champion Detroit Tigers and the National League champs, the St. Louis Cardinals, opened today. The game featured the dream match-up between 31-game winner Denny McLain of the Tigers and 1.12 E.R.A. man Bob Gibson of the Cardinals.

Gibson won Round One of the battle in decisive fashion, shutting Detroit out on five hits and setting a new World Series record by striking out 17 batters. McLain was the loser, giving up three runs in five innings of work. As a result, St. Louis won the opening game of the series, 4-0.

Both teams had made runaways of their respective pennant races. But the Cardinals entered the series as heavy favorites. For one thing, they had more experience, being the defending champions. But perhaps their biggest advantage was seen as the person of their pitching ace, Gibson.

Today he showed casual observers of baseball what followers of the game already knew: that he could be one of the most dominating performers in sports. He also showed the Tigers, and they were mightily impressed. Sure, they had heard about his rising fastball. But they weren't ready for his sharply breaking slider. They were clearly overmatched, and every man in the starting lineup struck out at least once. Gibson threw 144 pitches, including 53 breaking balls.

On a beautiful day, 54,692 people filled St. Louis's downtown Busch Stadium. Many sat in their shirtsleeves. The Cardinals presented exactly the same batting order that they had used in all seven games of the 1967 World Series. The Tigers made one important change in their lineup. Their manager, Mayo Smith, shifted his best fielding outfielder, Mickey Stanley, to shortstop, opening a spot for veteran Al Kaline in the outfield. Stanley had played short in a few late-season games, but this was his first "money game" at the position. The first Cardinal batter hit a fairly difficult bouncer to him, and Stanley handled the chance well. After that, he made all the plays.

The strikeout parade began early. In the first inning, the Tigers' leadoff man, Dick McAuliffe, chased a low fastball for strike three. Stanley singled on a full count but was thrown out trying to steal second. Gibby then fanned Kaline.

The Cardinals went down in order in the bottom of the first.

Gibson struck out the side in the second.

McLain got a clutch strikeout in the Cards' half. After Tim McCarver tripled with one out, Mike Shannon fanned on a 2-2 fastball. Javier then was called out on strikes, and McCarver was left stranded.

Gibson struck out Bill Freehan to open the third, making it five straight "K's." With a 1-2 count, Don Wert broke the string with a line single to center. McLain tried to bunt him over but fouled off the third attempt for an easy strikeout. McAuliffe then bounced softly to first base for the third out.

The Cards once again left a man on third on the bottom of the inning.

Gibson got only one strikeout in the fourth, getting the other two batters on fly balls.

Aided by McLain's wildness, the Cardinals broke the scoreless tie with three runs in the fourth. Roger Maris, first up, walked on four pitches. Orlando Cepeda fouled out on a full count. McCarver walked, also on four pitches. With a 2-and-2 count, Shannon ripped a high, inside fastball into left field, scoring Maris. When Willie Horton fumbled the hit, McCarver and Shannon got to third and second, respectively. With the infield playing in, Javier punched the first pitch to him through the right side for a two-run single.

Three runs were more than enough for Gibson today. He kept mowing the Tiger hitters down. His only real trouble came in the sixth. With one out in that inning,

McAuliffe singled. Stanley struck out, but Kaline golfed a breaking ball into the left field corner for a double. Fast fielding by Lou Brock kept McAuliffe from scoring. Gibson then put a little extra on a 2-2 fastball to Norm Cash, ending the threat with his eleventh strikeout.

McLain went out for a pinch-hitter in that inning, and Pat Dobson pitched for the Tigers in the sixth and seventh. Brock lined one of his serves into the bleachers for a home run in the seventh.

Gibson had 14 strikeouts going into the ninth inning, one short of the series record set by Sandy Koufax in 1963. Bob wasn't aware of the act, however. The first hitter, Stanley, singled, so Gibby bore down a little harder. He fanned Kaline on a fastball, tying the record, and the St. Louis crowd was on its feet. When Cash chased a breaking ball for strike three, the cheering nearly brought the house down. Gibson knew he still had one out to get to win the game, and he didn't know what all the fuss was about. But catcher McCarver pointed to him to turn around and look at the message board above the bleachers, which announced the new record. After a brief glance, Gibson turned back around and, a little peevishly, motioned for the ball. He wanted that last out. Strikeouts were not what mattered, winning the game was. When Horton took a called third strike (strikeout #17) the victory was completed.

Detroit (AL)	ab	r	h	bi	o	a	e		St. Louis (NL)	ab	r	h	bi	o	a	e
D. McAuliffe, 2b	4	0	1	0	4	0	0		L. Brock, lf	4	1	1	1	2	0	0
M. Stanley, ss	4	0	2	0	3	2	0		C. Flood, cf	4	0	1	0	1	0	0
A. Kaline, rf	4	0	1	0	2	0	0		R. Maris, rf	3	1	0	0	1	0	0
N. Cash, 1b	4	0	0	0	6	1	1		O. Cepeda, 1b	4	0	0	0	1	1	0
W. Horton, lf	4	0	0	0	2	0	1		T. McCarver, c	3	1	1	0	17	1	0
J. Northrup, cf	3	0	0	0	2	0	0		M. Shannon, 3b	4	1	2	1	0	0	0
B. Freehan, c	2	0	0	0	4	1	1		J. Javier, 2b	3	0	1	2	2	0	0
D. Wert, 3b	2	0	1	0	0	1	0		D. Maxvill, ss	2	0	0	0	2	0	0
E. Mathews, ph8	1	0	0	0	-	-	-		B. Gibson, p	2	0	0	0	1	0	0
D. Tracewski, 3b8	0	0	0	0	0	0	0									
D. McLain, p	1	0	0	0	0	2	0									
T. Matchick, ph6	1	0	0	0	-	-	-									
P. Dobson, p6	0	0	0	0	0	0	0									
G. Brown, ph8	1	0	0	0	-	-	-									
D. McMahon, p8	0	0	0	0	1	0	0									
	31	0	5	0	24	7	3			29	4	6	4	27	2	0

Detroit   000 000 000 - 0
St. Louis 000 300 10x - 4

	ip	h	r-er	bb	so
McLain (L 0-1)	5	3	3-2	3	3
Dobson	2	2	1-1	1	0
McMahon	1	1	0-0	0	0
Gibson (W 1-0)	9	5	0-0	1	17

Time - 2:29

LOB: Detr 5, StL 6. BE: StL 1.
2B: Kaline. 3B: McCarver.
HR. Brock. SH: Gibson.
SB: Brock, Javier, Flood.
CS: Stanley, Javier.
Attendance - 54,692
Umpires: T. Gorman, J. Honochick,
S. Landes, B. Kinnamon,
D. Harvey, & B. Haller

The Tigers won the second game of the series, 8-1, behind the pitching of Mickey Lolich.

The Cardinals won the next two games: 7-3 behind Ray Washburn and Joe Hoerner, and 10-1 with Gibson winning again.

The Tigers and Lolich rallied to win the fifth game, 5-3.

Then with McLain pitching, Detroit massacred St. Louis in Game #6, 13-1.

In the decisive seventh game, the Tigers and Lolich beat the Cardinals and Gibson, 4-1, thereby winning the series.

Chapter XII

Red's East Division Blues
1969-1976

1969—September 15th at Busch Memorial Stadium
Carlton Strikes Out 19 for New Record but Loses, 4-3

1970—August 11th at Busch Memorial Stadium
Carl Taylor's Pinch Grand Slam Caps Come-From-Behind Victory

1971—August 14th at Pittsburgh
Gibson Pitches No-Hitter, Cuts Pirates' Lead to 5 Games

1972—September 20th at Busch Memorial Stadium
Carlton Bests Wise and Cardinals, 2-1, for 25th Win

1973—July 22nd at Busch Memorial Stadium
Late Rally Wins for Cards, 5-4, St. Louis Takes Division Lead

1974—September 25th at Busch Memorial Stadium
Four-Run Rally in 11th Puts Red Birds Back Into First Place

1975—July 12th at Busch Memorial Stadium
"Mad Hungarian" Gets Win On "We Hlove Hrabosky Hbanner Day"

1976—May 22nd at Philadelphia
Smith's Three Homers & Great Catch Bring Victory to Cards, 7-6

The National League expanded to twelve teams for the 1969 season and put the Cardinals in the East Division.

Things began to change for the Red Birds after the 1968 World Series. Roger Maris retired. Orlando Cepeda, one of the team's morale boosters, was traded. The holdovers, after back-to-back pennants, got enough in salary boosts to give the team the first $1,000,000 player payroll in baseball history. When the Player's Association staged a work stoppage in spring training, Cardinal president Busch went down to training camp and spoke to the players about their obligations to the fans.

The upshot of it all was a bitterly disappointing season. Typical of the year was a game in mid-September when Steve Carlton set a new single-game strikeout record but lost to the Mets, and the Cardinals dropped farther out of the race. They finished fourth in the six-team division.

In 1970, the pitching staff was suddenly ineffective, and the Cards were a sub-.500 team. It sometimes took heroics like a ninth-inning grand slam to beat even the worst teams in the league, like the San Diego Padres. The Red Birds again finished fourth.

In 1971, some of the newer pitchers began to come around, and some veterans acquired to fill the lineup did well. Joe Torre, acquired in the Cepeda trade, had a great season, leading the league in batting and RBI's. And Matty Alou and Ted Sizemore helped. Carlton led the pitchers with 20 wins, although the nominal ace, Bob Gibson, was the star when he pitched a no-hitter against the first-place Pirates. The various improvements added up to a second-place finish.

In 1972, the Cardinals were optimistic at the start of the year, but Red Schoendienst's team was a big disappointment again. Carlton was traded to avoid his holding out for more salary than the club was willing to give him. The team got off to a terrible start, had one good stretch in June, then fell hopelessly out of the race in July. High-salaried veterans like Alou and Dal Maxvill were sold, and young prospects were force-fed into the lineup. St. Louis wound up back in fourth place. To make it seem even worse, Carlton compiled a 27-10 record with the last-place Phillies and beat the Red Birds four times.

In 1973, the Cards got off to another horrendous start. But they turned things around in May and climbed into first place on the day before the All-Star break. But they played poorly in August and September and finished second, just 1½ games out of first.

In 1974, St. Louis was again in the thick of the race down the stretch. With Lou Brock setting the pace with a record-breaking stolen base performance, the Cardinals had an exciting team. On their last home date of the season, the Cards won an epic, thirteen-inning battle with the Pirates to move ½ game ahead. But then they lost two games in the last week and again had to settle for second place, 1½ games out of first.

In 1975, St. Louis did not do as well at the start. The only really bright spot in the first half was the relief pitching of Al "The Mad Hungarian" Hrabosky. When he was left off the All-Star team, the Cardinal front office arranged for a banner day to honor the pitcher. To make the day complete, Hrabosky got the win.

The Cardinals made a run at first place in August, but then fell back and finished tied for third place.

In 1976, nothing went right. The team lacked power and was weak on defense. Reggie Smith, despite one three-home run game, did poorly and was traded to Los Angeles. The team finished a dismal fifth. The poor showing finally led to the removal of Red Schoendienst as manager after 12 years at the helm.

1969 — Monday Night, September 15th, at Busch Memorial Stadium

Carlton Strikes Out 19 for New Record but Loses to Mets, 4-3

Swoboda Hits Two Two-Run Home Runs

Strikes Out the Side in Ninth to Beat Old Modern Record by One

Steve Carlton broke one of baseball's more prestigious records tonight when he struck out 19 batters. The appreciative St. Louis fans gave the lefthander his first standing ovation ever when he broke the record. Only one detail marred an otherwise perfect evening for Carlton and the fans: the Cardinals lost the game to the amazing New York Mets, 4-3.

The Mets' runs came on a pair of two-run home runs by Ron Swoboda, whom Carlton struck out two other times. So, despite 19 strikeouts and four errors, the incredible Mets managed to win their eleventh decision in twelve games. They upped their lead in the National League East Division race to 4½ games over the Cubs and 10 games over the third-place Cardinals.

Today's Results
New York 4 - ST. LOUIS 3
Montreal 8 - Chicago 2
Philadelphia 2 - Pittsburgh 1 (1st)
Philadelphia 4 - Pittsburgh 3 (2nd)

Standings	W-L	Pct.	GB
New York	89-58	.605	-
Chicago	85-63	.574	4½
ST. LOUIS	79-68	.537	10
Pittsburgh	77-69	.527	11½
Philadelphia	59-87	.404	29½
Montreal	48-100	.324	41½

Carlton became the first major league pitcher to strike out more than 18 batters since 1884. Way back in that year, a couple of hurlers had struck out 19, but the rules allowed them to start about 4½ feet closer to the plate and to take a hop, skip, and jump in their delivery. Since then, 18 had been the best mark.

Carlton's previous career high in strikeouts was 16, set in a losing game on the road, meaning that he only pitched eight innings.

Tonight he again had 16 strikeouts after eight innings, and he was losing the game. Luckily he was pitching at home. When he saw an announcement about his 16 strikeouts on the stadium message board in the bottom of the eighth, Carlton decided to go after the record in the ninth. He struck out the side. Of his 19 strikeout victims, 10 were called out, and 9 went down swinging.

Carlton fanned three in the first inning. Bud Harrelson, batting first, and Swoboda, hitting fifth, both swung at third strikes. Amos Otis, second up, was called out. An error and a single were thrown in.

Three more victims went down in the second. Ed Charles and Gary Gentry going swinging, whereas Jerry Grote was called out.

Carlton picked Bud Harrelson, who had bunted safely, off base in the third. Otis popped out, and Tommy Agee fanned on a high, inside fastball.

The Cardinals scored the first run of the game in the bottom of the third. Questionable base running kept them from scoring more. Lou Brock walked with one out. With a full count on Curt Flood, Brock took off for second. Flood rolled a single to center, and the ball died on the wet outfield grass. Brock tried to come all the way home, but he was thrown out at the plate. Flood went to second on the play and scored on a hit by Vada Pinson.

Carlton added three more strikeouts in the fourth, but he lost the lead. He walked the first batter, Donn Clendenon. His first two pitches to the next man, Swoboda, were strikes. Then he tried to slip a fastball past him in tight. But the pitch was not in as far as Carlton had wanted, and Swoboda lined it into the mezzanine in left field for a two-run homer. Grote later singled in the inning, but Charles, Al Weis, and Gentry struck out.

In the fifth, Harrelson popped out, and Otis and Agee watched third strikes.

In the bottom half, the Cardinals went ahead. They scored two runs on two-out singles by Brock, Flood, Pinson, and Joe Torre.

Swoboda was the only Met to strike out in the sixth.

And only one Met struck out in the seventh. That was Otis, who looked at a called third strike with two on and two out.

Tug McGraw went in to pitch for the Mets in the seventh. He pitched three scoreless innings, although errors in the seventh and ninth made his job difficult.

The Mets took the lead again in the eighth, despite two strikeouts. Agee opened with a single. Clendenon was called out on a fastball at the knees. Swoboda worked the count to 2-and-2. Carlton then hung a slider, and Swoboda rode it into the stands for another homer run, putting New York ahead, 4-3. Charles flied out, Grote singled, and Weis was called out on strikes.

Through eight innings, Carlton had thrown 138 pitches, including 84 fastballs, 22 curves, and 32 sliders. In the ninth inning, when he was trying for the record, he threw 12 fastballs and 2 sliders. He was tiring, but two rain delays, totalling 81 minutes, had helped him.

He started the ninth needing three strikeouts to break the record. With the Mets ahead, McGraw got to bat for himself, and Carlton fanned him on four pitches. The first pitch to Harrelson was a ball. But the next three were fastballs over the plate, Harrelson being called out on the last one. Carlton had tied the record. Amos Otis was the next batter, and he had already struck out three times. Carlton wanted the record badly, and he poured five fastballs up to the plate. Two were balls, two were strikes, and the fifth was fouled. Carlton then tried a slider. The pitch was in the dirt, but Otis was fooled by the breaking ball, and he chased it for strike three. Carlton had the record, although catcher Tim McCarver had to throw to first to get the out. The fans gave the tall, 24-year-old pitcher a great hand as he walked off the mound.

The Cardinals got two men on base in the bottom of the ninth but failed to score. So, the Mets won the game, 4-3.

In the St. Louis clubhouse, Carlton was elated with the record. Over in the visitors' clubhouse, the Mets were elated with their victory. "Three cheers for Otis," they yelled, "Send his bat to Cooperstown."

New York	ab	r	h	bi	o	a	e
B. Harrelson, ss	4	0	1	0	1	3	1
A. Otis, lf	5	0	0	0	2	0	0
T. Agee, cf	4	1	1	0	4	1	0
D. Clendenon, 1b	3	1	1	0	7	0	1
R. Swoboda, rf	4	2	2	4	4	0	0
E. Charles, 3b	4	0	0	0	0	2	2
J. Grote, c	4	0	2	0	7	0	0
A. Weis, 2b	4	0	1	0	2	1	0
G. Gentry, p	2	0	0	0	0	2	0
B. Pfeil, ph7	1	0	1	0	-	-	-
J. Gosger, pr7	0	0	0	0	-	-	-
T. McGraw, p7	1	0	0	0	0	0	0
	36	4	9	4	27	9	4

St. Louis	ab	r	h	bi	o	a	e
L. Brock, lf	4	1	2	0	2	0	0
C. Flood, cf	5	2	2	1	1	0	0
V. Pinson, rf	4	0	3	1	1	0	0
J. Torre, 1b	4	0	1	1	4	0	0
T. McCarver, c	4	0	0	0	18	1	0
M. Shannon, 3b	4	0	0	0	0	1	0
J. Javier, 2b	4	0	0	0	0	0	1
D. Maxvill, ss	3	0	0	0	1	0	0
B. Browne, ph9	1	0	0	0	-	-	-
S. Carlton, p	3	0	0	0	0	1	0
P. Gagliano, ph9	1	0	0	0	-	-	-
J. Nossek, pr9	0	0	0	0	-	-	-
	37	3	8	3	27	3	1

New York	000	200	020	-	4
St. Louis	001	020	000	-	3

	ip	h	r-er	bb	so
Gentry	6	7	3-3	1	3
McGraw (W 8-3)	3	1	0-0	1	3
Carlton (L 16-10)	9	9	4-4	2	19

WP: Carlton

LOB: NY 7, StL 9. BE: NY 1, StL 4.
DP: Charles-Weis-Clendenon.
HR: Swoboda 2.
SB: Pinson, Brock 2.
Picked Off: Harrelson.
Time - 2:23 Attendance - 13,086
Umpires: D. Stello, A. Donatelli, M. Steiner, & B. Engel

The Cardinals slipped to fourth place by the end of the season. Their record was a respectable 87-75, but after two consecutive pennants, the 1969 season was a big disappointment.

The Mets went on to win the division pennant, the league championship playoff, and the World Series.

1970 — Tuesday Night, August 11th, at Busch Memorial Stadium
Carl Taylor's Pinch Grand Slam Caps Come-From-Behind Victory
Winning Blow Comes with Two Out in Ninth, Cards Win, 11-10
Both Bullpens Fail, Padres Lose 8-1 Lead

The St. Louis Cardinals, trying to battle back from a disastrous slump in July, continued their recent winning ways with a dramatic, come-from-behind victory over the San Diego Padres tonight, 11-10. The final four runs of their comeback came on a two-out, bases-loaded home run in the ninth inning by pinch-hitter Carl Taylor. The victory was the Red Birds' 13th in their last 16 games. Immediately before this hot streak, the Cards had lost 18 of 21, which had dropped them from third place, 3 games out of first, to last place, 13 games behind. Tonight's triumph kept St. Louis in fourth place and edged the team to 9 games behind the division-leading Pirates.

The Cardinals' biggest problem has been pitching, especially relief pitching.

Today's Results
ST. LOUIS 11 - San Diego 10
Los Angeles 5 - Pittsburgh 4
Cincinnati 8 - New York 1
Chicago 4 - San Francisco 1
Philadelphia 6 - Houston 5
Atlanta 1 - Montreal 0

Standings	W-L	Pct.	GB
Pittsburgh	64-52	.552	-
New York	60-53	.531	2½
Chicago	59-56	.513	4½
ST. LOUIS	54-60	.474	9
Philadelphia	53-60	.468	9½
Montreal	49-67	.422	15

The Padres' pitching, including their bullpen, has been as bad as or worse than the Cardinals'.

As might be expected, these two teams staged a slugfest in the opening game of their three-game series tonight. The St. Louis starter, Nelson Briles, entered the game with a whopping 6.71 E.R.A. He left with it at 7.19. Earl Wilson, who started for San Diego, reduced his E.R.A. from 4.61 to 4.50, but the Padre bullpen let the game get away after he left.

Briles started badly, hitting Jose Arcia with the very first pitch of the game. Arcia was caught stealing. But with two out, Briles walked Clarence Gaston and Al Ferrara. Then he gave up three straight singles, and the Padres had three runs.

The Cardinals got one run in their first ups. Lou Brock, Julian Javier, and Joe Torre singled for the score.

The Pads knocked Briles out of the game with two runs in the third. The key blow was a long fly to deep left field by Ferrara, which Brock grabbed with a leap but dropped when his glove hit the wall. It went for a double.

An error by Javier paved the way for another Padre run in the fourth against reliever Frank Linzy.

Ollie Brown homered against Linzy in the fifth, the ball going into the area between the two sections of the bleachers.

Brown got his fourth RBI of the game in the seventh with a single off Bob Chlupsa. Ferrara, who had tripled, scored the run.

The Cardinals came up in the bottom of the seventh, trailing, 8-1. Wilson had allowed just six hits and one walk. But he was tiring. With one out, Jim Beauchamp delivered a pinch single. Brock doubled, sending Beauchamp to third. Jim got home on an infield out, and Lou scored on Joe Hague's single. Padre manager Preston Gomez then decided to take Wilson out before any more damage was done. Tom Dukes came in and struck Richie Allen, the Cards' big RBI man, out to end the inning.

Chuck Taylor shut San Diego out in the top of the eighth.

In the bottom, St. Louis battled back into the game with three runs. Torre started off with a home run, his 13th of the year. Dukes retired Jose Cardenal and Mike Shannon, but utility man Ed Crosby, who had taken over as shortstop after Dal Maxvill left for a pinch-hitter, tripled to right. Manager Red Schoendienst then sent up hit ace pincher, Vic Davalillo. Vic beat out an infield tap, but Crosby had to hold third. When Brock delivered a double, both Crosby and Davalillo scored. Side-armer Ron Willis was brought in by the Pads to pitch, and he got Javier to line out.

The Cardinals had cut the Padre lead to 8-6, and the crowd, which included many Straight-A students, was hopeful. But young Harry Parker, the rookie from Collinsville, Illinois, couldn't hold San Diego down in the top of the ninth. Ed Spezio delivered a two-out, bases-loaded single to make the score 10-6.

Hague opened the bottom of the ninth with a hit. Allen forced him at second. Torre and Cardenal singled for a run.

With the tying run coming to the plate, Gomez reluctantly called in his overworked ace reliever, Ron Herbel. Herbel got Shannon to hit into another force play for the second out of the inning. Schoendienst had only one pinch-hitter left on the bench, Carl Taylor, and Crosby and Parker due up. Since Crosby had tripled already tonight, he was allowed to bat for himself, and Taylor went on deck. Crosby worked a walk to load the bases.

That brought up Taylor. He represented the potential winning run, and he had hit his first major league home run off of Herbel in 1969. But Carl was not known as a home run hitter. Indeed, teammates had nicknamed him "Warning Track" for his ability to hit drives that fell just short. And he had never hit a grand slam in his life, not even in Little League. Besides, he also represented the potential game-losing out, so he went to the plate just looking for a hit. After missing with the first pitch to Taylor, Herbel came in with a fastball. Carl was looking for one and swung hard. The ball was hit a little bit too far toward the end of the bat, and Taylor at first thought it would just be another shot to the track. But the drive, although not very high, carried just over the fence and into the left field runway for a game-winning grand slam.

The stadium went bonkers. The youthful fans gave Taylor a standing ovation. And his Cardinal teammates charged to the plate to greet him just like he had won the World Series or something.

San Diego	ab	r	h	bi	o	a	e
J. Arcia, ss	4	0	1	1	3	3	1
D. Campbell, 2b	5	0	1	0	5	4	0
C. Gaston, cf	4	3	2	0	4	0	0
A. Ferrara, lf	3	2	2	0	0	0	0
I. Murrell, pr7-lf	1	1	0	0	0	0	0
O. Brown, rf	3	3	4	0	0	0	0
N. Colbert, 1b	5	0	3	2	7	1	0
E. Spezio, 3b	5	0	2	3	1	2	0
C. Cannizzaro, c	5	0	1	0	5	0	0
E. Wilson, p	3	1	0	0	1	1	0
T. Dukes, p7	1	0	0	0	0	0	0
R. Willis, p8	0	0	0	0	0	0	0
R. Herbel, p9	0	0	0	0	0	0	0
	39	10	15	10	26	11	1

St. Louis	ab	r	h	bi	o	a	e
L. Brock, lf	5	2	4	2	1	0	0
J. Javier, 2b	5	0	2	1	3	3	0
J. Hague, rf	5	0	2	1	2	0	0
R. Allen, 1b	5	1	0	0	12	0	0
J. Torre, c	5	2	4	2	4	1	0
J. Cardenal, cf	4	0	1	1	0	0	0
M. Shannon, 3b	5	1	0	0	1	4	0
D. Maxvill, ss	2	0	0	0	3	3	1
T. Simmons, ph7	1	0	0	0	-	-	-
E. Crosby, ss8	1	2	1	0	0	0	0
N. Briles, p	1	0	0	0	0	0	0
F. Linzy, p3	0	0	0	0	0	0	0
L. Lee, ph5	1	0	0	0	-	-	-
B. Chlupsa, p6	0	0	0	0	0	2	0
J. Beauchamp, ph7	1	1	1	0	-	-	-
Ch. Taylor, p8	0	0	0	0	0	1	0
V. Davalillo, ph8	1	1	1	0	-	-	-
H. Parker, p9	0	0	0	0	0	0	0
Ca. Taylor, ph9	1	1	1	4	-	-	-
	43	11	17	11	27	14	1

San Diego   302 110 102 - 10
St. Louis   100 000 235 - 11
two out when winning run scored

	ip	h	r-er	bb	so
Wilson	6.2	9	3-3	1	3
Dukes	1	4	3-3	0	1
Willis	.2	3	3-3	0	0
Herbel (L 6-5)	.1	1	2-2	1	0
Briles	2.1	6	5-5	2	1
Linzy	2.2	2	2-1	0	1
Chlupsa	2	3	1-1	0	1
Ch. Taylor	1	1	0-0	0	0
Parker (W 1-0)	1	3	2-2	1	0

HBP: by Briles (Arcia)

LOB: SD 7, StL 8. BE: SD 1, StL 1.
DP: Javier-Maxvill-Allen, Spezio-Campbell-Colbert, Chlupsa-Maxvill-Allen.
2B: Ferrara, Arcia, Brock 2, Cannizzaro. 3B: Ferrara, Crosby.
HR: Brown, Torre, Ca. Taylor.
SF: Brown.
SB: none. CS: Arcia.
Time - 2:44 Attendance - 16,734
Umpires: A. Donatelli, C. Pelekoudas, J. Kibler, S. Davidson
WP: Ch. Taylor

The Cardinals won again the next day on a bases-loaded walk to Taylor. But on August 14th, Richie Allen was sidelined with a pulled hamstring muscle, and the team lost its hottest hitter.

Thereafter, they played under-.500 ball. They finished in fourth with a 76-86 record.

1971—Saturday Night, August 14th, at Three Rivers Stadium, Pittsburgh

Gibson Pitches No-Hitter, Cuts Pittsburgh's Lead to 5 Games

Torre & Simmons Lead Cardinal Attack in 11-0 Victory Over Pirates

Gibby Actually a Bit Nervous Toward the End!

Tonight Bob Gibson did something he never thought he would do: pitch a no-hitter. "I'm a high-ball pitcher, and high-ball pitchers don't throw no-hitters," had always been his stated feeling. Over 13 seasons in the National League, Gibby had pitched two one-hitters and eight two-hitters but never a "no-no." A couple of times he had gotten into the eighth inning with a no-hitter, only to have it broken up.

But tonight, pitching against the hard-hitting, league-leading Pittsburgh Pirates, Gibson made it all the way through without giving up a hit. The prospect of the actual achievement made the usually impassive hurler a bit nervous, he later confessed. "I couldn't believe it," he said, "I never got nervous before, even in the World Series." His biggest scare came in the eighth inning, when the speedy Dave Cash hit a high chop off the artificial turf, which third baseman Joe Torre had to leap to snare. Torre then whipped the ball across the diamond to nip Cash at first base. That was the closest the Pirates came to a hit.

Today's Results
ST. LOUIS 11 - Pittsburgh 0
Chicago 3 - Cincinnati 1
San Francisco 6 - New York 5 (10 inn.)
Montreal 3 - Los Angeles 0
   Philadelphia not scheduled

Standings	W-L	Pct.	GB
Pittsburgh	71-49	.592	-
ST. LOUIS	66-54	.550	5
Chicago	64-53	.547	5½
New York	58-59	.496	11½
Philadelphia	53-65	.449	17
Montreal	47-71	.398	23

Gibson got through the ninth without incident and became the first National League pitcher to hurl a no-hitter in Pittsburgh since 1907. The victory was also the 201st of Gibson's career. He won Number 200 on August 4th, beating the Giants, 7-2. In his next start, he was hit for 14 safeties and six runs in seven innings against the Dodgers. But he was back on the beam tonight. His fastball was not as fast as it may have been on some previous occasions, but it was jumping. And his breaking balls were very sharp. In all, Gibson threw 124 pitches. His control was good, giving three balls to only six batters, three of whom walked. He struck out ten, including one who fanned on a wild pitch and reached first base. "It was the greatest game I've ever pitched anywhere," Gibson candidly volunteered.

It was also one of his easier victories. His teammates scored five runs in the top of the first inning and went on to win, 11-0. The victory was the third straight for the second-place Cardinals over the first-place Pirates, and it reduced Pittsburgh's lead to 5 games. Just 25 games ago, St. Louis was 14 games out of first.

The Pirates did not present their strongest lineup against the righthanded Gibson. Roberto Clemente and Manny Sanguillen, righthanded hitters, were given the night off. So was lefthanded Richie Hebner, who had struck out six times in the last two nights. But the Bucs still presented an impressive lineup, headed by Willie Stargell, who held the league lead with 39 home runs and 101 RBI's.

Pittsburgh starting pitcher Bob Johnson put his team in a deep hole in the first inning. He walked Cardinal leadoff man Matty Alou. After Ted Sizemore flied out, Jose Cruz and Joe Torre singled for one run. Ted Simmons singled home another run. Then Joe Hague blasted a three-run homer to right, making the score 5-0 and knocking Johnson out of the box.

The Cardinals added three runs in the fifth off of Johnson's replacement, Bob Moose. Torre singled, Simmons doubled, and Hague walked, loading the bases. Ted Kubiak doubled two men home, and Gibson hit a sacrifice fly.

Bob Veale was on the hill when the Red Birds added their final three markers in the eighth. Dal Maxvill "batted" in one run with a bases-loaded walk, and Gibson singled two men home.

The Cardinals totaled 16 hits and seven walks. Simmons and Torre each made four hits. Gibby and Hague each wound up with three runs-batted-in. Hague and Simmons each scored three times. The big night for Torre raised his league-leading average to .359, and his first-inning RBI gave him a season total of 95, second in the league to Stargell.

But the big story was Gibson's pitching. The first Pirate to reach base was Milt May, who struck out in the second inning on a wild pitch that got past catcher Simmons. Jackie Hernandez walked in the third, and Stargell walked in the fourth.

The Bucs went down in order in the fifth and sixth innings.

There was a bid for a hit in the seventh. After Stargell fanned for the second time, May lifted a towering fly to deep left center. For a moment it looked like the ball might clear the fence for a home run. But it didn't, and Cruz made a nice running catch on the warning track, 390 feet from the plate. Bob Robertson walked, but Bill Mazeroski lined softly to shortstop for the final out of the inning.

In the eighth, Hernandez bounced out to first, and pinch-hitter Gene Clines struck out. Then came Gibson's biggest scare, the high bouncer by Cash.

The determined pitcher was bearing down extra hard in the ninth, going for his no-hitter. He got Vic Davalillo on a roller to short. The Pittsburgh crowd was now in Gibson's corner, and it roared its approval. The best that Al Oliver could do was an easy bouncer to Kubiak at second for out number two. Gibson was throwing as hard now as he had been at any time during the game.

Willie Stargell was the next batter, and Gibson got a couple of fastballs by him. Then he snapped off a slider, which nipped the outside corner, and plate umpire Harry Wendelstedt called it strike three! The fans screamed. Ted Simmons charged to the mound to mob Gibson, and soon all his teammates joined in. But there was no one more thrilled than Gibson himself.

St. Louis	ab	r	h	bi	o	a	e
M. Alou, 1b	4	1	0	0	7	0	0
T. Sizemore, lf	6	0	2	0	2	0	0
J. Cruz, cf	6	1	1	0	2	0	0
J. Torre, 3b	6	2	4	1	0	1	0
T. Simmons, c	6	3	4	1	9	0	0
J. Hague, rf	3	3	2	3	3	0	0
T. Kubiak, 2b	4	1	2	2	1	1	0
D. Maxvill, ss	3	0	0	1	3	2	0
B. Gibson, p	4	0	1	3	0	1	0
	42	11	16	11	27	5	0

Pittsburgh	ab	r	h	bi	o	a	e
D. Cash, 3b	4	0	0	0	1	1	0
V. Davalillo, rf	4	0	0	0	5	0	0
A. Oliver, cf	4	0	0	0	4	0	0
W. Stargell, lf	3	0	0	0	0	0	0
M. May, c	3	0	0	0	9	0	0
B. Robertson, 1b	2	0	0	0	7	0	0
B. Mazeroski, 2b	3	0	0	0	0	4	1
J. Hernandez, ss	2	0	0	0	1	2	0
B. Johnson, p	0	0	0	0	0	0	0
B. Moose, p1	1	0	0	0	0	0	1
C. Sands, ph5	1	0	0	0	-	-	-
B. Veale, p6	0	0	0	0	0	0	0
G. Clines, ph8	1	0	0	0	-	-	-
N. Briles, p9	0	0	0	0	0	0	0
	28	0	0	0	27	7	2

St. Louis	500	030	030	-	11
Pittsburgh	000	000	000	-	0

	ip	h	r-er	bb	so
Gibson (W 11-10)	9	0	0-0	3	10
Johnson (L 7-5)	.1	4	5-5	1	0
Moose	4.2	6	3-3	3	4
Veale	3	5	3-3	3	3
Briles	1	1	0-0	0	0

WP: Gibson

LOB: StL 12, Pitts 4. BE: StL 1.
Base on Missed 3rd Strike: Pitt 1.
DP: Briles-Hernandez-Robertson.
2B: Simmons, Kubiak.
HR: Hague. SF: Gibson.
Attendance - 30,678
Umpires: H. Wendelstedt, A. Olsen, T. Gorman, & C. Pelekoudas
Time 2:22

The Cardinals completed the sweep of the four-game series on Sunday, scoring five runs in the eight inning to win, 6-4.

They left Pittsburgh just 4 games behind, but then they lost five games in a row. Thereafter, they were never able to get closer than 5 games from the top. St. Louis finished in second place, 7 games behind, with a 90-72 record.

Gibson finished the season with a 16-13 mark.

1972 — Wednesday Night, September 20th, at Busch Memorial Stadium

Carlton Bests Wise and Cardinals, 2-1, for 25th Win

Twelfth One-Run Loss for Wise

Lefty Beats Former Teammates for Fourth Time

Neither the St. Louis Cardinals nor the Philadelphia Phillies have achieved very much of what they set out to do at the beginning of the 1972 season. But at least Philly pitcher Steve Carlton has.

The Cardinals had finished in second place in 1971 and hoped to be strong contenders for the division pennant this year. But except for one good stretch in June, they have played poorly and have spent most of the campaign in fourth place. Recently, they abandoned hope for this year, unloaded a few high-salaried veterans, and have been giving their young prospects a long look.

Today's Results
Philadelphia 2 - ST. LOUIS 1
New York 4 - Pittsburgh 1
Chicago 6 - Montreal 2

Standings	W-L	Pct.	GB
Pittsburgh	90-53	.629	-
Chicago	79-65	.549	11½
New York	74-68	.521	15½
ST. LOUIS	70-75	.483	21
Montreal	65-78	.455	25
Philadelphia	53-90	.371	37

The Phillies were looking for a rebound by their offense this year, and they wanted to find out which of their young pitchers could become winners. Instead, they entered the last two weeks of the season last in the league in runs scored per game, and only the most experienced member of their pitching staff had a winning record.

The lone winner on the Philly staff, Carlton, tonight reached the major goal he had set for himself at the beginning of the year: he won his 25th game. That achievement was all the more remarkable considering that Carlton did it while pitching for the worst team in the league. The Phillies have rung up a terrible .371 winning percentage. Without Carlton's 25-9 record, the figure would be incredibly dismal (.257). Luckily for Philadelphia, Carlton has been super, leading the league in wins, games started, complete games, innings pitched, strikeouts, and shutouts. Even pitching for the Phillies, he has ranked second in personal winning percentage. It's no wonder that he has been nicknamed "The Franchise" in Philadelphia.

Steve Carlton was with the St. Louis franchise until last February. He won 20 games for the Cardinals in 1971, and he wanted a big pay raise as a result. But the St. Louis management did not meet his $65,000 asking price. Instead, they traded him to the Phillies for Rick Wise, who was having contract troubles of his own in Philadelphia.

Wise has pitched good ball for St. Louis, but he has little to show for some of his fine work. Today he suffered his 16th loss (against 15 wins). Twelve of those defeats have been by just one run, all by scores of 1-0, 2-1, 3-2, or 4-3.

Today was the first time since the trade that Carlton and Wise had pitched against one another. Each did well, allowing six hits (Wise only pitched seven innings, however). Three of the hits today were doubles, and the rest were singles. But the three men who hit for two bases all scored. The Phillies got two of the doubles and won the game, 2-1.

Carlton had beaten his old team three times previously. Back in April, he beat Bob Gibson with a three-hitter, 1-0. In August he shut the Cardinals out on five hits, 5-0. And earlier in September, he edged Al Santorini and the Red Birds, 2-1.

The loss tonight was Wise's first decision against the Phillies.

The crowd tonight was very small. Only one previous Cardinal game in Busch Memorial Stadium had ever attracted less than the 5,569 admissions paid tonight. The night was warm and unpleasantly muggy. The two starting pitchers lost 8 to 10 pounds during the game.

Denny Doyle started things right off in the top of the first inning by ripping a double to right field. Larry Bowa sacrificed him to third. Tommy Hutton then brought him home with a single to right. Greg Luzinski walked later in the inning, but two men were left on base.

The Cardinals got the run right back in their half of the first. Lou Brock opened by chopping a hit past shortstop and speeding around to second with a double. A quick steal of third and a single to center by Ted Sizemore brought him home. Sizemore also stole a base, but the next three batters flied out.

Carlton and Wise both sailed through the next four innings with no real trouble.

Each side threatened in the sixth, but only the Phillies could score. As it turned out, their one run was the difference in the game.

Hutton opened the Phils' sixth with a double to right. He went to third on an infield tap by Willie Montanez. Luzinski followed with a shot toward right field. First baseman Joe Torre made a diving stop of the ball, preventing Hutton from scoring. But pitcher Wise, not wishing to get in the way of a possible throw to the plate, did not cover first, and Luzinski reached safely. When Bill Robinson hit into a force play at second and beat the throw to first, Hutton scored. Robinson stole second, and Mike Schmidt walked. But John Bateman flied to right for the third out.

Brock led off the bottom of the sixth with a hit to left. Sizemore flied out. Luis Melendez hit into a force out at second. Torre singled Melendez to second, and a wild pitch moved the runners to second and third. Ted Simmons was intentionally walked, loading the bases. But rookie Ken Reitz flied to right field, stranding the runners.

The Cardinals got hits by Bill Stein (in the seventh) and Sizemore (in the eighth) but could not get a man as far as second base for the rest of the game. So they lost, 2-1.

Carlton did not have his best fastball tonight, and he struck out only two batters, his lowest total of the year. But he pitched efficiently, making only 115 deliveries. This year, much to the chagrin of the St. Louis fans, he has shown that he can win even if his team is not strong and he does not have his best stuff. He's got 25 wins to help prove it.

Philadelphia	ab	r	h	bi	o	a	e	St. Louis	ab	r	h	bi	o	a	e
D. Doyle, 2b	3	1	2	0	4	2	1	L. Brock, lf	4	1	2	0	1	0	0
L. Bowa, ss	3	0	0	0	2	2	0	T. Sizemore, 2b	4	0	2	1	2	4	0
T. Hutton, rf	4	1	2	1	6	0	0	L. Melendez, rf	4	0	0	0	3	0	0
W. Montanez, 1b	4	0	0	0	6	0	0	J. Torre, 1b	4	0	1	0	11	0	0
G. Luzinski, lf	3	0	2	0	2	0	0	T. Simmons, c	3	0	0	0	5	2	0
B. Robinson, cf	4	0	1	1	4	0	0	K. Reitz, 3b	4	0	0	0	0	3	0
M. Schmidt, 3b	2	0	0	0	0	1	0	J. Roque, cf	3	0	0	0	3	0	0
D. Money, 3b8	1	0	0	0	0	0	0	M. Kelleher, ss	2	0	0	0	2	1	0
J. Bateman, c	4	0	0	0	2	1	0	B. Stein, ph7	1	0	1	0	-	-	-
S. Carlton, p	3	0	0	0	1	0	0	J. Cruz, pr7	0	0	0	0	-	-	-
								E. Crosby, ss8	0	0	0	0	0	1	0
								R. Wise, p	2	0	0	0	0	2	0
								S. Jutze, ph7	1	0	0	0	-	-	-
								D. Durham, pr7	0	0	0	0	-	-	-
								R. Folkers, p8	0	0	0	0	0	0	0
	31	2	7	2	27	6	1		32	1	6	1	27	13	0

Philadelphia	100	001	000	-	2
St. Louis	100	000	000	-	1

	ip	h	r-er	bb	so
Carlton (W 25-9)	9	6	1-1	2	2
Wise (L 15-16)	7	6	2-2	3	5
Folkers	2	1	0-0	0	0

WP: Carlton

LOB: Phil 6, StL 6. BE: StL 1.
DP: Bowa-Doyle-Montanez.
2B: Doyle, Brock, Hutton.
SH: Bowa.
SB: Brock, Sizemore, Robinson.
CS: Luzinski, Roque, Robinson.
Time - 2:20 Attendance - 5,569

Umpires: B. Froemming, A. Donatelli, S. Landes, & S. Davidson

The Cardinals won five games and lost six games after this to finish the season with a 75-81 record.

Wise continued to pitch with little support. He had to go ten innings to win his next start, 2-1. In his final start, he gave up only one run in eleven innings but got no decision.

Carlton lost his next outing, 2-1, on an unearned run, then won his final two games to give him a season record of 27-10. The Phillies finished with an overall mark of 59-97.

1973—Sunday, July 22nd, at Busch Memorial Stadium
Late Rally Wins for Cardinals, 5-4, St. Louis Takes Division Lead
Three Runs in Eighth Inning Send Dodgers to Defeat
After Being Last on Memorial Day, Cards in First at All-Star Break

Fully recovered from a disastrous start this season, the St. Louis Cardinals moved into first place in the National League East Division today. Their rise from the depths was culminated by a 5-4 victory over the Los Angeles Dodgers, leaders in the N.L. West. Combined with the Chicago loss to San Francisco, the Red Birds' triumph put them into the lead in the East by ½ game. St. Louis rallied for three runs in the bottom of the eighth to win today's game.

Considering that the Cards started the season by losing 15 of their first 17 games and trailed the Cubs by 11 games on May 14th, the turnabout has been remarkable. Since mid-May, they have won 43 games and lost just 22. The Cards did not move out of last place until the day after Memorial Day, but they made it to second place by June 29th. Even then they trailed the Cubs by 8 games. But Chicago slumped badly in July, and St. Louis continued to rise. Today the Cardinals took over first place on the final date before the All-Star break.

Today's Results
ST. LOUIS 5 - Los Angeles 4
San Francisco 4 - Chicago 1 (13 inn.)
Pittsburgh 3 - San Diego 1 (1st game)
Pittsburgh 13 - San Diego 7 (2nd)
Philadelphia 6 - Atlanta 5 (1st game)
Philadelphia 5 - Atlanta 1 (2nd)
Cincinnati 6 - Montreal 0
New York 3 - Houston 2

Standings	W-L	Pct.	GB
ST. LOUIS	51-45	.531	-
Chicago	51-46	.526	½
Pittsburgh	46-48	.489	4
Philadelphia	46-51	.474	5½
Montreal	44-51	.463	6½
New York	42-51	.452	7½

It was Old-Timers Day at Busch Stadium, and a crowd of over 40,000 came out for a touch of nostalgia. They also got a healthy case of pennant fever. The pre-game festivities included a three-inning game between old-time All-Stars. Paced by two hits by Stan Musial, the National League Old-Timers won, 7-0, beating an A.L. team which included two DiMaggios (Joe and Dom) and two Ferrells (Wes and Rick).

Then the 1973 athletes went at it, and it was All-Star reliever Jim Brewer of the Dodgers who was charged with the loss. Joe Torre and Ted Simmons, both of whom were also to play in this year's mid-summer classic, scored the tying and winning runs.

Reggie Cleveland was the starting pitcher for the Cards. He was making his first appearance in two weeks, having pulled a hamstring muscle on July 7th. He was fast but wild today, striking out eight and walking five in six innings of work.

Thanks to a pair of St. Louis errors, the Dodgers got a run in the first inning. With one out, Bill Buckner reached base on a fumble by first baseman Tim McCarver. Willie Davis followed with a hit to right field. Outfielder Bernie Carbo's throw to third was very high, and Buckner scored on the error. Not trusting his defense, Cleveland confined the rest of the action in the inning to the battery, walking one and striking out two.

Los Angeles upped its lead to two runs in the fourth. Willie Crawford led off with a single to left. Steve Garvey forced him at second. Ken McMullen then cracked a double to left, and Garvey scored.

Cleveland's fielding got him both into and out of a tight spot in the next inning. Davey Lopes singled to open the inning. Cleveland tried to pick him off but threw wildly past first, allowing the Dodger speedster to go all the way to third. After Buckner lined out, Davis was intentionally walked. Joe Ferguson then hit a smash up the middle, which Cleveland speared. Lopes was caught between third and home and run down. A walk to Crawford loaded the bases, but Garvey struck out, ending the threat.

Andy Messersmith, the Dodger starter, had the Cardinal bats neutralized until the fifth. Then with two out, Carbo scratched a single off shortstop Bill Russell's glove to become the first St. Louis base runner. Carbo scored moments later when Jose Cruz slashed a double to left.

The Birds tied the score with another run in the sixth. With one gone, Lou Brock extended his hitting streak to 10 games by beating out a grounder to short. Messersmith imitated Cleveland, throwing wildly on a pick-off attempt, and Brock went to third. Ted Sizemore was at bat, and he lifted a foul behind the plate. Catcher Ferguson ran under it but dropped it as he hit the screen. Sizemore then made the Dodgers pay for the mistake by singling to center, plating Brock.

Rick Folkers replaced Cleveland in the seventh. He got through one inning without trouble. And he had two out in the eighth before walking Tom Paciorek, who batted for Messersmith. Lopes then singled. With men on first and second and righthanded Manny Mota announced as a pinch-hitter, Cardinal manager Red Schoendienst called veteran righty Diego Segui in to pitch. Nevertheless, Mota stroked a hit to left. The ball got past Brock, and two runs scored, putting the visitors ahead, 4-2.

Dodger manager Walter Alston put his top reliever, Jim Brewer, in to protect the lead. He struck out the first Cardinal hitter in the eighth. Sizemore then singled to left. Luis Melendez, pinch-hitting, forced Sizemore at second. Then the big St. Louis hitters began teeing off on Brewer's screwballs. Torre rammed a double to left, sending Melendez to third. Simmons shot a solid single to center. The ball was bobbled in the outfield, two runs scored, and Simmons took second on the play. Carbo was next, and he bounced one into the bleachers for a ground-rule double, sending Simmons home with the go-ahead run. Tommy John relieved Brewer and struck out Cruz, but the Cardinals had the lead, 5-4.

Al Hrabosky blanked the Dodgers in the ninth to gain the first save of his career, and the Cardinals were winners.

Since the Cubs' game was already over, they were also division leaders. The St. Louis fans went home ready and willing to see the pennant come back to town.

Los Angeles	ab	r	h	bi	o	a	e	St. Louis	ab	r	h	bi	o	a	e
D. Lopes, 2b	4	1	2	0	2	3	0	L. Brock, lf	4	1	1	0	1	0	1
B. Buckner, lf	4	1	0	0	2	0	0	T. Sizemore, 2b	4	0	2	1	2	0	0
M. Mota, ph8	1	0	1	1	-	-	-	T. McCarver, 1b	2	0	0	0	3	0	1
J. Brewer, p8	0	0	0	0	0	0	0	R. Folkers, p7	0	0	0	0	0	0	0
T. John, p8	0	0	0	0	0	0	0	D. Segui, p8	0	0	0	0	0	0	0
W. Davis, cf	3	0	1	0	2	0	1	L. Melendez, ph8	1	1	0	0	-	-	-
J. Ferguson, c	5	0	1	0	8	0	0	A. Hrabosky, p9	0	0	0	0	0	0	0
W. Crawford, rf	2	0	1	0	1	0	0	J. Torre, 3b-1b7	4	1	1	0	4	2	0
R. Cey, ph9	1	0	0	0	-	-	-	T. Simmons, c	4	1	1	2	11	0	0
S. Garvey, 1b	5	1	0	0	6	1	0	B. Carbo, rf	4	1	3	1	2	0	1
K. McMullen, 3b	5	0	1	1	1	1	0	J. Cruz, cf	4	0	1	1	0	0	0
B. Russell, ss	4	0	0	0	1	1	0	M. Tyson, ss	3	0	0	0	3	3	0
A. Messersmith, p	2	0	1	0	1	0	1	R. Cleveland, p	1	0	0	0	0	1	1
T. Paciorek, ph8-lf	0	1	0	0	0	0	0	J. Dwyer, ph6	1	0	0	0	-	-	-
								K. Reitz, 3b7	1	0	0	0	0	2	0
	36	4	8	2	24	6	2		33	5	9	5	27	8	4

Los Angeles	100	100	020	-	4
St. Louis	000	011	03x	-	5

	ip	h	r-er	bb	so
Messersmith	7	5	2-2	1	6
Brewer (L 4-3)	.2	4	3-2	0	1
John	.1	0	0-0	0	1
Cleveland	6	5	2-1	5	8
Folkers	1.2	2	2-1	1	1
Segui (W 4-3)	.1	1	0-0	1	0
Hrabosky (sv #1)	1	0	0-0	0	1

LOB: LA 12, StL 5. BE: LA 1
2B: McMullen, Cruz, Torre, Carbo.
Time - 2:29
Attendance - 41,879
Umpires: T. Gorman, B. Williams, D. Stello, & J. Dale

The Cardinals built up a 5-game lead in early August, then went into a tailspin. They lost eight in a row. But no one else in the division was able to make a concerted drive, so St. Louis was able to hang on to first place until as late as September 11th, when they lost the lead for good.

The Mets, who were last as late as August 30th, ran past the rest of the division in September and won the title.

The Cardinals maintained a mathematical chance for the pennant right up until the end of the season, but wound up in second place, 1½ games behind. Their record was an even .500 (81-81).

1974 — Wednesday Night, September 25th, at Busch Memorial Stadium

Four-Run Rally in 11th Wins Game, 13-12, Puts Cards Back Into First

Cards Overcome Deficits of 5-0 and 12-9 to Beat Pirates

41,345 See Cardinals Close Home Season with Incredible, Clutch Victory

The Cardinals played some memorable games this September. There was the night that Lou Brock broke Maury Wills's stolen base record. And, on the very next night, it took St. Louis 25 innings to beat the Mets.

But tonight they topped all the rest. In a game of tremendous tension and incredible rallies, the St. Louis Cardinals overcame the Pittsburgh Pirates in extra innings to regain the lead in the National League East Division pennant race. The Pirates had come to St. Louis on Monday trailing the Cardinals by 1½ games. Pittsburgh won the first two games of the series to go into the lead. But St. Louis bounced back to win the final game of the set tonight and regain first place.

Today's Results

ST. LOUIS 13 - Pittsburgh 12 (11 inn.)
Philadelphia 6 - New York 2 (1st game)
Philadelphia 6 - New York 3 (2nd)
Montreal 7 - Chicago 1 (1st game)
Montreal 3 - Chicago 2 (2nd)

Standings	W-L	Pct.	GB
ST. LOUIS	83-73	.532	-
Pittsburgh	82-73	.529	½
Philadelphia	78-78	.500	5
Montreal	75-81	.481	8
New York	69-86	.445	13½
Chicago	65-91	.417	18

The Cardinals not only bounced back in the race, they bounced back in the game twice. They spotted the Pirates a 5-0 lead in the first inning. But they rallied with six runs in the third to take the lead. St. Louis led by as much as 9-6, but Pittsburgh came back to tie the score and send the game into extra innings. In the eleventh, the Pirates broke through with three runs. The task seemed impossible, but the Cardinals did it: they came up with four runs in the bottom of the eleventh to win the game, 13-12!

Tonight was the last game on St. Louis's home schedule, and 41,345 rooters came to Busch Stadium to urge the Cardinals on. Just about all of them were hoping for a chance to come see the Red Birds in the playoffs.

Before thousands of the customers had settled into their seats, the Pirates jumped out to what could have been a decisive lead. They racked up five runs before the second out of the game. Rookie pitcher Bob Forsch was the victim. A three-run home run by Manny Sanguillen was the biggest blow.

The fans were dejected until the bottom of the third. Then the Cards got five straight singles off of Pirate starter Ken Brett. Lou Brock, Ted Sizemore, Reggie Smith, Ted Simmons, and Joe Torre made up the parade, which plated three runs. After a force out, side-arming Larry Demery was brought on to relieve Brett. Ken Reitz hit Demery's first pitch for a two-run double. With the score suddenly tied, Jose Cruz was sent up to bat for Mike Tyson. He rapped a hit off second baseman Rennie Stennett's glove. The ball trickled into short right field, and Reitz plowed home from second. That put the Cardinals into the lead and sent the crowd into ecstasy.

The Pirates tied the score in the fifth. Richie Hebner singled and scored on Al Oliver's double. After Willie Stargell walked, manager Red Schoendienst decided to bring in his bullpen ace, Al Hrabosky, to pitch. The fifth inning was pretty early to bring in a short reliever, but this was no ordinary game. Hrabosky retired the next three batters, and he remained in the game until the eleventh inning.

The Cardinals quickly regained the lead, scoring three runs off John Morlan in the bottom of the fifth. Simmons opened with a single, Torre was hit by a pitch, and a wild pitch followed. Bake McBride's sacrifice fly drove home the lead run. Reitz added two more runs with a home run that just barely cleared the left field fence. St. Louis led, 9-6.

Pittsburgh cut the difference to 9-8 in the next inning on Oliver's two-run single..

A fielding error helped the Pirates tie the score in the ninth. After striking Stargell out to start the inning, Hrabosky hit Parker with a pitch. Sanguillen followed with a hit to center. Outfielder McBride tried to throw Parker out at third, but his heave bounced past both the third baseman and the pitcher, allowing Parker to score.

The game remained tied until the eleventh. Then the Pirates routed a tiring Hrabosky and scored three runs. Art Howe opened with a bunt single. Stargell singled the pinch-runner to third.

Parker fanned. But Sanguillen bounced a hit over shortstop for a run. Ed Kirkpatrick then drove two more men in with a double. Mike Garman came in and retired the side.

With the clock approaching midnight and their team down by three, the fans started streaming for the exits.

Pirate manager Danny Murtaugh gambled and sent a rookie, Juan Jimenez, out to hold the lead. Sizemore opened for the Cards with a hit. Smith walked, and some of those who were leaving sat back down. Simmons pounded an RBI double, and there was a sudden feeling that the game could be won.

Murtaugh called in another rookie, Jim Minshall, to pitch. Like Jimenez, he was appearing in only his third major league game. He got Torre to ground to second. Stennett, usually a sure fielder, had trouble getting the ball out of his glove, then he threw wildly past first. Two runs scampered home, tying the score, and Torre went to second. Larry Herndon took Torre's place on base. McBride bunted Herndon to third and beat the throw to first himself. So now the winning run was on third with just one out. Jim Dwyer, pinch-hitting, lifted a fly to deep right. Herndon tagged up and scored easily.

The players exploded out of the Cardinal dugout and began a mad, leaping celebration at home plate. Delirious fans danced in the aisles. The Cardinals had won! The Cardinals were in first place!

The exhausted players soon quieted down, but they felt great. As Hrabosky said in the clubhouse, "That's got to be the greatest game ever played."

Pittsburgh	ab	r	h	bi	o	a	e
R. Stennett, 2b	5	2	2	0	5	5	2
R. Hebner, 3b	6	2	3	0	1	0	1
A. Oliver, cf	4	0	2	4	3	0	0
D. Guisti, p8	0	0	0	0	0	0	0
A. Howe, ph11	1	0	1	0	-	-	-
M. Dilone, pr11	0	1	0	0	-	-	-
J. Jimenez, p11	0	0	0	0	0	0	0
J. Minshall, p11	0	0	0	0	0	0	0
W. Stargell, lf	4	2	1	0	3	0	0
D. Parker, rf-cf8	5	2	1	1	0	0	0
M. Sanguillen, c	5	2	3	4	4	1	0
E. Kirkpatrick, 1b	6	0	1	2	10	2	0
F. Taveras, ss	3	0	0	0	3	4	0
B. Robertson, ph8	1	0	0	0	-	-	-
M. Mendoza, ss8	0	0	0	0	0	1	0
P. Popovich, ph9-ss	2	0	0	0	0	0	0
K. Brett, p	1	0	1	0	0	1	0
L. Demery, p3	0	0	0	0	0	0	0
G. Clines, ph4	1	0	0	0	-	-	-
J. Morlan, p4	0	0	0	0	0	0	0
K. Macha, ph6	1	1	1	0	-	-	-
R. Hernandez, p6	0	0	0	0	0	2	0
R. Zisk, ph8-rf	3	0	0	0	2	0	0
	48	12	16	11	32	16	3

St. Louis	ab	r	h	bi	o	a	e
L. Brock, lf	5	1	1	0	1	0	0
T. Sizemore, 2b	6	2	3	0	2	4	0
R. Smith, rf	5	2	3	1	4	0	0
T. Simmons, c	5	2	3	2	10	0	0
J. Torre, 1b	5	2	1	2	7	2	0
L. Herndon, pr11	0	1	0	0	-	-	-
B. McBride, cf	4	1	1	1	6	0	1
K. Reitz, 3b	6	2	2	4	0	1	0
M. Tyson, ss	1	0	1	0	1	1	0
J. Cruz, ph3	1	0	1	1	-	-	-
J. Heidemann, ss4	3	0	1	0	1	2	0
J. Dwyer, ph11	0	0	0	1	-	-	-
B. Forsch, p	0	0	0	0	0	0	0
R. Folkers, p1	0	0	0	0	1	0	0
D. Godby, ph2	1	0	0	0	-	-	-
C. Osteen, p3	1	0	0	0	0	0	0
A. Hrabosky, p5	2	0	0	0	0	0	0
M. Garman, p11	0	0	0	0	0	0	0
	45	13	17	12	33	10	1

Pittsburgh   500 012 001 03 - 12
St. Louis   006 030 000 04 - 13
two out when winning run scored

	ip	h	r-er	bb	so
Brett	2.1	7	5-5	0	0
Demery	.2	2	1-1	0	0
Morlan	2	3	3-3	0	1
Hernandez	2	0	0-0	0	0
Giusti	3	2	0-0	2	0
Jimenez	*0	2	3-2	1	0
Minshall (L 0-1)	.2	1	1-0	0	1
Forsch	.1	3	5-5	2	0
Folkers	1.2	1	0-0	0	0
Osteen	#2	2	1-1	2	1
Hrabosky	6.1	10	6-5	0	9
Garman (W 7-2)	.2	0	0-0	0	0

*faced three batters in eleventh

LOB: Pitts 9, StL 8. BE: StL 3.
DP: Taveras-Kirkpatrick,
Sanguillen-Taveras,
Mendoza-Stennett-Kirkpatrick.
2B: Parker, Reitz, Oliver,
Stennett, Kirkpatrick, Simmons.
HR: Sanguillen, Reitz.
SH: Hrabosky, Simmons.
SF: Oliver, McBride, Dwyer.
HBP: by Morlan (Torre),
by Hrabosky (Parker).
SB: none. CS: Sizemore.
WP: Morlan.
Time - 3:41 Attendance - 41,345
Umpires: D. Harvey, J. Dale,
A. Williams, & H. Wendelstedt
#faced three batters in fifth

The euphoria did not last. The Cards lost two of their remaining six games, and one was rained out. Meanwhile, the Pirates lost only one of seven to win the division title by 1½ games.

1975—Saturday, July 12th, at Busch Memorial Stadium

"Mad Hungarian" Gets the Win on "We Hlove Hrabosky Hbanner Day"

Fans Cheer Hrabosky, Boo Alston and Marshall

Cardinals Beat Dodgers, 2-1, with Runs in Ninth and Tenth

For Al Hrabosky, the All-Star Game came three days early this year. Despite an impressive set of statistics and an unorthodox and well-known psychological ritual, Hrabosky was not named to the National League All-Star team by manager Walter Alston. So the St. Louis Cardinal front office arranged a promotional day to honor him. Choosing the Saturday game before the All-Star break between the Cardinals and Alston's Los Angeles Dodgers, the club offered free tickets to subsequent games to people who would bring banners on "Hrabosky Hbanner Hday."

Today's Results
ST. LOUIS 2 - Los Angeles 1 (10 inn.)
Pittsburgh 6 - San Diego 4
Philadelphia 14 - Houston 2
Cincinnati 3 - New York 2
Atlanta 9 - Montreal 4 (1st game)
Montreal 7 - Atlanta 3 (2nd)

Standings	W-L	Pct.	GB
Pittsburgh	55-32	.632	-
Philadelphia	49-39	.557	6½
New York	43-41	.512	10½
ST. LOUIS	41-44	.482	13
Chicago	42-47	.472	14
Montreal	35-47	.427	17½

"The Mad Hungarian," as Hrabosky is known, has become very popular in St. Louis in the last season and a half. Automobile bumper stickers declaring, "Hwe Hlove Hrabosky" have become widespread in the area. After an erratic first half of 1974, Al finished strongly and had an 8-1 record, 9 saves and a 2.97 E.R.A. for the season. He also introduced his psyching ritual: he turns his back to the hitter, screws his face up into a mean expression, slams the ball into his glove, and then marches to the rubber to pitch to the hitters. This serves both to increase Hrabosky's concentration and to distract the batters. He does this at the tensest moments of the game, and has been quite successful with it lately. The St. Louis fans have come to love it.

His psyching act notwithstanding, Al has owed much of his success to his fastball. Hitters around the league have had a lot of trouble with his herky-jerky left arm and the speed it imparts upon the pitches he has sent up to the plate. Very occasionally, he also throws a forkball.

This year he has rung up a fine set of numbers: 14 saves, 4 wins and 2 losses, and a 1.84 earned-run average. Those stats were easily the best among National League relief pitchers for this season. But Dodger manager Alston, who picked the players for the All-Star squad, chose two longer-established relief stars, Mike Marshall and Tug McGraw.

To publicize the snub and Hrabosky's abilities, today's promotion was arranged. Since the game was on network television, the banners praising Hrabosky and panning Alston got widespread publicity, as did the reliever's Fu Manchu mustache. And just like in Hollywood, Hrabosky pitched two perfect innings, and his teammates rallied to give him a 2-1 victory.

For a long time, the Dodgers' Al Downing stole the show. Don Sutton, an All-Star designate, was scheduled to start. But he suffered a muscle pull on Tuesday, and it was decided to give him some additional rest. So Downing got the call. St. Louis had only beaten him once, back in the 1964 World Series. In the National League, Downing was 7-0 versus the Cardinals.

For eight innings, he shut the Red Birds out on just four hits. His only obvious mistake came on a fastball to Reggie Smith in the fourth inning. The pitch was over the middle of the plate, belt high, and Smith creamed it. Luckily for Downing, it was pulled foul. Reggie then singled and stole second, but Downing struck out Ted Simmons and Ron Fairly.

The next time Smith came up, Ted Sizemore was on second with a double, and two were out. The lefthander wisely pitched around Reggie, then retired Simmons on a fly out to right.

Lynn McGlothen, starting for the Cardinals, also pitched a fine game. In eight innings, he also allowed just four hits. But his bad mistake, a curveball to Davey Lopes in the fifth, was hit just over the fence in left center for a home run.

McGlothen left for a pinch-hitter in the eighth, and the fans' favorite, Hrabosky, pitched the ninth. He set the Dodgers down in order.

The score was still 1-0 when Smith came up to lead off the bottom of the ninth. Downing fell behind on the count, 3-and-1, then threw a nice, fat fastball. Smith was ready but not too anxious, and he hit this one fair and deep into the mezzanine seats in left for his twelfth home run of the year.

That tied the game and brought Alston out to the mound. As soon as he emerged from the dugout, he was greeted by a chorus of boos. When he called Marshall in to relieve Downing, the booing increased. Unruffled by the crowd, Marshall set the next three hitters down in order.

Marshall was replaced by pinch-batter Lee Lacy in the top of the tenth. Hrabosky got Lacy on a grounder to short. Al also retired the next two hitters. In fact, he was working so effectively that he didn't have much need to go behind the mound to psych himself up.

Rick Rhoden came in to pitch for Los Angeles in the bottom of the tenth. He got a fastball up too high to Ken Reitz, and Kenny singled to left. Buddy Bradford went in to run for the slower Reitz. Mike Tyson followed with a neat sacrifice bunt down the first base line, moving Bradford to second. Rhoden almost had Bake McBride struck out, but catcher Steve Yeager could not quite hold onto a foul tip with the count 0-and-2. Reprieved, McBride chopped a bouncer past the mound and barely through the Dodger infield. Bradford raced home on the hit, and the Cardinals and Hrabosky were winners, 2-1.

After the game, the normally exuberant Hrabosky was especially exultant. Talking about all the banners and hoopla, he said, "It was probably the most rewarding feeling I've ever had.... This game today was my All-Star game."

Los Angeles	ab	r	h	bi	o	a	e	St. Louis	ab	r	h	bi	o	a	e
D. Lopes, 2b	5	1	2	1	3	5	0	L. Brock, lf	4	0	0	0	1	0	0
B. Buckner, lf	2	0	0	0	1	0	0	T. Sizemore, 2b	4	0	1	0	2	3	0
T. Paciorek, lf8	1	0	0	0	0	0	0	R. Smith, rf	3	1	2	1	2	0	0
J. Wynn, cf	3	0	0	0	1	0	0	T. Simmons, c	4	0	0	0	9	0	0
S. Garvey, 1b	4	0	1	0	14	0	0	R. Fairly, 1b	3	0	0	0	7	0	0
J. Hale, rf	3	0	1	0	3	0	0	L. Melendez, cf	4	0	1	0	5	0	0
R. Cey, 3b	4	0	0	0	0	3	0	K. Reitz, 3b	4	0	1	0	1	2	0
B. Russell, ss	4	0	0	0	0	5	0	B. Bradford, pr10	0	1	0	0	-	-	-
S. Yeager, c	4	0	0	0	6	1	0	M. Tyson, ss	3	0	1	0	3	3	0
A. Downing, p	3	0	0	0	0	1	0	L. McGlothen, p	1	0	0	0	0	0	0
M. Marshall, p9	0	0	0	0	0	0	0	W. Davis, ph8	1	0	0	0	-	-	-
L. Lacy, ph10	1	0	0	0	-	-	-	A. Hrabosky, p9	0	0	0	0	0	0	0
R. Rhoden, p10	0	0	0	0	0	0	0	B. McBride, ph10	1	0	1	1	-	-	-
	34	1	4	1	28	15	0		32	2	7	2	30	8	0

Los Angeles   000 010 000   0 - 1
St. Louis   000 000 001   1 - 2
one out when winning run scored

	ip	h	r-er	bb	so
Downing	*8	5	1-1	2	5
Marshall	1	0	0-0	0	0
Rhoden (L 1-1)	.1	2	1-1	0	0
McGlothen	8	4	1-1	4	7
Hrabosky (W 4-2)	2	0	0-0	0	1

*faced one batter in ninth

LOB: LA 7, StL 6.
DP: Cey-Lopes-Garvey.
2B: Sizemore.
HR: Lopes, Smith.
SH: McGlothen, Tyson.
SB: Smith.
PB: Simmons.
Time - 2:27
Attendance - 31,606
Umpires: P. Runge, E. Vargo, B. Froemming, & A. Williams

On the following day, Hrabosky was again the winning pitcher in a 2-1 victory over the Dodgers. McBride and Smith were again the hitting heroes, combining for a ninth-inning run to win the game.

Hrabosky finished the season with a league-leading total of 22 saves, a 13-3 record, and a 1.67 E.R.A.

The Cardinals made a run at the lead, getting to within 2 games of the Pirates in mid-August, but then they fell back. St. Louis finished tied for third, 10½ games behind, with an 82-80 record.

1976 — Saturday Night, May 22nd, at Veterans Stadium, Philadelphia

Smith's Three Homers & Great Catch Bring Victory to Cards, 7-6

Third Homer, in Ninth Inning, Breaks Tie

Three Great Plays in Infield Save Game in Bottom of Ninth

Led by the heroics of Reggie Smith, the St. Louis Cardinals stopped the red-hot Philadelphia Phillies tonight, 7-6. The first-place Phils had won six games in a row and 15 of their previous 17 before losing tonight. They held the lead on two different occasions tonight, but three home runs by Smith overcame them both times. His first circuit clout, a three-run job, took the Cardinals from behind, 2-1, to ahead, 4-2. The Phillies rallied to regain the lead, 6-4. But the Cards got one run, then Smith hit two solo homers, one to tie the score

Today's Results
ST. LOUIS 7 - Philadelphia 6
Pittsburgh 4 - Chicago 3 (16 inn.)
New York 4 - Montreal 1

Standings	W-L	Pct.	GB
Philadelphia	22-9	.710	-
Pittsburgh	21-14	.600	3
New York	22-16	.579	3½
Chicago	15-20	.429	9
ST. LOUIS	16-22	.421	9½
Montreal	13-19	.406	9½

and one to give the Cardinals a 7-6 lead in the ninth inning. Smith then made a great diving catch in the bottom of the ninth, and Don Kessinger made two fine plays at shortstop. So the Phillies' rally failed and the Cardinals won the game.

The triumph was only the Cards' fourth in 13 games. Their pitching had been spotty, and the offense had been unproductive. The team had hit just 11 home runs (fewest in the league) in 37 games before tonight. But tonight they erupted with four round trippers. Smith doubled his personal total and raised his batting average from .168 to .189. He also increased his RBI total from 13 to 18.

Smith's productivity had been limited by a shoulder injury, which had also led to moving him into the infield. But today he had a good meditation before coming to the park, and he went out and played a great game.

In the first inning, however, he failed in the clutch. Two bases on balls put men on base, but Smith, batting with two out, bounced into an inning-ending force out.

St. Louis got onto the board with a run in the second. Hector "Heity" Cruz did the job with a home run to left center off of Phillies' starter Jim Kaat. St. Louis pitcher John Curtis doubled with two out, but he was thrown out trying to score on Lou Brock's single to right field.

In the third, the Phillies scored two runs against Curtis. Dave Cash led off with a hit and stole second. With one out, Mike Schmidt walked, and Greg Luzinski singled, loading the bases. Ollie Brown then delivered a two-run single to center, and the Phils led, 2-1.

That lead lasted until the top of the fifth. An infield hit by Mike Tyson and a walk by Ted Simmons put two men on with two out. With Smith at the plate, Kaat fell behind on the count, 2-and-0, then came inside with a slider. Reggie got the thick part of the bat on it and drove it over the left field fence for a three-run home run.

The St. Louis lead did not last through the inning, however. The Phillies scored four runs in their half of the fifth to take a 6-4 advantage. A single by Larry Bowa and a double by Schmidt routed Curtis. Eric "Harry" Rasmussen came in to pitch. An infield hit by Luzinski and a sacrifice fly by Jay Johnstone tied the score, and a two-run homer by Richie Allen put Philadelphia ahead.

Ron Reed came in to pitch for the Phils in the sixth. The Cards scored a run off him in that round. The first two men went out, but Keith Hernandez, pinch-hitting, walked, and Lou Brock tripled him home.

Reed was still on the mound when Smith came up with two out in the seventh. With one ball, the tall righthander tried to fool Reggie with a change-up. But Smith was ready and pulled the ball over the fence in right. Having homered righthanded against Kaat, this became the sixth time that Smith had hit a home run from each side of the plate in the same game. More importantly, the clout tied the score, 6-6.

The Cards knocked Reed out of the box in the eighth with a two-out double by Jerry Mumphrey and a walk. Lefthander Tug McGraw was brought on, and he retired pinch-hitter Ron Fairly on a ground ball.

Mike Wallace pitched the sixth and seventh for St. Louis. Al Hrabosky took over in the eighth. Both men held the Phillies scoreless.

Vic Harris opened the top of the ninth with a single. But Simmons followed by grounding into a double play. So Smith once again was up with two out. McGraw's first pitch was a strike. Then he delivered a fastball away. Reggie jumped on it and hit it over the wall in straightaway center for his third home run in as many at bats. It was the first time in history that a switch-hitter had hit three straight home runs in a game while alternating sides of the plate each time. And the Cardinals had a 7-6 lead.

Bowa, leading off the bottom of the ninth, shot a liner toward left field. Smith, who had moved from first base to third in the eighth inning, had been shading Bowa toward the hole. He lunged to his left and caught the ball in the tip of his glove. Hrabosky walked the next batter, Schmidt. Luzinski followed with a liner through the box, which Hrabosky got in front of with his glove and his mid-section. The ball deflected toward short. Kessinger charged, bare-handed it, and threw to first base to nip the slow-footed Luzinski by half a step. Hrabosky then hit pinch-hitter Bobby Tolan in the back with a pitch, putting the potential winning run on base. Garry Maddox, up next, hit the ball hard, sending a liner toward left. But Kessinger, who was shifted in that direction, came up with another big play, lunging to his right and spearing the ball for the final out.

The Cardinals won the game, 7-6. But it took some outstanding slugging by Reggie Smith and some outstanding fielding in the ninth inning to do it.

St. Louis	ab	r	h	bi	o	a	e
L. Brock, lf	3	0	2	1	0	0	0
M. Tyson, 2b	4	1	1	0	1	1	0
R. Fairly, ph8-1b	1	0	0	0	3	0	0
V. Harris, cf-2b8	5	0	1	0	5	0	0
T. Simmons, c	3	1	0	0	4	1	0
R. Smith, 1b-3b8	5	3	3	5	7	1	0
M. Anderson, rf	5	0	1	0	1	0	0
H. Cruz, 3b	3	1	1	1	0	1	0
W. Crawford, ph8	1	0	0	0	-	-	-
A. Hrabosky, p8	0	0	0	0	0	1	0
D. Kessinger, ss	4	0	1	0	6	5	0
J. Curtis, p	2	0	1	0	0	0	0
H. Rasmussen, p5	0	0	0	0	0	0	0
K. Hernandez, ph6	0	1	0	0	-	-	-
M. Wallace, p6	0	0	0	0	0	1	0
J. Mumphrey, ph8-cf	1	0	1	0	0	0	0
	37	7	12	7	27	11	0

Philadelphia	ab	r	h	bi	o	a	e
D. Cash, 2b	5	1	1	0	2	2	0
L. Bowa, ss	4	1	1	0	0	2	0
M. Schmidt, 3b	3	2	1	0	0	5	0
G. Luzinski, lf	5	1	2	1	2	0	0
O. Brown, rf	2	0	2	2	0	1	0
J. Johnstone, ph5-rf	1	0	1	1	0	0	0
T. McGraw, p8	0	0	0	0	0	0	0
B. Tolan, ph9	0	0	0	0	-	-	-
G. Maddox, cf	5	0	1	0	4	0	0
R. Allen, 1b	4	1	1	2	10	0	0
B. Boone, c	4	0	2	0	9	1	0
J. Kaat, p	1	0	0	0	0	1	0
T. McCarver, ph5	1	0	0	0	-	-	-
R. Reed, p6	0	0	0	0	0	0	0
J. Martin, rf8	1	0	0	0	0	0	0
	36	6	12	6	27	12	0

```
St. Louis      010 031 101 -  7
Philadelphia   002 040 000 -  6
```

	ip	h	r-er	bb	so
Curtis	*4	8	4-4	3	2
Rasmussen	1	3	2-2	0	0
Wallace	2	1	0-0	0	2
Hrabosky (W 1-3)	2	0	0-0	1	0
Kaat	5	7	4-4	3	3
Reed	2.2	3	2-2	2	3
McGraw (L 2-3)	1.1	2	1-1	0	1

*faced two batters in fifth
Umpires: J. Crawford, T. Tata, D. Harvey, & J. Kibler

LOB: StL. 8. Phil 9.
DP: Kessinger-Smith, Bowa-Cash-Allen.
2B: Curtis, Schmidt, Mumphrey.
3B: Brock.
HR: Cruz, Smith 3, Allen.
SF: Johnstone.
SB: Brock, Brown, Cash. CS: Boone.
Attendance - 39,098
Time - 2:37
HBP: by Hrabosky (Tolan)

On June 15th, Smith, who was hitting .218 with eight home runs, was traded to Los Angeles for Joe Ferguson and a couple of minor leaguers.

Although the Cardinals' offense shook out of its early-season slump, their pitching and fielding were poor.

St. Louis never got higher than fourth place and finished in fifth. The Cardinals' final record was 72-90, for a .444 percentage, their worst since 1955.

Chapter XIII

On to Whitey Ball
1977-1981

1977—August 29th at San Diego
Brock Steals Two Bases to Pass Cobb, Red Birds Lose, 4-3

1978—April 16th at Busch Memorial Stadium
Forsch No-Hits Phillies, Controversy Over Scoring Call

1979—May 1st at Busch Memorial Stadium
Freed's Dramatic Grand Slam Wins Game for Cards in 11th, 7-6

1980—May 28th at Busch Memorial Stadium
Bullpen Fails Again, Blows 5-0 Lead, Mets Beat Cards, 6-5

1981—September 29th at Busch Memorial Stadium
Big Crowd Sees Cards Win Final Home Game & Regain First Place

Tough-guy Vern Rapp was hired to replace the soft-spoken Red Schoendienst as manager in 1977. The team showed a substantial improvement on the field, finishing third. Young players like Garry Templeton, Keith Hernandez, Jerry Mumphrey, Tony Scott, and Buddy Schultz all contributed to the rise. Ted Simmons (.318) and Bob Forsch (20-7), both more established, also had good years. Veteran Lou Brock began to show signs of slowing down, but he was still proficient enough to pass the immortal Ty Cobb's modern lifetime stolen base record on August 29th.

In 1978, Forsch started out well, winning his first three starts. The third one was a somewhat controversial no-hitter against the hard-hitting Phillies. But the Cards quickly dropped to last place, and Rapp was replaced as manager by Ken Boyer in late April. The Red Birds edged up into fourth place before diving to the cellar again with an 11-game losing streak.

The pitching was weak and the defense was porous. Shortstop Templeton led the league with 40 errors for the season. And Forsch went nearly two months without a victory.

The batting also dropped off dramatically. George Hendrick, who was picked up in a trade with San Diego, led St. Louis with a .288 average.

The Mets fell past the Cardinals in August, and St. Louis finished fifth. But their percentage was the club's worst since 1924.

After the season, Boyer was rehired as manager, but general manager Bing Devine was replaced by John Claiborne.

The 1979 season saw an upswing by the Cardinals. Lou Brock, who had announced that this would be his final year, made a dramatic comeback. He had hit just .221 in 1978, but he wound up at .304 in 1979. On August 13th, he reached 3,000 career hits.

There were other hitting stars, too. Hendrick, Templeton, Hernandez, and Ken Oberkfell all hit over .300, Hernandez winning the league batting title. Even bench-warmer Roger Freed contributed a dramatic, game-winning grand slam early in the year.

But bullpen ineffectiveness kept the team from finishing any higher than third place.

In 1980, the Cardinals quickly fell hopelessly out of the race. A 10-game losing streak in late May ruined their chances. When the cold streak reached 4 wins and 18 losses, Boyer was fired by Claiborne. The biggest problem with the team was relief pitching. The bullpen held the opposition scoreless only 7 times in the first 51 games of the season. One of the worst examples came on May 29th, when the Mets were given six runs in the eighth inning, and the Cards lost, 6-5.

Whitey Herzog succeeded Boyer as manager, and the team showed some improvement. The ownership decided to fire Claiborne in August, and Herzog became general manager, with Red Schoendienst taking over as interim manager. The Cardinals finished the season in fourth place.

Herzog made a flurry of trades at the winter meetings, picking up relief ace Bruce Sutter. Herzog was also made manager for 1981.

With a team molded to his personal style of aggressive play and sound fundamentals, Herzog led the Cards to a revival in 1981. They were on or near the top of the division most of the season. They fell behind the Phillies just four days before the players' strike interrupted play on June 11th. St. Louis was second, 1½ games back.

When play resumed 59 days later, the owners had decided to split the season, with playoffs between the two split-season winners. This really hurt St. Louis. The Red Birds finished the second half just ½ game behind Montreal. So, although St. Louis had the best overall record in the division, it didn't get into the playoffs. Still, the Cards might have won the second half. They suffered through losing streaks of five and four games in September and still bounced back into first place by beating the Expos in their last two home games. But two losses on the road in the last week doomed the Cardinals to second place.

1977—Monday Night, August 29th, at San Diego Stadium
Brock Steals Two Bases to Break Cobb's Record, Cards Lose, 4-3
Two-Run Homer Off Hrabosky in Eighth Gives Padres the Victory
Lou Steals #892 in First Inning to Tie, #893 in Seventh to Break Mark

Although the St. Louis Cardinals lost to the San Diego Padres tonight, 4-3, Lou Brock finally got over the hump and broke Ty Cobb's modern record for lifetime stolen bases. After failing to reach first base in his previous three games, Brock reached three times tonight and stole second twice, tying and breaking Cobb's mark of 892 steals.

Cobb played in the American League from 1905 through 1928. Billy Hamilton, who played in the majors from 1888 to 1901, was credited with 937 stolen bases. But the rules for counting steals were slightly different before 1898, as were many other things like field conditions and playing equipment.

Today's Results
San Diego 4 - ST. LOUIS 3
Philadelphia 3 - Atlanta 2 (14 inn.)
Los Angeles 4 - Chicago 1
Montreal 7 - Cincinnati 2
no other games scheduled

Standings	W-L	Pct.	GB
Philadelphia	79-50	.612	-
Pittsburgh	76-55	.580	4
Chicago	70-59	.543	9
ST. LOUIS	71-60	.542	9
Montreal	60-70	.462	19½
New York	51-78	.395	28

Like Cobb and Hamilton, Brock was blessed with exceptional running speed. But unlike the two older Hall-of-Famers, Lou continued to be a proficient base thief well after age 30. His biggest single season total, 118, was set at age 35. He hadn't really dropped off significantly until this year, when he turned 38.

Tonight's accomplishment ended two pretty frustrating weeks for Lou. When the Cardinals opened a 13-game homestand on August 12th, he needed only seven stolen bases to pass Cobb. But a batting slump (9-for-47) kept him from reaching base very often, and the homestand ended with him still one short at 891. Disappointed that he didn't break the record in St. Louis, Lou at least hoped to do it in Los Angeles, the Cardinals' next stop. But he went hitless in 11 at bats in L.A. The usually amiable Brock became curt and irritable with the press.

Leading off tonight's series opener in San Diego, Lou uncharacteristically watched six pitches go by and walked to first base. Padres' pitcher Dave Freisleben, obviously aware of what might happen, stared over at the base for a long while. When he finally got onto the pitching rubber, he threw over. Brock had taken a very short lead and stepped back easily.

Now certain that he had established the psychological advantage that had enabled him to steal so many bases before, Brock took off for second on the first pitch to the batter. He got a great jump. Catcher Dave Roberts hurried his throw, and it tailed away from shortstop Bill Almon, who tried to grab the ball and make the tag at the same time. He missed, and the ball went into center field. Brock, who had slid into second feet first, got up and scooted to third on the error. He had tied Cobb's record. The San Diego ground crew came out and removed second base. It was presented to Brock, who handed it to third base coach Jack Krol.

Jerry Mumphrey singled Brock home, starting the Cardinals to three runs in the first inning. Mumphrey stole second and scored on a hit by Ted Simmons. A throwing error by Mike Ivie and a double by Mike Phillips brought Simmons around.

Brock broke his hitless slump in the second inning with a double to deep center. He didn't steal this time because a quick single by Mumphrey sent him to third. He was left stranded there.

San Diego got two runs off Cardinal starter John Urrea in the third inning, cutting the St. Louis lead to 3-2. Roberts led off with a single and scored on a one-out triple by Gene Richards. Richards counted on Almon's infield out.

Brock grounded out in the fourth.

In the seventh, Urrea led off with a single. Brock bounced back to the mound and reached first while Urrea was being forced at second. The San Diego crowd suddenly came to life, hoping for the record-breaking steal.

Freisleben threw to first once. Then he delivered to the plate. But Brock had called time out. He thought someone had said something to him, but everyone around him at the base denied it. After the game, Cardinal publicist Marty Hendin conjectured that Lou might have heard the ghost of Ty Cobb.

When play resumed, Brock took off on the next pitch, again getting a good jump. Roberts made a strong throw, but it was a little off line, and Lou barreled into Almon ahead of the tag.

Number 893! A new record! Players rushed out of both dugouts to congratulate Brock at second base. Once again, the sack was removed from the ground, and Padres' player representative Randy Jones presented it to Brock, telling the crowd (Jones had brought a microphone out with him) that Lou "deserved every ovation," and exhorting the fans with "Let's hear it for Lou Brock!"

After being left on base in the top of the inning, Brock went out to his position in left field. Manager Vern Rapp sent Rick Bosetti out to replace Lou, and the greatest base stealer in baseball history trotted to the dugout amid tumultuous applause.

The lesser event (the ballgame) continued.

The Cards still led, 3-2, until the bottom of the eighth. Pinch-hitter Gene Tenace opened the frame with a walk. Al Hrabosky was brought in to relieve Urrea. Richard and Almon flied out, but Mike Ivie drove an 0-1 pitch over the fence in left center for a two-run homer, putting San Diego ahead, 4-3. Home runs had plagued the St. Louis pitching staff all season.

Relief ace Rollie Fingers shut the Cardinals out in the ninth, and the Padres won the game.

But the big event, Lou Brock's record-breaking stolen bases, seemed to overshadow the outcome of the game.

St. Louis	ab	r	h	bi	o	a	e	San Diego	ab	r	h	bi	o	a	e
L. Brock, lf	3	1	1	0	0	0	0	G. Richards, 1b-lf9	4	1	1	1	13	0	0
R. Bosetti, lf7	0	0	0	0	0	0	0	B. Almon, ss	4	0	0	1	2	8	0
D. Iorg, ph9	0	0	0	0	-	-	-	M. Ivie, 3b-1b9	4	1	3	2	1	0	1
J. Mumphrey, cf	5	1	2	1	2	0	0	G. Hendrick, cf	4	0	2	0	2	0	0
K. Hernandez, 1b	2	0	0	0	12	0	0	D. Winfield, rf	3	0	0	0	2	0	0
T. Simmons, c	4	1	1	1	5	1	0	J. Turner, lf	3	0	0	0	2	0	0
K. Reitz, 3b	4	0	0	0	0	1	0	T. Ashford, 3b9	0	0	0	0	0	0	0
H. Cruz, rf	4	0	0	0	1	0	0	B. Champion, 2b	2	0	0	0	1	3	0
A. Hrabosky, p8	0	0	0	0	0	0	0	D. Roberts, c	3	1	1	0	4	1	1
M. Phillips, ss	4	0	1	1	2	4	0	D. Freisleben, p	2	0	0	0	0	1	0
M. Tyson, 2b	2	0	0	0	1	5	0	G. Tenace, ph8	0	1	0	0	-	-	-
G. Templeton, ph9	1	0	0	0	-	-	-	R. Fingers, p9	0	0	0	0	0	0	0
J. Urrea, p	3	0	1	0	0	2	0								
M. Anderson, rf8	1	0	0	0	1	0	0								
	33	3	6	3	24	13	0		29	4	7	4	27	13	2

St. Louis   300 000 000 - 3
San Diego   002 000 02x - 4

	ip	h	r-er	bb	so
Urrea	*7	6	3-3	2	4
Hrabosky (L 6-5)	1	1	1-1	0	1
Freisleben (W 6-7)	8	6	3-2	4	4
Fingers (sv #29)	1	0	0-0	1	0

*faced one batter in eighth

LOB: StL 8, SD 3. BE: StL 1.
DP: Tyson-Phillips-Hernandez.
2B: Phillips, Brock. 3B: Richards.
HR: Ivie.
SB: Brock 2, Mumphrey.
CS: Mumphrey, Champion.
Time - 2:20
Attendance - 19,656
Umpires: J. Quick, B. Williams,
D. Stello, & B. Froemming

With the record finally broken, Brock got his average up to .272 by the end of the season. He also added seven more steals.

The Cardinals, plagued by pitching problems, slumped in September and finished the season 18 games behind the Phillies. St. Louis wound up in third place with a final record of 83-79.

1978 — Sunday, April 16th, at Busch Memorial Stadium

Forsch No-Hits Phillies, 5-0, Controversy Over Scoring Call

Two Phillies Walk

Reitz Can't Come Up With Bouncer in Eighth, Ruled an Error

Bob Forsch of the St. Louis Cardinals pitched a brilliant game today, shutting out the Philadelphia Phillies. He did not allow a single clean hit, and only one ball was difficult for his fielders. That was a bouncer down the third base line in the eighth inning, which Ken Reitz missed trying to backhand. The Phillies unanimously thought the ball was a hit. But the Cardinals all thought it was definitely an error. Official scorer Neil Russo ruled it an error, and Forsch was credited with a no-hitter.

Today's Results
ST. LOUIS 5 - Philadelphia 0
Chicago 5 - Pittsburgh 1
Montreal 4 - New York 1

Standings	W-L	Pct.	GB
Philadelphia	4-3	.571	-
ST. LOUIS	5-4	.555	-
Chicago	5-4	.555	-
Montreal	4-4	.500	½
New York	5-5	.500	½
Pittsburgh	3-6	.333	2

The Cardinals won the game, 5-0. Reitz drove in the first St. Louis run with a single in the fourth inning. Roger Freed doubled home three tallies in the sixth. And a bases-loaded walk gave the Red Birds their final run in the eighth.

The controversial play opened the eighth inning. Garry Maddox, leading off, hit the first pitch down the line toward third. Reitz, well-known for his fielding ability, got over and tried to backhand the ball. It was not hit quite as hard as he expected, and he brought his glove up an instant too soon. The ball skipped under it, just ticking the edge of the fingers. The shivering crowd groaned, thinking that the no-hitter was lost. Reitz slapped his glove in disgust. But the scoreboard flashed "E-5," indicating an error, and the fans let out a tremendous cheer.

After the game, opinions on the call were perfectly divided by which clubhouse the questions were asked in. Reitz, who had led the league's third basemen in fielding four times, thought he had made an error. The Phillies, however, thought it was a hit. Acknowledging that Reitz usually made those kinds of plays, they pointed out that it was a hard-hit ball, which usually are called hits even if the fielder gets a glove on the ball. "Home cooking" was how one Philly analyzed the ruling. But Reitz had been charged with an error on Friday on another ball that could have been ruled a hit, and no pitching gem was on the line then. So, the controversy raged, but the no-hitter was on the books.

Forsch pitched two no-hitters in the minor leagues, one in 1972 and one in 1973. He made the big league club in the middle of the 1974 season. In the National League, he pitched three two-hitters before today's gem. Last year his won-lost record was 20-7.

Today's win was his third in three starts in 1978. He was not overpowering, but his fastball was moving very well, and his control was excellent on all of his pitches. He mixed his deliveries well, fooling the Phillies with both his junk and his speed. It took him 96 pitches to complete the game.

With two out in the first inning, Mike Schmidt hit a tremendous fly to center field. But he had gotten a little bit too far under it, and Tony Scott hauled the ball down 400 feet from the plate. Schmidt flied deep to center again in the fourth.

In the bottom of the fourth, St. Louis broke the scoreless tie. With one out, Ted Simmons got a hit to left center and boldly raced around first. He slid into second just ahead of Maddox's throw with a double and the first hit of the game. He moved to third on an infield tap. Reitz then delivered an opposite-field single to right, sending Simmons home.

Greg Luzinski bounced out to the right side leading off the fifth, giving Forsch 13 batters set down in order. But then he walked Richie Hebner. Hebner stole second as Maddox was striking out (Forsch's first "K"). Bob Boone also fanned.

Philly starter Randy Lerch also fanned two in the St. Louis fifth.

But Lerch's error gave the Cardinals three runs in the sixth. Garry Templeton led off with a double to left center. The next two batters went out on the infield, and Keith Hernandez hit a bouncer to first baseman Hebner. Hebner flipped to Lerch covering first, but the pitcher dropped the ball. Upset, Lerch hit Reitz with a pitch, loading the bases. Cardinal skipper Vern Rapp sent Freed up to hit for Scott. He connected with a fastball and drove it into the gap in right center, clearing the bases.

With one out in the top of the seventh, Schmidt hit his third long fly to center. It was caught without much difficulty. Luzinski walked, and Hebner popped to short.

In the eighth, Maddox got a base on the much-discussed error by Reitz. Three pitches later, Boone hit into a 6-4-3 double play. Ted Sizemore lined out to end the inning.

The Cardinals added a final run in the bottom of the eighth. Jerry Morales opened with a hit. Simmons grounded to deep short, and Bowa's throw to first was wild, putting men on second and third. Simmons was credited with a single on the play. Gene Garber then relieved Lerch. An intentional walk filled the bases. With two out, an unintentional walk to Dane Iorg forced a run home.

In the ninth, pinch-hitter Jay Johnstone bounced to short and was thrown out. Bake McBride, going after one of Forsch's slow breaking balls, grounded out to second. Bowa could not get around on a fastball, and he grounded out, third to first, completing the no-hitter.

Simmons rushed to the mound to give his pitcher a bear hug. His teammates soon joined in. After staying out for several broadcast interviews and a lot of autographs, Bob Forsch made it into the clubhouse, where a white carpet, champagne, and a beer shampoo awaited him.

Philadelphia	ab	r	h	bi	o	a	e
B. McBride, rf	4	0	0	0	1	0	0
L. Bowa, ss	4	0	0	3	3	1	
M. Schmidt, 3b	3	0	0	0	1	2	0
G. Luzinski, lf	2	0	0	0	0	0	0
R. Hebner, 1b	2	0	0	0	7	1	0
G. Maddox, cf	3	0	0	0	5	0	0
B. Boone, c	3	0	0	0	5	0	0
T. Sizemore, 2b	3	0	0	0	2	1	0
R. Lerch, p	2	0	0	0	0	2	1
G. Garber, p8	0	0	0	0	0	0	0
J. Johnstone, ph9	1	0	0	0	-	-	-
	27	0	0	0	24	9	2

St. Louis	ab	r	h	bi	o	a	e
L. Brock, lf	3	0	0	0	1	0	0
G. Templeton, ss	4	1	1	0	2	3	0
J. Morales, rf	3	1	1	0	1	0	0
T. Simmons, c	4	1	2	0	3	1	0
K. Hernandez, 1b	3	1	0	0	12	1	0
K. Reitz, 3b	3	1	1	1	0	2	1
T. Scott, cf	2	0	0	0	5	0	0
R. Freed, ph6	1	0	1	3	-	-	-
J. Mumphrey, pr6-cf	1	0	0	0	1	0	0
M. Tyson, 2b	3	0	0	0	1	4	0
D. Iorg, ph8	0	0	0	1	-	-	-
M. Phillip, 2b9	0	0	0	0	0	1	0
B. Forsch, p	4	0	0	0	1	1	0
	31	5	6	5	27	13	1

Philadelphia   000 000 000 - 0
St. Louis   000 103 01x - 5

	ip	h	r-er	bb	so
Lerch (L 1-1)	*7	6	5-2	2	4
Garber	1	0	0-0	2	0
Forsch (W 3-0)	9	0	0-0	2	3

*faced two batter in eighth
HBP: by Lerch (Reitz)

LOB: Phil 2, StL 7.
BE: Phil 1, StL 1.
DP: Templeton-Tyson-Hernandez.
2B: Simmons, Templeton, Freed.
SB: Hebner.
Time - 1:56
Attendance - 11,495
Umpires: L. Weyer, H. Wendelstedt, D. Rennert, & E. Montague

This was pretty much the high point of the 1978 season for the Cardinals. They lost their next six games and never got to the .500 mark again. An eleven-game losing streak dropped them to last place in May. They stayed there until mid-August and finished in fifth. Their final record was 69-93, for their worst percentage since 1924.

Forsch went from July 1st to August 29th without a win, and his won-lost record for the season was 11-17.

1979 — Tuesday Night, May 1st, at Busch Memorial Stadium

Freed's Dramatic Grand Slam in 11th Wins Game for Cardinals, 7-6

Roger's First Hit of the Year

Blow Comes with Two Outs, Three Balls and Two Strikes

It is the ultimate situation for a baseball game. Bottom of the eleventh inning, the home team is trailing by three runs. The well-traveled pinch-hitter is facing the visitors' ace reliever with two out and the bases loaded. The count goes to three balls and two strikes. The runners are running with the pitch. Here it comes, a fastball. The big man swings. The ball soars up and into the bleachers for a grand slam home run to win the game.

Right out of juvenile fiction, Roger Freed won tonight's game for the St. Louis Cardinals in exactly that situation. His grand slam provided the Cards with the runs needed to overcome a three-run rally by the Houston Astros in the eleventh inning, and St. Louis won, 7-6. "Something like this really makes me feel like part of the ballclub," Freed said afterwards.

Today's Results

ST. LOUIS 7 - Houston 6 (11 inn.)
Montreal 7 - Los Angeles 3
San Francisco 7 - Philadelphia 0
Chicago 5 - Cincinnati 1
San Diego 10 - New York 5
Atlanta 5 - Pittsburgh 2

Standings	W-L	Pct.	GB
Montreal	15-5	.750	-
Philadelphia	14-6	.700	1
ST. LOUIS	10-10	.500	5
Chicago	9-9	.500	5
New York	8-11	.421	6½
Pittsburgh	7-12	.368	7½

This spring, Freed began his third year in St. Louis, the longest stay in any one town since he began his professional career back in 1966. He worked his way up through the Baltimore farm system and was named Minor League Player of the Year in 1970. But then he quickly passed from the Orioles to the Phillies, to the Indians, to the Mexican League, and to the Expos. The Cardinals drafted him out of the minor leagues before the 1977 season. That year he hit .398 with 21 RBI's, mostly as a pinch-hitter. In 1978 he had 20 RBI's, but his average slipped to .239.

This year he survived spring training but sat on the bench when the regular season started. He only had five at bats and no hits before tonight.

The starting pitchers in the game were J.R. Richard for the Astros and Silvio Martinez for the Cardinals. They both retired the opponents in order in the first inning.

Both sides scored one run in the second. Houston counted on a double by Jose Cruz and a single by Enos Cabell. Ted Simmons quickly tied the game by leading off the bottom of the inning with a home run to right field.

Richard held the Cardinals down for three innings.

St. Louis broke the tie in the sixth. Lou Brock opened with a one-base hit. He broke for second on a pitch to Keith Hernandez, and Hernandez hit the ball right up the middle. Shortstop Craig Reynolds, who had come over to cover against the steal, was in perfect position to get the ball, and he started a double play. Simmons then singled to right and came home on a double to right center by George Hendrick.

The Cardinals added another run in the seventh. Ken Reitz led off with a single. Mike Tyson fanned. Martinez forced Reitz. Garry Templeton then came through with a triple into the gap in right center for a run.

The Astros rallied to tie the game in the eighth. Alan Ashby opened with an opposite-field double to left. Jimmy Sexton went in to run for him. Martinez struck out pinch-batter Denny Walling. Terry Puhl lined out. Reynolds pulled a two-out double to right, bringing Sexton home. Cesar Cedeno walked. A single by Cruz tied the score and knocked Martinez out of the game. Mark Littell was brought in, and he struck out Cabell to end the rally.

Joaquin Andujar set six straight Cardinal batters down in the eighth and ninth innings. And Littell retired the Astros in order in the ninth and tenth.

Against Joe Sambito in the tenth, St. Louis loaded the bases. But Hendrick left the three men on by flying to center for the third out.

Tom Bruno was sent in to pitch for St. Louis in the eleventh. He walked Cedeno on four pitches. The runner quickly stole second and moved to third on Cruz's infield out. Cabell bounced to shortstop, and Templeton's throw to the plate was wide, allowing Cedeno to slide home safely. Cabell then stole second. Bob Watson was given an intentional pass. Art Howe flied out. Then light-hitting catcher Bruce Bochy singled, scoring Cabell. And pitcher Sambito drove in another run with a double. With the score 6-3 and many fans leaving, Darold Knowles came in and retired Puhl on a grounder for the third out.

The Cardinals came in needing three runs to tie and four to win. Tony Scott gave St. Louis some hope by beating out a hit to short. After Reitz fanned, Sambito walked both Ken Oberkfell and Steve Swisher. Then he struck Templeton out.

Sambito was nearly out of the woods, needing only one more out. St. Louis manager Ken Boyer decided to send Freed up to bat for Jerry Mumphrey. He went up looking for hard stuff from the Houston lefthander. The first pitch was a fastball on the outside corner for strike one. The next two fastballs missed. Sambito then changed speeds, and Freed looked bad missing the pitch. Roger fouled the next pitch off. Ball three came in very high. With the count full, Sambito tried to put a fastball over the outside corner. But he got more of the plate than he wanted, and Freed got good wood on the ball. The result was a home run.

Suddenly, instead of being one strike away from a three-run loss, the Cardinals were winners, 7-6. The happy players were all at the plate to greet Freed when he finished circling the bases. It sure made Roger feel like part of the team.

Houston	ab	r	h	bi	o	a	e
T. Puhl, rf	6	0	0	0	0	0	0
C. Reynolds, ss	5	1	1	1	3	3	0
C. Cedeno, cf	2	1	1	0	5	0	0
J. Cruz, lf	4	1	2	1	1	0	0
E. Cabell, 3b-1b11	5	1	1	2	2	1	0
B. Watson, 1b	4	0	1	0	11	1	0
R. Landestoy, pr11-2b	0	1	0	0	0	0	0
A. Howe, 2b-3b11	5	0	0	0	1	3	0
A. Ashby, c	3	0	1	0	5	0	0
J. Sexton, pr8	0	1	0	0	-	-	-
B. Bochy, c8	2	0	1	1	4	0	0
J. Richard, p	2	0	0	0	0	2	0
D. Walling, ph8	1	0	0	0	-	-	-
J. Andujar, p8	0	0	0	0	0	2	0
J. Alou, ph10	1	0	0	0	-	-	-
J. Sambito, p10	1	0	1	1	0	1	0
	41	6	9	6	32	13	0

St. Louis	ab	r	h	bi	o	a	e
G. Templeton, ss	6	0	2	1	2	4	0
L. Brock, lf	4	0	1	0	1	0	0
J. Mumphrey, lf8	1	0	0	0	2	0	0
R. Freed, ph11	1	1	1	4	-	-	-
K. Hernandez, 1b	5	0	0	0	14	1	0
T. Simmons, c	3	2	2	1	4	2	0
T. Bruno, p11	0	0	0	0	0	1	0
D. Knowles, p11	0	0	0	0	0	0	0
G. Hendrick, rf	5	0	2	1	4	0	0
T. Scott, cf	5	1	1	0	3	0	0
K. Reitz, 3b	5	0	1	0	1	1	0
M. Tyson, 2b	2	0	0	0	1	2	0
D. Iorg, ph9	1	0	0	0	-	-	-
K. Oberkfell, 2b10	0	1	0	0	0	1	0
S. Martinez, p	3	1	0	0	0	1	0
M. Littell, p8	0	0	0	0	1	2	0
T. Grieve, ph10	0	0	0	0	-	-	-
M. Phillips, pr10	0	0	0	0	-	-	-
S. Swisher, c11	0	1	0	0	0	0	0
	41	7	10	7	33	15	0

Houston   010 000 020 03 - 6
St. Louis   010 001 100 04 - 7
two out when winning run scored

	ip	h	r-er	bb	so
Richard	7	7	3-3	2	4
Andujar	2	0	0-0	0	1
Sambito (L 2-1)	1.2	3	4-4	4	3
Martinez	7.2	7	3-3	3	2
Littell	2.1	0	0-0	0	2
Bruno	.2	2	3-3	2	0
Knowles (W 1-0)	.1	0	0-0	0	0

Umpires: D. Pallone, R. Freels, J. Bendekovits, & J. Jones

LOB: Hou 7, StL 8.
DP: Reynolds-Watson.
2B: Cruz, Hendrick 2, Cedeno, Ashby, Reynolds, Sambito.
3B: Templeton.
HR: Simmon, Freed.
SB: Tyson, Cedeno 2, Cabell.
CS: Cabell. Picked Off: Watson.
Time - 3:09
Attendance - 6,349

Freed had only five hits and six RBI's in late July and was shipped to Springfield in the American Association. He was recalled in September, but cut in spring training in 1980.

The Cardinals did pretty well in 1979. They finished in third place with an 86-76 record. Lou Brock's revival in his final season, which saw him get his 3,000th hit, was an inspiration. And Hernandez and Templeton led a potent batting attack.

1980 — Wednesday, May 29th, at Busch Memorial Stadium
Cards' Bullpen Fails Again, Blows 5-0 Lead, and Mets Win, 6-5
Fulgham Pitches Seven Shutout Innings, Then is Removed
Relievers Walk Five Men in Eighth Inning

After the New York Mets had done their best to give the St. Louis Cardinals today's game, the Red Bird bullpen gave the game right back to the New Yorkers. With a couple of desperate St. Louis rallies failing, the Mets were able to hold onto a 6-5 victory.

For the Cardinals, the game was their 12th defeat in 13 games, and the team's won-lost record slipped to 15-27, the worst in the major leagues. Although the club boasted the three leading hitters in the National League (with Ken Reitz heading the list at .367), the offense has been ineffectual in the clutch. And the bullpen has been a disaster area. Today's performance lowered the cumulative record of the St. Louis relievers to 3 wins and 12 losses and raised their E.R.A. to a whopping 6.14.

Today's Results
New York 6 - ST. LOUIS 5
Philadelphia 6 - Pittsburgh 3
Chicago 3 - Montreal 3 (10 inn.)
(game suspended - darkness)

Standings	W-L	Pct.	GB
Philadelphia	22-16	.579	-
Pittsburgh	23-17	.575	-
Montreal	20-18	.526	2
Chicago	18-20	.474	4
New York	18-22	.450	5
ST. LOUIS	15-27	.357	9

Cardinal manager Ken Boyer took a tiring John Fulgham out of today's game after seven innings. Before the Mets had been retired in the eighth, Boyer had changed pitchers three more times, and New York had taken the lead. The Cards then left five men on base in their last two innings and lost the game by one run.

A sun-baked "Businessman's Special" crowd of 12,161 witnessed today's demonstration of big league baseball at its worst. The Mets failed to hit, and they gave runs away with terrible fielding. But the Cardinals gave the game away by presenting the visitors with 11 bases on balls. In addition, both managers employed unorthodox strategies, giving the second-guessers plenty of material to rake over.

Fulgham walked six men in seven innings, but the Mets got only two hits off him. St. Louis turned two double plays behind him, and New York failed to score. A blood blister on the middle finger of his pitching hand contributed to Fulgham's wildness. Having suffered from an inflamed shoulder earlier in the season, and having made 97 pitches in the heat, he was removed after seven innings by manager Boyer. With a 5-0 lead, it looked like a prudent thing to do.

The Cardinal lead came mostly as a result of poor fielding by the Mets.

The first three runs, all unearned, were scored in the second inning. A walk and a two-base error by Doug Flynn put Terry Kennedy and Mike Ramsey on third and second, respectively, with one out. Fulgham failed to bring them home, but Garry Templeton came through with a RBI single. Third baseman Elliott Maddox's error on the throw allowed a second run to score and put Templeton on third. Tony Scott singled Tempy home.

Templeton and Scott singled again in the fifth, and an error by Lee Mazzilli allowed a run to score.

Shoddy fielding also helped the Cardinals score their final run in the sixth. Kennedy opened with a single. With one out, Ramsey hit one to left center that skipped under Joel Youngblood's glove and went to the fence for a triple, scoring Kennedy.

Facing the Cards' new pitcher, Jim Otten, to lead off the eighth, rookie Jose Moreno fanned. That made Moreno's lifetime major league batting record 0-for-3. Otten, who was pitching in only his second game for St. Louis, then walked Mazzilli and Frank Taveras, both on 3-and-2 counts. Mike Jorgensen popped out, but Youngblood was also passed. That loaded the bases and brought Boyer out to the mound.

With just one more out needed to retire the side, Mark Littell was called in. He threw just five pitches. John Stearns lined the first one into right field for a two-run single.

Steve Henderson watched the next four miss the plate, and he took his base on balls.

With the score now 5-2 and the tying runs filling the bases, Boyer brought George Frazier in. Maddox jumped on his first pitch and sent it deep to left center. Ted Simmons, hardly the fastest available outfielder, was unable to get under the ball, and it bounced off the fence for a three-run double, tying the game. Ron Hodges, pinch-hitting for pitcher Kevin Kobel, was walked intentionally to bring Moreno to the plate. The rookie worked the count full, then he smacked a line single to right for his first big league hit. Maddox raced around from second and scored the go-ahead run.

Boyer then brought in Jim Kaat, the fourth pitcher of the inning. The veteran lefty retired Mazzilli on a fly to right, ending the round.

New York manager Joe Torre put his ace reliever, Neil Allen, out to try and hold the lead. In the eighth, Kennedy singled with one out, and Dane Iorg, pinch-hitting, singled with two out. George Hendrick was sent to bat, and Allen pitched around him, walking the bases loaded. But Templeton bounced out to second baseman Moreno, and the Cardinals were turned back.

Roy Thomas pitched the ninth inning for St. Louis, and he shut the Mets out on one harmless single.

In the bottom of the ninth, Scott opened with a hit. He moved to third on a sacrifice and an infield ground out. With Simmons up and two out, Torre ordered an intentional walk, putting the potential winning run on base. But Bobby Bonds, who had been bothered by a hand injury, was unable to get around on Allen's fastballs, and he flied out to center field.

That ended the game, and the Cardinals lost by a final score of 6-5.

Oh, for a relief pitcher who could throw strikes!

New York	ab	r	h	bi	o	a	e
L. Mazzilli, 1b	3	1	0	0	10	2	1
J. Morales, cf8	0	0	0	0	2	0	0
F. Taveras, ss	2	1	0	0	2	1	0
M. Jorgensen, rf-1b8	5	0	0	1	1	1	0
J. Youngblood, cf-rf8	4	1	1	0	0	0	0
J. Stearns, c	4	1	2	2	5	1	0
S. Henderson, lf	3	1	1	0	1	0	0
E. Maddox, 3b	3	1	1	3	1	0	1
D. Flynn, 2b	2	0	0	0	4	1	
K. Kobel, p7	0	0	0	0	0	0	0
R. Hodges, ph8	0	0	0	0	-	-	-
N. Allen, p8	0	0	0	0	1	1	0
R. Burris, p	1	0	0	0	2	0	0
J. Pacella, p6	0	0	0	0	0	0	0
J. Moreno, 2b7	2	0	1	1	2	2	0
	29	6	6	6	27	12	3

St. Louis	ab	r	h	bi	o	a	e
G. Templeton, ss	5	2	2	1	2	0	0
T. Scott, cf	4	0	3	1	6	0	0
L. Durham, rf	3	0	0	1	3	0	0
K. Hernandez, 1b	5	0	1	0	8	1	0
T. Simmons, lf-c9	4	0	0	0	1	0	0
T. Kennedy, c	3	2	2	0	4	1	0
B. Bonds, pr8-lf	1	0	0	0	0	0	0
K. Reitz, 3b	3	0	0	0	0	1	0
M. Phillips, 3b7	1	0	0	0	0	0	0
M. Ramsey, 2b	3	1	1	1	3	2	0
D. Iorg, ph8	1	0	1	0	-	-	-
T. Herr, pr8-2b	0	0	0	0	0	2	0
J. Fulgham, p	3	0	0	0	0	1	0
J. Otten, p8	0	0	0	0	0	0	0
M. Littell, p8	0	0	0	0	0	0	0
G. Frazier, p8	0	0	0	0	0	0	0
J. Kaat, p8	0	0	0	0	0	0	0
G. Hendrick, ph8	0	0	0	0	-	-	-
R. Thomas, p9	0	0	0	0	0	0	0
	36	5	10	4	27	8	0

New York	000	000	060	-	6	
St. Louis	030	011	000	-	5	

	ip	h	r-er	bb	so
Burris	5.1	7	5-2	2	3
Pacella	*.2	0	0-0	1	2
Kobel (W 1-4)	1	0	0-0	0	0
Allen (sv #9)	2	3	0-0	2	0
Fulgham	7	2	0-0	6	2
Otten	.2	0	3-3	3	1
Littell	#0	1	2-2	1	0
Frazier (L 0-1)	**0	2	1-1	1	0
Kaat	.1	0	0-0	0	0
Thomas	1	1	0-0	0	0

Umpires: J. Quick, J. Dale, B. Engel, & P. Runge

LOB: NY 8, StL 10. BE: StL 2.
DP: Reitz-Ramsey-Hernandez-Kennedy, Hernandez (unassisted), Moreno-Taveras-Mazzilli.
2B: Maddox. 3B: Ramsey.
SH: Burris, Durham.
SB: Scott, Youngblood.
CS: Mazzilli, Scott.
Time - 3:00
Attendance - 12,161
*faced one batter in seventh
#faced two batters in eighth
**faced three batters in eighth

Lack of a "stopper" helped cause Boyer and general manager John Claiborne to lose their jobs before the season was over. Whitey Herzog replaced them both. The Cardinals played at just over a .500 pace after Herzog arrived. They finished fourth with a lackluster 74-88 record.

Over the winter, Herzog acquired a certified bullpen ace, Bruce Sutter, from the Chicago Cubs.

1981—Tuesday Night, September 29th, at Busch Memorial Stadium
Big Crowd Sees Cardinals Regain First Place in Final Home Game
Beat Expos, 8-4, Lead by ½ Game with Five to Play
Oberkfell, Tenace Lead Hitting on "Fan Appreciation Night"

Before the largest home crowd of the season, the St. Louis Cardinals moved back into first place in the second half of the National League East Division's split season with an 8-4 victory over the Montreal Expos. The Expos had come to town leading by 1½ games with just seven games remaining, but St. Louis won both games of the short series. The Red Birds left town tonight to finish the season on the road.

It was "Fan Appreciation Night," with the club offering a voucher good for a free ticket to a game next year to each of tonight's paying customers. The fans came in droves, and the start of the game was delayed about 15 minutes to allow more spectators to get into the park. Even so, people were still standing in line at the ticket windows during the third inning. With the temperature around 80°F and first place at stake, the attendance was the largest of the season (40,488), and it brought the club's season total to over one million, despite the loss of 27 home dates cancelled by the mid-season strike.

Today's Results
ST. LOUIS 8 - Montreal 4
New York 7 - Philadelphia 0
Pittsburgh 10 - Chicago 6

Standings	W-L	Pct.	GB
ST. LOUIS	26-21	.553	-
Montreal	26-22	.542	½
Chicago	22-25	.468	4
Philadelphia*	22-25	.468	4
New York	22-26	.458	4½
Pittsburgh	20-29	.408	7

*Philadelphia was first half winner

Unfortunately for the late arrivals, the action of the game was concentrated in the early innings. By the end of the third frame, the Cardinals held a decisive, 6-3 lead. St. Louis pitchers Joaquin Andujar and Doug Bair held off the Expos, and, for the second night in a row, the Cardinals won the game without having to use their bullpen ace, Bruce Sutter. Gene Tenace (2-for-2) and Ken Oberkfell (4-for-4) lead the St. Louis batting attack.

Montreal struck for two quick runs against Andujar in the first. Warren Cromartie led off with a double into the gap in left center. On the very next pitch, Rodney Scott smashed a single to right field, and Cromartie headed for home. George Hendrick's throw came in on the fly, and catcher Darrell Porter applied a crunching tag. Umpire Jerry Crawford called Cromartie safe, much to the displeasure of Porter. Scott went to second on the play, and Cromartie was shaken up. When a pitch trickled away from Porter, Scott took third. He scored on an infield out by Andre Dawson. Gary Carter added a double off the top of the left field fence, but he was left on base.

The Cardinals countered with a three-run burst in the bottom of the first. After Tommy Herr and Garry Templeton had been retired, Keith Hernandez shot a grounder into left. Hendrick hit a pop fly that landed just fair and bounded off Tim Wallach's glove into the seats for a ground-rule double. Expo pitcher Bill Lee fell behind Gene Tenace on the count, 2-and-0, then came in with a fastball out over the plate. Tenace, normally a dead pull hitter, cracked it hard off the right field fence for a two-run double. Ken Oberkfell followed with a ground single to right, and Tenace just beat the throw to home, putting the Cardinals ahead, 3-2. Porter followed with a hit, but David Green bounced into a force out to end the inning.

After Montreal was retired in order, St. Louis added another run in the second. Herr's drive got between the right and center fielders for a triple, and Templeton drove him in with a sacrifice fly.

In the third inning, the Expos scored one. Cromartie lined a hit to right and limped to first base. He was replaced by Rowland Office. Scott and Dawson followed with singles to bring the runner in. Andujar was looking shaky on the mound, especially after Carter just missed a home run on a long foul ball. But the Expo slugger fanned on the next pitch, and Scott was thrown out trying to steal third. Larry Parrish then bounced out to end the rally.

As in the first inning, St. Louis came in to bat and outdid the Montreal rally, getting two runs. With one out, Tenace pulled a single into the left field corner. Oberkfell tripled just past Dawson in right center, scoring Tenace. After Porter was intentionally passed, young Bryn Smith replaced Lee on the mound for the Expos. The first man he faced, Green, laid down a squeeze bunt, which Smith fielded and threw toward first base. Unfortunately, no one was covering, and the ball sailed into foul ground. Oberkfell scored on the bunt, but Porter was out at home trying to come all the way around from first base on the error. Andujar struck out, but the Cardinals led, 6-3.

Andujar, who had been acquired in June from Houston, breezed through the fourth and fifth innings, but he aggravated a pulled hamstring muscle jumping for a high chop.

In the home half of the fifth, the Cardinals added two runs off Expo relievers Grand Jackson and Elias Sosa.

Doug Bair, acquired from Cincinnati earlier in the month, replaced Andujar as the St. Louis pitcher in the sixth. The first two men he faced hit the ball hard on the ground: Dawson's rap went past Herr for a single, but Oberkfell snared Carter's shot and turned it into a double play. Parrish then struck out of three pitches.

Bair breezed through the next two innings, then gave up a run in the ninth. With one out in the last frame, Carter and Parrish hit doubles. Sutter went trotting down to the Cardinal bullpen, but before he needed to get heated up, Bair retired the next two batters to end the game.

The final score was 8-4, and many of the delirious fans stayed around to chant "We're Number One!" All were hoping to see the Cardinals play again in the divisional playoffs.

Montreal	ab	r	h	bi	o	a	e		St. Louis	ab	r	h	bi	o	a	e
W. Cromartie, 1b	2	1	2	0	2	0	0		T. Herr, 2b	5	1	2	0	1	1	0
R. Office, pr3-rf	2	1	0	0	1	0	0		G. Templeton, ss	4	0	0	1	0	5	0
R. Scott, 2b	4	1	2	1	2	5	0		K. Hernandez, lf-1b6	3	1	1	0	4	0	0
A. Dawson, cf	4	0	2	2	4	0	0		G. Hendrick, rf	4	2	2	0	3	0	0
G. Carter, c	4	1	2	0	4	1	0		G. Tenace, 1b	2	2	2	2	6	0	0
L. Parrish, 3b	4	0	1	1	0	0	0		T. Landrum, pr5-lf	1	0	0	0	1	0	0
T. Wallach, rf-1b3	4	0	0	0	7	0	0		K. Oberkfell, 3b	4	2	4	3	1	1	0
T. Francona, lf	4	0	0	0	1	0	0		D. Porter, c	2	0	1	0	8	1	0
C. Speier, ss	3	0	0	0	3	6	0		D. Green, cf	4	0	1	1	3	0	0
B. Lee, p	1	0	0	0	0	0	0		J. Andujar, p	2	0	0	0	0	2	0
B. Smith, p3	0	0	0	0	0	0	1		D. Iorg, ph5	0	0	0	1	-	-	-
B. Mills, ph5	1	0	0	0	-	-	-		D. Bair, p6	1	0	0	0	0	0	0
G. Jackson, p5	0	0	0	0	0	0	0									
E. Sosa, p5	0	0	0	0	0	0	0									
W. Johnson, ph8	1	0	0	0	-	-	-									
T. Gorman, p8	0	0	0	0	0	0	0									
	34	4	9	4	24	12	1			32	8	13	8	27	10	0

Montreal	201	000	001	-	4	
St. Louis	312	020	00x	-	8	

	ip	h	r-er	bb	so
Lee (L 4-6)	2.1	8	6-6	1	0
Smith	1.2	1	0-0	1	1
Jackson	*0	2	2-2	2	0
Sosa	3	1	0-0	0	0
Gorman	1	1	0-0	0	1
Andujar (W 8-4)	5	6	3-3	0	3
Bair (sv #1)	4	3	1-1	0	4

*faced four batters in fifth

WP: Jackson. PB: Porter.

LOB: Mont 3, StL 6. BE: none.
DP: Oberkfell-Herr-Hernandez, Scott-Speier-Wallach
2B: Cromartie, Carter 2, Hendrick 2, Tenace, Parrish.
3B: Herr, Oberkfell.
SF: Templeton, Iorg.
SB: none. CS: Scott.
Picked Off: Hernandez
Time - 2:23
Attendance - 40,488 paid
43,104 total
Umpires: J. Crawford, E. Vargo, S. Davidson, & T. Tata

The Cardinals failed to hold their ½-game lead. They finished ½ game behind the Expos in the second-half standings. So, even though they had the best overall record in the division, there was no playoff berth for the Cardinals.

APPENDIX A
Season Statistics

Year-	(League no. of teams & schedule)	—Finish	Won-Lost	Pct.	GB	(Ties)	Home Record W-L-T	Days in 1st + days tied
1882-	(AA-6-80)	—Fifth	37-43	.462	-18	(1)	24-20-1	2+3
1883-	(AA-8-98)	—Second	65-33	.663	-1		35-14	12
1884-	(AA-12-110)	—Fourth	67-40	.626	-8	(3)	37-15-1	13+7
1885-	(AA-8-112)	—First	79-33	.705	+16		44-11	152+1
1886-	(AA-8-140)	—First	93-46	.669	+12		52-18	162+1
1887-	(AA-8-140)	—First	95-40	.704	+14	(3)	58-15	157+2
1888-	(AA-8-140)	—First	92-43	.681	+6½	(2)	60-21-1	98+6
1889-	(AA-8-140)	—Second	90-45	.667	-2	(6)	51-18-4	128+6
1890-	(AA-8-140)	—Third	78-58	.574	-12	(3)	45-25-2	0+1
1891-	(AA-8-140)	—Second	85-51	.625	-8½	(2)	52-21	5+3
1892-	(NL-12-77	—Ninth	31-42	.425	-20½	(1)	19-19-1	0
first half of split season								
1892-	(NL-12-77	—Eleventh	25-52	.325	-28½	(4)	*17-15-1	0+1
second half of split season								
1893-	(NL-12-132)	—Tenth	57-75	.432	-30½	(3)	40-30-2	4+5
1894-	(NL-12-132)	—Ninth	56-76	.424	-35	(1)	32-30	1+7
1895-	(NL-12-132)	—Eleventh	39-92	.298	-48½	(4)	25-41-1	0
1896-	(NL-12-132)	—Eleventh	40-90	.308	-50½	(1)	27-34	0+1
1897-	(NL-12-132)	—Twelfth	29-102	.221	-63½	(1)	18-41-1	0
1898-	(NL-12-154)	—Twelfth	39-111	.260	-63½	(4)	20-44-2	0
1899-	(NL-12-154)	—Fifth	84-67	.556	-18½	(4)	50-33-4	33+4
1900-	(NL-8-140)	—Fifth (tie)	65-75	.464	-19	(2)	40-31-1	1+3
1901-	(NL-8-140)	—Fourth	76-64	.543	-14½	(2)	@40-31-1	2
1902-	(NL-8-140)	—Sixth	56-78	.418	-44½	(6)	28-38-4	0
1903-	(NL-8-140)	—Eighth	43-94	.314	-46½	(2)	22-45-2	0+1
1904-	(NL-8-154)	—Fifth	75-79	.487	-31½	(1)	39-36-1	0
1905-	(NL-8-154)	—Sixth	58-96	.377	-47½		32-45	0
1906-	(NL-8-154)	—Seventh	52-98	.347	-63	(4)	28-48-1	0
1907-	(NL-8-154)	—Eighth	52-101	.340	-55½	(2)	31-47-1	0
1908-	(NL-8-154)	—Eighth	49-105	.318	-50		28-49	0
1909-	(NL-8-154)	—Seventh	54-98	.355	-56	(2)	26-48-2	0
1910-	(NL-8-154)	—Seventh	63-90	.412	-40½		35-41	0
1911-	(NL-8-154)	—Fifth	75-74	.503	-22	(9)	36-38-5	2+1
1912-	(NL-8-154)	—Sixth	63-90	.412	-41		37-40	0+6
1913-	(NL-8-154)	—Eighth	51-99	.340	-49	(3)	25-48-1	0+5
1914-	(NL-8-154)	—Third	81-72	.529	-13	(3)	43-34-3	0+1
1915-	(NL-8-154)	—Sixth	72-81	.471	-18½	(4)	42-36-3	0
1916-	(NL-8-154)	—Seventh(tie)	60-93	.392	-33½		36-40	0+1
1917-	(NL-8-154)	—Third	82-70	.539	-15	(2)	38-38-2	1
1918-	(NL-8-*WW)	—Eighth	51-78	.395	-33	(2)	32-40-1	0+2
1919-	(NL-8-140)	—Seventh	54-83	.394	-47½	(1)	34-35	0
1920-	(NL-8-154)	—Fifth(tie)	75-79	.487	-18	(1)	#38-38	0
1921-	(NL-8-154)	—Third	87-66	.569	-7	(1)	48-29-1	0
1922-	(NL-8-154)	—Third(tie)	85-69	.552	-8		43-34	7+4
1923-	(NL-8-154)	—Fourth	79-74	.516	-16	(1)	42-35-1	0
1924-	(NL-8-154)	—Sixth	65-89	.422	-28½		40-37	0+1
1925-	(NL-8-154)	—Fourth	77-76	.503	-18		48-28	0
1926-	(NL-8-154)	—First	89-65	.578	+2	(2)	47-30-2	25+5
1927-	(NL-8-154)	—Second	92-61	.601	-1½		55-25	10
1928-	(NL-8-154)	—First	95-59	.617	+2		42-35	104+3
1929-	(NL-8-154)	—Fourth	78-74	.513	-20	(2)	43-32-2	14+5
1930-	(NL-8-154)	—First	92-62	.597	+2		53-24	20+2
1931-	(NL-8-154)	—First	101-53	.656	+13		54-24	154+10
1932-	(NL-8-154)	—Sixth(tie)	72-82	.468	-18	(2)	42-35-2	0+2
1933-	(NL-8-154)	—Fifth	82-71	.536	-9½	(1)	47-30	4
1934-	(NL-8-154)	—First	95-58	.621	+2	(1)	48-29	11+5
1935-	(NL-8-154)	—Second	96-58	.623	-4		53-24	20
1936-	(NL-8-154)	—Second(tie)	87-67	.565	-5	(1)	43-33-1	82+3

264

Year	League	Finish	Record	Pct.	GB	(x)	Home	Away
1937-	(NL-8-154)	—Fourth	81-73	.526	-15	(3)	45-33-2	5+4
1938-	(NL-8-154)	—Sixth	71-80	.470	-17½	(5)	36-41-4	0
1939-	(NL-8-154)	—Second	92-61	.601	-4½	(2)	51-27-1	15+4
1940-	(NL-8-154)	—Third	84-69	.549	-16	(3)	41-36	0
1941-	(NL-8-154)	—Second	97-56	.634	-2½	(2)	53-24-2	70+11
1942-	(NL-8-154)	—First	106-48	.688	+2	(2)	60-17-1	15+1
1943-	(NL-8-154)	—First	105-49	.682	+18	(3)	58-21-2	121
1944-	(NL-8-154)	—First	105-49	.682	+14½	(3)	54-22-1	155+8
1945-	(NL-8-154)	—Second	95-59	.617	-3	(1)	48-29-1	0
1946-	(NL-8-154)	—First	##98-58	.628	+2		49-29	45+25
1947-	(NL-8-154)	—Second	89-65	.578	-5	(2)	46-31	0
1948-	(NL-8-154)	—Second	85-59	.552	-6½	(1)	44-33	21+5
1949-	(NL-8-154)	—Second	96-58	.623	-1	(3)	51-27-2	58+6
1950-	(NL-8-154)	—Fifth	78-75	.510	-12½		48-27	17+13
1951-	(NL-8-154)	—Third	81-73	.526	-15½	(1)	44-34-1	7+3
1952-	(NL-8-154)	—Third	88-66	.571	-8½		48-29	0+2
1953-	(NL-8-154)	—Third(tie)	83-71	.539	-22	(3)	48-30	0+1
1954-	(NL-8-154)	—Sixth	72-82	.468	-25		33-44	4
1955-	(NL-8-154)	—Seventh	68-86	.442	-30½		41-36	0
1956-	(NL-8-154)	—Fourth	76-78	.494	-17	(2)	43-34-1	2+2
1957-	(NL-8-154)	—Second	87-67	.565	-8		42-35	24+2
1958-	(NL-8-154)	—Fifth(tie)	72-82	.468	-20		39-38	0
1959-	(NL-8-154)	—Seventh	71-83	.461	-16		42-35	0
1960-	(NL-8-154)	—Third	86-68	.558	-9	(1)	51-26	0
1961-	(NL-8-154)	—Fifth	80-74	.519	-13	(1)	48-29-1	0+4
1962-	(NL-10-162)	—Sixth	84-78	.519	-17½	(1)	44-37	1+11
1963-	(NL-10-162)	—Second	93-69	.574	-6		53-28	21+11
1964-	(NL-10-162)	—First	93-69	.574	+1		48-33	4+2
1965-	(NL-10-162)	—Seventh	80-81	.497	-16½	(1)	42-39	0
1966-	(NL-10-162)	—Sixth	83-79	.512	-12		@@43-38	0
1967-	(NL-10-162)	—First	101-60	.627	+10½		49-32	114+7
1968-	(NL-10-162)	—First	97-65	.599	+9		47-34	153+7
1969-	(NLE-6-162)	—Fourth	87-75	.543	-13		42-38	0
1970-	(NLE-6-162)	—Fourth	76-86	.469	-13		34-47	5+9
1971-	(NLE-6-162)	—Second	90-72	.556	-7	(1)	45-36-1	16
1972-	(NLE-6-162)	—Fourth	75-81	.481	-21½		40-37	0
1973-	(NLE-6-162)	—Second	81-81	.500	-1½		43-38	51
1974-	(NLE-6-162)	—Second	86-75	.534	-1½		44-37	69+14
1975-	(NLE-6-162)	—Third(tie)	82-80	.506	-10½	(1)	45-36-1	0
1976-	(NLE-6-162)	—Fifth	72-90	.444	-29		37-44	0+1
1977-	(NLE-6-162)	—Third	83-79	.512	-18		52-31	15+6
1978-	(NLE-6-162)	—Fifth	69-83	.426	-21		37-44	2+1
1979-	(NLE-6-162)	—Third	86-76	.531	-12	(1)	42-39-1	5+5
1980-	(NLE-6-162)	—Fourth	74-88	.457	-17		41-40	0+1
1981- first half of split season	(NLE-6-*PS)	—Second	30-20	.600	-1½	(1)	20-11	33+2
1981- second half of split season	(NLE-6-*PS)	—Second	29-23	.558	-½		12-10	40+2

*PS 1972 and 1981 seasons shortened by players' strikes
* does not include three "home" games played in Kansas City (1W-2L)
@ includes one game played (and lost) at Athletic Park, Grand Av. at Sullivan
*WW season cut short by World War I
record at Cardinal Field: 16-13; record at Sportsman's Park: 22-25
@@ record at old Busch Stadium: 3-7; record at Busch Memorial Stadium: 40-31

WORLD SERIES Record

1885 - TIED, 3 games to 3 (with 1 tie), vs. Chicago White Stockings (NL)
1886 - WON, 4 games to 2, vs. Chicago White Stockings (NL)
1887 - LOST, 5 games to 10, vs. Detroit Wolverines (NL)
1888 - LOST, 4 games to 6, vs. New York Giants (NL)
1926 - WON, 4 games to 3, vs. New York Yankees (AL)
1928 - LOST, 0 games to 4, vs. New York Yankees (AL)
1930 - LOST, 2 games to 4, vs. Philadelphia Athletics (AL)
1931 - WON, 4 games to 3, vs. Philadelphia Athletics (AL)
1934 - WON, 4 games to 3, vs. Detroit Tigers (AL)
1942 - WON, 4 games to 1, vs. New York Yankees (AL)
1943 - LOST, 1 game to 4, vs. New York Yankees (AL)
1944 - WON, 4 games to 2, vs. St. Louis Browns (AL)
1946 - WON, 4 games to 3, vs. Boston Red Sox (AL)
1964 - WON, 4 games to 3, vs. New York Yankees (AL)
1967 - WON, 4 games to 3, vs. Boston Red Sox (AL)
1968 - LOST, 3 games to 4, vs. Detroit Tigers (AL)

CITY SERIES Record versus St. Louis Browns (AL)

1903 - LOST, 2 games to 5
1904 - TIED, 3 games to 3
1905 - LOST, 3 games to 4 with one tie
1906 - LOST, 1 game to 4 with three ties
1907 - WON, 5 games to 2
1911 - LOST, 3 games to 4 with one tie
1912 - WON, 4 games to 3 with one tie
1913 - TIED, 3 games to 3 with two ties
1914 - LOST, 1 game to 4 with one tie
1915 - LOST, 1 game to 4 with one tie
1916 - LOST, 1 game to 4
1917 - WON, 4 games to 2 with one tie

APPENDIX B
The Ballparks

Over the first hundred years of its existence, the St. Louis club has played its home games at three sites.

The first was the original Sportsman's Park, which was located on the west side of Grand Avenue, south of the corner of Sullivan Avenue. This site was originally laid out as a baseball field in 1866. In 1881, the grounds were expanded to include most of the present block surrounded by Grand, Sullivan, Dodier, and Spring Avenues (Dodier was not put through to Spring until 1889, however).

The Browns played here during their ten years in the American Association (1882-1891) and their first year in the National League (1892). At the time, home plate was located in the southeast corner of the lot.

In 1893, the Browns moved to a new park, located on the south side of Natural Bridge Avenue, between Vandeventer and Prairie. Home plate was in the northwest corner. This park was the home of National League baseball in St. Louis from 1893 to 1920. It was at first called Sportsman's Park, but that name was changed to League Park in 1899. In 1912, it was renamed Robison Field, and in 1917, the name was again changed, this time to Cardinal Field. The wooden stands suffered two serious fires, one in 1898 and one in 1901. After the 1901 fire, the Cardinals played one home game at Athletic Field, which was located on the site of the first Sportsman's Park (Grand and Sullivan).

In the middle of the 1920 season, the Cardinals moved in as tenants of the American League St. Louis Browns in their park, known as Sportsman's Park. This stadium was located on the same ground as the first Sportsman's Park (1882-1892), but home plate was located in the southwest corner (Dodier and Spring).

The Cardinals rented this park through 1952. Shortly after Anheuser-Busch, Inc., bought the ballclub, the company also purchased the park. The plant was remodeled and renamed Busch Stadium. The Cardinals continued to play here through May 8, 1966.

On May 12, 1966, the team moved from old Busch Stadium to the new Busch Memorial Stadium, located downtown between Broadway, Walnut, Eighth, and Spruce Streets. The Cardinals have played there ever since 1966.

Bibliographical Note

The basic sources of information used in this book were the accounts of the games in the daily newspapers. The St. Louis papers, naturally, were used most extensively. These included the *Globe-Democrat*, the *Post-Dispatch*, the *Times*, the *Star-Times*, and the *Republican*. Out-of-town newspapers were also consulted for specific games. The papers used included the Chicago *Tribune*, the Los Angeles *Times*, the New York *Times*, the New York *Daily News*, the New York *Herald-Tribune*, the San Diego *Union*, the San Francisco *Chronicle*, the San Francisco *Examiner*, and the Louisville *Courier*.

Also consulted, both for background research and for specific games were the sporting weeklies *The Sporting News* and *Sporting Life*.

For biographical and statistical material, the Macmillan Publishing Company's standard work, *The Baseball Encyclopedia*, Grosset & Dunlap's *The Sports Encyclopedia—Baseball*, and *The World Series*, by Sports Products, Inc., were major sources. Also consulted were *The Sporting News's Official Baseball Guides* and *Official World Series Records*.

Several prose works were also used for background information. Frederick G. Lieb's history, *The St. Louis Cardinals*, Alfred H. Spink's *The National Game*, and Bob Broeg's *Redbirds* were all very helpful. Harold Seymour's two volume history, *Baseball*, also contributed information about the early development of the franchise.

And a few autobiographical books were also consulted. These included works about Bob Gibson *(From Ghetto to Glory)*, Lou Brock *(Stealing Is My Game)*, Curt Flood *(The Way It Is)*, and Stan Musial *(Stan Musial—"The Man's" Own Story)*.

The St. Louis National Baseball Club, Inc., generously provided photographs and play-by-play information.

And the Missouri Historical Society's photographic files were also used.